Brooks Peninsula: An Ice Age Refugium on Vancouver Island

Occasional Paper No. 5 April 1997

Edited by
Richard J. Hebda[1]
James C. Haggarty[2]

1 Botany and Earth History, Royal British Columbia Museum, Victoria, BC and
Biology and School of Earth and Ocean Sciences, University of Victoria
2 Shoreline Archaeological Services, Victoria, BC

Published by BC Parks, Ministry of Environment, Lands and Parks, Victoria, BC, in association with the Royal British Columbia Museum, with funding provided by Forest Renewal British Columbia.

Printed in Canada.

Cover photo by Robert A. Cannings.
Cover design by Chris Tyrell, Royal British Columbia Museum.
Occasional Paper Series edited by Mona Holley, BC Parks

Canadian Cataloguing in Publication Data
Main entry under title:
Brooks Peninsula

(Occasional paper ; no. 5)

ISBN 0-7726-3139-5

1. Brooks Peninsula (B.C.). 2. Natural history - British Columbia - Brooks Peninsula. I. Hebda, Richard Joseph, 1950- . II. Haggarty, James C., 1943- III. British Columbia. Ministry of Environment, Lands and Parks. IV. Series: Occasional paper (BC Parks) ; no. 5.

QH106.2.B7B76 1997 508.711'2 C97-960012-X

Dedicated to

Bill H. Mathews
and
Wilf B. Schofield

Pioneers in the scholarly study of
British Columbia's natural history.

These tireless field scientists first
recognized the possibility of
an ice age refuge on Brooks Peninsula.

Foreword

You are reading a book about an expedition that explored a very special place. Even on a map, Brooks Peninsula stands out. Its peculiar rectangular shape reaches southwestward from Vancouver Island for about 18 kilometres. It looks different, but is even more different than it looks.

The peninsula's reputation as a different kind of place has been well deserved. Craggy peaks stand in odd relief from the rest of the rounded landscape. Rare plants there are found in only a few other places. Bogs occur where bogs shouldn't be. The peninsula's rocks "sailed" painfully slowly from elsewhere millions of years ago to join North America. Then thousands of years ago, while most of British Columbia was being crushed and polished under glacial ice, parts of Brooks Peninsula appear to have been ice-free. These features identify it as an area holding information of high scientific value. This was the reason for the expedition, and for this book.

When Brooks Peninsula was declared a provincial park, BC Parks' dedication to preserving the province's biodiversity took a long stride forward. The peninsula's location and features may not rate it in the top ten for public recreation, but it could be at the top for conserving rare species and abundant evidence of our province's complex prehistory.

This book is about a museum-organized expedition which found much information, but it was successful in other ways too. It enlarged existing friendships and created new ones. Professionally, it brought scientists together to exchange information and ideas, the mix being more productive than had the individuals worked alone. From these connections in the field there were lasting ones after everyone returned to offices and laboratories.

In especially complicated areas such as biodiversity and ecology it is often necessary that scientists work in teams. The essential relationships between kinds of life as well as their associations with rock, water and air are best unravelled by different kinds of experts in teams. Museums have been a source of such teams for over a century.

What is "Brooks" like? I was a brief part of the expedition, more an observer than a scientist. It was a memorable experience. Silent remoteness and its absolute wildness are memories of the place, along with the richness of vegetation in its storm twisted rainforest, its adjacent sea alive with many kinds of life, and the beaches of sand which recorded the imprints of passers by.

There were killer whales blowing offshore, and fresh wolf tracks in the sand. A family of river otters in a nearby estuary was in perpetual motion with the constant playful interactions characteristic of otters. The forest was almost impenetrable, a rich tangle of trees, logs and low brush that challenged invaders. Bogs were there, spongy wet, some animated with numerous half grown frogs; and pools were home to salamanders and their tadpoles still with gills. Sandpipers were the most numerous birds, migrants enroute from the Arctic and ready to rest and feed on the peninsula before moving on, some with destinations deep into Latin America.

Places like Brooks Peninsula reinforce the fact that our small planet and its life are our only wealth. All else is at most secondary. It is easy to forget this if you are not in touch with expert explorers on their voyages of discovery, such as those working in unusual places like Brooks Peninsula.

Yorke Edwards
Victoria, BC
January, 1997

Table of Contents

Acknowledgements

As with any project of this size and scope, the number of individuals, agencies, and institutions that supported this project is large. Heading this list are the many individuals who freely donate their time and energy to the museum through the auspices of the Friends of the Royal British Columbia Museum (FORM). The FORM obtain funds so that projects like this one move from being dreams in curators' minds, to reality. The Brooks Peninsula project, from field work well into the publication process, was made possible by grants from the FORM. On behalf of all of the project participants, we thank you. We especially thank Mrs. Ede Ross, Gift Shop Manager (retired), for her many years of devoted service to the museum and its staff. Ede and her staff made many projects possible through their work in the Museum gift shop.

We thank all of the participants in the project for their support. It is never easy to get twenty or so colleagues committed to a single set of objectives, let alone headed in a single direction. We deeply appreciate their commitment to research and to the goals of this project. We thank you also for your patience as we sought to bring our joint efforts to completion with the publication of this volume.

We gratefully acknowledge and thank the institutions and agencies who provided support for the participants. Thanks are due the University of British Columbia; the University of Calgary; BC Environment; Research Branch, Ministry of Forests; BC Parks; and the Royal British Columbia Museum (RBCM). Without the support provided by these institutions and agencies, the project would have remained small and narrow in scope.

In addition, we acknowledge the fine work performed on the project by Ruth and the late Louis Kirk, filmmakers from Tacoma, Washington, Ross Brand and Mary-Lou Florian, RBCM for logistical support, and Bjorn Simonsen, base camp coordinator, logistic boss, and camp cook. We thank all of you for the contribution of your energy and skill.

In the field, the project received support and assistance from a variety of sources. We wish to acknowledge and thank the Ministry of Transport of the Government of Canada for in-field logistics; Carl and Jeanette Stout for transportation aboard the Northern Rider to and from Winter Harbour and the Brooks Peninsula base camp; and Bob Moore for overnight accommodation in Winter Harbour. All projects seem to receive assistance at crucial times, and this project was no exception. We also wish to acknowledge the fine service provided by staff of Vancouver Island Helicopters, Port Hardy base. Thanks also to Harry Hole and Alfred Ilstead of Coal Harbour for advice and historical information regarding the Brooks Peninsula area.

Each chapter except Chapter 1 was reviewed by at least two colleagues within the respective discipline prior to final copy editing. To all reviewers we extend our sincere appreciation for your support and assistance with this volume. Reviewers of specific chapters are acknowledged in the appropriate chapter.

A number of different stenographers have typed and corrected various drafts and the final version of this manuscript. We appreciate the excellent work of Pam Giacomello, Carolyn Kenzie, Barbara Kuluah, and Sally Watson and extend our sincere thanks for the assistance provided us in the production of this volume. Tara Steigenberger (RBCM) marshalled together the manuscript on its way to BC Parks.

We acknowledge the dedicated work of Kathryn Bernick, the multi-talented assistant editor of the volume. A great deal of credit for guiding this volume through the various stages of publication to its near-final form go to Kitty. We thank her for a truly remarkable and professional piece of work. As co-editors, however, we accept full responsibility for any errors of fact.

As in all multi-authored, multi-subject publications, the task of producing an index can be a daunting and arduous task. We are most grateful to Annette Lorek of Infoplex Information Inc., Vancouver, BC, for undertaking this task.

We are indebted to the Friends of the Royal British Columbia Museum for their financial support of this publication. This support includes grants for editorial assistance provided by Kathryn Bernick. BC Parks provided much of the funding to publish the volume.

Mona Holley (editor, Occasional Paper Series), Patti Findlay and Nancy Chave of BC Parks put together the final form of the volume. To them we owe a great debt of thanks for completing this difficult task. BC Parks played the critical role in the final appearance of the Brooks Peninsula volume by providing the funds for its publication in the Occasional Paper Series. This support was augmented by funds from the Forest Renewal British Columbia (FRBC) Biodiversity Publications initiative. We thank Rob Cannings (RBCM) and Evelyn Hamilton, Ministry of Forests, for their efforts on our behalf.

Chapter 1

Brooks Peninsula Refugium Project

Richard J. Hebda[a]
James C. Haggarty[b]
Richard I. Inglis[c]

[a] Botany and Earth History, Royal British Columbia Museum
Victoria, BC and
Biology and School of Earth and Ocean Sciences, University of Victoria
Victoria, BC
[b] Shoreline Archaeological Services Inc.
Victoria, BC
[c] Ministry of Aboriginal Affairs
Victoria, BC

Abstract

Brooks Peninsula, Vancouver Island, British Columbia, exhibits physical and biological characteristics of a region which may have escaped the last glaciation. Its high peaks perch at the edge of the continental shelf, near the limit of the last ice sheet, and support rare endemic plant species. Historically the area has received little study. A multidisciplinary research team from the Royal British Columbia Museum, government agencies, universities and the private sector collected specimens and data on the human and natural history of the peninsula. The objectives of the expedition were to determine the age of the land surface and describe its environmental history, determine the degree to which the plant and animal populations differ from adjacent glaciated areas, and document past use of the landscape by people. This volume presents results on the bedrock and Quaternary geology and soils, vascular and non-vascular plants, cytogeography, vegetation and late Quaternary paleoecology, invertebrate and vertebrate fauna, archaeology and ethnographic history. Each contribution discusses the significance of results with respect to the question of a glacial refugium on the peninsula. Two concluding chapters consider the question of a refugium on the basis of the collective results and interpretations, and highlight the value of expeditions in museum research.

Acknowledgements

We thank Laurance Donovan, Okanagan University College, for comments on this chapter and Mona Holley, BC Parks, for information on provincial park status. Brian Young, BC Archives and

Records Service, helped get Figure 1.5 and Jo Matthews, Public Records Office, Great Britain, acquired Figures 1.3 and 1.4.

Introduction

For hundreds of years museums have dispatched expeditions to distant lands in quest of specimens either to be stored in musty basements for eventual study or to be displayed to the curious public. The objective of many expeditions was to discover and retrieve strange and exotic creatures, plants or objects isolated and forgotten in mythical lost worlds. These areas, whether they were high plateaus, mountain valleys or distant islands inexorably drew scientists with the thrill of adventure and discovery—the anticipation of being the first to see, record and collect an entity unknown to science. Even today in a world shrunken by intercontinental air travel such "lost worlds" still exist. One of these, virtually on our own doorstep, is the Brooks Peninsula of northwest Vancouver Island (Figure 1.1).

Brooks Peninsula qualifies well as a classic lost sector of the globe. It is geographically isolated, has a spectacular landscape (Figure 1.2), and is currently uninhabited. The nearest roads end many miles away blocked by rugged mountains, forests, and fiords. Access is by boat, float plane, or helicopter, only if fog and winds permit.

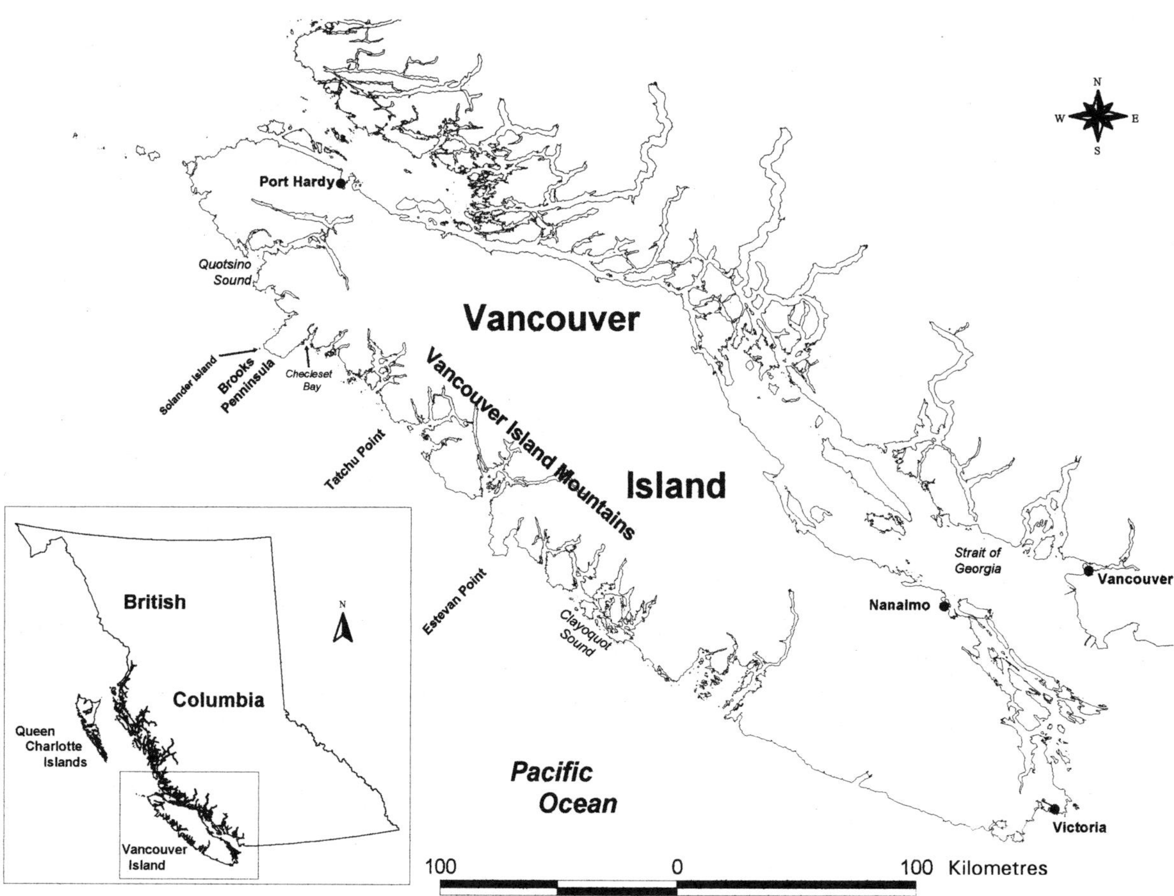

Figure 1.1 Vancouver Island showing the location of Brooks Peninsula

Figure 1.2 View of Brooks Peninsula (Photo: R.J. Hebda)

The peninsula consists of a craggy range of mountains which protrude into the Pacific Ocean from Vancouver Island. On the west shore the slopes plunge into the ocean scarcely leaving a foothold upon which to land. The north slope drops abruptly to an irregular lowland before diving under the sea. Conifer forests clothe the peninsula except on the windblown peaks and on the lowlands of the north shore where respectively subalpine heaths and boglands occur.

Traces of historic activity are restricted to remnants of a few decaying cabins of long-forgotten trappers and prospectors and a few abandoned hearths. There are only shadows of an earlier native occupation—a low shoreline terrace, shells eroding from a bank, planks in a cave.

It is the isolation of the peninsula, however, that is of major scientific interest. Its geographic position and imposing terrain suggest that it may have escaped the last or Vashon ice advance of the Fraser glaciation. Brooks Peninsula might have served as a glacial refuge and preserved plants, animals, and traces of human activity from a time before northwestern North America was scraped clear by ice 15 000 years ago.

Non-Aboriginal History

As far as the authors know, the first recorded European sighting of Brooks Peninsula was on the morning of 29 March 1778. As Captain James Cook approached Vancouver Island from the southwest, he perceived a bay demarcated by two points of land. The point to the south, which he named "Breakers Point", is known today as Estevan Point (Figure 1.1). Cook wrote that the point to the north "projects pretty much out to the SW and is high land" (Beaglehole ed. 1967: 294). This point he named "Woody Point"; today we call it Cape Cook on the Brooks Peninsula.

Brooks Peninsula is a prominent coastal feature, hence it serves as an ideal landmark for mariners. Following Cook's footsteps, many maritime traders encountered Brooks Peninsula. In September 1786, George Dixon on the *Queen Charlotte* named today's Solander Island as "Split Rock". James Colnett, captain of the *Princess of Wales* and Charles Duncan commanding the *Princess Royal* explored the region in 1787 (Colnett, 1788). Notably, Colnett named the waters off the south shore as Port Brooks, after one of his expedition's supporters and prepared three coastal profiles and one chart (Figures 1.3 and 1.4). From that time on the name "Brooks" became associated with the area.

Figure 1.3 Profile of Brooks Peninsula (Split Rock off Woody Point) drawn by James Colnett, Captain of the Princess of Wales in 1787 (Colnett 1788: 131)

Curiously, the name Port Brooks or Brooks Bay, as it is now known, applies to the north side of Brooks Peninsula. How this change occurred is not clear, but by the early 1790s both British and Spanish maps (Figure 1.5) had transposed Port Brooks to the north side of the peninsula[1]. The first accurate maps of the area were made by Captain George Richards aboard *HMS Hecate* during 1862, 1863. He formally assigned the name, Brooks Peninsula, to our study area, as well as several place names in current use (Great Britain, Admiralty Hydrographic Office 1865, 1866).

In the 1790s American trading ships[2] visited Columbia's Cove, located on the south shore of Brooks Peninsula, because it was well protected and presented a good beach for hauling out

[1] One of Colnett's unpublished maps has Woody Point located south of Brooks Peninsula in the area of Tatchu Point, and Split Rock off a large peninsula to the north. This may be the source of the error copied by both British and Spanish cartographers.

[2] The *Columbia* in 1791 and 1792, the *Adventure* in 1792, the *Margaret* in 1794 and the *Union* in 1795.

Figure 1.4 Profile of Brooks Peninsula (entrance to Port Brooks) drawn by James Colnett captain of the *Princess of Wales* in 1787 (Colnett 1788: 130)

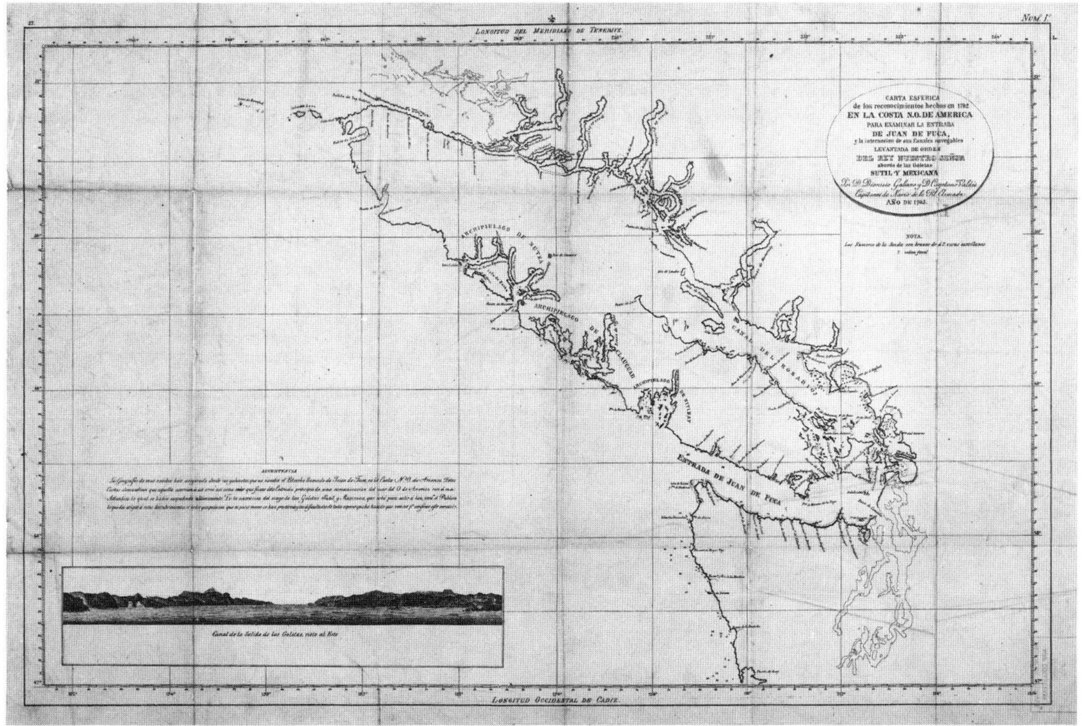

Figure 1.5 A 1795 Spanish map showing the waters to the north of Cabo Frondoso (Woody Point) ón Brooks Peninsula as "Puerto Bruks" (Galiano and Cayelano Valdes 1795)

vessels for repair[3]. The cove was also relatively remote from native settlement. The Americans obtained sea otter pelts and land mammal furs from the local inhabitants in exchange for copper, iron, and cloth. Beads, fishhooks and other trinkets were exchanged for foodstuffs.

For much of the 1800s, there are few references to Brooks Peninsula. Toward the end of the century and into the early 1900s the area was perhaps best known as part of the "Graveyard of the Pacific". The barque *Thos. R. Foster* was beached near Cape Cook in 1886 (Nicholson 1962). The crew survived for 21 days on mussels, crows, mice and seaweed until they were rescued by the Chicklesaht people (Canada, Department of Indian Affairs 1890). Less fortunate were 36 of the 61 people on board the whaling schooner *Jane Gray* who perished off Cape Cook in 1893 (Nicholson 1962). The government constructed an emergency shelter, at a place today known locally as "shelter sheds" by the locals, in a small bight east of Clerke Point. The rough, unpredictable waters of Brooks Peninsula continue to claim mariners' lives.

Interest in Brooks Peninsula was rekindled by mineral exploration at the turn of this century. In 1899 an extensive iron capping was discovered near Cape Cook, but never exploited (British Columbia, Mines Department 1900). In 1913, Messrs. Moerman, Falconer, Jackson, Nordstrom, H. Malmberg and A. Malmberg apparently prospected for gold near Cape Cook and six mining leases were staked on Amos and Gold Creeks (British Columbia, Mines Department 1915:283). Mineral exploration on Brooks Peninsula continued almost to the present without success.

Aside from occasional visits by fishermen, trappers, mainly from Quatsino Sound, have been the principal users of the peninsula in the 20th century. Alfred Ilstead and his father trapped, especially for mink, and built a cabin at Cape Cook Lagoon (A. Ilstead personal communication, April 1981). In the 1980s there was a small independent logging operation at Johnson Lagoon.

Preliminary plant collections from the peninsula in the 1970s led to an ecological reserve proposal for the unique upland and bog ecosystems. A provincial recreation area was created on the peninsula in 1986, and this was upgraded to a provincial park in 1995.

The lack of historic human visitation and use of Brooks Peninsula has left it as an ideal place for the study of landscapes and biota in their natural state. These attributes further enhanced the value of the Brooks Peninsula as the destination for a museum expedition.

Glacial Refugia

The continental glaciations of the last 70 000 years and their climatic and geomorphic after-effects obliterated life from huge areas of the globe. Most affected were the biota of northern climates—arctic, subarctic, boreal, and cool temperate regions—where the ice sheets were centered. Yet upon retreat of the ice a well-developed northern biota rapidly occupied vast stretches of newly emergent terrain.

Many of these organisms survived, or found refuge, in patches of suitable habitat south of the ice margins called "gross refugia" by Lindroth (1969). In North America such refugia would likely have occurred in the Cordillera, in the Appalachians, in disjunct pockets along the ice-front in the centre of the continent, and possibly on now inundated continental shelves. From these refugia,

---

3 In 1791, Captain Gray of the *Columbia* intended to use this anchorage as his winter quarters. Adverse winds prevented him from approaching the harbour, forcing him to choose Adventure Cove on Meares Island, Clayoquot Sound instead.

populations expanded and evolved to colonize newly available landscapes as ice melted. These gross refugia were open to invasion and change receiving an "uninterrupted influx" of species, species more or less in the mainstream of biotic action (Lindroth 1969).

The concept of a second type of refugium, an unglaciated "closed refugium" within the northern ice caps, was advanced by Scandinavian botanists (Lindroth 1969; Ives 1974). Plants and animals survived either on peaks, called nunataks[4], which poked above the ice surface or in sections of the coast missed by the continental ice sheet, called coastal refugia. The role of these refugia in the postglacial development of northern ecosystems is not yet clear, but the concept of these unglaciated "islands" explained disjunct patterns of distribution for arctic-subarctic species (Ives 1974).

Fernald (1925) proposed "closed refugia" in eastern North America to explain plant distributions. More recently the concept of a "closed refugium" was applied to the Queen Charlotte Islands to explain the occurrence of plants (Calder and Taylor 1968) and endemic animals (Foster 1965). The Queen Charlotte Islands had characteristics of both a "coastal refugium" perched at the edge of the continental ice-sheet and a "nunatak" with high peaks that likely rose above the ice surface.

It was these geographic and physiographic characteristics that led W.H. Mathews, Department of Geological Sciences, University of British Columbia, to identify the Brooks Peninsula as a possible glacial refugium. To test this supposition, W.B. Schofield, also of the University of British Columbia, sent four botanists (R. Hebda, G. Godfrey, J.D. Godfrey, J. Pinder-Moss) to Brooks Peninsula to collect bryophytes and vascular plants in July 1975. The plant specimens collected and geomorphic observations made during this trip clearly indicated that certain aspects of the Brooks Peninsula were peculiar. Significant collections included *Ligusticum calderi* Mathias and Constance (Calder's lovage), at that time known only as an endemic of the Queen Charlotte Islands and Banks Island along the coast, *Gentiana platypetala* Griseb. (broad-petalled gentian) a first record on Vancouver Island, and the type specimen of a new species of liverwort *Jungermania schusterana* (Godfrey and Godfrey 1979).

During the next five years further visits were made by British Columbia botanists to determine more precisely the nature of the flora and vegetation of Brooks Peninsula and to assess the suitability of the peninsula as an ecological reserve. More of the Queen Charlotte Island endemic plant species were found, strongly suggesting that the Brooks Peninsula was indeed a glacial refugium.

The Expedition

In 1980, Richard Hebda, a member of the 1975 botanical field trip, broached the idea of a return visit to the Brooks Peninsula with Jim Haggarty of the Archaeology Division, British Columbia Provincial Museum (now Royal British Columbia Museum). He suggested that a proposal be prepared for the Friends of the British Columbia Provincial Museum (now Friends of the Royal British Columbia Museum or FORM) for a large-scale, inter-disciplinary expedition to study in detail this unique area. The focus of the expedition would be to determine whether the Brooks Peninsula, or parts of it, escaped glaciation during the last major ice advance on the coast. During the last 60 000 years, ice accumulated to various depths, then melted several times (Clague 1981). The most widespread of these glaciations, known as the Vashon advance, occurred between about 12 000 and 17 000 years ago (Clague 1981; Hicock et al. 1982).

---

4 "Nunatak" is an Eskimo term for a mountain peak that is surrounded completely by glacial ice (see Ives 1974).

Concept and Objectives

The general objectives of the project were to:

1. collect geological and paleoecological data that would determine the age of the land surface and record the environmental history of the peninsula,
2. collect biological specimens to determine the degree to which Brooks Peninsula populations differed from surrounding glaciated areas, and
3. document past use of the landscape by people.

The range of expertise required to achieve these objectives was available, for the most part, at the British Columbia Provincial Museum. Additional expertise was solicited from organizations and agencies with specific research expertise or experience on and around the Brooks Peninsula. Table 1.1 lists participants on the Brooks Peninsula Refugium Project.

Table 1.1 Participants on the 1981 Brooks Peninsula refugium project

Participant	Affiliation at Time of Expedition	Specialization
Allen Banner	BC Ministry of Forests	Botany
Ross Brand	Royal British Columbia Museum	Logistics
R. Wayne Campbell	Royal British Columbia Museum[a]	Vertebrate Zoology
Robert A. Cannings	Royal British Columbia Museum	Entomology
Sydney G. Cannings	University of British Columbia[b]	Entomology
C.C. Chinnappa	University of Calgary	Botany, Cytology
John Cooper	Royal British Columbia Museum[c]	Vertebrate Zoology
Mary-Lou Florian	Royal British Columbia Museum	Conservation, Logistics
R. Yorke Edwards	Royal British Columbia Museum	Vertebrate Zoology
James C. Haggarty	Royal British Columbia Museum[d]	Archaeology
Richard J. Hebda	Royal British Columbia Museum	Paleoecology, Botany
Donald E. Howes	BC Environment[e]	Geology
Grant Hughes	Royal British Columbia Museum	Aquatic Zoology
Richard I. Inglis	Royal British Columbia Museum[f]	Archaeology
Louis Kirk	Private Consultant	Filmmaker
Ruth Kirk	Private Consultant	Filmmaker
William H. Mathewes	University of British Columbia	Geology
Robert Maxwell	BC Environment	Pedology
Robert T. Ogilvie	Royal British Columbia Museum	Botany, Ecology
Hans Roemer	BC Parks	Botany, Ecology
Wilfred B. Schofield	University of British Columbia	Botany, Ecology
Bjorn O. Simonsen	Private Consultant	Base camp co-ordinator
Elizabeth Taylor	Royal British Columbia Museum	Vertebrate Zoology

[a] Now with BC Environment.
[b] Now with BC Environment.
[c] Now a private consultant.
[d] Now with Shoreline Archaeological Services, Inc.
[f] Now with BC Land Use and Coordination Office.
[e] Now with BC Ministry of Aboriginal Affairs.

Assembly of this diverse team was part of another objective. We wanted to demonstrate that it was possible to put together an inter-disciplinary research team, based principally at the museum, to tackle problems of a broad scope. If this objective was achieved, further projects of similar scope could be attempted.

In addition to the general objectives of the project, individual participants were to achieve the following specific research objectives pertinent to their field of study:

1. core shallow lakes and bogs and generate a series of pollen profiles to reconstruct vegetation, environmental, and climatic history (Hebda),
2. survey and map terrain features to determine:
   a) extent of glacial activity,
   b) extent of possible non-glacial terrain, and
   c) terrain context of organic deposits and features (Howes, Mathews),
3. survey and describe soils of selected areas to:
   a) document soil relationships,
   b) identify possible paleosols, and
   c) determine age of soils (Maxwell),
4. collect materials suitable for radiocarbon dating from:
   a) organic sediment sequences (lake sediments, bogs), and
   b) geomorphic features associated with glacial history, and past sea levels (Howes, Mathews, Hebda),
5. locate and record native archaeological sites:
   a) along the present shoreline, and
   b) at selected inland locations related to higher sea levels (Haggarty, Inglis),
6. collect botanical specimens to:
   a) expand known vascular plant collections (Ogilvie, Roemer),
   b) expand known bryophyte collections (Schofield, Hebda),
   c) determine frequency and extent of populations of rare and endemic species (Ogilvie, Roemer, Banner),
   d) compare Brooks Peninsula flora to that of high peaks of adjacent western Vancouver Island (Ogilvie, Roemer), and
   e) investigate the role of geological substrates, such as limestones, associated with concentrations of Queen Charlotte Island disjunct and endemic plants (Roemer, Ogilvie),
7. study plant chromosome numbers and structure to:
   a) determine if differences exist between north Vancouver Island populations and those on the peninsula, and
   b) establish whether peninsula populations have long been separated from other populations during the latest ice advance (Chinnappa),
8. compile a generalized description of vegetation from aerial photos and ground reconnaissance (Banner, Hebda, Ogilvie, Roemer),
9. observe, record, and collect zoological specimens for comparative study to:
   a) compile a species inventory for the Brooks Peninsula,
   b) determine if small rodent, reptile, and amphibian populations differ from those of adjacent Vancouver Island, and
   c) inventory and describe small fishes (particularly sticklebacks) and aquatic invertebrates (other than insects), with the purpose of looking for endemic taxa (Hughes, Edwards, Campbell, Cooper, Taylor),
10. collect insects and related arthropods from plant and freshwater communities to:
    a) augment collections of outer coast arthropods,

b) determine extent of possible endemic forms, especially those that have low rates of dispersal (e.g., soil organisms, carabid beetles), and

c) determine if any unusual insects are associated with rare or endemic plants (R. Cannings, S. Cannings),

11. prepare a photographic record of the Brooks Peninsula area, including landforms, biota, and past human use and photograph specific activities of the project (R. Kirk, L. Kirk).

Funding

In some respects, funding of the Brooks Peninsula Refugium Project was as unique as the project itself. Total estimated cost for the project was approximately $250 000. This figure reflects both field and laboratory costs, including the writing of final reports for publication, and salary estimates for all participants. With good organization and efficient scheduling of activities during the field work, we believed that we could undertake the project with core funding of approximately $24 000 or 9% of the total estimated cost of the project. All other costs were to be borne by the participants' institutions or agencies. The Friends of the British Columbia Provincial Museum awarded a research grant to the project co-directors to cover costs that could not be borne by a single museum division or institution. This grant was to cover only those expenses that would be shared by all participants and, as such, made the project possible.

Field Strategy

The scope and diversity of the Brooks Peninsula expedition required an efficient, well organized logistic strategy. In April 1981, project co-directors (Haggarty and Hebda), along with Richard I. Inglis, visited Brooks Peninsula to determine a suitable location for the base camp and possible subcamps. A videotape record was made of the Brooks Peninsula shoreline and selected inland terrain. The aerial survey identified obvious archaeological sites and likely localities for paleoecological study. The advance survey helped estimate travel time to and from the peninsula and between selected points on the peninsula.

Preliminary preparations such as ordering and packing food and equipment were carried out in July. Upon arrival on Brooks Peninsula in late July a base camp was established adjacent to Cape Cook Lagoon on the northwest shore of the peninsula. Researchers established short-term upland camps at strategic locations, as required for their specific projects.

Transportation of personnel and equipment to and from the base camp was by power launch or helicopter, and from the base camp to upland camps by helicopter. Shoreline surveys were carried out by inflatable boat operating out of the base camp. Temporary shoreline subcamps were established, as required.

All research personnel were in radio communication with base camp from temporary camps at regular, specified intervals. A full-time logistics coordinator/cook was stationed at base camp during the project. The coordinator maintained regular contact with field parties and the museum. A weekly helicopter link was established with Port Hardy. The last people left in late August, ensuring the camp area was left in a natural state. Upon completion of the field phase, a joint meeting was planned in Victoria to discuss the expedition and to begin preparation of participant summaries of research activities and detailed reports.

The expedition grant provided the funding necessary in four major categories: transportation, communication equipment, food and camp supplies, and salary for a base camp coordinator/ cook. The major expense of the project was for helicopter time. Brooks Peninsula is extremely rugged with dense coastal forest at low elevation. Whereas helicopter trips may last only 10 minutes, hiking to study localities, especially at the tip of the peninsula, requires at least a day. Heavy equipment, such as coring devices and animal traps, needed to be transported to specific locations.

The isolation, rugged terrain, and numerous mobile parties made an effective radio communication system mandatory. The system employed enabled the participants to use helicopter and working time efficiently and to provide a quick response in case of emergency. Low cloud, fog, and rough seas often disrupted established plans, so the team needed the ability to communicate rapidly and to alter arrangements when necessary. Also for safety reasons, project personnel did not work alone in the isolated environment of Brooks Peninsula. Researchers travelled in groups of two or more people.

The short duration and intense research activity of the expedition required assistance at base camp. The team worked 14 to 16 hour days collecting specimens and data during daylight and packaging material in the evenings. Biological material required particularly rapid attention.

The coordinator's position was crucial to the success of the expedition. Research participants were very mobile and frequently away from base camp for several days. Regular communication with base camp helped coordinate activities and efficient use of transport. The coordinator also cooked meals for up to 15 researchers per sitting. This task required wise organization and planning in advance of the field operation.

Place Names

Brooks Peninsula, due to its uninhabited state, had few gazetted place names. This at first may not seem to be a serious problem. However, at a practical level it means that there was no simple way of communicating where a person or party was, or where a collection was made.

In advance of the expedition, a set of names derived from plant genera, mainly in the Heather family (Ericaceae), was prepared by R. Hebda for all the principal geographic features (Figure 1.6). Heather family plants predominate in many habitats on Brooks Peninsula and seemed appropriate to use. Names were copied onto maps for use of participants. The study area also was divided into 5 km by 5 km quadrants, each with its own name so that positions could be referred to by quadrant if there was no named feature nearby to serve as a reference point.

Several informal names were applied during the expedition. These names usually related to the occurrence of a plant or animal at a specific site. During the analytical and writing stages of the project it was realized that the place names needed to be registered in the British Columbia Gazetteer. In the process of doing this a few unrecorded local names in use and one non-gazetted, native name were uncovered. These place names (the native name translated approximately into English) were submitted to the gazetteer. Many of the names are now formally accepted and published in the gazetteer of British Columbia place names (Canadian Permanent Committee on Geographical Names 1985) and appear on the current National Topographic Series map for Brooks Peninsula. These names are used consistently throughout the text. Individual authors use several informal names for the convenience of precise reference. These names are for features too small to merit formal publication and are indicated on maps in the appropriate chapters.

Organization and Content

Following the introduction, three chapters describe and interpret the physical environment of Brooks Peninsula. Chapter 2, Geology of the Brooks Peninsula, outlines the characteristics of the

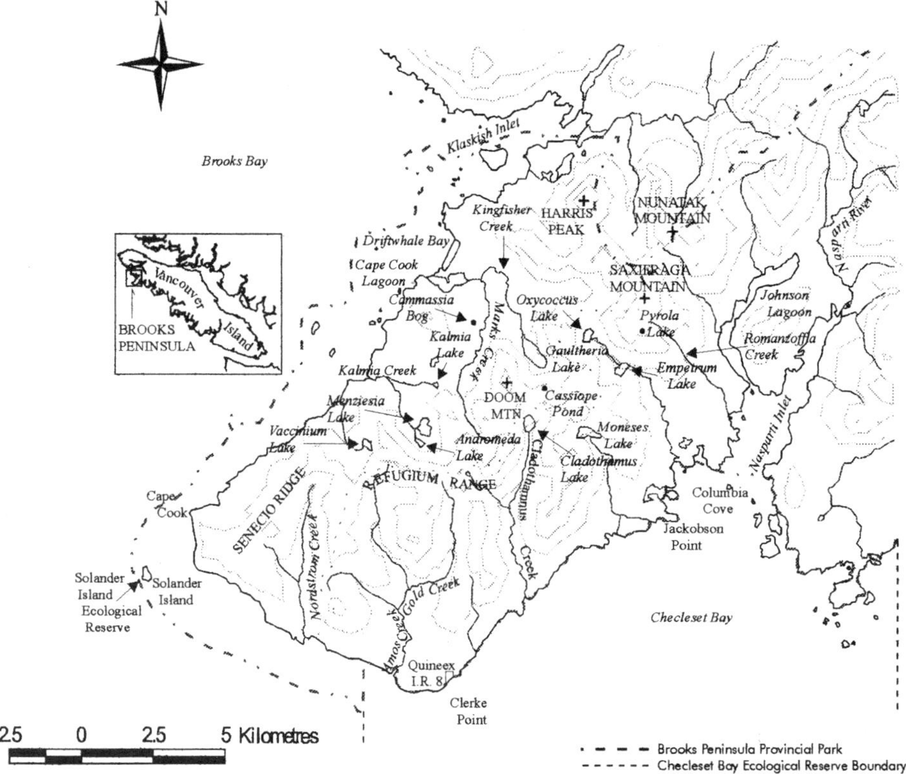

Figure 1.6 Place names of Brooks Peninsula

bedrock, discusses its history and comments on aspects of economic potential. This chapter is based on work in 1984, after the original expedition, by Ron Smyth. It explains why Brooks Peninsula is there, and describes the stage upon which more recent physical and biological developments took place.

Chapter 3, Quaternary Geology of Brooks Peninsula by Don Howes, addresses directly the question of a glacial refugium from the perspective of surface features, sediments, and their relative and absolute ages. Howes includes an outline of the regional Quaternary history which provides a framework within which to interpret the Brooks Peninsula story. Included is a detailed description of landform features and surficial sediments studied during the course of the project. Using these observations and theoretical considerations, Howes outlines the possible extent of glaciation on the peninsula. An overview of the peninsula's Quaternary history of the area follows.

Finally, the controversial question of a refugium and its possible extent is discussed. The chapter serves to set the physical stage on which biological and cultural events were played out to yield today's plant, animal and human distributions.

The chapter on Quaternary history provides the setting for Chapter 4, a descriptive account of the soils of Brooks Peninsula by Bob Maxwell. Soils, the product of the interaction between physical (land surface, climate) and biologic components of the environment, not only provide insight into plant and animal distribution today, but also record aspects of the history of the landscape.

After setting out the principles and methods used in the study of Brooks Peninsula soils, Maxwell describes the soils as they developed along the lowland landscape of Brooks Peninsula focusing on the nature of the underlying or parent material and on the age of soil profiles. Next, the nature of soil landscapes is discussed to provide a basis of soil descriptions from the high elevations of the central ridge of Brooks Peninsula. These unusual soils form the basis for the conclusions drawn regarding the question of a possible glacial refugium. The chapter concludes with a brief discussion of anthropogenic soils—soils formed under the influence of human activity. These are of significance because they occur in scattered locations along the shore in direct association with past sites of human activity.

The vascular plants of Brooks Peninsula are described by Bob Ogilvie in Chapter 5, the first of biological contributions. The list includes species of various postulated origins. Ogilvie also addresses geographical aspects of the flora (phytogeography), such as to what geographical element the individual species belong and what geographical elements are represented. Following this "floristic" analysis, which provides insight into the origin of the flora, the implications for a refugium are discussed.

Chromosome numbers of plants provide important insight into the geographic and evolutionary origins of the plants and their degree of isolation from other populations of the same or similar species. In Chapter 6, C.C. Chinnappa presents the results of chromosome studies of plants collected from the peninsula. This study, although not extensive, reveals features of the vascular flora which bear on the issue of a glacial refugium.

Chapter 7 consists of a list of mosses and liverworts compiled by Wilf Schofield, University of British Columbia. This list is based on material from his own collections on Brooks Peninsula and from the collections of others.

The vegetation of Brooks Peninsula, described in Chapter 8 by Richard Hebda, Bob Ogilvie, Hans Roemer and Allen Banner, has several distinctive characteristics because of the peninsula's exposed oceanic setting and because of the presence of several rare plants. The account begins with descriptions of the physical setting and the climate of the area. After a summary of the regional vegetation, Hebda, et al. discuss the problems of classifying Brooks Peninsula plant communities and explain the classification system. Each vegetation category, beginning with the most broad type and working down to the smallest recognizable unit, is described in detail. Each description includes a commentary on characteristic plants, layer by layer (stratum by stratum), derived from hundreds of field observations, and an account of the ecological factors responsible for the structure and composition of the vegetation unit. Brooks Peninsula plant communities are compared and contrasted with those of adjacent areas. The chapter concludes with a discussion of the vegetation character and pattern with respect to the question of a glacial refugium.

Chapter 9, by Richard Hebda examines the late Quaternary history of the environment (landscapes) on Brooks Peninsula. As with most of the chapters the story begins with an account of the regional framework. The setting of five principle study sites is described with emphasis on local vegetation. Following, there is an account for each site of the sediments and their age. The chapter consists mainly of descriptions and interpretation of the sequence of pollen and plant macrofossil assemblages at each site. These results and interpretations serve as the basis for describing the Late Quaternary environmental history of Brooks Peninsula. This history is then considered within the regional framework and the question of a glacial refugium.

In Chapter 10 the volume returns to the present and examines animal life of the peninsula. Rob and Syd Cannings describe and discuss the terrestrial anthropods of the area. Results generated by two weeks of field collecting and subsequent identification by North American experts, serve as the basis for an annotated list of arthropod species. Annotations include collection locality, habitat data, specimen and other information. The data are used to describe arthropod communities of the peninsula. Several new taxa and major range extensions are noted and discussed. Dragonflies receive special attention because of the expertise of the authors. The characteristics of the terrestrial arthropod fauna are used at the end of the chapter to consider questions of glacial refugia in general and the possibility of such a refugium on Brooks Peninsula.

From insects the volume moves to fishes in Chapter 11. The fish fauna of freshwater and inshore marine habitats was sampled and studied by Grant Hughes. The chapter begins with a discussion of endemism in freshwater fish with particular reference to northwestern North America. After a brief explanation of methods, Hughes gives measurements for numerous anatomical and morphological features for freshwater fishes. He uses the results to discuss the question of a glacial refugium from the perspective of the fish fauna and to suggest the origins of the freshwater fish fauna of Brooks Peninsula.

Wayne Campbell, Yorke Edwards, Elizabeth Taylor, and John Cooper observed the vertebrates of Brooks Peninsula and adjacent lands during the 1981 expedition. In Chapter 12, Wayne Campbell and Keith Summers of Aldergrove, British Columbia compile and analyze the results from 1981 and observations made during other visits. There is a comprehensive annotated list of vertebrate species including reptiles, amphibians, birds, and mammals of Brooks Peninsula and immediately adjacent areas. Each species entry includes comments on seasonal status, and specific occurrence. Also, there are observations of the biology of selected local species. Campbell and Summers address the characteristics of the vertebrate fauna with emphasis on species range. The relationship of vertebrate fauna to the question of refugia is discussed in general terms in the context of the coastal northwest North America setting. An assessment of the Brooks Peninsula fauna with respect to the refugium issue follows.

Chapter 13, by Richard Inglis, describes the ethnographic history of the Brooks Peninsula region. During the late 1700s and early 1800s significant political changes occurred among the peoples of the area, brought on by disease and indigenous warfare. By the end of the 1800s only two peoples occupied the area, the Kwakwala speaking Klaskino and the Nootka speaking Chicklesaht. Cape Cook on the tip of the peninsula was the recognized boundary.

Chapter 14, by Jim Haggarty and Richard Inglis describes the archaeology of the Brooks Peninsula region, including the research design and survey methods employed on shoreline and inland areas. Archaeological sites found and recorded during the study are classified by site type and described in detail. Site data from Brooks Peninsula are incorporated with site survey results obtained during an overview survey of the Chicklesaht area in 1984 to provide a regional perspective for understanding Chicklesaht settlement. Limited discussion on the role archaeological data may play in addressing the question of a glacial refugium is presented.

The final two chapters concern the principal objectives of the project. Chapter 15 addresses the question of whether or not all or part of Brooks Peninsula functioned as a glacial refugium. Evidence for and against the glacial refugium question is marshalled so that readers may draw their own conclusions. One view on the question is provided after weighing the evidence. Some of the problems inherent in trying to establish whether an area was or was not a glacial refugium are discussed. The issue of how long such an area may have been a refugium is considered. The chapter concludes with suggestions for future study on Brooks Peninsula and adjacent areas, in particular emphasizing those studies which might yield critical information.

In the final Chapter 16, the second objective, centred on museum expeditions and interdisciplinary research, is addressed. Several aspects of such projects are evaluated from the perspective of the experience of the 1981 expedition and subsequent activity. Budget, logistics, setting goals and objectives, and communicating scientific results are examined. Consideration is given to the importance of interdisciplinary expeditions in making collections especially from scientifically unknown areas. Special attention is paid to the role of a principal research focus or question as part of an interdisciplinary study. The chapter addresses a less tangible but extremely important issue, that of the intellectual synergistic benefits of interdisciplinary studies and the costs of these in terms of organization and compromise.

The chapters that follow are each a technical contribution to the knowledge about Brooks Peninsula. Several chapters contain a glossary to help the non-specialist reader understand their technical content. Yet these descriptions are no more than a set of translations by humans of a remarkable physical and biological experiment. Think not of Latin names; think of trees, flowers, birds, mice and bugs. Think not of geological features and bedrock types; imagine instead graceful slopes, deep chasms, and barren rocks. Feel the wind, the rain, and see the mist sliding down a mountainside. Focus not on archaeological site numbers and stratigraphic descriptions, but imagine people, hunting, fishing, eating, talking...living their lives generation after generation for thousands of years.

As you read, try to envisage how all these wonderful things came to be. Do they owe their origins, in part, to some happenstance of geological history whereby they came to live on a land the ice-age missed?

References Cited

Beaglehole, J.C. (ed.). 1967. The journals of Captain James Cook. Vols. Cambridge University Press, Cambridge, MA.

British Columbia Mines Department. 1900. Report of Minister of Mines for the year 1899. Victoria, BC.

______ . 1915. Report of Minister of Mines for the year 1914. Victoria, BC.

Calder, J.A. and R.L. Taylor. 1968. Flora of the Queen Charlotte Islands. Part 1. Systematics of Vascular Plants. Can. Dept. Agric. Monogr. 4, Pt. 1.

Canada Department of Indian Affairs. 1890. Letters from Peter O'Reilly, Indian Reserve Commission, Victoria to L. Van Koughnet, Deputy Superintendent General of Indian Affairs, Ottawa re: Chicklesaht reserves. British Columbia Archives and Records Service (Victoria, BC), Microfilm RG10B-1393, file 1277. Pp. 289-291 (14 April 1890).

Canadian Permanent Committee on Geographical Names. 1985. Gazetteer of Canada. British Columbia. 3rd ed. Geographical Services Division, Surveys and Mapping Branch, Department of Energy, Mines and Resources Canada. Ottawa.

Clague, J.J. 1981. Late Quaternary geology and geochronology of British Columbia. Geological Survey of Canada, Paper 80-35. 41 pp.

Colnett, J. 1788. The log of the Prince of Wales 1786-1788. Adm. 55-146. Public Record Office, London, U.K. (Microfilm copy on file British Columbia Archives and Records Service. Victoria, BC.)

Fernald, M.L. 1925. Persistence of plants in unglaciated areas of boreal America. Memoir of the Gray Herbarium of Harvard University II. Cambridge, MA.

Foster, J.B. 1965. The evolution of the mammals of the Queen Charlotte Islands, British Columbia. BC Provincial Museum (Victoria, BC.) Occas. Paper 14.

Galiano, D.D. and D. Cayelano Valdes. 1795. Carta Esferica de los reconocimientos hechos en 1792 En la Costa N. O. de America para examinar la entrada de Juan de Fuca, y la internacion de sus Canales navegables Levantada de Orden del Rey Nuestro Señor abordo de las Goletas Sutil y Mexicana. Map.

Godfrey, J.D. and G.A. Godfrey. 1979. *Jungermannia schusterana*, a new hepatic from the Pacific coast of North America. J. Hattori Bot. Lab. 46: 109-117.

Great Britain, Admiralty Hydrographic Office. 1865. Klaskino and Klaskish inlets and anchorages surveyed by Captain G.H. Richards in 1862. Chart 590. Nautical scale 1:36, 480. Admiralty, London.

______ . 1866. Nasparti and Ou-ou-kinsh inlets. Surveyed by Captain G.H. Richards in 1863. Chart 716 scale 1:36, 480. Admiralty, London.

Hicock, S.R., R.J. Hebda and J.E. Armstrong. 1982. Lag of the Fraser glacial maximum in the Pacific Northwest: pollen and macrofossil evidence from western Fraser Lowland, British Columbia. Canadian Journal of Earth Sciences 19: 2288-2296.

Ives, J.D. 1974. Biological refugia and the nunatak hypothesis. Pp. 605-636 in J.D. Ives and R.G. Berry (eds.) Arctic and alpine environments. London. Methuen.

Lindroth, C.H. 1969. The biological importance of Pleistocene refugia. Pp. 7-17 in T.N.V. Karlstrom and G.E. Ball (eds.). The Kodiak Island refugium, its geology, flora, fauna and history. The Boreal Institute, University of Alberta, Edmonton, AB.

Nicholson, G. 1962. Vancouver Island's West Coast 1762-1962. George Nicholson, Victoria, BC.

Chapter 2

Bedrock Geology of Brooks Peninsula

W.R. Smyth
Geological Survey Branch, Ministry of Employment and Investment
Victoria, BC

Abstract

Brooks Peninsula, lying on the outermost edge of Vancouver Island, is underlain by two distinct rock units: an inboard unit of Jurassic (170 my) gneiss and associated igneous rocks, and an outboard unit of Cretaceous (130 my) melange (tectonic mixture) composed predominantly of oceanic sedimentary rocks. The contact between these two units is a major northwest-trending fault. The peninsula is separated from Vancouver Island by a second major fault, known as the Westcoast Fault, which can be traced along the west coast of the island. A small area of younger conglomerates and sandstones of Tertiary (40 my) age unconformably overlies the older rock units in the area of Quineex Indian Reserve 8 and represents the on-land edge of a thicker sedimentary basin that extends offshore from the peninsula. There has been no bedrock mining on Brooks Peninsula and few mineral occurrences are known, probably reflecting the area's isolation and inaccessibility. Placer gold occurs in gravels near the junction of Amos and Gold creeks. The gravels were worked in the 1910s but there are no records of production.

Introduction

The geology of an area and its geological structures, such as faults and fractures, play an important role in determining the topography of an area and in shaping plant and animal communities and their evolution.

This paper presents a basic description of the bedrock geology of Brooks Peninsula set within the context of the geological history of Vancouver Island. The distribution and character of the major rock units that underlie the peninsula are described.

General Geology of Vancouver Island

Most of Vancouver Island, including the inboard part of Brooks Peninsula, is part of a large exotic terrane, a far-travelled piece of the earth's crust. This terrane, known by geologists as Wrangellia, began to form 380 million years ago in what is now the deep eastern Pacific Ocean. It was brought from the southwest some 90 million years ago and pasted onto the outermost edge of ancient North America by plate tectonic processes.

The outermost tip of Brooks Peninsula comprises a younger terrane, named the Pacific Rim Terrane, that collided with Wrangellia some 70 million years ago. The contact between the two is a major fault zone. The terranes have vastly different rock types and probably formed at different times in widely separated areas.

Today the Wrangellia terrane stretches from Vancouver Island through the Queen Charlotte Islands into the Yukon and Alaska. It comprises three distinct periods of volcanic eruption built on each other to raise a land mass above the surface of the sea. In the long interludes between eruptions, limestone and sediments accumulated on the tops of the volcanoes. The Upper Paleozoic Sicker Group volcanics (~365 my) are the oldest rocks exposed on Vancouver Island. These volcanics probably formed on a volcanic island arc, like the Japan Archipelago. The volcanic rocks are overlain by thinly bedded sandstones and limestones. Deformed and metamorphosed equivalents of the Sicker Group are called "the Westcoast Complex" and, as the name implies, occur on the western margin of the island and on Brooks Peninsula (Muller et al. 1974).

Upper Triassic (220 my) Vancouver Group volcanics form a thick basaltic lava pile, dominated by pillowed flows at the base and massive flows at the top. It constitutes the main stratigraphic and structural unit on Vancouver Island. The lavas formed extensive flat plains or broad, gently sloping shield volcanoes like those on the islands of Hawaii. The lavas are succeeded by shallow-water limestones and shales.

The Lower Jurassic (200 my) Bonanza Group volcanics overlie the older rocks in the western part of the island, probably having formed as a continental arc. Subaerial intermediate to felsic pyroclastics predominate, though a lower marine facies is developed in several places. Voluminous granodioritic intrusions accompanied the volcanism comprising the Island Plutonic Suite and, where intimately mixed with older metamorphic rocks, the Westcoast Complex.

Conglomerates, sandstones, argillites, and coal measures of the Upper Cretaceous (80 my) Nanaimo Group accumulated in a fore-arc basin along the east side of Vancouver Island and unconformably overlie older sequences.

The structural fabric of Wrangellia shows a predominant northwesterly grain with the rocks folded into a series of geanticlinal culminations. The older fabric is disrupted by a system of steep, northeasterly dipping reverse faults.

The Pacific Rim Terrane occurs outboard of Wrangellia. It comprises a mixture of Upper Triassic to Lower Cretaceous marine sedimentary and volcanic rocks. On Brooks Peninsula, rocks of this terrane are named the "Pacific Rim Complex" and correlate with similar rocks exposed at Pacific Rim National Park. Stratigraphic and metamorphic evidence suggests that the Pacific Rim Terrane is related to sequences in the San Juan Islands and was emplaced along the western edge of Vancouver Island during Late Cretaceous to Paleocene (70 my-60 my) (Brandon 1985).

A younger terrane, the Crescent Terrane, underlies the Coast Ranges of Washington and Oregon to the south and outcrops on the southern tip of Vancouver Island. It consists of an oceanic complex that formed as an island in a probable transform marginal basin during the early Eocene (55 my) (Brandon and Massey 1985). Related basaltic lavas are known from drill hole and geophysical evidence to extend northwestwards offshore, where they are overlain by younger Eocene to Recent sediments of the Tofino basin. On-land expressions of these younger basinal sediments are thin and occur close to sea level, such as at Quineex Indian Reserve 8 on Brooks Peninsula. These offshore sediments were the focus of petroleum exploration in the late 1960s.

Outboard of the Crescent Terrane lies a plate of modern oceanic crust known as the Juan de Fuca plate. This plate is presently descending beneath Vancouver Island causing tectonic instability and uplift of the island, and volcanic activity farther inland (for example, at Mt. St. Helens, Mt. Baker, and Mt. Rainier in Washington, and at Mt. Meager in British Columbia). Seismic studies offshore and across Vancouver Island have imaged the descending slab, but have also revealed other layers of crust beneath Wrangellia. One interpretation is that the present situation of a slab of oceanic crust descending below Vancouver Island was mirrored in the past so that a vertical slice through Vancouver Island would reveal a slab of older oceanic rocks wedged beneath it. The major fault zone exposed near the tip of Brooks Peninsula may represent a fossilized contact zone between oceanic rocks of the Pacific Rim Terrane and older, melted and deformed rocks of the Westcoast Complex.

Detailed Geology of Brooks Peninsula

Brooks Peninsula is underlain by five distinct geological elements (Figure 2.1). From northeast to southeast these are:

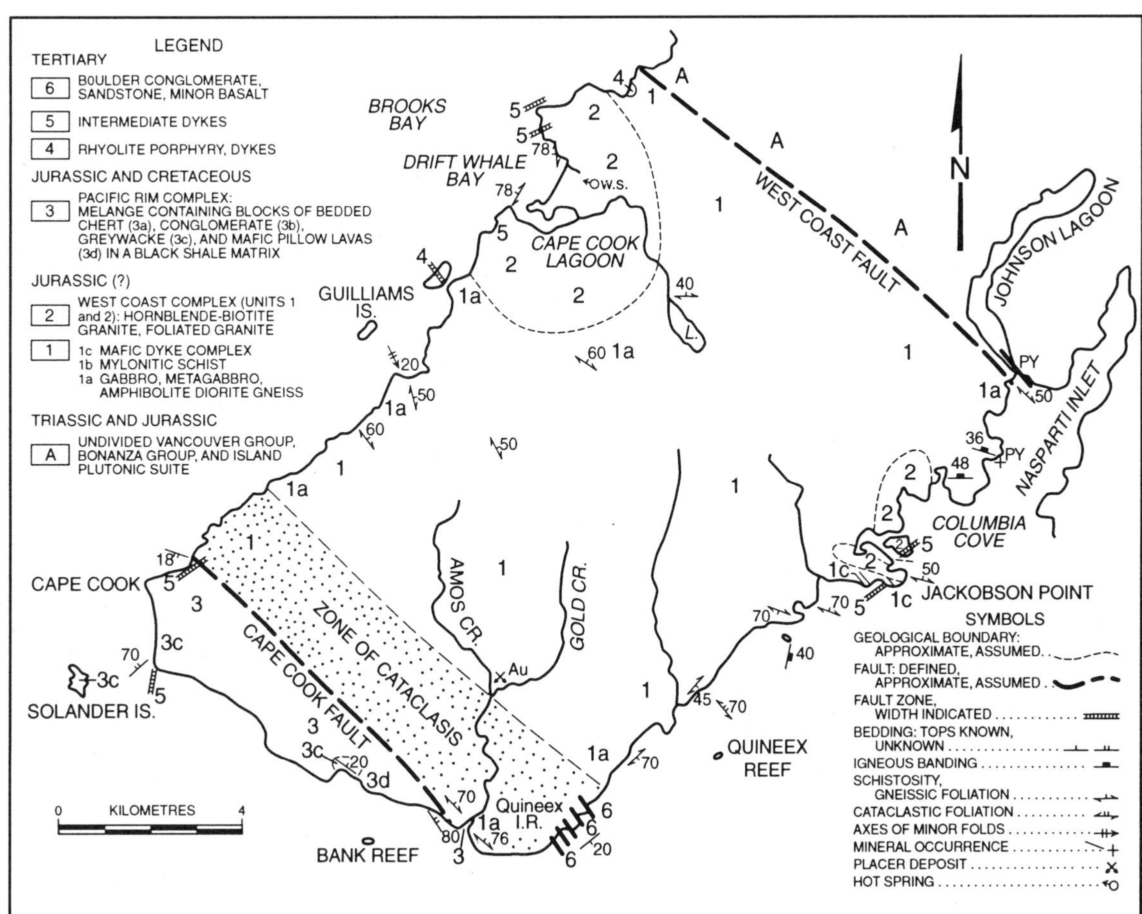

Figure 2.1 Geology of Brooks Peninsula

1) The Westcoast Fault. A major fault that separates the peninsula from Vancouver Island. The adjacent Vancouver Island area is underlain by rocks of the Wrangellia terrane; a sequence of Triassic and Jurassic volcanic and sedimentary rocks, and granitic rocks of the Island Plutonic Suite.
2) The Westcoast Complex. A variously deformed and metamorphosed mixture of gabbroic, dioritic, and granitic rocks that underlies 95% of the peninsula and represents the deeper levels or melted root zone of Wrangellia.
3) The Cape Cook Fault. A major northwest-trending structure that juxtaposes the Westcoast Complex and the outboard Pacific Rim Complex.
4) The Pacific Rim Complex. A mixture of oceanic slope and trench sedimentary and volcanic rocks confined to the outermost part of the peninsula.
5) Tertiary conglomerates and sandstones. These crop out on the southwest edge of the peninsula around Quineex Indian Reserve 8.

Westcoast Complex (Units 1 and 2)

"Westcoast Crystalline Complex" is the term proposed by Muller and Carson (1969) for a complex of amphibolite, basic migmatite, and gneissic quartz diorite and gabbro that outcrops on the west coast of Vancouver Island and in inlets in the Alberni map-area. Muller et al. (1974) subsequently applied the name to similar rocks that outcrop on Brooks Peninsula. Two rock units comprise the complex on the peninsula (units 1 and 2).

Unit 1: Gabbro, Metagabbro, Mylonitic Schists, and Mafic Dikes

Unit 1 consists of the non-granitic rocks of the Westcoast Complex. It comprises variably deformed and metamorphosed gabbro with minor amounts of schists and mafic dikes.

Undeformed to weakly deformed gabbro constitutes less than 10% of this unit. It is exposed mostly on the southeast side of the peninsula, away from the Westcoast Fault. A crude mineralogical banding, defined by a concentration of dark mafic minerals on a 3-5 cm scale, is developed locally on the north shore of Nasparti Inlet. The banding is discontinuous over two metres and may be the result of magmatic flowage differentiation.

In most places, the unit consists of foliated gabbros and amphibolites. In zones of high strain, such as south of Guilliams Island, they are converted to banded amphibolite gneiss. Migmatite and agmatite are locally developed adjacent to granitic intrusions as, for example, south of Cape Cook Lagoon.

The gabbros are everywhere intruded by granitoid dikes and pegmatites and, in at least two localities, by granitoid intrusions (unit 2) up to 4 km across. Foliated intrusion breccia with aligned xenoliths of gabbro is exposed at the northern contact of a granite stock at Columbia Cove.

A narrow unit (approximately 350 m) of banded mylonitic schist outcrops at the southern entrance to Columbia Cove. The mylonite varies in composition from granitic to calc-silicate. Thin amphibolite bands are also present. Isolated, lens-shaped granitic fragments up to 50 cm across occur in calc-silicate schists. These superficially resemble a metamorphosed conglomerate, but are more likely highly sheared and flattened intrusion breccia. The northern contact of the mylonitic schists is not exposed. The southern contact is obscured by a swarm of mafic dikes that cut the schists.

A narrow zone of fine-grained and porphyritic mafic dikes outcrops on the south shore of Jackobson Point. The dikes are undeformed to mildly deformed in contrast to the schists that they intrude. They trend 160° and are dark green, grey to black. Rare blocks of medium-grained gabbro are present.

Unit 2: Granitoid Intrusions

Numerous granitic dikes and pegmatites, and two granitoid intrusions cut unit 1. The intrusions are informally referred to as "Columbia Cove granite" and "Cape Cook Lagoon granite."

The Columbia Cove granite is medium- and coarse-grained, hornblende-biotite granite. It is massive in the centre, but towards the eastern contact with the gabbros a 25 m wide zone of intrusive breccia with a strong schistosity is developed.

The Cape Cook Lagoon granite is a deformed hornblende-biotite granite. It contains numerous aligned and flattened inclusions of gabbro, diorite, and pyroxenite, indicating syntectonic intrusion.

Locally, granitoid dikes are more deformed than the gabbro host rocks; they probably intruded into active shear or fault zones.

Pacific Rim Complex (Unit 3)

Muller et al. (1974) assigned the name "Pacific Rim Complex" to a highly disturbed and faulted sequence of argillite, greywacke, sandstone, and quartzite near Cape Cook. The unit is a melange containing isolated blocks or "knockers" set in a matrix of black and green shale. Some of the knockers are as large as 50 m across. The complex forms most of the southwest coast of Brooks Peninsula. The numerous rocks, reefs, and shoals that extend up to 1 km offshore are isolated, resistant knockers, standing above the eroded shale matrix.

A tectonic block containing bedded ribbon cherts is well-exposed on the coast about 1 km northeast of Cape Cook. The ribbon cherts occur in a sequence of greywacke, chert, breccia, and lesser black shale melange. The cherts are up to 20 m thick and are tightly and complexly folded. Individual ribbons are commonly 3-5 cm thick; they are separated by thin laminae of black argillite. The cherts are light-green to grey and weather white.

The greywackes that outcrop adjacent to the ribbon cherts and as knockers throughout the melange, are fine-grained, dark-green to grey, massive, and indistinctly bedded. Small rip-up clasts of black shale are common. Greywackes also underlie Solander Island (C. Yorath personal communication, 1984), which lies 2 km southwest of Cape Cook.

Knockers consisting of bedded and graded cobble conglomerate and sandstone occur in the melange 2 km south of Cape Cook. The clasts are subrounded and consist of sandstone, chert, black argillite, quartzite, gabbro, and granite. One large knocker 5 m across contains a sequence of beds—each up to 1 m thick—of sandstone, conglomerate, and black shale.

Blocks of mafic pillow lava occur in the melange on the shore north of Banks Reef. The melange also contains a thinly laminated, dark grey, fine-grained, calcareous siltstone towards the southern contact with the Cape Cook Fault. The siltstones are extensively brecciated close to the fault.

Rhyolite Porphyry and Dikes (Unit 4)

Two small, post-tectonic rhyolite porphyry intrusions cut the Westcoast Complex on the northwest coast of Brooks Peninsula. The top of a porphyritic rhyolite intrusion, 5 m across, cuts deformed gabbro south of the Westcoast Fault. The rhyolite is compositionally banded parallel to the domed contact. The rhyolite contains phenocrysts of quartz, K-feldspar, and biotite; it weathers white.

A 2 m wide, flow-banded porphyritic rhyolite dike cuts migmatic gneisses on a small island southwest of Cape Cook Lagoon. It is similar in composition to the rhyolite intrusion.

The rhyolites postdate major deformation and faulting in the area and are believed to be of Tertiary age.

Intermediate Dikes (Unit 5)

A number of northeast-trending, mafic to intermediate dikes cut both the Westcoast Complex and the Pacific Rim Complex. The dikes parallel the structural grain of the peninsula. The dikes are dark grey, fine-grained to porphyritic. These dikes are unaffected by the intense deformation associated with the Cape Cook Fault and are assumed to postdate the fault and be Tertiary in age. One such dike 2 km south of Cape Cook was dated by the potassium-argon dating method at 8.0 ± 0.7 million years (University of British Columbia).

Boulder Conglomerate, Sandstone, and Minor Basalt (Unit 6)

A thin sequence of cobble to boulder conglomerate that passed upwards into grits and sandstones unconformably overlies deformed gabbro of the Westcoast Crystalline Complex in the immediate vicinity of Quineex Indian Reserve 8.

The conglomerates are exposed at low tide in a narrow graben (approximately 25 m wide) that defines the Quineex canoe run as well as on islands and headlands 1 km to the northeast and 0.5 km to the southwest. The unit is undeformed, and beds dip 20° oceanward. Only about 50 m of strata are exposed.

The surface of the unconformity is exposed in many places and has a relief up to one metre. Boulders of gabbro breccia up to 1 m across occur on the unconformity surface. The conglomerate contains rounded cobbles and boulders of foliated gabbro, greenschist, granite, and cobbles and pebbles of rounded quartz.

A fine-grained, dark brown basalt flow or sill is interlayered with the basal conglomerate in the Quineex graben. The basalt is exposed at low tide and is at least 2 m thick. The basalt tongues into the underlying conglomerates, and isolated conglomerate fragments are caught up in the basalt.

The conglomerate is correlated with the Eocene/Oligocene Escalante Formation, which occupies a similar lithostratigraphic position in the Nootka Sound map-area 75 km to the south (Muller 1981). These outcrops on Brooks Peninsula are the most northerly known onshore exposures of this formation.

Structure

The Cape Cook Fault is a major structure in Brooks Peninsula. It separates the Pacific Rim Complex and the Westcoast Crystalline Complex and trends northwesterly across the southwest tip of the peninsula. The fault is exposed northwest of Amos Creek, where it is marked by tectonically interleaved thin slices of limestone and chert (which are up to 50 cm thick) with brecciated gabbros. At this locality, sedimentary rocks of the Pacific Rim Complex dip steeply to the northeast under the Westcoast Complex, and the gabbros of the Westcoast Complex are broken and brecciated. Extensive brecciation of the gabbros continues as far as 3 km from the fault. The breccias consist of angular fragments of gabbro, generally from 3 to 10 cm across, in a comminuted groundmass. This cataclasis, or deformation, is interpreted to have been caused by underthrusting of the Pacific Rim Complex beneath the Westcoast Complex.

The Westcoast Fault also trends northwest and is exposed at the entrance to Johnson Lagoon. It is marked by a 700 m wide zone of mylonitized, or deformed, granite. The mylonite dips moderately to the northwest. Brecciated and foliated gabbros and foliated greenschists of the Westcoast Complex are juxtaposed against the mylonite.

The dominant structures on Brooks Peninsula are a series of northeast trending faults and fractures that extend across Vancouver Island and are collectively known as the Brooks Peninsula Fault Zone. The fault zone is best observed on satellite imagery and is not easily identified on the ground. Displacement on the faults is small and essentially vertical. The faulting is contemporaneous with the Tertiary intermediate dikes.

Mineralization

Mylonites associated with the Westcoast Fault at Johnson Lagoon contain thin stringers of pyrite. Large, rusty, pyrite-bearing boulders of fine-grained granite were observed on the headland 1.5 km southwest of Johnson Lagoon. Also, disseminated pyrite occurs in volcanic rocks of the Karmutsen Formation 1.6 km northeast of the Westcoast Fault at Brooks Bay.

Coarse and fine-grained placer gold has been reported from the vicinity of the junction of Amos and Gold creeks (MINFILE 92L/248). This area was worked in the 1910s but there is no record of production (Neave 1913). The source of the placer gold has not been determined.

Summary

Brooks Peninsula offers two excellent coastal cross sections of a major tectonic boundary between two terranes of the Canadian Cordillera—the boundary between the older deformed and metamorphosed, largely plutonic, rocks of the Wrangellia Terrane, and the younger sedimentary and volcanic rocks of the Pacific Rim Terrane. On Brooks Peninsula the contact is a fault zone characterized by a 1.5 km wide zone of brecciated (broken) rocks. The area remains tectonically active; two major earthquakes with epicentres just west of Cape Cook occurred in 1978.

References Cited

Brandon, M.T. 1985. Mesozoic melange of Pacific Rim Complex, western Vancouver Island. Pp. 1-28 in D. Templeman-Kluit (ed.) Field guides to geology and mineral deposits of the southern Cordillera. Proc. Geological Society of America, Cordilleran Section Meeting, Vancouver, BC.

______ and N.W.D. Massey. 1985. Early tertiary tectonics of the Pacific Northwest: truncation and rifting within a transform plate boundary (abstr.) Programme and abstracts, Geological Association of Canada, Pacific Section. Proc. Symposium April 19, 1986, Victoria, BC.

BC Ministry of Energy, Mines and Petroleum Resources. 1983. MINFILE, File 92L/248, Victoria, BC.

Muller, J.E. 1981. Geology, Nootka Sound, British Columbia, map 1537A. Geological Survey, Canada.

_____ and D.J.T. Carson. 1969. Geology and mineral deposits of Alberni map-area, British Columbia (92F). Geological Survey Canada. 19 pp.

———, K.E. Northcote, and D. Carlisle. 1974. Geology and mineral deposits of Alert Bay-Cape Scott map area, Vancouver Island, British Columbia. Geological Survey Canada. 5 pp.

Neave, H.E. 1913. Auriferous gravels -- Brooks Peninsula, B.C. Ministry of Energy, Mines and Petroleum Resources, Victoria, B.C. Private assessment report.

Chapter 3

Quaternary Geology of Brooks Peninsula

D.E. Howes
BC Land Use and Coordination Office
Victoria, British Columbia

Abstract

The oldest radiocarbon-dated sediment on Brooks Peninsula is a mudflow deposit containing wood dated at 30 800 ± 510 B.P. (GSC-3449). Pollen collected from the sediment indicates that the climate at the time of deposition was cooler than present and possibly denotes climatic deterioration accompanying the beginning of the Fraser Glaciation on the peninsula. During the early stages of the Fraser Glaciation, Brooks Peninsula was subject to an extended period of cirque glaciation that probably commenced prior to 25 000 years ago and continued until sometime after 20 000 B.P.

Geological evidence indicates that at the Fraser maximum, about 15 000 years ago, ice covered low to mid elevations, but the high peaks and mountain ridges on the peninsula stood as nunataks above the ice surface. Estimates of the size of this ice-free area range from 7 km^2 to 9 km^2. The peninsula, located on the western margin of the ice front, a few tens of kilometres from the open sea, is tentatively thought to have had a local climate modified by maritime air at this time. Thus, these ice-free areas may have been able to support biotic communities.

Deglaciation of Fraser ice commenced prior to 12 250 ± 790 B.P. (WAT-924). The maximum observed level of marine inundation during the close of this glaciation was 20 m above mean sea level. Sea levels during the early Holocene are unknown. However, during the past 4000 years, the peninsula has been rising relative to the sea at an average rate of 1 mm to 2 mm per year. Most of this uplift is attributed to tectonic forces.

Acknowledgements

The author would like to thank J.J. Claque of the Geological Survey of Canada for his excellent review of the manuscript, R. Walker of the British Columbia Ministry of Environment, Lands and Parks who drafted the figures, and R. and L. Kirk who provided some of the photographs. In addition, the author would like to thank W.H. Mathews for his valuable comments in the field and concerning the manuscript, R. Hebda for the use of some of the radiocarbon dates, and B. Maxwell who provided the soils information.

Introduction

This chapter has three purposes: 1) to describe the Quaternary sediments and stratigraphy of Brooks Peninsula and relate this information to the regional framework established for northern Vancouver Island; 2) to detail the geomorphologic and sedimentary evidence used to determine the extent of ice on the peninsula at the Fraser Glaciation maximum; and 3) to indicate the extent of bare ground that could have supported biotic communities at the maximum extension of ice.

Physiography

Brooks Peninsula, located on the west coast of northern Vancouver Island, encompasses an area of 210 km^2 (Figure 3.1). It is part of the rugged Vancouver Island Ranges (Holland 1976) and is characterized by cool, wet winters and cool, moist summers. Annual precipitation, most of which falls between October and March, exceeds 3000 mm. Snow is usually confined to the mountains and is ephemeral at sea level (see Chapter 8). The climate favours a dense conifer forest over much of the landscape.

The peninsula is a rectangular, uplifted block dominated by Refugium Range with peaks that trend in a southwest to northeast direction along the central portion of the peninsula. This central ridge increases in elevation from about 420 m above sea level near Cape Cook to a maximum of 909 m in the northeast (3 km northwest of Johnson Lagoon). Summits and ridges lower than about 600 m tend to have rounded and smoothed forms, whereas higher peaks are typically jagged and angular (Figure 3.2).

Deeply incised cirques occur on northwest and southeast facing slopes of this central ridge (Figures 3.1 and 3.3). Elevations of cirque floors of the northwest-facing cirques are at least as low as 60 m to 90 m (their true elevations are hidden by tarns). In contrast, cirque floor elevations on the southeast facing slopes vary from 300 m to 370 m. The cirques are characterized by steep, high headwalls that can extend to 700 m upwards from their floors to the central mountain ridge. Narrow and short U-shaped valleys extend seawards from the cirques and usually terminate at a coastal plain. Valley side slopes are mantled by a thin cover of colluvium and/or till and are commonly undergoing modification by shallow, rapid mass movements.

Coastal lowlands occur along the northwest and southeast coasts. These areas of low relief are narrow, less than 3 km wide, and are overlain by a variety of unconsolidated sediments (e.g., till, fluvial and ice-contact gravels, and glaciomarine silts) of unknown depths. The continental shelf immediately adjacent to the northwest and southeast lowlands is characterized by U-shaped valleys less than 90 m below sea level, separated by gently rolling ridge crests. These features are submerged extensions of valleys originating in the Vancouver Island Ranges inland from Brooks Peninsula. In contrast, the continental shelf adjacent to the southwest coast has a moderately sloping surface that extends 4 km to 5 km off shore to the -100 m isobath.

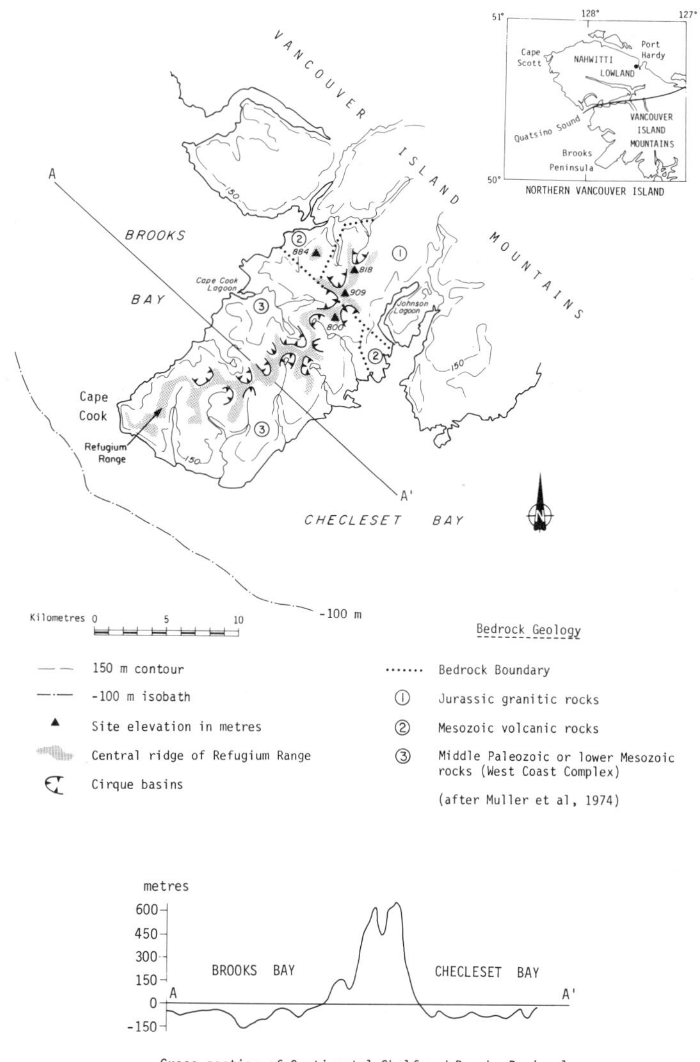

Figure 3.1 Physiography of Brooks Peninsula

Figure 3.2 Serrated and jagged peaks (⮋) standing above smoothed, rounded ridges (⬇) of the central spine of Refugium Range

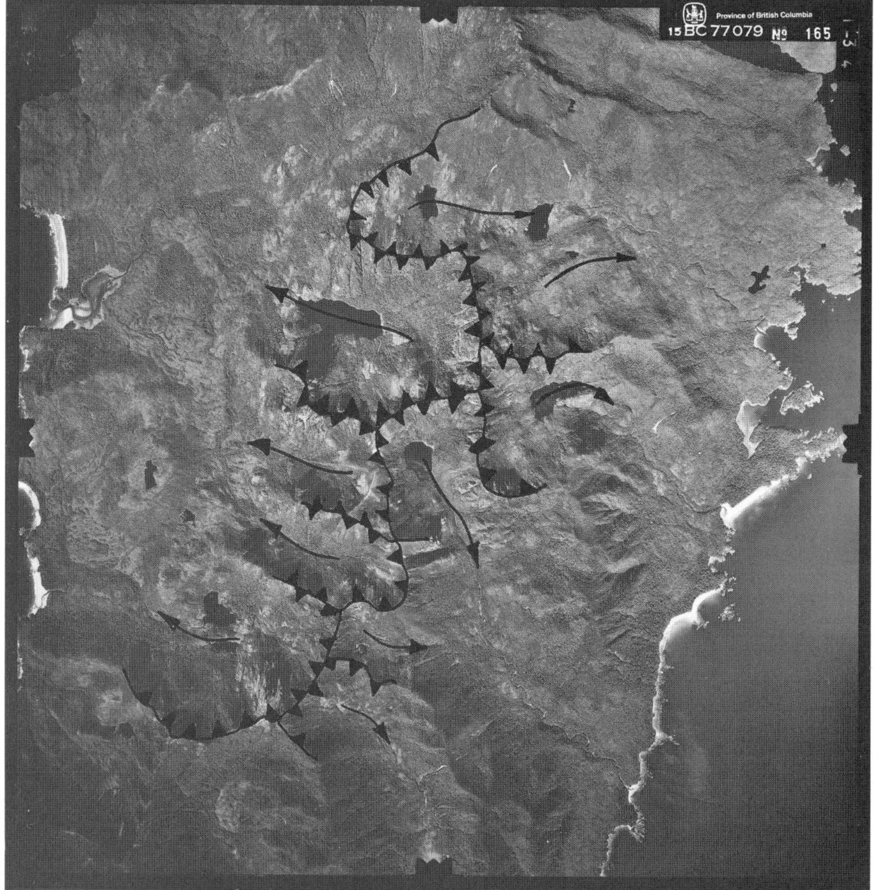

Figure 3.3 Deeply incised cirques adjacent to the central spine of Refugium Range (arrows indicate orientation of headwalls) (BC 77079-165)

Bedrock Geology

Most of the peninsula is underlain by granitoid rocks of the West Coast Complex (Muller et al. 1974). These middle Paleozoic or lower Mesozoic rocks are made up predominantly of quartz diorite, but vary from leuco-granodiorite to quartz gabbro. They are rarely homogeneous and typically display agmatitic or gneissic structure. The northeastern part of the area, however, consists of Mesozoic volcanic rocks and Jurassic granitic rock types. The former are made up of the Karmutsen Formation (basaltic lava) and Bonanza Volcanics (andesitic to rhyodacitic lava). The Jurassic rocks consist of the Island Intrusives, which are made up of quartz diorite and granodiorite (see Chapter 2).

Regional Quaternary History: Vancouver Island

Introduction

Two glacial and two non-glacial geologic-climate units have been identified from the Quaternary sediments on Vancouver Island (Table 3.1) (Alley 1979; Armstrong and Clague 1977; Fyles 1963; Howes 1981a, 1983). The units span a period of time greater than 50 000 years; from oldest to youngest they include: Semiahmoo Glaciation, Olympia non-glacial interval, Fraser Glaciation, and Recent. For the purpose of the Brooks Peninsula study only the last three units on northern Vancouver Island require review.

Table 3.1 Time-distance charts and Quaternary stratigraphic sequences for Vancouver Island, British Columbia

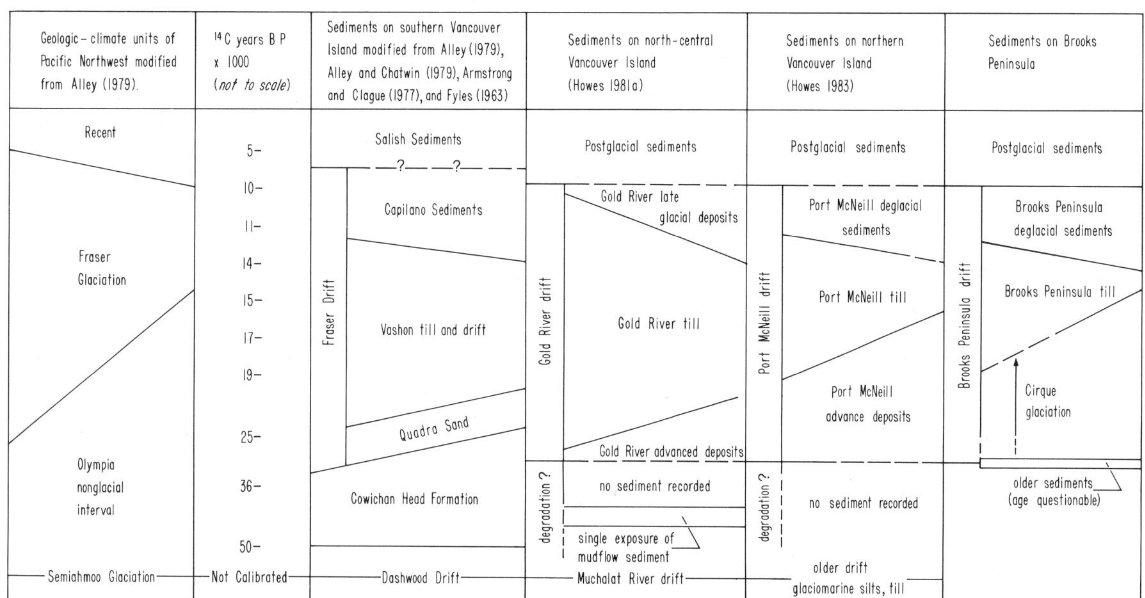

Geologic – climate units of Pacific Northwest modified from Alley (1979).
¹⁴C years B P x 1000 (*not to scale*)
Sediments on southern Vancouver Island modified from Alley (1979), Alley and Chatwin (1979), Armstrong and Clague (1977), and Fyles (1963)
Sediments on north-central Vancouver Island (Howes 1981a)
Sediments on northern Vancouver Island (Howes 1983)
Sediments on Brooks Peninsula
Recent
Fraser Glaciation
Olympia nonglacial interval
Semiahmoo Glaciation
5–
10–
11–
14–
15–
17–
19–
25–
36–
50–
Not Calibrated
Salish Sediments
Capilano Sediments
Fraser Drift
Vashon till and drift
Quadra Sand
Cowichan Head Formation
Dashwood Drift
Postglacial sediments
Gold River late glacial deposits
Gold River drift
Gold River till
Gold River advanced deposits
degradation ?
no sediment recorded
single exposure of mudflow sediment
Muchalat River drift
Port McNeill deglacial sediments
Port McNeill drift
Port McNeill till
Port McNeill advance deposits
no sediment recorded
older drift glaciomarine silts, till
Brooks Peninsula deglacial sediments
Brooks Peninsula drift
Brooks Peninsula till
Cirque glaciation
older sediments (age questionable)

Olympia Non-glacial Interval

The Olympia non-glacial interval commenced in southwestern British Columbia possibly as early as 58 800 B.P. (Clague 1981). Deposits of this interval on southern Vancouver Island are represented by the Cowichan Head Formation, which is made up of marine and fluvial sediments (Table 3.1). The only Olympia-age sediment on northern Vancouver Island is a single mudflow deposit, radiocarbon dated at 40 900 ± 2000 B.P. (Howes 1981a). Thus, it has been postulated that this interval on northern Vancouver Island was characterized by a period of degradation in which Olympia-age materials were deposited in transient sedimentary environments (Howes 1981a, 1983). Climatic conditions during the Olympia non-glacial interval are not completely understood. Studies from southern Vancouver Island and the adjacent mainland suggest the climate was at times similar to, but usually cooler than present (Alley 1979; Armstrong and Clague 1977; Hebda et al. 1983).

Fraser Glaciation

The Fraser Glaciation commenced about 29 000 years ago with the climatic deterioration at the end of the Olympia non-glacial interval (Alley 1979; Armstrong and Clague 1977). Accompanying this climatic shift, glaciers formed in the cirques of the Vancouver Island Ranges (Howes 1981a). Initially, glacier growth was slow; however, with continued ice accumulation the glaciers began to flow into the valleys. Valley glaciation on northern Vancouver Island had commenced prior to 25 000 years ago (Howes 1981a) and was well advanced about 20 000 years ago. At this time, valley glaciers probably extended westwards into the fiords on the west coast, and eastwards and northwards where they coalesced with the Coast Mountain glaciers to form an ice stream that flowed northwest along Queen Charlotte Strait (Figure 3.3; see Clague 1981; Howes 1983). The northern tip of the island was ice-free at this time (Clague et al. 1980). During this prolonged valley glaciation stage, outwash gravels and glaciolacustrine and glaciomarine silts were formed in a variety of depositional environments in front of the advancing ice on northern Vancouver Island (Howes 1981a, 1983).

The Fraser Glaciation maximum probably occurred about 15 000 years ago on northern Vancouver Island (Clague et al. 1980; Howes 1981a, 1983). Radiocarbon dates on marine shells, wood, and peat from both the east and west coasts of northern Vancouver Island indicate that deglaciation had commenced prior to 13 000 years ago (Howes 1981a, 1981b, 1983; Hebda 1983). Clague et al. (1980) noted that the Tofino area, located on the west coast of southern Vancouver Island, was not overridden by Fraser ice until sometime after 16 700 years ago. This date, coupled with the observation that Fraser ice did not advance over the northern tip of Vancouver Island until sometime after 20 000 years ago, indicates that the period of maximum extension of ice on northern Vancouver Island was a short-lived event, less than 7000 years and possibly as short as 3500 years (Howes 1983).

At the Fraser maximum, Coast Mountain ice coalesced with and overtopped Vancouver Island ice (Howes 1981a, 1981b, 1983). Regional flow directions and minimum elevations of the ice surface are presented in Figure 3.4. The northern tip of the island was completely covered by ice (Howes 1983). On north-central Vancouver Island, the ice surface was at least 1550 m; possibly 1820 m high at Victoria Peak; 1370 m at Pinder Peak and 1112 m at Garibaldi Peaks (about 55 km and 34 km due east of Brooks Peninsula, respectively); and 1335 m near Gold River (Howes 1981a).

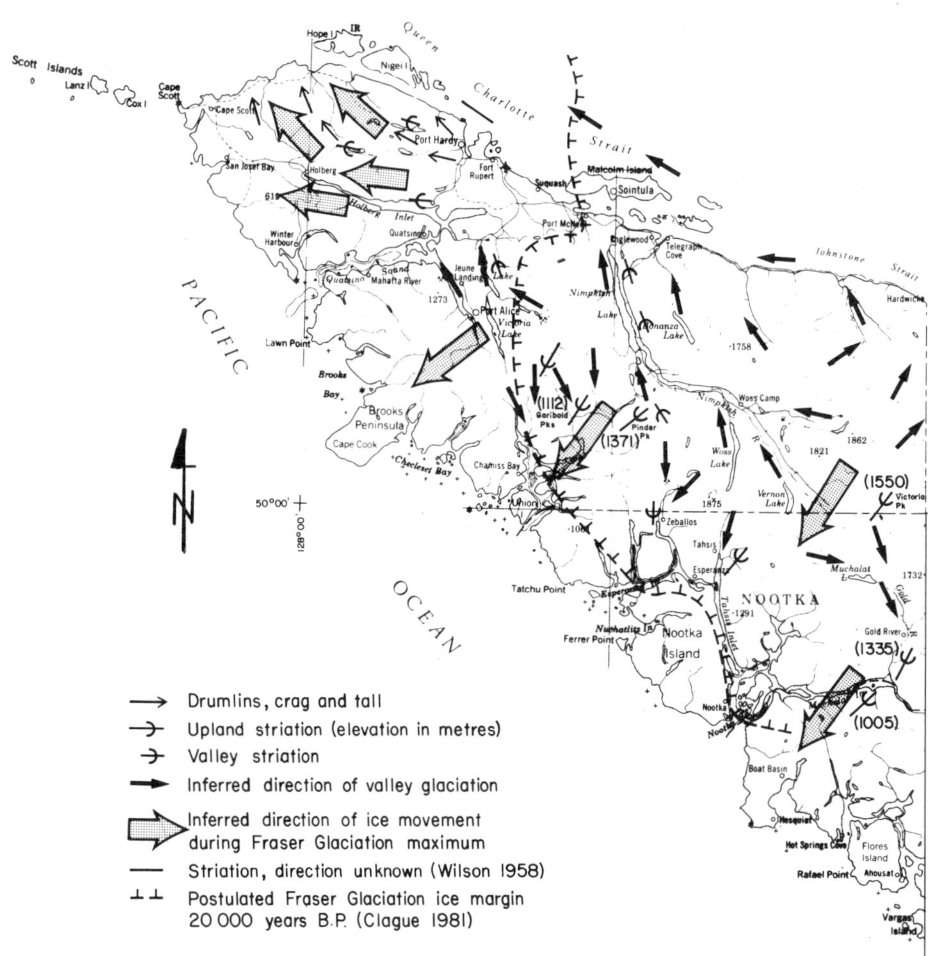

Figure 3.4 **Ice flow directions and minimum ice surface elevations during the Fraser glaciation on northern Vancouver Island (after Howes 1981a, 1983)**

The pattern of deglaciation of Fraser ice on northern Vancouver Island is complex. The ice surface lowered by downwasting and stagnation accompanied by frontal retreat of the glaciers up their respective valleys (Howes 1983). Due to isostatic and eustatic effects, sea levels were higher than present during and immediately following deglaciation. The limit of marine inundation for various coastal sites on northern Vancouver Island includes: 32-34 m at Hesquiat Harbour, 19-20 m at Brooks Peninsula, 27 m at Cape Scott, and 92 m at Port McNeill (Howes 1981b). A variety of ice-contact deposits of sand, gravel, and silt were deposited during this deglaciation (Howes 1981a, 1983).

Recent

Recent, or postglacial, conditions commenced about 10 000 years ago following the retreat of the ice to a few high-elevation cirques in the Vancouver Island Ranges (Howes 1981a). During this epoch, northern Vancouver Island has been subject to a variety of geological processes including sea level changes, fluvial erosion, alluvial fan deposition, and landslides.

The pattern of sea level change on western Vancouver Island from the end of the Pleistocene to about 5000 years ago is presently unknown. During the last 5000 years, however, the land has been rising relative to the sea at an average rate of 1 mm to 2 mm per year (Clague et al. 1982). Most of this emergence is thought to have resulted from tectonic uplift.

Major river systems have dissected the late Pleistocene sediments and bedrock to form multi-level terraces. Deltas have formed where these rivers discharge into the sea. Alluvial fan deposition commenced during deglaciation and continues today. Fans commonly occur where mountain streams debouch into broad, flat-lying valley floors.

Postglacial modification of slopes by rapid mass movement is a frequent event on the glacially oversteeped valley walls. These processes are far more active on the west coast than elsewhere on northern Vancouver Island (Howes 1981b).

Brooks Peninsula: Quaternary Sediments

Thick exposures of late Quaternary sediments do not occur on Brooks Peninsula. Most exposures are up to a few metres thick and usually outcrop in stream banks. Important sites and their locations are presented in Figure 3.5. Radiocarbon dates for these sites are listed in Table 3.2. The sediments have been informally grouped into two units, in order of decreasing age: Brooks Peninsula drift and postglacial sediments (Table 3.1).

Brooks Peninsula Drift

Brooks Peninsula drift comprises three units: "older" sediments, Brooks Peninsula till, and Brooks Peninsula deglacial sediments.

"Older" Sediments

"Older" sediments outcrop in an escarpment of a river terrace of Amos Creek, approximately 2 km from its mouth (Figure 3.5: Amos Creek site-BP1). The exposure consists of alternating beds of compact, silty to sandy diamicton, and dense, thinly bedded, lacustrine silt with discontinuous organic lenses. Pebble lithologies of the diamicton are dominated by local granitic rock types. The contacts between the beds are sharp and wavy. The "older" sediments are overlain by one metre of well-rounded, pebble cobble gravel that underlies the terrace surface.

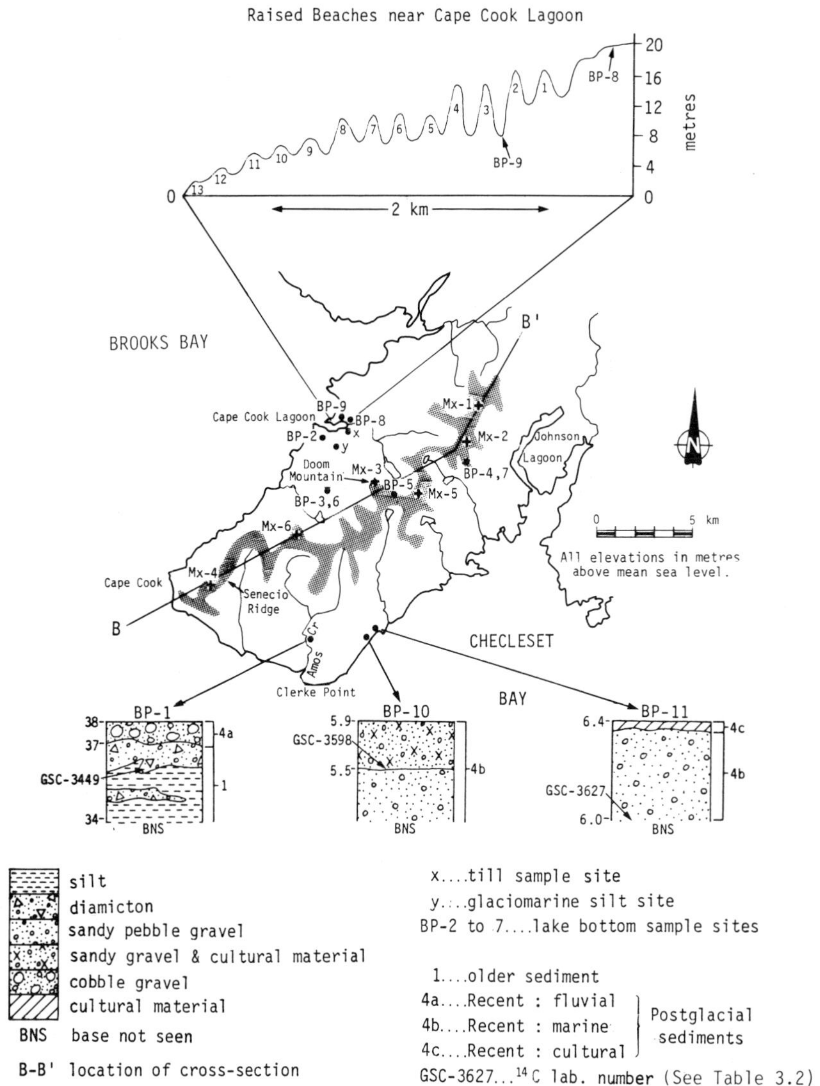

Figure 3.5 Locations of sites and stratigraphic columns of late Quarternary sediments on Brooks Peninsula

Compressed, coniferous wood not otherwise identifiable (R. Mott personal communication, September 1984), collected from the upper diamicton, has been radiocarbon dated at 30 800 ± 510 B.P. (GSC-3449). The pollen assemblage of the upper silt bed consists of 56% tree pollen, predominantly *Picea,* and diverse herbaceous types (see Chapter 9). It indicates that the temperature at the time of deposition was cooler than present.

The diamicton is thought to represent mudflow material that descended from the adjacent slopes into a lake situated in the lower part of Amos Creek valley. The origin of the lake is unknown. It may have formed by temporary damming of the creek by an earlier landslide, or by ice that flowed out of Nasparti Inlet during the advance of Fraser Glaciation ice.

Table 3.2 Radiocarbon dates for Brooks Peninsula, British Columbia

Site[a]	Latitude	Longitude	Material	Metres[b]	Years B.P.	Lab No.	Collector
Amos Creek (BP-1)	50°06'10"N	127°48'30"W	wood	36	30 800±510	GSC-3449	D.E. Howes W.H. Mathews
Panicum Pond (BP-2)	50°11'40"N	127°47'20"W	wood	25	12 250±790	WAT-924	R.J. Hebda
Kalmia Lake (BP-3)	50°10'20"N	127°48'W	peat	150	12 100±480	SFU-213	R.J. Hebda
Pyrola Lake (BP-4)	50°1'20"N	127°41'40"W	gyttja	535	11 400±480	SFU-214	R.J. Hebda
Cassiope Pond (BP-5)	50°10'N	127°45'W	peat	550	10 460±550	SFU-215	R.J. Hebda
Kalmia Lake (BP-6)	50°10'20"N	127°48'W	peat	150	10 390±370	WAT-927	R.J. Hebda
Pyrola Lake (BP-7)	50°11'20"N	127°41'40"W	gyttja	535	9950±260	SFU-217	R.J. Hebda
Kingfisher Creek (BP-8)	50°12'N	127°47'W	peat	20	8460±460	WAT-917	R.J. Hebda
Cottongrass Hollow (BP-9)	50°12'N	127°47'W	wood	6.6	3900±140	SFU-140	R.J. Hebda
Cottongrass Hollow (BP-9)	50°12'N	127°47'W	peat	6.5	1980±70	WAT-926	R.J. Hebda
Quineex Cave 2 (BP-11)	50°06'N	127°46'W	shell	5.5	1640±50	GSC-3598	D.E. Howes
Quineex Cave 1 (BP-10)	50°06'15"N	127°45'30"W	shell	6.0	1560±50	GSC-3627	D.E. Howes

[a] Refer to Figure 3.5 of site locations.
[b] Metres above mean sea level.

Evidence for a landslide origin includes: 1) the major advance of ice of the Fraser Glaciation on northern Vancouver Island occurred after 20 000 years ago; and 2) the lacustrine deposit is of limited local extent, though it may have, in part, been eroded by Fraser ice.

There is, however, the possibility that the dated wood has been reworked and redeposited. The wood, in this case, would be older than the deposit. This favours a glacial dam origin of the lake. Support for this alternative is provided by the process that deposited the diamictons (i.e., mudflow), the occurrence of active mass movements today and probably in the past on the peninsula (Howes 1981b), and numerous past examples of reworked and redeposited radiocarbon dated wood collected from sediments on northern Vancouver Island (Howes 1981a, 1983).

Although the origin of these materials is unknown, the age of the sediments and the pollen assemblage, which indicate that climate at the time of deposition was cooler than present, suggest that the Fraser Glaciation may have started at this time. Therefore, in this paper, the sediments have been included, tentatively, as part of the Brooks Peninsula drift. Future studies, however, may indicate that they are part of the Olympia non-glacial interval.

Brooks Peninsula Till

Few good exposures of Brooks Peninsula till were observed in the study area. The till is a massive, compact diamicton with a silty sand matrix. Till thicknesses typically vary from a few metres on lower mountain slopes to three or more metres in valley bottoms. A local origin of the till is suggested by the till matrix and clast lithologies. For example, the matrix of a till sampled in the lowlands (Figure 3.5: site x), consists of a high proportion of sand (77% sand, 21% silt, 2% clay) and is dominated by local "granitic" clasts. These characteristics of the till suggest a local origin, since Brooks Peninsula is dominated by granitic rock types, whereas the adjacent Vancouver Island Ranges consist of Mesozoic volcanic rocks (Muller et al. 1974).

Numerous large boulders rest on and in the till, mantling the lowlands adjacent to Cape Cook Lagoon. The boulders are of local origin, mainly quartz diorite and diorite, and their surfaces are etched and pitted 1 mm to 2 mm deep. It is thought that the boulders represent a local deposit laid down during deglaciation as the ice downwasted and stagnated in the lowlands. The boulders probably were transported on and in the ice that flowed in a northwesterly direction from the cirques facing Brooks Bay. This interpretation is supported by the local lithology of the boulders and the steep, high headwalls of the cirque basins, which likely acted as source areas.

The Brooks Peninsula till has been tentatively correlated with Vashon till (see Table 3.1), though the stratigraphic relationship and age of the till are not known. This interpretation is based upon the soil development on the till, which is similar to soil development on known Vashon tills on Vancouver Island (Jungen and Lewis 1978; see Chapter 4), and on the degree of surface weathering on the boulders in the lowlands. Surface weathering of 1 mm to 2 mm is not uncommon on exposed granitic bedrock overridden by Fraser Glaciation ice on Vancouver Island.

Brooks Peninsula Deglacial Sediments

Deglacial sediments include glaciomarine silt and sand. Glaciomarine silts are exposed at the head of Cape Cook Lagoon in the upper tidal zone (Figure 3.5: site y). They contain marine shells, dropstones (pebble size), and fragments of wood. Unfortunately, insufficient organic debris was collected for radiocarbon dating.

Sands, of probable marine origin, are overlain by peat on the lowlands immediately inland from a series of strandlines adjacent to the north shore of Cape Cook Lagoon (Figure 3.5: Kingfisher Creek site-BP8). The contact is at about 20 m above mean sea level. The peat is approximately 1 m thick and 8460 ± 460 years old near its base (Table 3.2).

The sedimentary character of the glaciomarine silts, which are similar to radiocarbon-dated glaciomarine silts on western Vancouver Island (Howes 1981b), and the age of the peat overlying sand, tentatively suggest that these materials were deposited during deglaciation of Fraser ice. They were deposited prior to 8500 years ago, and probably commenced deposition about 13 000 years ago (Howes 1981b). The Kingfisher Creek site defines the known limit of marine inundation, 20 m above mean sea level, during the close of the Fraser Glaciation.

Postglacial Sediments

Postglacial sediments on Brooks Peninsula include raised littoral materials, lake-bottom sediments, and other deposits, such as colluvium and organic deposits.

Raised Littoral Materials

Raised littoral materials include a series of strandlines immediately north of Cape Cook Lagoon and wave-derived deposits on cave floors presently located above high tide level on the southeast shoreline (Figure 3.5).

Thirteen strandlines, numbered in Figure 3.5, occur from 17 m to about 2 m above mean sea level adjacent to Cape Cook Lagoon. An exposure in strandline 2 (adjacent to the Cottongrass Hollow site-BP9), about 17 m high, and exposures in holes up to 1 m deep dug in several other strandlines, indicate that these ridges consist of thin to moderately thick beds (4-15 cm) of well-sorted, medium sand with marine shells and the occasional well-rounded pebble clast.

A core taken at 8 m above mean sea level, in the hollow between strandlines 2 and 3 (Figure 3.5), revealed 1.4 m of terrestrial peat overlying 10 cm of peaty sand that rests on clean sand (Figure 3.5: Cottongrass Hollow site). Pollen assemblages from the peaty sand layer indicate that it was deposited in the upper intertidal zone (see Chapter 9). Two radiocarbon dates have been obtained from the core. Wood collected from the base of the peat at 6.6 m above sea level and thought to be contemporaneous with the peaty sand is 3900 ± 140 years old. The other date, determined from peat collected from the peaty sand layer, is 1980 ± 70 B.P. (WAT-926) and is considered to be unreliable as root contamination is suspected. This site suggests that by 3900 years ago sea level was between 4.5 m and 5.5 m above present mean sea level (based on a 1 m to 2 m elevation for the upper intertidal zone), and records an equivalent amount of uplift in about 4000 years.

On the southeast coast of the peninsula, two sea-carved caves, now elevated above high tide, contain littoral pebble gravels in coarse sand that are overlain by cultural deposits (Figure 3.5: Quineex Cave sites 1-BP10, 2-BP11). The cultural materials at Quineex Cave 2 are waterworn and mixed with beach sediments. Shells from the base of this unit have been radiocarbon dated at 1640 ± 50 B.P. (GSC-3598; Table 3.2), whereas marine shells collected from the littoral deposits at Quineex Cave 1 have been dated at 1560 ± 50 B.P. (GSC-3627). The elevations of the cave floors are 5.5 m and 6.0 m above mean sea level (about 3.5 m and 4.0 m above the present high tide line), respectively. The occurrence of waterworn artifacts at Quineex Cave 2 suggests that the littoral deposits were probably deposited above what was then the high water line, by storm waves. Thus, these materials more than likely formed when the cave floors were about 1 m to 2 m above the high tide line, or 2 m to 3.4 m above present high tide. Hence, 2 m to 3.5 m of emergence in the past 1600 years is indicated for Brooks Peninsula.

The rates of emergence of these sites vary from 1.1 mm to 2.2 mm per year. These rates are similar to other observed rates determined for the west coast of Vancouver Island (Clague et al. 1982).

Lake-bottom Sediments

A number of lakes and ponds on Brooks Peninsula, ranging in elevation from about 25 m to 550 m, were cored and dated (Figure 3.5: Panicum Pond, Pyrola Lake, Kalmia Lake, and Cassiope Pond sites-BP 2 to 7). Most of the bottom sediments consist of limnic peat overlying a thin layer of silty gyttja and/or silt (see Chapter 9). Core depths varied from 2.4 m to 8.4 m. Radiocarbon dates obtained at or near the bases of these cores range from 12 250 ± 790 B.P. to 9950 ± 260 B.P. (Table 3.2). All six dates postdate Fraser Glaciation and indicate that these lakes formed during or after deglaciation of Fraser ice. The small volume of deltaic deposits formed by streams feeding these lakes is a further indication of recent origin. The 12 250 B.P. date from the lowlands indicates that deglaciation had commenced prior to this time on Brooks Peninsula.

Other Deposits

Other deposits that have formed on Brooks Peninsula during the Recent epoch include colluvium and organic sediment. Postglacial modification of slopes by weathering and rapid mass movements has resulted in the formation of talus slopes, debris flow fans, and a mantle of bedrock-derived colluvium on steep valley slopes.

Organic deposits are widely distributed. They occur locally in poorly drained, shallow depressions overlying till or glaciomarine silts and on a few slopes. The sediments are thin, usually less than 1 m thick, and contain lenses of sand and pebbles. These lenses probably represent slope wash materials transported by surface runoff from adjacent slopes.

Fraser Glaciation: Maximum Ice Elevations

A number of geomorphic features and Quaternary sediments—some radiocarbon dated—have been used to determine the maximum height of ice on Brooks Peninsula (Table 3.3). These features and sediments are known, or believed, to date from the Fraser Glaciation. The data indicate that the ice probably stood up to 640-670 m in the northeastern portion of the peninsula, 609 m in the central part, and possibly up to 365 m near the southwest coast. Evidence that supports this interpretation follows:

1) Late glacial and postglacial dates of lake-bottom sediments collected from lakes situated on the central ridge (Figure 3.4 and Table 3.3) suggest that the surface of the ice was at least 535-550 m above sea level in the central part of the study area. The topography surrounding the lakes is rounded and smoothed.

2) Well-preserved stoss and lee forms (whalebacks) and large perched boulders (Figures 3.6 and 3.7) occur in two cols on the northeastern part of the central ridge (Table 3.3: sites Mx-1, Mx-2). Both sites are located between and above cirque basins, at 580 m. The stoss and lee features are oriented due west. The perched boulders are subrounded in shape, of local origin, and are either too big to have been transported by local agencies, or too far from cliffs to be the products of rockfalls or landslides. That is, they were probably transported by glacial ice. The surfaces of these boulders and the exposed bedrock are weathered to a depth of 2 mm, which is not unusual for granitic rocks overridden by Fraser ice elsewhere on Vancouver Island. Thus, these features are probably a result of the Fraser Glaciation.

3) A distinct trimline on several peaks of the central ridge separates rounded and smoothed ridges and peaks from higher, jagged and angular summits. At sites Mx-1 and Mx-2, the trimline occurs at 670 m and 640 m, respectively. The line decreases in elevation to about 609 m in the central portion of the central ridge (near Doom Mountain) and to 580 m at site Mx-6, about 7 km north-northeast of Cape Cook (Figure 3.5 and Table 3.3). The distinct change in surface topography at these sites is thought to represent the maximum elevation of Fraser Glaciation ice.

4) Physical and chemical properties of a podzolic soil observed at 760 m on the central ridge tentatively suggest that this soil may be older than Recent soils on Vancouver Island (Figure 3.5: Mx-5 site). Some clasts within the profile disintegrate when crushed by hand, the percent of clay in the weathered portion of the profile is about ten times as great as the clay content in soils developed on the till in the lowlands, and the total free iron is higher than in Recent soils (see Chapter 4). Although these results can be due to factors other than time, the marked contrast between this soil and soils developed at lower elevations (below 600 m), and the location of the site well above the nearest observed trimline of 609 m, suggest an older age.

Table 3.3 Evidence for Fraser Glaciation maximum ice limits on Brooks Peninsula

Site[a]	Elevation[b]	Features
Mx-1	670 (max)	trimline marking change from rounded to steep, jagged topography
Mx-1	580 (min)	perched boulders; stoss and lee forms; bedrock surface weathered up to 2 mm
Mx-2	640 (max)	trimline
Mx-2	580 (min)	perched boulders; stoss and lee forms; bedrock surface weathered up to 2 mm
Mx-3	609 (max)	trimline
Pyrola Lake (BP-9, 7)	35 (min)	lake-bottom sediments; ^{14}C dated at 11 400 B.P. and 9950 B.P.
Cassiope Pond (BP-5)	550 (min)	lake-bottom sediments; ^{14}C dated at 10 460 B.P.
Mx-4	365 (min)	possible striated bedrock on Senecio Ridge
Mx-5	760 (>max)	possible old soil
Mx-6	550 (max)	trimline (determined from topographic base map, 1:50 000 scale)

[a] Refer to Figure 3.5 for site locations.
[b] Metres above sea level.

5) A maximum elevation of Fraser ice of 670 m in the northeastern part of the study area is consistent with minimum regional ice surface elevations observed elsewhere on northern Vancouver Island (see Regional Quaternary History section, this chapter).

6) A profile representing the assumed ice surface at the Fraser Glaciation maximum is presented in Figure 3.8. It has been constructed under the following assumptions: 1) the ice terminated near the -100 m isobath (Figure 3.1); and 2) the ice surface was close to present sea level due to the combined effects of eustatic drop of sea level (-100 m) and isostatic depression of the land due to a local ice mass. The curve that best fits these assumptions and that uses the trimline elevations (Table 3.3: sites Mx-1, Mx-2, Mx-3, Mx-6) is $\underline{Y} = 24.89 \pm 4.539\underline{X}^{1/2}$, where $\underline{Y}$ is the height of the ice sheet in metres and $\underline{X}$ is the distance inland from the ice front. This profile is very similar to the parabolic profiles of the Antarctic and Greenland ice caps that are grounded on their continental shelves (Mathews 1974) and clearly separates the lower, rounded ridges and peaks from the angular crests and summits.

Figure 3.6 **Westward trending stoss and lee forms (whalebacks) in col on central ridge (site Mx-1 in Figure 3.5) (Photo by R. and L. Kirk)**

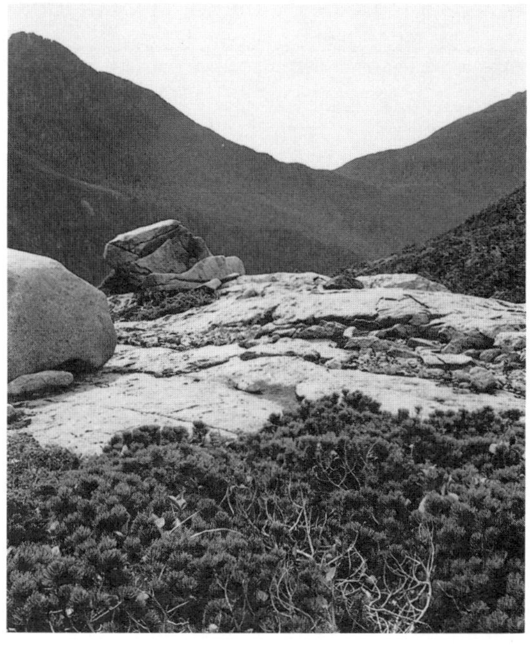

Figure 3.7 **Perched boulder on "granitic" bedrock in a col (site Mx-1 in Figure 3.5) at 580 m (Photo by R. and L. Kirk)**

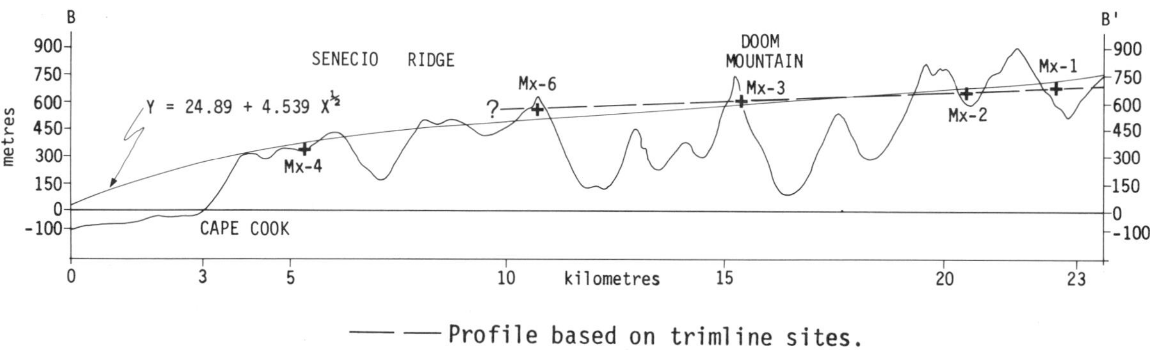

Figure 3.8 **Projected profiles of Fraser glaciation ice at the maximum (for profile location refer to Figure 3.5)**

The collective sum of this evidence strongly suggests that areas on the central and northeastern portion of the ridge and on the upper portion of Harris Peak remained ice free during the Fraser Glaciation maximum (Figure 3.9). These areas probably projected as nunataks above the ice surface and covered a total area of about 7 km^2.

The elevation of the ice surface on Senecio Ridge (Figure 3.5), however, is not known. There is some question as to whether the crest of the ridge was covered by Fraser ice. Striations, of possible glacial origin, were observed at three localities on the summit of this ridge. They are well-preserved under a veneer of soil (Figure 3.10), occur at about 365 m, and trend in a northeasterly direction. The location of these features near the theoretical upper limit of glaciation (Figure 3.8), and their orientation, which can be reconciled with local ice flow during the Fraser Glaciation (Figure 3.9), suggest that the ice covered the ridge. Further support for a Fraser origin includes several well-preserved grooves, oriented in a northeasterly direction, on exposed bedrock near sea level at the base of Senecio Ridge near Cape Cook (R. Smith personal communication, September 1985), and an ice profile (based on observed trimline points) that tentatively suggests that the ice may have been thicker than suggested by the theoretical parabolic profile for this part of the peninsula (Figure 3.8).

Alternatively, there is limited evidence that the ridge crest remained ice-free during the Fraser Glaciation. This is supported by: 1) the possibility that the striations were formed by an earlier glaciation and subsequently preserved under a soil mantle, or by tectonic activity (fault movement); and 2) the presence of small tors on the ridge crest. Earlier glacial origin of the striations implies that they are older than 58 000 years (see Regional Quaternary History section, this chapter) and that the tors commenced formation prior to postglacial time. This argument, however, is weakened by: 1) studies by Dahl (1966) and Watts (1979, 1981) that have demonstrated that tors can form in postglacial time and are not always indicative of non-glaciated terrain; and 2) the weathering pattern developed on exposed and buried surfaces of the striated bedrock on the ridge, which is similar to that of late Wisconsin granitic boulders partially buried in till in the Rocky Mountains (Birkland 1974: 156). Exposed bedrock surfaces on the ridges are commonly weathered along joints and fractures in the rock up to 2 mm and 3 mm deep, whereas surfaces of bedrock protected by a thin mantle of soil are smooth and show little evidence of physical weathering. The two zones are marked by a sharp boundary (Figure 3.10). Exposed surfaces of boulders partially buried in till are weathered to a similar degree as the exposed bedrock on the ridge, whereas the buried portions are weathered similar to the buried striated surfaces. In contrast, partially buried granitic clasts in early Wisconsin till are extensively weathered on both sides. This comparison of weathering patterns suggests a late Wisconsin origin for the striations.

Moreover, in order for the buried striations to have remained unweathered for at least 60 000 years, they would have had to have been protected from surface and subsurface weathering processes by a thick drift-cover. The sediments would have to be at least 1.5 m to 3 m thick, which is the average observed depth of weathering in late Wisconsin till on the northwestern coast of Vancouver Island (Howes 1981b). There are, however, no remnant areas of thick sediments on the gently sloping ridge, nor evidence of mass movements operating on the ridge crest that could have removed such a volume of material. Deflation, an active process on the ridge, is not considered to have been sufficient to have removed a thick overburden. Hence, the possibility of burial beneath a thick drift mantle appears to be remote. A tectonic origin of the striations is possible, though difficult to prove.

Future studies should address this intriguing problem—the age of the tors, weathering rates on granitic surfaces on the west coast of Vancouver Island, and whether Senecio Ridge was covered by Fraser Glaciation ice. If the striations were formed by Fraser ice, the ice surface was at least 365 m above sea level at the maximum. The inclusion of Senecio Ridge with other ice-free areas, however, would increase the extent of unglaciated terrain during the Fraser Glaciation maximum by approximately 2.5 km^2. Based on the evidence presented, a Fraser Glaciation origin of the striations is tentatively favoured.

Quaternary History: Brooks Peninsula

The oldest Pleistocene sediment recorded on Brooks Peninsula is the "older" drift outcropping of

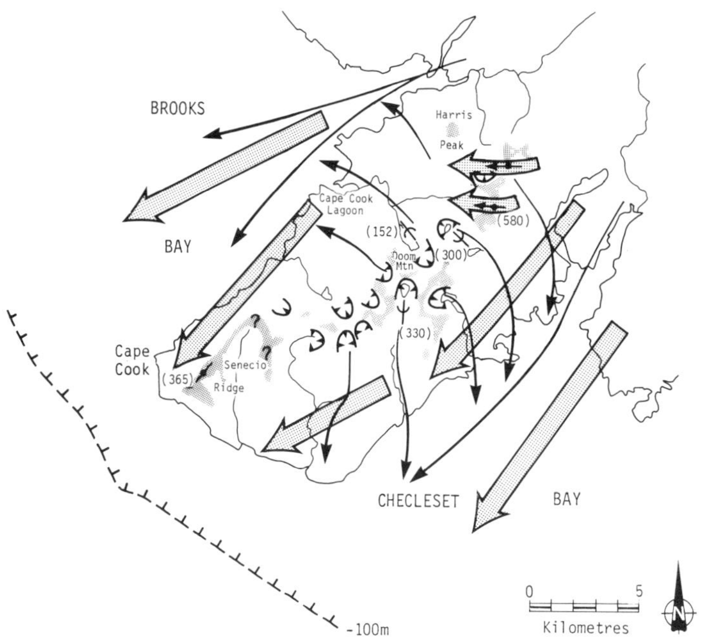

Cirque

Striations, whalebacks on cirque basin floor

Striations, whalebacks on central ridge (direction unkown, known)

(306) Elevation in metres

Inferred ice flow at Piedmont stage (prior to the maximum)

Inferred ice flow at Fraser Glaciation maximum (about 15000 years ago)

Inferred ice margin at Fraser Glaciation, (≈ -100m Isobath)

Ice-free terrain at Fraser Glaciation maximum

Figure 3.9 Inferred ice flow directions during the Fraser Glaciation and ice-free terrain (nunataks) at the Fraser Glaciation maximum

Figure 3.10 Striations on bedrock on Senecio Ridge (note the difference in degree of weathering between exposed and buried bedrock surfaces)

the Amos Creek site. These interbedded mudflow and lacustrine materials are thought to have been deposited about 30 000 years ago, though a younger age for the sediment is possible. Pollen collected from the sediment indicates that the climate at the time of deposition was cooler than present and possibly signals cooling at the beginning of the Fraser Glaciation. The sediments, thus, have been tentatively correlated with drift of the Fraser Glaciation, though the possibility of an Olympia non-glacial origin does exist (Table 3.1).

It is proposed that during the early stages of the Fraser Glaciation, Brooks Peninsula was subject to an extended period of cirque glaciation that probably commenced prior to 25 000 years ago and continued until sometime after 20 000 years ago. This is supported by: 1) valley glaciation had commenced prior to 25 000 years ago on north-central Vancouver Island and, hence, ice had likely started to build up in cirques on Brooks Peninsula; 2) northern Vancouver Island was ice-free until sometime after 20 000 years ago; and 3) cirque basins on the peninsula are well-developed with steep, high headwalls. Prior to the Fraser maximum, about 15 000 B.P., cirque glaciers on Brooks Peninsula flowed out from their valleys and coalesced with valley glaciers that extended onto the continental shelf from the Vancouver Island Ranges. Together they formed a piedmont-type glacier on the floors of Brooks and Checleset bays. At the Fraser maximum, as Coast Mountain ice coalesced with Vancouver Island ice, glaciers flowed in a southwesterly direction across Brooks Peninsula (Figure 3.9). Two streams of ice probably existed—both flowing in a southwesterly direction and separated by the central ridge of the peninsula—one to the north, in Brooks Bay, the other to the south, in Checleset Bay. Ice, flowing in a westerly direction from the Checleset Bay area, spilled through cols and saddles of the central ridge and coalesced with Brooks Bay ice. High peaks and ridges on the central spine stood as nunataks above the ice surface. On the southwest coast, the ice is thought to have extended to the edge of the continental shelf, about 5 km southwest of the present shoreline, where it calved into the sea. During this major ice advance, most of the Brooks Peninsula till was deposited. This till is equivalent to the Vashon till of the Fraser Glaciation.

Deglaciation of Fraser ice commenced prior to 12 250 years ago and more than likely prior to 13 500 years ago. While the ice downwasted and stagnated large boulders were deposited in the lowlands behind Cape Cook Lagoon. At the close of the glaciation, sea levels were higher than present due to isostatic depression of the land surface by ice. The maximum observed level of marine inundation was about 20 m above mean sea level. During this period, when the sea flooded the land, the Brooks Peninsula deglacial sediments (glaciomarine silts and sands) were deposited. These materials have been tentatively correlated with the Capilano sediments of the Fraser Drift (Table 3.1).

From the end of the Pleistocene, about 10 000 years ago, until 3900 years ago, the pattern of sea level change on Brooks Peninsula is unknown. At the end of this interval, sea level was probably between 4.5 m and 5.5 m above present mean sea level. Littoral cave deposits, located on the south coast of the peninsula and at present above high tide, indicate that sea level was 2 m to 3.5 m above present mean sea level about 1600 years ago. These data suggest that the land has been rising relative to the sea at an average rate of 1 mm to 2 mm per year for the past 4000 years. Most of this uplift is probably due to tectonic forces.

In addition to the deposition of beach materials during the Recent epoch, debris flow materials have been transported from the glacially oversteepened slopes and deposited on the valley floors, and streams have dissected Pleistocene sediments and the underlying bedrock at least up to 10 m. Organic materials have accumulated in poorly drained depressions and on some slopes.

Implications for a Refugium

Geological evidence from Brooks Peninsula indicates that the higher parts of Refugium Range and Harris Peak remained ice free during the Fraser Glaciation. From the beginning of the Fraser Glaciation to its maximum, a decreasing amount of bare land was available for the growth of vegetation. At the Fraser Glaciation maximum, however, the only ice-free land occurred as nunataks. Estimates of the size of this area range from 7 km^2 to 9.5 km^2. In order for vegetation to have survived at these sites, the local climate around the nunataks could not have been too severe. Although climatic conditions at the maximum are unknown, the location of the peninsula on the western margin of the ice front, a few tens of kilometres from the (then) open sea, suggests that the local climate at that time may have been moderated by maritime air. Hence, the climate may have been suitable for supporting plants.

A modern analogue to Brooks Peninsula exists in the Coast Mountains of Alaska. Flora collected from nunataks of the Juneau Ice Field, located on coastal Alaska, includes lichens, bryophytes, and vascular plants (Heusser 1954). Some indication of the climate on these nunataks is provided by temperature and snowfall data for 1951 from the Taku Glacier (Heusser 1954). Average January and July temperatures and annual snowfall at 1160 m are -24°C, 8°C, and 609 cm, respectively.

In summary, the evidence suggests that limited areas of bare ground (nunataks) existed on Brooks Peninsula at the Fraser Glaciation maximum. The location of the peninsula near the western margin of the ice front, and only a few tens of kilometres from open water, probably resulted in a local climate moderated by maritime air, suitable for vegetation growth.

References Cited

Alley, N.F. 1979. Middle Wisconsin stratigraphy and climate reconstruction, southern Vancouver Island, British Columbia. Quat. Res. 11: 213-237.

Alley, N.F. and S.C. Chatwin. 1979. Late Pleistocene history and geomorphology, southwestern Vancouver Island, British Columbia. Canadian Journal Earth Science 16: 1645-1657.

Armstrong, J.E. and J.J. Clague. 1977. Two major Wisconsin lithostratigraphic units in southwest British Columbia. Canadian Journal Earth Science 14: 1471-1480.

Birkland, P.W. 1964. Pleistocene glaciation of the northern Sierra Nevada, north of Lake Tahoe, California. Journal of Geology 72: 810-825.

______ . 1974. Pedology, weathering and geomorphological research. Oxford University Press, London.

Clague, J.J. 1981. Late Quaternary geology and geochronology of British Columbia. Part 2. Summary and discussion of radiocarbon-dated Quaternary history. Pp. 80-85, Geological Survey Canada.

______ , J.E. Armstrong, and W.H. Mathews. 1980. Advance of the late Wisconsin Cordilleran ice sheet in southern British Columbia since 22,000 B.P. Quat. Res. 13: 322-326.

______ , J.R. Harper, R.J. Hebda, and D.E. Howes. 1982. Late Quaternary sea levels and crustal movements, coastal British Columbia. Canadian Journal Earth Science 19: 597-618.

Dahl, R. 1966. Block fields, weathering pits and tor-like forms in the Narvik Mountains, Nordland, Norway. Geografiska Annaler Stockholm 48: 55-85.

Fyles, J.G. 1963. Surficial geology of Horne Lake and Parksville map areas, Vancouver Island, British Columbia. Mem. 318, Geological Survey Canada.

Hebda, R.J. 1983. Lateglacial and postglacial vegetation history at Bear Cove bog, northeast Vancouver Island, British Columbia. Canadian Journal of Botany 61: 3172-3192.

______ , S.R. Hicock, R.F. Miller, and J.E. Armstrong. 1983. Paleoecology of mid-Wisconsin sediments from Lynn Canyon, Fraser Lowland, British Columbia. Abstract. In Program with abstracts, volume 8. Geological Association of Canada and Mineralogical Association of Canada, Victoria, BC. Pp. A31.

Heusser, C.J. 1954. Nunatak flora of the Juneau Ice Field, Alaska. Bull. Torrey Botany Club 81(3): 236-250.

Holland, S.S. 1976. Landforms of British Columbia: a physiographic outline. Bull. 48, B.C. Department of Mines and Petroleum Resources.

Howes, D.E. 1981a. Late Quaternary sediments and geomorphic history of north-central Vancouver Island. Canadian Journal Earth Science 18: 1-12.

______ . 1981b. Terrain inventory and geological hazards: northern Vancouver Island. British Columbia Ministry of Environment (Victoria), APD Bulletin 5.

. 1983. Late Quaternary sediments and geomorphic history of northern Vancouver Island, British Columbia. Canadian Journal Earth Science 20: 57-65.

Jungen, J.R. and T. Lewis. 1978. The Coast Mountains and islands. Pp. 101-120 in K.W.G. Valentine, P.N. Sprout, T.E. Baker, and L.M. Lavkulich (eds.). The soil landscapes of British Columbia. Resource Analysis Branch, B.C. Ministry of Environment, Victoria, BC.

Mathews, W.H. 1974. Surface profiles of the Laurentide ice sheet in its marginal areas. Journal of Glaciology 13: 37-43.

Muller, J.E., K.E. Northcote, and D. Carlisle. 1974. Geology and mineral deposits of Alert Bay-Cape Scott map-area, Vancouver Island, British Columbia. Pp. 74-8, Geological Survey Canada.

Watts, S.H. 1979. Some observations on rock weathering, Cumberland Peninsula, Baffin Island. Canadian Journal Earth Science 16: 977-983.

______ . 1981. Bedrock weathering features in a portion of eastern high Arctic Canada: their nature and significance. Annals of Glaciology 2: 170-175.

Chapter 4

Soils of Brooks Peninsula

R.E. Maxwell
Wildlife Branch, Ministry of Environment, Lands and Parks
Victoria, BC

Abstract

Soil investigation on Brooks Peninsula, Vancouver Island, revealed three distinct soil phenomena. First, progressive pan formation (placic and duric) over time restricted soil drainage and appears to have influenced forest succession leading to paludification (bogging). The conditions were observed on one lowland area consisting of uplifted marine, glaciomarine, and glacial drift materials. Second, a soil investigated on a coastal fluvial terrace shows distinct evidence of structural modification (black, charcoal-rich organic surface). Chemical analyses of this site, when compared to archaeological deposits, show similarities in humic and fulvic acid ratios and in phosphorous, sulphur, and carbon levels. Unusually high boron levels were also found. Third, and most significant to the ice refugium question, is a soil located at 760 m on the central ridge. This soil has characteristics common to older unglaciated terrain—the clay mineral gibbsite, 20% (or more) clay content, a very high talc level, low calcium to magnesium ratio, and easily broken stones that are weathered to the core. Possible relict solifluction lobes on the headlands contain soil horizons with >30% clay. This third phenomenon provides evidence that an ice-free zone may have existed on Brooks Peninsula.

Acknowledgements

Soil analyses were done by Hong Chuah and staff, BC Environment, Kelowna, BC. Geological information was provided by D.E. Howes. Vegetation correlation was provided by R. Hebda, H. Roemer, and R.T. Ogilvie, and archaeological correlation by J. Haggarty and R. Inglis.

Manuscript review was by A.J. Green, Agriculture Canada Research Station, Vancouver, BC. X-ray diffraction analysis was by Dr. L.M. Lavkulich, University of British Columbia. Dr. N. Miles performed soil chemical and clay analysis at the Soil Research Institute, Ottawa. I thank

Lyle Ottenbriet for drafting the figures, and Dorothy Oldridge and Carolyn Kenzie for typing this report. The manuscript was edited by Kathryn Bernick, Tara Steigenberger and Mona Holley.

Introduction

The purpose of the soil studies on Brooks Peninsula was to explore the possible existence of relict soils[1]. Once on the peninsula, questions were raised as to the probable location and duration of glacial ice in the deep cirques, on the headlands, and along the central mountainous spine. The soil weathering processes that contributed to the formation of the unique bogs and scrublands were questioned. Are these features the products of old soils on relict landscapes or of more recent soils with severe drainage restrictions? Where are the most suitable sites for early human habitation? Are there distinctive soil features associated with the recently discovered archaeological deposits along the coastline?

To answer some of these questions, two approaches were taken. The first was to describe and classify soils along a transect from the coastline to the central ridge—to clarify the relict soil and vegetation questions. The second approach was to describe and classify soils thought to be significant to the geological and archaeological history of the area and to the soil-vegetation relationships.

This chapter is divided into four sections. The first, "Soil Landscape Descriptions", is intended to provide a broad ecological overview of the peninsula via brief soil-landscape descriptions. The second section, "Soil Development across a Lowland Landscape", is presented in two parts: 1) the Sandy Beach Ridge Sequence discusses the progression of soil development over time on a series of raised sandy beach ridges; and 2) the Glacial Drift Surface documents and compares a number of soil profiles that serve as a guide to the nature of recently glaciated surfaces. The third section discusses two unique soils located on the central ridge, which appears to have been unglaciated. The fourth section discusses and compares some black anthropogenic soils on a gravelly stream terrace. Definitions of technical soil science terms are given in Appendix 4.1.

Brooks Peninsula is part of the Insular Mountain Physiographic Region on the west coast of Vancouver Island (Holland 1976). The rectangular block of land projects into the Pacific Ocean 14 km, and is approximately 10 km wide. The area is characterized by a series of moderately to extremely sloping mountains and ridges that rise in elevation from 300 m to 800 m (Figure 4.1). At lower elevations, gently sloping to level terrain occurs in the form of subdued marine and fluvial terraces and drift-covered mountain slopes (Howes and Pattison 1978). The soils are mainly extremely well-developed podzols, and most are saturated during the wet portion of the year; they contain cemented pan formations, are extremely acid, and are virtually devoid of bases (water soluble elements and compounds, salts).

Soil-forming processes are dominated by the effects of a very high mean annual precipitation and a relatively high mean annual temperature. The Spring Island weather station (50° 00' N, 127° 25' W), located approximately 33 km southeast of Brooks Peninsula, records a mean annual precipitation of 3155 mm, almost all occurring as rain (Atmospheric Environment Service 1982). Mean annual daily temperature is 9.1°C. The winters are mild, the soils are wet for most of the year and rarely freeze. The character of the climate is discussed in greater detail in Chapter 8.

[1] Relict soils are those formed on pre-existing landscapes and not subsequently buried by younger materials (Lavkulich 1969: 25).

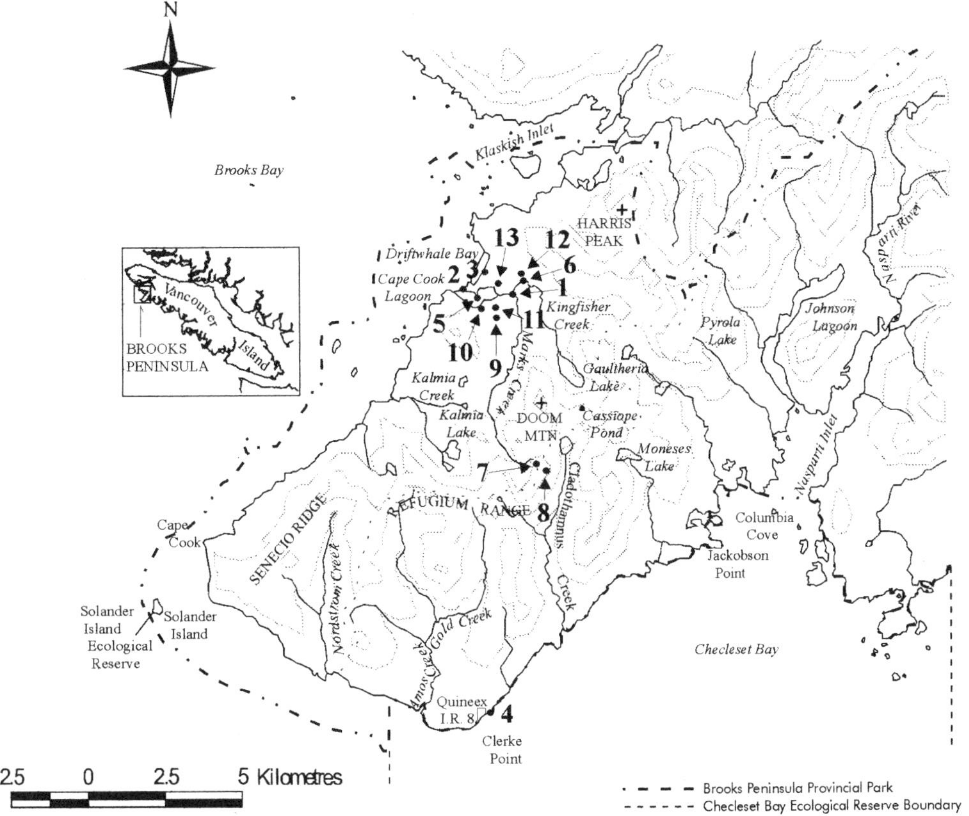

Figure 4.1 Brooks Peninsula study area and location of soil profile sites in Appendix 4.2

The soils of Brooks Peninsula have been classified into the Ferro-Humic Podzol Soil Landscape as described by Valentine et al. (1978). Excess moisture and the high incidence of poorly drained soils typify the landscape. Soils on recently glaciated terrain are characterized by the accumulation of complexes of amorphous organic matter, iron, and aluminum and are soils with exceptionally strong podzolic B horizons (i.e., rust stained, reddish-black surface soils).

"The soils may or may not have thin eluvial (Ae) horizons (whitish surface layer); are dominated by thick dark reddish B horizons of ± 1 m rich in iron, aluminum and organic matter; have strong indications of turbic activity, are medium to coarse textured and generally lack horizons in which clay has accumulated (Bt). Leaching is intense in these soils" (Valentine et al. 1978:108).

Most soils investigated on Brooks Peninsula are similar to descriptions of soils elsewhere along the coast of Vancouver Island, with occasional exceptions with regard to unusual chemical and clay contents.

The mineral soils have a low fertility status, the sum of the exchangeable bases is extremely low, usually less than 0.3 milliequivalents per 100 g of soil, and an extremely acid pH (3.5-4.0) is common to about 1 m deep. The surface organic matter (forest litter) is a major supplier of nutrients.

Soils are developed mainly in colluvial, morainal (or till), fluvioglacial, fluvial, and marine deposits. These deposits consist of ice-worn and weathered acidic igneous rock, which includes granodiorite, quartz diorite, and granite with some associated inclusions (Muller et al. 1974).

The terrain (surficial deposits) and soils of Brooks Peninsula were mapped at a 1:50 000 scale as part of a northern Vancouver Island study (Chatterton and Senyk 1976, 1977, 1978, 1979; Howes and Pattison 1978). During that reconnaissance survey no attempt was made to differentiate between glaciated and possibly unglaciated areas. The terrain and biophysical (ecosystem) resources were mapped in more detail in 1992 under contract by BC Parks, BC Ministry of Environment, Lands and Parks. The soil investigation during the "refugium expedition" generally confirms the soil descriptions of the earlier survey, however, a number of unique soils were identified.

Field Methods

To maximize the five days of fieldwork it was decided to run a transect from the coastline north of Cape Cook Lagoon to the low mountain slopes. This provided comparative information on marine, fluvial, organic, fluvioglacial, and morainal parent materials, which were identified on the 1:50 000 reconnaissance soil maps. The raised sandy marine ridges had created a soil chronosequence. New surfaces are gradually being exposed to soil weathering processes as a result of coastal tectonic uplift and indications of soil weathering rates could be explored.

Sites were selected on the basis of distinct changes in soil drainage regimes, topographic and morphological features, and vegetation physiognomy. Soil profile descriptions and laboratory analyses of significant soils could be used for comparative analyses with respect to the refugium question. From a total of 20 soil profiles, 14 were described and analysed. The soils were sampled by horizon, based on maximum expression of soil genesis as reflected in the morphological characteristics at each site according to McKeague (1978) and Walmsley et al. (1980). Appendix 4.2 contains the 14 soil profile descriptions with chemical and physical analyses. All soils, except those from archaeological sites, were located on the northwest portion of the peninsula (Figure 4.1).

Laboratory Methods

The standard soil chemical and physical analyses were according to McKeague (1978). Organic material analyses were based on Lowe (1980). Total macro- and micro-nutrient analyses were measured by an Inductively Coupled Plasma Emission Spectrometer ARL 3400 (I.C.P.) following a total nitric-perchloric digest (W. van Lierop personal communication, March 1983). See Appendix 4.3 for details of analysis methods.

Soil Landscapes

A soil landscape, as described in Table 4.1, consists of a relatively uniform geomorphic surface; the topography, genetic material, modifying processes, soil drainage, texture, and soil classification are within definable ranges. The soil landscape usually consists of one major forest community. For example, a moderately well-drained lowland forest on a gravelly fluvial terrace with Gleyed Ortstein Humo Ferric Podzol soil development, represents a soil landscape.

In some cases, a soil landscape may be complex; it can encompass a variety of soils and drainage patterns with two or more forest communities. In other cases, small, relatively homogeneous soil landscapes are described—for example, a single sandy beach ridge covered by only one or two vegetation types. The soil landscapes are, therefore, presented at various scales. Table 4.1 provides correlations of dominant terrain, vegetation, and soil features on Brooks Peninsula. The soil landscape names are derived from the respective terrains and their modifying processes, the vegetation types correlate to those listed in Chapter 8, and the soil descriptions list significant features. In some cases, detailed descriptions exist for some sites. Most soil descriptions are from Chatterton and Senyk (1976, 1977, 1978, 1979). Most landscapes are also outlined on photographs (Figures 4.2, 4.3, 4.4, 4.5, 4.6, 4.7).

Table 4.1 Soil landscape descriptions

Figure No.	Landscape No.	Soil Landscape	Vegetation[a]	Soil Description
4.2	1	Marine sediments, active littoral	(A) unvegetated	Gleyed Regosol, saline phase; poorly drained; gravelly to sandy loam texture; subject to wave and tidal influence; saline, base rich, neutral pH range.
-	-	Marine sediments, intertidal	(B) 4.2.1, lower salt marsh herbaceous vegetation	(Site 1, Appendix 4.2)
-	-	Marine sediments, intertidal	(C) 4.2.2, upper salt marsh herbaceous vegetation	(Site 1, Appendix 4.2)
4.2	2	Marine sediments, active	(A) 4.1.1 and 4.1.2, beach strand herbaceous vegetation; beach dune herbaceous	Orthic Regosol; well to moderately well drained; sand to gravelly sand texture; subject to wind erosion and sea spray; moderate to high base saturation, strongly acid, pH 5.0-5.5.
4.2	3	Marine sediments	(B) 3.1 beach shrub vegetation	Orthic Regosol-Orthic Dystric Brunisol; well to moderately well drained; sand to gravelly sand texture; subject to wind and sea spray; base saturation moderate to high, extremely acid, pH 3.6 to 5.0 (Site 2, Appendix 4.2).
4.3	4	Marine sediments, raised beaches, beach ridges; rock terraces	(A) 1.1 shoreline forest	Sombric Humo Ferric Podzol, Folisol inclusions; moderately well drained with imperfectly drained inclusions; sand and gravelly sand texture; subject to sea spray; low base saturation, extremely acid, pH, 4.0 (Site 3, Appendix 4.2).
-	-	Marine sediments, anthroprogenic mound over raised beaches	(B) 1.1 shoreline forest	Regosol anthroprogenic phase; well to rapidly drained; shelly matrix including sand and gravels; subject to sea spray; high base saturation, slightly acid to neutral, pH 6 to 7 (Site 4, Appendix 4.2).
4.5	5	Marine sediments, raised beaches, beach ridges, rock terraces	(A) Lowland forest, moderately well drained	Placic Humo Ferric Podzol, imperfectly to moderately well drained, extremely low base saturation, extremely acid, pH 4.5 (Site 5, Appendix 4.2).
4.4	6	Fluvial terrace, marine terrace	(B) Lowland forest, moderately well drained	Variable, Gleyed Ortstein Humo Ferric Podzol most common; imperfectly to moderately well drained; gravelly to very gravelly loamy sand texture; extremely low base saturation, extremely acid, pH 4.5.
4.3	7	Colluvial, mid to lower mountain slopes	(A) Lower mountain slope forest, moderate to steep slopes	Variable, Orthic Ferro Humic Podzol, lithic phases common; well to moderately well drained with imperfectly drained inclusions; gravelly loamy sand to sandy loam textures; extremely acid, pH 4 to 5.

[a] For vegetation details refer to Chapter 8.

Table 4.1 Continued

Figure No.	Landscape No.	Soil Landscape	Vegetation[a]	Soil Description
4.3 & 4.4	8	Till-Colluvial complex, lower mountain slopes	(B) Lowland forest, moderately well drained, gentle to moderate slopes	Variable, Gleyed Ferro Humic Podzol; placic, ortstein and duric horizons common; imperfectly drained with poorly drained inclusions; gravelly loamy sand to sandy loam; extremely low base saturation, extremely acid, pH 4.0 (Site 10, Appendix 4.2).
4.3	9a	Fluvioglacial-Till-Bog complexes and Till-Colluvial-Bog complexes. Inclusions of marine sediments at <20 m A.S.L.	(A) 3.2 bog shrub 4.4 shallow herbaceous vegetation 2.2 shallow bog scrub forest (minor inclusions)	Variable, Placic Ferro Humic Podzol, Gleyed Humo Ferric Podzol, peaty phases, ortstein and placic horizons common; gravelly loamy sand to sandy loam; extremely low to low base saturation; extremely acid to strongly acid, pH 4.4 to 5.5 (Site 9, Appendix 4.2).
4.3	9b	(similar to 9a above, most specific to bog inclusions)	(B) 2.2 shallow bog scrub forest	Variable, Placic Humo Ferric Podzol, peaty phases, ortstein horizons common; poorly drained; gravelly loamy sand; extremely low base saturation, very strongly acid, pH 4.5 to 5.0 (Site 10, Appendix 4.2)
4.3	9c	(similar to 9a above, most specific to bog inclusions)	(C) 2.2 bog scrub forest	Variable, Typic Humisol, Terric Humic Mesisol, Humic Fibrisol; very poorly drained; humic, mesic and fibric organic textures; extremely low base saturation, extremely acid, pH 3.7 to 4.5.
4.3	10	Colluvial veneer-rock complex with pockets of deep residual material on ridges and peaks	2.3 timberline scrub forest 3.3 timberline shrub	Gleyed Ferro Humic Podzol, lithic and peaty phases; imperfectly drained, gravelly sandy loam to gravelly loam texture; subject to intense wind and rain; extremely low base saturation, extremely acid, pH 3.8 to 4.4 (Site 7, Appendix 4.2).
4.11	10a	Similar to 10 above; some sites may include ancient soil surfaces	4.7 well-drained alpine meadow 4.8 windblown ridge herb	Complex soils, Orthic Ferro Humic Podzol, lithic phases; well to moderately well drained; gravelly and very gravelly loam (20% clay content); subject to intense wind and rain; extremely low base saturation, extremely acid, pH 3.8 to 4.4 (Site 8, Appendix 4.2).
4.6	11	Debris slide scar, revegetated	2.5 slide scrub forest 3.4 slide shrub	Soils variable depending upon age of disturbance; very recent slides have Regosolic soil development, revegetated slides have Brunisolic and Podzolic soil development; rapidly to imperfectly drained; stones and cobbles variable, gravelly to very gravelly loamy sand textures; strongly to extremely acid, pH 5.5 to 4.4.
4.7	12	Debris slide scar, partially revegetated		

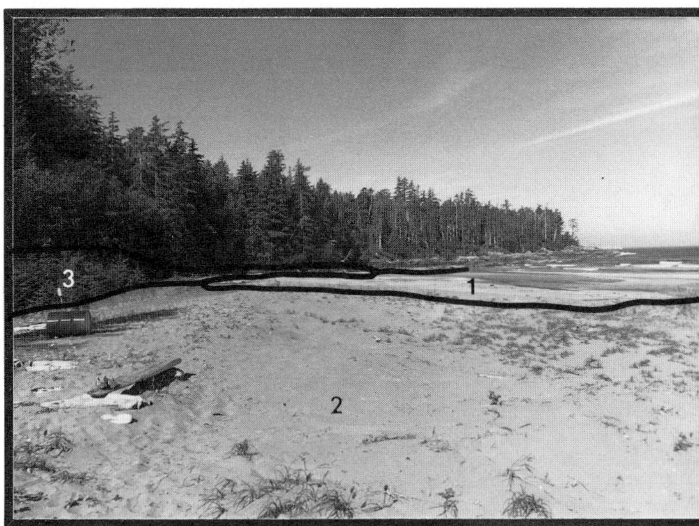

Legend

1	Marine sediments, active littoral
2	Marine sediments, active sand dunes
3	Marine sediments, sand dunes on raised beaches

Figure 4.2 **Beach deposits fronting Cape Cook Lagoon and facing Brooks Bay, showing landscapes (Photo: R.E.M.)**

Legend

1	Marine sediments, active littoral
2	Marine sediments, active sand dunes
3	Marine sediments, sand dunes on raised beaches
4	Marine sediments, raised beaches
7	Colluvial mid-lower slopes
8	Till-colluvial complex, lower slope
9a	Fluvioglacial, till, bog complexes
9b	Bog complexes
7&10	Colluvial ridges and mid-slope complex

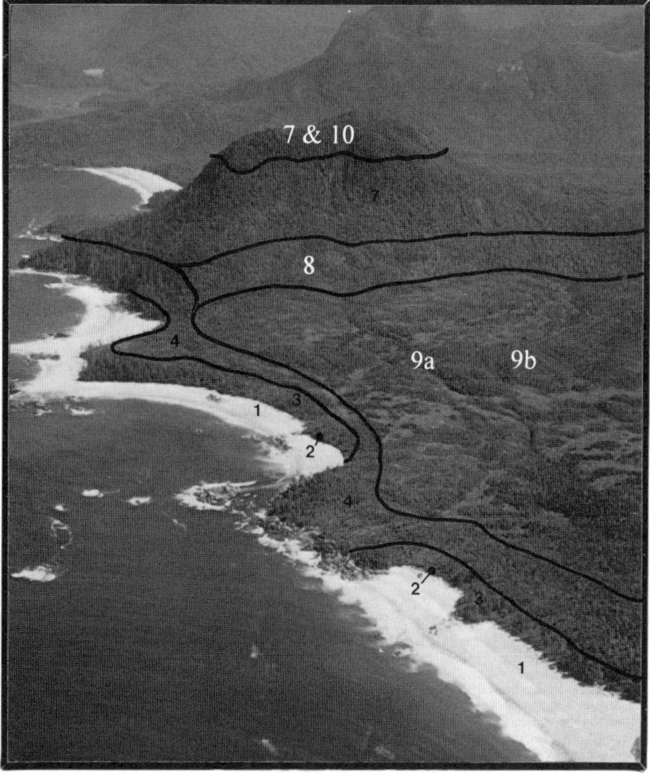

Figure 4.3 **Coastline and lowlands facing Brooks Bay (Photo: Hedi Kootner, "Beautiful BC")**

Legend
6 Fluvial terrace, marine terrace
7,8 Till-colluvial complex

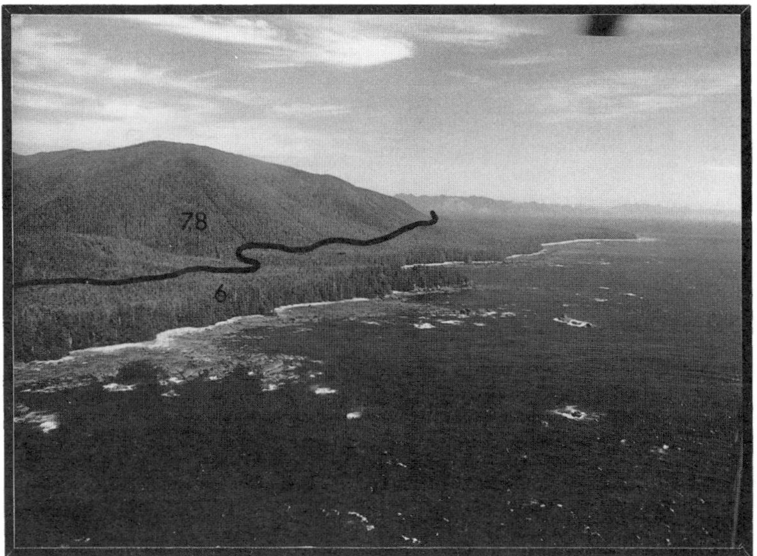

Figure 4.4 Brooks Peninsula headlands at Nordstrom Creek, showing landscapes (Photo: Heidi Kottner)

Legend
5,4 Marine sediments, rock ridges (shoreline forest), raised beaches
9a Till-colluvial and bog complexes
9b Glaciofluvial-till and bog complexes

Figure 4.5 Senecio Ridge east of Cape Cook (Photo: R.E.M.)

Figure 4.6 Brooks Peninsula headlands. Landscape 11, debris slide scar, revegetated (Photo: R.E.M.)

Legend	
8	Till-colluvium complex
12	Debris slide scar, partially vegetated

Figure 4.7 Landslide on tributary draining southards to Checleset Bay, showing landscapes (Photo: R.E.M.)

Soil Development Across a Lowland Landscape

General Characteristics

Exploratory soil investigations along a transect, from a series of raised beaches to an inland glacial-drift-covered surface, found that progressive development of placic (iron) pan formation probably influences forest succession (Figure 4.8). Placic pans are very common in this lowland area of Brooks Peninsula, where they are the dominant cemented horizon within the normal rooting-depth of approximately 70 cm.

Soils developed in raised beaches, inferred to be younger than 1200 B.P., generally did not exhibit strong, continuous placic horizons, though 8000-12 000-year-old beach ridge soils at a slightly higher elevation did exhibit strong, well-developed placic pans. The soils developed in drift materials that are older than 12 000 B.P. (see Chapters 3 and 9) contained both shallow placic pans and combinations of deep cemented layers known as duric, fragic (fragipan), and ortstein horizons (Figure 4.8).

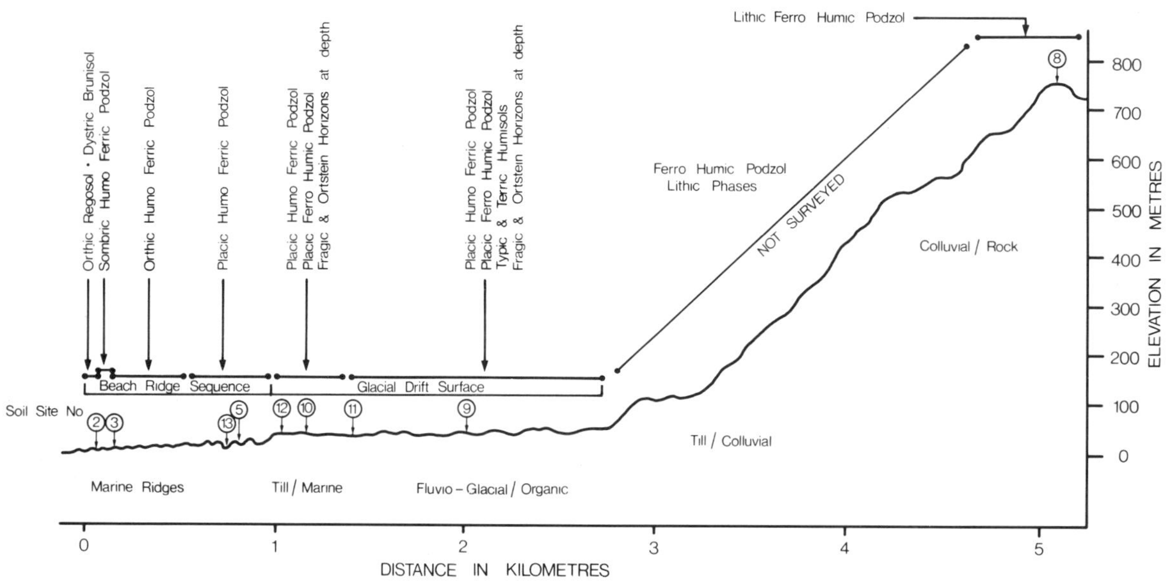

Figure 4.8 **Soil development across a lowland landscape on the northern corner of Brooks Peninsula**

Sandy beach ridge sequence

The series of raised beach ridges located just north of Cape Cook Lagoon provided a unique landscape in which to explore a soil chronosequence. Howes (Chapter 3) describes the geological history of the raised beach formation. All 13 raised beaches consist of deep, stone-free sand to loamy sand textures. The general sequence of soil development across this marine landscape may span approximately 13 000 years (Figures 4.9 and 4.10). Each soil pit, of a total of six, was located on the crest of the ridge; not all ridges were sampled. Detailed soil and site descriptions are in Appendix 4.2.

At the tide line (mean sea level) recent beach deposits subject to intertidal marine processes are classified as Orthic Regosols, saline eroded phases. These young soils contain no pans, are unvegetated, and have not experienced constant soil weathering.

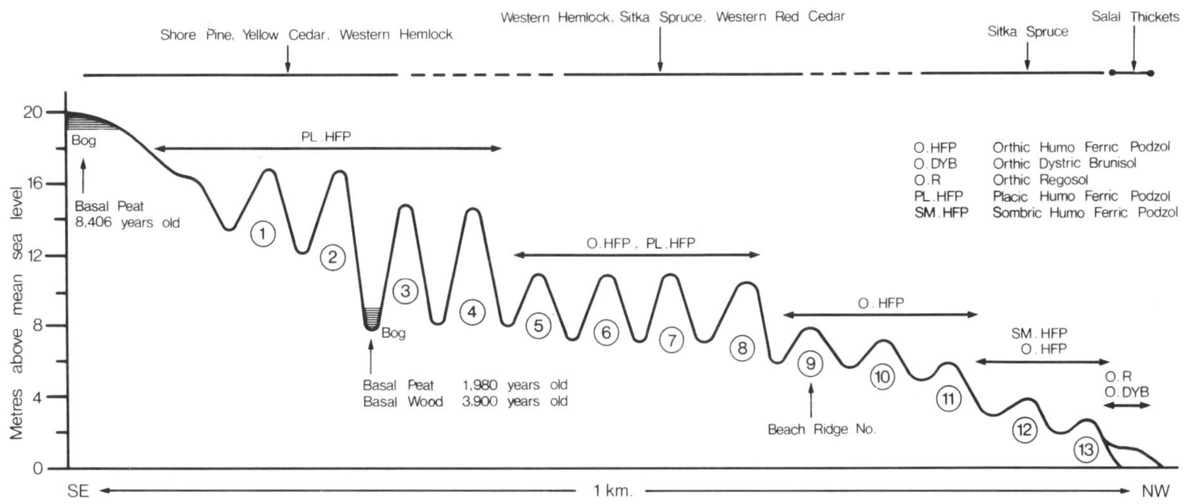

Figure 4.9 Soil development and forest cover relationships across a sandy beach ridge sequence near Cape Cook Lagoon

Figure 4.10 Part of lowland landscape east of Cape Cook Lagoon (The raised beach ridges are outlined.) (Photo: R.E.M.)

At approximately 2-3 m above mean sea level, recently stabilized, aeolian modified beaches have soils with a slight yellowish colour in the surface B horizon. These are classified as Orthic Regosols and Orthic Dystric Brunisols (Appendix 4.2: site 2). The vegetation consists mainly of dense thickets of *Gaultheria* (salal) and occasional young *Picea sitchensis* (Sitka spruce). These soils are estimated to be less than 200 years old.

At approximately 3-4 m above mean sea level, raised beach ridges have soils with humic-rich surface A and podzolic B horizons. They are classified as Sombric Humo Ferric Podzol with inclusions of Orthic Humo Ferric Podzols. Placic pan formation was not evident. A coastal Sitka spruce forest (Shoreline Forest) covered the ridges (Figure 4.9: ridges 12, 13). The age of the soils is estimated to be between 600 and 1200 years old (see Appendix 4.2: site 3).

At approximately 6-8 m, the beach ridges had soils classified as Orthic Humo Ferric Podzol. The surface soils to 50 cm deep had a slightly blotchy mottled appearance, indicating a slightly wetter soil moisture regime than the previous 2 m to 4 m ridges. These soils had no placic pans within the top 50 cm of soil—the depth of excavation. The ridges were covered by a *Tsuga heterophylla-Picea sitchensis* forest (Lowland Forest), and the soils are inferred to be older than 1200 years old.

At approximately 11 m (Figure 4.9: ridges 5-8), the soils are classified as both Orthic Humo Ferric Podzol and Placic Humo Ferric Podzol. Placic pans appeared intermittently. They were vegetated by *Tsuga heterophylla* (western hemlock), *Picea sitchensis* (Sitka spruce), and *Thuja plicata* (western redcedar). These soils are inferred to be older than 1200 years (an estimated range is 3000-5000 years old).

At approximately 15 m (Figure 4.9: ridges 3, 4), there are two ridges that are distinctly higher than the previously described seaward ridges. Placic Humo Ferric Podzol soil development is dominant, and surface mineral soil horizons are moist and exhibit blotchy, mottled patterns. The placic horizons appear to restrict drainage. Forest growth (Wet Lowland Forest) appears to be less vigorous—*Tsuga heterophylla* (western hemlock) and *Thuja plicata* (western redcedar) are comparatively low, the trees are widely spaced, and the moss layers are thick and very moist. The age of the soils is inferred to be older than the estimated range of 3000 to 5000 years.

A large swale that served as a drainage route is located between ridges 2 and 3. It contains a moderately deep sphagnum bog. The date of basal material is approximately 4000 B.P. (see Chapter 9; Appendix 4.2: site 13).

The oldest beach strands occur at about 17 m (Figure 4.9: ridges 1, 2). The soils are classified as Placic Humo Ferric Podzols, and the mineral horizons exhibit distinct, large, blotchy mottles indicating temporarily saturated soil conditions. The placic pans are continuous, approximately 3-5 mm thick, and are located at about 50 cm depth. These pans appear to restrict the penetration of both water and roots. The vegetation cover does not change even on the steep slopes of 15-30%. It consists of a suppressed, open forest, predominantly *Pinus contorta* (lodgepole pine) and *Chamaecyparis nootkatensis* (yellow cedar), and sphagnum carpets the surface. The soils are inferred to be older than 8000 B.P.

Detailed studies on the ecology of Sitka spruce, conducted 220 km south of Brooks Peninsula, at Tofino, showed a similar trend of soil development across raised sandy beach ridges (Cordes 1972; Sondheim et al. 1981). Cordes found Orthic Regosols under a *Picea sitchensis-Eurhynchium oreganum* (Sitka spruce-feather moss) community and soils inferred to be less than 200 years old (dated from the oldest standing tree). Orthic Humo Ferric Podzols with a thin surface eluvial horizon (Ae) are classified in *Picea sitchensis-Rubus spectabilis* (Sitka spruce-salmonberry) communities. The more weakly expressed podzols are correlated to younger stands. These soils were inferred to be

250-350 years old. Placic Humo Ferric Podzols are described for the *Tsuga heterophylla-Picea sitchensis* community, and the soils are noted as the "oldest" found on that particular beach plain. Cordes does state, however, that "although an iron pan is present in this profile, it is not always present in the soils belonging to this type" (Cordes 1972: 208).

Tofino beach deposits that contain inclusions of Placic Humo Ferric Podzols, range in elevation from approximately 8 m to 12 m (Cordes 1972). On Brooks Peninsula, the beach ridge sequence on which Placic Humo Ferric Podzols begin to appear, is at approximately 9 m. It should be noted that postglacial coastal emergence rates and elevations are probably different at these locations.

Cordes also found throughout the profiles an increase in moisture, from younger to older soils. He states "this factor appears to be related to a reduction in internal drainage due to cementation" (Cordes 1972: 209). Studies by Baker (1974) and Valentine (1971) on the Tofino lowland have also found that placic horizons appear impermeable enough to prevent the passage of water and roots.

Glacial Drift Surface

Sites 9, 10, and 11 along the transect (see Appendix 4.2 and Figure 4.8) revealed soils developed in three distinct parent materials. The till, or possible glaciomarine deposit, located at approximately 18 m, is of particular interest because it can be compared to other Holocene tills. The organic deposit (bog) is of interest as it is one of numerous small bogs on Brooks Peninsula associated with scrub forest communities. The fluvioglacial deposit provides some insight to soil-weathering features. All three sites were investigated to discover soil characteristics responsible for restricted drainage that results in a poorly drained landscape and suppressed forest growth.

The soil formed in the till parent material is located near "Panicum Pond", dated as older than 12 250 B.P. (see Chapter 9). The podzolization processes in this soil are well expressed by the strong podzolic B horizon and the distinct placic and fragic pan formations (Appendix 4.2: site 10). Table 4.2 shows that the till soil (site 10) tends to reflect a greater degree of podzolization than does the oldest raised beach (site 5), even with consideration of the different parent materials. This is inferred from the different iron and aluminum values extracted with both pyrophosphate and dithionite. The percent of organic carbon is also significantly higher in site 10 than in site 5. The base saturation values and, to some degree, the exchangeable bases are also lower in the till soil. The stronger podzolization, increased organic matter through depth, and lower base status tend to indicate that the till (glaciomarine) soil may have been exposed to weathering longer than the oldest raised beaches. The till soil is also subject to relatively intense lateral seepage and overland flow due to restricted soil infiltration caused by pan formations. It is suspected that the high organic matter levels may be, partially, the result of downslope transport of organic colloids, in addition to physical mixing and biological cycling. It is likely that, under the current climatic regime, this soil has reached its maximum stage of development—possibly an irreversible stage—and will maintain poorly drained, acidic, low-base conditions.

Comparisons of chemical and physical analyses of this till soil to analyses of other podzolic soils formed in till and derived from the granite-rhyolite family, show that most soil characteristics are similar and within comparable ranges. A notable consistency in soils investigated below 100 m, is low clay content—less than 2%. This feature appears to be characteristic of most Holocene tills on Vancouver Island—of generally less than 10% clay (Jungen 1985; Lewis 1976). At the present stage of soil investigation, the lowland till site appears to be developed on late Wisconsin glacial and/or glaciomarine materials.

Site 11, a bog dated at 12 250 B.P. (see Chapter 9), is located at approximately 20 m above sea level on a pitted outwash plain and is classified as a Typic Humisol. The advanced stage of peat

Table 4.2 Selected soil data for transect sites[a]

Depth	Horizon	Sand	Silt %	Clay	O.C. %	N	Pyrophosphate Fe %	Pyrophosphate Al	Dithionite Fe %	Dithionite Al	Ext. Bases meg/100g	CEC	Base Sat. %	pH $CaCl_2$
SITE 2, ORTHIC REGOSOL - sandy beach, active (<100 years est.), 1 m elevation														
0-10	C1	99.4	0.3	0.3	0.55	0.03	0.12	0.05	0.45	0.10	1.58	2.81	56.2	4.6
10-25	C2	99.4	0.2	0.4	0.26	0.12	0.07	0.04	0.43	0.09	2.89	1.20	100.0	5.6
SITE 3, SOMBRIC HUMO FERRIC PODZOL - sandy beach ridge (700-2000 years est.), 4 m elevation														
3-15	Ah	88.5	11.0	0.5	2.96	0.10	0.88	0.22	1.10	0.22	0.78	15.42	5.1	3.9
15-35	Bf	94.5	5.4	0.1	1.77	0.04	0.58	0.22	0.81	0.21	0.47	10.50	4.5	4.0
15-60	Bm	98.0	1.7	0.3	0.57	0.15	0.16	0.17	0.50	0.21	0.55	4.01	13.7	4.4
SITE 5, PLACIC HUMO FERRIC PODZOL - sandy beach ridge (5000-12 000 years est.), 17 m elevation														
0-10	Ah	79.8	15.4	4.8	1.64	0.18	0.70	0.27	0.76	0.17	0.82	16.38	5.0	-
10-22	Bfc	92.4	6.5	1.1	1.75	0.15	0.70	0.43	0.75	0.25	0.32	10.46	3.1	4.2
40-60	Bf	98.6	0.6	0.8	0.42	0.02	0.15	0.28	0.58	0.36	0.25	6.44	3.9	4.7
200-210	Cl	99.7	0.1	0.2	0.14	0.04	0.07	0.07	0.50	0.12	0.32	0.80	40.0	4.7
SITE 10, PLACIC HUMO FERRIC PODZOL - silty sand till blanket (12 250 years adjacent to bog date), 18 m elevation														
0-8	Ahe	52.1	39.3	8.6	5.24	0.20	0.34	1.00	-	-	0.48	26.08	1.8	4.0
8-15	Bfg	70.5	27.9	1.6	3.25	0.07	2.16	1.25	3.80	1.23	0.28	26.03	1.1	4.5
15-19	IIBfcc	68.0	30.7	1.3	3.39	0.08	1.08	1.17	1.90	1.23	0.26	23.83	1.1	4.7
19-30	IIBfg1	63.4	34.8	1.8	4.28	0.14	1.14	1.36	-	-	0.36	29.38	1.2	4.8
30-45	IIBfg2	70.9	28.6	0.5	2.86	0.10	1.08	1.06	-	-	0.31	18.69	1.7	4.7
45-62	IIBfg	77.8	21.3	0.9	2.86	0.10	0.24	0.54	0.81	0.71	0.36	13.15	2.7	5.0
SITE 8, ORTHIC FERRO HUMIC PODZOL - silty sand residual veneer (age not determined, soils appear "older"), 760 m elevation														
0-10	Bhf	48.1	34.5	17.4	12.75	0.60	0.88	1.16	2.65	0.86	1.63	32.62	5.0	4.5
10-20	Bf1	53.5	28.0	18.5	5.03	0.23	0.74	1.12	2.90	0.78	0.60	19.87	3.0	3.5
20-40	Bf2	57.9	23.1	19.0	3.67	0.16	0.66	0.98	3.04	0.75	0.43	17.75	2.4	3.2

[a] See Canada Dept. of Agriculture (1976) for an explanation of chemical terms.

decomposition is quite different from the organic soils at sites 12 and 13. Site 12, a Terric Humisol, located at approximately 18 m elevation over a silty marine terrace, is shallower, consists predominantly of sphagnum and sedge peat, and is considerably less decomposed throughout. Site 13, a bog classified as a Humic Fibrisol, is located at approximately 5 m elevation, between beach ridges 2 and 3. The date of the basal (130-140 cm) peat is approximately 2000-4000 B.P. (see Chapter 9). This young bog (site 13) has only 32 cm of basal peat below the sphagnum-sedge derived surface and middle tiers, whereas the 12 000-year-old bog (site 11) has more than 80 cm of well-decomposed basal peat, as well as humified peat throughout the middle tier. The stepped pond-like environment of site 11 is, probably, a major reason for the predominance of well-humified organic material—the site suggests that a significant proportion of the humic material originated as washed-in sediments.

Throughout this local landscape, particularly upslope of site 11, surface accumulations of well-humified organic matter (10-30 cm thick) occur in patchwork fashion, with mineral soil exposures. These exposures exist as intermittent surface drainage channels and very small, active deltas and fans located particularly at the edges of bogs. Other active surface erosion includes constant undercutting and erosion of the humic veneer, a process enhanced by restricted soil water infiltration.

The reason for the general lack of deep (>50 cm), undecomposed sphagnum deposits on these poorly drained sites is unknown. Three possible soil-related explanations are: 1) the soil drainage and soil chemistry have never been conducive to sphagnum accumulation; 2) constant surface erosion, enhanced by progressively restricted drainage, physically removes or channels sphagnum accumulations; 3) the large amounts of divalent iron, aluminum, and associated compounds with sulphur present, in the extremely acid environment (pH 3.7), may be toxic to sphagnum. (These elements were high in the mineral soils of sites 9 and 10; see Appendix 4.2.) Periodically, patches of surface mineral soil are dispersed over organic deposits during storm-induced erosion. Exposed, mixed mounds of grey-green subsoil have been noted along seepage zones, and thin buried horizons of mineral soil have been observed in the humic veneer profiles. The cause of the turbation (boil-like mounds) is not known; water-saturated soils with hydraulic pressure originating upslope may have an influence.

Site 9, a glaciofluvial deposit with postglacial fluvial deposition, is classified as a Placic Humo Ferric Podzol. The degree of weathering, as indicated by iron and aluminum values, is comparatively lower than the till site located downslope. This is probably the result of more recent deposition at site 9. Deeper into this soil (40 cm deep), a number of discontinuous, thin placic pans occur. These pans appear to be partially responsible for the poor drainage in the shallow bog herbaceous vegetation, and they also concentrate surface runoff. The uppermost 15 cm of the soil profile exhibits a weakly stratified sequence of fluvial sediments (silt loam to sandy loam) with lens-like inclusions of dark greyish brown organic matter. The terrace-like deposit that supports this small floodplain also indicates that the local landscape is subject to moderately active erosion and deposition.

Discussion

The transect across Brooks Peninsula lowland shows characteristics of soil development and forest succession similar to those found by other, more detailed, coastal soil studies. It must be realized that this discussion is based on very limited fieldwork in only one area of Brooks Peninsula. These studies and those of Brooks Peninsula show that a number of features of soil formation may occur consistently with increasing soil age. The following features (also see Table 4.2) relate mainly to the sandy beach ridge sequence, with the glacial drift sequence representing the relatively well-weathered soils of late Wisconsin age (± 10 000 years):

1) progressive increase in organic matter as surface accumulations and throughout the mineral soil solum;
2) increased pyrophosphate and dithionite extractable iron plus aluminum;
3) progressive decrease in exchangeable bases;
4) progressive increase in cation exchange capacity;
5) general decrease in percent base saturation;
6) consistently low (very strongly acid) pH;
7) progressive increase in pan formation, particularly placic (iron) pans, coupled with progressive increase in soil moisture status as soil drainage and soil permeability decrease;
8) consistent relatively low clay content for all soils except surface soil horizons, where clay content increases.

Ugolini (1968) studied soil development along a transect of recently deglaciated terrain in Glacier Bay, Alaska. The soils range only to 250 years old, but show the following trends with age: a decrease in pH from 8 to 4.5; a decrease in carbonates through the surface horizons, accumulating at greater depths; an increase in free iron oxides; an increase in cation exchange capacity; a progressive increase in organic carbon, in both forest litter and mineral soil; and an increase in the depth of the weathered solum.

Ugolini and Mann (1979) studied a soil chronosequence across uplifted marine terraces near Lituya Bay, Alaska. The terraces range from 9 m to 80 m above sea level and date from 400 to 2000-3000 years old. They propose that the formation of peatlands there is caused by the deterioration of the internal soil drainage as an iron cemented pan develops during podzolization.

Gently sloping lowland soils, which are prone to progressive pan formation, experience gradual reduction in internal soil drainage. This causes water-saturated soil conditions, perched water tables, and extensive overland flow. As a result, forest growth becomes poor and suppressed, and some sites experience progressive bogging (paludification). This process of landscape evolution has been described for other locations in British Columbia and in Alaska (Ugolini and Mann 1979; Valentine 1971). Brooks Peninsula provides unique, virgin landscapes in which to study the effects of soil genesis on plant succession, particularly as it relates to decreased productivity of some coastal forest lands.

Soil Development on the Central Ridge

General Characteristics

The area investigated on the central ridge, at 760 m, is one of the highest centrally located points of moderate relief on Brooks Peninsula. It is situated above the upper mountain shoulders, above and adjacent to steep cirque basins. The ridge area is characterized by a generally consistent macro-form that includes a blend of strongly rolling, weathered rock outcrops, steep cliff faces, and moderate to very steep colluvial slopes (Figure 4.11). The few solifluction lobes observed are confined to the lowermost portion of the slope; some lobes show evidence of activity—slightly flattened and buried vegetation along their snouts. Other deflated lobes have lost their distinct lobe-like forms, are vegetated, and may be relict periglacial features.

The ridge is subject to intense, driving rains and very strong, constant winds. Wind-sculptured mountain hemlock occurs on the northwest-facing leeward slopes. Most soil surfaces are vegetated, except for scattered exposures of mineral soil and stone pavement subject to deflation. The slope movement processes associated with some solifluction lobes appear to result from periodically saturated soil conditions. Present climatic conditions are thought to be favourable only for minor freeze-thaw-induced soil erosion. Occasional extreme temperatures recorded near sea level at Estevan Point (-13.9°C, -10.6°C and -7.8°C) do document freezing conditions. During cold winters it is likely that an initial snow cover helps insulate the soils from the freeze. The bedrock includes granodiorite, quartz-diorite, and minor inclusions of rhyolite.

Physical and Chemical Soil Properties

The primary soil profile was excavated to a depth of 40 cm; rubble precluded further digging. Five other exploratory holes were dug at various locations—solifluction lobes, flat-shallow to bedrock positions, and vegetated steep slopes. One shallow profile was excavated beneath a dense stand of mountain hemlock. Most profiles exhibited coarse fragments and similar field textures and colours.

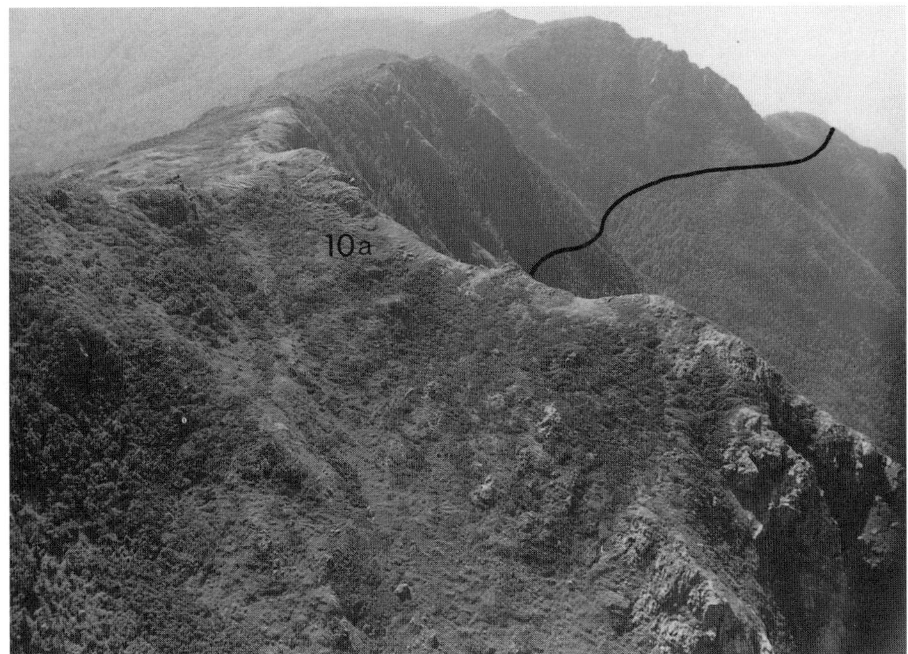

Figure 4.11 Soil landscapes of the central ridge of Brooks Peninsula (The black line approximates a possible glacial trim line. The upslope portion may have remained ice-free for an unknown time, 10a see Table 4.1.)

Several soil features at the ridge location, site 8, stand out as being distinct from other comparable granodiorite-derived soils. The large angular and subangular gravels, cobbles, and stones have extensively and deeply pitted surfaces. A well-weathered rind is common to most clasts on deflated soil surfaces and also to those throughout the soil profile. Most stones break easily and show weathering to the core. Similar clasts excavated from a nearby concave site, site 7, had very soft rinds that could be scraped off with a knife—the clasts were often rotten throughout, and some could be broken by hand.

Analytical results that signify a long period of weathering include: relatively high clay content (19%), relatively high dithionite extractable iron (3.04%), high organic carbon (12.7%), relatively low calcium to magnesium ratio (0.66%), and high copper (174 ppm), zinc (84 ppm), and molybdenum (24 ppm) levels[3] (Table 4.3; Appendix 4.2: sites 7, 8).

Published comparative data on residual colluvium derived from granodiorite or associated rock are rare for British Columbia. For general comparative purposes four morainal deposits from the BC. Cordillera (Green 1976; Luttmerding and Shields 1976) and from two Pleistocene surfaces—one each from Oregon and California—were selected (Table 4.3). The author's experience that

[3] The copper, zinc, and molybdenum values are comparatively high, but the soils could be derived from a weathered, mineralized dike. A dike sample taken from a cave wall (on Brooks Peninsula) shows similar chemical values.

Table 4.3 Selected chemical and physical properties of Holocene and Pleistocene soils

Depth	Horizon	Sand	Silt	Clay	O.C. %	Pyro Phosphate Fe	Pyro Phosphate Al	Dithionite Citrate Fe	Dithionite Citrate Al	CaC12 pH	Ratio Ca/ Mg	Ratio FeA1/ Clay %	Ratio O.M./ Fe (pyro) %
ORTHIC FERRO HOMIC PODZOL-silty sand residual veneer-Brooks Peninsula @ 760 metres													
0-10	Bhf1	48.1	34.5	17.4	12.75	0.88	1.16	2.65	0.86	4.50	0.75	0.12	27.50
10-20	Bhf2	53.5	28.0	18.5	5.03	0.74	1.12	2.90	0.78	3.47	0.64	0.10	11.35
20-40	Bf	57.9	23.1	19.0	3.67	0.66	0.98	3.04	0.75	3.19	0.66	0.08	3.32
[a] ORTHIC HUMO FERRIC PODZOL-rubbly silty sand Moraine (#3) Dunn Peak Shuswap Highlands @ 1900 m (10 000-8000 yrs. B.P.)													
1 (0-40)	Ae	57	41	3.0	2.1	0.02	0.04	-	-	3.4	-	0.02	175.35
2 (10-25)	Bf1	59	35	6.0	3.2	0.40	0.77	-	-	3.8	-	0.19	13.36
3 (25-50)	Bf2	63	34	3.0	1.8	0.18	0.66	-	-	4.2	-	0.34	16.70
4 (50-100)	Bf3, C	65	33	2.0	1.2	0.13	0.56	-	-	4.2	-	0.34	15.41
[b] ORTHIC HUMO FERRIC PODZOL-silty sand Moraine (#3) Germansen Mt. @1585 metres (10 000-8000 years B.P.)													
1 (0-5)	Ae	59.7	35.6	4.7	1.53	0.04	0.04	0.09	0.06	3.25	5.5	0.01	66.25
2 (5-18)	Bhf	57.7	36.0	6.3	4.65	1.03	0.39	1.38	0.45	3.60	5.2	0.22	7.78
3 (18-25)	Bfl	61.1	34.2	4.7	2.09	0.45	0.44	1.02	0.71	4.15	10.75	0.18	8.00
4 (25-56)	Bfg, Bm	59.9	36.1	4.0	1.04	0.22	0.33	0.42	0.31	4.43	22.20	0.13	8.18
5 (56-102)	BCg, C	71.0	26.1	2.9	0.20	0.03	0.15	0.18	0.06	4.70	37.00	0.06	12.33
[c] ORTHIC HUMO FERRIC PODZOL-silty sand till, Site 5 Fitzsimmons Range @ 1950 metres (approx. 12 000 years B.P.													
0-10	Ae	43.6	46.2	10.2	10.4	-	-	0.58	0.59	4.0	1.61	0.11	29.8
10-21	Bf1	66.5	24.0	9.5	3.1	-	-	0.53	1.42	4.6	2.44	0.62	6.9
21-36	Bf2	54.6	36.5	8.9	1.2	-	-	0.28	0.75	4.8	2.76	0.11	-
36+	C	56.3	34.2	9.5	0.3	-	-	0.19	0.27	4.9	1.55	0.04	1.9
[d] DURIC HUMO FERRIC PODZOL-silty sand till, "Golden Ears" soil association, Mount Seymour @870 metres (approx. 12 000 years B.P.)													
0-4	Ae	55	39	6.0	5.63	0.2	0.1	-	-	2.8	4.4	0.05	48.0
4-12	Bf	-	-	-	6.95	0.9	0.5	-	-	3.4	2.5	-	13.3
12-17	Bhf1	67	29	4.0	7.87	0.8	2.2	-	-	4.0	7.6	0.75	16.9
27-42	Bhf2	62	35	3.0	5.51	0.6	1.4	-	-	4.3	9.0	0.66	15.8
42-59	Bfg1	71	27	2.0	3.64	0.2	0.8	-	-	4.5	6.5	0.50	31.3
59-95	BCg1	59	38	3.0	0.53	0.1	0.3	-	-	4.7	2.0	0.13	9.1
[e] JOEY TAXADJUNCT AERIC HAPLAQUOD, fine silty, marine sediments mixed mesic, ortstein-Seven Devils Surface-Oregon coast @ 120 m (middle Pleistocene)													
0-15	Ae21	27.1	69.2	3.7	2.03	tr	tr	tr	tr	3.3	-	-	-
15-25	A22	28.4	65.6	6.0	0.99	tr	tr	tr	tr	3.5	-	-	-
25-30	B21H	39.0	55.0	6.0	3.36	tr	0.3	tr	0.3	3.7	-	-	-
30-43	B22ir	26.7	60.4	12.9	0.69	0.3	0.3	1.8	0.4	4.1	-	0.04	3.95
43-61	B23ir	48.1	41.9	10.0	1.03	0.2	0.5	3.7	5.0	4.7	-	0.10	8.85
61-86	11C1	16.9	44.7	35.4	0.19	0.3	0.2	2.1	0.5	4.0	-	0.01	1.08
86-104	11C2	18.8	48.7	32.5	0.12	0.1	0.1	0.9	0.3	3.9	-	0.006	2.06
[f] PEDON 115, Xeric HAPLOHOMULT silty clay Colluvium (Residual Weathering) Nevada County, California @ 829 m (late Pleistocene or older)													
0-18	A1	23.2	39.4	37.4	6.69	0.4	0.7	41.3	1.0	5.3	3.36	0.029	16.72
18-36	B1†	19.3	35.3	45.4	2.16	-	-	9.5	1.0	4.8	1.06		
36-46	B21†	17.8	31.1	51.1	1.39	-	-	10.7	1.1	4.8	0.83		-
46-84	V22†	18.6	30.8	50.6	0.84	-	-	11.4	1.2	4.8	0.31		-
84-120	B31†	22.1	28.2	49.7	0.85	-	-	12.8	1.5	4.6	1.20		-
120-155	B32†	26.8	32.8	40.4	0.42	-	-	12.3	1.1	4.5	1.00		-
155-185	C	26.7	34.7	38.6	0.37	-	-	12.2	1.2	4.4	1.00		-

[a] Values are averages from three soil profiles; horizons have been grouped into four depth intervals. K.W.G. Valentine, 1977

[b] Values are representative of one soil profile; horizons have been grouped into five depth intervals. K.W.G. Valentine et al. 1977.

[c] Fe and A1 values have been determined by pyrophosphate-dithionite procedure developed by Franzmeier, this solution is weaker than dithionite-citrate, hence the values are not totally comparable, they are intended as a relative guide only. Age approximation is derived from Clague 1981 GSC Paper 80-35 (Figure 4, Decay of the Cordilleran Sheet).

[d] Age approximation derived from Clague 1981. Soil profile by A.J. Green, in Luttmerding 1981 Volume 6.

[e] Profile data extracted from Nettleton et al. 1982.

[f] Profile data extracted from USDA 1975.

See Appendix 4.5 for geographical information concerning each of the above soils.

morainal (till) deposits derived from the granite-rhyolite family generally consist of an equal or greater proportion of clay than do their upslope colluvial counterparts, particularly in high elevation environments. Therefore, a comparison of Brooks Peninsula residual soil to morainal deposits seems reasonable.

Table 4.3 also shows that Brooks Peninsula site 8 has a substantially higher clay content throughout the upper 40 cm as compared to other Holocene granitic tills. Located near the apex, this site does not appear to have been subject to slope-wash deposition.

The ridge soil has approximately 20% clay throughout its depth. Even the estuarine, marine, and glaciomarine soils at lower elevations on Brooks Peninsula, consist of less than 3% clay throughout the depths investigated. However, some surface horizons subject to slope-wash deposition are comprised of up to 8% clay. Lewis (1976), who studied many podzolic soils derived from tills on Vancouver Island, found the clay-size fraction to be generally below 10%. Analyses of a soil in California (Table 4.3) with similar site characteristics, show that high clay content is often associated with relict soils. The high silt content in those soils included in Table 4.3 that are located in alpine and krummholz environments, is largely a result of frost weathering. Sneddon et al. (1972) and others have reported similar trends in Cordilleran soils. If clays are not inherent, or easily derived from parent materials originating from fine-grained rock such as slate or phyllite, a relatively long period of time is required to chemically weather granodiorite silt and sand particles into a clay-size fraction.

Soil samples collected by Richard Hebda and Robert Powell in 1984, from an exposure on Brooks Peninsula at Nordstrom Creek, on the headlands at approximately 350 m, show very high clay content. Many of their soil horizons were analysed, and at the 6-20 cm and 75-100 cm depth intervals a 30% clay content was found. It is classified as a clay loam texture. Thirty per cent is an unusually high clay content for coastal soils at this elevation.

Exploratory X-ray diffraction analyses performed by Dr. L. Lavkulich on the three major soil horizons of the ridge site are recorded in Table 4.4 The most notable mineral found is gibbsite, unknown in Canadian soils until it was described by Miles et al. (1978). Their study found gibbsite in an Orthic Dystric Brunisol near Port Alberni, Vancouver Island, and they concluded that the gibbsite there was inherited (presumably either from older soil or rocks). Soil samples from the central ridge site were also analysed by Dr. Norman Miles at the Soil Research Institute in Ottawa. He confirmed gibbsite from the Central Ridge sample. He did not find the mineral in the low elevation till (site 10) located at about 10 m elevation (N. Miles personal communication, January 1989).

A.J. Green of Agriculture Canada (personal communication, October 1985) states, "according to Ross (1980) the nature of mineralogy in Spodzols or Podzols is the disappearance of chlorite or chlorite-like minerals from the E (eluvial) horizon clay, and the dominance of a dioctohedral expanding layer silicate either beidellite or vermiculite or both." This is not the case in the central ridge soil where chlorite is the most abundant mineral in the clay fraction, from the surface down to at least 40 cm. Green goes on to say, in reference to Ross (1980) that gibbsite is not usually present in podzols, and that if it is present, it is usually in low horizons.

Gibbsite is a fairly stable mineral commonly associated with Ultisols, soils of the mid to low latitudes, mainly on Pleistocene or older surfaces. Kaolin, gibbsite, and aluminum interlayed clays are common in the mid to low latitudes, in the clay fraction (U.S. Dept. of Agriculture 1975).

Table 4.4 X-ray diffraction analyses of the central ridge soil by Dr. L. Lavkulich, Soil Science Department, University of British Columbia

Soil Horizon	Depth cm	Clay and Sand Mineralogy[a]
Bhf1	0-10	Chlorite, Kaolinite, Gibbsite, Mica (trace), Sand: Chlorite, Mica, Amphibole, Gypsum, Gibbsite?, Anatase?, Quartz (trace).
Bhf2	10-20	Chlorite, Kaolinite, Vermiculite (trace), Gibbsite, Quartz (trace), Feldspar (probably K and trace). Sand: Quartz, Chlorite, Amphibole, Gibbsite?, Feldspar, Gypsum?, Calcite?
Bf	20-40	Chlorite, Mica, Amphibole, Vermiculite (trace), Gibbsite?, Quartz (high), Feldspar. Sand: Quartz, Chlorite, Amphibole, Feldspar (both), Calcite?

[a] In general, the order listed is the order of abundance except for the sand fraction. For this fraction a random mount was used and the result means only that a mineral is likely present.

Birkeland (1974) states that an extensive surface soil sampling study by Barshard, over a large part of California, found kaolinite, halloysite, montmorillonite, illite, vermiculite, and gibbsite to be the major minerals present.

Chemical analyses of the central ridge soil by N. Miles (personal communication, January 1989) showed an extremely high level of talc. Miles stated this was amongst the highest level he has found in Canadian soils. Talc, a basic magnesium silicate, may be responsible, in part, for the lack of vegetation on some high elevation soils. The dominance of magnesium may restrict uptake of other bases, such as calcium, that may otherwise be available. Miles found very little talc in the low elevation till site.

The organic carbon content of 12.7% in the upper 10 cm, is surprisingly high, as the soil had virtually no vegetative cover. High organic carbon contents commonly exist deep into the solum of soils located in the coastal Ferro Humic Podzol landscape, but these particular soils are usually under a dense cover of hemlock and cedar. It appears that this site was vegetated at one time, for a relatively long period. An adjacent site located beneath mountain hemlock, site 7, contained a deep, black, very well-humified organic surface that extended for some depth into the mineral soil. The cool, moist, acid soil environment of Brooks Peninsula would have limited microbial degradation and oxidation of organic matter, and high organic-matter levels would be expected in a relict soil landscape. Warmer soils in Oregon and California (Table 4.3) experience a more rapid decomposition of organic matter, which tends to lower the levels in that bioclimatic environment.

Pyrophosphate treatment extracts organically-complexed iron and aluminum from soil. These two elements provide a measurement of the nature and degree of podzolization. There is usually a strong correlation between the percentage of organic carbon and pyrophosphate-extractable iron and aluminum. Therefore, relatively young soils under forest cover in a coastal marine climate may exhibit moderately high values of iron and aluminum. Considering the organic carbon content of the central ridge soil, the pyrophosphate iron and aluminum are somewhat lower than expected (Table 4.3). This suggests that the organic complexes may be breaking down partly, with a subsequent release of free iron oxides. High amounts of these oxides are usually common in podzolic soils, particularly those with a long history of weathering.

The dithionite-citrate extract procedure removes both free iron oxides and organically bound iron. The values for the central ridge soil at least point in the direction of more intensive, or longer, periods of weathering. There is, however, a local source of iron-bearing hornblende and biotite minerals.

The pH of granodiorite-derived soils in coastal environments is generally extremely acidic; the few bases originally in the soil are leached downwards. Such soils that are more than 500 years old usually become extremely acid.

The small exchangeable calcium to magnesium ratio (0.66) of the central ridge soil also points in the direction of intensive or long periods of weathering. The ratios are much smaller through depth than the ratios for Holocene soils in Table 4.3, as well as for other mineral soils on Brooks Peninsula. The older California soil, which is the most similar, shows only a slightly higher calcium to magnesium ratio. However, this southern area experiences a net summer moisture deficit, which may encourage upward migration of salts; also, the diabase rock is higher in calcium feldspar. Foth and Riechen (1954) state that some studies indicate that exchangeable calcium to magnesium ratios tend to diminish with increased profile development or age, in certain Wiesenboden and Brunizen soils in northwestern Iowa.

Discussion

The strongest soil evidence that suggests Brooks Peninsula's central ridge may not have been glaciated during the Fraser advance, comes from the deeply weathered clasts, the relict periglacial features, and the relatively high clay content in the upper 40 cm. Soil analyses from the ridge site show 18% and 20% average clay content. Analysis of a headlands site shows soil horizons with 30% clay content. This is up to three times the amount found in other comparable Holocene locations in British Columbia (Table 4.3), particularly sediments derived from coarse-grained bedrock. The occurrence of the clay mineral gibbsite, which is almost unknown in Canadian soils, but well-known in pre-Wisconsin soils of the southern United States, is very significant and deserves further study. Because the sampled site is on a ridge, it is unlikely that the gibbsite was inherited from older sediment; most probably it is of pedogenic (soil process) origin. Detailed geological studies should be undertaken to resolve the petrology questions.

Chemical factors provide little insight into the relict soil question, due to the lack of comparative data. Nevertheless, the high talc levels, the moderately high organic carbon and dithionite extractable iron and aluminum, as well as the small calcium to magnesium ratio do indicate older soils subject to intensive weathering. Also, the disappearance of chlorite, or chlorite-like minerals, from the surface horizons of the ridge soil is not normal for podzolic soils.

Anthropogenic and Archaeological Soils

During the expedition, anthropogenic soils (human-influenced soils) became of particular interest because a black charcoal-rich horizon was discovered near the mouth of Kingfisher Creek. The site of the horizon bore little indication of human activity. To ascertain whether this black soil was the product of human activity (Figure 4.12 and Table 4.5), samples from this site, from Shelter Sheds

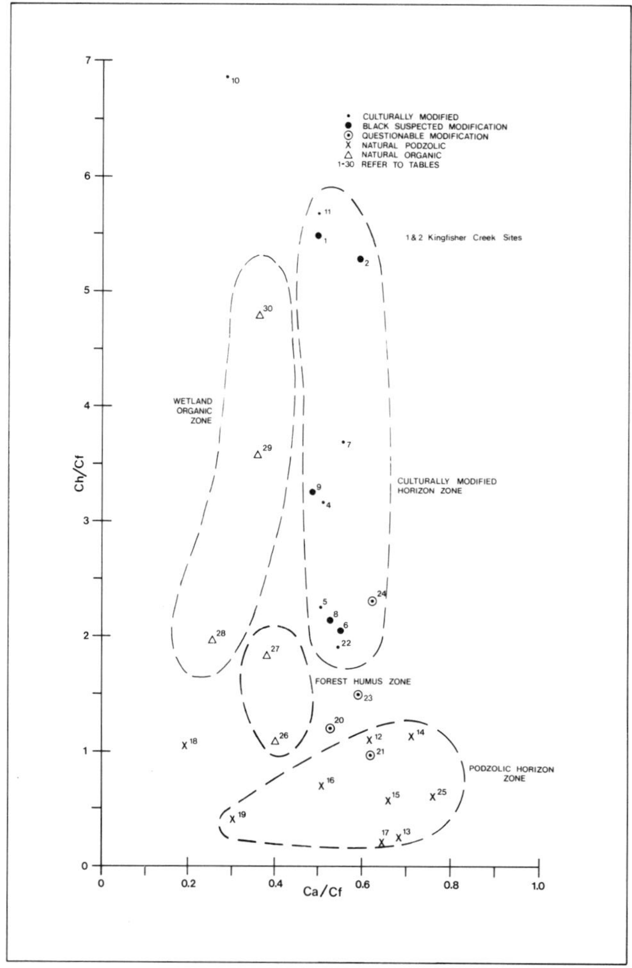

Figure 4.12 Ratios of acids extracted from humus materials (humic [Ch] and fulvic [Cf] acid ratios are thought by Lowe (1980) to be effective in differentiating organic rich soil horizons.)

(EaSw 1) and Nordstrom Cave (EaSx 1) were compared. They were also compared to soils from other coastal archaeological sites.

Shelter Sheds

The midden at Shelter Sheds has a comparatively thick surface forest litter horizon. Stratification of the deposit is clear. The Ap2 horizon has less shell and appears to have more humic forest litter, than the horizons above and below it, indicating possible abandonment of the site or a portion of the site for a period of time (Site 4, Appendix 4.2). Biological mixing of forest humus with the well-humified cultural surface is evident from arthropod tubules and frass. The midden also contains a moderate volume of sand, possibly wind blown from the now deflated beach. The humic fraction ratios of the surface Ap1 and Ap2 horizons correlate well with other anthropogenic surface horizons. These horizons fit into the "culturally modified horizon zone" on Figure 4.12.

Kingfisher Creek Terrace

Soil investigated on the second terrace of Kingfisher Creek, at approximately 12 m elevation, consists of a black, charcoal-rich humic surface. This surface was not noted on adjacent terraces located at approximately 9 m and 15 m elevation. Initial investigations showed that the black

Table 4.5 Selected data for anthropogenic and natural soils

SITE	HORIZON	DEPTH	%C	Ch/Cf	Ca/Cf	Ch	Cf	C/N	$CaCl_2$ pH	Exchangeable Me/100 grams Ca	Mg	K	Na	TOTAL PPM P	S	NOTES
								ANTHROPOGENIC COASTAL SOILS AND MIDDEN DEPOSITS								
Kingfisher Terrace	1. Hp1	23-10	21.5	5.50	0.45	7.64	1.39	37.2	-	0.66	1.11	0.11	0.52	975.0	586.0	1. No shell, no seaspray
Brooks Peninsula	2. Hp2	10-0	23.2	5.38	0.60	14.03	2.61	19.6	3.8	0.15	0.20	0.07	0.79	1584.0	556.6	2. No shell, no seaspray
Kingfisher Terrace (suspected cultural)	3. Hp	20-5	21.2	10.32	1.58	14.55	1.41	46.3	3.5	0.17	0.74	0.06	0.50	776.0	373.7	3. No shell, no seaspray
Shelter Sheds (EaSw1)	4. Ap1	11-22	10.38	3.12	0.54	3.56	1.14	13.4	6.3	25.01	13.51	0.33	5.33	12 363.0	800.7	4. Shell and seaspray
Midden (Brooks Peninsula)	5. Ap2	25-35	10.27	2.29	0.50	3.48	0.70	15.5	4.6	3.53	4.80	0.40	5.04	26 583.0	322.2	5. Shell
Sandpoint (potential midden)	6. Ap1	8-25	10.40	2.15	0.55	-	-	22.9	5.9	40.25	6.71	0.13	1.45	24 400.0	915.0	6. Shell - minor sea spray
Washington	7. Ap2	38-58	6.82	3.76	0.55	-	-	15.3	7.3	39.57	1.75	0.05	0.62	55 500.0	525.0	7. Bones and shell
Anton Point	8. Ap1	0-25	16.18	2.28	0.53	-	-	36.3	4.4	11.29	4.68	0.09	1.24	548.5	770.0	8. No shell, some seaspray
Hesquiat (Suspected cultural)	9. Ap2	25-50	14.34	3.20	0.47	-	-	36.8	5.4	41.12	7.26	0.86	1.15	401.0	455.0	9. White, shell-like fragments
Skull Rock Midden	10. Hp1	0-15	25.23	6.98	0.27	-	-	24.1	5.2	50.42	17.31	0.52	2.52	188.1	990.0	10. Shell and bone - very minor seaspray
Hesquiat	11. Hp2	15-37	25.82	5.73	0.50	-	-	24.5	5.7	84.60	15.74	0.27	2.78	318.2	1120.0	11. Shell and bone
								NATURAL COASTAL PODZOLIC SOILS								
Deep beach section	12. Ah	0-10	4.64	1.10	0.62	1.18	1.07	8.9	-	0.22	0.36	0.05	0.19	252.6	310.8	12. Natural podzol with
(Brooks Peninsula)	13. Bfc	10-22	1.75	0.36	0.69	0.44	1.22	11.5	4.2	0.14	0.08	0.02	0.08	170.7	84.8	13. minor seaspray
2nd beach strand	14. Ah	3-5	2.96	1.15	0.71	0.88	1.31	0.106	3.9	0.27	0.26	0.04	0.21	198.7	187.9	14. Natural podzol with
(Brooks Peninsula)	15. Bf	15-35	1.77	0.54	0.66	0.44	0.82	0.048	4.0	0.13	0.18	0.03	0.13	207.2	104.3	15. minor seaspray
Sandy marine terrace	16. Ahe	0-7	5.57	0.70	0.51	-	-	43.5	3.5	1.08	0.55	0.16	0.14	200	45.5	16. Natural brunisol, very minor
Hesquiat	17. Bm	7-20	0.54	0.66	0.65	-	-	38.6	4.9	0.19	0.08	0.04	0.06	400	40.0	17. seaspray
Gravelly marine	18. Ahe	0-10	11.18	1.05	0.19	3.42	3.25	35.62	5.3	0.57	0.32	0.15	0.29	680	600	18. Natural podzol
(Nettle Island) Broken group	19. Bhf	10-25	6.22	0.44	0.31	0.88	2.00	38.31	5.7	0.12	0.06	0.05	0.11	760	540	19. very minor seaspray

surface soil covers an area at least 200 m x 30 m. The site supports a mature stand of hemlock and cedar. This soil appears to be derived from forest litter, fine charcoal, and, possibly, cultural materials. The black humic horizon contains well-dispersed fine charcoal throughout, with inclusions of fire-cracked gravels. The major visual differences between this organic horizon and the forest floors on the adjacent terraces are that the black surface contains a dominant black humic (H) horizon with only a very thin surface litter (L) horizon, and no intermediate fibric (F) horizon, whereas the other forest floors usually exhibit distinct L, F, and H horizons (Klinka et al. 1981). The black layer ranges from 20 cm to 30 cm deep, down to mineral soil contact; it was not observed extending into the mineral soil. Detailed chemical analyses are found in (Appendix 4.2: site 6).

Chemical analyses of the Kingfisher Creek terrace soil were compared to other "black" surface soils and to black sandy matrices in coastal midden deposits. They show many similar characteristics

(Table 4.5). The other archaeological sites, mainly on Hesquiat Peninsula and the Broken Group Islands, were usually within 500 m of known native habitation locations. They were near tide water, as well as a fresh water source, usually at low elevation (<15 m), on well-drained coarse-textured marine or fluvial deposits, and were usually under a mixed hemlock-cedar, or pure Sitka spruce, forest.

The chemical comparisons (of points 1 to 5 on Table 4.5) show phosphorus, sulphur, and carbon values equal to, or, in some cases, higher than comparable unmodified forest humus (points 12 to 19, Table 4.5). For a discussion of forest humus form analyses, see Klinka et al. (1981). The relatively high calcium and magnesium levels are characteristic of many (shelly) midden deposits[4] as compared to coastal Podzolic soils (Table 4.5). Higher pH levels correlate with the shell fragments in each horizon, and organic carbon appears to correlate with the incidence of humified forest accumulations (Table 4.5).

The most notable similarity of the Kingfisher Creek terrace site to other known anthropogenic soils is found in humic acid and fulvic acid comparison. Lowe (1980) suggests that humus fraction ratios (Ch/Cf and Ca/Cf) may be effective in separating distinct sub-populations with Ah horizons and Bf horizons, based on the qualitative differences in organic matter present.

A plot of Ch/Cf versus Ca/Cf (Figure 4.11), is used to separate the "cultural" from the "natural" horizons. (Table 4.5 gives further information on the plotted components.) This exploratory plot seems to place the Kingfisher Creek terrace site in the culturally modified horizon zone. This terrace may have been the site of human activity, where fire was used. The natural forest floor appears to have been somewhat chemically enriched and periodically compacted. Note, the zones on Figure 4.12 are empirical groupings for illustration only, they have not been collaborated extensively. Further site and soil relationships are provided in Appendix 4.4.

Summary

The Kingfisher Creek terrace site contained soils that do not have, as yet, archaeological evidence of cultural activities or habitation. However, the distinctly black charcoal-rich surface horizons share many soil characteristics with the soil matrices of coastal midden deposits. Exploratory soil analyses show that humic and fulvic acid ratios (Ch/Cf vs. Ca/Cf) fit graphically with those of known cultural soil deposits. Carbon, phosphorus, sulphur, and calcium values are all more closely associated with the cultural group as compared to the natural soils. It is highly probable this terrace was a human activity site with extensive use of fire.

The EaSw 1 midden site at Shelter Sheds has a near-surface soil horizon, which indicates that natural forest deposits accumulated directly from the tree canopy. Oxidation (iron staining) on shells and mineral grains is due to weathering. These observations may indicate abandonment of the site or local area, by aboriginal people, for a period of time.

Aboriginal people's activities, particularly those that concentrated fire and debris, appear to have left a strong, characteristic (black) signature in the surfaces of (natural) soils.

---

[4] The Nordstrom Cave site on Brooks Peninsula is an archaeological deposit with virtually no tree litter fall as compared to the Shelter Sheds midden, which has a 15 cm humic surface. As expected, the predominance of mussel shell and charcoal in the cave have resulted in extremely high calcium and magnesium levels (Appendix 4.2: site 14), as compared to the Shelter Sheds deposits with low shell volumes and low levels of calcium and magnesium. The higher amount of humic components in the Shelter Sheds horizons, however, resulted in higher levels of carbon and sulphur (Appendix 4.2: site 4), when compared to the Nordstrom Cave site.

Conclusions

Besides providing a basic description of soils from several elevations and settings on Brooks Peninsula, this chapter leads to the following conclusions:

1) Periodically saturated sandy soils, developed across a lowland landscape, reveal that placic pans develop progressively within the rooting zone as the soils age.
2) Restricted soil drainage that results from pan formation influences forest succession and leads to paludification.
3) Soils from Brooks Peninsula archaeological sites are similar to those of other archaeological sites on Vancouver Island.
4) Physical and chemical characteristics of Podzolic soils developed on Brooks Peninsula glacial drift surface, are similar to those on other Vancouver Island tills of presumed late Wisconsin age.
5) Soils from high elevations on the central ridge are unlike lowland soils. Features such as high clay content, thoroughly weathered stones, the clay mineral gibbsite, and other similarities to old soils on unglaciated terrain, suggest that these soils are relict from a time before the last major ice advance.

It would be instructive to know more about the rate of weathering and general erosional processes in an environment with such intensive weathering—extremely acid soils and annual rainfall of more than 3300 mm. Clay mineralogy studies, carbon dating, the study of deep critically located soil pits, and additional rock-weathering and mineralogical analysis should provide more conclusive statements about Brooks Peninsula soil history.

Assuming that the soils are relic, the high elevations of Brooks Peninsula provide a unique landscape for studies in soil genesis on very old sites. The long-term (more than 10 000 years) of weathering effects on soil pan formation, textural change, and the dynamics of soil chemistry in coastal soils are largely unknown for British Columbia. Such studies may provide insight into the long-term dynamics of soil-biota relationships as well as into forest soil management decisions.

References Cited

Atmosphere Environment Service. 1982. Canadian climate normals: temperature and precipitation, 1951-1980. British Columbia. Environment Canada, Ottawa.

Baker, T. 1974. The major soils of the Tofino area of Vancouver Island and implications for land use planning and management. Ph.D. thesis. Department of Agriculture, University of British Columbia, Vancouver, BC.

Birkeland, P.W. 1974. Pedology, weathering, and geomorphological research. Oxford University Press, NY.

Buol, S.W., F.D. Hole, and R.J. McCracken. 1973. Soil genesis and classification. Iowa State University Press, Ames, IA.

Canada Dept. of Agriculture. 1976. Glossary of terms in soil science. Canadian Department of Agriculture. Publ. 1459 (revised). Ottawa.

Canada Soil Survey Committee. 1978. The Canadian system of soil classification. Canadian Department of Agriculture. Publ. 1646. Ottawa.

Chatterton, A. and J.P. Senyk. 1976-1979. Soils of northern Vancouver Island [map and expanded legend]. Terrestrial Studies Branch, BC Ministry of Environment, Victoria, BC. 92L/3, 4, 5, 6. 1:50 000.

Clague, J.J. 1981. Late Quaternary geology and geochronology of British Columbia. Part 2. Pap. 80-25, Geological Survey of Canada.

Cordes, L.D. 1972. An ecological study of the Sitka spruce forest on the west coast of Vancouver Island. Ph.D. thesis. Department of Botany, University of British Columbia, Vancouver, BC.

Day, P.R. 1965. Particle fractionation and particle size analysis. In C.A. Black (ed.). Methods of soil analysis. Pt. 1. Agronomy. American Society of Agronomy, Madison, WI.

Dumanski, J. (ed.). 1978. The Canada soil information system (CanSIS): manual for describing soils in the field. (Revised ed.). Land Resource Research Institute, Ottawa.

Foth, H.D. and F.F. Riecken. 1954. Properties of the Galva and Moody series of northwestern Iowa. Soil Sci. Soc. Am. Proc. 18: 206-211.

Green, A.J. 1976. Soil analysis of the Germansen Mountain moraines. Unpublished manuscript. Agriculture Canada, 6660 N.W. Marine Drive, Vancouver, BC.

Howes, D.E. 1981. Terrain inventory and geological hazards: northern Vancouver Island. BC Ministry of Environment, APD Bull. 5, Victoria, BC.

______ and A. Pattison. 1978. Terrain map and legend 92L/4 [map]. Terrestrial Studies Branch, BC Ministry of Environment, Victoria, BC.

Holland, S.S. 1976. Landforms of British Columbia, a physiographic outline. Bull. 48, BC Dept. Mines and Petroleum Resources.

Jungen, J.R. 1985. Soil resources of southern Vancouver Island. Surveys and Resource Mapping Branch, BC Ministry of Environment, MOE Tech. Rep. 17, Victoria, BC.

Klinka, K., R.N. Green, R.L. Trowbridge, and L.E. Lowe. 1981. Taxonomic classification of humus forms in ecosystems of British Columbia. Land management report 8. BC Ministry of Forests, Victoria, BC.

Laboratory Equipment Corporation. 1974. Leco, Model 325-300, serial no. 2194 [instruction manual]. 3000 Lake View Ave., St. Joseph, MI, 49085.

Lavkulich, L.M. 1969. Soil dynamics in the interpretation of paleosols. In S. Pawluk (ed.). Pedology and Quaternary research. Symposium held at Edmonton, AB, May 13-14, 1969. Alberta Institute of Pedology, Edmonton, AB.

Lewis, Terence. 1976. Till-derived podzols of Vancouver Island. Ph.D. thesis. Department of Soil Science, University of British Columbia, Vancouver, BC.

Lowe, L.E. 1980. Humus fraction ratios as a means of discriminating between horizon types. Can. J. Soil Sci. 60: 219-229.

______ . 1983. Organic horizons in British Columbia, their chemical properties and classification. Unpublished manuscript. Study sponsored by the working group on Organic horizons, humus forms, and Folisols, Department of Soil Science, University of British Columbia, Vancouver, BC.

Luttmerding, H.A. 1981. Soils of the Langley-Vancouver map area. Vol. 3, Description of the soils. Vol. 6, Technical data-soil profile descriptions and analytical data. BC Ministry of Environment, RAB Bull. 18, Kelowna, BC.

______ . and J.A. Shields (eds.). 1976. Proceedings of the workshop on alpine and subalpine environments. Resource Analysis Branch, BC Ministry of Environment, Victoria, BC.

McKeague, J.A. (ed.). 1978. Manual on soil sampling and methods of analysis. 2nd edition. Canadian Society of Soil Science, Ottawa.

Miles, N.M., G.C. Scott, and A.J. Green. 1978. The occurrence of gibbsite in a British Columbia soil. Can. J. Soil Sci. 58: 529-533.

Muller, J.E., K.E. Northcote, and D. Carlisle. 1974. Geology and mineral deposits of Alert Bay-Cape Scott map area on Vancouver Island, British Columbia. Pap. 74-8, Geological Survey of Canada.

Nettleton, W.D., R.B. Parsons, A.O. Ness, and F.W. Gelderman. 1982. Spodosols along the southwest Oregon coast. Soil Sci. Soc. Am. J. 46: 593-598.

Ross, G.J. 1980. Soils with variable charge. Pp. 127-147 in B.K.G. Phenge (ed.). Mineralogy of soils. New Zealand Society of Soil Science, Lower Hutt, New Zealand.

Ryder, J.M. 1993. Terrain maps for Brooks Peninsula 1:50,000. Under contract by Norecol, Dames & Moore, Inc. Richmond, B.C. BC Parks South Coast Region, Ministry of Environment, Lands and Parks. Victoria, BC.

Sondheim, M.W., G.A. Singleton, and L.M. Lavkulich. 1981. Numerical analysis of a chronosequence, including the development of a chronofunction. Soil Sci. Am. J. 45: 558-563.

Ugolini, F.C. 1968. Biology of alder: soil development and alder invasion in a recently deglaciated area of Glacier Bay, Alaska. Pp. 115-148 in J.M. Trappe, J.F. Franklin, R.F. Tarrant, and G.M. Hansen (eds.). Biology of alder. Pacific Northwest Forest and Range Experiment Station, Forest Service, U.S. Dept. Agriculture, Portland, OR.

______ . and D.H. Mann. 1979. Biopedological origin of peatlands in south east Alaska. Nature (London) 281: 366-368.

U.S. Department of Agriculture. 1975. Soil taxonomy: a basic system of soil classification for making and interpreting soil surveys. Agriculture Handbook 436. Washington, DC.

Valentine, K.W.G. 1971. Soils of the Tofino-Ucluelet lowland of British Columbia. Research Branch, Canadian Department of Agriculture. British Columbia Soil Survey Report 11. Ottawa.

______ , N.F. Alley, A.J. Green, G.A. Singleton, and R.K. Jones. 1977. Complex soil history on Holocene moraines in British Columbia, Canada. Paper presented at the 10th International INQUA Congress, University of Birmingham, England, August 1977.

______ , P.N. Sprout, T.E. Baker, and L.M. Lavkulich (eds.). 1978. The soil landscapes of British Columbia. Resource Analysis Branch, BC Ministry of Environment, Victoria, BC.

Walmsley, M., G. Utzig, T. Vold, D. Moon, and J. van Barnveld (eds.). 1980. Describing ecosystems in the field. BC Ministry of Environment, RAB Tech. Pap. 2, Victoria, BC.

Appendix 4.1. Glossary

This glossary contains selected soil science and related terms frequently used in this chapter. For definitions of technical terms consult Glossary of Terms in Soil Science (Canada Dept. of Agriculture 1976).

Brunisol	A soil order that usually lacks intensely weathered (strongly leached) horizons or very young horizons as in fresh river deposits. The soils may be "old" and are found under a variety of climatic and vegetative conditions.
chronosequence	A series of related soils that differ from each other because of factors associated with their ages.
dithionite	A chemical extract ($Na_2S_2O_4$) used to remove organically bound aluminum and iron from particles of soil. For method see McKeague (1978).
duric	A strongly cemented zone within the B horizon of soils. The zone is most strongly cemented at the abrupt upper boundary.
eluvial (horizon)	A soil horizon from which soil materials have been leached downwards. See illuvial.
Fibrisol	A category of soils (great group) within the organic order characterized by abundant, weakly decomposed plant fibres. Fibrisols are saturated for much of the year.
Folisol	A category of soils (great group) within the organic order characterized by thick (10 cm or more) horizons of decomposed forest litter and upland forest floor plants. Folisol horizons overlie mineral horizons within 160 cm of surface and commonly overlie bedrock and rubble. Folisols are rarely saturated throughout the year.
fragic	A dense, firm-to-hard zone within the B horizon of a soil. A fragic horizon resembles the parent material in colour, but has very different consistency. The upper boundary is normally clear and abrupt.
fulvic acids	A term with various meanings that usually refers to the mixture of organic substances that remains in solution when a dilute alkali extract from the soil has been acidified.
gibbsite	A hydrous aluminum clay mineral [Al_2 $(OH)_6$] which is commonly associated with advanced stages of weathering (Boul et al. 1973).
gleying	A soil process that occurs under conditions of poor drainage. Iron and other elements are reduced resulting in a grey soil with brownish mottles.

Humisol	A category of soils (great group) within the organic order characterized by a dominance of well-decomposed humified organic matter horizons. Humisols are saturated throughout most of the year.
humic acids	A mixture of various dark-colored organic substances precipitated by acidifying a dilute alkali extract from the soil. The term is used by some workers to designate only the alcohol-insoluble part of this precipitate.
illuvial (horizon)	The zone within which mineral or organic soil materials are deposited after transport from overlying horizons; usually in B horizon. See eluvial.
ortstein	A hard layer in the B horizon of podzols. The layer is cemented by illuviated sesquioxides and organic matter.
paludification	The progressive development of wetlands (such as bogs) because of gradually decreasing drainage.
pan	Hard, compacted or very clay-rich soil layers.
pedogenic	Soil-forming process responsible for the development of the soil profile.
placic (horizon)	A hard impervious dark reddish brown soil horizon that is cemented by iron-organic complexes, iron oxides, or iron and manganese oxides. A placic horizon may consist of one or more layers, each about 3 mm to 7 mm thick.
Podzol	A soil order in which amorphous organic matter, aluminum, and iron accumulate in the B horizons. Podzols are acidic.
pyrophosphate	A solution of sodium pyrophosphate ($Na_4P_2O_7$) used to extract and quantify organically bound iron and aluminum.
Regosol	A category of soils (great group) with little or no weathered soil horizon (profile) development; a young soil.
solum	The upper layers of a soil modified by soil process into A and B horizons. Most plant roots grow in the solum.
spring line	A zone from which a series of water sources (springs) flow. Spring lines often occur in association with changes in geological materials along a slope.
turbation/turbated	Mixed or disturbed by natural processes such as root-throw and frost action.

Appendix 4.2 Soil profile descriptions and their associated chemical and physical data. Fourteen soil profiles from the Brooks Peninsula, their locations are plotted on Figure 4.1.

Site 1: 0 m elevation, level; developed in sandy marine delta; poorly drained; **salt marsh**, Cape Cook Lagoon.

Soil Profile Description
Orthic Humic Regosol-Saline Phase

Horizon	Depth (cm)	Description
Ahs 1	0-15	Dark grayish brown (10YR 4/2 m) sandy loam, extensive fibrous root mat, in matrix of mesic to humic organic matter; moderate, very coarse, angular block structure breaking to moderate medium subangular blocky structure; subject to tidal influence at high high tide; pH 4.9, very strongly acid.
Ahs 2	15-60	Very dark grayish brown (10YR 3/2 m) sandy loam, extensive fibrous root mat in a matrix of humic organic matter; moderate coarse subangular blocky structure; subject to daily tidal influence; pH 5.3, very strongly acid.
Cgs	60-100	Olive gray (5Y 4/2 m) sand; single grain structure; 30% gravels, cobbles, and stones; subject to daily tidal influence.

STANDARD CHEMICAL AND PHYSICAL SOIL ANALYSIS

Lab No.	Horizon	Depth	H_2O	% C LECO/W.B.	% N	C/N	Exchangeable Bases (me/100g) Ca	Mg	K	Na	Sum	C.E.C.	Base Sat. %	Pyrophos. % Fe	Al	Dithionite % Fe	Al	Hydrometer % Sand	Silt	Clay	pH H_2O	$CaCl_2$
81/4223	Ahs 1	0-15	1.77	7.56/8.07	0.46	17.4	3.42	9.14	1.22	44.33	58.11	24.42	100	0.33	0.21	0.57	0.17	81.6	17.3	1.1	5.1	4.9
81/4224	Ahs 2	50-60	1.84	5.00/5.05	0.40	12.4	3.5	9.18	0.93	25.08	38.69	23.00	100	0.60	0.48	0.73	0.35	73.2	23.7	8.1	5.6	5.3

TOTAL MACRO AND MICRO NUTRIENTS IN PPM

Lab No.	Horizon	Depth (cm)	CA	P	S	NA	K	MN	MG	FE	ZN	CU	MO	B
81/4223	Ahs1	0-15	13 085	547.2	1216	5415	1768	313.2	11 453	>10 000	35.96	14.48	8.02	<0.157
81/4224	Ahs2	50-60	8440	776.8	1413	5060	1171	259.1	11 367	>10 000	35.67	16.61	11.69	<0.157

Comments: Due to tidal influence sodium levels are comparatively high. Sulphur levels are also high due to the periodically reduced and oxidized intertidal marine conditions.

BROOKS PENINSULA

Site 2: 0.5 m elevation, facing 300° NW, 3% slope; developed in windblown **marine sands** overlying sand; well-drained; Beach Shrub to Shoreline Forest transition, Cape Cook Lagoon.

Soil Profile Description
Orthic Regosol

Horizon	Depth (cm)	Description
F-H	10-0	Fibrihumimor. Very dark grayish brown (10YR 3/2 m), mesic to fibric loosely matted; well- to semi-decomposed Sitka spruce and *Gaultheria* litter; scattered sands throughout matrix; abrupt, smooth boundary; pH 3.6, extremely acid.
C1	0-10	Light olive gray (5Y 6/2 m), medium sand; single grain structure; no shell fragments or gravels; gradual, smooth boundary; pH 4.6, extremely acid.
C_2	10-25	Olive gray (5Y 5.2 m), medium sand; single grain structure; no shell fragments or gravels; pH 5.6, very strongly acid.

STANDARD CHEMICAL AND PHYSICAL SOIL ANALYSIS

Lab No.	Horizon	Depth	H_2O	% C LECO/W.B.	% N	C/N	Exchangeable Bases (me/100g) Ca	Mg	K	Na	Sum	C.E.C.	Base Sat. %	Pyrophos. % Fe	Al	Dithionite % Fe	Al	Hydrometer % Sand	Silt	Clay	pH H_2O	$CaCl_2$
81/4207	F-H	10-0	7.76	40.05/39.08	1.043	37.5	13.71	9.12	2.22	1.53	26.58	100.86	26.4	0.04	0.11	0.34	0.11	64.9	34.1	1.0	4.3	3.6
81/4209	C1	0-10	0.25	0.54/0.55	0.034	16.2	0.64	0.76	0.04	0.14	1.58	2.81	56.2	0.12	0.05	0.45	0.10	99.4	0.3	0.3	5.6	4.6
81/4209	C2	10-25	0.14	0.26/0.26	0.127	2.0	2.19	0.47	0.03	0.20	2.89	1.20	100.0	0.07	0.04	0.43	0.09	99.4	0.4	0.4	6.4	5.6

ORGANIC MATTER ANALYSIS

Lab No.	Horizon	Depth	% C W.B.	Von Post	Pyrophosphate Index	Fibre Rubbed	Fibre Unrubbed	Ch/Cf	Ca/Cf	% C Humic	% C Fulvic	% C PVP-Fulvic	C14 Date
81/4209	C2	10-25	-	-	-	-	-	0.67	1.0	0.04	0.06	0.06	-

TOTAL MACRO AND MICRO NUTRIENTS IN PPM

Lab No.	Horizon	Depth (cm)	CA	P	S	NA	K	MN	MG	FE	ZN	CU	MO	B
81/4207	F-H	10-0	10 562	782.7	1146	298.4	984.9	151.8	4633	8727	30.71	6.517	3.006	15.33
81/4208	C1	0-10	24 863	278.9	26.36	749.2	1005.0	352.0	12 539	>10 000	35.62	11.02	8.667	<0.157
81/4209	C2	10-25	19 180	258.8	62.52	412.9	878.0	317.2	12 454	>10 000	36.32	12.39	7.257	<0.157

Comments: The higher Boron level in the F-H horizon is relatively unique; it compares to the Hp_1 horizon on the Kingfisher Creek terrace anthroporogenic site.

Site 3: 6 m elevation, facing 315°NW, 8% slope; developed in **ridge of marine sands (beach ridge),** moderately well-drained; Shoreline Forest, Cape Cook Lagoon.

Soil Profile Description

Sombric Ferric Podzol with thick coniferous Fibrimor surface

Horizon	Depth (cm)	Description
L	25-23	Raw conifer needles, twigs, *Gaultheria* leaves on surface; partially decomposed surface on litter fragments; fibric.
F	23-4	Partly decomposed needles and leaves, grading to unrecognizable fragments in matrix of humic to mesic fine mor; mesic.
H	4-0	Completely decomposed matrix of fine humic mor with partially decomposed needles and twigs throughout horizon; humic.
Ahe	0-3	Dark gray (5YR 4/1 m) sand; moderate medium subangular blocky structure; clear wavy boundary; extremely acid.
Ah	3-15	Dark reddish brown (5YR 2.5/2 m) sand; moderate medium subangular blocky structure; clear wavy boundary; pockets of humic-rich sand throughout horizon; pH 3.9, extremely acid.
Bf	15-35	Dark reddish brown (2.5YR 3/4 m) sand; weak fine subangular blocky structure; diffuse smooth boundary; pH 4.0, extremely acid.
Bm	35-60	Light olive brown (2.5YR 5.4 m) sand; very weak fine subangular blocky structure; pH 4.4, extremely acid.

STANDARD CHEMICAL AND PHYSICAL SOIL ANALYSIS

Lab No.	Horizon	Depth	H_2O	% C LECO/W.B.	% N	C/N	Exchangeable Bases (me/100g) Ca	Mg	K	Na	Sum	C.E.C.	Base Sat. %	Pyrophos. % Fe	Al	Dithionite % Fe	Al	Hydrometer % Sand	Silt	Clay	pH H_2O	$CaCl_2$
81/4218	Ah	3-15	1.43	2.34/2.96	0.106	27.9	0.27	0.26	0.04	0.21	0.78	15.42	5.1	0.88	0.22	1.10	0.22	88.5	11.0	0.5	4.9	3.9
81/4219	Bf	15-35	0.92	1.84/1.77	0.048	36.9	0.13	0.18	0.03	0.13	0.47	10.50	4.5	0.58	0.22	0.81	0.21	94.5	5.4	0.1	5.0	4.0
81/4220	Bm	35-60	0.35	0.57/0.57	0.158	3.6	0.26	0.03	0.01	0.25	0.55	4.01	13.7	0.16	0.17	0.50	0.21	98.0	1.7	0.3	5.2	4.4

ORGANIC MATTER ANALYSIS

Lab No.	Horizon	Depth	% C W.B.	Von Post	Pyrophosphate Index	Fibre Rubbed	Fibre Unrubbed	Ch/Cf	Ca/Cf	% C Humic	% C Fulvic	% C PVP-Fulvic	C14 Date
81/4218	Ah	3-15	2.96	-	-	-	-	1.15	0.71	0.88	1.31	0.93	-
81/4219	Bf	15-35	1.77	-	-	-	-	0.54	0.66	0.44	0.82	0.54	-
81/4220	Bm	35-60	0.57	-	-	-	-	0.33	0.42	0.08	0.24	0.10	-

TOTAL MACRO AND MICRO NUTRIENTS IN PPM

Lab No.	Horizon	Depth (cm)	CA	P	S	NA	K	MN	MG	FE	ZN	CU	MO	B
81/4218	Ah	3-15	17 030	198.7	187.9	160.1	427.9	221.7	7706	>10 000	25.10	5.127	6.193	<0.157
81/4219	Bf	15-35	16 100	207.2	104.3	210.3	534.7	278.3	10 275	>10 000	31.50	6.899	6.486	<0.157
81/4220	Bm	35-60	24 365	190.2	25.94	532.3	1209	360.0	12 864	>10 000	31.43	10.14	8.395	<0.157

Comments:

Site 4: 3 m elevation, facing 225° SW, 30% slope; developed in shelly sands of anthropogenic origin over marine sandy gravel; rapidly to well-drained; Shoreline Forest, shelter sheds.

Soil Profile Description

Regosol, anthropogenic phase

Horizon	Depth (cm)	Description
Hi	15-0	Dark reddish brown (5YR 3/2 m) humic matrix with subdominant components of fibric and mesic material, sand grains common. Humimor.
Ap1	0-22	Black (5YR 2.5/1 m) sand, with roughly equal components of shell and well-decomposed humus; fine charcoal throughout matrix; matrix smears charcoal black with a greasy feel; abrupt wavy boundary; pH 6.3, slightly acid.
Ap2	22-35	Black (5YR 2.5/1 m) loamy sand, loose single grain structure, varied proportions of shell, sand, and humic components; fine charcoal throughout matrix, matrix smears charcoal black with a gritty feel; gradual smooth boundary; pH 4.6, very strongly acid.
Ap3-4	35-90	Similar in appearance and composition to the Ap$_2$ horizon (above) but the shells do not have the same weathered appearance.
Ap5	90-100	Black (5YR 2.5/1 m) loamy sand, loose single grain structure, varied proportions of shell, sand, and humic components; fine charcoal throughout matrix, matrix smears charcoal black with a gritty feel; pH 7.1, neutral.

STANDARD CHEMICAL AND PHYSICAL SOIL ANALYSIS

Lab No.	Horizon	Depth	H_2O	% C LECO/W.B.	% N	C/N	Exchangeable Bases (me/100g) Ca	Mg	K	Na	Sum	C.E.C.	Base Sat. %	Pyrophos. % Fe	Al	Dithionite % Fe	Al	Hydrometer % Sand	Silt	Clay	pH H_2O	$CaCl_2$
81/4189	Ap1	11-22	3.06	10.45/10.38	0.775	13.4	25.01	13.51	0.33	5.33	44.18	46.79	94.4	0.52	0.24	0.52	0.16	93.0	1.4	5.0	6.7	6.3
81/4190	Ap2	25-35	4.06	10.68/10.27	0.662	15.5	3.53	4.80	0.40	5.04	13.77	53.07	25.9	1.35	1.75	1.31	0.80	82.0	17.4	0.6	5.2	4.6
81/4191	Ap5	90-100	1.93	8.95/4.28	0.427	10.0	22.49	5.61	0.10	2.02	30.22	24.06	100	0.06	0.11	0.13	0.05	69.2	27.0	3.8	7.7	7.1

ORGANIC MATTER ANALYSIS

Lab No.	Horizon	Depth	% C W.B.	Von Post	Pyrophosphate Index	Fibre Rubbed	Fibre Unrubbed	Ch/Cf	Ca/Cf	% C Humic	% C Fulvic	% C PVP-Fulvic	C14 Date
81/4218	Ap1	11-22	10.38	6	10YR 2/1 (1)	35.84	65.84	3.12	0.54	3.56	1.14	0.61	
81/4219	Ap2	25-35	10.27	5	7.5YR 3/4 (1)	17.50	51.67	2.29	0.50	3.48	1.52	0.76	
81/4191	Ap5	90-100	4.28	6	10YR 2/1 (1)	49.17	68.34	2.80	0.36	0.70	0.25	0.09	

Note: Composition of materials throughout matrix of midden is greatly different from that of a natural soil. The materials consisted of a shell fraction, sand fraction and organic fraction.

TOTAL MACRO AND MICRO NUTRIENTS IN PPM

Lab No.	Horizon	Depth (cm)	CA	P	S	NA	K	MN	MG	FE	ZN	CU	MO	B
81/4189	Ap1	11-22	60 504	12 363	800.7	1530	1003	561.2	7363	>10 000	213.2	38.09	7.204	<0.157
81/4190	Ap2	25-35	32 710	14 183	662.1	1570	890.2	697.2	5887	>10 000	99.87	34.62	9.951	<0.157
81/4191	Ap5	90-100	159 849	26 593	332.2	1750	667.9	423.6	5171	>10 000	114.8	32.30	4.776	<0.157

Site 5: 15 m elevation, facing 200° SW, 6% slope; developed in **inactive marine and dune sands,** moderately to imperfectly drained; Mesic Lowland Forest, Cape Cook Lagoon.

Soil Profile Description
Placic Humo Ferric Podzol

Horizon	Depth (cm)	Description
F	15-5	Partly decomposed needles and leaves grading to unrecognizable fragments in a matrix of humic to mesic fine mor; mesic.
H	5-0	Completely decomposed matrix of fine humic mor with partially decomposed needles and twigs throughout the horizon; humic.
Ae	(0-6)	White (7.5YR 8/1 m) sand; very weak, fine subangular blocky structure; discontinuous pockets of Ae may be associated with root churning and tree throws along escarpment.
Ah	0-10	Very dusky red (2.5YR 2.5/2 m) loamy sand; moderate medium subangular blocky structure; pockets containing a high percentage of humic material randomly mixed with lighter coloured Ahe lens; abrupt wavy boundary determined by a thin placic band; extremely acid pH.
Bfc	10-22	Dark brown (7.5YR 3/4 m) sand; consisting of a medium to thin (2-5 cm) placic band above a weakly cemented coarse platy strong brown (7.5YR 5/6 m) sand; discontinuous thin placic bands are located below and roughly parallel to the uppermost placic band; gradual wavy boundary; pH 4.2, extremely acid.
Bf	22-60	Light olive brown (2.5Y 5/4 m) sand; single grain structure; wavy pockets of reddish-yellow (7.5YR 6/8 m) sand following root channels; gradual wavy boundary; pH 4.7, very strongly acid.
BC	60-200	Olive yellow (2.5Y 6/6 m) sand; single grain structure; wavy reddish yellow (7.5YR 6/8 m) oxidized weathering fronts randomly located throughout horizon; pH 4.7, very strongly acid.
C1	200-400	Light olive gray (5Y 6/2 m) sand; single grain structure; laminated wave-set bedding; pH 5.0, very strongly acid.
C2	400-800 (est.)	Light olive gray (5Y 6/2 m) sand; single grain structure; laminated wave-set bedding; pH 5.0, very strongly acid.
C3	800-1000 (est.)	Light olive gray (5Y 6/2 m) sand; single grain structure; laminated wave-set bedding; pH 5.0, very strongly acid.
C4	1000-1020 (est.)	Light olive gray (5Y 6/2 m) sand; single grain structure; fine to very fine charcoal fragments common; very fine shell fragments common; pH 5.0, very strongly acid.
C5	1020-1100	Light olive gray (5Y 6/2 m) sand; single grain structure; laminated wave-set bedding; pH 5.0, very strongly acid.

Site 6: 12 m elevation, facing 180° S, 3% slope; developed in a **sandy gravel fluvial terrace**; moderate to imperfect drainage; Mesic Lowland Forest, Kingfisher Creek.

Soil Profile Description
Sombric Humo Ferric Podzol, anthropogenic phase

Horizon	Depth (cm)	Description
H	27-23	(Humimor) reddish black (10YR 2.5/1 m) humic matrix with minor fibric fibres and sand particles; gravels common; smears reddish black; occasional very fine charcoal particles; extremely acid.
Hp1	23-10	Black (5Yr 2.5/1 m) humic matrix with no fibric particles; horizon appears as a charcoal black contact zone, smears charcoal black with silty feel, very fine and fine charcoal particles common, fire cracked gravels and fine gravel content ca. 25%; extremely acid.
Hp2	10-0	Black (5YR 2/5/1 m) humic matrix incorporated with a sandy loam mineral soil; very high organic matter; gravels common, 20%, some fire-cracked; smears charcoal black; very fine charcoal particles common; pH 3.8, extremely acid. (This is the most humified horizon with the most evidence of human activity on the fluvial terrace.)
(B)	0-(20)	Podsolized gravels in a sandy matrix; not described or sampled.

STANDARD CHEMICAL AND PHYSICAL SOIL ANALYSIS

Lab No.	Horizon	Depth	H_2O	% C LECO/W.B.	% N	C/N	Exchangeable Bases (me/100g)					C.E.C.	Base Sat. %	Pyrophos. %		Dithionite %		Hydrometer %			pH	
							Ca	Mg	K	Na	Sum			Fe	Al	Fe	Al	Sand	Silt	Clay	H_2O	$CaCl_2$
81/4198	H	27-23	9.00	53.45/51.15	1.528	33.5	1.35	17.40	0.59	1.90	79.65	163.94	48.6	0.12	0.15	0.26	0.12	11.2	80.2	8.6	-	-
81/4199	Hp1	23-10	3.45	22.29/21.5	0.578	37.2	0.66	1.11	0.11	0.52	2.40	54.00	4.4	0.30	0.53	0.41	0.46	-	-	-	-	-
81/4200	Hp2	10-0	9.31	22.64/23.17	1.185	19.6	0.15	0.20	0.07	0.79	1.21	44.16	2.7	2.32	1.91	2.13	1.56	49.0	45.6	5.4	4.2	3.8
Second sample taken on same terrace, approximately 400 metres east																						
81/4225	Hp	20-5	5.43	22.08/21.22	0.458	46.3	0.17	0.74	0.06	0.50	1.47	100.37	1.51	1.21	1.66	1.85	1.17	46.4	48.8	4.8	4.2	3.5

ORGANIC MATTER ANALYSIS

Lab No.	Horizon	Depth	% C W.B.	Von Post	Pyrophosphate Index	Fibre Rubbed	Fibre Unrubbed	Ch/Cf	Ca/Cf	% C Humic	% C Fulvic	% C PVP-Fulvic	C14 Date
81/4198	(insufficient sample)												
81/4199	Hp1	23-10	21.50	10	7.5 Y 3/2 (1)	2.50	40.00	5.50	0.45	7.64	1.39	0.63	-
81/4200	Hp2	10-0	23.17	10	10 YR 2/2 (0)	6.67	31.67	5.38	-	14.03	2.61	1.56	-
Second sample taken on same terrace, approximately 400 metres to east													
81/4225	Hp	20-50	21.22	10	10 YR 2/1 (1)	4.17	30.00	10.32	1.0	1.58	1.41	0.89	-

TOTAL MACRO AND MICRO NUTRIENTS IN PPM

Lab No.	Horizon	Depth (cm)	CA	P	S	NA	K	MN	MG	FE	ZN	CU	MO	B
81/4198	H	27-23	2624	678.4	1409	620.2	458.4	35.67	3384	5523	9.758	7.639	2.228	36.89
81/4199	Hp1	23-10	6964	975.0	586.0	339.4	1852	89.10	2098	9601	12.32	9.256	6.346	14.45
81/4200	Hp2	10-0	10 339	1584	556.6	195.0	674.1	197.0	6064	>10 000	37.24	46.87	11.0	<0.157
Second sample taken on same terrace, approximately 400 metres to east														
81/4225	Hp	20-5	4514	776.0	373.7	30.07	922.1	70.84	1315	>10 000	16.66	27.41	5.621	<0.157

Comments: Considering the depth of sample, there is a very close correlation between sample No. 4225 and No. 4199. Boron levels in the H and Hp1 horizons are comparatively very high.

Site 7: 712 m elevation, facing 310° NW, 8% slope; developed in **sandy gravelly colluvial veneer**; imperfect drainage; Krummholz, mountain hemlock, Central Ridge.

Soil Profile Description

Gleyed Ferro-Humic Podzol; shallow lithic, peaty phase

Horizon	Depth (cm)	Description
H	30-0	Humimor. Black (5YR 2.5/1 m) humic; well-decomposed litter from *Tsuga mertensiana*; very high organic matter; coarse subangular blocky structure; no mineral soil or gravel in horizon; diffuse irregular boundary; pH 3.5, extremely acid.
$Bhfg_1$	0-10	Dark brown (7.5YR 3/2 m) sandy loam; with many medium, prominent diffuse dark gray (5Y 4/1 m) mottles; pockets of humic (H) material located randomly throughout horizon; moderate, medium, coarse angular blocky structure; 30% moderately well decomposed subangular gravels (4-30 mm); 40% angular, subangular, and subrounded cobbles and stones that are deeply weathered. Diffuse irregular boundary; pH 3.8, extremely acid.
(Bhfg)	10-50	Approximately 80% cobbles and stones that are deeply weathered; matrix consisting of material similar to horizon $Bhfg_1$ (above).

STANDARD CHEMICAL AND PHYSICAL SOIL ANALYSIS

Lab No.	Horizon	Depth	H_2O	% C LECO/W.B.	% N	C/N	Exchangeable Bases (me/100g) Ca	Mg	K	Na	Sum	C.E.C.	Base Sat. %	Pyrophos. % Fe	Al	Dithionite % Fe	Al	Hydrometer % Sand	Silt	Clay	pH H_2O	$CaCl_2$
81/4195	H	30-0	2.63	17.07/15.94	0.416	38.3	-	-	-	-	-	-	-	0.72	0.37	0.78	0.19				4.0	3.5
81/4196	Bhfg1	0-10	1.64	5.58/5.14	0.147	35.0	-	-	-	-	-	-	-	0.45	0.51	0.92	0.85				4.3	3.8

TOTAL MACRO AND MICRO NUTRIENTS IN PPM

Lab No.	Horizon	Depth (cm)	CA	P	S	NA	K	MN	MG	FE	ZN	CU	MO	B
81/4195	H	30-0	2389	385.0	413.5	195.6	887.0	103.3	1929	>10 000	16.65	16.67	4.011	<0.157
81/4196	Bhfg	0-10	1483	225.9	202.4	547.2	1161	85.98	1535	>10 000	21.04	21.04	5.567	<0.157

Site 8:	760 m elevation, facing 135° SE, 60% slope; developed in **colluvial veneer; well drained; Alpine** Meadow Vegetation, Central Ridge.

Soil Profile Description
Orthic Humo Ferric Podzol; shallow lithic phase

Horizon	Depth (cm)	Description
Bhf1	0-10	Dark brown (10 YR 4.3 d) to dark yellowish brown (10YR 3/3 m) loam, subangular blocky structure, 40% gravel content (4-12 mm); ca. 15% stone-size clasts, predominantly angular and subangular with extensively pitted surfaces; pH 4.2, extremely acid.
Bhf2	10-20	Light yellowish brown (10YR 6/4 d) to yellowish brown (10YR 5/3 m) loam; weak, very fine subangular blocky structure; ca. 40% gravel (dominant size 4-12 mm); ca. 15% stone and cobble size clasts, predominantly angular and subangular with extensively pitted surfaces; pH 4.4, extremely acid.
Bf	20-40	Brownish yellow (10YR 6/6 d) to yellowish brown (10YR 5/6 m) loam to sandy clay loam, weak very fine subangular blocky structure, ca. 60% gravel content (dominant size 5-30 mm); ca. 20% stone and cobble size clasts predominantly angular with pitted surfaces; pH 4.4, extremely acid.
Bf	40+	Well weathered, subangular cobble-sized clasts; depth to bedrock estimated at 70-100 cm.

STANDARD CHEMICAL AND PHYSICAL SOIL ANALYSIS

Lab No.	Horizon	Depth	H_2O	% C LECO/W.B.	% N	C/N	Exchangeable Bases (me/100g) Ca	Mg	K	Na	Sum	C.E.C.	Base Sat. %	Pyrophos. % Fe	Al	Dithionite % Fe	Al	Hydrometer % Sand	Silt	Clay	pH H_2O	$CaCl_2$
81/4192	Bhf1	0-10	4.54	11.46/12.75	0.604	21.1	0.44	0.58	0.38	0.23	1.63	46.79	5.0	0.88	1.16	2.65	0.86	48.1	34.5	17.4	5.0	4.2
81/4193	Bhf2	10-20	3.47	4.47/5.03	0.230	21.9	0.11	0.17	0.12	0.20	0.60	53.07	3.0	0.74	1.12	2.90	0.78	53.5	28.0	18.5	5.2	4.4
81/4194	Bhf3	20-40	3.19	3.31/3.67	0.165	22.2	0.08	0.12	0.08	0.15	0.43	24.06	2.4	0.66	0.98	3.04	0.75	57.9	23.1	19.0	5.2	4.4

ORGANIC MATTER ANALYSIS

Lab No.	Horizon	Depth	% C W.B.	Von Post	Pyrophosphate Index	Fibre Rubbed	Fibre Unrubbed	Ch/Cf	Ca/Cf	% C Humic	% C Fulvic	% C PVP-Fulvic	C14 Date
81/4192	Bhf1	0-10	12.75	-	-	-	-	0.86	0.41	1.92	2.22	0.92	
81/4193	Bhf2	10-20	5.03	-	-	-	-	0.48	0.46	0.70	1.47	0.68	
81/4194	Bh	20-40	3.67	-	-	-	-	0.40	0.47	0.48	1.19	0.56	

TOTAL MACRO AND MICRO NUTRIENTS IN PPM

Lab No.	Horizon	Depth (cm)	CA	P	S	NA	K	MN	MG	FE	ZN	CU	MO	B
81/4192	Bhf1	0-10	1898	560.3	781.2	252.0	896.1	354.0	8938	>10 000	63.40	98.78	18.14	<0.157
81/4193	Bhf2	10-20	2623	399.4	462.5	369.9	1072	417.8	10 994	>10 000	74.23	149.4	23.08	<0.157
81/4194	Bf	20-40	2296	392.8	377.4	453.4	990.4	457.0	12 735	>10 000	84.61	174.8	24.15	<0.157

Site 9: 20 m elevation, level; developed in **sandy fluvioglacial blanket** capped by silt; poorly drained; Bog Herbaceous Vegetation, Cape Cook Lagoon.

Soil Profile Description
Gleyed Placic Humo Ferric Podzol

Horizon	Depth (cm)	Description
Hi	8-0	Very dark grayish brown (10YR 3/2 m) humic matrix with minor inclusions of silts and sands.
Ah	0-5	Dark grayish brown (10YR 4/2 m) silt loam, inclusions of discontinuous humic lenses common; prominent olive (2.5Y 6/6 m) mottles common, fine to medium subangular structures; soil matrix feels slick and smears easily due to 7% carbon content and 72% silt content; horizon consists primarily of fluvial or slope wash sediments; pH 4.4, extremely acid.
IIBgs	5-15	Dark yellowish brown (10YR 4/4 m) sandy loam; prominent olive brown (2.5Y 4/4 m) mottles common; fine to medium subangular blocky structure; discontinuous lenses of humic-rich matrix adjacent to weakly gleyed sands common; approximately 30% gravel content; pH 4.7, very strongly acid.
IIBg	15-28	Greenish gray (5GY 6/1 m) sandy loam, many coarse prominent light yellowish brown (2.5Y 6/4 m) mottles; moderate medium subangular blocky structure; ca. 35% gravel content; pH 5.2, very strongly acid.
IIIBCg1	28-40	Greenish gray (5GY 6/1 m) sand; many coarse prominent light yellowish brown (10YR 6/4 m) mottles; single grain stucture; discontinuous lens of fine sand; 40% gravel content; very strongly acid pH.
IIIBCg2	40-50	Greenish gray (5GY 5/1 m) sand; many coarse prominent strong brown (7.5YR 5/6 m) mottles; discontinuous thin, dusky red placic bands throughout horizon; pH 5.5, strongly acid.

STANDARD CHEMICAL AND PHYSICAL SOIL ANALYSIS

Lab No.	Horizon	Depth	H_2O	% C LECO/W.B.	% N	C/N	Exchangeable Bases (me/100g) Ca	Mg	K	Na	Sum	C.E.C.	Base Sat. %	Pyrophos. % Fe	Al	Dithionite % Fe	Al	Hydrometer % Sand	Silt	Clay	pH H_2O	$CaCl_2$
81/4233	Ah	0-5	1.70	6.64/7.20	0.186	38.7	0.29	0.10	0.02	0.13	0.54	24.41	2.2	0.15	0.91	0.97	0.60	19.2	72.5	8.3	4.7	4.4
81/4234	IIBfgj	5-15	1.54	2.45/2.36	0.086	27.4	0.48	0.12	0.02	0.17	0.79	12.79	6.2	0.38	0.56			66.0	31.3	2.7	5.5	4.7
81/4236	IIBg	15-28	1.13	0.93/0.91	0.031	29.4	0.30	0.08	0.01	0.16	0.55	7.89	7.0	0.05	0.37			58.9	40.8	0.3	5.8	5.2
81/4236	IIIBCg2	40-50	1.54	0.94/0.67	0.024	27.9	0.26	0.13	0.01	0.19	0.59	8.73	6.8	0.06	0.31	1.43	0.46	87.6	11.1	1.3	6.0	5.5

ORGANIC MATTER ANALYSIS

Lab No.	Horizon	Depth	% C W.B.	Von Post	Pyrophosphate Index	Fibre Rubbed	Fibre Unrubbed	Ch/Cf	Ca/Cf	% C Humic	% C Fulvic	% C PVP-Fulvic	C14 Date
81/4234	IIBfgj	5-15	2.36	-	-	-	-	0.24	0.59	0.22	0.90	1.53	-

TOTAL MACRO AND MICRO NUTRIENTS IN PPM

Lab No.	Horizon	Depth (cm)	CA	P	S	NA	K	MN	MG	FE	ZN	CU	MO	B
81/4233	Ah	0-5	4465	310.0	425.7	416.2	1470	91.61	1470	8519	10.21	4.259	6.326	<0.157
81/4234	IIBfgj	5-15	7858	178.4	163.0	1514	856.0	275.3	7180	>10 000	28.89	15.61	7.743	<0.157
81/4235	IIBg	15-28	7838	495.1	161.4	495.4	642.3	261.9	6852	>10 000	30.25	24.70	6.113	<0.157
81/4236	IIIBCg2	40-50	5974	391.5	159.0	484.1	667.5	254.3	6745	>10 000	36.92	27.26	7.490	<0.157

Site 10: 15 m elevation, facing 300° NW, 9% slope; developed in **silty sand till; poorly drained; Wet** Lowland Forest, Cape Cook Lagoon.

Soil Profile Description
Gleyed Placic Humo Ferric Podzol

Horizon	Depth (cm)	Description
L-F	8-0	A thin litter layer of needles and weakly decomposed mosses rests upon a dark brown (10YR 4/3 m) moderately decomposed mat of coniferous needles and mosses.
Ahe	0-8	Very dark grayish brown (10YR 3/2 m) with discontinuous pockets of light brownish gray (10YR 6/2 m) loam; prominent mottles (10YR 4/2 m) (10YR 4/6 m); moderate, medium, subangular blocky structure. Soil matrix feels slick and smears easily due to 5% organic carbon content and 39% silt content. Horizon may consist primarily of slope wash materials; pH 4.0, extremely acid.
Bfgj	8-15	Dark brown (7.5YR 3/4 m) sandy loam; many medium prominent olive (5Y 5/4 m) mottles; moderate, fine to medium, subangular blocky structure; approximately 15% gravel. Pockets of very dark brown soil throughout horizon. Matrix is predominantly loose, not compacted; horizon has been influenced by slope wash processes; pH 4.5, extremely acid.
IIBfccgj	15-19	Dark brown (10YR 3/3 m) sandy loam; many medium prominent olive (5Y 5/4 m) mottles; moderate, medium subangular blocky structure; ca. 20% gravel, slightly more (10%) cobbles and stones than the Bfgj horizon (above). Matrix is slightly more compacted with local concentrations of platelike placic (iron cemented) bands consisting primarily of sand; pH 4.7, extremely acid.
IIBfgj1	19-30	Very dark grayish brown 10YR 3/2 m) sandy loam; many coarse, brown (7.5YR 5/6 m) mottles; moderate medium subangular blocky structure; ca. 20% gravel, 10% cobbles and stones. Matrix slightly compacted, with no form of cementation; pH 4.8, extremely acid.
IIBfgj2	30-45	Dark brown (10YR 4/3 m) loamy sand; many coarse light yellowish brown (2.5Y 6/4 m) mottles, moderate medium subangular blocky structure; ca. 20% gravel, 10% cobbles and stones. Matrix slightly compacted with no form of cementation; pH 4.7, extremely acid.
IIBfg	45-62	Olive (5Y 5/4 m) loamy sand; many coarse strong brown (7.5YR 4/6 m) mottles; moderate medium subangular blocky structure; ca. 20% gravel, 10% cobbles and stones. Matrix slightly compacted with no form of cementation; pH 5.0, extremely acid.

STANDARD CHEMICAL AND PHYSICAL SOIL ANALYSIS

Lab No.	Horizon	Depth	H_2O	% C LECO/W.B.	% N	C/N	Exchangeable Bases (me/100g) Ca	Mg	K	Na	Sum	C.E.C.	Base Sat. %	Pyrophos. % Fe	Al	Dithionite % Fe	Al	Hydrometer % Sand	Silt	Clay	pH H_2O	$CaCl_2$
81/4237	Ahe	0-8	1.87	4.97/5.24	0.206	25.4	0.08	0.16	0.05	0.05	0.48	26.08	1.8	0.34	1.41	0.41	0.24	52.1	39.3	8.6	4.7	4.0
81/4239	Bfgj	8-15	2.80	3.71/3.25	0.079	41.1	0.04	0.11	0.01	0.01	0.28	26.30	1.1	2.16	1.25	3.80	1.23	70.5	27.9	1.6	5.0	4.5
81/4240	IIBfccgj	15-19	2.72	3.89/3.39	0.085	40.0	0.05	0.10	0.01	0.01	0.26	23.83	1.1	2.16	1.25	3.80	1.23	68.0	30.7	1.3	5.1	4.7
81/4241	IIBfgj1	19-30	3.44	4.40/4.28	0.140	30.6	0.17	0.12	0.01	0.01	0.36	29.38	1.2	1.14	1.36	1.96	1.78	63.4	34.8	1.8	5.1	4.8
81/4242	IIBfgj2	30-45	2.71	2.98/2.86	0.100	28.6	0.13	0.11	0.01	0.01	0.31	18.69	1.7	1.08	1.06	1.90	1.36	70.9	28.6	0.5	5.2	4.7
81/4243	IIBfg	45-62	1.93	2.98/1.86	0.100	28.6	0.16	0.12	0.01	0.01	0.36	13.15	2.7	0.24	0.54	0.81	0.71	77.8	21.3	0.9	5.2	5.0

TOTAL MACRO AND MICRO NUTRIENTS IN PPM

Lab No.	Horizon	Depth (cm)	CA	P	S	NA	K	MN	MG	FE	ZN	CU	MO	B
81/4237	Ahe	0-8	3058	212.3	216.8	226.4	1972	72.07	1068	7677	7.883	3.089	4.383	0.712
81/4239	Bfgj	8-15	5248	269.2	291.1	132.8	1048	256.3	6183	<10 000	28.71	17.49	8.255	<0.157
81/4240	IIBfccgj	15-19	4826	318.4	280.3	309.0	964	253.5	6247	>10 000	27.66	19.55	8.122	<0.157
81/4241	IIBfgj1	19-30	4361	462.8	437.6	205.2	1009	266.0	6866	>10 000	31.55	26.34	10.62	<0.157
81/4242	IIBfgj2	30-45	4436	328.8	328.8	179.8	1017	266.0	6750	>10 000	29.55	22.42	8.581	<0.157

Extremely acid with virtually no exchangeable bases.

Site 11: 20 m elevation, facing 0° N, 2% slope; developed on **humic organics over gravel and sand**; poorly drained; Bog Shrub, Cape Cook Lagoon.

Soil Profile Description
Terric Humisol

Horizon	Depth (cm)	Description
Of	0-10	Reddish brown (2.5YR m) fibric raw moss; not decomposed.
Oh1	10-20	Dark brown (10YR 3/3 m) humic with inclusions of mesic zones; strongly to moderately decomposed; pH 3.7, extremely acid.
Oh2	20-40	Very dark grayish brown (10YR 3/2 m) humic; very strongly decomposed; pH 3.7, extremely acid.
Oh3	40-70	Very dark brown (10YR 2/2 m) humic; almost completely decomposed; pH 3.7, extremely acid.
Oh4	70-90	Very dark grayish brown (10YR 3/1 m) humic; very strongly decomposed; pH 3.7, extremely acid.
IIOh	90-110	Dark yellowish brown (10YR 3/4 m) humic muck with a moderate inclusion of sandy loam mineral soil incorporated into matrix; random small grandiorite gravels; muck almost completely decomposed; pH 4.0, extremely acid.

STANDARD CHEMICAL AND PHYSICAL SOIL ANALYSIS

Lab No.	Horizon	Depth	H_2O	% C LECO/W.B.	% N	C/N	Exchangeable Bases (me/100g) Ca	Mg	K	Na	Sum	C.E.C.	Base Sat. %	Pyrophos. % Fe	Al	Dithionite % Fe	Al	Hydrometer % Sand	Silt	Clay	pH H_2O	$CaCl_2$
81/4228	Of	0-10	7.86	44.70/53.07	1.68	31.5	2.54	3.32	0.56	1.01	7.43	160.06	4.6	1.29	0.53						4.4	3.7
81/4229	Oh1	10-20	6.29	45.36/50.88	0.40	-	3.42	1.34	0.13	0.6	5.55	123.30	4.5	0.10	0.75						4.4	3.7
81/4230	Oh2	20-40	9.23	53.86/58.69	2.32	25.3	0.81	0.68	0.04	0.39	1.92	107.04	1.8	0.05	1.89						4.7	3.7
81/4231	Oh3	40-70	7.74	54.33/57.90	1.63	35.4	0.75	0.60	0.04	0.54	1.93	122.39	1.6	0.02	1.53						4.4	3.7
81/4232	IIOh	90-110	4.90	22.70/21/80	0.55	39.1	0.47	0.15	0.02	0.19	0.83	72.17	1.2	0.07	1.81						4.4	4.0

ORGANIC MATTER ANALYSIS

Lab No.	Horizon	Depth	% C W.B.	Von Post	Pyrophosphate Index	Fibre Rubbed	Fibre Unrubbed	Ch/Cf	Ca/Cf	% C Humic	% C Fulvic	% C PVP-Fulvic	C14 Date
81/4228	Of	0-10	53.07	02	10YR 6/3 (3)	39.17	8.34						
81/4229	Oh1	10-20	50.88	07	10YR 5/4 (1)	27.50	6.67						
81/4230	Oh2	20-40	58.69	08	10YR 2/2 (0)	29.17	3.33						
81/4231	Oh3	40-70	57.90	09	7.5YR 3/4 (1)	45.00	6.67						
81/4232	IIOh	90-110	21.80	09	(sandy loam mineral matrix)								

TOTAL MACRO AND MICRO NUTRIENTS IN PPM

Lab No.	Horizon	Depth (cm)	CA	P	S	NA	K	MN	MG	FE	ZN	CU	MO	B
81/4228	Of	0-10	1544	753.8	2565	297.4	673.6	17.75	744.0	9293	7.109	5.278	2.335	14.19
81/4229	Oh1	10-20	1816	573.8	3807	337.0	795.7	23.88	525.8	2180	4.741	5.967	3.366	1.733
81/4230	Oh2	20-40	771.2	531.3	4858	87.93	420.9	13.41	298.0	1172	2.339	11.64	3.738	16.41
81/4231	Oh3	40-70	537.7	560.9	5177	70.23	555.4	22.45	506.2	1636	4.958	12.82	3.971	<0.157
81/4232	IIOh	90-110	5231	623.7	1822	328.3	1316	260.80	6963	>10 000	30.29	18.51	6.891	<0.157

Site 12: ca. 20 m elevation, level; developed on **organic veneer over sandy silt**; poorly to very poorly drained; Bog Scrubforest, Cape Cook Lagoon.

Soil Profile Description
Terric Humic Mesisol

Horizon	Depth (cm)	Description
Of	0-20	Raw sphagnum moss; fibric; slightly decomposed.
Om	20-50	Moderately decomposed; mesic.
Oh	50-70	Very strongly decomposed; humic.
IIBCg	70-80	Dark greenish gray (5GY 5/1 m) silt loams with many medium prominent clear olive brown (2.5Y 4/4 m) mottles; pH 4.4, extremely acid.
IICBcg	80-105	Grayish green (5G 5/2 m) silt loam, with many medium prominent dark brown (7.5YR 4/2 m) mottles; placic pan(s) occur in horizon (soil probe tends to distort true pan position); pH 5.0, very strongly acid.

STANDARD CHEMICAL AND PHYSICAL SOIL ANALYSIS

Lab No.	Horizon	Depth	H_2O	% C LECO/W.B.	% N	C/N	Exchangeable Bases (me/100g) Ca	Mg	K	Na	Sum	C.E.C.	Base Sat. %	Pyrophos. % Fe	Al	Dithionite % Fe	Al	Hydrometer % Sand	Silt	Clay	pH H_2O	$CaCl_2$
81/4201	IIBCg	70-80	3.21	3.77/4.50	0.119	14.7	0.31	0.10	0.01	0.12	0.54	20.64	2.6	0.05	1.26	0.10	0.82	20.5	76.8	2.7	5.2	4.4
81/4202	IICBcg	80-105	1.91	1.52/1.55	0.048	32.3	0.14	0.08	0.02	0.10	0.34	9.78	3.5	0.03	0.40	0.75	0.39	24.6	74.1	1.3	5.6	5.0

TOTAL MACRO AND MICRO NUTRIENTS IN PPM

Lab No.	Horizon	Depth (cm)	CA	P	S	NA	K	MN	MG	FE	ZN	CU	MO	B
81/4201	IIBCg	70-80	8783	1002	524.6	323.8	860.2	406.2	11 316	>10 000	51.48	48.11	8.787	<0.157
81/4202	IICBcg	80-115	8585	790.5	199.8	439.3	790.5	436.7	11 428	>10 000	57.48	63.95	8.408	<0.157

Site 13:	ca. 8 m elevation, level; developed on organic veneer over sand; Bog Herbaceous Vegetation--Deep Bog, Cape Cook Lagoon.	

Soil Profile Description
Humic Fibrisol

Horizon	Depth (cm)	Description
Of1	0-18	Dark brown (7.5YR 4/4 m) raw fibric sphagnum moss; not decomposed; pH 3.7, extremely acid.
Of2	18-48	Very dark grayish brown (10YR 3/2 m) fibric, sphagnum moss and sedge roots; weakly to moderately decomposed; pH 3.5, extremely acid.
Of3	48-88	Very dark grayish brown (10YR 3/2 m) fribric to mesic, sedge roots with sphagnum moss inclusions; weakly to moderately decomposed; extremely acid.
Of4	88-108	Very dark grayish brown (10YR 3/2 m) fibric to mesic, sedge roots with sphagnum moss inclusions; weakly to moderately decomposed; water lily root in matrix; extremely acid.
Oh	108-128	Very dark brown (10YR 2/2 m) humic to mesic, mesic components are similar to the overlying horizons; strongly to very strongly decomposed; pH 3.7, extremely acid.
Oh2	128-140	Very dark brown (10YR 2/2 m) muck and humic peat, almost completely decomposed; (difficult to identify all material in horizon due to water table and depth--log felt with probe), branch fragments extracted; extremely acid.
IIC	140-150	Very dark brown (10YR 2/2 m) medium sand, (no strong indication of gleying at this depth--may be masked by organic colloids); pH 4.0, extremely acid. .

STANDARD CHEMICAL AND PHYSICAL SOIL ANALYSIS

Lab No.	Horizon	Depth	H_2O	%	%	C/N	Exchangeable Bases (me/100g)					C.E.C.	Base Sat.	Pyrophos. %		Dithionite %		Hydrometer %			pH	
				C LECO/W.B.	N		Ca	Mg	K	Na	Sum		%	Fe	Al	Fe	Al	Sand	Silt	Clay	H_2O	$CaCl_2$
81/4214	Of1	0-18	9.52	47.64/58.84	1.29	45.3	8.56	10.23	1.71	1.91	22.41	161.20	13.9	-	-	0.00	0.00	-	-	-	4.2	3.7
81/4215	Of2	18-48	8.33	47.46/59.94	1.88	31.9	6.09	5.7	0.39	1.17	13.35	158.60	8.4	-	-	0.15	0.26	-	-	-	4.1	3.5
81/4216	Oh	108-128	3.74	27.29/24.17	0.89	27.1	1.39	1.16	0.02	0.27	2.84	63.90	4.4	-	-	0.05	0.61	-	-	-	4.3	3.7
81/4217	IIC	140-150	1.31	3.00/2.30	0.094	24.5	0.51	0.13	0.01	0.20	0.85	15.20	5.6	0.04	0.29	0.10	0.27	92.7	7.2	0.1	4.7	4.0

TOTAL MACRO AND MICRO NUTRIENTS IN PPM

Lab No.	Horizon	Depth (cm)	CA	P	S	NA	K	MN	MG	FE	ZN	CU	MO	B
81/4214	Of1	0-18	3456	554.5	1897	554.6	962.1	27.30	1949	1760	11.62	6.413	1.337	28.89
81/4215	Of2	18-48	1548	569.1	2761	69.48	312.2	11.16	772.1	1158	3.898	3.618	1.364	16.88

Site 14: **Nordstrom cave floor surface,** 6 m elevation, opening faces 190o SSW, level; **anthropogenic debris over sand and gravel,** underlain by bedrock; rapidly drained; unvegetated.

Soil Profile Description
Regosol, anthropogenic phase

Horizon	Depth (cm)	Description
Cp1 & Cp2	0-80	Black (10YR 2/1 m) fine loose humic matrix; consists primarily of a shell mixture with a subdominant component of gravels, sands, wood fragments, and fine charcoal; loose structureless deposit generally consistent through 80 cm depth; pH 7.1, neutral.
Cp3	85-105	Black (7.5YR 2/0 m) fine loose humic matrix; predominant materials are shells, gravels, and sands; fine fraction has a moderate medium granular structure.
Cp4	105-120	Black (7.5YR 2/0 m) fine loose humic matrix with a moderate medium granular structure; predominant materials are shells, gravels, and sands; pH 7.1, neutral.

A second surface horizon at 2 m distant from profile described above:

Horizon	Depth (cm)	Description
Cp1	1-7	Light yellowish brown (10YR 6/4 m) loamy sand ash-like material with inclusions of fine dark humic material; some shells and gravels; pH 7.4, mildly alkaline.

STANDARD CHEMICAL AND PHYSICAL SOIL ANALYSIS

Lab No.	Horizon	Depth	H_2O	%	%	C/N	Exchangeable Bases (me/100g)					C.E.C.	Base Sat.	Pyrophos. %		Dithionite %		Hydrometer %			pH	
				C LECO/W.B.	N		Ca	Mg	K	Na	Sum		%	Fe	Al	Fe	Al	Sand	Silt	Clay	H_2O	$CaCl_2$
81/4187	Cp1-Cp2	0-80	2.31	13.02/7.94	0.453	17.5	37.39	4.56	0.21	2.26	44.42	34.99	100	0.02	0.04	0.31	0.04	-	-	-	7.7	7.1
81/4184	Cp3	85-105	2.30	11.90/8.51	0.486	17.5	39.88	3.13	0.20	0.74	43.95	37.54	100	0.02	0.05	0.05	0.25	-	-	-	-	-
81/4185	Cp4	105-120	2.87	13.43/9.05	0.547	16.5	44.21	3.04	0.27	0.81	48.33	41.97	100	0.03	0.06	0.23	0.05	-	-	-	7.6	7.1
Surface horizon 2 metres distance from soil profile above																		-	-	-		
81/4182	Cp1	1-7	1.08	5.66/1.50	0.098	15.3	17.03	4.41	0.37	0.82	22.63	12.53	100	0.01	0.03	0.66	0.06	-	-	-	8.1	7.4

TOTAL MACRO AND MICRO NUTRIENTS IN PPM

Lab No.	Horizon	Depth (cm)	CA	P	S	NA	K	MN	MG	FE	ZN	CU	MO	B
81/4184	Cp3	85-105	181 908	18 145	247.0	1931	514.7	516.8	14 002	>10 000	74.23	40.81	5.474	<0.157
81/4185	Cp4	105-120	>200 000	17 180	<2.03	2201	605.8	534.1	10 979	>10 000	79.37	43.96	5.235	<0.157
Surface horizon 2 metres distance from soil profile above														
81/4182	Cp1	1-7	186 667	10 198	367.0	5377	1669	985.5	18 328	>10 000	128.1	69.15	8.282	<0.157

Appendix 4.3 Methods of soil profile descriptions and laboratory analysis

Soil profile descriptions

The soils are described according to methodologies and procedures provided in:

Walmsley, M., G. Utzig, T. Vold, D. Moon and J. van Barneveld (eds.). 1980. Describing ecosystems in the field. RAB Technical Paper No. 2, Resource Analysis Branch, British Columbia Ministry of Environment and Research Branch, British Columbia Ministry of Forests, Victoria, BC.

Dumanski, J. (ed.) Revised 1978. The Canadian Soil Information System (CanSIS). Manual for describing soils in the field. Land Resource Research Institute, Agriculture Canada, Central Experimental Farm, Ottawa, ON (compiled by the Working Group on Soil Survey Data, Canada Soil Survey Commission).

They are classified according to the Canadian Soil Classification System which is described in:

Canada Soil Survey Committee, Subcommittee on Soil Classification. 1978. The Canadian System of Soil Classification. Publication 1646, Resource Branch, Canada Department of Agriculture. Supply and Services Canada, Ottawa, ON.

Chemical and physical analyses

A variety of laboratory analyses have been performed on the soils described in Chapter 6. The analytical method(s) or appropriate literature reference(s) for each analysis follows.

Chemical analysis

Soil reaction (pH): method 1 (1:1 soil-water ratio), method 2 (1:5 soil-water ratio) and method 4 (in 0.01M$CaC1_2$) are described in J.A. McKeague (ed.) 1978. Manual on Soil Sampling and Methods of Analysis. 2nd edition. Prepared by Subcommittee (of Canada Soil Survey Committee) on Methods of Analysis. 2nd edition. Canadian Society of Soil Science. Pp 61-62.

Organ carbon (%) "Leco" carbon analyses are according to Laboratory Equipment Corporation. 1969, Carbon Analysis by Leco Analyser. Leco instruction manual for induction furnace and carbon analyser. St. Joseph's, Michigan. Modified Walkley-Black method is described in J.A. McKeague (ed.) (1978). Method 3.613.

Nitrogen (%) analyses are done by Semi-micro Kjeldahl method without precautions to include NO3 and NO2, 3.622; in J.A. McKeague (ed.) (1978). Pp 125.

Cation Exchange Capacity (me/100gm): the CEC is determined by NH_4 displacement and macroKjeldahl distillation as described in J.A. McKeague (ed.) (1978). Method 3321. Pp 78-80.

Exchangeable Cations-Ca, Mg, K, Na (me/100 gm): are done by atomic absorption spectrophotometry as described in J.A. McKeague (ed.) (1978). Method 3311. Pp 73-75.

Iron and aluminum (%), pyrophosphate extraction and diothinite-citrate-bicarbonate method of extraction are both described in J.A. McKeague (ed.) (1978). Pp 98-105.

Total macro and micro nutrients (PPM) were measured by a ARL 24000 inductively coupled agron plasma analyses (35:1 dilution), following a total digest with nitric-perchloric acid (3:1).

Humus fraction analyses. (PPMC) are according to Lowe, L.E. 1980. Humus fraction ratios as a means of discriminating between horizon types. Canadian Journal Soil Science. 60:219-229.

Physical analysis

Particle size distribution: analyses are according to sieving methods described in J.A. McKeague (ed.) (1978) and P.R. Day (1965). Pp. 26. Particle Fractionation and Particle Size Analysis. Pp 545-567 in Methods of soil analysis, C.A. Black, editor. Agronomy, No. 9, Part 1. American Society of Agronomy, Madison, Wisconsin.

Mechanical analysis (% sand, silt, clay, fine clay): analyses are according to the pipette method in J.A. McKeague (ed.) (1978). Pp 6-15.

Appendix 4.4 Kingfisher Creek: the identification of a culturally modified soil

The plot of Ch/Cf versus Ca/Cf (figure 4.12) is used in an attempt to separate the "cultural" from the "natural" horizons. Ch represents the carbon content in humic acid; Cf represents the carbon content in fulvic acid and Ca represents the carbon content in the strongly coloured polyphenolic component of the fulvic acid fraction. Fraction distribution is described by the ratios of Ch/Cf and Ca/Cf.

Site and horizon identification of numbered points on figure 4.12

Point No.	Geographic Area	Site	Horizon Depth cm	Soil Horizon
1	Brooks Peninsula	Kingfisher Creek terrace	23-10	Hp1
2	" "	" " "	10-0	Hp2
(3)	" "	(point located off of figure)	20-5	Hp
4	" "	Shelter Sheds (EaSW1)	11-22	Ap1
5	" "	" "	25-35	Ap2
6	Olympic Peninsula (USA)	Sandpoint	8-25	Ap1
7	" "	"	38-58	Ap2
8	Hesquiat Peninsula	Anton Point (DiSo 2)	0-25	Ap1
9	" "	" "	25-50	Ap2
10	" "	Skull Rock (DiSo 22)	0-15	Hp1
11	" "	" "	15-37	Hp2
12	Brooks Peninsula	Raised beach ridge No. 12	0-10	Ah
13	" "	" " " " "	10-22	Bfc
14	" "	" " " " 2	3-15	Ah
15	" "	" " " " "	15-35	Bf
16	Hesquiat Peninsula	Sandy marine terrace	0-7	Ahe
17	" "	" " "	7-20	Bm
18	Broken Island Group	Gravelly marine terrace	0-10	Ahe
19	" "	" " "	10-25	Bhf
20	Hesquiat Peninsula	Gravelly beach (DiSo 9)	0-4	Ahe
21	" "	" " "	4-10	Ah
22	" "	" " "	10-13	A(p)b
23	" "	" " "	13-33	A(hp)b
24	" "	" " "	33-49	Bhf
25	" "	" " "	49-63	Bf1
26	(from Lowe 1983)	B.C.	(composite of)	F
27	" "	" "	" "	H
28	" "	" "	" "	Of
29	" "	" "	" "	Om
30	" "	" "	" "	Oh

Appendix 4.5 Geographic information of soils on Table 4.3

Brooks Peninsula Site

Location:	West coast of N. Vancouver Island, B.C.
Elevation:	760 metres.
Parent material:	rubbly silty sand colluvium, primarily derived from granodiorite, igneous rock of the granite-rhyolite family
Slope and topography:	60% near apex, steeply sloping moderately mounded mountain ridge; southeast aspect; well drained.
Climate:	(3,300 mm rainfall, mean annual temperature 9.0° C) soils subject to only minor freeze.[1]
Vegetation:	Mountain hemlock *Tsuga mertensiana.*

Dunn Peak Site

Location:	Dunn Peak Shuswap Highl., B.C.
Elevation:	1900 metres.
Parent material:	rubbly silty and morainal ridge, primarily derived from medium to coarse grained gradiorite.
Slope and topography:	20%, low rubbly mass on cirque floor; well drained soils.
Vegetation:	Subalpine fir (*Abies lasiocarpa*), Rhododendron (*Rhododendron albiflorum*) (*Vaccinium membranaceum*).

Germansen Mountain

Location:	Germansen Range, B.C.
Elevation:	1585 metres.
Parent material:	rubbly silty sand morainal ridge primarily derived from medium to coarse grained granodiorite.
Slope and topography:	20%, low rubbly mass on cirque floor; well drained soils.
Vegetation:	Subalpine fir (*Abies lasiocarpa*), *Cassiope mertensiana* and *Phyllodoce empetriformis.*

Site 5, Fitzsimmons Range

Location:	N. of Vancouver, B.C. 50°02'N, 127°51'W.
Elevation:	1950 metres.
Parent material:	gravelly silty sand and locally derived drift from the underlying fractured phaneritic fine to medium grained quartz, diorites, gneisses and granites.
Slope and topography:	6-8% north northeast aspect; well drained soils.
Vegetation:	Krummholz *Abies lasiocarpa* sedges (*Carex spp.*) (*Juncus spp.*) (*Poa arctica*).

Golden Ears soil

Location:	N. of Vancouver, B.C. 49°21'N, 122°20'W.
Elevation:	670 metres.
Parent material:	gravelly silty sand glacial till derived mainly from granitic bedrock.
Slope and topography:	18%, severely moulded south southwest slope; moderately well drained soils.
Vegetation:	Pacific silver fir, Western hemlock, Yellow cedar.

<u>Seven Devil's surface</u>

Location:	near Coos Bay, Oregon.
Elevation:	120 metres.
Parent material:	Pleistocene beach and offshore sediments with probably increments of eolian sand overlying a wave cut platform of soft sandstone or siltstone.
Vegetation:	Western hemlock and Western red-cedar.

<u>USDA Pedon 115</u>

Location:	Nevada County, California.
Elevation:	829 metres.
Parent material:	clayey silt colluvium, residual material derived from diabase and metabasic rock-plutonic rock known as diorite or microgabbro higher in calcium plagioclase.
Vegetation:	Ponderosa pine.

[1] Environment Canada, Canadian climatic normals, 1951-80, closest rainfall data Kyuquot 50°02'N by 127°22'W at 3 metres elevation; closest coastal temperature data Estevan Point 49°23'N by 126°33'W at 7 metres elevation

Chapter 5

Vascular Plants and Phytogeography of Brooks Peninsula

R.T. Ogilvie
Biology Department, University of Victoria
Victoria, BC

Abstract

The vascular flora of Brooks Peninsula consists of 350 taxa, 330 (94%) of which are native. Sixty percent of the flora are North American, 35% are Pacific Coastal, 21% are Cordilleran, and 25% are Circumpolar.

An annotated species list is given, describing for each taxon its abundance, occurrence, habitat, and vegetation type on Brooks Peninsula.

Important distributional patterns in the flora are: 9 taxa endemic to the Queen Charlotte Islands and Vancouver Island, 2 taxa endemic to the Olympic Peninsula and Vancouver Island, 7 southern disjunct taxa, and 10 northern disjunct taxa.

The literature on glacial refugia and floristic distribution is reviewed and discussed in terms of Brooks Peninsula and the northwest coast of North America. It is concluded that the high proportion of endemic and disjunct taxa, having diverse geographic affinities, provides support for the idea of a glacial refugium on Brooks Peninsula. The Brooks Peninsula refugium is one of a series of refugia extending from the Olympic Peninsula, to northwestern Vancouver Island, the Queen Charlotte Islands, and the Alexander Archipelago of Coastal Alaska.

Solutions to these phytogeographic questions and the refugium problem will come from many more intensive floristic inventories on northern Vancouver Island and the northwestern coast, and more dated palynological and macrofossil series of plant species extending back to glacial times.

Acknowledgements

I would like to thank the following botanists for checking the identifications of certain plant groups: T.C. Brayshaw (*Salix, Potamogetonaceae, Ranunculaceae*), Adolf Ceska (*Pteridophyta, Juncaceae, Cyperaceae*), G.W. Douglas (*Asteraceae*). I also thank the curators of the University of

British Columbia and University of Victoria herbaria for permission to consult their collections for distribution records. Finally, I thank Adolf Ceska, Rolf Mathewes, and Wilf Schofield for their discussions of these floristics and refugia problems of the North Pacific Coast.

Introduction

The most westerly projection of Vancouver Island, exposed to the open ocean on the north, west, and south, and bounded by high mountains to the east, Brooks Peninsula is remote and difficult of access. Botanical exploration of the peninsula has taken place only during the last 20 years.

Even the land adjoining the peninsula has had meagre floristic attention. In 1955 a small plant collection consisting of 42 vascular species was made on the Bunsby Islands, approximately 15 km to the southeast (Carl and Guiguet 1956). Collections on Kains Island at the entrance to Quatsino Sound, ca. 33 km to the north, were made in 1968 by Gordon Carr; they included two species of phytogeographic interest: *Douglasia laevigata* and *Lomatium martindalei*. Complete floristic inventories have been made of Mt. St. Patrick at the northern tip of Vancouver Island, and of six other mountain peaks to the southeast of the study area (Ogilvie and Ceska 1984). A number of plant collections have been made from the Port Hardy and Nahwitti Lowland area of northeastern Vancouver Island.

For Brooks Peninsula, information on the vascular flora is based on surveys and collections begun in 1975. The discovery of a number of the Queen Charlotte Islands' endemic plants on Brooks Peninsula by R. Hebda and J. Pinder-Moss in 1975, and J. Pojar and F. Boas in 1977 provided the foundation for the idea of a Brooks Peninsula glacial refugium (Pojar 1980). The botanical survey of the 1981 expedition was planned as a complete floristic inventory to provide further information related to the refugium hypothesis. The following is a summary of the various plant collections and surveys which have been made:

1975, August. Six days of collecting were done by Richard Hebda, John Pinder-Moss, Judy Godfrey, and Geoffrey Godfrey. Collecting was done at Cape Cook Lagoon, the peatlands adjacent to the lagoon, and the lower slopes of Doom Mountain. The specimens are deposited at University of British Columbia (UBC).

1976, Summer. Jim Pojar carried out a brief floristic survey of the intertidal zone of Cape Cook Lagoon.

1977, June 23-29. Jim Pojar and Frank Boas made collections from the Cape Cook Lagoon shore, the peatlands adjacent to the lagoon, and the slopes and summit of Doom Mountain. The specimens are at UBC and Royal British Columbia Museum (V). A floristic list of the vegetation was compiled from the 1976 and 1977 surveys by Jim Pojar.

1978, June 7. Robert K. Scagel made plant collections near Cape Cook. The specimens are at UBC.

1978, July 22-23. Hans Roemer made collections from the southeast shore of Brooks Peninsula, ascending Cladothamnus Creek to the central mountain ridge and to near the summit of Doom Mountain. A floristic list was compiled and the specimens are deposited at V.

1981, July 19-August 25. During the Royal British Columbia Museum's expedition, floristic collections were made over most of Brooks Peninsula by R.T. Ogilvie, R. Hebda, Hans Roemer, and W.B. Schofield. Approximately 690 specimens were collected; they are deposited at V.

1984, August 6-14. Supplementary collecting was done by R.T. Ogilvie, R. Hebda, W.B. Schofield, and Bob Powell. Collections were made along the southeast shore of the peninsula: Moneses Creek, Amos Creek, Quineex Creek, and Nordstrom Creek, in addition to Senecio Ridge, Harris Peak and adjacent ridges, Oxycoccus Ridge, and Doom Mountain. Approximately 260 specimens were collected; they are deposited at V.

The following floristic list is compiled from these collections and surveys. The numbered specimens cited are primarily those collected in 1981 by R.T. Ogilvie, Hans Roemer, Richard Hebda, W.B. Schofield, and A. Banner; and in 1984 by R.T. Ogilvie, W.B. Schofield, and Richard Hebda. Additional collections from earlier trips are cited with the collector's name(s).

Taxa without specimen citations were not collected, but were recorded in field notes.

The taxonomic treatments of main relevance to the Brooks Peninsula flora are: Calder and Taylor (1968), Hulten (1967, 1968, 1973), and Hitchcock et al. (1955-1969).

Except where superseded by more recent taxonomic studies, the author has primarily followed Calder and Taylor (1968), since this more readily allows floristic comparison of the two areas.

In the floristic list, the sequence of families follows Hitchcock and Cronquist (1973) and the common names are primarily based on Taylor and MacBryde (1977).

The author has indicated the frequency of occurrence of the taxa in the study area by the following qualitative terms: very rare, rare, occasional, frequent, common. This is a continuous series ranging from "very rare" for a single occurrence to "common" for wide occurrence, e.g., from sea level to timberline. A brief statement is given of the vegetation and habitat of each taxon. The relevant detailed vegetation data are presented in Chapter 8.

List of Vascular Plants

Lycopodiaceae

Huperzia selago (L.) Bernh. Fir clubmoss
8173035, 8173115, 818110, 818911, 8181448, 8481317. Common; alpine, montane, and bogs.

Lycopodium annotinum L. Stiff clubmoss
848114. Rare; a single collection from Senecio Ridge, krummholz.

Lycopodium clavatum L. Running clubmoss
8173034, 8173117, 818426, 818522, 848113. Common; in alpine, krummholz, and bogs.

Lycopodium inundatum L. [*Lycopodiella inundata* (L.) Holub] Bog clubmoss
8181237, 8181434. Occasional; in bogs.

Lycopodium obscurum L. [L. *dendroideum* Michx.] Ground-pine
8481318, 8481319. Rare; in bogs along Moneses Creek.

Lycopodium sitchense Rupr. [*Diphasiastrum sitchense* (Rupr.) Holub] Alaska clubmoss
8173110, 818741, 8481030. Occasional; alpine and montane.

Selaginellaceae

Selaginella selaginoides (L.) Link Mountain clubmoss
818224, 818427, 818510, 8181298, 8182030, 84894B, 8481017, 8481032. Occasional; in bogs and alpine seepage.

Selaginella wallacei Hieron. Wallace's clubmoss
8181621, 84887. Rare; on rock headlands and alpine outcrops.

Isoetaceae
Isoëtes echinospora Dur. Bristle-like quillwort
818225, 818226, 81852, 818164, 818172, 818191, 8481047, 8481048. Occasional; in ponds and lakes.

Isoëtes flettii (A.A. Eat.) N.E. Pfeiffer [*I. occidentalis* Henderson] Western quillwort
818152, 818153, 818154. Rare; a single occurrence in water of Ledum Lake. These specimens are large and coarse, compared with *I. echinospora* in the study area. The megaspores are relatively large (0.5-0.7 mm in diameter) and the surface is covered with spines (A. Ceska, personal communication).

Equisetaceae
Equisetum arvense L. Common horsetail
8181219, 8181447, 818423, 8481325, 8481326. Infrequent; beaches, bogs, and alluvial forest.

Equisetum hyemale L. Scouring-rush
8481110. Rare; a single collection from Jackobson Point beach.

Equisetum telmateia Ehrh. Giant horsetail
8182364, HR (s.n.). Rare; upper beach and alluvial forest.

Ophioglossaceae
Botrychium multifidum (Gmel.) Rupr. ssp. *multifidum* Leathery grape-fern
818124. Rare; Menziesia Creek, bog streamlet.

Polypodiaceae
Adiantum pedatum L. var. *aleuticum* Rupr. Northern maidenhair fern
818721. Occasional; alpine cliffs, coastal surge channels.

Adiantum pedatum L. var. *subpumilum* W.H. Wagner in Wagner & Boydston Dwarf maidenhair fern
Pojar & Boas 770191 (type). Cape Cook Lagoon headland, surge channel cliff; very rare, a single collection. The specimen of Pojar & Boas is the basis for this new variety described by Wagner (Wagner and Boydston 1978); thus, Brooks Peninsula is the type locality for this fern. Since its discovery on Brooks Peninsula it has been found at several other localities on the outer west coast of Vancouver Island. It also occurs on the outer northwest coast of the Olympic Peninsula.

Asplenium trichomanes L. Maidenhair spleenwort
81837, 8181295, 848105. Occasional; alpine cliffs and chasms, rock headlands.

Asplenium viride Huds. Green spleenwort
818714, 818715, 8181294, 848103, 848104. Rare; Doom Mountain, alpine cliffs and chasms.

Athyrium filix-femina (L.) Roth ssp. *cyclosorum* (Rupr.) C. Christens. Common lady fern
Frequent; alluvial and montane forests.

Blechnum spicant (L.) Roth Deer fern
8481212. Common; forests and bogs.

Cryptogramma crispa (L.) R.Br. var. *acrostichoides* (R.Br.) Clarke [*C. acrostichoides* R.Br.] Parsley fern
8181610. Rare; Doom Mountain, alpine outcrops.

Cystopteris fragilis (L.) Bernh.   Fragile fern
848913, 848914, 8481015, 8481016. Very rare; Harris Peak, Doom Mountain, alpine cliffs and outcrops.

Dryopteris expansa (Presl) Fraser-Jenkins & Jermy   Spiny shield fern
817302, 817303, 818116, 81875, 81876, 848916, 848917, 848918, 848919, 848920, 848921. Frequent; alluvial to montane forest, mountain cliffs.

Gymnocarpium dryopteris (L.) Newman   Oak fern
817312, 818173. Frequent; coniferous forest and mountain cliffs.

Polypodium amorphum Suksd.   Pacific polypody fern
81878. Rare; Doom Mountain, alpine ledges.

Polypodium glycyrrhiza D.C. Eaton   Licorice fern
8181296, 848833, 848842, 848108. Frequent; headlands, coniferous forest, and alpine.

Polypodium hesperium Maxon   Western polypody fern
8181413, 8481022. Occasional; coniferous forest and alpine.

Polypodium scouleri Hook. & Grev.   Leathery polypody fern
8181275, 8182021, 8182362, 848116. Rare; sea stacks, headlands and upper beach.

Polystichum braunii (Spenner) Fee   Braun's holly fern
Very rare; recorded from Doom Mountain, shaded chasm walls, 427 m and 550 m elevation.

Polystichum lonchitis (L.) Roth   Mountain holly fern
848915. Very rare; a single occurrence, on Harris Peak, alpine cliffs.

Polystichum munitum (Kaulf.) Presl   Sword fern
81877, 818122, 8181287, 8181611, 818251. Common; from beach scrub to montane forest, mountain cliffs.

Pteridium aquilinum (L.) Kuhn ssp. *aquilinum* var. *pubescens* Underw.   Western bracken fern
81843, 81844, 848820. Rare; upper beach scrub and headlands.

Thelypteris limbosperma (Allioni) H.P. Fuchs   Mountain wood fern
817311, 81871, 81872, 81874, 81891, 818101, 818102, 818129, 8181210, 8181211, 8181212, 818165, 818166, 818167, 818168, 818169, 848106, 848109, 8481010, 8481011, 8481012, 8481013, 8481014. Occasional; alpine cliffs and chasms.

Thelypteris phegopteris (L.) Slosson   Beech fern
81873, 818121, 818125, 848107, Roemer 7883. Rare; alpine cliffs and ledges, alluvial forest.

Taxaceae
Taxus brevifolia Nutt.   Western yew
818740. Occasional; montane forest.

Pinaceae
Abies amabilis (Dougl.) Forbes   Pacific silver fir
8173022, 8173023, 8173024, 8173131, 818517, 848922. Common; shore forest to timberline.

Picea sitchensis (Bong.) Carr. Sitka spruce
8181276. Common; shore forest and lower montane.

Pinus contorta Dougl. ex Loud. var. *contorta* Shore pine
848958, 848959. Common; bogs, montane and krummholz.

Pseudotsuga menziesii (Mirbel) Franco var. *menziesii* Coast Douglas-fir
817294, 84886A, 84886B, 84886C. Rare; Cape Cook Lagoon and Jackobson Point shore forest.

Tsuga heterophylla (Raf.) Sarg. Western hemlock
Common; shore forest and montane, occasionally to timberline.

Tsuga mertensiana (Bong.) Carr. Mountain hemlock
Common; montane forest and krummholz.

Cupressaceae
Chamaecyparis nootkatensis (D.Don) Spach Yellow-cedar
Common; bogs, montane, and krummholz.

Juniperus communis L. var. *saxatilis* Pall. Rock juniper
Occasional; montane and alpine outcrops, bogs.

Thuja plicata Donn ex D. Don in Lamb. Western red-cedar
Common; shore forest to montane, rarely to timberline

Salicaceae
Salix babylonica L. Weeping willow
818231. Rare; escaped from cultivation at Quineex Indian reserve cabin.

Salix scouleriana Barratt in Hook. Scouler willow
818412, 8481113, 8481114, 8481345, 8481346, 8481347, 8481348, 8481349, 8481350, 8481351.
Occasional; upper beach scrub.

Salix sp. Willow
818201. A single sterile specimen, growing in sand on Guilliams Bay beach. The specimen belongs to the *Salix commutata* group, but cannot be assigned to a species.

Myricaceae
Myrica gale L. Sweet gale
Common; in bogs.

Betulaceae
Alnus crispa (Aiton) Pursh ssp. *sinuata* (Regel) Hult. Sitka alder
8173130, 818151, 818161, 848935. Occasional; montane, krummholz, streamside, bogs, and rockslide scrub.

Alnus rubra Bong. Red alder
Common; beach scrub, shore forest, and alluvial forest.

Loranthaceae
Arceuthobium campylopodum Engelm. in A. Gray Western dwarf mistletoe
Occasional; parasitizing *Tsuga heterophylla* in low elevation forests.

Polygonaceae
Polygonum fowleri Robins. Fowler's knotweed
8182367, 8182368. Rare; a single occurrence at Quineex beach.

Rumex maritimus L. Seaside dock
8481337. Rare; a single collection from the marine beach at the mouth of Moneses Creek.

Rumex transitorius Rechinger f. Narrow-leaved dock
8182351, 8182352, 8182353, 8182013. Rare; upper beach sand at Quineex Indian Reserve beach and Guilliams Bay beaches.

Chenopodiaceae
Atriplex patula L. var. *obtusa* (Cham.) C.L. Hitchc. Orache
8173038, 818414, 8182012. Occasional; upper tidal flats at Cape Cook Lagoon and Guilliams Bay beaches.

Chenopodium album L. Lamb's-quarters
8182370. Rare; upper shore, Quineex Indian Reserve beach. Introduced.

Salicornia virginica L. American glasswort
Occasional; tidal flats at Cape Cook Lagoon and Jackobson Point.

Nyctaginaceae
Abronia latifolia Eschsch. Yellow sandverbena
818206, 818207. Very rare; a single occurrence on Guilliams Bay beach sand dune.

Portulacaceae
Montia parvifolia (Mocino) Greene Small-leaved montia
81832, 8181618. Occasional; rock headlands and alpine ledges.

Montia sibirica (L.) Howell [*Claytonia sibirica* L.] Siberian miner's-lettuce
8181291, 8181619, 8182024, 8182310. Occasional; beach scrub and alpine ledges.

Caryophyllaceae
Cerastium arvense L. Field chickweed
8182319, 8182330, 84888, 848834. Occasional; Quineex Indian Reserve beach and Jackobson Point, rock headlands.

Honckenya peploides (L.) Ehrh. ssp. *major* (Hook.) Hult. [*Arenaria peploides* L.] Seabeach sandwort
8182019, 8481338. Occasional; on sand beaches of Cape Cook Lagoon, Guilliams Bay and at the mouth of the creek draining Moneses Lake.

Lychnis coronaria (L.) Desr. Rose campion
818233, 8182325. Rare; escaped from cultivation around Quineex Indian Reserve cabin.

Sagina crassicaulis S. Wats. Sticky-stemmed pearlwort
81846, 8181261, 8182011, 8182028, 8182311, 8182363, 848816, 848839. Occasional; on rock headlands and beaches.

Spergularia marina (L.) Griseb. Saltmarsh sand-spurrey
84861. Very rare; a single occurrence at Jackobson Point, salt marsh. Introduced.

Stellaria crispa Cham. & Schlecht. Crisped starwort
8173026, 81836, 8181620, 8182016, 848924. Occasional; disturbed patches on beaches, forests, and cliffs.

Stellaria humifusa Rottb. Saltmarsh starwort
818413, 8182369. Occasional; cobble beaches.

Nymphaeaceae
Brasenia schreberi Gmelin Watershield
81862, 81863. Rare; ponds of Cape Cook Lagoon bogs.

Nuphar polysepalum Engelm. Yellow pond-lily
Common; bog pools, ponds, and lakes.

Ranunculaceae
Anemone narcissiflora L. ssp. *alaskana* Hult. Narcissus anemone
8173132, 8173133, 818541, 818104, 8181428, 8181029, Roemer 7824, 7896.
Rare; Cassiope Lake, Doom Mountain, Andromeda Ridge, Senecio Ridge, alpine ledges and cliffs.

Aquilegia formosa Fisch. in DC. Red columbine
848944, 848945, 8481215, 8481320, 8481321. Occasional; bogs, streamside, alpine cliffs, chasms and ledges.

Caltha biflora DC. White marsh-marigold
818725, 818742, 848911, 848912. Occasional; alpine seepage and snowbeds.

Coptis aspleniifolia Salisb. Spleenwort-leaved goldthread
8173012, 818514, 818537, 8182035, 848128. Common; bogs, wet forests, and alpine.

Coptis trifolia (L.) Salisb. ssp. *trifolia* Three-leaflet goldthread
818428, 818616. Occasional; bogs.

Isopyrum savilei Calder & Taylor Queen Charlotte isopyrum
818710, 8181015, 818176, 848102, Roemer 7825. Very rare; Doom Mountain and Andromeda Ridge, alpine cliffs and ledges. Previously known only as endemic to the Queen Charlotte Islands; extended to Brooks Peninsula in this study; and most recently to Porcher Island, southwest of Prince Rupert (RTO) (Figure 5.1).

Ranunculus cooleyae Vasey & Rose Cooley's buttercup
818126. Rare; alpine cliffs, Doom Mountain

Ranunculus uncinatus D.Don. var. *parviflorus* (Torr.) Benson Small-flowered buttercup
81849, 818410, 8181238, 8182315, 8182340, 8182341. Occasional; upper beach and beach scrub.

Trautvetteria caroliniensis (Walt.) Vail. var. *occidentalis* (Gray) C.L. Hitchc. False bugbane
848135. Rare; streamside and alluvial forest.

Brassicaceae
Arabis hirsuta (L.) Scop. ssp. *eschscholtziana* (Andrz.) Hult. Hairy rockcress
817298, 817299, 818209, 818237. Rare; beach sand and dunes, Cape Cook Lagoon beach, Guilliams Bay beach, Quineex Indian Reserve beach.

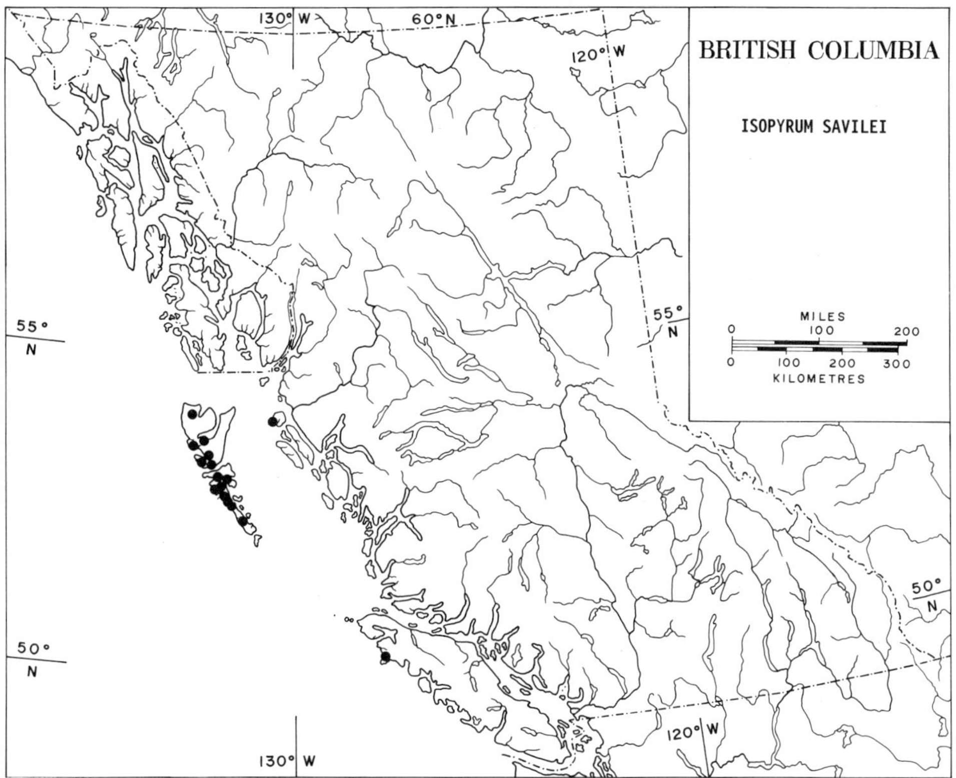

Figure 5.1 Distribution of *Isopyrum savilei*

Barbarea orthoceras Ledeb. American wintercress
818208. Rare; sand dunes at Guilliams Bay beach.

Cakile edentula (Bigel.) Hook. American searocket
8181251, 8181252, 8481339. Occasional; beach sand, Guilliams Bay beach, Jackobson Point beach, and the marine beach at the mouth of the creek draining Moneses Lake; introduced. Barbour and Rodman (1970) discuss the introduction and spread along the Pacific Coast of *Cakile*.

Cakile maritima Scop. European searocket
8181253, 8181254, 8182365, 8182366 8481340, 8481341, 8481342, 8481344. Occasional; beach sand, Guilliams Bay beach, Quineex Indian Reserve beach, and the marine beach at the mouth of the creek draining Moneses Lake beach; introduced.

Cardamine oligosperma Nutt. var. *oligosperma* Few-seeded bittercress
8181836, 8182015, 8182023. Rare; beach sand and headland, Guilliams Bay beach.

Cochlearia officinalis L. ssp. *oblongifolia* (DC.) Hult. Scurvygrass
Not known on Brooks Peninsula, but collected on Solander Island in 1916, by Newcombe (No. 287).

Rorippa islandica (Oeder) Borbas var. *hispida* (Desv.) Butters & Abbe Bristly yellowcress
8182384. Rare: a single collection from Quineex Indian Reserve beach; introduced.

Droseraceae
Drosera anglica Huds. Great sundew
8182210. Rare; in bogs.

Drosera rotundifolia L. Round-leaved sundew
8182211. Common; in bogs.

Crassulaceae
Sedum oreganum Nutt. Oregon stonecrop
8182334. Very rare; a single collection from Quineex Indian Reserve, on beach rock.

Saxifragaceae
Boykinia elata (Nutt.) Greene Coast boykinia
818217, 848132, 848133, 848134. Rare; stream edge, upper Cape Cook Lagoon and creek draining Moneses Lake.

Heuchera glabra Willd. ex R. & S. Smooth alumroot
8173128, 818719, 818720, 8181639, 848123, 848124, 848125, 848126, 848127.
Occasional; outcrops, alpine cliffs and ledges.

Saxifraga ferruginea Grah. Alaska saxifrage
818117, 818724, 818743, 8181513, 8182031, 84898, Roemer 7868. Common; rock headlands and alpine outcrops.

Saxifraga mertensiana Bong. Mertens' saxifrage
818726, 818727. Rare; alpine outcrops, Doom Mountain.

Saxifraga punctata L. ssp. *cascadensis* Calder & Savile [*S. nelsoniana* D. Don] Dotted saxifrage
848926, Roemer 7867, 7882. Rare; shaded alpine cliffs and ridges, Harris Peak and Doom Mountain.

Saxifraga taylori Calder & Savile Taylor's saxifrage
818910, 8181016, 8181293, 8181638, 818710, Roemer 7846, 7892. Occasional; alpine cliffs and outcrops, Doom Mountain, Cladothamnus Ridge, Andromeda Ridge, Pyrola Peak. One of the species previously considered as endemic to the Queen Charlotte Islands, now known from the above collections and four other localities on Vancouver Island. L.R. Goertzen (1996) has just completed research on the genetic diversity of this species (Figure 5.2).

Tellima grandiflora (Pursh) Dougl. Tall fringecup
81835. Rare; Cape Cook Lagoon headland, and beach scrub.

Tiarella laciniata Hook. Cutleaved foamflower
818723. Occasional; forest and montane.

Tiarella trifoliata L. Three leaflet foamflower
818529. Frequent; forest and montane.

Tolmiea menziesii (Pursh) T. & G. Piggy-back plant
Occasional; alluvial forest.

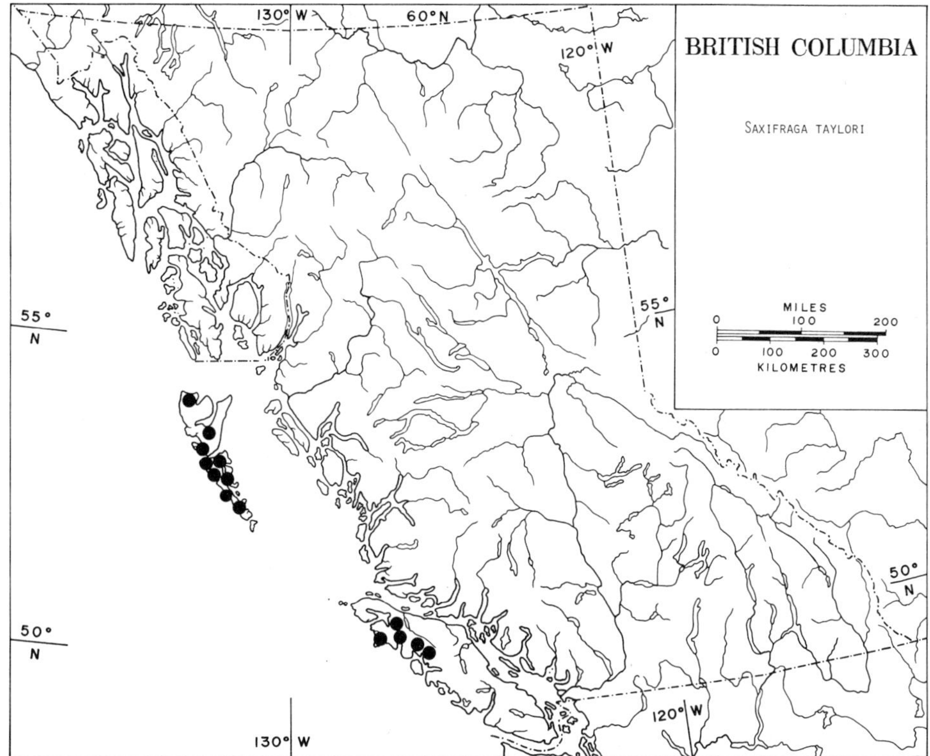

Figure 5.2 Distribution of *Saxifraga taylori*

Grossulariaceae
Ribes bracteosum Dougl. ex Hook. Stink currant
818157, 848143, 848144. Occasional; beach scrub and alluvial forest.

Ribes divaricatum Dougl. Coast black gooseberry
8181713. Occasional; beach scrub.

Rosaceae
Amelanchier alnifolia Nutt. Saskatoon
8181712, 848827. Occasional; headlands and promontories, and upper beach scrub.

Aruncus sylvester Kostel. [*A. dioicus* (Walter) Fernald] Sylvan goatsbeard
Rare; upper beach scrub and alluvial forest.

Fragaria chiloensis (L.) Duchesne Pacific coast strawberry
Frequent; headlands and beach meadows.

Geum calthifolium Menzies ex J.E. Smith Caltha-leaved avens
817317, 8173129, 818533, 818711, 818712, 818713, 818175. Occasional; alpine heath, meadows, and outcrops.

Geum schofieldii Calder & Taylor Queen Charlotte avens
Pojar & Boas 770221: "small unnamed drainage south of Orchard Point, 500-800 m altitude, wet more or less subalpine cliffs, crevices, ledges, niches, gullies and rock ledges, much moss, heath

and krummholz." Very rare; this plant was collected on the upper slopes of Doom Mountain, the only occurrence of it on Brooks Peninsula. This is one of the species previously considered as endemic to the Queen Charlotte Islands, and the Doom Mountain collection is the only record of it outside of the Queen Charlotte Islands. Ogilvie (1994) discovered two more small populations on Moresby Island, Queen Charlotte Islands (Figure 5.3).

Luetkea pectinata (Pursh) Kuntze   Partridgefoot
818525, 818116. Common; krummholz, alpine heath, outcrops and meadows.

Potentilla pacifica Howell   Pacific silverweed
Occasional; beach meadow and salt marsh.

Potentilla villosa Pallas ex Pursh   Woolly cinquefoil
Occasional; shore rocks and headlands.

Pyrus fusca Raf. [*Malus fusca* (Raf.) Schneid.]   Pacific crabapple
Occasional; beach scrub and scrub forest, alluvial forest.

Rosa gymnocarpa Nutt. in T. & G.   Baldhip rose
8181615, 8181616, 848826, 8481217. Occasional; shore scrub, alluvial and montane forest.

Rosa nutkana Presl var. *nutkana*   Nootka rose
818912, 8181265, 8181266. Occasional, beach shrub and scrub forest.

Rubus laciniatus Willd.   Cutleaf evergreen blackberry
8182332, 8182358. Rare; introduced near Quineex Indian Reserve cabin.

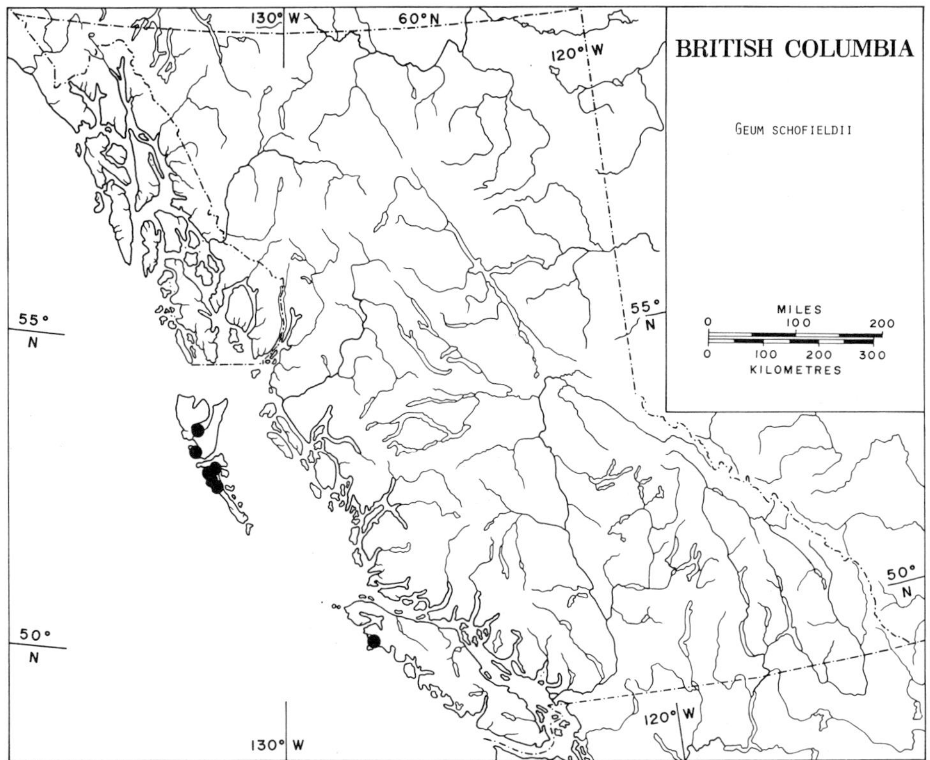

Figure 5.3   Distribution of *Geum schofieldii*

Rubus parviflorus Nutt. Thimbleberry
Occasional; beach shrub and scrub forest.

Rubus pedatus J.E. Smith Five-leaflet creeping raspberry
8173011, 8173027, 818538. Common; lowland forest, shore forest, slope forest, timberline scrub forest, and krummholz.

Rubus procerus P.J. Mueller ex Boulay Himalayan blackberry
8182333. Rare; introduced near Quineex Indian Reserve cabin.

Rubus spectabilis Pursh Salmonberry
818532. Common and widespread; from beach scrub to krummholz.

Sanguisorba officinalis L. ssp. *microcephala* (Presl) Calder & Taylor Great burnet
818223, 8181218, 8181229, 818148, 8481313. Occasional; bogs and alluvial forest.

Sorbus sitchensis Roemer var. *grayi* (Wenzig) C.L. Hitchc. Sitka mountain-ash
818113, 818107, 818174. Occasional; timberline scrub and krummholz.

Fabaceae
Hedysarum occidentale Greene Western hedysarum
84894, 84895, 84896. Very rare; from a single locality, the summit of Harris Peak, on alpine ledges. This is a southern cordilleran species that extends into Canada only on a few mountain peaks on Vancouver Island; Ogilvie and Ceska (1984).

Lathyrus japonicus Willd. Beach-pea
8481112. Rare; upper beach and beach shrub.

Lupinus nootkatensis Donn ex Sims Nootka lupine
817315, 818528. Occasional; alpine meadow, heath, and ledges.

Trifolium wormskioldii Lehm. Springbank clover
848119. Occasional; headlands, beach meadow, and upper estuary meadow.

Vicia gigantea Hook. Giant vetch
81842, 8181453. Occasional; upper beach herb and beach shrub.

Empetraceae
Empetrum nigrum L. Crowberry
817309, 818530, 8181013, 8181860, 848936, 8481039. Common; bog scrub and scrub forest, krummholz, alpine heath, outcrops, and meadows.

Rhamnaceae
Rhamnus purshiana DC. Cascara
848141, 848142. Rare; a single occurrence at forest edge at Jackobson Point beach. There is a seasonal midden site (EaSw 6) at this location, which suggests that the cascara might have been introduced there by the aboriginal people. In this connection, the few specimens of this species from the Queen Charlotte Islands are considered by J.A. Calder to have been introduced by humans (Calder and Taylor 1968; and specimens annotated by Calder at V).

Violaceae

The determination of the Brooks Peninsula Violas is problematic, since we found no flowering material, and identification had to be based on fruiting and vegetative characters. Under V. *sempervirens* we have placed the specimens that are stoloniferous with cordate-ovate, purple-maculate leaves and lanceolate, brown, membranous stipules. A few of our specimens conform to Calder and Taylor's (1968) description of V. *biflora* ssp. *carlottae*: these plants are non-stoloniferous, leaves obtuse, reniform, with coarse pubescence on the margins and upper surface; stipules broad-ovate; and sepals blunt, ciliate-margin, with a prominent purple mid-stripe.

Viola biflora L. ssp. *carlottae* Calder & Taylor   Queen Charlotte violet
8181017, 8181419, 8181429, 848115. Very rare; restricted to Senecio Ridge and Andromeda Ridge; exposed alpine ridges and cliffs. Listed by Calder and Taylor (1968) as endemic to the Queen Charlotte Islands; this is its only known occurrence outside of there (Figure 5.4).

Viola glabella Nutt. in T. & G.   Yellow wood violet
8181220, 848954, 8481024, 848129, 8481210. Occasional; alluvial and mountain slope forests.

Viola palustris L.   Marsh violet
Rare; wet lowland forest.

Viola sempervirens Greene   Trailing evergreen yellow violet
8173031, 818543, 818617, 818746, 8181213, 8181221, 8181229, 8181913, 848930, 8481023. Occasional; alluvial forest, mountain slope forest, and montane outcrops.

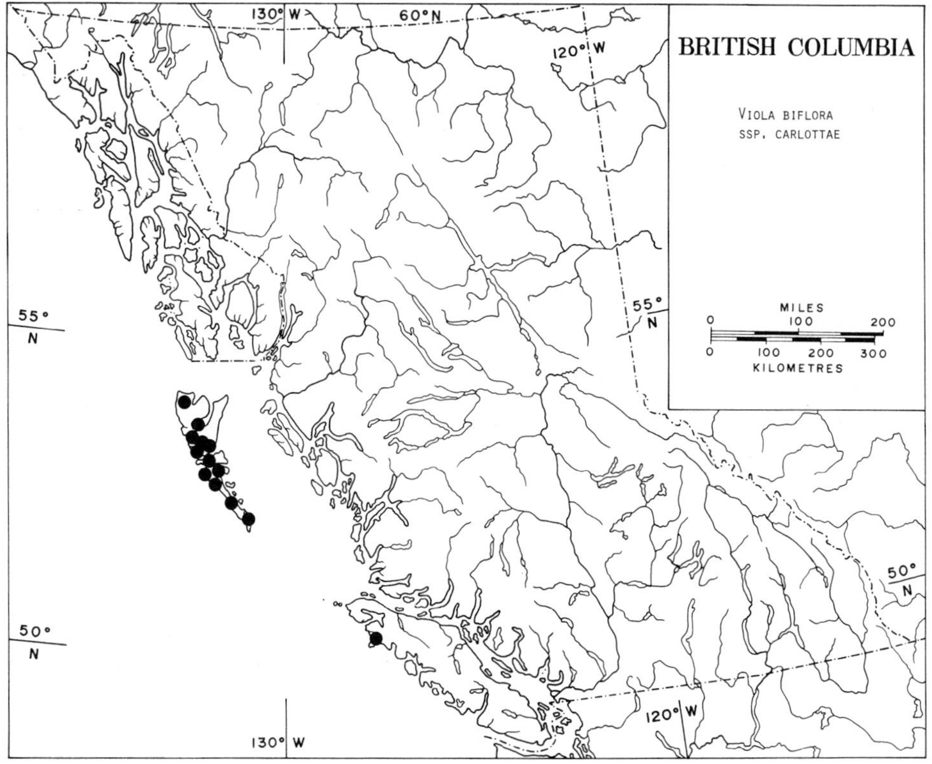

Figure 5.4   Distribution of *Viola biflora* ssp. *carlottae*

Onagraceae
Epilobium adenocaulon Hausskn. Tall annual willow-herb
8181725. Rare; mountain slope.

Epilobium alpinum L. Alpine willow-herb
Roemer 78100; Doom Mountain, chasm, 24 July 1978. Rare; alpine and alluvial forest.

Epilobium glandulosum Lehm. var. *glandulosum* Sticky willow-herb
8182014, 848136, 848137. Rare; beach headland and streamside.

Epilobium glandulosum Lehm. var. *tenue* (Trel.) C.L. Hitchc. Sticky willow-herb
8181244, 8181250, 818231. Rare; upper beach, Guilliams Bay beach and Quineex Indian Reserve beach.

Hippuridaceae
Hippuris montana Ledeb. Mountain mare's-tail
84899, 848910. Very rare; a single occurrence on Harris Peak, alpine snowbed.

Araliaceae
Oplopanax horridus (Smith) Miq. Devil's club
Occasional; alluvial and montane forest.

Apiaceae
Angelica genuflexa Nutt. Bentknee angelica
8182371, 8182372, 8182373. Rare; upper beach herb, Quineex Indian Reserve beach.

Angelica lucida L. Seacoast angelica
818515, Roemer (s.n.). Rare; beach meadow, Quineex Indian Reserve, Jackobson Point and Guilliams Bay beaches.

Conioselinum pacificum (S. Wats.) Coult. & Rose Hemlock-parsley
818516, 8181717, 8181718. Frequent; beach herb, beach shrub, and headland.

Glehnia littoralis Schmidt. ssp. *leiocarpa* (Mathias) Hult. American glehnia
Rare; beach sand and dunes, Cape Cook Lagoon and Guilliams Bay beaches.

Heracleum lanatum Michx. Cow-parsnip
Occasional; upper beach meadow and beach shrub.

Ligusticum calderi Mathias & Const. Calder's lovage
Pojar & Boas 770166, Pinder-Moss 1201, 1231, 1255, R.K. Scagel 7505703 ("near Cape Cook"), 8173039, 8173040, 817316, 818214, 818536, 818744, 81895, 81896, 81897, 8181018, 8181223, 8181223, 8181225, 818147, 8181424, 8181514, 8181627, 8181912, 848943, 848962, 848963, 848964, 848965, 848966, 848967, 848968, 848969, Roemer 7873, 7877, 7897. Occasional; alpine heath, meadows and ridges, krummholz, timberline scrub forest, alluvial and shore forest, bogs. In 1995 two new large populations of this species were found on northwestern Vancouver Island low elevation peatlands, by Ogilvie and Ceska (Figure 5.5).

Lilaeopsis occidentalis Coult. & Rose Western lilaeopsis
8173037. Rare; tidal flats and salt marsh.

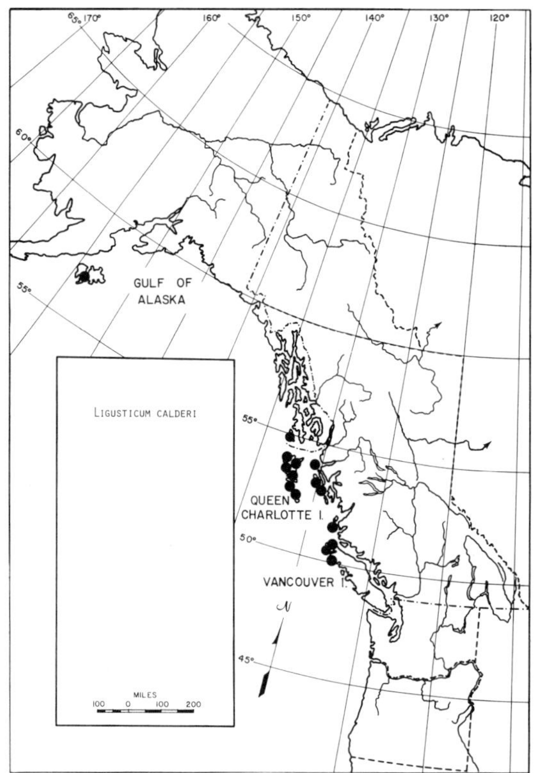

Figure 5.5 Distribution of *Ligusticum calderi*

Lomatium martindalei Coult. & Rose Few-fruited lomatium
84892, 84893. Very rare; a single occurrence, Harris Peak, alpine ridge rock. A southern coastal species; the Brooks Peninsula population is near its known northern limit at Quatsino Sound.

Oenanthe sarmentosa Presl in DC. Pacific oenanthe
8182316, 8182327, 8182359, 8182360, 8182361. Occasional; upper beach meadow, Quineex Indian Reserve and Jackobson Point beaches.

Osmorhiza chilensis Hook. & Arn. Mountain sweetcicely
Rare; montane forest and alpine.

Osmorhiza purpurea (Coult. & Rose) Suksd. Purple sweetcicely
81815, 81816, 818737, 818738. Occasional; montane forest, timberline scrub, ledges.

Cornaceae
Cornus unalaschkensis Ledeb. Pacific coast bunchberry
818529, 818149, 848938. Common; timberline scrubforest, krummholz, alpine heath.

Pyrolaceae
Hemitomes congestum A. Gray Gnome plant
818216. Rare; a single collection from alluvial forest along Marks Creek.

Hypopitys monotropa Crantz Pinesap
8173019, 8181721. Rare; Lagoon Peak and Pyrola Lake, lowland forest and scrub forest.

Moneses uniflora (L.) A. Gray Single delight
8173032, 848923. Occasional; lowland forest, mountain slope forest, timberline scrub forest, and krummholz.

Pyrola secunda L. One-sided wintergreen
Occasional; mountain forest and timberline.

Ericaceae
Andromeda polifolia L. Bog-rosemary
81865, 8181862. Occasional; bogs.

Arctostaphylos uva-ursi (L.) Spreng. Kinnikinnick
818114. Occasional; alpine ridges and outcrops, shore headlands and promontories.

Cassiope lycopodioides (Pall.) D. Don ssp. *cristapilosa* Calder & Taylor Crinkle-haired mountain-heather.
81858, 81879, 818722, 8181011, 818179, 8481019, 8481020, 8481035, 8481036, 8481037. Occasional; alpine outcrops and ridges. One of the taxa previously considered as endemic to the Queen Charlotte Islands; it has been found also on one other mountain peak southeast of Brooks Peninsula. Plant systematists do not agree on the status to give ssp. *cristapilosa*. More familiarity with, and detailed analyses of, field populations are needed (Figure 5.6).

Cassiope mertensiana (Bong.) G. Don Mertens' mountain-heather
8181632. Occasional; alpine heath and meadow.

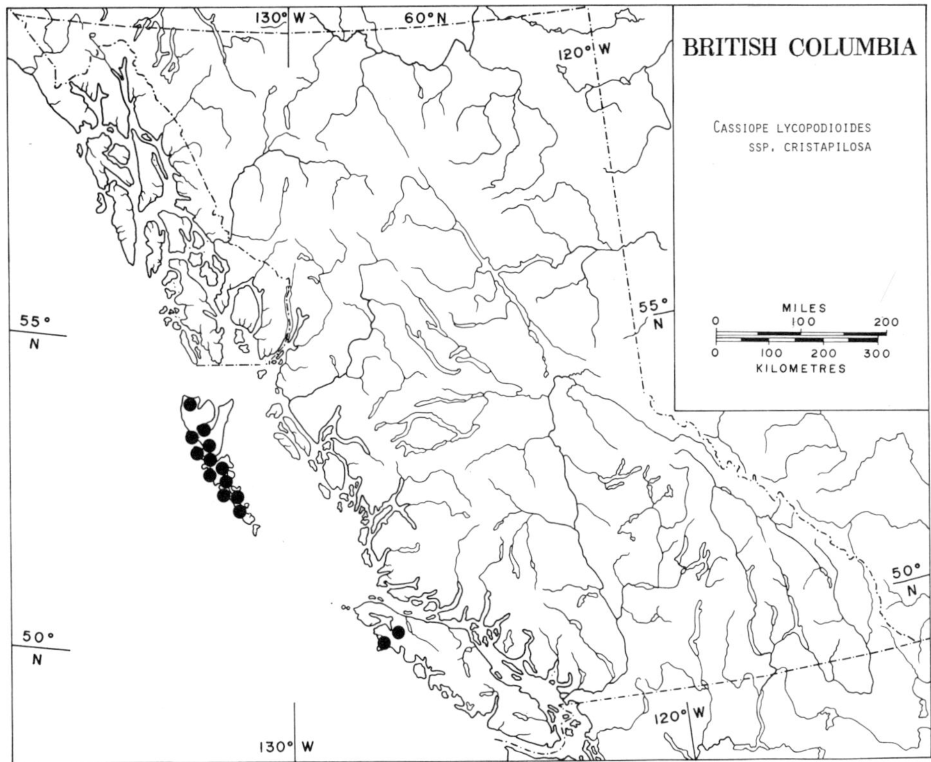

Figure 5.6 Distribution of *Cassiope lycopodioides* ssp. *cristapilosa*

Cassiope stelleriana (Pall.) DC. Steller's mountain-heather
8173116, 81857, 818531, 8181010, 8181410, 8181633, 8481018, 8481034. Occasional; krummholz, alpine heath, ridges, and outcrops.

Cladothamnus pyroliflorus Bong. Copperbush
8173036. Common; shore forest, alluvial forest, bog scrub, and krummholz.

Gaultheria shallon Pursh Salal
Common and widespread; from beach shrub up to timberline krummholz.

Kalmia polifolia Wang. var. *microphylla* (Hook.) Rehd. Alpine-laurel
Occasional; bogs and bog scrub forest.

Ledum groenlandicum Oeder Labrador-tea
Occasional; bogs and bog scrub forest.

Loiseleuria procumbens (L.) Desv. Alpine-azalea
8173118, 848956, 8481038. Frequent; krummholz, alpine heath, meadows and outcrops, bogs.

Menziesia ferruginea J.E. Smith ssp. *ferruginea* False-azalea
Common and widespread; from shore forest up to timberline krummholz.

Phyllodoce empetriformis (J.E. Smith) D. Don Red mountain-heather
817308, 818527, 8181012, 8181631, 8481329. Common; alpine heath, krummholz, timberline scrub forest, and bog scrub forest.

Vaccinium alaskaense Howell Alaska blueberry
8181636, 8181719, 8181720, 8181914. Frequent; timberline scrub forest and krummholz, lowland and mountain slope forest.

Vaccinium caespitosum Michx. Dwarf bilberry
8173111, 818425, 81855, 818534, 848937. Frequent; alpine heath and outcrops, krummholz, and bogs.

Vaccinium deliciosum Piper Cascade blueberry
Occasional; timberline scrub forest and krummholz.

Vaccinium membranaceum Dougl. ex Hook. Black huckleberry
Occasional; timberline scrub forest and mountain slope forest.

Vaccinium ovalifolium J.E. Smith Oval-leaf blueberry
8181511. Common and widespread; lowland and mountain slope forest, timberline scrub forest, and krummholz.

Vaccinium ovatum Pursh Evergreen huckleberry
818155, 818156. Rare; Cook Lagoon and Jackobson Point, bog scrub forest and beach shrub.

Vaccinium oxycoccos L. ssp. *oxycoccos* Bog cranberry
818432, 818145. Rare; bogs and scrub forest.

Vaccinium parvifolium J.E. Smith in Rees   Red huckleberry
8173010. Common and widespread; from shore forest to timberline scrub forest and krummholz.

Vaccinium uliginosum L.   Bog blueberry
8173119. Frequent; alpine heath and meadows, krummholz, and bog scrub forest.

Vaccinium vitis-idaea L. ssp. *minus* (Lodd.) Hult.   Mountain cranberry
818144. Occasional; krummholz and bog scrub forest.

Primulaceae
Dodecatheon jeffreyi van Houtte   Jeffrey's shootingstar
848946, 8481045. Occasional; bogs, bog scrub forest, streamside, alpine meadow and heath.

Douglasia laevigata A. Gray ssp. *ciliolata* (Constance) Calder & Taylor   Smooth douglasia
Pojar & Boas 770218, south of Orchard Point, 500-800 m. Very rare; Doom Mountain, alpine cliffs. A southern species of the Olympic, Coast, and Cascade Mountains; it is known from several mountains on Vancouver Island, three localities on the Queen Charlotte Islands, and a suspect report from the southern Cascade Mountains on the mainland. The Calder and Taylor (1968) record from the Queen Charlotte Islands, is from "a few sterile rosettes" on Mt. Moresby; in 1980 a second population of this species was found on Tasu Ridge, Moresby Island by Roemer, Ogilvie and Mersereau; and a third population was discovered in 1994 on southern Graham Island by Goertzen and Ogilvie.

Glaux maritima L.   Sea milkwort
Rare; tidal marsh, Cape Cook Lagoon and Jackobson Point beach.

Trientalis arctica Fisch. ex Hook.   Northern starflower
818539. Occasional; alpine meadows, heath and krummholz, shore outcrops, and bog scrub forest.

Gentianaceae
Gentiana douglasiana Bong.   Swamp gentian
8173013, 8173014, 81827, 818513, 848949A. Common; bogs, bog scrub forest, alpine meadows and heath.

Gentiana platypetala Griseb. in Hook.   Broad-petalled gentian
818519, 848934, 848960, 8481031A, 8481211. Occasional; alpine heath and meadows. This is a north coast species, ranging from Alaska southward to Bella Coola and the Queen Charlotte Islands; it is known from one other location on northwestern Vancouver Island.

Gentiana sceptrum Griseb. in Hook.   King gentian
8181230, 8181451, 8481031B, 8481310, 8481311, 8481312. Occasional; bogs and bog scrub forest.

Swertia perennis L.   Alpine bog swertia
8181452. Rare; a single collection in bog scrub forest below Senecio Ridge.

Menyanthaceae
Fauria crista-galli (Menzies) Makino   Deer-cabbage
8173121, 81811, 81812. Common; bogs and bog scrub forest, wet alpine meadows, heath, and krummholz.

Polemoniaceae

Phlox diffusa Benth. ssp. *longistylis* Wherry   Spreading phlox
Rare; dry meadow slope of Doom Mountain. A species of the southern Coast and Cascade Mountains, this is its northernmost record on Vancouver Island.

Hydrophyllaceae

Romanzoffia sitchensis Bong.   Sitka mistmaiden
8181290, 8181723. Occasional; montane and alpine moist ledges and cliffs.

Lamiaceae

Galeopsis tetrahit L.   Common hemp-nettle
Rare; introduced weed, a single record from Cape Cook Lagoon Beach.

Mentha arvensis L. var. *villosa* (Benth.) Stewart   Field mint
8181248. Rare; a single occurrence in beach meadow on Crabapple Islet.

Prunella vulgaris L. var. *lanceolata* (Barton) Fern.   Self-heal
8181432, 848818, 8481216, 8481327. Occasional; headlands, beach meadow, streamside, and bogs.

Stachys cooleyae Heller   Cooley's hedge-nettle
818158, 818411. Occasional; alluvial forest, beach shrub, and upper beach meadow.

Stachys mexicana Benth.   Mexican hedge-nettle
8181241. Rare; upper beach meadow.

Scrophulariaceae

Castilleja miniata Dougl. ex Hook.   Common paintbrush
8181267, 8182017, 8182326. Occasional; beach meadow and headlands.

Digitalis purpurea L.   Foxglove
8182328. Rare; introduced, around Quineex Indian Reserve cabin.

Mimulus guttatus DC. ssp. *guttatus*   Yellow monkey flower
8182029, 8182331. Rare; moist headlands and beach meadow.

Pedicularis bracteosa Benth. in Hook.   Bracted lousewort
818171, 8181722. Rare; alpine meadows and ravines.

Pedicularis bracteosa Benth. in Hook. var. *atrosanguinea* (Pennell & Thompson) Cronq.
Dark-red lousewort
818108, 818109, 8181411. Rare; Senecio Ridge and Andromeda Ridge, alpine meadow and krummholz. One of the taxa considered endemic to the Olympic Mountains, it is now known from two other mountain peaks on northwestern Vancouver Island.

Pedicularis ornithorhyncha Benth. in Hook.   Bird's beak lousewort
8481043, 818171, 8481044, Roemer & Carson 7849. Occasional; moist alpine meadow and heath, krummholz.

Penstemon davidsonii Greene var. *menziesii* (Keck) Cronq.   Davidson's penstemon
8173122, 818114. Occasional; alpine outcrops, meadows, heath, and krummholz.

Scrophularia californica Cham. & Schlecht. var. *oregana* (Pennell) Cronq. California figwort
8182022. Rare; upper beach herb.

Veronica americana Schwein. ex Benth. in DC. American speedwell
8182348, 8182349, 8182350. Rare; a single occurrence in upper beach herb at Quineex Indian Reserve.

Orobanchaceae
Boschniakia hookeri Walpers. Ground-cone
8173018, 818419, 8181454. Rare; headlands, beach shrub, beach scrub forest, and timberline scrub forest.

Lentibulariaceae
Pinguicula vulgaris L. ssp. *macroceras* (Link.) Calder & Taylor Butterwort
817318, 8173125, 818745, 8481046. Occasional, but widely distributed; moist alpine meadow and heath.

Utricularia minor L. Lesser bladderwort
818123, 8181287, 818222. Rare; bog ponds and streamlets.

Utricularia vulgaris L. Common bladderwort
Rare; bog ponds and streamlets.

Plantaginaceae
Plantago macrocarpa Cham. & Schlecht. Alaska plantain
8181022. Occasional; tidal marsh, shore meadow, bogs.

Plantago maritima L. Seaside plantain
Common; tidal marsh, headlands, shore outcrops, beach meadows.

Rubiaceae
Galium aparine L. Common cleavers
8181243, 8181258. Occasional; beach meadow.

Galium kamtschaticum Steller ex R. & S. Boreal bedstraw
8181292, Roemer 78104. Very rare; Doom Mountain, alpine scree meadow, ledges and chasms.

Galium trifidum L. Small bedstraw
8181918, 848840. Very rare; Cape Cook Lagoon and Jackobson Point, alluvial forest and beach promontories.

Galium triflorum Michx. Fragrant bedstraw
8181259, 8181260, 8182025, 818236, 8182312, 848121. Common; beach meadows and shrub, alluvial forest, mountain slopes and cliffs.

Caprifoliaceae
Linnaea borealis L. ssp. *longiflora* (Torr.) Hult. Western twinflower
818146, 8181861, 8182034. Frequent; krummholz, timberline scrub forest, alpine heath, bogs, and lowland forest.

Lonicera involucrata (Richards.) Banks ex Sprengel Black twinberry
Occasional; headlands and beach shrub, shore forest.

Lonicera periclymenum L. Woodbine honeysuckle
8182336. Rare; a single occurrence at Quineex Indian Reserve cabin where it was planted.

Sambucus racemosa L. ssp. *pubens* (Michx.) House var. *arborescens* (T. & G.) A. Gray Coastal red elder
818739. Occasional; Doom Mountain, mountain slopes and ledges.

Valerianaceae
Valeriana sitchensis Bong. Mountain heliotrope
818105, 818106, 8481026. Occasional; Doom Mountain and Andromeda Ridge, ravines, talus, and chasms.

Campanulaceae
Campanula rotundifolia L. Common harebell
8173124, 818213, 818103, 8181420, 848812. Frequent; alpine ridges, cliffs, heath and krummholz, headlands.

Campanula rotundifolia L. var. *alaskana* A. Gray Alaska harebell
817295, 817296, 8481322, 8481323, 8481324, Pinder-Moss 1267A: lagoon shoreline, rockwalls of runnels. Occasional; Cape Cook Lagoon, Jackobson Point, Moneses Creek, beach rocks and cliffs, bogs.

Lobelia dortmanna L. Water lobelia
818112, 818113. Rare; a single occurrence in stream entering Kalmia Lake.

Asteraceae
Achillea millefolium L. ssp. *borealis* (Bong.) Breitung Northern yarrow
818234. Occasional; beach meadows, headlands, promontories and sand dunes, alpine and krummholz.

Ambrosia chamissonis (Less.) Greene var. *bipinnatisecta* (Less.) J.T. Howell Sand-bur ragweed
81841, 8181264. Rare; sand beaches, dunes, and beach meadows.

Anaphalis margaritacea (L.) Benth. & Hook. Pearly everlasting
8181249, 8182010, 848927. Rare; Guilliams Bay beach meadow and dune, 1900 Peak alpine heath.

Apargidium boreale (Bong.) T. & G. [*Microseris borealis* (Bong.) Schulz-Bip] Apargidium
Common; in bogs and bog scrub forest, wet forest, wet alpine meadows, heath and krummholz.

Arnica amplexicaulis Nutt. ssp. *amplexicaulis* Streambank arnica
818728, 8181284, 8181285, 8181417, 8181617, 8181857, 848101. Occasional; streamside, alluvial forest, moist alpine ledges and cliffs.

Arnica latifolia Bong. var. *gracilis* (Rydb.) Cronq. Slender arnica
818524, 818119, 84891. Rare; Doom Mountain, Harris Peak, Andromeda Ridge, exposed alpine ridges and rock.

Arnica latifolia Bong. var. *latifolia* Mountain arnica
8181110, 8181637. Rare; Doom Mountain, Pyrola Peak, Andromeda Ridge, alpine heath, krummholz, and scree meadow.

Artemisia arctica Lessing ssp. *arctica* Mountain sagewort
(= *Artemisia norvegica* Fries ssp. *saxatilis* (Besser in Hook.) Hall & Clements)
Roemer 7894. Very rare; a single occurrence, Doom Mountain, 760 m, south-facing cliff. The distribution of this taxon is eastern Asia and the cordillera of Alaska, the Yukon, Mackenzie, British Columbia, and Alberta, south to California and Colorado. Its nearest occurrences are on the Queen Charlotte Islands, the Coast Mountains of the adjacent mainland, and the Olympic Mountains. On the Queen Charlotte Islands, Calder and Taylor (1968) report two small, rare populations; and Ogilvie (1994) reported two new populations which are small and "very scarce".

Artemisia furcata Bieb. var. *heterophylla* (Besser) Hult. (= *Artemisia trifurcata* Steph.) Three-forked mugwort
818548, 8181297, 818178, Pojar 770228. Very rare; found only on Doom Mountain, 760 m, sunny exposed summit. The species occurs in eastern Asia and the mountains of Alaska, the Yukon, and Mackenzie, with southern disjunctions in the Selkirk and northern Rocky Mountains, and the Olympic and Cascade Mountains of Washington. The southern disjunct populations of the Olympic and Cascade Mountains and Brooks Peninsula are distinguished taxonomically as variety *heterophylla*.

Artemisia suksdorfii Piper Coastal mugwort
8181245, 8181246. Rare; a single occurrence at Guilliams Bay beach, upper beach.

Aster eatonii (A. Gray) Howell [*A. bracteolatus* Nutt.] Eaton's aster
8182354, 8182355, 8182356, 8182357. Rare; a single occurrence, Quineex Indian Reserve upper beach.

Aster subspicatus Nees ssp. *subspicatus* Douglas' aster
817291, 817292, 817293, 8181450, 818159, 8181917, 848817, 848836, 8481315, 8481316. Occasional; beach meadow and shrub, headlands, alluvial and shore forest, bogs.

Cirsium brevistylum Cronq. Short-styled thistle
8181242, 8181247, 8182339. Rare; Guilliams Bay beach, Quineex Indian Reserve, upper beach and meadow. Calder and Taylor (1968) believe this species to be introduced at disturbed coastal sites on the Queen Charlotte Islands.

Erigeron peregrinus (Pursh) Greene ssp. *peregrinus* var. *dawsonii* Greene Dawson's fleabane
817313, 817314, 81823, 81824, 818212, 818512, 818542, 818615, 81898, 8181014, 8181425, 8181431, 8181436, 818163, 8181614, 848942, 848961, 8481328. Occasional; alpine ridges, cliffs, and pond edges; bogs and streamsides.

Erigeron peregrinus (Pursh) Greene ssp. *peregrinus* var. *peregrinus* Subalpine fleabane
81819, 81833, 8181628, 8481027. Occasional; headlands, mountain slopes and krummholz.

Eriophyllum lanatum (Pursh) Forbes var. *lanatum* Woolly-sunflower
848811, 848117, 848118. Very rare; restricted to Jackobson Point, south-facing slopes of headlands and sea-stacks. This is a southern coastal species that reaches its northern limit on Brooks Peninsula.

Hieracium albiflorum Hook. White hawkweed
Rare; Cape Cook Lagoon and Jackobson Point beach.

Hieracium gracile Hook. Alpine hawkweed
818115, 848929. Rare; Andromeda Ridge and 1900 Peak, krummholz and heath.

Lactuca biennis (Moench.) Fern. Tall blue lettuce
8181255, 8181256, 8181257. Rare; shore of Crabapple Islet, introduced weed.

Prenanthes alata (Hook.) D. Dietr. Western rattlesnake-root
8173127, 818540. Occasional; headlands, beach shrub, alluvial forest, timberline scrub forest, krummholz, alpine ledges and cliffs.

Senecio moresbiensis (Calder & Taylor) G.W. Dougl. & G. Ruyle-Dougl. Queen Charlotte butterweed
8181418, 8181430, 8181433, 8481213. Rare; Senecio Ridge and peatland, Nordstrom Creek, alpine heath and bogs. One of the taxa previously considered as endemic to the Queen Charlotte Islands; it is now known from Port Hardy and six islands along the northern coast of the mainland. Two new large populations were found in low elevation peatlands of northwestern Vancouver Island by Ogilvie and Ceska, 1995 (Figure 5.7).

Solidago multiradiata Ait. var. *scopulorum* A. Gray Northern goldenrod
818117, 818118, 848815, 848824, 848829, 848830, 848841. Occasional; alpine heath, krummholz and outcrops, beach rock headlands and promontories.

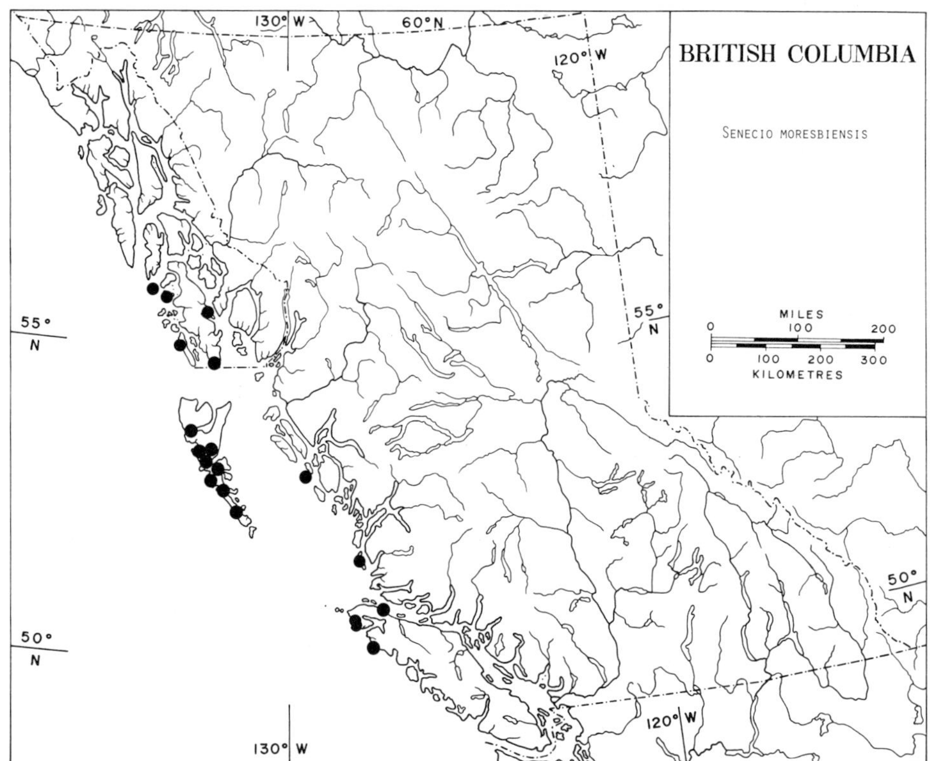

Figure 5.7 Distribution of *Senecio moresbiensis*

Sonchus asper (L.) Hill   Prickly sow-thistle
818202, 8182338. Rare; Guillams Bay and Quineex Indian Reserve beaches, upper beach, introduced weed.

Sonchus oleraceus L.   Annual sow-thistle
8182314. Rare; Quineex Indian Reserve beach, introduced weed.

Juncaginaceae
Triglochin maritimum L.   Seaside arrow-grass
818233. Occasional; tidal flats, saltmarsh meadow, bogs.

Triglochin palustre L.   Marsh arrow-grass
818194. Rare; Cape Cook Lagoon peatlands, along streamlets.

Potamogetonaceae
Potamogeton gramineus L.   Grass-leaved pondweed
81861, 818131, 818211. Occasional; bog pools and ponds.

Zosteraceae
Phyllospadix scouleri Hooker   Scouler's surf-grass
Five specimens of this species from the study area are at UBC. Cape Cook area, 11 June 1964, R. Lee & A. Mathieson, 8252, 8272; Cape Cook, mid intertidal tide pool, 27 August 1968, JM, PC, KB, DP, BB, PH, 22569; Jackobson Point, at diving station, 14 August 1968, JM, PC, KB, DP, BB, PH, 21149; Southwest of Orchard Point, mile-long beach, September 1975, J. Pinder-Moss, 1301.

Zostera marina L.   Eel-grass
817301, 818231, 818243. Common; lower tidal, bays and coves.

Zostera marina L. var. *stenophylla* Asch. & Graebn.   Narrow-leaved eel-grass
818242. A single collection from Cape Cook Lagoon bay.

Juncaceae
Juncus arcticus Willd. ssp. *ater* (Rydb.) Hult.   Arctic rush
8181235, 818212. Occasional; bogs and lagoon meadows.

Juncus articulatus L.   Jointed-leaved rush
8181445, 8182381, 8182382. Occasional; bogs and upper beach meadow.

Juncus bufonius L.   Toad rush
8182385. Very rare; a single collection from Quineex Indian Reserve beach. Introduced.

Juncus effusus L. var. *pacificus* Fern. & Wieg.   Pacific common rush
818610, 818195, 848940, 848941. Frequent; bogs.

Juncus ensifolius Wikstr. var. *ensifolius*   Sword-leaved rush
818219, 8181444, 8181856. Frequent; bogs, bog pools, and streamlets.

Juncus falcatus E. Meyer var. *sitchensis* Buch.   Sickle-leaved rush
81848, 8181232, 8181282, 8181442, 8181443, 818196, 818199, 818225, 8481330. Common; bogs, seepage, streamlets, and pools.

Juncus leseurii Boland. Salt rush
81847, 818203, 818204. Occasional; beach meadows and seepage.

Juncus nodosus L. Noded rush
8182383. Rare; upper beach seepage.

Juncus oreganus S. Wats. Oregon rush
81829, 818210, 818424, 81869, 8181233, 8181234, 8181283, 818143, 8181435, 8181852, 8181854, 8181855, 848953, 8481049. Common; bog pools and ponds, lakeshore.

Juncus stygius L. Stygian rush
818198, 818228. Rare; bog ponds and streamlets.

Luzula campestris (L.) DC. var. *congesta* (Thuill.) E. Meyer Compact wood-rush
8481111, 848131. Uncommon; beach seepage and streamside.

Luzula campestris (L.) DC. var. *frigida* Buch. Arctic wood-rush
81826, 818433, 818515, 818128, 8181414, 8181630. Frequent; alpine heath and outcrops; bogs.

Luzula campestris (L.) DC. var. *multiflora* Buch. Many-flowered wood-rush
8181278. Uncommon; headland herb and beach shrub.

Luzula parviflora (Ehrh.) Desv. Small-flowered wood-rush
817307. Common; mountain forest, krummholz and scree, alluvial forest.

Luzula parviflora (Ehrh.) Desv. ssp. *fastigiata* (E. Meyer) Hamet-Ahti Upright clumped wood-rush
81814, 818127, 8481025. Uncommon; mountain forest and scree.

Luzula spicata (L.) DC. Spiked wood-rush
818433, 8182018, 818238. Rare; headlands and bogs.

Cyperaceae
Carex anthoxanthea Presl Yellow-flowered sedge
817305, 817306, 818511, 8181019, 8181625, 8181626. Common; alpine lakeshore meadows and ravines.

Carex arenicola Schmidt Sand dune sedge
84882, 84883, 84884, 84885. Rare; upper beach, Jackobson Point.

Carex circinata C.A. Meyer Coiled sedge
8173120, 818112, 81851, 81853, 818177, 84897, 848111. Frequent; alpine outcrops, rock blocks, cliffs.

Carex deweyana Schweinitz Dewey's sedge
8182323, 8182324, 8182375. Rare; upper beach, Quineex Indian Reserve.

Carex kelloggii W. Boott Kellogg's sedge
81825. Rare; Cassiope Pond, lakeshore.

Carex laeviculmis Meinsh. Smooth-stemmed sedge
848139. Rare; lowland forest and streamside.

Carex livida (Wahlenb.) Willd. Pale sedge
818431, 8181441, 8182033, 848950. Frequent; bogs, bog pools, and bog scrub forest.

Carex lyngbyei Hornem. Lyngbye's sedge
818434, 818205, 8182026, 8182212, 8182213, 84865, 84866. Common; upper estuary and salt marsh, beach meadow and bog.

Carex macrocephala Willd. Big-headed sedge
Rare; sands and dunes of Cape Cook Lagoon, Orchard Point, and Guilliams Bay beaches.

Carex mertensii Prescott Mertens' sedge
817304, 818731, 8181512, 8181714. Occasional; scree meadow, ledges, beach shrub.

Carex obnupta Bailey Slough sedge
8181216, 8181850, 8182376. Common; upper estuary, beach meadow and shrub, lowland and alluvial forest.

Carex pauciflora Lightf. Few-flowered sedge
Pojar & Boas 770165. Rare; Cape Cook Lagoon peatlands, blanket bog.

Carex phyllomanica W. Boott Coastal stellate sedge
818613, 818614, 8181848, 818227, 848951, 848138. Common; bog pools and streamside, lowland and bog scrubforest.

Carex physocarpa Presl Russet sedge
8181613, 8181843, 8181846, 8181851, 8481050. Occasional; shores of ponds, pools, and lakes.

Carex scirpoidea Michx. Northern single-spiked sedge
8181412. Rare; Senecio Ridge, exposed alpine.

Carex sitchensis Prescott Sitka sedge
Occasional; beach shrub, alluvial forest, timberline scrub forest.

Carex spectabilis Dewey Showy sedge
818115, 818730, 8181629. Occasional; alpine ravines, ledges, and meadows.

Carex stylosa C.A. Meyer Long-styled sedge
8181226, 8181849. Occasional; bogs, lakeshore, and streambank.

Carex viridula Michx. Green sedge
818612, 8181228, 8181281, 8181438, 8181439, 8181440, 818224, 818229, 848952, 8481214. Common; bogs and pools.

Eriophorum angustifolium Honck. Narrow-leaved cotton-grass
81828, 818429, 8181844, 8182032, 848939. Frequent; bogs, bog scrub forest, wet alpine meadow, and lakeshore.

Rhynchospora alba (L.) Vahl White-tipped beak-rush
818221, 81867, 8181227. Occasional; bogs and bog scrub forest.

Scirpus cespitosus L. [*Trichophorum cespitosum* (L.) Hartm.] Tussock clubrush
8173114. Common; bogs and bog scrub forest, wet alpine meadow, heath, and krummholz.

Scirpus cernuus Vahl Low clubrush
818417, 818197. Rare; Cape Cook Lagoon, saltmarsh, and bog streams.

Scirpus maritimus L. Seacoast bulrush
8182378, 8182379, 8182380. Rare; Quineex Indian Reserve, tidal shore.

Scirpus subterminalis Torr. Water clubrush
8181612, 8181910. Rare; bog pools and streamlets.

Scirpus validus Torr. Tule
8182377. Rare; Quineex Indian Reserve, tidal shore.

Poaceae
Agrostis aequivalvis (Trin.) Trin. Alaska bent grass
81822, 818430, 818729, 8181415, 8181416, 8481051. Frequent; lakeshore, bog, alpine meadow, and heath.

Agrostis borealis Hartm. Northern bent grass
8181853. Rare; lakeshore.

Agrostis exarata Trin. ssp. *exarata* Spike bent grass
81845, 818416, 8181239, 8182020. Frequent; beach meadow, headlands, tidal shore.

Agrostis exarata Trin. ssp. *minor* (Hook.) C.L. Hitchc. Lesser spike bent grass
8182322, 8182337, 8182345, 848837, 848838A. Occasional; upper beach meadow.

Agrostis scabra Willd. Hair bent grass
848821, 848931. Occasional; lakeshore and alpine ridges.

Ammophila arenaria (L.) Link Beach grass
Occasional; introduced and established on sand beaches at Cape Cook Lagoon and Quineex Indian Reserve.

Bromus pacificus Shear. Pacific brome grass
8181915, 8182343, 8182344. Occasional; upper beach and headlands, alluvial forest.

Bromus sitchensis Trin. Alaska brome grass
8181272, 8181273, 8182320, 8182321. Occasional; beach sand and meadow.

Calamagrostis canadensis (Michx.) Beauv. var. *scabra* (Kunth) A.S. Hitchc. Bluejoint reed grass
8173126. Rare; moist mountain cliffs and meadow.

Calamagrostis nutkaensis (Presl) Steud. Nootka reed grass
8173015, 8173021, 8173025, 818420, 818523, 818545, 818547, 818732, 81893, 8181215, 8181622, 8181623, 8181624, 8181640, 8181847, 8182317, 8182342, 848932, 8481040. Common; widespread, from estuary meadow to alpine ledges.

Calamagrostis nutkaensis (Presl) Steud. X *Calamagrostis canadensis* (Michx.) Beauv.
Hybrid reed grass
818421. Rare; a single collection from upper beach at Orchard Point.

Calamagrostis purpurascens R.Br. ssp. *tasuensis* Calder & Taylor [*C. sesquiflora* (Trin.) Tzvelev]
Queen Charlotte reed grass
8173113, 818211, 818523, 818546, 818717, 81893, 81894, 8181711, Roemer 7884. Occasional, but widely occurring; alpine ridges, heath, and meadow. One of the taxa previously considered as endemic to the Queen Charlotte Islands; extended to Brooks Peninsula in this study and most recently found to be conspecific with diploid populations from Aleutian Islands and coastal Kamtchatka. The name C. *sesquiflora* has priority and should be used.

Danthonia intermedia Vasey Timber oat grass
8173123, 8181911, 848112. Occasional; alpine ridges, outcrops, and bogs.

Danthonia spicata (L.) Beauv. ex R. & S. Poverty oat grass
818611, 8181231, 8181421, 8181422, 8181858, 818226, 84889, 848822, 848823, 848933, 848947, 848948, 8481331. Occasional; bogs, alpine ridges, and shore rock headlands.

Deschampsia cespitosa (L.) Beauv. Tufted hair grass
818733, 818734, 818735, 818736, 8181426, 8181716. Common and widespread; from salt marsh to alpine.

Deschampsia cespitosa (L.) Beauv. ssp. *beringensis* (Hult.) Lawr. Bering hair grass
8173112. Rare; a single collection from alpine ridge meadow.

Deschampsia cespitosa (L.) Beauv. var. *longiflora* Beal Narrow hair grass
81811, 81854, 818520, 818544, 8182214, 8182215. Occasional; alpine ridges and beach headlands.

Distichlis spicata (L.) Greene var. *borealis* (Presl) Beetle Seashore saltgrass
Rare; a single occurrence in saltmarsh at Jackobson Point.

Elymus glaucus Buckl. ssp. *glaucus* Blue wild rye grass
8181240. Rare; a single collection from upper beach at Guilliams Bay beach.

Elymus hirsutus Presl Hairy wild rye grass
8181217. Occasional; sand beach, alluvial forest, and alpine ledges.

Elymus mollis Trin. Dune wild rye grass
Common; sand beach, beach herb and shrub.

Festuca rubra L. var. *littoralis* Vasey ex Beal [*F. rubra* var. *densiuscula* Hackel] Coastal red fescue
818422, 8181274, 8182027, 818213, 8182325, 84881, 84882, 848831, 848832, 848835. Common; beach headlands, meadows, and tidal marsh.

Festuca subulata Trin. in Bong. Bearded fescue
Occasional; headlands, alluvial forest, and alpine slopes.

Festuca subuliflora Scribn. Crinkle-awned fescue
Rare; alluvial forest.

Glyceria pauciflora Presl [*Torreyochloa pauciflora* (Presl) Church] False manna grass
8182318, 8182319. Rare; upper beach herb, Quineex.

Holcus lanatus L. Yorkshire fog
8182346, 8182347. Rare; introduced, Quineex Indian Reserve beach.

Hordeum brachyantherum Nevski Meadow barley grass
8181919. Occasional; headland herb, beach meadow, saltmarsh, and alluvial forest.

Melica subulata (Griseb.) Scribn. Alaska onion grass
8181715, 8181916, 848122. Occasional; headland shrub, alluvial forest, mountain scree meadow.

Panicum occidentale Scribn. Western panic grass
8181446, 818192, 818193, 8481332. Frequent; bogs.

Phleum sp. Timothy grass
8181271. A single collection from Crabapple Islet, sand beach. Morphologically this collection most closely fits *Phleum alpinum*, except for the exceptionally tall plants (60+ cm) and the narrow, elongated panicle. Ecologically, one would expect the widely introduced meadow timothy (*Phleum pratense*) growing in beach sand, rather than the alpine timothy (*Phleum alpinum*), which was not found on any of the mountains of the study area.

Poa macrantha Vasey Seashore blue grass
Rare; dunes and beach sand, Cape Cook Lagoon and Guilliams Bay beaches.

Poa palustris L. Meadow blue grass
818235, 818239. Rare; introduced at Quineex Indian Reserve cabin.

Puccinellia nutkaensis (Presl) Fern. & Weatherby Nootka alkali grass
818211, 8182374, 84868, 84869. Occasional; saltmarsh and upper tidal shore.

Puccinellia pumila (Vasey) A.S. Hitchc. Dwarf alkali grass
818415, 8181510, 84863, 84864, 84867. Occasional; tidal shore and salt marsh.

Trisetum cernuum Trin. Nodding trisetum
817297, 81817, 848838B. Occasional; edge of shore forest, alluvial forest, alpine ledges, and scree meadow.

Trisetum spicatum (L.) Richt. Spike trisetum
Rare; alpine heath and ridge, Doom Mountain and Cassiope Ridge.

Sparganiaceae
Sparganium angustifolium Michx. Narrow-leaved bur-reed
81821, 818111, 818141, 818142, 818162, 8181845. Frequent; lakes, ponds, and bog pools.

Araceae
Lysichiton americanum Hult. & St. John Skunk-cabbage
Occasional; alluvial and lowland forest.

Liliaceae
Allium cernuum Roth Nodding onion

8181262, 848810. Occasional; headlands, promontories, and beach meadows.

Camassia quamash (Pursh) Greene Common camas
818218, 8181236, 8481333, 8481334, 8481335, 8481336. Rare; along streamlets in bogs; Cape Cook Lagoon bogs, Moneses Creek, Menziesia Creek. This is the northernmost occurrence of this species, and it represents significant isolation from the rest of the species' range. The Brooks Peninsula plants are unusual in having narrower leaves and smaller flowers, and in occupying bog habitats.

Clintonia uniflora (Schult.) Kunth Bead lily
Rare; alpine heath.

Fritillaria camschatcensis (L.) Ker-Gawl. Indian riceroot
81834, 848819, 848825, Roemer 7866. Occasional; headlands, rock promontories, and alpine cliffs.

Lloydia serotina (L.) Reichenb. Alp lily
8481042. Very rare; Oxycoccus Ridge and Doom Mountain, moist alpine cliffs and ledges.

Lloydia serotina (L.) Reichenb. ssp. *flava* Calder & Taylor Queen Charlotte alp lily
Pojar & Boas 770222. Very rare; Doom Mountain, moist alpine cliffs and ledges. One of the taxa previously considered as endemic to the Queen Charlotte Islands. Plant systematists disagree over the status of ssp. *flava;* but DNA studies begun in 1995 on British Columbia populations (Queen Charlotte Islands, Vancouver Island, and Cascade Mountains) by Dr. B. Jones at University of Wales, will provide valuable information on this problem.

Maianthemum dilatatum (Wood) Nelson & Macbr. May lily
Common and widespread; from beach shrub and headlands up to krummholz.

Stenanthium occidentale A. Gray Western mountain bells
818618, 818716, Roemer 7853. Occasional; moist cliffs and ledges, bogs, and mountain slope forest.

Streptopus amplexifolius (L.) DC. Clasping-leaved twisted-stalk
8181515. Frequent; alluvial forest, lowland forest, mountain slope forest, timberline scrub forest.

Streptopus roseus Michx. Rosy twisted-stalk
Occasional; lowland and mountain slope forest, krummholz.

Streptopus streptopoides (Ledeb.) Frye & Rigg var. *brevipes* (Baker) Fassett Small twisted-stalk
818521, 8181635. Occasional; mountain slope forest, timberline scrub forest, and headlands.

Tofieldia glutinosa (Michx.) Pers. Sticky false asphodel
Frequent; wet mountain meadows and cliffs, bogs and heath.

Veratrum eschscholtzii A. Gray Green false hellebore
Occasional; alluvial and lowland forest, bog scrub forest, mountain slope forest, and timberline scrub forest.

Iridaceae
Sisyrinchium angustifolium Mill. Narrow-leaved blue-eyed-grass
Rare; beach meadows.

Sisyrinchium littorale Greene Shore blue-eyed-grass
8181267, 8181268, 8181269, 8181270, 8181279, 8181449, 8181859, 84862, 848813, 848814. Occasional; beach headlands and meadows, bogs.

Orchidaceae
Corallorhiza maculata Raf. ssp. *maculata* Spotted coralroot
8173028, 8181517, 8181634. Occasional; mountain slope forest.

Goodyera oblongifolia Raf. Giant rattlesnake orchid
Very rare; bog scrubforest.

Habenaria chorisiana Cham. [*Platanthera chorisiana* (Cham.) Reichenb.] Chamisso's rein-orchid
817319, 8181423, 8481028, 848955, 8481033. Occasional; bogs, alpine ledges, and heath.

Habenaria hyperborea (L.) R. Br. [*Platanthera hyperborea* (L.) Lindl.] Green-flowered rein-orchid
8173016, 8173017, 81813, 81892, 81899, 8181222, 8181516. Occasional; alluvial forest, bog scrub forest, krummholz, and alpine meadow.

Habenaria saccata Greene [*Platanthera stricta* Lindl.] Slender rein-orchid
Uncommon; lowland and bog scrub forest.

Listera borealis Morong Northern twayblade
8173030. Rare; timberline scrub forest.

Listera caurina Piper Northwestern twayblade
818215. Rare; mountain slope forest, lowland forest, and timberline scrub forest.

Listera cordata (L.) R. Br. Heart-leaved twayblade
8173029, 848925. Occasional; lowland and mountain slope forest, timberline scrub forest, krummholz.

Spiranthes romanzoffiana Cham. Hooded ladies-tresses
8181280, 8181299, 8181437, 848828. Occasional; bogs, bog scrub forest, and shore promontories.

List of the Vascular Plants from "Power Mountain"

During the 1981 expedition Hans Roemer and the author made a floristic survey on a mountain 15 km east of Brooks Peninsula. The unnamed peak is on the east side of Power River, and it is designated "Power Mountain" on the specimen labels. The map co-ordinates are 50°14' N, 127°29' W, and the elevation is 1200 m. In the following list the taxa that do not occur on Brooks Peninsula are marked with an asterisk (*).

Adiantum pedatum
Aquilegia formosa
**Athyrium distentifolium* Tausch ssp. *americanum* (Maxon) Hult. Alpine lady-fern; 818181, 818182
Athyrium filix-femina
Cardamine oligosperma 8181836
Carex circinata 8181837
**Carex nigricans* C.A. Meyer Black alpine sedge
Carex spectabilis
Cassiope mertensiana

Cassiope stelleriana
Castilleja miniata
Cladothamnus pyroliflorus
Coptis asplenifolia 8181830
Cryptogramma crispa var. *acrostichoides* 818187; on Brooks Peninsula occurs only on Doom Mountain
Cystopteris fragilis restricted to Doom Mountain and Harris Peak on Brooks Peninsula
Deschampsia cespitosa
Empetrum nigrum
Erigeron peregrinus ssp. *peregrinus* var. *dawsonii* 8181822
Gymnocarpium dryopteris 818186
Heuchera glabra
Hieracium gracile 8181826
Hippuris montana 8181816 restricted to Harris Peak on Brooks Peninsula
Huperzia selago 8181838
**Juncus drummondii* Meyer Drummond's rush
**Juncus mertensianus* Bong. Mertens' rush
Luetkea pectinata
Luzula parviflora ssp. *melanocarpa* 818183
**Luzula piperi* (Cov.) M.E. Jones Piper's wood-rush; 8181827, 8181832
**Mimulus lewisii* Pursh Great purple monkey flower; 8181821
**Mimulus tilingii* Regel Large mountain monkey flower; 8181820
**Mitella pentandra* Hook. Alpine mitrewort; 8181831
**Mitella trifida* Grah. Three-toothed mitrewort
Osmorhiza chilensis
Osmorhiza purpurea 818188
**Oxyria digyna* (L.) Hill Mountain sorrel; 8181835
Penstemon davidsonii
Phyllodoce empetriformis
**Poa nervosa* (Hook.) Vasey Nerved bluegrass; 8181842
**Polystichum andersonii* Hopkins Anderson's holly-fern; 8181810, 8181811, 8181812, 8181813, 8181814, 8181815
Polystichum lonchitis 818184, 818185; restricted to Harris Peak on Brooks Peninsula
Polystichum munitum 818189
Prenanthes alata
Ranunculus cooleyae 8181822, 8181833; restricted to Doom Mountain on Brooks Peninsula
Romanzoffia sitchensis 8181818
Rubus spectabilis
Saxifraga ferruginea var. *macounii* 8181817, 8181824
Saxifraga mertensiana restricted to Doom Mountain on Brooks Peninsula
Saxifraga punctata ssp. *cascadensis* 8181825; restricted to Harris Peak on Brooks Peninsula
**Saxifraga tolmiei* T. & G. Tolmie's saxifraga; 8181823
**Sibbaldia procumbens* L. Creeping sibbaldia
Sorbus sitchensis ssp. *grayi* 8181839
Stenanthium occidentale 8181819
Tiarella trifoliata
Vaccinium deliciosum
Vaccinium ovalifolium 8181841
**Vahlodea atropurpurea* (Wahlenb.) Fries Mountain hairgrass
Valeriana sitchensis
**Veronica wormskjoldii* Roem. & Schult. Alpine speedwell; 8181829, 8181834

Viola glabella
Viola sempervirens 8181840

Discussion

Phytogeographical Analysis

To provide a general view of the geographic composition of the Brooks Peninsula vascular flora it has been categorized into a number of broad distribution groups, or floristic elements. The following floristic elements are used: Introduced, alien taxa introduced by humans; Circumpolar, occurring at high latitudes in the Northern Hemisphere and extending southward down the major mountain systems; North American, restricted to the North American continent; Cordilleran, occurring from the Rocky Mountains westward to the Pacific Coast; and Pacific Coastal, from the Coast Range westward to the Pacific Coast. Within the final category, is a Northern Pacific Coast group occurring from British Columbia north to Alaska, and a Southern Pacific Coast group occurring from British Columbia south to Washington, or Oregon, and northern California.

Faegri (1963) has discussed some of the limitations to the concept of floristic elements, specifically in its application to the refugium problem. Although floristic elements are used to support the existence of glacial refugia, the floristic elements themselves need to be explained as to the basis for the concurrent distribution of their species. The floristic element does not behave as a collective unit, rather it is the individual plants of the component series that function individually, undergoing immigration, establishment, or emigration. "The more or less fortuitous occurring together... (of different species in the floristic element) ...may be the result of widely differing histories and ecologic demands" (Faegri 1963: 221).

The total number of vascular plant taxa on Brooks Peninsula is 350. These are primarily North American (ca. 60%), having a Pacific Coastal distribution (ca. 35%), or Cordilleran distribution (ca. 21%); the other major distributional element is Circumpolar (ca. 25%). Six per cent (20) of the taxa are introduced. This very low number of alien taxa may be compared to 21% for all of British Columbia (Taylor and MacBryde 1977), 20% for the Queen Charlotte Islands (Calder and Taylor 1968), and ca. 32% for the southern Gulf Islands (Janszen 1977, 1981). On Brooks Peninsula the alien taxa are confined to shoreline habitats with human disturbance on sand beaches and around the cabin at Quineex Indian Reserve. Comparing the native floras of Brooks Peninsula (330 taxa) and the Queen Charlotte Islands (486 taxa), the Index of Similarity (Sørensen 1948) is 65%.

Despite the high proportion of Pacific Coastal species, a number of the common species are absent, such as: *Achlys triphylla, Adenocaulon bicolor, Armeria maritima, Circaea pacifica, Dicentra formosa, Grindelia integrifolia, Petasites frigidus, Sedum divergens, S. spathulifolium, Spiraea douglasii*, and *Urtica lyallii*. Furthermore, a number of alpine species that occur frequently on the Vancouver Island Mountains are absent from Brooks Peninsula, for example: *Antennaria alpina, Draba* spp., *Epilobium angustifolium, Festuca saximontana, Poa alpina, Potentilla diversifolia, Ranunculus eschscholtzii, Saxifraga bronchialis, S. cespitosa, Silene acaulis*, and *Vahlodea atropurpurea*. The floristic list from "Power Peak", 15 km east of Brooks Peninsula, also shows similar absences, with 16 taxa that are unknown on Brooks Peninsula, and another seven taxa that are present in only a single locality there. Thus, the geographic isolation of Brooks Peninsula makes it similar to an island flora, in which some of the common members of the regional flora are absent.

The Brooks Peninsula flora consists of a number of taxa of special phytogeographic significance: taxa endemic to the Queen Charlotte Islands and Vancouver Island, taxa endemic to the Olympic Peninsula and Vancouver Island, southern disjunct taxa, and northern disjunct taxa.

1) Taxa endemic to the Queen Charlotte Islands and Vancouver Island—nine of the 13 taxa considered as endemic to the Queen Charlotte Islands occur here: *Calamagrostis purpurascens* ssp. *tasuensis*, *Cassiope lycopodioides* ssp. *cristapilosa*, *Geum schofieldii*, *Isopyrum savilei*, *Ligusticum calderi*, *Lloydia serotina* ssp. *flava*, *Saxifraga taylori*, *Senecio moresbiensis*, and *Viola biflora* ssp. *carlottae*.
2) Taxa endemic to the Olympic Peninsula and Vancouver Island—two of the 11 taxa considered as endemic to the Olympic Peninsula occur here: *Adiantum pedatum* var. *subpumilum*, and *Pedicularis bracteosa* var. *atrosanguinea*.
3) Southern disjunct taxa—included here are taxa that are separated from their main range, which is to the south, primarily along the coast: *Camassia quamash*, *Douglasia laevigata*, *Eriophyllum lanatum*, *Hedysarum occidentale*, *Lomatium martindalei*, *Phlox diffusa*, and *Saxifraga punctata* ssp. *cascadensis*.
4) Northern disjunct taxa—these are taxa that are separated from their main range to the north, primarily coastal Alaska and adjacent British Columbia: *Anemone narcissiflora* ssp. *alaskana*, *Artemisia trifurcata*, *Campanula rotundifolia* var. *alaskana*, *Carex circinata*, *Galium kamtschaticum*, *Gentiana platypetala*, *Geum calthifolium*, *Habenaria chorisiana*, *Hippuris montana*, and *Lupinus nootkatensis*.

The Vascular Flora and the Refugium Question

The glacial refugium theory explains the occurrence of disjunct and endemic taxa as a result of their survival in unglaciated areas when the surrounding terrain was overrun by glaciation. This concept was proposed a century ago by Scandinavian botanists, and much of the subsequent early research on the problem was carried out by them. There is now a voluminous literature on refugia, disjunctions and endemism, which has been reviewed in several symposia: Löve and Löve (1963), Hopkins (1967), Schofield (1969), Brassard (1971), Morisset (1971a, 1971b), Solbrig (1972), Ives (1974), Murray (1981), Hopkins et al. (1982).

Dahl (1946) describes models for glacial refugia, distinguishing between tundra refugia and coastal mountain refugia. Tundra refugia are situated distantly from the open sea, resulting in a continental climate with very low precipitation. Coastal mountain refugia have high mountains close to the continental shelf near the edge of deep oceans, and the climate is oceanic with high winter precipitation. The glacier ice breaks up in the deep sea waters, and from the edge of the glacier there is a maximum gradient that the ice can support. Mountains exceeding this gradient extend above the ice as potential refugia. According to Dahl (1946), coastal mountain refugia occur in "western Scandinavia, probably Scotland, Iceland, the southern half of Greenland, and possibly Labrador". Brooks Peninsula fits this model for coastal mountain refugia, as do other areas on the northern Pacific Coast such as western Queen Charlotte Islands and parts of coastal Alaska.

The disjunct and endemic plant taxa associated with the glacial refugia of Norway are discussed by Dahl (1946, 1955), Nordhagen (1963), and Gjaerevoll (1963); for Iceland by Steindorsson (1962, 1963); and for Greenland by Böcher (1963).

The possibility that plants can survive on mountain peaks exposed from the surrounding glacier (i.e., nunataks) has been demonstrated by floristic surveys of nunataks projecting above present-day ice-sheets in Greenland (Frederiksen 1971; Gjaerevoll and Ryvarden 1977), and in southwestern Alaska and adjacent Yukon (Heusser 1954; Neilson 1968; Murray 1968, 1971a, 1971b). In a survey of five nunataks in southwestern Greenland, Gjaerevoll and Ryvarden (1977) found a total of 62 vascular plant species. Heusser (1954) reported a total of 102 vascular plants on 25 nunataks of the Juneau Icefield in the Coast Range of southeastern Alaska. Based on the present occurrence of species above the upper limit of late-Wisconsin glaciation, as indicated by geomorphological features, Heusser estimated that 18 of the vascular plant species would have survived glaciation on the nunataks. Elven (1980) documented the immigration and establishment of plants on ten Norwegian nunataks exposed during the last 50 years. The primary features of the colonising plants were their prolific propagule production and short reproduction time, rather than morphological specialisations. The 50 immigrant vascular plant species included two endemic species, one rare species, and one rare genotype. Elven advised caution in using rare and restricted species as indicators of glacial refugia, because some rare species restricted in distribution and habitat are effective colonisers of open deglaciated terrain where interspecific competition is minimal.

There have been numerous alternatives to the refugium theory to explain disjunct distributions; summaries of these have been discussed by Ives (1974), Schofield (1969), and Morisset (1971a, 1971b). A common theme of these alternative views is that the occurrence of the disjunct and endemic taxa can be a consequence of postglacial migration of these species to areas of specialized habitats such as topographic microclimates, calcareous substrata, and cliffs. As a result of competition from the invading forest or other dominant vegetation, these species become eliminated except in the specialized habitats. These counterarguments have been applied to the refugia of northeastern North America (Wynne-Edwards 1937, 1939; Griggs 1940; Rousseau 1950; Drury 1969), to the Scandinavian refugia (Faegri 1963; Hoppe 1963; Berg 1963; Dahl 1963, 1966; Mangerud 1973), and to Greenland (Funder 1979).

Reviewing the Norwegian refugia, Mangerud (1973) states that recent plant collecting has extended the areas of the disjunct and endemic taxa, thus, they are less locally concentrated, and consequently less reliable as indicators of glacial refugia. The disjunct plant distributions are considered to be a result of frequent glacial and climatic oscillations during late-glacial and postglacial time. Mangerud (1973) concludes that all of Scandinavia was ice-covered, and that plant migration occurred after the last glacial maximum.

In a recent reevaluation of Greenland refugia, Funder (1979) states that geological evidence shows that all of Greenland was ice covered at least once, and that all supposed alpine refugia (nunataks) show signs of glaciation. The only areas that missed glaciation are lowlands on the outer east coast, which escaped the last two glacial advances and have been ice free for a minimum of 40 000 years. Funder believes that the disjunct plants of these areas are the result of random, long-distance dispersal by ocean currents and wind, and not the result of glacial fragmentation of a more widespread range. Although the palynological record is limited in time (10 000 years) and contains only 12 identifiable species, Funder concludes that the earliest immigrants were ubiquitous species having wide geographic and ecological ranges, that the southern-ranging species are postglacial immigrants, and that the northern-ranging species were the latest (6000 B.P.) postglacial immigrants.

Such arguments against glacial refugia do not adequately explain why the disjunct and endemic species are concentrated in highly localized areas and are absent from surrounding areas with similar habitats. Migration of these species along the receding edge of the ice sheet would require genotypic diversity, which should allow them to spread into many more of the specialized habitats, rather than being restricted to a few localities.

In most discussions of the refugium problem it is assumed that the ecological tolerances of species were similar in the past, though some of the genotypes of those species would have been exterminated during glaciation. On the Greenland nunataks, though the bedrock is gneiss and amphibolite, many of the species reported by Gjaerevoll and Ryvarden (1977) are calcicoles. These authors conclude that under low competition in the open nunatak habitats, the ecological tolerances of both calcicoles and calcifuges are much broader. Warner et al. (1982) report a diversity of alpine and low-elevation species from late glacial deposits near sea level on the eastern Queen Charlotte Islands. They infer that the late periglacial environment was able to accommodate a greater floristic diversity; it also implies that the ecotypic diversity of the species was greater then. In this respect, there are a number of the Vancouver Island plants with alpine-maritime tolerances, occurring in both seacliff and alpine habitats, and suggesting their ability to survive in refugia either at sea level or on nunataks. Some examples of these species are: *Potentilla villosa, Saxifraga cespitosa, Valeriana sitchensis, Arctostaphylos uva-ursi, Saxifraga bronchialis, Sedum integrifolium, Solidago multiradiata, Erigeron peregrinus, Anaphalis margaritacea,* and *Campanula rotundifolia.*

On the northwest coast of North America the problem of plant distribution and glacial refugia has long been the subject of discussion (Jones 1936; Hulten 1967, 1968; Heusser 1960; Calder and Taylor 1968; Schofield 1969; Taylor 1989). A common theme of these discussions is that the restricted distribution patterns of endemic and disjunct plant species cannot be explained alone by postglacial migrations, but must involve the survival of some of these species in unglaciated refugia.

A number of non-glaciated areas along the northwest coast has been documented: Olympic Peninsula (Heusser 1964, 1971, 1972, 1977; Florer 1972), eastern Graham Island (Warner et al. 1982; Mathewes 1989a, 1989b, Clague, 1989a), and Kodiak Island (Karlstrom and Ball 1969; Hultén 1969). Recent phytogeographic evidence supports the occurrence of refugia on the Queen Charlotte Islands, on the west coast headlands where glaciers were least thick and least able to coalesce and on south-facing mountain slopes with high summer temperatures (Heusser 1989), on the eastern coastal plain (Mathewes 1989a, 1989b; Warner et al. 1982), and on the west coast nunataks (Roemer and Ogilvie 1983).

Geological evidence for non-glaciated areas on western Vancouver Island is meagre, although Muller et al. (1974) and Muller (1977) state that ice levels ranged from 1220 m elevation in the south to 500 m in the north of the island. These data were used by Ogilvie and Ceska (1984) in support of glacial refugia for disjunct taxa on mountain peaks immediately southeast of Brooks Peninsula.

Turning now to the Brooks Peninsula vascular flora and its bearing on the question of a refugium, in the phytogeographic analysis at the beginning of this discussion it was shown that there are nine of the Queen Charlotte Islands-Vancouver Island endemic taxa, two of the Vancouver Island-Olympic Peninsula taxa, and a number of disjunct taxa with both northern and southern geographic affinities. The relatively low number of vascular plant taxa of Brooks Peninsula, in part, reflects impoverishment that occurred during full glacial conditions. Despite this impoverished flora, there is a relatively high proportion of endemic and disjunct species. And these rare taxa are of diverse geographic affinities: south coastal, north coastal, cordilleran, and circumpolar. These features—an impoverished flora, rich in rare species, and of diverse geographic affinities—together provide support for a glacial refugium. The most likely refugium habitats, based on the concentration of endemic and disjunct taxa, are on the western headlands and the summits, cliffs, and chasm walls of the central peaks of the peninsula. The Brooks Peninsula refugium should be viewed as one of a series of Pacific Coast refugia, as proposed by Heusser (1960, 1971, 1972, 1989), extending from the Olympic Peninsula, the west coast of Vancouver Island, and the Queen Charlotte Islands, to the coast of Alaska.

As is apparent from the literature discussed above, alternative interpretations from phytogeographic data can be made of the refugium question. For example, if the Brooks Peninsula flora is a result of postglacial immigration of species along the coast, a number of questions are unanswered: why are some of the widespread coastal species absent; what is the explanation for the large number of Queen Charlotte Islands' endemic taxa and two of the Olympic Peninsula endemic taxa; and how can the widely disjunctive species from the north and south be explained?

The phytogeographic data alone cannot provide firm evidence for the age of the present flora or of the refugium. Earlier discussions of the Queen Charlotte Islands refugium have variously suggested that it existed throughout the Pleistocene (Martin and Rouse 1966; Schofield 1969), or throughout the Wisconsin (Calder and Taylor 1968; Heusser 1960). Yet another possibility is that the refugium dates from the interglacial stage prior to the last glacial advance of the Wisconsin. Schofield (1969) states that the evolutionary relationships of five of the Queen Charlotte Islands' endemic taxa (*Isopyrum savilei, Saxifraga taylori, Geum schofieldii, Ligusticum calderi,* and *Senecio newcombei*) imply that they are pre-Pleistocene relicts. However, Packer (1971), using cytotaxonomic criteria, lists four of the endemic taxa (*Geum schofieldii, Ligusticum calderi, Viola biflora* ssp. *carlottae,* and *Senecio moresbiensis*) as polyploids recently derived from their more widespread relatives, implying either a lateglacial or postglacial origin for them. These interpretations are not necessarily conflicting, since the 13 endemic taxa differ considerably in the morphological distinctiveness and the distance of geographic separation from their nearest relatives, and their level of ploidy. Consequently, the different taxa differ in the time of their evolutionary origin. Dated fossil records are required to resolve all these problems of chronology.

Calder and Taylor (1968) presented a general schema for the survival and migration of the Queen Charlotte Islands' vascular flora:

1) survival of the endemic and some disjunct taxa in the refugium,
2) early postglacial immigration of southern littoral and lowland species following the recession of the main coastal glaciation,
3) a later postglacial immigration of northern species from the Beringian refugium,
4) a postglacial Hypsithermal immigration of more xerophytic species from the interior and southern mainland,
5) simultaneous with the last three immigrations were emigrations of some of the plants that persisted in the refugium to the areas along the coast.

Twenty-nine years later, we now have additional information to supplement and refine these ideas. Recent floristic collections along the north Pacific Coast have added considerably to the distributional data that were available to Calder and Taylor for their phytogeographic analyses (Ogilvie 1989). As discussed above, these recent collections support the view of a series of refugia along the outer west coast. This means that we now have to take into account the relationships of the floras of these different refugia: which species survived glaciation at one or several refugia, and which species have immigrated to other refugial areas following deglaciation.

Paleobotanical findings have provided substantiation for refugia on the Queen Charlotte Islands (Warner et al. 1982; Mathewes 1989a, 1989b), but have also required significant modifications in the above schema. Mathewes and Clague (1982) and Mathewes (1989a, 1989b) have shown that *Polemonium pulcherrimum,* considered by Calder and Taylor to be a Hypsithermal xerophytic immigrant from the eastern British Columbia Interior, was present on the Queen Charlotte Islands during late-glacial time, between ca. 12 000 and 13 000 B.P. Along with this species are fossil remains of several species of diverse floristic elements: Circumpolar Arctic-Alpine, Northern Pacific Coastal, Southern Pacific Coastal, and Cordilleran. This underlines the need for caution in inferring the routes and times of migration from the present distributional ranges of floristic elements. Mathewes and Clague (1982) also report late-glacial fossils of three plant species now absent from the Queen Charlotte Islands, and they conclude that their extinction may be a result of late glacial or postglacial rising sea level or climatic change. Thus, one other feature needs to be added to the Calder and Taylor schema: the extinction of a number of plant species during postglacial times.

Dated fossil series of plant species, such as those for the Queen Charlotte Islands (Mathewes 1989a, 1989b; Mathewes and Clague 1982), for *Ligusticum calderi* on Brooks Peninsula (see Chapter 9), and for several species on the Olympic Peninsula (Heusser 1989), are essential for providing the chronology and substantiating the indirect evidence of the phytogeographic data. And further detailed floristic studies on northwestern Vancouver Island, on the coastal islets, and along the northern coastal mainland are necessary for completing our knowledge of the phytogeography and glacial refugia on the North Pacific Coast.

Update

Recent research in Quaternary geology and paleobotany have contributed greatly to the understanding of North Pacific coast glacial refugia and post-glacial flora. An extensive summary of regional Quaternary geology is contained in the large compendium *Quaternary Geology of Canada and Greenland* (Fulton 1989).

Exposed sea cliffs on northeastern Graham Island, Queen Charlotte Islands, contain peat deposits of late glacial vegetation dated at 13 700 B.P., and basal organic deposits dated at 15 500 B.P. (Clague 1989a; Clague, Mathewes and Warner 1982; Mathewes and Clague 1982; Warner et al. 1982). These findings substantiate the evidence for a Queen Charlotte Islands glacial refugium. Cores of organic deposits from Hecate Strait have shown that a large area of the strait was exposed and supported terrestrial tundra vegetation between 13 200 and 10 000 B.P. (Barrie et al. 1993). A marine core from 95 m deep in Queen Charlotte Sound, 20 km off the north end of Vancouver Island has recovered an *in situ* tree root and pollen of pine, spruce, alder, and hemlock (Luternauer et al. 1989). These organic deposits range in age from 10 500 to 9900 B.P. This discovery indicates that Cook Bank was exposed down to ca. 100 m depth, and Vancouver Island extended northward ca. 60 km at ca. 11 000 to 10 000 B.P. With sea level ca. 100 m lower, a wide shelf along the west shore of Vancouver Island connected with the exposed shelf in Hecate Strait. This exposed shelf was of large enough extent to be considered as a late-glacial migration corridor for plants and animals.

At maximum glaciation the ice sheet on Vancouver Island coalesced with the massive ice sheet of the Coast Mountains, in contrast to the glaciers on the Queen Charlotte Islands and the Olympic Peninsula which were independent of the Cordilleran Ice Sheet (Clague 1989a, 1989b; Ryder and Clague 1989). Ice-flow in the vicinity of Brooks Peninsula was westerly and calved off abruptly at the edge of the continental shelf which is close to the western shore of Brooks Peninsula. On southeastern Vancouver Island the glacier ice coalesced with the ice from the mainland to form a massive ice lobe that flowed southward down the Strait of Georgia into the Puget lowland to south of Olympia, Washington. The ice field on the Olympic highlands was separate from this ice lobe, and was bordered on the west by an exposed coastal plain.

Sea levels in the vicinity of Brooks Peninsula were ca. 20 m higher than present, at the beginning of deglaciation (ca. 15 000 B.P.); as deglaciation progressed there was very rapid fall in sea level over 1000-2000 years (Clague 1989a, 1989c; Clague et al. 1982). Such sea level changes would have had profound effects on low elevation vegetation and flora. The effects on near-shore flora of more recent rapid sea level changes as a result of major earthquakes have been described from southern Vancouver Island and the lower Fraser Valley (Mathewes and Clague 1994; Atwater et al. 1995). Near-shore vegetation showed abrupt change from forest, shrubland, and fresh water bogs to brackish or saline vegetation as a result of subsidence at 3400 B.P. and also 2000 B.P. Three of the sites in the Fraser Valley showed a change from brackish to fresh water vegetation as a result of uplift.

A warm, dry interval (Hypsithermal or Xerothermic) has been frequently described for early to middle Holocene vegetation. It is now known that there was considerable variation in the occurrence and chronology of the warm dry interval (Anderson et al. 1989). A record from northern Vancouver Island dates the maximum warm dry conditions between ca. 8800 to 7000 B.P.; at this time there was a major decrease in hemlock and increase in Douglas-fir and bracken (Hebda 1983). It is possible that during this warm dry period southern xeric species such as *Camassia quamash, Eriophyllum lanatum, Phlox diffusa, Lomatium martindalei,* extended their range northward on Vancouver Island to the Brooks Peninsula area, but there are no macrofossil or pollen records to substantiate this.

Floristic inventories and phytogeographic analyses have been carried out on the Queen Charlotte Islands, northwestern Vancouver Island, and coastal islets such as Dewdney Island and Porcher Island (Roemer and Ogilvie 1983; Ogilvie and Roemer 1984; Ogilvie and Ceska 1984; Ogilvie et al. 1984; Ogilvie 1994). The proceedings of a symposium on the Queen Charlotte Islands—*The Outer Shores* (Scudder and Gessler 1989) gives a good summary of the state of knowledge of the islands at that time. Of specific relevance to Brooks Peninsula are the following chapters: Quaternary geology - John Clague (1989a), Paleobotany - Rolf Mathewes (1989a), Refugia - Calvin Heusser (1989), Bryoflora - W. Schofield (1989), Vascular flora - Roy Taylor (1989), Disjunct flora and refugia - R.T. Ogilvie (1989), Vegetation and soils - Banner, Pojar, Schwab and Trowbridge (1989), Birds and Mammals - I. McT. Cowan (1989) and Ground-beetle fauna - David Kavanaugh (1989).

Important floristic inventories of the Alaskan area immediately north of the Queen Charlotte Islands, the Alexander Archipelago and the adjacent mainland coast, have been carried out jointly by the Nature Conservancy Natural Heritage Program and the U.S. Forest Service (DeLapp 1991; Duffy 1993). Some of the significant floristic elements recorded there are: *Senecio moresbiensis* - Prince of Wales Island, Coronation Island; *Ligusticum calderi* - Dall Island; *Lloydia serotina* - Prince of Wales Island; *Viola biflora* - Prince of Wales Island; *Cassiope lycopodioides* - Evans Island, Knight Island, Brilliant Glacier, Mt. Reid; *Primula cuneifolia* ssp. *saxifragifolia* - Montague Island. Further intensive floristic inventories of the islands and coastal mainland of northern British Columbia and southeastern Alaska are important for a full understanding of the phytogeography of the north Pacific Coast.

The recently published *Flora of the Olympic Peninsula* (Buckingham et al. 1996) provides a detailed annotated list of the plant taxa and a discussion of the postglacial phytogeography. Nine plant taxa are endemic to the Olympic Peninsula. Also, seven taxa are endemic to both the Olympic Peninsula and Vancouver Island: *Adiantum pedatum* var. *subpumilum, Abronia umbellata* ssp. *acutalata* (extinct), *Castilleja parviflora* var. *olympica, Aster paucicapitatus, Claytonia lanceolata* var. *pacifica, Pedicularis bracteosa* var. *atrosanguinea, Saxifraga tischii.* Other plant species on the Olympic Peninsula of phytogeographic significance are: *Artemisia arctica, Artemisia furcata, Douglasia laevigata, Galium kamtschaticum, Hedysarum occidentale, Hippuris montana, Lloydia serotina, Ranunculus cooleyi.* Geological and phytogeographical evidence are used in support of a glacial refugium on the Olympic Peninsula during the Fraser glaciation from 22 000 to 12 500 B.P. Ice-free areas occurred on the mountain peaks, ridges and upper slopes, and along a broad western coastal plain exposed during lower sea level. Species with a coastal distribution are thought to have survived on this coastal plain refugium, for example: *Gentiana douglasiana, Ranunculus cooleyae, Apargidium boreale.* Most of the Olympic Peninsula endemic plants survived glaciation on mountain nunataks, although one taxon is thought to have survived on the coastal plain. The evolutionary ages of endemic taxa are inferred from the geographic distance to their closest relatives: *Aster paucicapitatus* is thought to be a recently evolved species because its nearest relative (the *Aster engelmannii* complex) occurs in the nearby Cascade Mountains. However, *Campanula piperi* is believed to have evolved anciently because its nearest related species (*C. aurita*) occurs in the Alaska-Yukon-Mackenzie districts. Endemic taxa occurring in more than one of the island refugia (Vancouver Island, Queen Charlotte Islands, Alexander Archipelago) are thought to have originated on the mainland, dispersed to the nearby islands, and subsequently became extirpated on the mainland. However, the endemic taxa shared between the Olympic Peninsula and Vancouver Island may have migrated the short distance (20 km) across Juan de Fuca Strait, rather than from the mainland. *Hedysarum occidentale,* which occurs on high mountains of northwestern Vancouver Island, the Olympic Peninsula, Cascade Mountains, and 300 km eastward in Idaho and south in Montana, Wyoming, and Colorado, is cited as an example of a disjunct species that prior to glacial advance occurred more continuously further north and on intervening mountain ranges, but was subsequently eliminated except for its survival on the Olympic Peninsula. It is believed that the Olympic Peninsula was a reservoir of plants that survived glaciation, and subsequently re-invaded the Puget Trough and Vancouver Island following deglaciation.

Plant systematics provides the means for obtaining detailed floristic inventories which supply the basic data for phytogeographic analyses. New approaches in plant systematics using phytochemical analyses are providing information on phylogenetic relationships of endemic species and the genetic diversity of endemic and disjunct taxa.

Allen et al. (1996) made isozyme analyses of disjunct populations of *Erythronium montanum* from four different regions: two within the area covered by the Vashon advance of the Cordilleran Ice Sheet (Central Coast Mountains, British Columbia and San Juan Ridge, Vancouver Island), and two lying mainly south of glaciation (Olympic Peninsula and Cascade Mountains of Washington and Oregon). The population from the Coast Range had the least genetic variability, the lowest number of alleles per locus, the lowest heterozygosity, and contained only alleles present in all the other regions. The Vancouver Island population had intermediate variability, and had some alleles absent from the Coast Range population. The Olympic Peninsula population and the Cascade Mountains populations had the greatest variability and more alleles per locus. The Coast Range population had the highest similarity with the northern Olympic Peninsula population; and the Vancouver Island population had the highest similarity with the southern Olympic Peninsula population. The reproductive biology of *E. montanum* puts severe restrictions on its dispersal and migration: the plants are insect pollinated but with a short pollen dispersal distance (less than ca. 10 m), seed dispersal distance is very short (less than ca. 1 m), and vegetative propagation is negligible in relation to plant dispersal. The disjunct populations in British Columbia did not originate from glacial refugia because there are no known refugia close to them, and they show little genetic divergence from the main southern populations of the species which they should have if they had been separated since the glacial maximum 15 000 to 20 000 B.P. Nor did the disjunct British Columbia populations originate from rapid dispersal after deglaciation: the cold, dry postglacial climate was not congenial to this species, and there are no fragmentary populations in the intervening area. These authors concluded that the British Columbia populations originated via long-distance dispersal: the Coast Range population from the northern Olympic Peninsula, and the Vancouver Island population via repeated dispersal from the southern Olympic Peninsula. Biotic or abiotic agents are suggested for this long-distance dispersal.

A study of the phylogenetic relationships of North American *Aquilegia* species and related genera, including *Isopyrum,* was done using DNA sequence data (Hodges and Arnold 1994; Goertzen personal communication, 1997). The analyses showed that the North American species of *Isopyrum* group together, but *I. savilei* was the most remotely related to the other species. Calder and Taylor originally suggested that although the Oregon *I. hallii* and the Japanese *I. raddeanum* are closely related, *I. savilei* is most closely linked to other Japanese species, and appears to occupy an intermediate position between the North American and Asian species.

Goertzen (1996) has recently completed biosystematic studies on *Senecio newcombei* (endemic to the Queen Charlotte Islands) and *Saxifraga taylori* (endemic to the Queen Charlotte Islands, Brooks Peninsula, and northwestern Vancouver Island). Pollination experiments were made to determine the breeding systems of these species. In *Senecio newcombei* no seed developed from self-pollination, but cross-pollination resulted in abundant, fertile and viable seed. This species is self-incompatible and obligate out-crossed. In *Saxifraga taylori* all pollination experiments were unsuccessful: self-pollination and cross-pollination were unsuccessful, and crosses with the putative close relative *Saxifraga vespertina* were also unsuccessful. Allozyme analyses of four populations of *Senecio newcombei* showed low genetic diversity and low heterozygosity. Allozyme analyses of four populations of *Saxifraga taylori* from the Queen Charlotte Islands and three populations of *Saxifraga vespertina* from the Columbia River Gorge, Oregon showed low genetic diversity and low heterozygosity in *Saxifraga taylori*, but high polymorphic loci and high heterozygosity in *Saxifraga vespertina*. The analyses also show extremely low genetic identity between *Saxifraga taylori* and its putative close relative *Saxifraga vespertina*.

Barbara Jones (1997) is currently researching the systematics and genetics of disjunct populations of *Lloydia serotina*, from Wales, Colorado, British Columbia, and Olympic Peninsula. DNA analyses have shown that the populations from Wales and Colorado are different from the British Columbia and Olympic Peninsula populations. One of the British Columbia populations from the Cascade Mountains is most similar to the Olympic Peninsula population. The other British Columbia population from northwestern Vancouver Island has lowest similarity to the other populations and has the highest heterozygosity. This may be a result of its relationship to ssp. *flava*, the Queen Charlotte Islands endemic. Further analyses of populations from the Queen Charlotte Islands and Brooks Peninsula will provide important data on this question.

In conclusion, the recent research in Quaternary geology, paleobotany, floristic inventories, and phytochemical population studies, has made major contributions to the understanding of north Pacific coast refugia and phytogeography. Continued research in these disciplines are needed for solving the remaining problems.

References Cited

Allen, G.A., J. Antos, A.C. Worley, T.A. Suttill, R.J. Hebda. 1996. Morphological and genetic variation in disjunct populations of the avalanche lily *Erythronium montanum*. Can. J. Bot. 74: 403-412.

Anderson, T.W., R.W. Mathewes, C.E. Schweger. 1989. Holocene climatic trends in Canada with special reference to the Hypsithermal interval. Pp. 520-528 in R.J. Fulton (ed.). Quaternary Geology of Canada and Greenland. G.S.C., Ottawa.

Atwater, B.F., A.R. Nelson, J.J. Clague, G.A. Carver. 1995. Summary of coastal geologic evidence for past great earthquakes at the Cascadia subduction zone. Earthquake Spectra 11(1): 1-18.

Banner, A., J. Pojar, J.W. Schwab, R. Trowbridge. 1989. Vegetation and soils of the Queen Charlotte Islands: recent impacts of development. Pp. 261-279 in G.G.E. Scudder and N. Gessler (eds.). The Outer Shores. Queen Charlotte Islands Museum, BC.

Barbour, M.G. and J.E. Rodman. 1970. Saga of the west coast sea-rockets: *Cakile edentula* ssp. *californica* and *C. maritima*. Rhodora 72(791): 370-386.

Barrie, J.V., K.W. Conway, R.W. Mathewes, H.W. Josenhans, M.J. Johns. 1993. Submerged Late Quaternary terrestrial deposits and paleoenvironment of northern Hecate Strait, British Columbia, Continental Shelf, Canada. Quaternary International 20: 123-129.

Berg, R.Y. 1963. Disjunksjoner i Norges fjellflora og de teorier som er framsatt til forklaring av dem. Blyttia 21: 133-177.

Böcher, T.W. 1963. Phytogeography of Greenland in the light of recent investigations. Pp. 285-302. in A. Löve and D. Löve (eds.). North Atlantic biota and their history. Pergamon Press, Oxford, England.

Brassard, G.R. 1971. Endemism in the flora of the Canadian high arctic. Naturaliste canadien 98: 159-166.

Buckingham, N.M., E.G. Schreiner, T.N. Kaye, J.E. Burger, E.L. Tisch. 1996. Flora of the Olympic Peninsula. Northwest Interpretive Association and Washington Native Plant Society. Seattle, WA. 199 pp.

Calder, J.A. and R.L. Taylor. 1968. Flora of the Queen Charlotte Islands. Part 1. Systematics of the vascular plants. Canada Department of Agriculture Research Branch, Monogr. 4, Pt. 1.

Carl, G.C. and C.J. Guiguet. 1956. Notes on the flora and fauna of Bunsby Islands, BC. Provincial Museum of Natural History and Anthropology report for the year 1955. BC Department of Education, Victoria, BC. 14 pp.

Clague, J.J. 1989a. Quaternary geology of the Queen Charlotte Islands. Pp. 65-74 in G.G.E. Scudder and N. Gessler (eds.). The Outer Shores. Queen Charlotte Islands Museum, BC.

______ . 1989b. Cordilleran Ice Sheet. Pp. 40-42 in R.J. Fulton (ed.). Quaternary Geology of Canada and Greenland. G.S.C., Ottawa.

______ . 1989c. Quaternary sea levels (Canadian Cordillera). Pp. 43-47 in R.J. Fulton (ed.). Quaternary Geology of Canada and Greenland. G.S.C., Ottawa.

______ , J.R. Harper, R.J. Hebda, and D.E. Howes. 1982. Late Quaternary sea levels and crustal movements, coastal British Columbia. Can. J. Earth Sciences 19: 597-618.

______ , R.W. Mathewes, and B.G. Warner. 1982. Late Quaternary geology of eastern Graham Island, Queen Charlotte Islands, British Columbia. Can. J. Earth Sciences 19: 1786-1795.

Cowan, I. McT. 1989. Birds and mammals on the Queen Charlotte Islands. Pp. 175-186 in G.G.E. Scudder and N. Gessler (eds.). The Outer Shores. Queen Charlotte Islands Museum, BC.

Dahl, E. 1946. On different types of unglaciated areas during the ice ages and their significance to phytogeography. New Phytol. 45: 225-242.

______ . 1955. Biogeographic and geologic indications of unglaciated areas in Scandinavia during the glacial ages. Geol. Soc. Am. Bull. 66: 1499-1519.

Dahl, R. 1963. Shifting ice culmination, alternating ice covering and ambulant refuge organisms. Geogr. Ann. 45(2-3): 122-138.

_____ . 1966. Block fields, weathering pits and tor-like forms in the Narvik Mountains, Nordland, Norway. Geogr. Ann. 48, A(2): 55-85.

DeLapp, J. 1991. Rare vascular plant species of the U.S. Forest Service Alaska Region. The Nature Conservancy, Alaska Natural Heritage Program. Anchorage, AK.

Drury, W.H. 1969. Plant persistence in the Gulf of St. Lawrence. Pp. 105-148 in N.H. Greenidge (ed.). Essays in plant geography and ecology. Nova Scotia Museum, Halifax, NS.

Duffy, M. 1993. Results of the 1993 rare plant survey, U.S. Forest Service Alaska Region. Alaska Natural Heritage Program, Anchorage, AK.

Elven, R. 1980. The Omnsbreen glacier nunataks - a case study of plant immigration. Norwegian J. Botany 27: 1-16.

Faegri, K. 1963. Problems of immigration and dispersal of the Scandinavian flora. Pp. 221-232 in North Atlantic biota and their history. Pergamon Press, Oxford, England.

Florer, L. 1972. Quaternary paleoecology and stratigraphy of the sea-cliffs, western Olympic Peninsula, Washington. Quat. Res. 2: 202-216.

Frederiksen, S. 1971. The flora of some nunataks in Frederikshab district, West Greenland. Bot. Tidsskr. 66: 60-68.

Fulton, R.J. (ed.). 1989. Quaternary geology of Canada and Greenland. Geological Survey of Canada, Ottawa. 839 pp.

Funder, S. 1979. Ice-age plant refugia in east Greenland. Palaeogeogr. Palaeoclimatol. Palaeoecol. 28: 279-295.

Gjaerevoll, O. 1963. Survival of plants on nunataks in Norway during the Pleistocene glaciation. Pp. 261-283. in A. Löve and D. Löve (eds.). North Atlantic biota and their history. Pergamon Press, Oxford, England.

_____ . and L. Ryvarden. 1977. Botanical investigations on J.A.D. Jensens Nunatakker in Greenland. Kongelige Norske Videnskabers Selskab Skrifter 4: 1-40.

Goertzen, L.R. 1996. Genetic diversity and origin of two Queen Charlotte Islands plants: *Senecio newcombei* and *Saxifraga taylori*. M.Sc. thesis. Department of Botany, University of British Columbia, Vancouver, BC. 62 pp.

Griggs, R.F. 1940. The ecology of rare plants. Bull. Torrey Bot. Club 67: 575-594.

Hebda, R.J. 1983. Late-glacial and postglacial vegetation history at Bear Cove Bog, northeast Vancouver Island, British Columbia. Can. J. Bot. 61: 3172-3192.

Heusser, C.J. 1954. Nunatak flora of the Juneau Ice Field, Alaska. Bull. Torrey Botanical Club 81: 236-250.

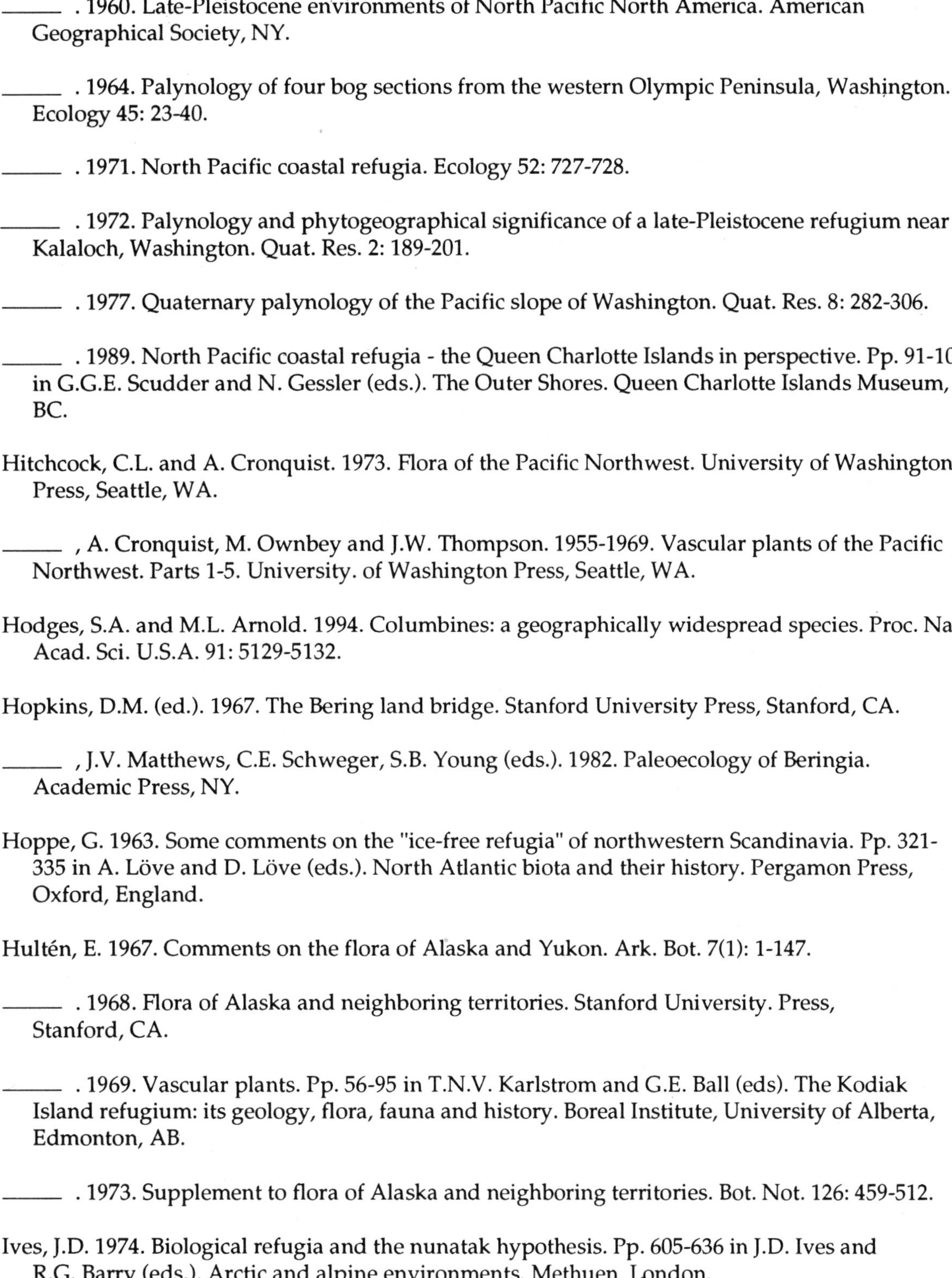

______ . 1960. Late-Pleistocene environments of North Pacific North America. American Geographical Society, NY.

______ . 1964. Palynology of four bog sections from the western Olympic Peninsula, Washington. Ecology 45: 23-40.

______ . 1971. North Pacific coastal refugia. Ecology 52: 727-728.

______ . 1972. Palynology and phytogeographical significance of a late-Pleistocene refugium near Kalaloch, Washington. Quat. Res. 2: 189-201.

______ . 1977. Quaternary palynology of the Pacific slope of Washington. Quat. Res. 8: 282-306.

______ . 1989. North Pacific coastal refugia - the Queen Charlotte Islands in perspective. Pp. 91-106 in G.G.E. Scudder and N. Gessler (eds.). The Outer Shores. Queen Charlotte Islands Museum, BC.

Hitchcock, C.L. and A. Cronquist. 1973. Flora of the Pacific Northwest. University of Washington Press, Seattle, WA.

______ , A. Cronquist, M. Ownbey and J.W. Thompson. 1955-1969. Vascular plants of the Pacific Northwest. Parts 1-5. University. of Washington Press, Seattle, WA.

Hodges, S.A. and M.L. Arnold. 1994. Columbines: a geographically widespread species. Proc. Nat. Acad. Sci. U.S.A. 91: 5129-5132.

Hopkins, D.M. (ed.). 1967. The Bering land bridge. Stanford University Press, Stanford, CA.

______ , J.V. Matthews, C.E. Schweger, S.B. Young (eds.). 1982. Paleoecology of Beringia. Academic Press, NY.

Hoppe, G. 1963. Some comments on the "ice-free refugia" of northwestern Scandinavia. Pp. 321-335 in A. Löve and D. Löve (eds.). North Atlantic biota and their history. Pergamon Press, Oxford, England.

Hultén, E. 1967. Comments on the flora of Alaska and Yukon. Ark. Bot. 7(1): 1-147.

______ . 1968. Flora of Alaska and neighboring territories. Stanford University. Press, Stanford, CA.

______ . 1969. Vascular plants. Pp. 56-95 in T.N.V. Karlstrom and G.E. Ball (eds). The Kodiak Island refugium: its geology, flora, fauna and history. Boreal Institute, University of Alberta, Edmonton, AB.

______ . 1973. Supplement to flora of Alaska and neighboring territories. Bot. Not. 126: 459-512.

Ives, J.D. 1974. Biological refugia and the nunatak hypothesis. Pp. 605-636 in J.D. Ives and R.G. Barry (eds.). Arctic and alpine environments. Methuen, London.

Jones, B. 1997. Conservation genetics and ecology of *Lloydia serotina*. Ph.D. thesis. University of Wales, Bangor, Wales.

Jones, G.N. 1936. A botanical survey of the Olympic Peninsula, Washington. Univ. Wash. Publ. Biol. 5: 1-286.

Janszen, H. 1977. Vascular plants of Saturna Island, British Columbia. Syesis 10: 85-96.

______ . 1981. Vascular plants of Mayne Island, British Columbia. Syesis 14: 81-92.

Karlstrom, T.N.V. and G.E. Ball (eds.). 1969. The Kodiak Island refugium. Boreal Institute, University of Alberta, Edmonton, AB.

Kavanaugh, D.H. 1989. The ground-beetle (Coleoptera: Carabidae) fauna of the Queen Charlotte Islands. Its composition, affinities, and origins. Pp. 131-146 in G.G.E. Scudder and N. Gessler (eds.) The Outer Shores. Queen Charlotte Islands Museum, BC.

Löve, A. and D. Löve (eds.). 1963. North Atlantic biota and their history. Pergamon Press, Oxford, England.

Luternauer, J.L., J.J. Clague, K.W. Conway, J.V. Barrie, B. Blaise, and R.W. Mathewes. 1989. Late Pleistocene terrestrial deposits on the continental shelf of western Canada: Evidence for rapid sea-level change at the end of the last glaciation. Geology 17: 357-360.

Mangerud, J. 1973. Isfrie refugier i Norge under istidene. (Unglaciated refugia in Norway during the ice ages.) Norges Geologiske Undersokelse 29(7): 1-23.

Martin, H.A. and G.E. Rouse. 1966. Palynology of Late Tertiary sediments from Queen Charlotte Islands, British Columbia. Can. J. Bot. 44: 171-220.

Mathewes, R.W. 1989a. Paleobotany of the Queen Charlotte Islands. Pp. 75-90 in G.G.E. Scudder and N. Gessler (eds.). The Outer Shores. Queen Charlotte Islands Museum, BC.

______ . 1989b. The Queen Charlotte Islands refugium: a paleoecological perspective. Pp. 486-491 in R.J. Fulton (ed.). Quaternary geology of Canada and Greenland. G.S.C., Ottawa.

______ and J.J. Clague. 1982. Stratigraphic relationships and paleoecology of a late-glacial peat bed from the Queen Charlotte Islands, BC. Can. J. Earth Sciences 19: 1185-1195.

______ and ______1994. Detection of large prehistoric earthquakes in the Pacific Northwest by microfossil analysis. Science 264: 688-691.

Morisset, P. 1971a. Endemism in the vascular plants of the Gulf of St. Lawrence region. Naturaliste canadien 98: 167-177.

______ . (ed.). 1971b. Endemism in the vascular flora of Canada: a symposium. Naturaliste canadien 98: 121-177.

Muller, J.E., K.E. Northcote, and D. Carlisle. 1977. Geology of Vancouver Island. Geol. Surv. Can., Ottawa. Open File 463.

______ , K.E. Northcote, and D. Carlisle. 1974. Geology and mineral deposits of Alert Bay-Cape Scott map-area on Vancouver Island, British Columbia. Pap. 74-B, Geol. Surv. Can.

Murray, D.F. 1968. A plant collection from the Wrangell Mountains, Alaska. Arctic 21: 106-110.

______ . 1971a. Comments on the flora of the Steele Glacier region, Yukon Territory. Pp. 178-181 in M. Fisher (ed.) Expedition Yukon. Thomas Nelson & Sons, Don Mills, ON.

______ . 1971b. Notes on the alpine flora of the St. Elias Mountains. Arctic 24: 301-304.

______ . 1981. The role of arctic refugia in the evolution of the arctic vascular flora—a Beringian perspective. Pp. 11-20 in G.G.E Scudder and J.L. Reveal (eds.). Evolution today: proceedings of the second International Congress of Systematic and Evolutionary Biology. Hunt Institute for Botanical Documentation, Carnegie-Mellon University, Pittsburgh, PA.

Neilson, J.E. 1968. New and important additions to the flora of the southwestern Yukon Territory, Canada. Can. Field-Naturalist 82: 114-119.

Nordhagen, R. 1963. Recent discoveries in the south Norwegian flora and their significance for the understanding of the history of the Scandinavian mountain flora during and after the last glaciation. Pp. 241-260 in A. Löve and D. Löve (eds.). North Atlantic biota and their history. Pergamon Press, Oxford, England.

Ogilvie, R.T. 1989. Disjunct vascular flora of Northwestern Vancouver Island in relation to Queen Charlotte Islands' endemism and Pacific Coast refugia. Pp. 127-130 in G.G.E. Scudder and N. Gessler (eds.). The Outer Shores. Queen Charlotte Islands Museum, BC.

______ . 1994. Rare and endemic vascular plants of Gwaii Haanas (South Moresby) Park, Queen Charlotte Islands, British Columbia. FRDA Report 214, Canadian Forest Service, Victoria, BC. 25 pp.

______ and A. Ceska. 1984. Alpine plants of phytogeographic interest on northwestern Vancouver Island. Can. J. Bot. 62: 2356-2362.

______ and H.L. Roemer. 1984. The rare plants of the Queen Charlotte Islands. BC. Naturalist 22(2): 17-18.

______ , R.J. Hebda, and H.L. Roemer. 1984. The phytogeography of *Oxalis oregana* in British Columbia. Can. J. Bot. 62(7): 1561-1563.

Packer, J.G. 1971. Endemism in the flora of western Canada. Naturaliste canadien 98: 131-144.

Pojar, J. 1980. Brooks Peninsula: possible Pleistocene glacial refugium on northwestern Vancouver Island. Abstract Bot. Soc. Am. Misc. Ser. Publ. 158: 89.

Roemer, H.L. and R.T. Ogilvie. 1983. Additions to the flora of the Queen Charlotte Islands on limestone. Can. J. Bot. 61: 2577-2580.

Rousseau, J. 1950. The value of botany as indicator of unglaciated areas. Mem. Jard. Bot. Montreal 69: 41-106.

Ryder, J.M. and J.J. Clague. 1989. Regional Quaternary stratigraphy and history of British Columbia. Pp. 48-58 in R.J. Fulton (ed.). Quaternary Geology of Canada and Greenland. G.S.C., Ottawa.

Schofield, W.B. 1969. Phytogeography of northwestern North America: Bryophytes and vascular plants. Madrono 20: 155-207.

———. 1989. Structure and affinities of the bryoflora of the Queen Charlotte Islands. Pp. 109-119 in G.G.E. Scudder and N. Gessler (eds.). The Outer Shores. Queen Charlotte Islands Museum, BC.

Scudder, G.G.E. and N. Gessler (eds.). 1989. The Outer Shores. Based on the proceedings of the Queen Charlotte Islands First International Symposium. Queen Charlotte Islands Museum Press, BC. 327 pp.

Solbrig, O.T. (ed.). 1972. Disjunctions in plants: a symposium. Ann. Missouri Bot. Gard. 59: 105-246.

Sørensen, T. 1948. A method of establishing groups of equal amplitude in plant sociology based on similarity of species content. Det Kongelige Danske Vidensk. Selsk. Biol. Skr. B.V. 4.

Steindorsson, S. 1962. On the age and immigration of the Icelandic flora. Societas Scientiorum Islandica 35: 1-157. Leiftur Publ., Reykjavik, Iceland.

———. 1963. Ice age refugia in Iceland as indicated by the present distribution of plant species. Pp. 303-320 in A. Löve and D. Löve (eds.) North Atlantic biota and their history. Pergamon Press, Oxford, England.

Taylor, R.L. 1994. Vascular plants of the Queen Charlotte Islands. Pp. 121-125 in G.G.E. Scudder and N. Gessler (eds.). The Outer Shores. Queen Charlotte Islands Museum, BC.

——— and B. MacBryde. 1977. Vascular plants of British Columbia: a descriptive resource inventory. Univ. BC. Bot. Gard. Tech. Bull. 4.

——— and G.A. Mulligan. 1968. Flora of the Queen Charlotte Islands. Part 2: Cytological aspects of the vascular plants. Canada Department of Agriculture Research Branch, Monograph 4, Pt. 2.

Wagner, W.H. and K.E. Boydston. 1978. A dwarf coastal variety of maidenhair fern, *Adiantum pedatum*. Can. J. Bot. 56: 1726-1729.

Warner, B.G., R.W. Mathewes, and J.J. Clague. 1982. Ice-free conditions on the Queen Charlotte Islands, British Columbia, at the height of late Wisconsin Glaciation. Science 218: 675-677.

Wynne-Edwards, V.C. 1937. Isolated arctic-alpine floras in eastern North America: a discussion of their glacial and recent history. Proc. Trans. R. Soc. Can., Sect. 5, Ser. 3, 31: 1-26.

———. 1939. Some factors in the isolation of rare alpine plants. Proc. Trans. R. Soc. Can., Sect. 5, Ser. 3, 33: 35-42.

Chapter 6

Cytogeographic Studies on the Vascular Plants of Brooks Peninsula

C.C. Chinnappa
Department of Biology, University of Calgary
Calgary, Alberta

Abstract

Chromosome numbers were determined for 30 taxa. Five species are represented as diploids on Brooks Peninsula: *Artemisia trifurcata, Franseria chamissonis, Gaultheria shallon, Melica subulata,* and *Vaccinium uliginosum. Ligusticum calderi* exhibits the same chromosome number ($2\underline{n} = 66$) as on the Queen Charlotte Islands. The counts suggest the possibility of a refugium on Brooks Peninsula, however, more species need to be examined, especially members of the Ericaceae.

Acknowledgements

I am grateful to Dr. Richard Hebda for inviting me to participate in the expedition. Part of the funds for travel were provided by a University of Calgary research grant.

Introduction

The refugia idea evolved to explain plant distributions that could not be reasonably accounted for by postglacial dispersal. Refugia are small, unglaciated enclaves in areas of otherwise total glaciation. They occur in two types: 1) generally low, coastal enclaves; and 2) high-elevation nunataks, or mountain tops (Packer and Vitt 1974).

It is reasonably well-recognized that a refugium existed on the Queen Charlotte Islands, though its extent is not clear (Warner et al. 1982). The Queen Charlotte Islands are geographically close to Brooks Peninsula, and there is speculation that similar refugia may have existed in both locations. The natural population of a new variety of the maiden-hair fern, *Adiantum pedatum* L. var. *subpumilum,* is one example of the many rare, disjunct or relict vascular and cryptogamic plants that have been noted on Brooks Peninsula (Pojar 1980; Wagner and Boydston 1978).

The purpose of this study was to find cytological evidence to support, or refute, the idea of the existence of a Pleistocene glacial refugium on Brooks Peninsula. A study of the genetic composition of the species presently found in the area, that is, chromosome counts, was done as a means of tackling the problem. If a refugium existed on Brooks Peninsula, there should be variation in the present species' chromosomal makeup. This would indicate the presence of parental forms, either diploid or low level polyploid (Packer 1971). Diploids still mark the approximate locations of the refugia in which they survived (Randhawa and Beamish 1972); it is generally understood that the polyploids evolved as colonizers.

Materials and Methods

Chromosomes from root tips were counted from living material, which was dug up with rootstocks intact, kept in self-sealing plastic bags, and brought into cultivation in the University of Calgary greenhouse. Chromosomes were also counted from flower buds, which were fixed in the field. Species collected for the chromosome studies are given in Table 6.1. Collection sites are plotted in Figure 6.1.

Table 6.1 Species collected on Brooks Peninsula for chromosome studies

Family	Species	UAC#[a]	Location	Map code[b]
Poaceae	*Deschampsia cespitosa* (L.) Beauv.	39617	Gentiana Lake	2
	Melica subulata (Griseb.) Scribn.	39620	Cassiope Pond	1
	Puccinellia nutkaensis (Presl.) Fern & Weath	39621	Cassiope Pond	1
Cyperaceae	*Carex circinata* C.A. Meyer	39622	Gentiana Lake	2
Juncaceae	*Juncus falcatus* E. Meyer	39624	Mouth of Cape Cook Lagoon	5
Liliaceae	*Allium cernuum* Roth	----	Quineex I.R. 8	3
	Fritillaria camschatcensis (L.) Ker-Gawl.	39625	Gentiana Lake	2
	Tofieldia glutinosa (Michx.) Pers.	39626	Cassiope Pond	1
	Veratrum eschscholtzii A. Gray	----	Cassiope Pond	1
Orchidaceae	*Habenaria chorisiana* Cham.	39627	Cape Cook Lagoon	4
Caryophyllaceae	*Stellaria humifusa* Rottb.	39629	Cape Cook Lagoon	4
Brassicaceae	*Cakile edentula* (Bigel.) Hook.	----	Cape Cook Lagoon	4
Droseraceae	*Drosera rotundifolia* L.	39630	Gentiana Lake	2
Saxifragaceae	*Heuchera glabra* Piper	39631	Cape Cook Lagoon	4
Fabaceae	*Lupinus nootkatensis* Donn ex Sims	----	Harris Peak	6
	Vicia gigantea Hook.	----	Cape Cook Lagoon	4
Apiaceae	*Ligusticum calderi* Math. & Const.[c]	39634	Gentiana Lake	2

Table 6.1 Continued

Family	Species	UAC#[a]	Location	Map code[b]
Ericaceae	*Gaultheria shallon* Pursh	----	Cassiope Pond	1
	Vaccinium uliginosum L.	39636	Cassiope Pond	1
Scrophulariaceae	*Pedicularis ornithorhyncha* Benth. in Hook.	39637	Cassiope Pond	1
Asteraceae	*Apargidium boreale* (Bong.) T. & G.	50027	Gentiana Lake	2
	Arnica latifolia Bong.	----	Doom Mountain	7
	Artemisia trifurcata Steph.	----	Doom Mountain	7
	Aster foliaceus Lindl.	----	Cape Cook Lagoon	4
	Aster subspicatus Nees ssp. *subspicatus*	39640	Gentiana Lake	2
	Erigeron peregrinus (Pursh) Greene	39641	Cassiope Pond	1
	Erigeron peregrinus (Pursh) Greene	39642	Cape Cook Lagoon tidal meadow	8
	Franseria chamissonis Les.	----	Mouth of Cape Cook Lagoon	5
	Hieracium albiflorum Hook.	----	Mouth of Cape Cook Lagoon	5
	Prenanthes alata D. Dietr.	----	Mouth of Cape Cook Lagoon	5

[a] Univ. of Calgary herbarium accession numbers.

[b] As indicated on map showing sampling locations (Figure 6.1).

[c] Endemic.

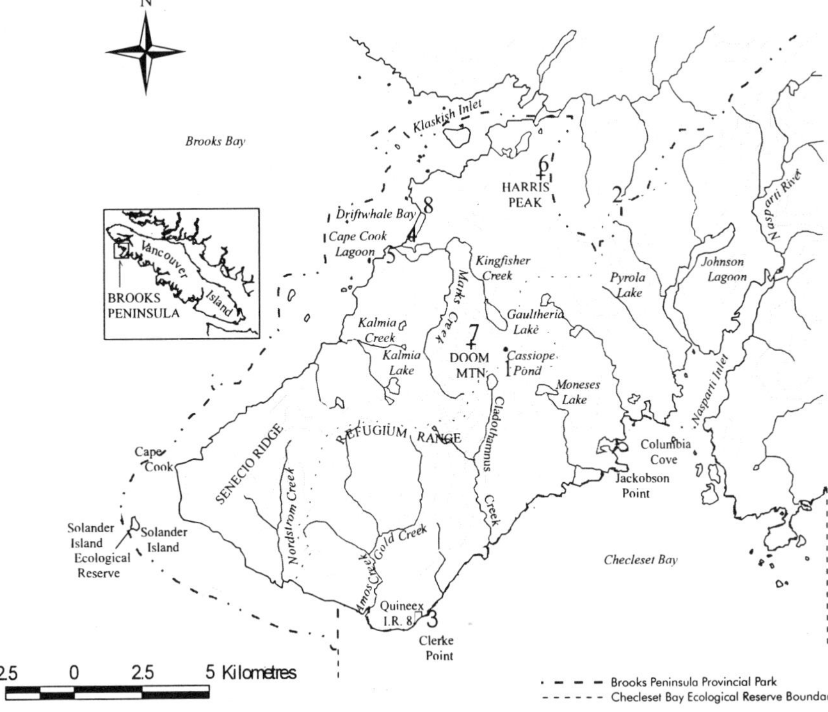

Figure 6.1 Sampling locations for plants used in chromosome counts. Numbers refer to map code in Table 6.1

Chromosome Counts From Root Tips

Root tips were treated with 0.05% colchicine for two hours and fixed in a mixture of ethyl alcohol and glacial acetic acid (3:1). They were hydrolyzed in 1N HC1 at 60°C for 10-12 minutes, and then squashed with 2% acetic orcein stain.

Chromosome Counts From Flower Buds

Flower buds were fixed in modified Carnoy's fixative (absolute alcohol: chloroform: glacial acetic acid = 3:4:1). The anthers were squashed with 1% acetic orcein stain. Slides were made permanent with the dry ice method. Photographs were taken with a Zeiss Universal photomicroscope, using Kodak high-contrast copy film.

Results and Discussion

The Queen Charlotte Islands are recognized as a reasonable site of a refugium. It is, therefore, instructive to compare the results determined for the vascular flora of Brooks Peninsula with chromosomal findings of the vascular flora of the Queen Charlotte Islands (Taylor and Mulligan 1968). The data are presented in Table 6.2.

Table 6.2 Chromosome numbers[a]

Species	Brooks Peninsula	Queen Charlotte Islands[b]	British Columbia[c]
Deschampsia cespitosa (L.) Beauv.	n = 13	2n = 26	2n = 26
Melica subulata (Griseb.) Scribn.	2n = 18	2n = 27	2n = 27
Puccinellia nutkaensis (Presl.) Fern & Weath	2n = 56	2n = 28, 42, 56	2n = 42
Carex circinata C.A. Meyer	2n = 58ca	2n = 60ca	2n = 60ca
Juncus falcatus E. Meyer	2n = 40ca	2n = 38	2n = 38
Allium cernuum Roth	2n = 14+6-11B's	nil	nil
Fritillaria camschatcensis (L.) Ker-Gawl	2n = 24	2n = 24	2n = 24
Tofieldia glutinosa (Michx.) Pers.	2n = 30	2n = 30	2n = 30
Veratrum eschscholtzii A. Gray	n = 16	2n = 32	2n = 32
Habenaria chorisiana Cham.	n = 21	2n = 42	2n = 42
Stellaria humifusa Rottb.	2n = 26	n = 13	2n = 26
Cakile edentula (Bigel.) Hook.	n = 9	n = 9	2n = 18
Drosera rotundifolia L.	2n = 20	n = 10	2n = 20
Heuchera glabra Piper	n = 7	n = 7	2n = 14
Lupinus nootkatensis Donn ex Sims	n = 24	n = 24	2n = 48
Vicia gigantea Hook.	n = 7	n = 7	2n = 14
Ligusticum calderi Math. & Const.	2n = 66	2n = 66ca	2n = 66, 66ca
Gaultheria shallon Pursh	n = 22	nil	2n = 88
Vaccinium uliginosum L.	2n = 24	nil	2n = 48
Pedicularis ornithorhyncha Benth. in Hook.	2n = 16	n = 8	2n = 16
Apargidium boreale (Bong.) T. & G.	2n = 18	2n = 18	2n = 18
Arnica latifolia Bong.	2n = 38	n = 19	2n = 38
Artemisia trifurcata Steph.	2n = 18	nil	nil
Aster foliaceus Lindl.	2n = 64	nil	n = 9
Aster subspicatus Nees ssp. *subspicatus*	2n = 90	nil	n = 9
Erigeron peregrinus (Pursh) Greene	2n = 18	n = 18	2n = 18

Table 6.2 Continued

Species	Brooks Peninsula	Queen Charlotte Islands	British Columbia
Erigeron peregrinus (Pursh) Greene	2n = 18	2n = 18	2n = 18
Franseria chamissonis Lees.	2n = 18	2n = 36	2n = 36
Hieracium albiflorum Hook.	n = 9	n = 9	2n = 18
Prenanthes alata D. Dietr.	n = 8	2n = 16	2n = 16

[a] n = pollen mother-cell count; 2n = root tip count.
[b] Taylor and Mulligan (1968).
[c] Taylor and MacBryde (1977).

Diploids and low levels of polyploids indicate the presence of refugia. *Melica subulata* (Griseb.) Scribn. was found in the diploid state (2n = 18) on Brooks Peninsula. Taylor and MacBryde (1977) and Taylor and Mulligan (1968) report this species as occurring in the triploid state. *Gaultheria shallon* Pursh is reported by Taylor and MacBryde as tetraploid (2n = 88); the count for Brooks Peninsula is n = 22 (diploid). The ploidy level is lower on Brooks Peninsula than elsewhere in British Columbia, which supports the idea of a refugium on Brooks Peninsula. *Vaccinium uliginosum* L. was also found in the diploid state (2n = 24) on Brooks Peninsula. Specimens from elsewhere in British Columbia (Table 6.2) are tetraploid (2n = 48). Both members of the Ericaceae show the diploid nature well. Chromosome counts are not available for the Queen Charlotte Islands population. *Franseria chamissonis* Less., collected on a lowland site, was determined to be a diploid (2n = 18). Taylor and MacBryde (1977) and Taylor and Mulligan (1968) report it to have a chromosome status of 2n = 36 (tetraploid). It is interesting that in this case the Queen Charlotte Islands material has a higher ploidy level than the Brooks Peninsula material. It may be the first indication of a diploid count for the species.

Artemisia trifurcata Steph. was determined to have a chromosome number of 2n = 18. This species is rare in British Columbia and does not occur on the Queen Charlotte Islands. Kawatani and Ohno (1964) report three numbers for the species: 18, 36, and 54. Taylor and MacBryde (1977) report the base number as 9. The Brooks Peninsula specimen is diploid and, therefore, is a significant indicator that a refugium once existed on the peninsula. The only other specimen collected from the province is from a disjunct population in northern British Columbia. This is also the first count for British Columbia material.

The endemic *Ligusticum calderi* Math. & Const. has the same chromosome count on Brooks Peninsula as it does on the Queen Charlotte Islands (Table 6.2). This count is also the same as the one reported for the species by Taylor and MacBryde (see Table 6.2). Most species of this genus are diploids. *Ligusticum calderi* Math & Const., though, is a hexaploid. Its occurrence on Brooks Peninsula, and the chromosome number, which is identical to the Queen Charlotte Islands population, are good indicators that Brooks Peninsula may have been a refugium.

Carex circinata C.A. Meyer (2n = 58ca) varies but slightly from Taylor and MacBryde's and Taylor and Mulligan's counts of 2n = 60ca. Since the base number for the species is 10 (Taylor and MacBryde 1977), there is probably no significance in this difference. *Juncus falcatus* E. Meyer also varies only slightly— 2n = 38, compared to the Brooks Peninsula count of 2n = 40ca [the base number is 5 (Taylor and MacBryde 1977)].

Puccinellia nutkaensis (Presl.) Fern & Weath. was counted as octoploid (2n = 56) on Brooks Peninsula. Taylor and MacBryde (1977) report the hexaploid count of 2n = 42. Taylor and Mulligan (1968) report three counts from the Queen Charlotte Islands: 2n = 28, 2n = 42, and 2n = 56. The populations on Brooks Peninsula have higher ploidy levels and could be recent introductions.

Taylor and Mulligan (1968) include *Aster foliaceus* Lindl. in with *Aster subspicatus* Nees, but do not report the chromosome number of either one. Taylor and MacBryde (1977) report the base chromosome number for both as n = 9. Brooks Peninsula specimens of these two species exhibit high levels of polyploidy. *Aster foliaceus* Lindl. was determined to have a chromosome count of 2n = 64 (Figure 6.2d). The chromosome number of *Aster subspicatus* Nees ssp. *subspicatus* was determined to be 2n = 90. *Aster foliaceus* Lindl. was collected on a lowland site.

Allium cernuum Roth is interesting as there is no count in Taylor and MacBryde (1977) and the plant is not listed as occurring on the Queen Charlotte Islands. The count for Brooks Peninsula is 2n = 14 + 6-11B's (Figure 6.2a).

There is reason to believe, based on other Brooks Peninsula data as well as on the present findings of five diploid (parent stock) species, that a refugium may have existed on Brooks Peninsula. According to Packer and Vitt (1974) these data should be given due consideration. "We are of the opinion that it is the irreducible minimum of species whose distribution cannot be explained that constitutes the problem. To simply subsume the minority under explanations that apply to the majority, for no better reason than the fact that they are a minority, is manifestly unscientific" (Packer and Vitt 1974:1394).

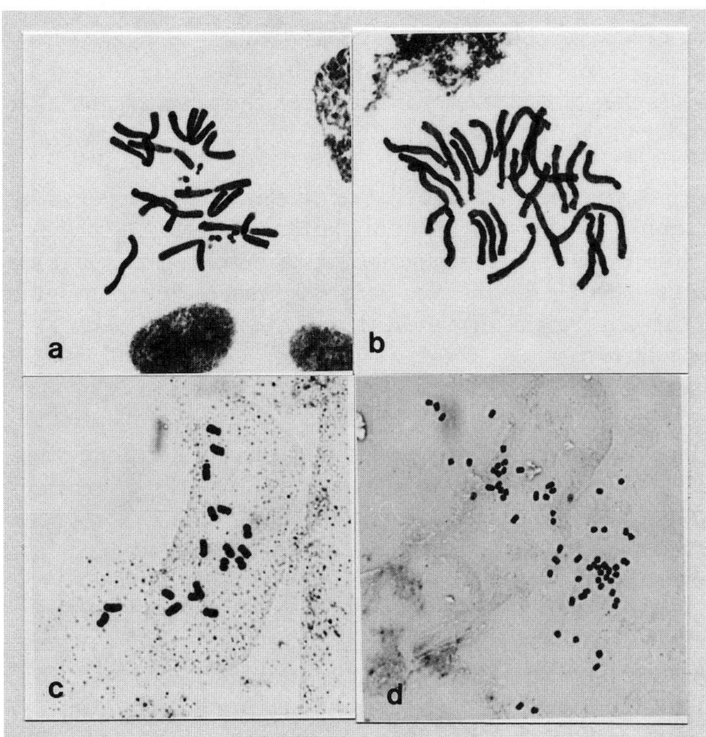

Figure 6.2 Mitotic chromosomes of four species: a) *Allium cernum* 2n = 14 + 6 B-chromosomes; b) *Fritillaria camschatcensis* 2n = 24; c) *Erigeron peregrinus* 2n = 18; d) *Aster foliaceus* 2n = 64

Diploids present on Brooks Peninsula, but not in other areas of British Columbia (excepting, in some cases, the Queen Charlotte Islands), include the following species: *Melica subulata* (Griseb.) Scribn., *Gaultheria shallon* Pursh, *Vaccinium uliginosum* L., *Artemisia trifurcata* Steph., and *Franseria chamissonis* Less. Evidence contradicting the tendency towards diploid levels of chromosomes is indicated by the high levels of ploidy in *Puccinellia nutkaensis* (Presl.) Fern & Weath., *Aster foliaceus* Lindl., and *Aster subspicatus* Nees ssp. *subspicatus* (only *P. nutkaensis* has reported chromosome counts from the Queen Charlotte Islands).

It is also interesting that the chromosome numbers of *Ligusticum calderi* Math & Const. from both the Brooks Peninsula and the Queen Charlotte Islands locations agree. This species is endemic to the two areas.

In conclusion, there is a distinct possibility that a refugium once existed on Brooks Peninsula, though this study gives no clear-cut answer. The theory cannot be proven without examining the genetic composition of a greater number of species from more varied locations, especially at high elevations. The Ericaceae might be of special importance in clarifying the problem.

References Cited

Kawatani, T. and T. Ohno. 1964. Chromosome numbers in *Artemisia*. Bulletin of National Institute Hyg. Science (Japan) 82: 183-193.

Packer, J.G. 1971. Endemism in the flora of western Canada. Naturaliste Canadien 98: 131-144.

——— and D.H. Vitt. 1974. Mountain Park: a plant refugium in the Canadian Rocky Mountains. Canadian Journal of Botany 52: 1393-1409.

Pojar, J. 1980. Brooks Peninsula: possible Pleistocene glacial refugium on northwestern Vancouver Island. Botanical Society Am. Misc. Ser. Publ. 158: 89.

Randhawa, A.S. and K.I. Beamish. 1972. The distribution of *Saxifraga ferruginea* and the problem of refugia in northwestern North America. Canadian Journal of Botany 50: 79-87.

Taylor, R.L. and B. MacBryde. 1977. Vascular plants of British Columbia: a descriptive resource inventory. University of British Columbia Bot. Gard. Technical Bulletin 4.

——— and G.A. Mulligan. 1968. Flora of the Queen Charlotte Islands. Part 2. Cytological aspects of the vascular plants. Canadian Department of Agriculture Research Branch, Monograph 4, Pt. 2.

Wagner, W.H., Jr. and K.E. Boydston. 1978. A dwarf coastal variety of maidenhair fern, *Adiantum pedatum*. Canadian Journal of Botany 56: 1726-1729.

Warner, B.G., R.W. Mathewes, and J.J. Clague. 1982. Ice-free conditions on the Queen Charlotte Islands, British Columbia, at the height of late Wisconsin glaciation. Science 218: 675-677.

Chapter 7

Hepaticae and Musci of Brooks Peninsula

W.B. Schofield
Botany Department, University of British Columbia
Vancouver, BC

This list is based on specimens housed at the herbarium of the University of British Columbia.

Hepaticae:
Anastrophyllum assimile (Mitt.) Steph.
Anastrophyllum minutum (Schreb.) Schust.
Aneura pinguis (L.) Dum.
Anthelia julacea (L.) Dum.
Apometzgeria pubescens (Schrank) Kuwah.
Apotreubia nana (Hatt. & H. Inoue) Hatt. & Mizut.
Bazzania denudata (Torrey *ex* Gott. *et al.*) Trev.
Bazzania pearsonii Steph.
Bazzania tricrenata (Wahlenb.) Lindb.
Blasia pusilla L.
Blepharostoma arachnoideum M.A. Howe
Blepharostoma trichophyllum (L.) Dum.
Calypogeia azurea Stotler & Crotz
Calypogeia fissa (L.) Raddi
Calypogeia integristipula Steph.
Calypogeia muelleriana (Schiffn.) K. Müll.
Cephalozia bicuspidata (L.) Dum.
Cephalozia lunulifolia (Dum.) Dum.
Cephaloziella divaricata (Sm.) Schiffn.
Chiloscyphus cuspidatus (Nees) Engel & Schust.
Chiloscyphus polyanthos (L.) Corda
Chiloscyphus pallescens (Ehrh.) Dum.
Conocephalum conicum (L.) Lindb.
Diplophyllum albicans (L.) Dum.
Diplophyllum imbricatum (M.A. Howe) K. Müll.
Diplophyllum plicatum Lindb.
Diplophyllum taxifolium (Wahlenb.) Dum.
Douinia ovata (Dicks.) Buch
Frullania tamarisci (L.) Dum. ssp. *nisquallensis* (Sull.) Hatt.
Geocalyx graveolens (Schrad.) Nees
Gymnocolea inflata (Huds.) Dum.
Gymnomitrion concinnatum (Lightf.) Corda
Gymnomitrion obtusum (Lindb.) Pears.
Gymnomitrion pacificum Grolle.
Gyrothyra underwoodiana M.A. Howe
Harpanthus flotovianus (Nees) Nees
Herbertus aduncus (Dicks.) S. Gray

Herbertus sakuraii Steph.
Hygrobiella laxifolia (Hook.) Spruce
Jungermannia obovata Nees
Jungermannia rubra Gott.
Jungermannia schusterana J. Godfr. & G. Godfr.
Kurzia makinoana (Steph.) Grolle
Kurzia setacea (Web.) Grolle
Lepidozia filamentosa (Lehm. & Lindenb.) Lindenb.
Lepidozia reptans (L.) Dum.
Lophozia floerkei Web. & Mohr
Lophozia gillmanii (Aust.) Schust.
Lophozia guttulata (Lindb. & Arn.) Evans
Lophozia incisa (Schrad.) Dum.
Lophozia opacifolia Culm.
Lophozia ventricosa (Dicks.) Dum.
Lophozia wenzelii (Nees) Steph.
Marsupella alpina (Gottsche) Bernet
Marsupella aquatica (Schrad.) Schiffn.
Marsupella commutata (Limpr.) H. Bern.
Marsupella emarginata (Ehrh.) Dum.
Marsupella sparsifolia (Lind.) Dum.
Marsupella sphacelata (Gieseke) Dum.
Marsupella stableri Spruce
Metzgeria conjugata Lindb.
Metzgeria temperata Kuwah.
Moerckia blyttii (Moerck.) Brockm.
Moerckia hibernica (Hook.) Gott.
Mylia taylori (Hook.) S. Gray
Nardia scalaris S. Gray
Odontoschisma denudatum (Nees. *ex* Mart.) Dum.
Odontoschisma elongatum (Lindb.) Evans
Pellia neesiana (Gott.) Limpr.
Plagiochila porelloides (Torrey *ex* Nees) Lindenb.
Plagiochila semidecurrens Lehm. & Lindenb., var *alaskana* (Evans) H. Inoue.
Pleurozia purpurea Lindb.
Porella navicularis (Lehm & Lindenb.) Lindb.
Porella roellii Steph.
Preissia quadrata (Scop.) Nees
Ptilidium californicum (Aust.) Underw.
Radula bolanderi Gott.
Radula complanata (L.) Dum.
Radula obtusiloba Steph., ssp. *polyclada* (Evans) Hatt.
Riccardia chamedryfolia (With.) Groble
Riccardia latifrons Lindb.
Riccardia multifida (L.) S. Gray
Riccardia palmata (Hedw.) Carruth.
Scapania americana K. Müll.
Scapania bolanderi Aust.
Scapania paludosa (K. Müll.) K. Müll.
Scapania umbrosa (Schrad.) Dum.
Scapania undulata (L.) Dum.
Sphenolobopsis pearsonii (Spruce) Schust.

Musci:
Amblystegium serpens (Hedw.) Schimp. *in* B.S.G.
Amphidium lapponicum (Hedw.) Schimp.
Amphidium mougeotii (Bruch & Schimp. *in* B.S.G.) Schimp.
Andreaea nivalis Web. & Mohr
Andreaea alpestris (Thed.) Schimp.
Andreaea megistospora B. Murray var. *megistospora*
Andreaea megistospora var. *epapillosa* (B. Murr.) Crum & Anderson
Andreaea rupestris Hedw.
Anoectangium aestivum (Hedw.) Mitt.
Antitrichia curtipendula (Hedw.) Brid.
Arctoa fulvella (Dicks.) Bruch & Schimp. *in* B.S.G.
Aulacomnium androgynum (Hedw.) Schwaegr.
Aulacomnium palustre (Hedw.) Schwaegr.
Barbula cylindrica (Tayl. *ex* Mackay) Schimp. *ex* Boul.
Bartramia pomiformis Hedw.
Bartramiopsis lescurii (James) Kindb.
Blindia acuta (Hedw.) Bruch & Schimp. *in* B.S.G.
Brachythecium albicans (Hedw.) Schimp. *in* B.S.G.
Brachythecium frigidum (C. Müll.) Besch.
Brachythecium plumosum (Hedw.) Schimp. *in* B.S.G.
Bryolawtonia vancouverensis (Kindb. *ex* Macoun) Norris & Enroth
Bryum capillare Hedw.
Bryum erythroloma (Kindb.) Syed
Bryum miniatum Lesq.
Bryum pseudotriquetrum (Hedw.) Gaertn., Meyer & Scherb.
Campylium stellatum (Hedw.) C. Jens.
Campylopus atrovirens De Not.
Campylopus fragilis (Brid.) Bruch & Schimp. *in* B.S.G.
Campylopus schimperi Milde
Campylopus schwarzii Schimp.
Ceratodon purpureus (Hedw.) Brid.
Claopodium bolanderi Best
Claopodium crispifolium (Hook) Ren. & Card.
Claopodium whippleanum (Sull. *in* Whipple & Ives) Ren. & Card.
Cratoneuron filicinum (Hedw.) Spruce
Cynodontium jenneri (Schimp. *in* Howie) Stirt
Dichodontium pellucidum (Hedw.) Schimp.
Dicranella heteromalla (Hedw.) Schimp.
Dicranella pacifica Schof.
Dicranella palustris (Dicks.) Crundw. *ex* Warb.
Dicranella rufescens (With.) Schimp.
Dicranodontium asperulum (Mitt.) Broth.
Dicranodontium denudatum (Brid.) Britt. *in* Williams
Dicranodontium uncinatum (Harv. *in* Hook.) Jaeg. & Sauerb.
Dicranoweisia cirrata (Hedw.) Lindb. *ex* Milde
Dicranum fuscescens Turn.
Dicranum majus Sm.
Dicranum pallidisetum (Bail. *in* Holz.) Irel.
Dicranum scoparium Hedw.
Distichium capillaceum (Hedw.) Bruch & Schimp. *in* B.S.G.

Ditrichum crispatissimum (C. Müll.) Paris
Ditrichum heteromallum (Hedw.) Britt.
Ditrichum zonatum (Brid.) Kindb. var *scabrifolium* Dix.
Drepanocladus exannulatus (Schimp. *in* B.S.G.) Warnst.
Dryptodon patens (Hedw.) Brid.
Eucladium verticellatum (Brid.) B.S.G.
Fissidens adianthoides Hedw.
Fissidens bryoides Hedw.
Fissidens grandifrons Brid.
Fissidens osmundioides Hedw.
Fontinalis antipyretica Hedw.
Funaria hygrometrica Hedw.
Grimmia torquata Hornsch. *in* Grev.
Gymnostomum aeruginosum Sm.
Herzogiella striatella (Brid.) Iwats.
Heterocladium macounii Best.
Heterocladium procurrens (Mitt.) Jaeg.
Homalothecium fulgescens (Mitt. *ex* C. Müll.) Lawt.
Hookeria acutifolia Hook. & Grev.
Hookeria lucens (Hedw.) Sm.
Hygrohypnum bestii (Ren. & Bryhn. *in* Ren.) Broth.
Hygrohypnum ochraceum (Turn. *ex* Wils.) Loeske
Hylocomium splendens (Hedw.) Schimp. *in* B.S.G.
Hypnum callichroum Funck. *ex* Brid.
Hypnum circinale Hook.
Hypnum cupressiforme Hedw.
Hypnum dieckii Ren. & Card. *in* Röll.
Hypnum subimponens Lesq.
Hypopterygium fauriei Besch.
Isothecium stoloniferum Brid.
Iwatsukiella leucotricha (Mitt.) Buck & Crum
Kiaeria starkei (Web. & Mohr) Hag.
Kindbergia oregana (Sull.) Ochrya
Kindbergia praelonga (Hedw.) Ochrya
Leucolepis acanthoneuron (Schwaegr.) Lindb.
Mnium thomsonii Schimp.
Neckera douglasii Hook.
Oedipodium griffithianum (Dicks.) Schwaeg.
Oligotrichum aligerum Mitt.
Oligotrichum parallelum (Mitt.) Kindb.
Oncophorus wahlenbergii Brid.
Orthotrichum lyellii Hook. & Tayl.
Paraleucobryum enerve (Thed. *ex* C.J. Hartm.) Loeske
Philonotis capillaris Lindb. *in* C.J. Hartm.
Philonotis fontana (Hedw.) Brid.
Plagiomnium insigne (Mitt.) Kop.
Plagiothecium cavifolium (Brid.) Iwats.
Plagiothecium denticulatum (Hedw.) Schimp. *in* B.S.G.
Plagiothecium laetum Schimp. *in* B.S.G.
Plagiothecium undulatum (Hedw.) Schimp. *in* B.S.G.
Platydictya jungermannioides (Brid.) Crum

Pleurozium schreberi (Brid.) Mitt.
Pogonatum contortum (Brid.) Lesq.
Pogonatum dentatum (Brid.) Brid.
Pogonatum urnigerum (Hedw.) P. Beauv.
Pohlia cruda (Hedw.) Lindb.
Pohlia longibracteata Broth *in* Röll
Pohlia nutans (Hedw.) Lindb.
Pohlia wahlenbergii (Web. & Mohr.) Andr.
Polytrichastrum alpinum (Hedw.) G.L.Sm.
Polytrichum formosum Hedw.
Polytrichum juniperinum Hedw.
Polytrichum piliferum Hedw.
Polytrichum strictum Brid.
Porotrichum bigelovii (Sull.) Kindb.
Pseudoleskea baileyi Best & Grout *in* Grout.
Pseudotaxiphyllum elegans (Brid.) Iwats.
Racomitrium aciculare (Hedw.) Brid.
Racomitrium aquaticum (Brid. *ex* Schrad.) Brid.
Racomitrium elongatum Ehrh. *ex* Frisvoll.
Racomitrium fasciculare (Hedw.) Brid.
Racomitrium lanuginosum (Hedw.) Brid.
Racomitrium lawtonae Irel.
Racomitrium microcarpon (Hedw.) Brid.
Racomitrium occidentale (Ren. & Card.) Ren. & Card.
Racomitrium sudeticum (Funck) Bruch & Schimp. *in* B.S.G.
Racomitrium varium (Mitt.) Jaeg.
Rhabdoweisia crispata (With.) Lindb.
Rhizomnium glabrescens (Kindb.) Kop.
Rhizomnium nudum (Britt. & Williams) Kop.
Rhytidiadelphus loreus (Hedw.) Warnst.
Rhytidiadelphus squarrosus (Hedw.) Warnst.
Rhytidiadelphus triquetrus (Hedw.) Warnst.
Rhytidiopsis robusta (Hedw.) Broth.
Schistidium apocarpum (Hedw.) Bruch & Schimp. *in* B.S.G.
Schistidium maritimum (Turn.) Bruch & Schimp. *in* B.S.G.
Schistidium rivulare (Brid.) Podp.
Scleropodium obtusifolium (Jaeg.) Kindb. *in* Mac. & Kindb.
Scleropodium tourettei (Brid.) L. Koch
Scouleria aquatica Hook. *in* Drumm.
Sphagnum austinii Sull. *in* Aust.
Sphagnum capillifolium (Ehrh.) Hedw.
Sphagnum compactum D.C. *in* Lam. & D.C.
Sphagnum fuscum (Schimp.) Klinggr.
Sphagnum girgensohnii Russ.
Sphagnum lindbergii Schimp. *in* Lindb.
Sphagnum magellanicum Brid.
Sphagnum mendocinum Sull. & Lesq. *in* Sull.
Sphagnum papillosum Lindb.
Sphagnum recurvum P-Beav. *sensu lato.*
Sphagnum rubellum Wils.
Sphagnum russowii Warnst.

Sphagnum squarrosum Crome
Sphagnum subnitens Russ. & Warnst *in* Warnst.
Sphagnum subsecundum Nees *in* Sturm.
Sphagnum tenellum (Brid.) Bory
Takakia lepidozioides Hatt. & Inoue
Tayloria serrata (Hedw.) Bruch & Schimp. *in* B.S.G.
Tetraphis pellucida Hedw.
Tetrodontium brownianum (Dicks.) Schwaegr.
Timmia austriaca (Hedw.) Limpr.
Tortella tortuosa (Hedw.) Limpr.
Trichostomum tenuirostre (Hook. & Tayl.) Lindb.
Ulota megalospora Vent. *in* Röll
Ulota obtusiuscula C. Müll. & Kindb.*in* Mac. & Kindb.
Ulota phyllantha Brid.
Zygodon baumgartneri Malta
Zygodon reinwardtii (Hornsch. *in* Reinw. & Hornsch.) A.Br. *in* Bruch & Schimp. *in* B.S.G.

Chapter 8

Vegetation of Brooks Peninsula

Richard J. Hebda[a]
R.T. Ogilvie[b]
Hans Roemer[c]
Allen Banner[d]

[a] Botany and Earth History, Royal British Columbia Museum
Victoria, BC
and
Biology and School of Earth and Ocean Sciences, University of Victoria
Victoria, BC
[b] Biology Department, University of Victoria
Victoria, BC
[c] Conservation Services, BC Parks
Victoria, BC
[d] BC Ministry of Forests
Smithers, BC

Abstract

Brooks Peninsula vegetation was studied at a reconnaissance level to provide a basis for describing habitats and interpreting vegetation history and to characterize communities with rare plants. Field observation included use of sample plots. Four major physiognomic types are recognized: Forest, Scrubforest, Shrub Vegetation, and Herbaceous Vegetation.

The Forest vegetation includes: Lowland Forest, Shoreline Forest, Alluvial Forest, and Mountain Slope Forest. Five Scrubforest types are recognized: Shoreline Scrubforest, Bog Scrubforest, Timberline Scrubforest, Krummholz, and Slide Scrubforest. Shrub Vegetation includes: Beach Shrub, Bog Shrub, Alpine Heath and Slide Shrub. Herbaceous Vegetation categories are: Beach Herbaceous Vegetation, Salt Marsh, Freshwater Marsh, Bog Herbaceous Vegetation, Herbaceous Aquatic Vegetation, Herbaceous Rock Vegetation, Alpine Meadow Vegetation, and Windblown Ridge Herb.

Lowland Forests on Brooks Peninsula are dominated by *Tsuga heterophylla* (western hemlock) and *Thuja plicata* (western redcedar) and resemble other forests of western Vancouver Island. Mature *Picea sitchensis* (Sitka spruce) forms a narrow band of Shoreline Forest. Alluvial Forests contain many species and exhibit many strata. Mountain Slope Forest is dominated by *Abies amabilis* (amabilis fir) and western hemlock with *Chamaecyparis nootkatensis* (yellow cedar) and *Tsuga mertensiana* (mountain hemlock) as important species. Scrubforests exhibit poorer growth and more open stands compared with adjacent forest types. Timberline occurs between 500 m and 800 m. Timberline Scrubforest and Krummholz resemble subalpine vegetation physiognomically, but lack many of the typical coastal subalpine species. Alpine shrub and herbaceous communities occupy high-elevation wind blown ridges, peaks, and cliffs and contain rare and disjunct species. Bog shrub and herb communities are widespread in lowlands, but are associated with only thin peat accumulations. Shoreline shrub and herb communities resemble those elsewhere on the coast of British Columbia.

Acknowledgements

Special thanks must go to Wilf Schofield, University of British Columbia, Vancouver, who identified several packets of mosses. Wilf Schofield also reviewed a draft of the manuscript. Bob Maxwell, BC Ministry of Environment, Lands and Parks, Victoria, provided valuable comments on the soils portion of this paper. Jim Pojar, BC Ministry of Forests, Smithers, and Adolf Ceska, Royal British Columbia Museum, Victoria, gave critical readings to the paper. Adolf Ceska ran the COENOS program on forest data on his computer. Andrew Niemann, Royal British Columbia Museum, prepared the photographs.

We thank Barbara Kuluah and Carolyn Kenzie for typing the full draft of the manuscript including the numerous tables and Pam Giacomello for converting and correcting disk versions. Finally, we thank the Friends of the Royal Museum (formerly Friends of the Provincial Museum) for granting us the financial support to study Brooks Peninsula.

Introduction

The vegetation of Brooks Peninsula merits description for several reasons. First, the vegetation of the northwest coast of Vancouver Island has had only limited study. It is of peculiar character, shaped by hyperoceanic climate, and has presented problems in classification (Pojar and Annas 1980). Second, the vegetation describes the setting in which plants and animals live. Third, a basic description of the vegetation and its dynamics is prerequisite to a study of vegetation history and past climate.

This study was not intended to be exhaustive, nor particularly systematic. Rather, it was intended to identify and describe the main plant communities and to uncover some of the factors shaping them.

The vegetation of Brooks Peninsula has anomalous features and the commonly used concepts of alpine, subalpine, and bog are difficult to apply. The plant communities are described according to a physiognomic classification, with subcategories based on dominant processes of the physical environment, that is, habitat features. The results are discussed in terms of regional vegetation types, soils, and vegetation history. Comment is then provided on the significance of the extant plant communities and the distribution of rare species.

Study Area

Physiography

Brooks Peninsula is located in the Vancouver Island Mountains of the Insular Mountains physiographic unit of British Columbia (Holland 1976). This is a rugged landscape consisting of mountain ridges and deep valleys.

In this context, Brooks Peninsula is unusual because it juts out from the main body of the Vancouver Island Ranges. As a consequence, though mountainous, Brooks Peninsula is surrounded on three sides by open ocean. The peninsula is about 10 km wide and 14 km long; no point is more than 5 km from shore.

The land mass consists of two types of terrain: (1) mountain ridges and slopes that form a backbone running the length of the peninsula, (2) rolling lowland terrain that forms an interrupted skirt around the base of the mountains.

The ridge system runs more or less southwest-northeast, but wanders sinuously. Numerous short spurs extend out from it. In general, the ridge system presents two contrasting exposures, one to the south and southeast, the other to the north and northwest. An exception to this is the Senecio Ridge area at the headlands of the peninsula, where there is significant western exposure (Figure 8.1).

The ridge system has a characteristic morphology. Slopes rise relatively steeply (30°) from marginal lowlands or from deeply incised glacial valleys. The heads of these valleys are abandoned cirques, cut deeply into the ridge system. Valley heads reach within 0.5-1.0 km of the ridge crests. Above 600-700 m the slopes steepen, in many cases becoming vertical cliffs with

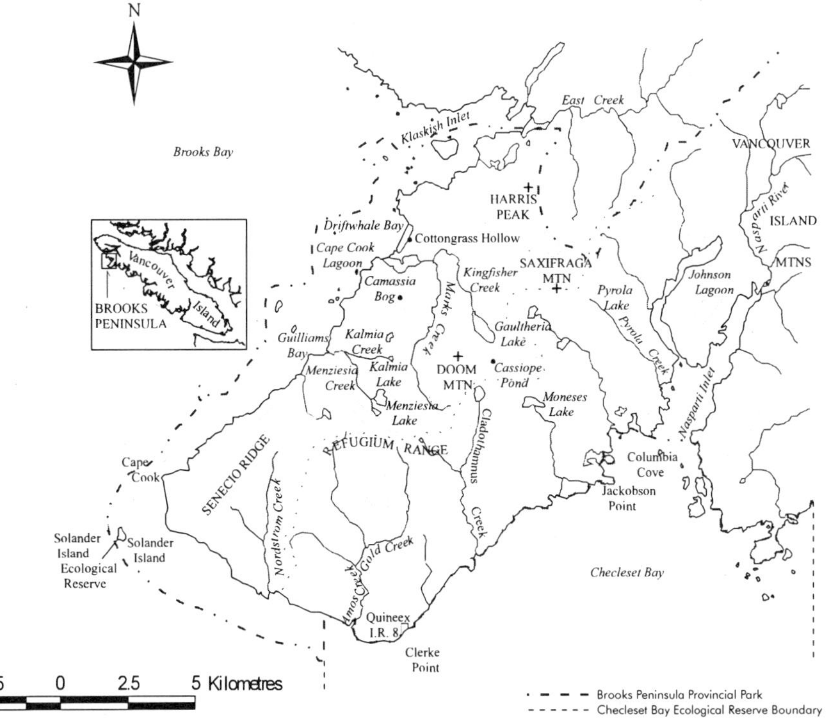

Figure 8.1 Brooks Peninsula and surrounding areas with locations mentioned in text

deeply incised clefts. Ridge crests are usually sharp. The Senecio Ridge area has much rounder crests, gentler, lower slopes, and upper slopes uncut by clefts. The elevation of the central ridge increases from about 350 m near the head of the peninsula to about 900 m at the northeast end, at Saxifraga Mountain and Harris Peak.

Lowland terrain is irregularly developed. It is most extensive between Cape Cook Lagoon and Guilliams Bay, in the Amos Creek-Nordstrom Creek drainage system at the south end, and on the west side of Nasparti Inlet. Near the shore, the terrain is generally flat or gently sloping. Inland, as west of Cape Cook Lagoon, the landscape consists of a rolling surface between 100-150 m, with hills to 250 m. Valleys extend as much as 4 km inland from these lowlands and usually contain a cirque lake with an effluent stream.

The shoreline is of two forms—steep rocky cliffs and beaches separated by rocky headlands. There is one major estuary, in Cape Cook Lagoon. Cliffs plunge into the ocean along nearly half of the coastline, leaving little or no space for beach development. This is characteristic of the northwest face of the peninsula adjacent to Cape Cook. The other half of the shoreline consists of beach and headland systems. These occur in two forms: (1) a broad rocky platform with a coarse cobble/boulder beach or exposed bedrock at the back, (2) a series of sandy beaches interrupted by rocky headlands or outcrops. Platform shorelines are well-developed at the south tip near Clerke Point. Sandy beach systems extend along the base of the northwest-facing shore and the southeast-facing shore.

Geology and Surficial Materials

Features of the geology and surficial materials of Brooks Peninsula are discussed in detail in other chapters of this volume (see Chapters 2 and 3). A summary is presented here.

Bedrock consists of four major units. Most of the peninsula, excluding the tip, is mapped as Westcoast Complex rocks, possibly of Jurassic age (Muller 1983). These rocks are of three types. Deformed and metamorphosed gabbros, schists, and mafic dikes underlie 80% of the study area. In general, these are very rich in iron and magnesium. Acidic granites occur, as far as is known, in the vicinity of Cape Cook Lagoon and Columbia Cove. Within the Westcoast Complex, but adjacent to the Pacific Rim Complex, there is a 2-3 km wide band consisting of gabbro fragments within a finer matrix. The Pacific Rim Complex, at the head of Brooks Peninsula, contains many rock types including limestones, cherts, shales, and conglomerates, as well as iron- and magnesium-rich basaltic pillow lavas.

Surficial materials fall into six categories: colluvium, morainal deposits, fluvial (that is, alluvial) deposits, marine sediments, organic deposits and bedrock. Colluvial blankets or veneers (less than 1 m thick) cover about 90% of the peninsula (Pattison 1980). This results from the combination of steep slopes, heavy rainfall, and frequent mass wasting. Several slopes show recent failure (landslides or debris flows). The colluvium is composed of non-sorted, occasionally poorly sorted, sediment containing particles ranging from clay to boulder size. Lenses of organic matter occur occasionally within colluvium.

Glacial materials such as ablation (melt-out) till or possibly end-moraine deposits occur upon some of the lowland surfaces around the base of the ridge system. Much of the till has been modified into colluvium by mass-wasting. The surface of the hummocky lowland extending from Cape Cook Lagoon to Guilliams Bay is mainly derived from glacial till, in either unmodified or slightly modified form. Scattered patches of these materials also occur along the southeast-facing slope. Morainal materials are heterogeneous in composition and contain mostly silt-to-boulder size particles. The deposits are usually compact.

River and stream derived deposits cover the floors of the large valleys, such as those adjacent to Kingfisher, Kalmia, Nordstrom, and Amos creeks. The bulk of these sediments is of fluvioglacial origin, that is, derived from melting glaciers. The sediments consist of poorly sorted sands and gravels. Active fluvial erosion in stream valleys has produced limited patches of well-sorted gravel and sand associated with narrow, shallow, silty or organic-silty alluvial zones in the floodplain.

Marine-derived deposits occur over a limited area adjacent to the shore. The medium-grained forest-covered sand dunes immediately north of Cape Cook Lagoon and the ridged marine deposits near the mouth of Amos Creek are notable. Marine sediments occupy discontinuous patches along the peninsula's southeast-facing shore. These may consist of well-sorted sand or gravel beds.

Exposed bedrock is scattered over much of the peninsula, but the most extensive areas are located along ridge crests, southeast-facing upper slopes, and the shoreline. Exposures occur where surfaces are actively shedding, or where strong southeasterly winds deflate products of weathering and prevent the establishment of vegetation.

On the rounded ridges of Senecio Ridge, there are areas of fine-to medium-sized angular rocks, often sorted into stripes. These are either presently active solifluction patterns, or perhaps relict periglacial features that are currently undergoing deflation and possibly further frost action.

Although large areas of organic surficial materials were not mapped by Pattison (1980), organic deposits occur abundantly on Brooks Peninsula. They occur as a continuous veneer of humus up to 0.5 m thick underlying many of the forested areas. In bogs, or bog-like terrain, the organic layer ranges from less than 0.5 m to more than one metre thick in exceptionally deep basins (see Chapter 9).

Climate

Brooks Peninsula is located in a cool, moist, oceanic climate that falls into Koeppen's Cfb classification (Chapman 1952). The winters are mild and the summers cool, though occasional warm spells occur. Precipitation is heavy, especially during the winter months. Clouds and fog are regular features of the weather, resulting in reduced solar radiation. There is considerable climatic variation on the peninsula because of differences in altitude (from 0 m to over 1000 m) and because of the contrast in aspect. This orientation is perpendicular to both the strongest wind and solar exposure.

The climate is dominated by the prevailing westerly air flow, which is seasonally modified by a summer high pressure system and a winter low pressure system. The North Pacific High system dominates the weather during the summer (mid-May to mid-September), promoting westerly and northwesterly winds, dry sunny conditions, and infrequent and weak storms. From mid-September to mid-May, a low pressure system, the Aleutian Low, is dominant and the weather is a succession of storms, dense clouds, heavy precipitation, and strong southeasterly winds.

There are no climatic records specifically for Brooks Peninsula. The description that follows is based on: (1) general climatic conditions of nearby regions (Chapman 1952; Technical Committee 1982); (2) climatic data for Spring Island, which is located off the exposed west coast of Vancouver Island, 30 km southeast of Brooks Peninsula; (3) records of a similar hyperoceanic climate on the Queen Charlotte Islands (Williams 1968). Spring Island climatic data should be applied with some caution because Brooks Peninsula is much more exposed.

There is little information on vertical climatic variation for this part of the coast, and the topography is complex.

Temperatures have a narrow range throughout the year. The mean daily temperature, for the year, is 9.1°C; with a mean January value of 4.6°C and a mean July value of 13.9°C (Figure 8.2). Extreme temperatures are rare; the coldest temperature recorded at Spring Island is -11.1°C and the warmest is 34.4°C. Presumably, the higher elevations of Brooks Peninsula are colder. On Mt. Cain, in interior north-central Vancouver Island, mean annual temperature decreases about 0.5°C per 100 m elevation (Technical Committee 1982).

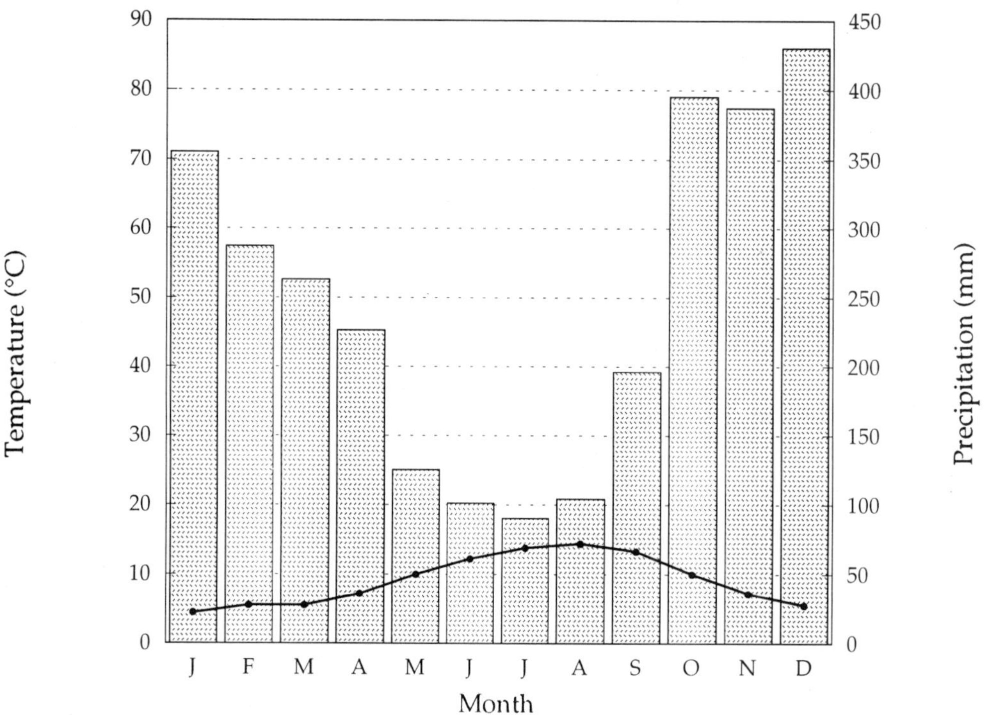

Figure 8.2 Climatic diagram for Spring Island station, Vancouver Island

Effective growing-degree-days (above 5°C) for Spring Island are estimated to be 740. The average frost-free interval is 240 days. The frost-free period decreases by about 8 days per 100 m increase in elevation on Vancouver Island (Technical Committee 1982).

The total mean annual precipitation at sea level on Spring Island is 3155.1 mm, consisting of 3110.6 mm of rain and 40.4 cm of snow, a typical distribution for coastal areas in the region (Chapman 1952). Precipitation increases dramatically inland on the west coast of Vancouver Island. For example, Estevan Point receives 25% less precipitation than Tahsis, ca. 30 km inland from the shore. Most rain falls between October and April—2343 mm at Spring Island compared to 617 mm from May to September (Technical Committee 1982). The wettest zone on Vancouver Island is a band located between 15 km and 20 km inland from the west coast. This suggests that Brooks Peninsula has lower precipitation than the highlands to the east of the peninsula (see Technical Committee 1982: Figure 7).

On the basis of limited data, annual precipitation appears to increase about 20% per 100 m elevation, to about 1200-1400 m (Technical Committee 1982). Thus, the upper slopes of Brooks Peninsula are probably considerably wetter than the lower slopes.

Snow amounts and duration-of-lie are important factors controlling vegetation. There are no data for these parameters on Brooks Peninsula. Based on snowfall data from maritime meteorological stations on western Vancouver Island, between 27 cm and 58 cm of snow would be expected at sea level.

The Queen Charlotte Islands have a climatic setting similar to that of Brooks Peninsula. Williams (1968) concludes that precipitation along the coast of the Queen Charlotte Islands usually falls as rain rather than snow, though small differences in temperature bring occasional heavy snowfalls. Nevertheless, snow cover rarely lasts long except high in the Queen Charlotte Mountains. In late spring, adjacent Vancouver Island peaks often bear much snow, whereas Brooks Peninsula peaks have little or no snow.

Wind plays an important role in the climate of Brooks Peninsula because the land mass is completely exposed to unencumbered air movements from all directions except the northeast. The strongest winter winds blow from the southeast off the open ocean where, unlike along much of the rest of the Vancouver Island coast, they are not slowed down by land masses and mountain peaks. At Spring Island, the wind recording station nearest to Brooks Peninsula, winds from the southeast are most frequent. The mean wind velocity is 15.6 km/h. Winter winds are strongest, averaging 18-20 km/h; summer winds are weakest, 10-12 km/h. Winter storm winds may blow faster than 100 km/h for extended periods, with a maximum recorded speed of 148 km/h. It is suspected, that wind velocity on Brooks Peninsula is greater than this on high elevation peaks, mountain cliffs and ridge crests. An example of this is the western end of the Refugium Range where plants survive in the lee of protective rocks (Figure 8.3), and southeast-facing slopes in saddles are denuded of plants, humus, and fine sediment. Wind speeds probably approach those recorded at the Cape St. James weather station located in an exposed setting on the southern tip of the Queen Charlotte Islands archipelago. There, mean winter wind speeds range from 35 km/h to 42 km/h. Wind speeds of 177 km/h have been recorded (Atmospheric Environment Service 1982).

Figure 8.3 Plants growing in the lee of protective rocks on Senecio Ridge (Photo: R.J. Hebda)

Cloudiness has a major influence on the amount of incident radiation available to plants. The west coast of Vancouver Island and, presumably, Brooks Peninsula are among the cloudiest localities in Canada. The climatic station at Estevan Point, 120 km southeast of Brooks Peninsula, registers an annual mean of 1690 hours of sunshine. The period from October to April is very cloudy (e.g., the 50 hours of sunshine in December represent 19% of the possible sunshine). Areas at high elevations and locations where clouds are trapped, such as in the upper parts of valleys, receive even less sun.

Fog, common in late summer and fall, further reduces sunshine. A large fog zone develops off the west coast of Vancouver Island in summer (Technical Committee 1982). The fog bank rolls onto the coast blanketing lowlands and penetrating valleys. The fog is usually less than 300 m thick, but winds tear off stringers and drive them up valleys to dissipate over ridges.

Incident radiation varies considerably on Brooks Peninsula because of a number of factors. There are very steep slopes oriented predominantly southeast and northwest. This topographic configuration could theoretically result in a major difference in radiation available to the opposite slopes of the peninsula. The predominantly southeast-facing side receives much more incident radiation. A 30° southeast-facing slope would receive, in January, twice as much total radiation as a northeast-facing side; in June, about 1.15 times as much (Technical Committee 1982). Much of Brooks Peninsula is steeply sloping terrain.

As might be expected in such a climate, there is no climatic moisture deficit (based on Spring Island data). High precipitation and very low evapotranspiration rates, typical of this hyperoceanic climate, maintain wet soil conditions throughout the year, even on many freely drained upland sites. However, minor soil-moisture deficits may occur on south-facing windy sites on Brooks Peninsula. Other sites with the potential for moisture deficits are south-facing cliffs, rock outcrops, and sand dunes.

Soils

In this chapter there are descriptions only of the general features of the soils on Brooks Peninsula. Regional affinities are emphasized to provide a setting in which the vegetation can be considered. The soils on the northern part of the peninsula are described in detail in Chapter 4.

According to the Canadian System of Soil Classification (Agriculture Canada Expert Committee on Soil Survey 1987), the soils of Brooks Peninsula are mainly classified in the Podzolic order, as Ferro-Humic Podzols. The U.S. equivalent is Humic Cryorthod or Humic Haplorthod (Jungen and Lewis 1978). Organic, Gleysolic, and Regosolic orders also occur within the study area. The soils are characteristic of the Coastal Western Hemlock Biogeoclimatic Zone (Jungen and Lewis 1978), and develop in regions of moist cool climate with abundant rainfall.

The major soil-forming processes on Brooks Peninsula include intensive podzolization and organic matter accumulation. The podsolized soils are characterized by the accumulation of amorphous organic matter combined with iron and aluminum compounds in the B, or illuvial, horizon. Heavy rainfall leaches dissolved or suspended minerals, iron and aluminum oxides, and humified organic matter from the surface and Ae horizons into the underlying B and BC horizons (Agriculture Canada Expert Committee on Soil Survey 1987). Organic matter in the form of raw and decomposed litter is abundant on the surface, and translocated colloidal humus decomposition products occur in the B horizon. A representative soil profile from mid-slope position may consist of 10-40 cm of coniferous litter and well-decomposed organic matter (LFH layer) on the surface. Humimors are the most common humus forms (Klinka et al. 1981). Beneath this LFH layer there is generally a light grey leached Ae horizon, but it may be absent. The diagnostic B horizon (Bhf, Bf) ranges from 10 cm to 40 cm in thickness and contains dark reddish brown organic matter accumulated in the B horizon. Often, on flat lowland terrain an iron-cemented horizon impedes the downward movement of water in the profile and restricts root penetration. Consequently, the active rooting zone is confined above this hardpan. The high ground-water is believed to be nutrient-poor and often to flow perched on top of the hardpan.

Wetland Organic soils are composed mainly of saturated peat derived primarily from sphagnum moss. Typically, the peat is more than 0.4 m thick and consists of layers of plant remains in various states of decomposition. The peat layer rests on a gleyed (a chemically-reduced state) mineral horizon (Bg or Cg). Although organic soils are widespread on the peninsula, deep peat soils (1.0-1.5 m thick) are restricted to small basins such as Cottongrass Hollow. Pockets of organic soil also occur in the most poorly drained situations across the lowlands. They are part of a complex pattern of Podzolic soils with pan formations, Organic soils, and Gleysolic soils, usually with peaty or folic (folisol-like) phases.

Folisols comprise a noteworthy Organic soil category on Brooks Peninsula. Folisols have a thick forest litter humus layer (LFH) in various stages of decomposition. Folisols drain better than wetland peat in depressions. The Brooks Peninsula Folisols may occur directly over bedrock or shallow layers of rock fragments, where the LFH is thicker than 10 cm; on high ridges; adjacent slopes; or shallow bedrock in lowlands. Folisols also occur where the LFH is thicker than 40 cm over mineral horizons. Many of the forest soils on the peninsula have more than 40 cm of LFH above a podzolic mineral horizon (Bfh) or gleysolic mineral horizons (Bg, Cg) (Agriculture Canada Expert Committee on Soil Survey 1987).

Gleysols are water-saturated throughout the soil profile for long periods, but are occasionally aerated during the dry season. The profile is characterized by a greyish green cast (reduced), and is often mottled with yellowish red pockets (oxidized). Peaty, organic matter may occur on the surface, or coniferous litter and humus up to 40 cm thick. Gleysols occur on floodplains, small basins, and hollows across the rolling lowland surface.

Regosols are weakly developed mineral soils with little or no A or B horizon or organic layers (O or LFH). These soils cover young surfaces, such as sandy beaches on emerging coastlines and on gravel bars in creeks. Regosols also occur on recent landslide surfaces and on active talus or other fresh bedrock rubble. The stony areas of Senecio Ridge consist of wind-deflated lag deposits or patterned frost-sorted features. Although the soil surface appears regosolic, the underlying fine-grained fraction testifies to intense podzolization.

Although Podzolic soils predominate over the upland areas of the peninsula, the rolling lowland terrain has complex patterns of Gleysolic, Podzolic, and Organic soils. The soils located on receiving slopes are subject to soil creep, minor surface wash, channel cutting, and occasional root throw. The soil forming processes and texture vary considerably over short distances and the active slope processes enhance the heterogeneity.

Regional Vegetation

The forests of the lowland and lower mountain slopes of the Brooks Peninsula are included within the North Pacific Coast section of Rowe's (1972) Coast Forest Region, within the wetter subzone of Krajina's (1965) Coastal Western Hemlock Biogeoclimatic Zone (CWH), and within the Very Wet Hypermaritime subzone of the Coastal Western Hemlock Zone (CWHvh) according to the BC Ministry of Forests (Meidinger and Pojar 1991). The CWH occurs at low to mid-elevation along the Pacific Coast from Oregon to Alaska and includes the western flanks of the mainland Coast

Mountains, the coastal lowlands and islands. The Very Wet Hypermaritime subzone (CWHvh) occurs northward from the most exposed western and northern fringe of Vancouver Island.

Several vegetation-environmental studies have been carried out within the CWH zone on western Vancouver Island (Bell 1972; Bell and Harcombe 1973; Cordes 1972; Cordes et al. 1974; Klinka et al. 1984; Klinka et al. 1979; Klinka et al. 1980; Kojima and Krajina 1975; Lewis 1985; Packee 1974; Technical Committee 1982; Wade 1965). Some of these describe closely related vegetation types to those on Brooks Peninsula. However, because of the geographic setting of Brooks Peninsula, its climate and vegetation patterns are distinct from adjacent areas of Vancouver Island and have close affinities with British Columbia's outer coast to the north.

For this area from northern Vancouver Island to southeastern Alaska, Pojar and Annas (1980; also see Pojar 1983) proposed a separate biogeoclimatic unit, initially named Coastal Cedars-Pine-Hemlock Zone, but this is now classified as part of the hypermaritime subzone of the CWH (CWHvh) in Pojar et al. 1988; Banner et al. 1990; Klinka et al. 1991; and Meidinger and Pojar 1991.

Forest and bog ecosystems within this CWHvh subzone resemble Brooks Peninsula ecosystems and have been described on the northern mainland coast (Banner 1983; Banner et al. 1988; Banner et al. 1990) and on the Queen Charlotte Islands (Banner et al. 1989; Banner et al. 1990; Calder and Taylor 1968; Lewis 1982). Neiland (1971) described similar ecosystems in southeast Alaska.

Major tree species in the CWHvh are *Thuja plicata* (western redcedar), *Chamaecyparis nootkatensis* (yellow cedar), *Tsuga heterophylla* (western hemlock), *Pinus contorta* (shore pine), *Picea sitchensis* (Sitka spruce), and *Abies amabilis* (amabilis fir). *Alnus rubra* (red alder), *Tsuga mertensiana* (mountain hemlock) and *Taxus brevifolia* (western yew) are relatively minor elements. Much of the subzone is covered by scrubby, low-productivity forests dominated by western redcedar, yellow cedar, western hemlock, and, in the poorest forests and woodlands, shore pine. The scrubby nature of these forests reflects several factors, including: (1) the prevalence of imperfectly to poorly drained soils, even on moderate slopes in this cool, perhumic subzone, (2) low nutrient availability in the cool, wet, acidic soils.

Throughout the most oceanic, exposed parts of the subzone, scrub forests form a mosaic with shore pine-yellow cedar bog woodland, and shrubby shore pine-*Ledum groenlandicum* (Labrador tea) blanket bog communities. In some areas, blanket bogs dominate the landscape even on moderate to steep slopes. These bogs are particularly interesting because, although they contain many of the plant species that characterize acid bogs in general, many have shallow or discontinuous peat deposits. Furthermore, they contain relatively little sphagnum compared with classic peat bogs of less maritime environments throughout the world. Deep ombrotophic (rain-fed) bogs also occur in the CWHvh subzone, for example, near Prince Rupert, but shallow minerotrophic (influenced by mineral seepage) bog types appear to be more typical of outer, exposed localities along the mainland coast and the western Queen Charlotte Islands—and also Brooks Peninsula.

Productive forests do occur in the CWHvh subzone. However, in contrast to other CWH subzones, they are restricted to edaphically-favourable sites and do not dominate the landscape. Vigorous mixtures of western hemlock, western redcedar, amabilis fir, and Sitka spruce occur on well-drained soils (generally Podzols) on steep colluvial slopes that usually have a recent history of disturbance by mass wasting or windfall. The most productive forests occupy well-drained fluvial landforms where vigorous spruce-dominated forests occur.

Shoreline ecosystems form an important and characteristic component of the vegetation along the coast of Vancouver Island and other parts of British Columbia (Bell 1972; Bell and Harcombe 1973;

Ceska 1978; Cordes et al. 1974; Dawe and White 1982; van Dieren 1982). Rocky shoreline plant communities on Vancouver Island consist of widely scattered herbaceous plants. Sandy beach and dune communities contain grasses and scattered herbs. Usually, between the upper beach and the forest edge there is dense shrub vegetation. Wind-sculptured Sitka spruce-salal forests border most of the shorelines on beach deposits, headlands, and colluvial slopes influenced by salt spray. Many of these vegetation types are well-represented on Brooks Peninsula. Several aquatic and semi-aquatic lagoon/tidal-marsh communities occur in sheltered pockets along the Vancouver Island coast.

Communities at and above timberline on Vancouver Island have received little study. Ogilvie and Ceska (1984) provide a phytogeographic analysis of some Vancouver Island alpine peaks. Klinka, Nuszdorfer and Skoda (1979) briefly describe the Alpine Tundra Biogeoclimatic Zone (AT) and open forms of the Pacific Coastal Subalpine Forest-Mountain Hemlock Biogeoclimatic Zone (MH) on Vancouver Island. The AT vegetation consists of herbs, mosses, liverworts, and lichens, and low-growing shrubs. There are occasional stunted conifers at the lower limits of AT. Wet snow-cover of long duration is characteristic. One MH parkland type, the Maritime Parkland Subzone, occurs on Vancouver Island. Scattered trees, mainly mountain hemlock, grow on topographic high points. Shrubs are abundant and form heath-like vegetation with few herbs.

Calder and Taylor (1968) recognize four categories of non-arboreal high elevation communities on the Queen Charlotte Islands: meadows, heaths, talus slopes, and cliffs, runnels and rock outcrops. Lush meadow communities grow along valley bottoms and on flats bordering creeks. They contain many herbaceous species, as well as grasses and sedges. Heath communities consist of shrubby ericaceous species. Heath communities are generally associated with rocky terrain. Talus communities are not abundant and generally include herbaceous species. Cliffs, runnels, and rock outcrops support a wide diversity of plant species. Two chief associations are recognized, one in runnels on wooded slopes, the other on cliffs and rock outcrops above tree line.

Methods

In the early phases of planning the expedition to Brooks Peninsula, the need to examine vegetation was recognized. However, it was clear that a comprehensive study was not possible with the relatively small work-group and limited time available. Vegetation analyses were carried out by four botanists on the team (A. Banner, R.J. Hebda, R.T. Ogilvie, and H. Roemer). By necessity, the vegetation sampling was done along with palaeobotanical, physiographic, and floristic studies. All of the main vegetation types were sampled, though not with equal intensity. A field-form consisting of a list of vascular plant species known to grow on Brooks Peninsula was used at many study sites. Beside each entry on the form there was space to record the percent cover of the respective species for the appropriate stratum (tree, shrub, herb). Observers used the scale with which they were most familiar to record species cover.

In some instances, especially where time was short, data were recorded in other ways (e.g., list of species in order of dominance). Most observations were later converted to approximate values on a modified Braun-Blanquet scale or modified Daubenmire coverage scale (Mueller-Dombois and Ellenberg 1974). Bryophyte data were recorded for some sites. Because observers had different skills in the identification of bryophytes, usually only the more abundant species were noted. In certain cases, bryophytes were collected and brought back to the field camp, where they were identified by W.B. Schofield. Lichens were collected, but few observations were made about their relationship to vegetation.

The Forest data were tabulated and ordinated using the COENOS program, provided by A. Ceska (Ceska and Roemer 1971). The vegetation tables were constructed to reveal synecological affinities of the species and sample-plots.

Voucher specimens of selected vascular plants are deposited in the herbarium of the Royal British Columbia Museum. Vouchers of selected bryophytes are at the herbarium of the University of British Columbia.

Results

Classification System

The Brooks Peninsula vegetation is classified on the basis of physiognomy, environmental factors, and species composition. The first level of classification is based on physiognomy, that is, the growth form of the dominant plants. Thus, four physiognomic categories are recognized: Forests, Scrubforests (stunted trees), Shrub Vegetation, and Herbaceous Vegetation. These categories are subdivided on the basis of environmental factors and species composition. For example, the forest vegetation is subdivided into Lowland Forest, Shoreline Forest, Alluvial Forest, and Mountain Slope Forest. The complete classification includes:

1. Forests
   - 1.1 Lowland Forest
     - 1.1.1 Wet Lowland Forest
     - 1.1.2 Mesic Lowland Forest
     - 1.1.3 Lowland Forest on Steep Slopes
   - 1.2 Shoreline Forest
   - 1.3 Alluvial Forest
     - 1.3.1 Alluvial Floodplain Forest
     - 1.3.2 Alluvial Fringe Forest
   - 1.4 Mountain Slope Forest

2. Scrubforests
   - 2.1 Shoreline Scrubforest
   - 2.2 Bog Scrubforest
   - 2.3 Timberline Scrubforest
   - 2.4 Krummholz
   - 2.5 Slide Scrubforest

3. Shrub Vegetation
   - 3.1 Beach Shrub
   - 3.2 Bog Shrub
   - 3.3 Alpine Heath
   - 3.4 Slide Shrub

4. Herbaceous Vegetation
   - 4.1 Beach Herbaceous Vegetation
   - 4.2 Salt Marsh
   - 4.3 Freshwater Marsh
   - 4.4 Bog Herbaceous Vegetation
     - 4.4.1 Shallow Bog
     - 4.4.2 Deep Bog

Vegetation Types

1. Forests

Criteria and Environmental Factors

The Forest vegetation falls into four broad divisions: Lowland Forest, Mountain Slope Forest, Alluvial Forest, and Shoreline Forest. In each of these divisions, distinct environmental factors give rise to the distinguishing features of the vegetation. Forests include vegetation dominated by trees higher than 8-12 m. The authors chose to distinguish Lowland Forest and Mountain Slope Forest instead of the conventional altitudinal zonation of lowland, montane, and subalpine forests. Altitudinal forest vegetation zones on Brooks Peninsula proved difficult to recognize because of the narrow range of elevation and the interfingering of typical lowland and montane forest types at low elevations. It appears that the distinct soil-forming processes on the generally steep slopes are more important than elevation in determining the forest vegetation. Colluvial processes on slopes yield loose, frequently rejuvenated, and generally more fertile soils without stagnant moisture, whereas stable till and marine parent materials on the gentle topography of the lowlands tend to give rise to highly podzolised or humified, poorly drained, and generally less fertile soils. These processes separate Lowland Forest from Mountain Slope Forest. Such trends are more pronounced under the hyperoceanic climate of Brooks Peninsula than under the less oceanic climate elsewhere on Vancouver Island.

The influence of salt spray and salt-laden air shapes the character of Shoreline Forest and distinguishes it ecologically from neighbouring Lowland Forest. Alluvial Forest is disturbed by flooding and is influenced by rapid ground water movement associated with watercourses. Alluvial Forest receives a higher flux of nutrients than adjacent forest types, especially Lowland Forest, from floodwaters and from the rejuvenation of the soil surface by erosion or sediment deposition. Sample plots of forest vegetation types are presented in Table 8.1.

1.1 Lowland Forest

The Lowland Forest on Brooks Peninsula is similar, both in appearance and in species composition, to other lowland forests along the west coast of Vancouver Island. It is a mature forest of western redcedar and western hemlock at or near climax stage. The cedar trees are typically large in diameter, but only of moderate height, of poor quality, frequently split into several leaders (candelabra-type), and usually with dead tops. Western hemlock also grows poorly, seldom taller than 20 m. Most hemlock trees are infected with *Arceuthobium tsugense* (dwarf mistletoe). The large, spike-topped cedars and the uneven hemlocks give this forest an irregular and patchy appearance when viewed from the air as well as from within the stand.

Features that help to distinguish the typical lowland forest of Brooks Peninsula from that of adjacent areas are the occasional presence of yellow cedar, the near absence of amabilis fir on gentle terrain, and generally smaller trees.

Table 8.1 Summary for Forest and Scrubforest Vegetation types on Brooks Peninsula (see Appendix 8.1 for abbreviations; Appendix 8.2 for detailed plot listings)

(Table entries: first number (roman) = presence class[a]; second number (arabic) = predominant cover value[b]; section 6[c])

table section	1	2	3	4	5	6	7	8	9	10
number of sample plots	9	5	21	11	7	4	6	8	6	6
major (minor) physiognom. type[d]	K	T(K)	T/M	L	S(L)	A	W	B(W)	B(P)	B
height of stand (m)	2	8	14	26	24	33	19	11	6	10
elevation (m)	550	542	563	76	64	25	36	53	188	263
slope (degrees)	5	23	21	12	11	0	1	6	1	9
Coptis aspleniifolia	II.2	II.2	V.3				I.+	II.+	IV.1	III.+
Tsuga mertensiana	IV.3	III.4	IV.3					II.1	III.2	II.2
Veratrum viride	II.+	I.x	III.1					IV.+		II.1
Moneses uniflora	I.+		III.1	I.+	I.x					
Streptopus streptopoides		I.+	III.+							
Tiarella trifoliata		I.x	IV.3	VI.1	III.+	4.x	IV.+			I.2
Vaccinium alaskaense			IV.3	III.1		3.2	III.x			
Tiarella laciniata			III.3	III.+	III.+	4.1	I.+			
Listera cordata	I.x	I.+	IV.1	III.+	II.+		I.+			
Polystichum munitum			I.+	I.x	V.3	4.x				
Picea sitchensis				I.x	V.3	3.x				
Festuca subulata						3.1				
Adiantum pedatum						3.x				
Aruncus dioicus						1.x				
Carex obnupta						2.+	V.2	II.x	I.x	
Lysichiton americanum				I.x		1.x	V.x	I.x		I.+
Alnus rubra						2.x	III.x			
Carex laeviculmis							III.x	I.x		
Pinus contorta	V.3	I.3		I.2			IV.2	V.2	V.2	V.3
Linnaea borealis	II.1	I.x	I.2				V.x	V.2	V.1	II.1
Lycopodium clavatum	II.+		II.1				II.x	V.1	IV.+	IV.1
Empetrum nigrum	IV.2		I.1					IV.2	V.3	V.2
Ledum groenlandicum								V.3	V.1	
Agrostis aequivalvis							I.x	V.1	II.x	
Trientalis arctica							I.x	IV.1	I.x	
Kalmia polifolia								II.+	V.+	
Carex phyllomanica							I.x	III.x	I.x	
Vaccinium uliginosum	III.2								IV.2	II.2
Cladothamnus pyroliflorus	III.2		I.2						I.2	III.2
Fauria crista-gallii	II.2		I.2						I.2	IV.2
Vaccinium caespitosum	III.1								III.1	II.1
Deschampsia caespitosa									V.+	III.2
Blechnum spicant	III.1	I.1	V.1	V.2	V.2	3.3	V.3	V.2	V.2	IV.3
Gaultheria shallon	V.3	II.4	IV.2	V.4	IV.3	3.4	V.4	V.3	V.2	V.2
Tsuga heterophylla	II.1	II.2	IV.2	V.3	V.2	4.4	V.2	V.3	V.2	V.2
Chamaecyparis nootkatensis	V.4	V.4	IV.4	II.2	I.+		V.2	V.2	III.1	V.3
Vaccinium parvifolium	II.2	II.2	IV.2	V.3	IV.+	4.2	V.2	V.2	V.3	III.2
Cornus unalaschkensis	V.2	IV.2	III.2	IV.1			V.1	V.2	III.+	III.2
Majanthemum dilatatum	III.1	IV.+	II.+	III.1	III.+	4.1	V.1	V.1	V.2	III.1
Thuja plicata	I.x	II.2	II.2	V.3	III.2	4.4	V.2	V.3	IV.+	IV.4
Menziesia ferruginea	I.2	II.2	IV.1	V.2	III.1	3.2	V.1	IV.2	I.+	III.1
Rhytidiadelphus loreus	II.4	II.x	IV.3	III.2	IV.2	3.1	V.3	V.2		I.3

Table 8.1 Continued

table section	1	2	3	4	5	6	7	8	9	10
number of sample plots	9	5	21	11	7	4	6	8	6	6
major (minor) physiognom. type[d]	K	T(K)	T/M	L	S(L)	A	W	B(W)	B(P)	B
height of stand (m)	2	8	14	26	24	33	19	11	6	10
elevation (m)	550	542	563	76	64	25	36	53	188	263
slope (degrees)	5	23	21	12	11	0	1	6	1	9
Calamagrostis nutkatensis	IV.2	II.x	III.2	II.1		1.x	III.x	V.3	V.2	IV.3
Hylocomium splendens	II.2	III.1	III.2	III.1	II.1	1.x	III.1	V.1		II.1
Abies amabilis	II.1	I.x	V.3	II.2	III.3	3.3				
Rubus pedatus	II.1	III.+	V.2	I.x			IV.x			
Plagiothecium undulatum			III.1	III.x	III.x	1.+	II.+		I.+	III.+
Rhizomnium glabrescens	II.+		III.+	III.x	III.x	2.2	II.+			II.+
Kindbergia oregana	I.x	I.x	I.1	III.1	V.4	3.3	III.+	II.1		I.+
Ligusticum calderi	I.+	I.x	III.2				II.+	I.1	I.x	IV.+
Rubus spectabilis		I.5	I.1	III.1	IV.2	4.3	III.x			I.1
Scapania bolanderi			III.2	I.+	I.x		I.1	III.+		I.2
Pellia neesiana		I.x	I.x	II.+	III.x	3.1	V.x	I.x		I.2
Phyllodoce empetriformis	III.x		II.1						V.2	IV.1
Vaccinium ovalifolium	II.1	III.2	II.3	II.2		1.1	I.2		I.1	
Cephalozia spp.			II.1	II.x	II.x	1.+	III.+	II.x		
Diplophyllum albicans		I.2	II.1	I.+	I.x	1.+	I.+	I.x		II.1
Sphagnum girgensohnii	I.x	I.x	II.2	II.x		1.2	III.x	II.x		I.1
Listera caurina	II.+	I.x	III.+	II.x	I.+		I.+			
Apargidium boreale								IV.+	V.+	III.1
Streptopus amplexifolius			II.1	I.+	I.+	2.x	IV.+			
Isothecium stoloniferum		I.1	II.+		III.1		I.1			I.2
Viola orbiculata/sempervirens		II.x	II.2	II.+		3.+	II.+			I.+
Calypogeia muelleri		I.+	I.+	II.x	II.x	1.+	II.+	I.r		
Taxus brevifolia				II.2			III.1	III.x	I.3	I.1
Habenaria saccata			I.+				I.x	V.x	II.+	III.+
Alnus sinuata	II.1	I.x	I.x	I.1				I.2	II.x	II.2
Sphagnum rubellum	I.x	I.x						V.2	III.1	I.x
Dicranum majus	I.2		I.1				II.+	III.1	II.2	
Gentiana douglasiana	II.1							II.1	III.+	IV.1
Sphagnum papillosum	I.x	I.x					III.x	II.x	III.1	
Plagiothecium asplenioides			II.+		I.1	2.1				
Huperzia selago	I.x		I.r	I.+		2.+		I.x		I.+
Herberta adunca		I.x	I.+				I.2	II.1	I.x	I.2
Dicranum scoparium			I.1				I.+	I.2		II.1
Mylia taylori			I.+	I.+			II.+	II.x		
Dryopteris assimilis			I.+	I.+	III.+					
Riccardia sp.			I.+	I.x	I.x		I.x	I.x		
Carex mertensiana		I.x	I.1			1.1		II.x		
Hypnum circinale			II.+		I.x					
Viola glabella			I.+			4.1				I.2
Drosera rotundifolia								II.+	II.+	I.+
Rhytidiadelphus triquetrus	I.x		I.+							I.x
Erigeron peregrinus	I.+							I.+	III.+	I.+
Cladonia mitis								IV.1	I.x	
Prenanthes alata		I.x	I.+			1.x				I.+
Bazzania sp.					II.x		I.x	II.+		
Pleurozia purpurea	I.1							I.2	III.2	
Habenaria hyperborea		I.x	I.r					I.x		
Scirpus caespitosus	I.4								II.+	II.2
Leucolepis menziesii			I.2	I.x	I.x	2.1				

a Presence classes I to V from 0 to 100% in 20% intervals.

b Braun-Blanquet cover/abundance scale: r = single or very few individuals, very low cover; + = few individuals, cover < 1%; 1 = 1-5%; 2 = 5-25%; 3 = 25-50%; 4 = 50-75%; 5 = 75-100%.

c Entries under section 6: Due to the low number of plots represented by this column, the first number is the number of actual occurrences instead of presence class.

d Physiognomic types: K = krummholz, T = timberline scrubforest, M = mountainslope forest, L = lowland forest, S = shoreline forest, A = alluvial floodplain forest, W = wet lowland forest, B = blanketbog scrubforest, P = peatbog scrubforest.

Lowland forests occur widely on the peninsula, however, not in large, continuous areas as is the case elsewhere on western Vancouver Island. This is because there are few suitable habitats under the extreme climatic and topographic conditions on Brooks Peninsula. The limiting circumstances are: (1) impeded drainage on gentle terrain, especially on the wet northwestern slope of the peninsula; (2) a small range in suitable elevations, commonly 0-100 m on the northwestern side and 0-300 m on the southeastern side of the peninsula; (3) little moderate terrain between the shorelines and the extremely steep mountain slopes; (4) few low-elevation valleys extending into the interior of the peninsula.

Three types of Lowland Forest may be distinguished: one on poorly drained sites of gentle, or nearly flat, terrain; one on moderate slopes (about 5°-15°); and one on well-drained, steep slopes. Tree height increases from under 20 m in the wet type, through 25 m to 30 m in the mesic type on moderate slopes, to over 35 m on steep slopes.

1.1.1 Wet Lowland Forest

Western redcedar is the predominant tree (Table 8.1). Virtually all older specimens show dead spike-tops. Western hemlock is equally common, but smaller and of very poor quality. Yellow cedar of medium size is scattered, and shore pine, red alder, and western yew occur occasionally. Amabilis fir is absent. The tree canopy is partly open and irregular.

The shrub layer is open, irregular, and restricted to slightly raised areas and mounds created by the upturned root bases of fallen trees. The three constant species are *Gaultheria shallon* (salal), *Menziesia ferruginea* (false azalea), and *Vaccinium parvifolium* (red huckleberry). Of these three, either *Gaultheria* or *Menziesia* may be dominant. *Vaccinium alaskaense* (Alaska blueberry) and *Rubus spectabilis* (salmonberry) occur, scattered, only in some sites.

The herb layer is dominated by *Blechnum spicant* (deer fern). Less common, but equally constant, are *Maianthemum dilatatum* (false lily-of-the-valley), *Cornus unalaschkensis* (bunchberry), and *Linnaea borealis* (twinflower). Important indicators of wet sites are *Carex obnupta* (slough sedge), *Lysichiton americanum* (skunk cabbage), *Carex laeviculmis* (smooth-stemmed sedge), and, occasionally, *Habenaria saccata* (swamp rein orchid); these occupy the frequent wet pockets and slight depressions.

Bryophytes occur in two microhabitats—raised areas and low, wet areas. *Rhytidiadelphus loreus* dominates the former, with associated *Hylocomium splendens*, *Kindbergia oregana*, *Bazzania denudata*, and *Mylia taylori*, whereas *Pellia neesiana*, *Sphagnum girgensohnii*, and *Riccardia* predominate in low, wet areas (moss and liverwort nomenclature follows Schofield, Chapter 6).

From the few examinations that were possible, it appears that the Wet Lowland Forest soils are mainly Orthic and Humic Gleysols, developed on marine and basal-till parent materials. Humic Folisols also occur.

1.1.2 Mesic Lowland Forest

This forest occupies better-drained sites than the Wet Lowland Forest and is dominated equally by western redcedar and western hemlock (Table 8.1). Western redcedar (Table 8.1) may attain large size, though it is represented by candelabra-type specimens that rarely exceed 30 m in height. Western hemlock growth is of poor quality. Yellow cedar, amabilis fir, and western yew occur infrequently.

The dense and tall shrub layer of this forest is dominated by *Gaultheria shallon*. *Menziesia ferruginea* and *Vaccinium parvifolium* are also frequent and vigorous, followed by *Vaccinium alaskaense*.

The dense shrub layer restricts the growth of the herb layer. *Blechnum spicant* is always most abundant, followed by *Cornus unalaschkensis*, *Maianthemum dilatatum*, *Tiarella trifoliata* (trifoliolate-leaved foam flower), *Tiarella laciniata* (cut-leaved foam flower), *Listera cordata* (heart-leaved twayblade), and *Listera caurina* (western twayblade). There is a species-poor variant in which the herb layer is composed solely of *Blechnum spicant*.

The bryophyte layer is often sparse, but when present, consists of the following species (in order of decreasing significance): *Rhytidiadelphus loreus*, *Kindbergia oregana*, *Plagiothecium undulatum*, *Rhizomnium glabrescens*, *Sphagnum girgensohnii*.

The soils are Gleyed Humo-Ferric and Ferro-Humic Podzols, developed mainly on till and on moderately well-drained marine and outwash parent materials.

1.1.3 Lowland Forest on Steep Slopes

This is the least uniform of the three Lowland Forest types. On stable soils and on poor rocky sites, the vegetation may be very similar to that of the Mesic Lowland Forest. Because of good drainage, amabilis fir and *Vaccinium alaskaense* play a greater role and western hemlock usually grows better (Table 8.1). On rich sites and young soils repeatedly disturbed by erosion and colluvial processes, the species composition may vary, with amabilis fir and *Polystichum munitum* (sword fern) dominant, or at least frequent. Some salt spray influence is indicated at these plots by the relatively high frequency of Sitka spruce. No detailed vegetation data are available from the very steep southwest-facing slopes (southeastwards from Cape Cook). On these slopes, which reach up to 350 m elevation, tree combinations are similar to Lowland Forest on Steep Slopes, but also contain Sitka spruce (Forest Inventory Division 1969). They are probably the highest upward extension of this type of lowland forest on Brooks Peninsula.

On steep slopes, relatively dense tree canopies make the shrub layer less vigorous as compared with the Mesic Lowland Forest, but the dominant species are generally the same. *Rubus spectabilis* is a more constant component on rich sites.

In the herb layer, *Polystichum munitum* and *Blechnum spicant* are most conspicuous, accompanied occasionally by *Dryopteris expansa* (spiny shield fern). A close relationship between Lowland Forest on Steep Slopes and Mountain Slope Forest is indicated by the presence of occasional montane components, such as *Moneses uniflora* (one-flowered wintergreen) and *Viola orbiculata* (evergreen yellow violet)[1].

The moss layer is similar to that of the Mesic Lowland Forest, but with greater proportions of *Kindbergia oregana*, *Plagiothecium undulatum*, *Rhizomnium glabrescens*, and *Scapania bolanderi*.

1.2 Shoreline Forest

Shoreline Forests form a narrow fringe along the entire coastline of Brooks Peninsula (Figure 8.4). The width of this fringe depends mainly on the reach of salt spray (Cordes 1972), which, in turn, is a function of coastline exposure to wind and waves. Thus, the band of Shoreline Forest is narrow along the protected shores of the indented coastline on the southeast side of the peninsula, whereas it reaches widths of 80 m to 300 m along the open west and northwest coasts.

Shoreline Forest is distinct, not only because the dominant tree species, Sitka spruce, rarely grows farther inland away from the salt spray zone, but also because the trees are taller than those

---

[1] Combined with *Viola sempervirens* in Table 8.1 because the two were difficult to differentiate in the field.

Figure 8.4 Shoreline Forest at Cape Cook Lagoon dominated by Sitka spruce (Photo: R.J. Hebda)

farther inland. Where a shoreline cliff or bluff occurs (a common feature on the peninsula), the better growth of Shoreline Forest—compared with forest vegetation farther inland—must be attributed to relatively better drainage. The species composition of the Shoreline Forest is simple: the tree layer is dominated by Sitka spruce with western hemlock the only regular associate (Table 8.1); western redcedar occurs occasionally. The dense shrub layer is dominated by vigorous *Gaultheria shallon*. *Rubus spectabilis* is always present as an associate. *Lonicera involucrata* (black twinberry) occurs, scattered, only in this forest type. In the herb layer, *Polystichum munitum* is prominent, with *Blechnum spicant*, *Maianthemum dilatatum*, *Tiarella trifoliata*, and *Tiarella laciniata* following in order of decreasing significance. The moss layer is similar to that of the Lowland Forest types, but *Kindbergia oregana* often predominates over *Rhytidiadephus loreus*.

Shoreline Forests occur on a wide variety of parent materials ranging from beach sands to small-scale floodplain deposits and colluvium. Soils range from Regosols to Dystric and Sombric Brunisols. For the species composition, soil variation may be less important than nutrient input by ocean spray.

1.3 Alluvial Forest

1.3.1 Alluvial Floodplain Forest

Except for the East Creek valley, which forms the eastern boundary of Brooks Peninsula, very few young floodplain deposits occur. Small pockets of alluvium are present in four drainages: Kingfisher, Menziesia, Amos, and Pyrola creeks. Though small, these sites have vegetation that contrasts sharply with that of surrounding areas.

The Alluvial Floodplain Forest is the most diverse forest type on Brooks Peninsula, both structurally and floristically. Physiognomic diversity is expressed by the presence of two or three distinct tree layers, two shrub layers, a comparatively luxuriant herb layer, and a rich moss layer.

The tall tree layer consists of Sitka spruce that reaches 40 m or more in height. The second tree layer contains, in order of dominance, western hemlock, western redcedar, and amabilis fir, and averages 30 m high. When present, the third, deciduous tree layer, consists of red alder and, occasionally, Pacific crabapple.

The upper shrub layer consists of *Rubus spectabilis* and the lower shrub layer contains, in order of dominance: *Gaultheria shallon*, *Vaccinium parvifolium*, *Vaccinium alaskaense*, and *Menziesia ferruginea*. *Ribes bracteosum* (stink currant) and *Oplopanax horridum* (devil's-club) occur occasionally.

In the herb layer, the more common species are *Polystichum munitum*, *Tiarella trifoliata*, *Tiarella laciniata*, *Viola glabella* (tall yellow violet), *Festuca subulata* (fescue), *Adiantum pedatum* (maidenhair fern), *Melica subulata* (melic grass), and *Galium triflorum* (three-flowered bedstraw). Less common, but also characteristic of alluvial sites, are *Stachys cooleyae* (hedge nettle), *Trautvetteria caroliniensis* (false bugbane), *Aruncus sylvester* (goat's beard), *Tolmiea menziesii* (youth on age), *Trisetum cernuum* (Trisetum grass), *Festuca subuliflora* (crinkle-awned fescue), and *Luzula parviflora* (small-flowered woodrush). Nearly all these species may be considered indicators of rich sites on Brooks Peninsula (compare to Klinka and Carter 1980 and Klinka et al. 1984).

The predominant bryophytes are *Leucolepis menziesii*, *Kindbergia oregana*, and *Rhytidiadelphus loreus* in well-drained microhabitats, and *Pellia neesiana* in poorly drained pockets. Also present and characteristic of alluvial sites, but less constant and dominant, are *Sphagnum squarrosum*, *Plagiochila porelloides*, and *Pogonatum alpinum*. *Plagiomnium insigne*, a characteristic moss of alluvial sites elsewhere on Vancouver Island, is absent.

Based on a few observations of soils in the Kingfisher Creek drainage, it appears that not only Regosols, but also gleyed Brunisols and Podzols occur. Presumably similar soils occur in the other drainage areas.

1.3.2 Alluvial Fringe Forest

On Brooks Peninsula, many of the small streams, and several of the large creeks have not formed alluvial floodplains. The banks of these watercourses show a number of species that are absent from the surrounding vegetation. On the peninsula, such alluvial fringe habitats exhibit a narrow band of tall trees because of good drainage on the banks and good nutrient supply in the running water. Where streams cross blanket-bog communities, the alluvial fringes would qualify as scrubforest vegetation on the basis of tree size. These were included with Alluvial Fringe Forest.

Diagnostic species are usually additions to, rather than replacements of, the usual species composition of the vegetation that is traversed by the streams. These species occur too erratically to allow a formal floristic definition of this community[2].

Alluvial Fringe Forest species include red alder and shrubs—*Rubus spectabilis*, *Vaccinium ovalifolium* (oval-leaved blueberry), and *Cladothamnus pyroliflorus* (copper bush)[3]. In the herb layer, *Boykinia elata* (Boykinia), *Viola glabella*, *Veratrum eschscholtzii* (false hellebore), *Prenanthes alata* (white lettuce), *Tolmiea menziesii*, *Arnica amplexicaulis* (clasping arnica), and *Dodecatheon jeffreyi* (Jeffrey's shooting star) often grow on rocks in streams along with several other wet habitat species, where light is sufficient.

---

2 Two samples of this forest type are included in Appendix 8.2, sections 7 and 10.

3 The last two are found mostly in a matrix of bog species.

1.4 Mountain Slope Forest

This category encompasses all forests on Brooks Peninsula that have trees taller than 8-12 m and occur on continuous slopes above the three previously described forest types. Mountain Slope Forests reach down to an elevation of 100 m and have been observed in small protected pockets as high as 700 m. The normal range is in the mid-elevations, between 200 m and 600 m. These forests grow on steep sites with colluvial materials and protected from strong, southeast winter storm winds. Apparent exceptions are the steep colluvial slopes facing the sea to the southeast and northeast of Cape Cook. These are covered with Shoreline and Lowland Forests.

Physiognomically, the Mountain Slope Forest is dense, relatively narrow-crowned, with a somewhat open, or absent, shrub layer, a moderately developed, species-rich herb layer, and a well-developed moss layer[4].

The predominant tree species in this forest are amabilis fir and western hemlock. Yellow cedar is not present in all stands and rarely assumes dominance. Based on the combination of species generally present, yellow cedar appears to grow mainly on poor sites. Western redcedar decreases and mountain hemlock increases with increased elevation and exposure to wind along the gradient from Lowland Forest through Mountain Slope Forest to Timberline Scrubforest.

The shrub layer is composed of about equal amounts of *Vaccinium alaskaense, Vaccinium parvifolium,* and *Gaultheria shallon. Menziesia ferruginea* is also present in most stands, but in small quantities.

In the herb layer, species that are always present are (in order of decreasing dominance): *Tiarella laciniata, Tiarella trifoliata, Coptis aspleniifolia* (goldthread), and *Blechnum spicant.* Also present in most stands, but usually with low cover, are: *Rubus pedatus* (five-leaved creeping raspberry), *Streptopus streptopoides* (small twistedstalk), *Moneses uniflora, Listera cordata, Veratrum eschscholtzii,* and *Listera caurina.*

The bryophyte layer is dominated by *Rhytidiadelphus loreus.* Other common species are *Rhizomnium glabrescens, Scapania bolanderi, Diplophyllum albicans, Plagiothecium undulatum, Isothecium stoloniferum* (mostly on rocks and tree bases), *Hylocomium splendens, Rhytidiadelphus triquetrus,* and *Plagiochila porelloides.*

The soils of the Mountain Slope Forest are Orthic Ferro-Humic and Humo-Ferric Podzols, developed on well- to moderately well-drained colluvial blankets and veneers. Organic surface horizons may be as thick as 30 cm.

This forest type covers a large portion of the mountainous terrain on Brooks Peninsula. It shows no sharp boundary with the Timberline Scrubforest, which is distinguished mainly by a shorter canopy. An area nearly as large as that ascribed to Mountain Slope Forest is occupied by stands that, according to tree size, could be classed either as forest or scrubforest.

2.0 Scrubforests

Criteria and Environmental Factors

Scrubforests include woody vegetation with tree species less than 8-12 m tall. They occur in sites where extreme climatic and edaphic conditions prevent normal tree development. Cross sections

---

[4] This description is based primarily on vegetation data and observations from the central ridge of Brooks Peninsula.

of tree stems from such sites indicate very slow growth rates, reaching extremes of, for example, 10 cm of trunk diameter in 400 years. The tree stems have very short internodes. On Brooks Peninsula, poor growth conditions are so common that stunted trees may be regarded as characteristic. It was estimated that about one-half of the tree vegetation on the peninsula occurs as scrub.

Five types of Scrubforest occur on Brooks Peninsula. Shoreline Scrubforest grows under the influence of salt spray and wind. Bog Scrubforest occupies lowland zones where growth is restricted by poor drainage and unfavourable soil properties. Timberline Scrubforest grows in the zone between Mountain Slope Forest and treeless vegetation of ridges where strong wind and relatively cool temperatures prevail. Krummholz is a very stunted derivative of Timberline Scrubforest, composed of trees stunted to prostrate shrub form by extreme wind. Slide Scrubforest occurs on unstable substrates in ravines and on very steep slopes. Composition of scrubforest vegetation types is presented in Table 8.1.

2.1 Shoreline Scrubforest

Extreme exposure to wind and salt spray produce a stunted and very dense "wind-sheared" growth of trees. Shoreline Scrubforest is particularly common on rocky headlands and is absent, or restricted to narrow bands, along sheltered beaches where Shoreline Forests occur. Landwards, Shoreline Scrubforests may grade into Lowland Forests or Bog Scrubforests.

The species forming this scrubby growth are essentially the same as in the Shoreline Forest. Sitka spruce always forms the outer edge of the stand, as it is the most tolerant of salt spray (Cordes 1972). Farther back, western hemlock or, less commonly, red alder, western redcedar, and Pacific crabapple, may occur.

The shrub layer consists of *Gaultheria shallon* and under moist conditions *Rubus spectabilis*. Shrub growth is extremely dense, particularly near the edges of stands. In the very shaded interior of the forest, shrubs may be nearly absent. The herb layer consists of *Maianthemum dilatatum* at, and near the edges, and of *Polystichum munitum* farther into the stand.

The soils are Folisols or Lithic Podzols with thick organic surface layers.

2.2 Bog Scrubforest

In this vegetation type, impeded drainage, restricted rooting-depth, and resultant low nutrient availability are the apparent reasons for stunted tree growth. Bog Scrubforest forms the link between the Wet Lowland Forest described previously and Bog Shrub vegetation where trees are absent, or small and scattered.

The most common image of the Bog Scrubforest is a 8-12 m tall, slender-stemmed, open forest with conspicuous shore pines and a partially open, low shrub layer (Figure 8.5). There is a diverse graminoid, fern, and low ericaceous cover and a diverse bryophyte and lichen layer. The trees, always present, include shore pine and yellow cedar. Western redcedar and western hemlock are also common, but frequently as depauperate specimens.

Gaultheria shallon is the only shrub that occurs commonly in all stands, even though it may not be dominant. Other shrubs are *Ledum groenlandicum*, *Vaccinium parvifolium*, and *Menziesia ferruginea*. *Phyllodoce empetriformis* (red mountain heather), *Vaccinium uliginosum* (bog blueberry), and *Kalmia polifolia* (western swamp kalmia) are less common. *Cladothamnus pyroliflorus* replaces *Ledum groenlandicum* where the surface peat is very thin.

Figure 8.5 Bog Scrubforest showing poor tree growth and open understory (Photo: R.J. Hebda)

The herb layer is dominated by a mixture of *Calamagrostis nutkaensis* (Pacific reed grass) and *Blechnum spicant*. Numerous other species, such as *Cornus unalaschkensis, Linnaea borealis, Empetrum nigrum* (crowberry), *Maianthemum dilatatum*, and *Lycopodium clavatum* (running club-moss), also grow in the herb stratum.

The bryophyte and lichen layer contains (in order of decreasing coverage): the mosses *Rhytidiadelphus loreus, Hylocomium splendens, Sphagnum rubellum, Sphagnum papillosum, Scapania bolanderi*, and *Dicranum majus*, and the lichens *Cladonia mitis* and *Cladonia impexa*.

Bog Scrubforests grow primarily on the gentle slopes in the lower third of Brooks Peninsula's north slope and parts of the south slope. Bog Scrubforests occur there in a mosaic pattern with bog shrubland and non-woody bog vegetation on slopes up to 8°.

Soils of the Bog Scrubforest habitat are Humic Gleysols, Orthic Gleysols, Gleyed Duric Ferro-Humic Podzols, and Folisols, all developed on till and some outwash parent materials. Rarely, Folisols occur on bedrock outcrops.

2.3 Timberline Scrubforest

This scrubforest normally occurs above the Mountain Slope Forest and below the treeless vegetation at 500-900 m elevation (Figure 8.6), but on exposed ridges it descends as low as 200 m. Probably, exposure to wind, combined with poor nutrients, poor soil drainage, and low temperature, shape this vegetation.

The overall appearance is that of a miniature forest with flattened, or umbrella-shaped crowns, a fragmentary shrub layer, and a well-developed herb layer.

Figure 8.6 The transition from Timberline Scrubforest to Krummholz on Senecio Ridge (Photo: R.J. Hebda)

The more common and dominant trees are mountain hemlock and yellow cedar. Amabilis fir occurs in about half of the stands and is occasionally dominant. Western hemlock is less common and is mainly confined to the shrub layer.

The shrub layer of the Timberline Scrubforest is neither uniform nor dense. *Gaultheria shallon* and *Menziesia ferruginea* are the most common dominants, but in some cases are replaced by *Vaccinium ovalifolium, V. parvifolium*, and *V. alaskaense*. The most conspicuous, and often dominant, species in the herb layer is *Calamagrostis nutkaensis*. Also very common are *Rubus pedatus* and *Cornus unalaschkensis*, followed by *Coptis aspleniifolia, Veratrum eschscholtzii, Ligusticum calderi* (Queen Charlotte lovage), *Blechnum spicant, Listera cordata, Linnaea borealis, Listera caurina*, and *Tiarella trifoliata*. The bryophyte layer is similar to that of the Mountain Slope Forest and is usually dominated by *Rhytidiadelphus loreus*.

The soils of the Timberline Scrubforest are bedrock-controlled and are developed on shallow and coarse rocky talus. The majority are classified as Lithic Ferro-Humic Podzols and Humic Folisols.

2.4 Krummholz

Krummholz[5] could be regarded as an extreme condition of Timberline Scrubforest. It represents the farthest advance of tree species towards the wind-exposed ridges of Brooks Peninsula. On Brooks Peninsula, Krummholz is positioned between Timberline Scrubforest and sparsely

[5] A German word meaning "crooked wood", "krummholz" designates prostrate, gnarled trees at timberline.

vegetated, deflated stone fields, between Timberline Scrubforest and Alpine Heath, and between Timberline Scrubforest and Alpine Meadow Vegetation. With regard to its low growth (.5 m to 2 m), this vegetation could have been treated as Shrub Vegetation, but the tree species composition places it in a continuum with Timberline Scrubforest.

The physiognomy of Krummholz is characterized by extremely gnarled, contorted mountain hemlocks, yellow cedars, and shore pines (Figure 8.7), which often creep along the ground for 5 m to 6 m without rising more than 1 m. These very old trees attain diameters of 30 cm to 40 cm at their bases. Trees have been shaped into streamlined forms snaking away from the southeasterly gales. In larger areas with similar exposures, they form impenetrable, dense mats that tend to level out irregularities of the ground surface. Branch layering is uncommon at the margins of Krummholz stands.

Figure 8.7 Krummholz shore pine and mountain hemlock on Senecio Ridge (Photo: R.J. Hebda)

In addition to the tree species previously mentioned, many shrubs occur, including: *Gaultheria shallon*, *Vaccinium ovalifolium*, *Cladothamnus pyroliforus*, *Vaccinium uliginosum*, *Phyllodoce empetriformis*, *Vaccinium caespitosum* (dwarf blueberry), and *Empetrum nigrum*. These shrubs and herbs grow only where the cover of large woody plants is irregular, where rocks protrude, and near the margins of the stands. Typical herbs include *Cornus unalaschkensis*, *Coptis aspleniifolia*, *Calamagrostis nutkaensis*, *Blechnum spicant*, *Rubus pedatus*, *Maianthemum dilatatum*, *Linnaea borealis*, *Listera cordata*, and *Lycopodium clavatum*. The moss layer consists mainly of *Hylocomium splendens* and *Rhytidiadelphus loreus*.

The soils are Lithic Ferro-Humic and Humo-Ferric Podzols.

2.5 Slide Scrubforest

Slide Scrubforests on Brooks Peninsula are deciduous stands of alder (Figure 8.8) that occupy chronically unstable sites and sites recently affected by catastrophic mass movements. There is little evidence that snow avalanches are a factor in their maintenance. These scrubforests occur primarily in steep, narrow ravines, at all elevations.

Figure 8.8 Pioneering stands of *Alnus sinuata* on recent slide debris in Moneses Lake valley (Photo: R.J. Hebda)

Both *Alnus rubra* and *Alnus sinuata* (Sitka mountain alder) stands have been observed, the former prevailing at low elevations and the latter at high elevations. Where *Alnus rubra* communities occur on older, now stable deposits of colluvium, tree heights may exceed the limits of scrubforests. The structure and species composition of the Slide Scrubforests grade into the Alluvial Floodplain Forest.

The vegetation of Slide Scrubforests shows great variation, because of diverse parent materials, such as loose talus, mud, and soil slide debris, variable exposure of bedrock, and the presence or absence of surface and subsurface water. Of the three stands observed, two had an *Alnus rubra-Rubus spectabilis-Polystichum munitum* combination, and one had an *Alnus sinuata-Calamagrostis nutkaensis-Rhytidiadelphus loreus* (moss) combination, with *Polystichum* and *Elymus hirsutus* (nodding rye grass).

The soils of Slide Scrubforests have not been examined in detail, but it may be assumed that a variety of Regosols and incipient Brunisols predominate.

3.0 Shrub Vegetation

Criteria and Environmental Factors

Shrub Vegetation includes plant communities dominated by shrubs or shrublike trees without single trunks. Generally, the vegetation is less than 2 m high. Many vegetation types, shaped by different ecological factors, fall into this category. Beach Shrub occurs in a narrow zone between the forest margin and the beach, on immature soils and under the influence of salt spray and strong wind. Bog Shrub occupies poorly drained lowland areas between Bog Scrubforest and Bog Herbaceous Vegetation or Aquatic Herbaceous Vegetation communities. Slide Shrub has developed on recently deposited or unstable landslide surfaces and is of limited extent. Alpine Heath occurs on the high mountain slopes and ridge crests often adjacent to Timberline Scrubforest, Krummholz, or alpine herbaceous communities. Extreme wind is probably the most important ecological factor in shaping this vegetation, though low temperatures and associated freeze-thaw cycles also play a role.

3.1 Beach Shrub

Beach Shrub vegetation forms a dense, often impenetrable, hedge, about .5-2 m high, between the Shoreline Forest and Beach Herbaceous Vegetation of the upper drift-log zone (Figure 8.9). Only a few shrub species, and even fewer herb species, comprise the vegetation (Table 8.2). The shrubs include *Gaultheria shallon*, *Rubus parviflorus* (thimbleberry), *Rubus spectabilis*, and *Lonicera involucrata* (twinberry honeysuckle). The few herbs that occur occasionally under the shrubs are *Maianthemum dilatatum* and *Vicia gigantea* (giant vetch). Growing at the edge of the shrub hedge, but usually not within it, are *Conioselinum pacificum* (Pacific hemlock parsley), *Heracleum lanatum* (common cow-parsnip), *Aster subspicatus* (Douglas' aster), *Campanula rotundifolia* (common harebell), and *Ranunculus uncinatus* (little-flowered buttercup).

3.2 Bog Shrub

Impeded drainage, occasionally associated with surface flow, erosion, and creep, shape this vegetation type. Lowland areas between Wet Lowland Forest or Bog Scrubforest and Bog

Figure 8.9 Beach Shrub vegetation at Cape Cook Lagoon (Photo: R.J. Hebda)

Table 8.2 Vascular plant cover[a] in sample relevés from Beach Shrub Vegetation

Plot No.	1	2	3	4	5	6
Gaultheria shallon	5	5	3	5-6	5	x
Rubus parviflorus	2	3	-	1	-	x
Rubus spectabilis	1	-	-	2	2	x
Lonicera involucrata	3	-	3	1	-	x
Rosa nutkana	-	2	-	-	+	-
Pyrus fusca	5	-	5	-	-	-
Ribes divaricatum	-	3	-	-	-	x
Salix hookeriana	-	-	-	3	-	-
Vicia gigantea	2	2	-	+	-	-
Maianthemum dilatatum	1	-	-	1	1	x
Galium triflorum	-	2	-	-	-	x
Elymus mollis	-	2	-	-	2	-
Heracleum lanatum	-	2	-	-	-	x
Stachys palustris	-	2	-	-	-	-
Polystichum munitum	1	-	-	-	1	-
Calamagrostis nutkaensis	-	-	-	2	1	x

Species with low constancy: *Athyrium filix-femina* (Plot 4: r)
Plot 5 *Pteridium aquilinum*: 2, *Lathyrus japonicus*: 1
Plot 6: x - *Aquilegia formosa, Deschampsia cespitosa*
Conioselinum pacificum, Prunella vulgaris, Fritillaria camschatcensis, Aster subspicatus, Campanula rotundifolia, Luzula campestris, Prenanthes alata, Aruncus sylvestris, Ranunculus uncinatus

[a] Cover estimates according to Braun-Blanquet scale, see Appendix 8.1. No quantitative estimates were made in plot 6, hence occurrence of species denoted by "x".

Herbaceous Vegetation provide the setting for the growth of Bog Shrub. Only seven stands of this vegetation were studied, yet two subcategories and intermediate types between them are evident: (1) communities dominated by cedars; (2) communities dominated by *Myrica gale* (sweet gale).

Bog Shrub most commonly appears as a knee-to-waist-high mosaic of mixed thickets of western redcedar, yellow cedar, and shore pine above a complex mosaic of ericaceous species, grasses, sedges, herbs, and bryophytes (Table 8.3). A less common community, dominated by *Myrica gale*, occurs in microalluvial sites (patches measuring only a few meters across) in boggy terrain. In these settings, there is occasional sheet or channelled flow and associated erosion and deposition of mineral and organic sediments.

In the typical yellow cedar-western redcedar Bog Shrub community, cedar and pine cover more than 50% of the ground with a dense tangle of branches. Shore pine occasionally rises to scrub-tree height, above the shrub layer. Scattered *Alnus sinuata* plants are evident, but they cover very little of the area. Western hemlock and mountain hemlock, which normally occur in adjacent Bog Scrubforests, are absent. Characteristic ericaceous shrubs, in order of decreasing abundance and cover, are: *Empetrum nigrum*, which forms patches of a low heath mat; *Kalmia polifolia* and *Ledum groenlandicum*, stems of which intermingle with cedar shrubs; and, less frequently, *Gaultheria shallon, Vaccinium uliginosum*, and *Vaccinium caespitosum. Myrica gale* and *Juniperus communis*

Table 8.3 Vascular plant cover[a] in relevés from Bog Shrub and Bog Herbaceous Vegetation

	Shrub								Herbaceaous		
Plot No.	1	2	3	4	5	6	7	8	9	10	11
Trees & Shrubs											
Chamaecyparis nootkatensis	3	3	3	2	2	2	+	-	+	2	-
Thuja plicata	2	2	3	2	2	-	-	+	+	-	-
Pinus contorta	2	2	2	2	1	2	-	-	+	-	-
Tsuga heterophylla	-	-	-	-	1	-	-	-	+	-	-
Alnus sinuata	+	+	-	+	-	-	-	-	-	-	-
Empetrum nigrum	2	2	2	2	1	1	1	+	+	-	-
Ledum groenlandicum	1	2	+	+	2	2	-	1	+	-	+
Kalmia polifolia	2	3	+	2	+	1	-	1	1	-	+
Gaultheria shallon	2	2	+	-	1	-	-	-	-	-	+
Vaccinium uliginosum	1	+	2	1	1	1	-	+	+	-	+
Vaccinium caespitosum	1	1	+	1	-	-	-	+	-	-	-
Vaccinium oxycoccus	1	1	-	1	-	1	-	-	-	-	+
Myrica gale	-	-	3	3	2	-	4	4	2	-	2
Juniperus communis	-	-	+	2	1	-	2	3	2	-	1
Loiseleuria procumbens	-	-	-	1	-	-	-	-	+	-	-
Andromeda polifolia	-	-	-	+	-	+	-	+	1	-	-
Vaccinium ovalifolium	-	-	-	-	-	-	-	1	-	-	-
Herbs											
Deschampsia cespitosa	2	2	1	2	1	-	3	2	+	3	1
Eriophorum angustifolium	1	1	2	2	2	3	+	+	-	2	-
Cornus unalaschkensis	2	2	-	2	+	-	-	+	-	-	-
Linnaea borealis	2	2	-	+	1	+	-	+	-	-	-
Apargidium boreale	1	1	-	1	-	2	1	+	-	-	-
Rhynchospora alba	+	+	2	2	1	-	2	+	2	-	1
Scirpus caespitosus	+	+	2	2	1	-	-	2	1	-	2
Dodecatheon jeffreyi	+	+	-	2	1	-	2	2	1	-	1
Drosera rotundifolia	1	1	+	1	1	1	-	+	1	-	+
Calamagrostis nutkaensis	1	1	-	1	+	-	-	+	-	-	-
Sanguisorba occidentalis	-	-	1	2	1	-	-	1	1	-	1
Selaginella selaginoides	-	+	-	-	-	+	-	+	-	-	-
Trientalis arctica	+	+	-	-	-	+	-	+	+	-	-
Caltha biflora	-	-	-	-	-	-	-	-	-	1	-
Aster foliaceus/subspicatus	-	-	-	-	1	-	-	-	-	-	1
Camassia quamash	-	-	-	+	-	-	2	-	-	-	-
Carex viridula	?	2	-	-	-	-	-	-	-	-	-
Carex pauciflora	-	-	+	-	-	-	-	-	-	-	-
Coptis aspleniifolia	-	-	-	+	1	+	-	-	+	-	-

[a] Cover values according to modified Braun-Blanquet scale (Appendix 8.1) where categories "r" and "+" are combined as "+".

Table 8.3 Continued

	Shrub								Herbaceous		
Plot No.	1	2	3	4	5	6	7	8	9	10	11
Danthonia spicata	-	-	-	-	-	-	-	2	3	-	-
Erigeron peregrinus	-	-	-	+	-	-	-	-	-	-	+
Equisetum sp.	-	-	-	-	+	-	-	-	-	-	-
Faura crista-galli	-	-	-	1	-	-	1	-	+	2	-
Geum calthifolium	-	-	-	+	-	-	-	-	-	-	-
Juncus cf. effusus	-	-	-	-	-	-	-	1	-	-	+
Juncus oreganus	-	+	-	-	-	-	-	-	-	-	-
Lycopodium clavatum	-	1	-	-	-	-	-	-	-	+	-
Prunella vulgaris	-	+	-	-	-	-	-	-	-	-	+
Pinguicula vulgaris	-	-	-	+	-	-	+	-	+	-	+
Panicum occidentale	-	-	+	-	-	-	-	-	-	-	-
Drosera anglica	-	-	-	-	-	-	-	-	+	-	-
Juncus sp.	-	-	-	-	-	-	-	-	1	-	-
Carex spp.	-	-	-	-	-	-	-	-	-	2	-

(common juniper) may be closely associated with cedar thickets. Typically, the two occur together and *Myrica* is notably dominant.

Herbaceous and graminoid species are numerous, covering about 30-50% of the ground in both cedar-dominated and *Myrica*-dominated thickets. *Deschampsia cespitosa* (tufted hair grass) is characteristic and abundant in both Bog Shrub subcategories. *Eriophorum angustifolium* (narrow-leaved cotton-grass) occurs in both types, but does not comprise extensive cover in *Myrica*-dominated thickets. Four other species regularly occur in Bog Shrub: *Dodecatheon jeffreyi, Drosera rotundifolia* (round-leaved sundew), *Rhynchospora alba* (white-topped beak-rush), and *Scirpus cespitosus* (tufted deer-grass). *Dodecatheon, Rhynchospora,* and *Scirpus* are characteristically associated with *Myrica* and *Juniperus*. *Calamagrostis nutkaensis, Cornus unalaschkensis,* and *Linnaea borealis* are characteristic of cedar-dominated thickets.

Many other herbaceous species also occur (Table 8.3), notably *Carex livida* (pale sedge), *Apargidium boreale* (apargidium), *Gentiana douglasiana* (swamp gentian), and *Tofieldia glutinosa* (sticky false asphodel) (Table 8.3). Two species, *Sanguisorba officinalis* (great burnet)—which occurs in significant quantities—and *Ligusticum calderi*, appear to be associated only with the *Myrica*-dominated phase.

Bryophyte cover varies considerably, being shaped by microtopographic features including hummocks, pools, and streamlets. Predominant mosses, which form hummocks, include *Sphagnum* spp. and *Racomitrium lanuginosum*. Although *Sphagnum* spp. were not always clearly distinguished in the field, it is apparent that several species are involved. *Sphagnum capillifolium, S. recurvum, S. compactum,* and *S. fuscum* all form significant patches. Other characteristic, though less abundant, bryophytes include *Pleurozia purpurea* and *Dicranum* spp. The lichen *Cladonia mitis* occurs frequently and abundantly in Bog Shrub vegetation.

A Terric Humisol soil is described by Maxwell (see Chapter 4) for Bog Shrub.

3.3 Alpine Heath

Above timberline, Alpine Heath vegetation prevails. These heath communities occur on mesic, well-drained ridges and upper mountain slopes. Alpine Heath usually adjoins Mesic Meadows, but may occur adjacent to Krummholz and Timberline Scrubforest. Alpine Heath appears as a nearly continuous carpet of dwarf shrubs 5-20 cm tall.

Important factors controlling heath communities are wind and cool temperatures. Strong winds buffet high ridges, and severely limit tree and tall-shrub growth. Along Senecio Ridge, Alpine Heath usually persists only in northwest-facing sites in the lee of rocks (Figure 8.3).

The dominant heath species are *Empetrum nigrum, Vaccinium uliginosum, Phyllodoce empetriformis,* and *Vaccinium caespitosum* (Table 8.4). Other heath species occur occasionally, covering small areas. These include *Cassiope mertensiana* (Merten's cassiope), *C. stelleriana* (Steller's cassiope), and *Loiseleuria procumbens* (alpine-azalea). The common herbaceous species are *Erigeron peregrinus* (subalpine fleabane), *Luetkea pectinata* (luetkea), and *Calamagrostis purpurascens* ssp. *tasuensis* (purple small reed grass). Less common herbaceous species include *Ligusticum calderi* and *Lupinus nootkatensis* (Nootka lupine).

3.4 Slide Shrub

Landslide habitats covered by shrubs are uncommon on Brooks Peninsula. One Slide Shrub stand was covered by shrubby *Alnus sinuata* under which grew a sparse herb layer of *Calamagrostis nutkaensis, Polystichum munitum,* and *Elymus hirsutus* (hairy wild rye grass), and the moss *Rhytidiadelphus loreus.*

4.0 Herbaceous Vegetation

Criteria and Environmental Factors

The Herbaceous Vegetation category includes a wide range of types, all dominated by non-woody species. Herbaceous Vegetation occurs in response to many ecological factors. Along the ocean shore, Herbaceous Vegetation communities occupy beaches, salt marshes, and rock headlands. Beach Herbaceous Vegetation covers unstable sand, pebble, cobble, or rocky shorelines subject to salt spray and occasional inundation and erosion.

Salt Marsh communities occupy protected embayments subject to regular inundation by salty, tidal water. Shore Headland Vegetation occurs along much of the coast, where rock outcrops predominate. Salt spray and strong wind influence the composition and structure of these plant communities.

The degree of inundation and substrate saturation by fresh water shape Bog Herbaceous Vegetation, Freshwater Marsh, and Herbaceous Aquatic Vegetation. Bog Herbaceous communities generally occupy the wettest and the most actively eroding zones in boggy lowlands. Freshwater Marsh vegetation occupies areas of standing water with fluctuating water tables, whereas Herbaceous Aquatic Vegetation, in part, is permanently submerged in pools and lake-margins.

Shallow soils and the exposed settings of rock outcrops restrict nutrient and substrate availability and confine the plant community of such sites to tenacious herbaceous species, the Rock Knoll and Cliff vegetation types.

The last two Herbaceous Vegetation types, Alpine Meadow Vegetation and Windblown Ridge Herb, occur on the high ridges of Brooks Peninsula. These sites are exposed to extremely strong winds, and probably also to frost action. They extend along the high ridges and peaks. Sample plots of selected herbaceous vegetation types are presented in Tables 8.5, 8.6, 8.7, 8.8, 8.9, 8.10, 8.11, 8.12.

Table 8.4 Vascular plant cover in relevés from Alpine Heath Vegetation

Elevation	700	608	600	790	550	640	792	730	550	600	550	790	579	470	427	600	580	600	600
Slope[a]	g	m	g	g	m	f	g	g	g	m	g	f	g	g	g	g	g	g	g
Aspect	–	ENE	–	SW	E	–	–	f	–	NNE	–	–	S	W	–	ENE	–	–	–
Stand Type	AH	AH	AH	AH	AH	AH	AH	AH	AH	AH	AH	AH	AH	AH	AH	AH	AH	AH	AH
Substrate	s	r	r	r	r	r	r	s	r	–	r	s	s	r	r	r	r	r	r
Analyst/Plot No.	091	092	093	094	095	096	097	098	H91	099	0911	R91	0912	0913	R92	R93	R924	H92	H93
Empetrum nigrum	1	2	3	2	3	2	2	5	2	2	x	x	2	x	x	2	x	3	2
Vaccinium uliginosum	3	3	1	2	2	3	2	3	1	2	x	-	3	-	x	2	x	1	1
Phyllodoce empetriformis	3	3	2	2	1	4	-	2	3	3	x	-	-	-	x	1	x	2	2
Luetkea pectinata	3	2	2	2	1	2	3	-	1	1	x	x	2	x	x	1	x	-	+
Erigeron peregrinus	1	2	1	1	+	2	2	3	1	2	x	-	1	-	-	1	x	+	1
Vaccinium caespitosum	1	-	1	1	1	1	3	3	-	1	x	x	3	-	x	-	x	-	-
Ligusticum calderi	1	+	1	1	-	1	1	4	1	+	x	x	-	x	x	1	-	-	+
Calamagrostis purpurascens	1	2	2	1	+	-	2	4	+	+	-	-	-	x	x	-	-	-	+
Deschampsia cespitosa	-	4	2	2	+	-	3	1	-	4	-	-	-	x	x	2	-	-	-
Lupinus nootkatensis	2	-	+	1	-	1	2	4	1	-	x	x	-	-	-	-	-	-	1
Cornus unalaschkensis	+	-	+	-	1	1	-	3	2	-	x	x	-	-	-	-	-	1	2
Loiseleuria procumbens	-	1	2	-	2	1	-	-	+	1	-	-	+	-	x	2	-	-	+
Geum calthifolium	+	1	-	-	-	1	-	-	1	1	x	-	-	x	x	2	x	-	1
Gentiana platypetala	+	-	r	+	-	+	1	+	1	-	x	-	-	-	x	-	x	-	1
Lycopodium clavatum	-	-	-	-	+	1	-	-	1	r	x	-	1	-	-	1	x	-	+
Carex circinata	-	-	2	2	+	1	1	-	-	-	-	-	1	-	x	-	-	-	-
Agrostis aequivalvis	-	2	-	-	-	-	-	-	1	2	x	-	-	-	-	1	x	-	+
Calamagrostis nutkaensis	4	-	-	-	-	3	-	-	-	-	x	x	3	-	-	-	-	-	-
Campanula rotundifolia	-	-	r	+	-	+	-	-	-	-	-	-	1	-	x	-	x	-	-
Habenaria chorisiana	-	+	-	-	-	-	-	-	+	+	x	-	-	-	x	-	-	-	+
Apargidium boreale	-	-	-	-	-	+	-	-	-	3	x	-	-	-	-	1	-	-	+
Fauria crista-galli	-	2	-	-	-	2	-	-	-	2	-	-	-	-	-	3	-	-	-
Cassiope mertensiana	-	1	-	-	-	2	-	-	-	1	x	-	-	-	-	-	-	-	-
Dodecatheon jeffreyi	-	1	-	-	-	+	-	-	-	+	-	-	-	-	-	1	-	-	-
Danthonia intermedia	-	-	-	-	+	1	-	-	-	-	x	-	1	-	-	-	-	-	-
Pedicularis ornithorhyncha	-	-	-	-	-	+	-	-	1	-	x	-	-	-	-	-	-	-	+
Lycopodium sitchensis	-	-	r	+	-	1	-	-	-	-	x	-	-	-	-	-	-	-	-
Cassiope stelleriana	-	-	-	-	-	2	-	-	-	-	x	-	-	-	-	-	-	1	-
Alnus crispa	r	-	-	-	-	-	-	-	+	-	-	-	-	-	-	-	-	-	+
Pinguicula vulgaris	-	-	-	-	-	-	-	-	+	-	x	-	-	-	x	-	-	-	+
Cladothamnus pyroliflorus	-	-	-	-	-	-	-	-	-	r	-	-	1	-	-	-	x	1	-

Species with low constancy - *Alnus crispa* (091: r, H91: +, H93: +); *Penstemon davidsonii* (096: 1, 0912: +); *Solidago multiradiata* (093: +, 094: +, 0912: 1); *Gentiana douglasiana* (096: 1, 0911: x, R93: 1); *Arctostaphylos uva-ursi* (094: 1): *Anemone narcissiflora* (093: +); *Scirpus cespitosus* (096: +, R93: 1); *Luzula campestris* (091: 1); *Linnaea borealis* (096: +, 0911: x, R91: x); *Rubus pedatus* (098: +, R91: x); *Trientalis arcticus* (098: +, R91: x, 0912: +), *Tofieldia glutinosa* (H91: +, 0911: x, H93: +); *Carex anthoxanthea* (099: 2); *Selaginella selaginoides* (099: +); *Coptis aspleniifolia* (0911: x, R91: x); *Anaphalis margaritacea* (0912: 2); *Viola biflora* (0912: +, R92: x); *Agrostis scabra* (0912: 1, R924: x); *Hieracium gracile* (0912: +); *Senecio moresbiensis* (0913: x, R92: x); *Clintonia uniflora* (R924: x); *Trisetum spicatum* (R924: x); *Lloydia serotina* (R924: x).

[a] See Appendix 8.1 for abbreviations.

4.1 Beach Herbaceous Vegetation

The beaches of Brooks Peninsula support herbaceous plant communities that occupy sand, gravel, and boulder substrates, or log debris along the shore. Herbaceous communities are confined usually to a narrow zone between Beach Shrub vegetation and the surf. However, extensive herb-dominated patches occur on the emergent parts of spits at the mouths of streams and embayments. Sample plots of Beach Herbaceous Vegetation are presented in Table 8.5.

Table 8.5 Vascular plant cover[a] in relevés from Beach Herbaceous Vegetation

Plot No.	1	2	3	4	5	6	7	8	9
Cakile edentula	-	x	r	2	-	-	-	-	-
Cakile maritima	-	x	r	1-2	-	-	-	-	-
Ambrosia chamissonis	-	x	r	2	-	+	x	-	-
Elymus mollis	x	x	-	1	5	3	-	5	3
Ammophila arenaria	x	-	-	-	-	-	-	-	-
Poa macrantha	x	-	1	-	-	-	-	-	-
Glehnia littoralis	x	-	+	-	-	+	-	-	-
Carex macrocephala	x	-	1	-	-	-	-	-	-
Arabis hirsuta	x	-	+	-	-	-	-	-	-
Abronia latifolia	-	-	2-3	-	-	-	-	-	-
Barbarea orthoceras	-	-	+	-	-	-	-	-	-
Achillea millefolium	x	-	+	-	-	-	-	-	2
Anaphalis margaritacea	-	-	+	-	-	-	-	-	+
Pteridium aquilinum	-	-	+	-	-	-	x	-	-
Rumex transitorius	-	-	r	-	-	-	-	-	-
Heracleum lanatum	-	-	-	+	-	-	-	3	-
Bromus sitchensis	-	-	-	-	2	-	-	-	2
Elymus hirsutus	-	-	-	-	1	-	-	-	-
Aster subspicatus	-	-	-	-	3	-	-	-	2
Galium triflorum	-	-	-	-	2	-	-	-	-
Mentha arvensis	-	-	-	-	2	-	-	-	1
Juncus leseurii	-	-	-	-	-	3	-	-	1
Festuca rubra	-	-	-	-	-	-	x	-	3

Species with low constancy: *Vicia gigantea, Ranunculus uncinatus, Stachys cooleyae, Calamagrostis nutkaensis* (Plot 7: x); Plot 8: *Angelica lucida*: 3; *Conioselinum pacificum*: 3; *Scrophularia californica*: 2; Plot 9: *Fragaria chiloensis*: 3; *Potentilla pacifica*: 2; *Prunella vulgaris*: +; *Sisyrinchium angustifolium*: 1; *Rhytidiadelphus triquetrus*: 5; *Gaultheria shallon*: 1; *Rubus parviflorus*: 1.

[a] Cover values according to Braun-Blanquet Scale, see Appendix 8.1. No quantitative estimates were made in plots 1, 2, and 7, hence occurrence of species denoted by "x".

Unstable sands of the lower beach zone are sparsely vegetated with *Cakile edentula* (searocket), *C. maritima* (European searocket), *Poa macrantha* (seashore bluegrass), *Glehnia littoralis* (American glehnia), *Ambrosia chamissonis* (sand-bar ragweed), *Arabis hirsuta* (hairy rock cress), and *Carex macrocephala* (big headed sedge). Colonies of *Elymus mollis* (dune wild rye grass) and *Ammophila arenaria* (European beachgrass) induce sand stabilization, and other species, such as *Achillea millefolium* (yarrow), *Aster subspicatus, Bromus sitchensis* (Alaska brome grass) and *Elymus hirsutus,* often accompany these two grasses. These plants thrive in areas such as the mouth of Cape Cook Lagoon where sand has been whipped into dunes. The upper beach drift-log zone consists, in order of decreasing coverage, of *Elymus mollis, Stachys cooleyae, S. mexicana* (Mexican hedge-nettle), *Artemisia suksdorfii* (Suksdorf's mugwort), *Scrophularia californica* (California figwort), *Conioselinum pacificum, Vicia gigantea, Ranunculus uncinatus, Galium aparine* (common cleavers), *Calamagrostis nutkaensis,* and *Prenanthes alata.*

At Quineex Indian Reserve 8, recent human disturbance has allowed Beach Herbaceous species and adventives to grow in openings among Sitka spruces (Figure 8.10). Native species, *Heracleum lanatum* (common cow-parsnip), *Stachys* sp., *Scrophularia californica,* and *Cirsium brevistylum* (short-styled thistle), dominate the herb stratum in this setting. Adventive species include the sow thistles *Sonchus asper* and *Sonchus oleraceus,* and *Phleum pratense* (common timothy grass). Several other introduced species persist in the area, notable among them *Lychnis coronaria* (rose campion), which clings to a rock outcrop. The native forest and beach vegetation largely exclude adventive species. The infrequent and presumed short duration of recent human occupancy would have provided little occasion for weeds to arrive and little chance for them to become established.

4.2 Salt Marsh

Salt Marsh vegetation consists of meadows growing on or near estuaries that are subjected to tidal flooding by saline and brackish water. The most extensive salt marsh on Brooks Peninsula has developed at the mouth of Kingfisher Creek in Cape Cook Lagoon and along the shores of the lagoon (Figure 8.11).

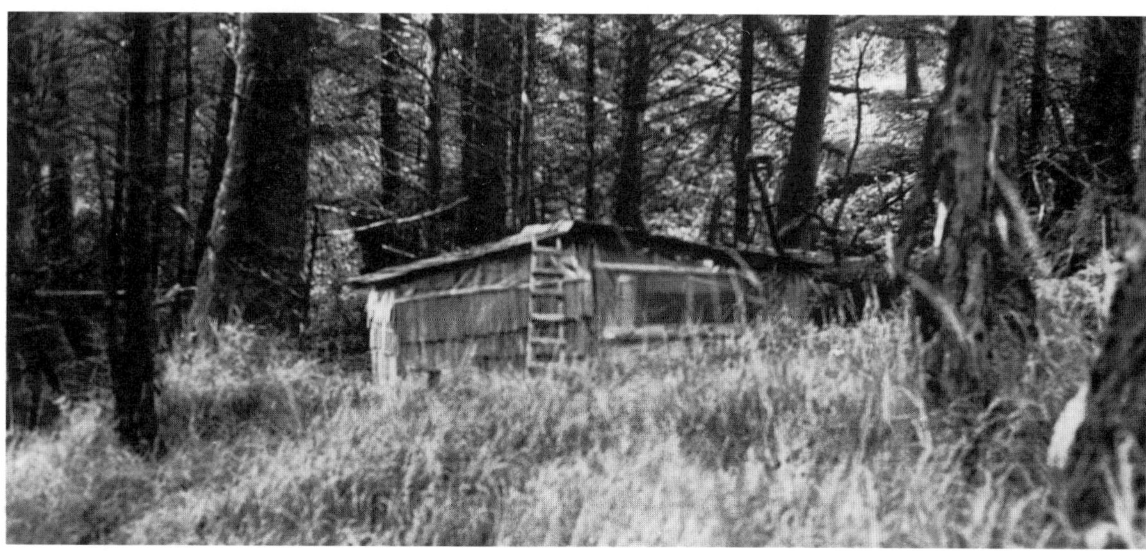

Figure 8.10 Adventive and native species growing in open disturbed Shoreline Forest near Quineex Indian Reserve 8 (Photo: R.J. Hebda)

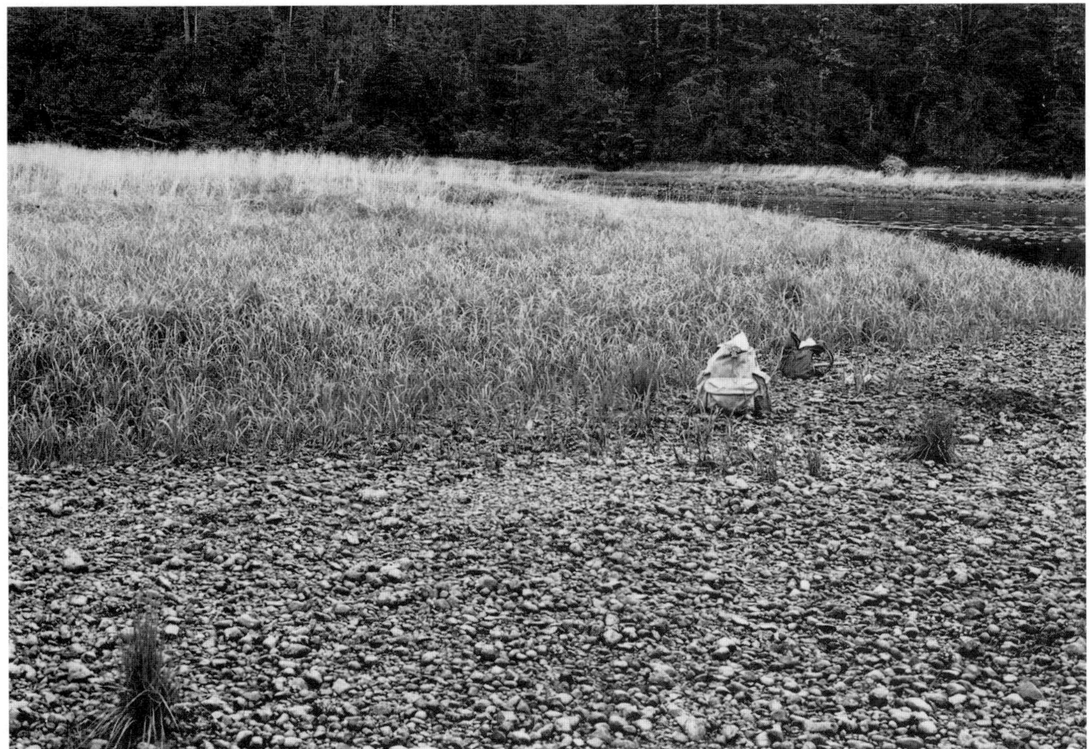

Figure 8.11 Salt Marsh vegetation in Kingfisher Creek estuary (Photo: R.J. Hebda)

Deschampsia cespitosa is the major species in this vegetation (Table 8.6). Other common species are *Potentilla pacifica* (Pacific silverweed), *Plantago maritima* (sea plantain), and *Carex lyngbyei* (Lyngbye's sedge). Among the widespread Pacific halophytes (salt-adapted plants), are: *Puccinellia nutkaensis* (Nootka alkali grass), *P. pumila* (dwarf alkali grass), *Glaux maritima* (sea milkwort), *Fucus* spp. (brown alga), *Lilaeopsis occidentalis* (western lilaeopsis), *Triglochin maritimum* (sea-side arrow-grass), and *Plantago macrocarpa* (Alaska plantain). In the upper parts of the estuaries, which have fresh-to-brackish waters, several upland herbs occur (Figure 8.12), including *Aster subspicatus, Achillea millefolium, Festuca rubra* (red fescue), *Calamagrostis nutkaensis, Carex obnupta, Trifolium wormskioldii* (springbank clover), and *Juncus balticus* (Arctic rush).

4.3 Freshwater Marsh

Marsh vegetation, in the strict sense, dominated by *Typha* spp. or large *Scirpus* spp. (see Wetzel 1975), does not occur on Brooks Peninsula. Rather, there are restricted wetland zones that emerge seasonally and are covered by herbaceous species. These sites occur only at lake margins. At the edge of Pyrola Lake (Figure 8.13) a grass-sedge meadow occupies a zone several metres wide at the edge of a very shallow sub-basin into which a stream flows. The meadow covers the emergent part of the stream delta and the adjoining flat-lying shore. *Deschampsia cespitosa*, two or three *Carex* species, and *Gentiana sceptrum* (king gentian) cover the ground. No other plant species were noted in the meadow.

4.4 Bog Herbaceous Vegetation

The boggy areas of Brooks Peninsula are covered by a mosaic of plant communities shaped by microtopographic features and local variations in hydrology. Bog Herbaceous Vegetation communities occupy areas that are too wet and nutrient-poor for shrubby communities to develop. Individual herbaceous patches are small, but, in aggregate, cover a considerable portion of the wet lowland and poorly drained upland sites. Typically, they are characterized by a

Table 8.6 Vascular plant cover[a] in relevés from Salt Marsh Vegetation

Analyst/Plot No.	OH16	OH13	OH17	OH18	OH19	R60	O20	R44	OH14	OH12	OH15
Deschampsia cespitosa	5	2	5	1	2	-	1	x	3	3	3
Potentilla pacifica	3	1	+	-	-	x	4	x	3	2	3
Plantago maritima	1	+	+	-	1	x	-	x	2	1	+
Carex lyngbyei	1	4	1	3	1	-	-	x	-	-	-
Hordeum brachyantherum	2	-	+	-	-	-	+	x	2	1	1
Glaux maritima	+	1	1	2	1	x	-	-	-	-	-
Fucus spp.	+	2	+	2	-	-	-	x	-	-	-
Plantago macrocarpa	-	-	-	-	+	x	-	-	2	1	2
Lilaeopsis occidentalis	-	+	-	4	2	-	-	-	-	-	-
Puccinellia pumila	+	+	+	-	-	-	-	-	-	-	-
Puccinellia nutkaensis	-	-	-	-	-	x	+	-	-	-	-
Triglochin maritimum	-	1	+	-	-	-	-	x	+	-	-
Scirpus cernuus	-	1	-	+	1	-	-	-	+	-	-
Juncus arcticus	-	1	-	-	-	-	-	-	3	-	-
Carex obnupta	-	-	-	-	-	-	4	x	-	-	-
Trifolium wormskioldii	-	-	-	-	-	x	-	-	2	2	+
Festuca rubra	-	-	-	-	-	-	-	x	1	1	-
Aster subspicatus	-	-	-	-	-	-	-	-	2	3-4	1
Calamagrostis nutkaensis	-	-	-	-	-	-	-	-	-	3	3
Ligusticum calderi	-	-	-	-	-	-	-	-	-	1	2
Achillea millefolium	-	-	-	-	-	-	-	-	-	3-4	-

Species with low constancy and coverage: *Honckenya peploides* (020: r); *Elymus hirsutus* (OH15: 1); *Maianthemum dilatatum* (OH15: 1); *Fritillaria camschatcensis* (OH15: +); *Galium* sp. (OH15: +); *Trientalis arctica* (OH15: +).

[a] Cover values according to modified Braun-Blanquet scale, see Appendix 8.1. No quantitative estimates were made in plots R60 and R44, hence occurrence of species denoted by "x".

Figure 8.12 Salt Marsh meadow in upper part of Kingfisher Creek estuary (Photo: R.J. Hebda)

Figure 8.13 Freshwater marsh community at the edge of Pyrola Lake. Stands of *Juncus oreganus* are in the foreground (Photo: R.J. Hebda)

well-developed graminoid layer (grasses, sedges, and rushes), numerous bog forbs, and sphagnum mats or hummocks. There are at least two non-woody bog communities, differing in composition because of the depth of the organic substrate.

4.4.1 Shallow Bog

Typically, there is a discontinuous plant cover, with either bare mineral soil, or exposed organic muck. Scattered low shrubs grow on small island-like hummocks formed by *Sphagnum* or by protruding rocks (Figure 8.14). *Chamaecyparis, Myrica,* and *Juniperus* occur occasionally. The herbaceous stratum is discontinuous, often bunched or clumped because of the growth habit of the principal species. No single species is characteristic, but an association of *Deschampsia cespitosa, Eriophorum angustifolium, Dodecatheon jeffreyi, Drosera rotundifolia, Rhynchospora alba, Scirpus cespitosus,* and, occasionally, *Carex* spp. is indicative of this vegetation type (Table 8.3). Many other bog species occur, though they never seem to be abundant, including *Pinguicula macroceras* (common butterwort).

Like the herbaceous cover, the bryophyte cover is patchy, ranging from a few scraps on barren soil to extensive hummock-mat complexes. Because vegetation plots did not involve detailed sampling of bryoflora, only general comments concerning the composition of this stratum are possible. The mosses *Racomitrium lanuginosum, Campylopus atrovirens,* and *Sphagnum* spp. predominate. *Racomitrium,* characteristic of cedar-dominated Bog Shrub, occupies hummocks where it forms little islands in association with scattered shrubs, *Sphagnum* hummocks, and rocks. *Sphagnum* spp. are ubiquitous and diverse, but rarely form continuous cover. *Sphagnum papillosum* and *Sphagnum fuscum* appear to be the more common species. *Campylopus atrovirens,* though a major species, is characteristic of minerotrophic situations in herbaceous bog communities. *Campylopus* usually grows on mineral soil or very shallow peat, especially where there is seasonal water flow. Of the liverworts, *Herbertus* spp. seem to occur regularly, but cover little surface area. *Pleurozia purpurea*

Figure 8.14 Shallow Bog Herbaceous Vegetation on a slope near Kalmia Lake (Photo: R.J. Hebda)

may occur, but seems more closely associated with shrub communities. Shallow, seasonally dry pools often contain well-developed patches of the lichen *Siphula ceratites*.

Gleyed Placic Humo Ferric Podzol soils were observed under this vegetation (see Chapter 4).

4.4.2 Deep Bog

In contrast to the widespread discontinuous shallow peat bog, there are few areas on Brooks Peninsula where peat is more than 50 cm deep. In such a setting, organic deposits restrict the contact of plant roots with mineral soil. Hence, the nutrient status of the community is ombrotrophic (rain- or cloud-fed), rather than minerotrophic (ground-water or mineral-fed) as in shallow peat bogs.

A deep bog has developed in the hollow between two ancient sand dunes adjacent to Cape Cook Lagoon ("Cottongrass Hollow", see Chapter 9). Scattered shrubs occur at this site, but are not prominent. Yellow cedar, *Ledum groenlandicum*, and *Kalmia polifolia* are abundant. The herbaceous cover ranges from about 40% to 50%. *Eriophorum angustifolium* covers much of the ground, and given its rather upright form, dominates the vegetation. Two other herbaceous species, *Apargidium boreale* and *Gentiana douglasiana*, are, in relative terms, extremely abundant in this setting. *Apargidium boreale*, which, except for its yellow inflorescence, is an inconspicuous plant, is more abundant in Deep Bog than in any other habitat on the peninsula. Other typical bog herbs include: *Drosera rotundifolia*, *Carex livida*, and *Gentiana sceptrum*. Many of the species dominant and characteristic of Brooks Peninsula's Bog Shrub vegetation and Shallow Bog vegetation are absent, including *Scirpus cespitosus*, *Dodecatheon jeffreyi*, and *Deschampsia cespitosa*. Presumably these species require nutrient levels, or specific nutrients, available only from moving ground water or from contact with mineral substrates.

The bryophyte stratum in Deep Bog vegetation is dominated almost exclusively by *Sphagnum* spp., mainly *Sphagnum* cf. *papillosum*, and occasionally *Sphagnum capillifolium*.

4.5 Herbaceous Aquatic Vegetation

Most of the lakes and ponds on Brooks Peninsula contain floating or submerged aquatic plants (Figure 8.15). The flora of these sites is not rich, nor is the vegetation robust. Usually, a few leaves float on the surface of the water, or a few stems rise above the water. The poor development of this vegetation is likely related to the relatively acidic water and the steep shore zones of many of the lakes.

Nuphar polysepalum (yellow pond-lily) is the most prominent aquatic plant. Floating leaves of this plant ring most of the smaller lakes, grow in shallower parts of larger lakes, and cover ponds. *Brasenia schreberi* (watershield) thrives in several ponds in the boggy lowlands on the north side of the peninsula. Notably, only one species of pondweed, *Potamogeton gramineus* (grass-leaved pondweed), grows in shallow ponds in boggy terrain.

Emergent vegetation favours shallow bog ponds, though it is encountered also along the margins of some small lakes. Monospecific stands of *Juncus oreganus* (spreading rush) are the most common emergent vegetation. These stands occupy zones of shallow water that dry out during mid to late summer. Plants of slightly deeper water include *Isoetes echinospora* (bristle-like quillwort) and *Scirpus subterminalis* (water club-rush). Other species of shallow ponds include: *Sparganium angustifolium* (narrow leaf bur-reed), *Eriophorum angustifolium* (narrow-leaf cotton grass) and *Juncus effusus* (common rush). One aquatic moss, *Drepanocladus exannulatus*, is especially abundant in Pyrola Lake, in water 2 m deep, and also occurs in other small lakes and ponds.

Figure 8.15 ***Brasenia schreberi*** **floating on a small pond in Camassia Bog; an example of Herbaceous Aquatic Vegetation (Photo: R.J. Hebda)**

4.6 Herbaceous Rock Vegetation

Shallow soils and exposure to wind and salt spray restrict plant growth on rock outcrops. Such rock outcrops support primarily herbaceous species that cling to bryophyte mats or lodge in crevices. Three rock habitats are described here: shore headlands, rock knolls, and cliffs. None of these habitats covers much terrain, yet they are home to the most distinctive plant species on Brooks Peninsula.

4.6.1 *Shore Headland Vegetation*

The rocky headlands bordering the sea are sparsely vegetated. Within reach of the breaking waves, only a few species are rooted in the rock crevices. The brown alga *Fucus* grows interspersed with rock-encrusting barnacles in the upper intertidal zone. From 0.5 m to 1.0 m above the *Fucus*, there is a band of contrasting colours—the black crustose lichen *Verrucaria* and the white crustose lichen, *Coccotrema maritimum*. The more salt-tolerant vascular plants first appear just beyond or just within the *Verrucaria* zone. The four commonly encountered species include *Potentilla villosa* (woolly cinquefoil), *Deschampsia cespitosa*, *Sagina crassicaulis* (sticky-stemmed pearlwort), and *Plantago maritima* (Table 8.7). The moss *Ulota phyllantha* also occurs in this habitat.

Table 8.7 Vascular plant cover[a] in relevés from Shore Headland Vegetation

Plot No.	1	2	3	4
Plantago maritima	2	x	-	+
Potentilla villosa	2	x	-	1
Festuca rubra	1	x	-	2
Achillea millefolium	+	-	-	+
Hordeum brachyantherum	1	-	-	3
Prunella vulgaris	+	x	-	-
Montia parvifolia	-	x	-	-
Sagina crassicaulis	-	x	x	-
Fragaria chiloensis	-	x	-	-
Stellaria crispa	-	x	-	-
Fritillaria camschatcensis	-	x	-	-
Agrostis exarata	-	-	x	-
Luzula campestris	-	x	-	-
Deschampsia cespitosa	-	x	-	-
Saxifraga ferruginea	-	x	-	-
Trifolium wormskioldii	-	-	-	5
Carex obnupta	-	-	-	3

[a] Cover values according to modified Braun-Blanquet scale, see Appendix 8.1. No quantitative estimates were made in plots 2 and 3, hence occurrence of species denoted by "x".

Farther onto the headlands, there is a gradual increase in plant cover and species diversity. *Festuca rubra*, *Achillea millefolium*, *Fragaria chiloensis* (Pacific Coast strawberry), and *Montia parvifolia* (small-leaved montia) grow well. Closer to the forest edge, where there is a thin accumulation of humus on the bedrock, a more continuous meadow is formed. Species in this habitat, in order of decreasing importance, include: *Trifolium wormskioldii*, *Carex obnupta*, *Hordeum brachyantherum* (meadow barley), *Fritillaria camschatcensis* (riceroot fritillary), *Saxifraga ferruginea* (Alaska saxifrage), *Campanula rotundifolia* var. *alaskana*, and *Castilleja miniata* (common red Indian paintbrush).

Many of the headlands feature eroded surge channels with vertical walls. The inner and upper sections of the surge channels are sheltered from the brunt of the tidal wash and salt spray, and are frequently very moist and shaded. Some typical plants of the headland walls are: *Aquilegia formosa* (Sitka columbine), *Maianthemum dilatatum*, *Adiantum pedatum*, *Polypodium glycyrrhiza* (licorice fern), *P. scouleri* (leathery polypody), *Prenanthes alata*, *Tellima grandiflora* (tall fringecup), *Aruncus sylvester*, *Blechnum spicant*, and *Galium triflorum*.

Rocky headlands are widespread along the shore, hence, Shore Headland Vegetation occurs frequently, albeit in small separated patches.

4.6.2 Rock Knoll Vegetation

Throughout the Brooks Peninsula lowlands and on some of the ridges, bedrock knolls are exposed to sun, wind, and rain. Soils are shallow and restricted to pockets or crevices. Mineral particles produced by chemical and physical weathering are blown away in strong winds.

Plants occur singly or in small patches (Figure 8.16). Herbaceous species predominate, though wherever there is sufficient footing shrubs take hold. Little data was collected from this vegetation type, but a relevé recorded from a windblown rock knoll near Kalmia Lake at 300 m provides an example.

Luetka pectinata and the mosses *Racomitrium* spp. form patches in protected pockets. Tufts of an undetermined grass poke out of rock cracks. Associated with mats, there is often good cover of *Pinguicula macroceras* (common butterwort), and prostrate shrubs as *Vaccinium uliginosum* and *Juniperus communis*.

Figure 8.16 Rock Knoll Vegetation communities on Doom Mountain (Photo: R.J. Hebda)

4.6.3 Cliff Vegetation

Mountain cliffs provide a wide range of habitats for hardy and tenacious herbs. Cliff habitats occur along the rugged ridges of Brooks Peninsula.

(a) Cliffs and Chasm Walls

The high mountain peaks have rugged topography with steep rock faces and deep, narrow, vertical-walled chasms with steep colluvial floors. These localized habitats contain many of the rare plant species on Brooks Peninsula. Moisture regime is a major ecological factor separating these habitats. Aspect, and relative amount of shade vs. direct sun, are especially important in determining moisture conditions. Variations in microhabitat are reflected in the high floristic diversity of this vegetation.

The north- and northeast-facing walls of chasms and cliffs of peaks such as Doom Mountain are strongly shaded and provide humid habitats for plants. Common species (Table 8.8) are: *Isopyrum savilei* (Queen Charlotte isopyrum, Figure 8.17), *Saxifraga ferruginea*, *S. taylori* (Taylor's saxifrage), and *Anemone narcissiflora* (narcissus anemone). Less abundant, but notable, are *Geum calthifolium* (caltha-leaved avens), *Thelypteris phegopteris* (beech fern), *Heuchera glabra* (smooth alumroot), *Saxifraga mertensiana* (Merten's saxifrage), *Aquilegia formosa*, and *Aruncus sylvester*.

The south- and southwest-facing chasm walls and cliffs are sunny and drier than the north- and northeast-facing walls (Figure 8.18). Typical species (Table 8.9) of these habitats include: *Carex circinata* (coiled sedge), *Penstemon davidsonii* (Davidson's penstemon), *Calamagrostis purpurascens* ssp. *tasuensis*, *Geum calthifolium*, *Ligusticum calderi*, and *Saxifraga taylori* (Taylor's saxifrage). Other species are *Artemisia furcata* (three-forked mugwort), *Solidago multiradiata* (northern goldenrod), *Cryptogramma crispa* (parsley fern), *Anemone narcissiflora*, and *Montia parvifolia*.

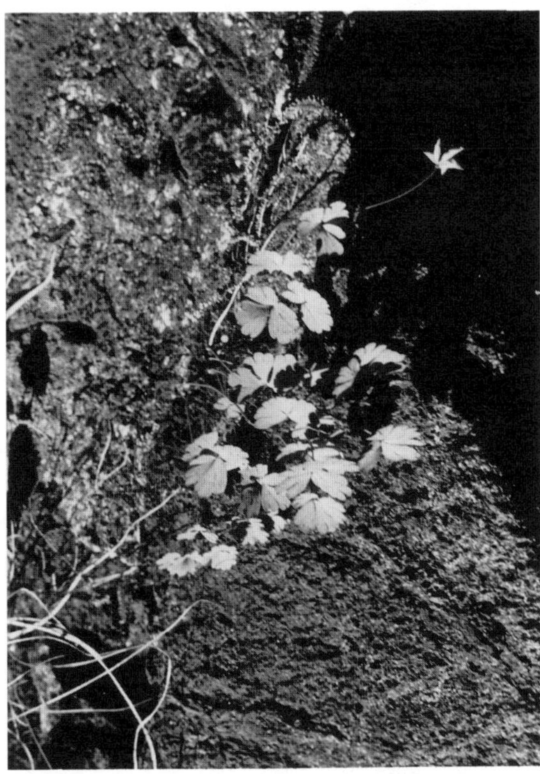

Figure 8.17 *Isopyrum savilei* **growing on a cliff face on Doom Mountain (Photo: R.J. Hebda)**

Table 8.8 Vascular plant occurrence in shaded habitats of Cliffs and Chasm Walls

Elevation	609	675	609	520	609	670	550	600
Slope[a]	ch	cl	cl	ch	cl	cl	ch	cl
Aspect	N	NW	NW	N	--	--	N	N
Stand Type	ACu	ACu	ACu	ACu	ACu	ACu	ACu	ACu
Substrate	R	R	R	R	R	R	R	R
Analyst/Plot No.	R94	R95	R96	R97	R98	R99	R911	0917
Isopyrum savilei	x	x	x	x	x	-	x	x
Saxifraga ferruginea	x	x	x	-	x	-	x	-
Anemone narcissiflora	-	x	-	x	x	-	x	x
Saxifraga taylori	x	-	-	-	x	x	x	x
Heuchera glabra	-	x	x	x	-	-	-	x
Thelypteris phegopteris	x	x	-	x	-	-	x	-
Geum calthifolium	x	-	-	x	-	x	-	x
Saxifraga mertensiana	-	-	-	x	x	-	x	x
Aquilegia formosa	-	-	-	-	x	-	x	x
Aruncus sylvester	-	x	-	x	x	-	-	-
Valeriana sitchensis	x	-	x	-	-	-	-	-
Carex circinata	x	-	-	-	-	x	-	-
Adiantum pedatum	-	x	-	x	-	-	-	-
Cassiope stelleriana	-	x	-	-	x	-	-	-
Ligusticum calderi	-	x	-	-	-	x	-	-
Montia parvifolia	-	x	-	-	-	-	x	-
Luetkea pectinata	-	-	x	-	-	x	-	-
Erigeron peregrinus	-	-	-	x	-	x	-	-
Calamagrostis purpurascens	-	-	-	-	x	x	-	-
Penstemon davidsonii	-	-	-	-	x	x	-	-
Cassiope lycopodioides	-	-	-	-	-	x	-	x
Campanula rotundifolia	-	-	-	-	-	-	x	x

Species present (x) in a single plot: *Lloydia serotina, Romanzoffia sitchensis, Stenanthium occidentalis* (R94); *Montia sibirica, Prenanthes alata, Cystopteris fragilis, Rubus spectabilis* (R95); *Gymnocarpium dryopteris, Carex spectabilis, Athyrium filix-femina, Tiarella trifoliata* (R96); *Alnus crispa, Cladothamnus pyroliflorus, Pinguicula vulgaris (R97); Ranunculus cooleyae, Pedicularis ornithorhyncha* (R98); *Lupinus nootkatensis, Artemisia furcata, Gentiana platypetala, Solidago multiradiata* (R99); *Boykinia elata, Selaginella wallacei* (R911); *Thelypteris limbosperma* (0917).

[a] See Appendix 8.1 for abbreviations.

(b) Cliff Ledges and Chasm Floors

Cliff bases and broad ledges have deep pockets of soil and receive seepage from water draining down the rock walls. Some plants of this habitat (Table 8.10) are *Thelypteris limbosperma* (mountain wood fern), *Prenanthes alata, Viola glabella*, and *Huperzia selago* (fir club-moss).

Steeply sloping chasm floors consist of consolidated colluvial rubble and provide a slightly different habitat. Some of the common species of this habitat (Table 8.10) include *Epilobium alpinum* (alpine willow herb), *Viola glabella, Calamagrostis nutkaensis, Luzula parviflora* (small-flowered wood-rush), and *Stellaria crispa* (crisp starwort).

Figure 8.18 Vegetation of sunny cliffs and ledges on Doom Mountain (Photo: R.J. Hebda)

Table 8.9 Vascular plant occurrence in sunny habitats of Cliffs and Chasm Walls

Elevation	609	675	790
Slope[a]	cl	cl	cl
Aspect	S	W	W
Stand Type	ACs	ACs	ACs
Substrate	R	R	R
Analyst/Plot No.	R919	R921	R922
Carex circinata	x	x	x
Penstemon davidsonii	x	x	x
Geum calthifolium	x	x	x
Calamagrostis purpurascens	-	x	x
Ligusticum calderi	-	x	x
Saxifraga taylori	x	-	x
Anemone narcissiflora	x	-	x
Montia parvifolia	x	x	-
Cryptogramma crispa	x	x	-
Cladothamnus pyroliflorus	-	x	x

Species present (x) in a single plot: *Solidago multiradiata, Phlox diffusa, Achillea millefolium, Fritillaria camschatcensis* (R910); *Saxifraga ferruginea, Luetkea pectinata, Alnus crispa* (R921); *Cassiope stelleriana, Cassiope lycopodioides, Campanula rotundifolia, Caltha biflora, Sorbus sitchensis* (R922).

[a] See Appendix 8.1 for abbreviations.

Table 8.10 Vascular plant occurrence of Cliff Ledges and Chasm Floors

	Chasm Floor				Cliff Ledge		
Elevation	580	600	609	550	600	600	790
Slope[a]	st	st	st	st	g	g	g
Aspect	N	N	N	N	N	N	N
Stand Type	ACh	ACh	ACh	ACh	ACl	ACl	ACl
Substrate	R	R	R	R	R	R	R
Analyst/Plot No.	R915	R916	R917	R918	R912	R913	R914
Viola glabella	x	x	x	x	x	-	x
Epilobium alpinum	x	x	x	x	-	-	-
Calamagrostis nutkaensis	x	-	x	x	x	-	-
Luzula parvifolia	x	x	x	-	-	x	-
Prenanthes alata	x	x	x	-	-	x	x
Stellaria crispa	-	x	x	x	-	-	-
Valeriana sitchensis	x	-	x	x	-	-	-
Carex spectabilis	x	x	x	-	-	-	-
Rubus spectabilis	-	x	x	x	-	-	x
Thelypteris limbosperma	-	x	x	-	x	x	x
Saxifraga ferruginea	x	-	x	-	-	-	-
Ligusticum calderi	-	x	x	-	-	-	-
Elymus hirsutus	-	x	x	-	x	-	-
Osmorhiza chilensis	x	x	-	-	x	-	-
Galium kamtschaticum	x	x	-	-	x	-	-
Luzula campestris	x	-	x	-	-	-	-
Heracleum lanatum	-	x	x	-	-	-	-
Deschampsia cespitosa	-	x	x	-	-	-	-
Melica subulata	-	x	x	-	-	-	-
Fritillaria camtschatcensis	-	-	x	x	-	-	-
Huperzia selago	-	-	-	-	-	x	x

Species with low constancy: *Romanzoffia sitchensis, Saxifraga taylori, Ranunculus cooleyae* (R915); *Isopyron savilei* (R915, R914); *Saxifraga mertensiana, Erigeron peregrinus, Agrostis* sp. (R916); *Heuchera glabra* (R916, R914); *Aruncus sylvester* (R916, R913); *Tiarella trifoliata, Campanula rotundifolia, Carex mertensii, Carex stylosa, Tellima grandiflora; Caltha biflora, Pedicularis bracteosa* (R917); *Aquilegia formosa, Veratrum eschscholtzii, Athyrium filix-femina* (R917, R912); *Cystopteris fragilis, Montia sibirica* (R917, R913); *Arnica latifolia, Trisetum cernuum, Polystichum munitum* (R917, R914); *Asplenium trichomanes, Asplenium viride, Polypodium glycyrrhiza, Polypodium amorphum, Galium triflorum, Viola sempervirens, Maianthemum dilatatum* (R913); *Habenaria hyperborea, Dryopteris disjuncta* (R914).

[a] See Appendix 8.1 for abbreviations.

4.7 Alpine Meadow Vegetation

Herb-dominated Alpine Meadow Vegetation is relatively uncommon and forms comparatively small stands on Brooks Peninsula. Such alpine meadow communities occur at the same elevation as heath vegetation, and indeed, some heath species are present, with very low coverage, in most meadow stands. Two Alpine Meadow Vegetation types are recognized: Mesic Meadow and Moist Meadow (Table 8.11).

Table 8.11 Vascular plant cover in sample relevés from Alpine Meadow Vegetation

	Mesic Meadow			Moist Meadow						
Elevation	457	600	600	600	600	500	600	500	600	335
Slope[a]	10%	45%	40%	m	m	g	f	f	f	f
Aspect	SE	NNE	N	S	S	--	--	--	--	--
Stand Type	AM	AM	AM	AM	AM	AM	AM	AM	AM	AM
Substrate	g	s	s	s	s	s	r	r	r	r
Analyst/Plot No.	R913	0914	0915	0916	0919	0918	H8/2	R38	R78	R76
Deschampsia cespitosa	x	3	4	3	2	2	2	-	x	x
Erigeron peregrinus	-	3	3	2	1	-	1	x	-	-
Calamagrostis purpurascens	-	3	4	-	-	-	-	-	-	-
Fauria crista-galli	-	2	2	3	4	3	3	x	x	x
Scirpus cespitosus	x	-	-	4	5	3	3	x	x	-
Gentiana douglasiana	x	1	-	2	3	3	2	x	-	-
Apargidium boreale	x	-	-	3	2	1	2	x	-	x
Dodecatheon jeffreyi	-	+	-	1	1	+	2	-	-	x
Tofieldia glutinosa	-	+	-	1	+	+	1	-	x	-
Carex anthoxanthea	-	2	1	1	-	-	-	-	-	x
Geum calthifolium	-	1	r	1	+	+	+	-	-	-
Agrostis aequivalvis	-	1	1	1	-	-	1	x	-	x
Ligusticum calderi	-	1	2	-	-	-	-	-	-	x
Empetrum nigrum	x	+	-	2	+	1	2	x	x	-
Phyllodoce empetriformis	-	+	1	-	+	-	1	-	-	-
Vaccinium uliginosum	-	-	-	2	1	1	2	x	x	x
Blechnum spicant	-	1	1	-	-	-	-	-	-	-
Habenaria hyperborea	-	+	+	-	-	-	+	-	-	-
Viola biflora	x	-	r	-	-	-	-	-	-	-
Rhytidiadelphus loreus	-	2	1	-	-	-	-	-	-	-
Pellaea sp.	-	2	2	-	-	-	-	-	-	-
Racomitrium lanuginosum	x	-	-	4	3	-	-	-	-	-
Sphagnum compactum	-	2	-	+	1	-	-	x	-	-
Sphagnum girgensohnii	-	+	3	-	-	-	-	-	-	-
Siphula ceratites	x	-	-	+	r	-	-	x	x	-
Cephalozia sp.	-	2	+	-	-	-	-	-	-	-
Drosera rotundifolia	-	-	-	-	-	1	1	-	-	-
Eriophorum angustifolium	-	-	-	-	-	1	1	x	-	-

Species with low Constancy: *Vaccinium cespitosum* (0915: +, 0916: r); *Cassiope mertensiana* (R923: 1); *Cassiope stelleriana* (R923: +); *Cornus unalaschkensis* (R923: +); *Luetkea pectinata* (0914: 1, 0918: +); *Gentiana platypetala* (0915: 1, H8/2: +, R76: x); *Cladothamnus pyroliflorus* (0915: +, 0918: +); *Loiseleuria procumbens* (0916: 1); *Rubus pedatus* (0914: 1); *Pinguicula vulgaris* (0914: +, H8/2: +); *Coptis aspleniifolia* (0914: 1); *Thelypteris limbosperma* (0915: 2); *Valeriana sitchensis* (0915: +); *Pedicularis bracteosa* (0915: +); *Lycopodium clavatum* (0915: r); *Tiarella laciniata* (0915: r); *Juniperus communis* (R923: x); *Carex circinata* (R923: x); *Campanula rotundifolia* (R923: x); *Sisyrinchium angustifolium* (R923: x); *Lycopodium sitchense* (0916: +, 0919: +); *Carex kelloggii* (0919: 2); *Calamagrostis canadensis* (0918: 1, H8/2: +); *Luzula campestris* (0918: 1, H8/2: +); *Lophozia* sp. (0914: 1); *Diplophyllum* sp. (0914: +, 0915: 1); *Cetraria islandica* (0916: r, 0919: r); *Cladina mitis* (0916: +, 0919: r); *Sphagnum papillosum* (0914: 3); *Rhizomnium glabrescens* (0914: 2); *Dicranum majus* (0914: 2); *Dicranum fuscescens* (0915: 2); *Mylia taylorii* (0914: 1); *Herbertus* sp. (0914: 1); *Peltigera polydactyla* (0914: +); *Scapania* sp. (0914: +); *Hylocomium splendens* (0914: 1); *Hypnum* sp. (0914: r); *Bazzania* sp. (0914: +); *Calypogeia* sp. (0915: +);

Table 8.11 Continued

Ctenidium molluscum (0915: 1); *Plagiothecium undulatum* (0915: 1); *Cladina impexa* (R923: x); *Habenaria chorisiana* (H8/2: +); *Agrostis scabra* (R76: x); *Carex stylosa* (R76: x); *Carex physocarpa* (R76: x); *Veratrum eschscholtzii* (R76: x).

[a] See Appendix 8.1 for abbreviations.

4.7.1 Mesic Meadow

Mesic Meadow communities occur on well-drained slopes and ridges with stony soil. The overall impression is of a grass and herb sward (Figure 8.19). The dominant species are *Deschampsia cespitosa, Erigeron peregrinus*, and *Calamagrostis purpurascens* ssp. *tasuensis*. Other species include *Fauria crista-galli* (deer cabbage), *Carex anthoxanthea*, and *Ligusticum calderi* (Table 8.11).

4.7.2 Moist Meadow and Stream Margins

Moist meadows occur in poorly-drained habitats with fine soils. They are commonly found around pond margins. *Scirpus cespitosus, Fauria crista-galli*, and *Deschampsia cespitosa* are dominant species (Table 8.11). Typical species with low coverage include: *Gentiana douglasiana, Apargidium boreale, Dodecatheon jeffreyi, Tofieldia glutinosa, Vaccinium uliginosum*, and *Agrostis aequivalvis* (Alaska bent grass).

A similar assemblage, but containing more wetland species, occupies the margins of streamlets and drainage channels. Common species are: *Dodecatheon jeffreyi, Tofieldia glutinosa, Panicum occidentale* (western panicum), *Lycopodium inundatum* (bog club-moss), *Carex stylosa* (long-styled sedge), *C. phyllomanica* (coastal stellate sedge), *Juncus ensifolius* (sword-leaved rush), *J. oreganus*, and *J. falcatus* (sickle-leaved rush).

Figure 8.19 Alpine Meadow Vegetation adjacent to Cassiope Pond (Photo: R.J. Hebda)

4.8 Windblown Ridge Herb

Along the crest of Senecio Ridge, the vegetation and habitat features are different from those of other high ridges on Brooks Peninsula. This habitat is covered in loose rock, occasional bedrock outcrops, and scattered plants or patches of plants (Figures 8.20 and 8.21). Plants often occur singly, widely separated, and low. Adjoining, occasionally intermixed, vegetation includes Krummholz and Alpine Heath. Strong winds and possibly frost action and solifluction render the substrate unstable. Wind erosion is pronounced, as a result of the exposure to southeasterly winds in winter and westerly winds in summer. Human disturbance associated with building a telephone repeating station may have exacerbated erosion.

Figure 8.20 Vegetation of Windblown Senecio Ridge (Photo: R.J. Hebda)

Figure 8.21 Windblown ridge herb vegetation with *Senecio moresbiensis* in centre (Photo: R.J. Hebda)

Shrubs are rare and usually cover less than 5% of the ground. Shrubs are restricted to small heath or Krummholz patches, or are plastered over and among bedrock and loose gravel. Typical shrubs include *Vaccinium uliginosum*, *Vaccinium caespitosum*, *Phyllodoce empetriformis*, *Loiseleuria procumbens*, and *Empetrum nigrum* (Table 8.12).

Herbaceous cover ranges from 5% to 20%. *Ligusticum calderi* is most prominent in very stony zones, with typical coverage 3-5% (Figure 8.22). Other regularly occurring species include *Senecio moresbiensis* (Queen Charlotte butterweed), *Viola biflora* ssp. *carlottae* (Queen Charlotte violet), *Carex circinata*, *Luetkea pectinata*, and *Deschampsia cespitosa*. Each of these plants usually covers less than 1% of the ground. Bryophytes are absent or rare, tucked away against the prostrate shrubs. Floristically, Windblown Ridge Herb is related to Alpine Heath—many of the same species are present in both of these vegetation types.

The soils are deep, but very stony. Angular rocks and stones mantle the surface to a depth of 5-10 cm. Often, the stones are sorted into stripes. Red silty clay or fine silt, usually containing some stones, occurs to a depth of at least 40-50 cm.

Table 8.12 Vascular plant and moss cover[a] in relevés from Windblown Ridge Herb Vegetation

Elevation	450	450	450	450	450
Slope[b]	f	g	g	g	st
Aspect	--	--	--	--	ENE
Stand Type	RH	RH	RH	RH	RH
Substrate	R	R	R	R	TOR
Analyst/Plot No.	HO88-7	HO88-8	HO88-10	HO88-11	HO88-6
Ligusticum calderi	1-2	1	1-2	-	1
Carex circinata	+	+	1	1-2	1
Deschampsia cespitosa	+	+	1	1-2	-
Vaccinium caespitosum	-	+	+	1	1
Vaccinium uliginosum	+	1	+	1	-
Senecio moresbiensis	+	+	1	1	+
Viola biflora	+	+	1	1	-
Luetkea pectinata	+	+	+	1	4
Phyllodoce empetriformis	-	+	+	1	1
Racomitrium sp.	+	-	+	+	2
Empetrum nigrum	1	+	-	2	-
Campanula rotundifolia	-	r	+	-	+
Loiseleuria procumbens	-	+	-	1	-
Geum calthifolium	-	+	-	-	1
Erigeron peregrinus	-	+	-	+	-
Gentiana platypetala	-	+	-	+	-
Pinguicula vulgaris	-	-	-	+	+

Species with low Constancy: *Viola sempervirens* (HO88-6: 3); *Polytrichum* sp. (HO88-6: 3); *Gaultheria shallon* (HO88-6: 2); *Blechnum spicant* (HO88-6: 1); *Anemone narcissiflora* (HO88-6: 1); *Alnus crispa* (HO88-6: 1); *Apargidium boreale* (HO88-6: 1); *Pinus contorta* (HO88-11: 1); *Lycopodium clavatum* (HO88-11: +); *Huperzia selago* (HO88-6: +).

[a] Cover values according to modified Braun-Blanquet scale see Table 8.1.
[b] See Appendix 8.1 for abbreviations.

Figure 8.22 *Ligusticum calderi* growing on deflated gravel on Senecio Ridge (Photo: R.J. Hebda)

Discussion

The intent of this chapter is to describe vegetation types on Brooks Peninsula, to relate them to environmental factors, and to compare them with vegetation described for other places on Vancouver Island and the outer coast of British Columbia. Consequently, the character and relationships of Brooks Peninsula forests, subalpine and alpine vegetation, bog vegetation, and communities with rare and endemic species will be discussed in this context.

Forest Classification and Gradients

From the outset, the authors did not expect forest vegetation to provide many answers about a glacial refugium on Brooks Peninsula[11]. Indeed, with the possible exception of bryophytes no disjunct, rare, or endemic plant species were found to be restricted to typical forest habitats. However, the character of forest vegetation illustrates the exceptional conditions on the peninsula in comparison to the rest of Vancouver Island.

Four questions in this connection are:

(1) How distinct are the physiognomic classes of forest vegetation in terms of species composition?
(2) Which environmental factors are responsible for these physiognomic features and to what extent?

---

[11] See Hulten (1969: 84) on the "poor trivial coastal flora" of the lowlands of Kodiak Island.

(3) How do Brooks Peninsula forests relate to forest ecosystems elsewhere in coastal British Columbia?
(4) Is it warranted to speak of a subalpine zone on Brooks Peninsula?

Floristic Versus Physiognomic Types

Table 8.1 represents a computer-aided classification based entirely on floristic composition (the methodology is described in Ceska and Roemer 1971). Most of the physiognomic types (abbreviated at the head of the table) correspond well with the computer-generated classification, that is, all or most stands labelled as a specific type also sorted together on the basis of species combinations. However, Mountain Slope Forest, Timberline Scrubforest, and some Krummholz stands form a relatively homogeneous class in the table—they exhibit few differences in species combination. The same combination of montane species is characteristic of stands ranging from 4 m to 40 m tall.

The Krummholz, so distinct physiognomically with its dwarfed, gnarled growth, may vary greatly in the number and combination of species present in addition to the common trees. Some particularly dense stands are species-poor, whereas others may have many species, including ericaceous shrubs and dwarf shrubs that are also found in Bog Scrubforests at low and mid elevations. In regard to species composition, most Krummholz stands only differ marginally from these Bog Scrubforests, though a gradual shift in dominance occurs, with more western redcedar in Bog Scrubforest and more mountain hemlock in Krummholz.

Physiognomic Expressions and Environment

When average elevations are compared with species combination (Table 8.1), there is little difference between Mountain Slope Forest, Timberline Scrubforest, and Krummholz. Mountain hemlock is the only tree species that appears to be positively correlated with higher elevations on Brooks Peninsula; dominance of mountain hemlock increases, starting at about 200 m. Many of the characteristic snow-bed subalpine species are absent from Brooks Peninsula. In the absence of these species, the authors have concluded that wind exposure is, to a large degree, responsible for the appearance of the extreme forest types on Brooks Peninsula.

Examination of alternative arrangements in Table 8.1 suggests that these arrangements or vegetation continua are correlated with three gradients: soil moisture (section sequence 3-4-7-8), nutrient levels (section sequence 4-5-6 or 4-7-6), and wind exposure (section sequence 3-2-1).

Relationships to Previously Described Forest Vegetation

The floristic and edaphic ecosystem characteristics of the Hypermaritime Subzone of the Coastal Western Hemlock Biogeoclimatic Zone (CWHvh of Banner et al. 1990; CWHd of Klinka, Green, Courtin and Nuszdorfer 1984) apply well to the ecosystems found on Brooks Peninsula. Thus, even in the absence of on-site climatic records, ecosystem similarities suggest climatic similarities between Brooks Peninsula and other areas classified within CWHvh.

Table 8.13 compares ecosystem units proposed by various investigators of forest and forest-bog vegetation along the coast of British Columbia with those described in this chapter. The comparison reveals that all Brooks Peninsula types have equivalents elsewhere along the British Columbia coast. On Vancouver Island, however, clear equivalents of Brooks Peninsula forest vegetation can be found only for the Mesic Lowland Forest, the Shoreline Scrubforest, the Shoreline Forest, and the Alluvial Floodplain Forest. Wet Lowland Forest and Bog Scrubforest have better equivalents on British Columbia's north coast and the Queen Charlotte Islands.

Table 8.13 Previously described forest types comparable to those on Brooks Peninsula and their distinctions

Brooks Peninsula types	Wade 1965	Bell 1972	Cordes 1972	Bell and Harcombe 1973	Cordes et al. 1974
Mountain Slope Forest					
Lowland Forest on Steep Slopes		*Abies amabilis* *Climax Forest* Absent: *Picea* (wider definition, poor fit)		*Thuja p.-Tsuga* h. Forest Type Absent: *Picea*	*Picea s.-Rubus s.-Polystichum m.* and *Tsuga h.-Blechnum s.* Forests, both in part
Typical Lowland Forest		*Thuja-Tsuga* Forest		*Thuja plicata* and *Thuja plicata-Vaccinium ovatum* Forest Types Absent: *Chamaecyparis* Present: *Vaccinium o.*	*Thuja plicata-Tsuga heterophylla* Forest Absent: *Chamaecyparis*
Wet Lowland Forest		Absent: *Chamaecyparis* Present: *Rubus spectabilis* (wider definition)		*Thuja plicata* Bog Forest Type Absent: *Chamaecyparis* Present: *Vaccinium ovatum*	*Thuja plicata* Muskeg Forest Absent: *Chamaecyparis*, *Carex obnupta*
Bog Scrubforest	*Pinus c.-Chamaecyparis n.-Sphagnum r.* Assocation Absent: *Carex anthoxanthea*, *Cladothamnus*, *Phyllodoce* (wider definition)	*Pinus contorta* Muskeg Absent: *Carex anthoxanthea*, *Cladothamnus*, *Phyllodoce* (wider definition)			*Pinus c.* Bog Forest Absent: *Carex anthoxanthea*, *Cladothamnus*, *Phyllodoce*, (*Calamagrostis nootkaensis?*)
Shoreline Scrubforest			*Picea s.-Maianthemum d.* and *Picea s.-Gaultheria s.* Forest Types		
Shoreline Forest		*Picea sitchensis* Fringe (wider definition)	*Picea s.-Rubus s.* Forest Type *Blechnum* replacing *Polystichum*	*Picea s.-Gaultheria s.* Forest Type	*Picea s.-Gaultheria s.-Maianthemum d.* Forest (wider definition)
Alluvial Flood-plain Forest			*Picea s.-Polystichum m.-Leucolepis m.* Forest Type		*Picea s.-Tsuga h.* (Riverine) Forest

Table 8.13 Continued

Brooks Peninsula types	Klinka et al. 1980 (Biogeocoenotic Associations)[a]	Banner et al. 1982	Banner, Pojar and Yole 1983	Banner, Pojar and Trowbridge 1983
Mountain Slope Forest	*Rhytidiadelpho l.-Vaccinio p. & a. (Piceo s.) & Abieto a.-Tsugetum h.* Absent: *Coptis a., Chamaecyparis;* Present: *Picea* (poor fit)		Hemlock-Cedar-Moss Assocation Present: *Picea, Thuja;* (transitional between this and Lowland F.)	Montane Zonal Hemlock-Moss Association Absent: *Abies* Present: *Picea*
Lowland Forest on Steep Slopes	*Polysticho m.-Blechno s.-Abieto a.-Tsugetum h.* Absent: *Picea*		Hemlock-Cedar-Spruce-Fern Association Present: *Gymnocarpium, Athyrium*	Montane Zonal Hemlock-Moss and Montane Oakfern Association Absent: *Abies;* Present: *Picea, Gymnocarpium, Athyrium*
Typical Lowland Forest	*Gaultherio s.-Vaccinio a. & p.-Thujo p. Tsugetum h.* Absent: *Chamaecyparis*		Submesic Cedar-Hemlock-Salal-Moss Association Absent: *Tiarella;* Present: *Picea, Pinus,* (*Chamaecyparis* more common)	Zonal Hemlock-Moss Association, Cedar-Dominated Subassociation Present: *Rubus pedatus, Coptis; Gaultheria* less dominant
Wet Lowland Forest	*Sphagno g.-Copteto a.-Thujo p. & Chamaecypareto n.-Tsugetum h.* Absent: *Carex obnupta & laeviculmis;* Present: *Carex hendersonii, Coptis aspleniifolia*	Bog Forest (intermediate to our bog scrub forest; very similar)	Cedar-Spruce-Skunk Cabbage Association Absent: *Habenaria s.,* Present: *Luzula parviflora*	
Bog Scrubforest	*Caltho b,-Lysichito a.-Tsugo h. & m.-Thujetum p. & Chamaecyparetum n.* Absent: *Pinus, Carex anthoxanthea;* Present: *Caltha b., Carex nigricans*	Bog Woodland Absent: *Calamagrostis nootkaensis* (very similar)	Pine-Cypress-Cedar Bog Woodland Association Absent: some bog spp., however these are pres. in a unit "Blanket Bogs"	Cedar-Cypress Scrub (similar and intermediate to both these units
Shoreline Scrubforest				
Shoreline Forest				
Alluvial Flood-plain Forest	*Leucolepido m.-Polysticho m.-(Tsugo h.) & Abieto a.-Piceetum s.* (very similar)		Spruce Alluvial Forest (fewer species)	Alluvial Spruce Association, Grass Subassociation Absent: *Polystichum, (Abies);* Present: *Gymnocarpium, Athyrium, Circaea, Mnium insigne*

[a] Specific names (here abbreviated) appear in the latin genitive case.

It appears significant that northern vegetation types of the outer coast and the western Queen Charlotte Islands are similar to Brooks Peninsula's vegetation. Of the large number of ecosystems in the CWHvh subzone on the eastern Queen Charlotte Islands (Banner et al. 1989; Banner et al. 1990), few have equivalents on Brooks Peninsula. Most CWHvh ecosystems appear to reflect richer, more productive sites than those found on Brooks Peninsula. However, much of this species richness may be a result of the much larger sample area and much larger flora, as compared to the very limited area of Brooks Peninsula.

Mountain Slope Forest, Timberline Scrubforest, and Krummholz have some equivalents in the montane and subalpine forests on the Queen Charlotte Islands and the outer mainland coast. Although few detailed descriptions of these forest and scrub communities are available, similar timberline vegetation has been observed by A. Banner, H. Roemer, and R.T. Ogilvie on the Queen Charlotte Islands, and by A. Banner and R.T. Ogilvie on other islands of the north coast.

Brooke et al. (1970) describe vegetation and environments for the Subalpine Mountain Hemlock Zone north of Vancouver. Their classification unit that is most like the Krummholz vegetation type in this chapter, with regard to tree species and physiognomy, is "*Nano-Tsugetum mertensianae*" (order *Phyllodoco-Cassiopetalia*). However, as only one of 11 species listed as characteristic for this order is present in the Krummholz, it should be clear that any resemblance is superficial. Krummholz, and particularly Timberline Scrubforest, should also be compared with the adjacent order of Brooke et al. (1970), "*Vaccinietalia membranacei*". Only one association of this order, *Streptopo rosei-Abietetum amabilis*, has features in common with high elevation forests of Brooks Peninsula. Some constant species of the order, such as *Rhytidiopsis robusta* and *Rhizomnium nudum* are not present on Brooks Peninsula.

The authors conclude that the well-drained lowland forest types of Brooks Peninsula are very similar to those found elsewhere on Vancouver Island's west coast, that the characteristic bog scrubforests closely resemble those on outer coastal areas to the north, and that plant communities on the mountain slopes, including wind-blown vegetation, are similar to the high-elevation vegetation of the exposed outer coast to the north.

Stunted Forest and Environment

On Brooks Peninsula, stunted woody vegetation types composed of tree species are of two kinds, those on wet soils at low elevation and those on well-drained soils at high elevations. The latter, Timberline Scrubforest and Krummholz, owe only some of their poor growth to elevation-induced cool temperatures, as demonstrated by small pockets of tall trees in protected settings and on deep colluvial materials of steep slopes. A major environmental factor shaping Timberline Scrubforest and Krummholz is strong wind—southeasterly fall and winter gales to which Brooks Peninsula is exposed.

Stunted growth in the Bog Scrubforests is explained by wet soil and poor nutrition, both the result of a humid macroclimate. For similar situations in southeastern Alaska, Zach (1950) discusses how cool temperatures, and high precipitation and its even distribution throughout the seasons, together with a high incidence of clouds and fog and resulting low evapotranspiration, inhibit decomposition and favour accumulation of organic matter. Banner et al. (1990) found, for areas with vegetation similar to that of the Brooks Peninsula, that evapotranspiration values were generally lower than those in the adjacent Maritime Coastal Western Hemlock Subzones. This, together with cool, wet soils is bound to reduce organic matter decomposition, assimilation processes, rate of growth, and total productivity (Banner et al. 1983). Available rooting depth is restricted because of poor aeration in water-saturated soils. Ugolini and Mann (1979) point out that paludification of forest sites in similar situations in southeastern Alaska proceeds from initial formation of iron-cemented impermeable pans in the soil profile. Similar hardpans were observed in Bog Scrubforest soils on Brooks Peninsula (see Chapter 4), but the samples are too few to indicate how common this mechanism for restricting available rooting space and nutrition may be. Impermeable pans would explain stunted growth where only very shallow surface layers of organic matter are present in bog forests and blanket bogs on Brooks Peninsula.

Coastal Modifications Versus Subalpine Conditions

In a review of the terms "subarctic" and "subalpine", Löve (1970: 69) defines the subalpine belt as the "natural belt below the treeless belt from the upper altitudinal tree line to the closed montane forest". In the same review, she describes both the subarctic zone and the subalpine belt as the "forest-tundra ecotone". The Krummholz and Timberline Scrubforest vegetation types of Brooks Peninsula certainly satisfy Löve's definition—they are part of the belt below the highest treeless zone. Thus, on this physiognomic basis, there is a subalpine zone on Brooks Peninsula.

There are, however, structural differences between this zone and the typical subalpine of adjacent areas on Vancouver Island and the mainland coast. In the transition to non-forested alpine vegetation, typical subalpine areas consist of islands of coniferous trees and Krummholz colonies surrounded by meadows or heath. The configuration of this vegetation is shaped largely by the distribution of snow-hollows and persistent snow patches. Tree islands are uncommon on Brooks Peninsula, where, in general, there is an abrupt boundary between scrubforest and Krummholz and heath. The boundary is usually associated with ridge crests. Discontinuous woody patches occur, but these often occupy hollows protected from the wind. In the adjacent mountains, such hollows collect and retain snow well into the growing season and would be free of trees.

The tree line position is an interesting feature on Brooks Peninsula. Over a distance of 16 km, the tree line rises from 300 m to 800 m, between exposed Senecio Ridge near Cape Cook and the highest ridges on the peninsula. Farther into the Vancouver Island Ranges, about 30 km, the tree line reaches 1300 m. Even in the absence of detailed climatic data for the peninsula, it appears that cold temperatures alone are not responsible for limiting tree growth. Notably, the lapse rate in most climates is only 6°C/1000 m of elevation (MacArthur 1972: 7). Complete absence of snow-bed communities, both above and below tree line, is significant in this connection. On the other hand, the distinctly-shaped vegetation associated with Brooks Peninsula's treeless ridges provides strong evidence that high winds are a major factor responsible for the position and structure of the tree line. Löve (1970: 68) acknowledges that "wind most likely has as much a decisive role as temperature on the limits of tree growth and Krummholz formation at high altitude".

Another way of viewing this problem, is to examine the vegetation for subalpine species, that is, species usually associated with subalpine ecosystems in southwestern British Columbia. On Brooks Peninsula, an upper timberline forest is formed by *Tsuga mertensiana*, *Chamaecyparis nootkatensis*, and *Abies amabilis*, as in other mountain ranges of the northern Pacific Coast (Brooke et al. 1970). Dwarfed, stunted trees and Krummholz colonies of these species make up the timberline vegetation. Between the colonies, and at higher elevations, there are heath and meadow communities.

The shrubs *Cladothamnus pyroliflorus*, *Phyllodoce empetriformis*, and, rarely, *Vaccinium deliciosum* (Cascade blueberry) are typical subalpine species that occur in some of the Krummholz stands, but they are never dominant. These species may be significant in identifying subalpine conditions, but they are equally common (possibly more common) in the Bog Scrubforest at lower elevations (Table 8.1). The Queen Charlotte Islands exhibit a similar phenomenon (Calder and Taylor 1968). There, as on Brooks Peninsula, a cloudy, cool, moist climate and winds favour the growth of montane species in open habitats near sea level.

On the basis of species composition and typical structural features it is not possible to recognize differences among the communities in Krummholz, Timberline Scrubforest, and Mountain Slope Forest, despite their different physiognomies. Though there are physiognomic and floristic similarities to typical coastal subalpine vegetation, upper elevation forest communities are different from other coastal subalpine communities described to date. Rather, they are similar to some of the oceanic mountain communities of the Queen Charlotte Islands.

On Brooks Peninsula, the alpine zone differs from that on adjacent mountains. The anomalous features are: the relatively low elevation of timberline and alpine, the impoverished alpine flora, and absence of widespread typical alpine species. Some examples of common alpine species that are absent from Brooks Peninsula include *Silene acaulis* (moss campion), *Sibbaldia procumbens* (creeping sibbaldia), and several alpine species of *Saxifraga*, *Draba*, *Erigeron*, *Potentilla*, and *Carex*. Brooks Peninsula alpine plant species are typical of the low alpine to subalpine habitats of other mountain ranges; none are mid-alpine or high-alpine species (Ogilvie 1978). The highest peak on Brooks Peninsula reaches approximately 900 m, and most ridges and summits range between 600 m and 900 m. Since high alpine habitats are lacking, this at least in part can explain the impoverished alpine flora, and the absence of high alpine and mid-alpine species.

The low elevation of Brooks Peninsula's timberline and alpine zone results from the extreme oceanic climate and wind exposure. A similar phenomenon exists in Norway and in northern Britain. In the more continental climate of eastern Norway, timberline occurs at 1000 m, in the more maritime central Norway it occurs at 750 m, and on the oceanic west coast of Norway, timberline is at 500 m. The pattern in Scotland is even more dramatic. In the more continental climate of eastern Scotland, timberline is at 650 m, in oceanic western Scotland it occurs at 375 m. On the strongly oceanic Isle of Skye, timberline occurs at 310 m (Birks 1973; McVean and Ratcliffe 1962; Poore and McVean 1957).

Little information is available on timberline ecology in southern hyperoceanic climates. For the southern hemisphere, Mark and Bayliss (1963) and Wardle (1971, 1974) report timberline altitudes of ca. 900 m on Secretary Island (45° S) and 200 m on Campbell Island (53° S), both south of New Zealand; and at 450 m on Hermite Island (56° S) south of Chile. On the islands of northern Japan (44-45° N), timberline occurs at 450 m on Rebrun Island and at ca. 400 m in the southern Kurile Islands (Numata 1974; Numata et al. 1972; Tatewaki 1963). In the Japanese Islands, though there are distinct timberlines and extensive alpine floras, both Kojima (1979) and Hamet-Ahti et al. (1974) question the existence of alpine vegetation, on the grounds that it does not conform to their theoretical ecological zonal concepts. From these geographic data from northern coastal Europe, northern coastal Asia, and southern oceanic New Zealand and Chile, it can be seen that the occurrence of timberline and alpine vegetation at extremely low elevations is a widespread phenomenon associated with strongly oceanic environments comparable to the conditions on Brooks Peninsula.

Relationships of Alpine Vegetation

Comparison with alpine and subalpine vegetation of other mountain systems is difficult because the mountain flora of Brooks Peninsula is impoverished. Perhaps most comparable is the mountain vegetation of the Queen Charlotte Islands. There too, the flora is poor and restricted, and many of the species range over diverse habitats (Calder and Taylor 1968).

Rock habitats on the Queen Charlotte Islands include cliffs, runnels, crevices, ledges, and outcrops, and several plant species that grow in them have similar habitats on Brooks Peninsula, as for example *Cryptogramma crispa* (parsley fern), *Saxifraga ferruginea* (Alaska saxifrage), *S. taylori*, and *Carex circinata*. The meadow vegetation types of the two areas also show some similarities, for example, both include *Deschampsia cespitosa, Erigeron peregrinus, Dodecatheon jeffreyi,* and *Eriophorum angustifolium.*

Throughout the mountains of western North America, alpine heath vegetation is widespread. The distinctive features of this vegetation are its physiognomy and its dominance by *Phyllodoce and Cassiope*. Beyond these common features, there is considerable geographic variation in the particular species of these genera that are dominant, in their associated species composition, and in their habitat relationships. In general, *Phyllodoce empetriformis* and *Cassiope mertensiana* occur in mountain ranges having more oceanic climates, *Phyllodoce glanduliflora* (yellow mountain-heather) and *Cassiope tetragona* (four-angled cassiope) grow in more continental climatic conditions, and *Cassiope lycopodioides* (club-moss cassiope) and *C. stelleriana* are primarily species of the northern coastal mountains. Communities of *Phyllodoce empetriformis-Cassiope mertensiana* have been described for the southern Coast Mountains of British Columbia (Brooke et al. 1970), the Olympic Peninsula (Kuramoto and Bliss 1970), and the western North Cascade Range of Washington (Douglas 1972; Franklin and Dyrness 1973). Heath vegetation in the Queen Charlotte Mountains is composed of *Cassiope lycopodioides* ssp. *cristapilosa, C. mertensiana, C. stelleriana,* and *Phyllodoce glanduliflora; Phyllodoce empetriformis* is absent from the archipelago. On Vancouver Island, except for Brooks Peninsula, *Phyllodoce empetriformis* and *Cassiope mertensiana* are the major heath species; *Phyllodoce glanduliflora* is less common, and *Cassiope stelleriana* and *C. lycopodioides* are rare. Brooks Peninsula heath communities, characterized by *Empetrum, Phyllodoce empetriformis, Vaccinium uliginosum,* and *V. caespitosum*, resemble heath vegetation of islands off British Columbia's central and northern mainland coast, such as Pitt, Princess Royal, and Calvert Islands (J. Pojar personal communication, February 1988).

The Moist Meadow and Stream Margins communities on Brooks Peninsula show some similarity to the *Leptarrhena-Caltha* community in the southern Coast Mountains (Brooke et al. 1970), and to Streamside Communities in the Washington Cascade Mountains (Franklin and Dyrness 1973).

In summary, on Brooks Peninsula, the mountain vegetation does have a pattern of altitudinal zonation, albeit different from that on adjacent mountain ranges of Vancouver Island and coastal mainland. The trees of the upper subalpine forest form a distinct timberline of Krummholz and stunted growth forms. The meadows and heaths at and above timberline are similar physiognomically, if only partly floristically, to those of other western Canadian mountain ranges. The low elevation of the timberline and the alpine zone is attributable to an extreme oceanic climate and is consistent with the occurrence of these zones in other hyperoceanic environments.

Bog Vegetation

The plant communities of Brooks Peninsula's bogs, specifically Bog Scrubforest, Bog Shrub, and Bog Herbaceous Vegetation, are intriguing. They include a rich assemblage of species with obvious bog affinities, yet are unlike most other bogs on Vancouver Island. Perhaps, the most interesting feature is that these bogs occur on very shallow peat, usually less than .5 m deep.

Banner et al. (1988) classify the extensive bogs of the rolling lowlands of Brooks Peninsula as "Slope Bogs", within the Pacific Oceanic Wetland Region. Examples of their two slope bog types, each containing two subtypes, can be found on Brooks Peninsula. The "Coniferous Forest Type" is mainly equivalent to Bog Scrubforest Vegetation, but probably also includes part of our Wet Lowland Forest. Their "Tall Shrub Type" is equivalent to Bog Shrub and Bog Herbaceous Vegetation. Bog Shrub communities more or less conform to the characteristics of the "deep phase" of the Tall Shrub Type, both in species composition and in physiognomy. However, peat depth in this bog type on Brooks Peninsula rarely exceeds one metre. The "shallow phase" of the Tall Shrub Type encompasses some vegetation that we classify as Bog Shrub and Bog Herbaceous Vegetation.

Many of the bogs on Brooks Peninsula develop over very shallow peat, usually less than .5 m deep. Patches of mineral soil are exposed throughout this vegetation and provide substrates for a variety of herbs. However, even in these settings predominantly bog or bog-associated species grow. Why do these boggy areas not support more vigorous plant growth? The answer may lie with three factors: soil chemistry, hydrology, and climate.

The role of soil chemistry may be viewed as follows. The upper layers of the soil profile have been leached of important nutrients, especially calcium and magnesium. Limited sampling reveals that the pH of these soils is very low (see Chapter 4), with some mineral-dominated horizons yielding pH values as low as 3.2. In some cases, the peat has higher pH and more available cations than the underlying mineral horizons. However, it makes little difference to the plant whether its roots are in contact with peat or mineral soil or a combination thereof--serious nutrient deficiencies exist.

Ground water moves in abundance through most of the slope bogs, thus the bogs are not truly ombrotrophic, or rain-fed, in the classic raised-bog sense. The ground water, however, is very poor in nutrients, especially because it may flow above the cemented iron or placic pan. This pan occurs at shallow depths, restricting the potential nutrient source to a very small volume. Only along streamlets where the flux of water is great, is there a sufficient rate of nutrient supply to favour non-bog plants such as alder and salmonberry.

The role of climate is two-fold. High rainfall results in soils that are intensively leached and have low nutrient concentrations. It also results in waterlogged conditions, which together with very low pH inhibit solubility and availability of nutrients. Combined with low soil temperatures these factors result in low availability and low uptake of nutrients by the plants. Low temperatures and high relative humidity also imply very low transpiration rates. Plants are covered in dew and surrounded by mist for long intervals. Water and nutrients from the soil may be drawn slowly since moisture is not lost from leaf surfaces. Such a phenomenon needs to be tested under natural field conditions.

Marsh Vegetation

Freshwater marshes occur infrequently along the west coast of Vancouver Island. These marshes are usually associated with freshwater deltas or estuaries and are typically dominated by grasses, usually *Deschampsia*. Brooks Peninsula conforms to this pattern and does not have extensive estuarine systems or freshwater deltas where there is sufficient flow of nutrient-rich water associated with water-table draw-down during the growing season. Furthermore, the pH of most of the ground water is sufficiently acidic that only acidophilic, or bog, species are favoured in potential marsh habitats.

Calder and Taylor (1968) give detailed descriptions of salt marsh vegetation on the Queen Charlotte Islands. Their species lists for marshes of high and low salinity contain most of the species that grow on Brooks Peninsula, as well as many more that do not. Most salt marsh plants on Brooks Peninsula are wide-ranging Pacific Coast species. On Vancouver Island, *Deschampsia cespitosa* communities, *Carex lyngbyei* communities, and *Glaux maritima* communities similar to those on Brooks Peninsula are described for the Somass River estuary (van Dieren 1982), Little Qualicum River estuary (Dawe and White 1982), and the Nanoose estuary (Dawe and White 1986).

Vegetation and the Refugium Question

Does the vegetation provide any information on the question of a refugium on Brooks Peninsula? To discuss this question, we need to examine the origin of Brooks Peninsula plant communities. The present plant communities originated from separate migrations of individual species at different times. In addition to the postglacial immigrants, some of these species are believed to have survived glaciation, as discussed in Chapters 5 and 9. Climatic changes during postglacial time have resulted in contractions and extensions of species' ranges, producing further changes in the species composition of the vegetation. Consequently, rather than speak of relict communities, it is more meaningful to think of relict species and their habitats.

The endemic and disjunct species occur in a few specialized habitats of the high mountains. The mountain cliff habitat has high concentrations of such species, including *Isopyrum savilei, Saxifraga taylori, Geum schofieldii, Ligusticum calderi, Calamagrostis purpurascens* ssp. *tasuensis, Artemisia trifurcata*, and *Artemisia arctica*. The plants of this habitat are confined to crevices and ledges and are free from strong competition from surrounding forest and wetland vegetation. It is very likely that this cliff habitat and some of the species in it survived the last glaciation.

The windblown ridge habitat supports the rare species *Ligusticum calderi, Senecio moresbiensis*, and *Viola biflora* ssp. *carlottae*, which occur on exposed mineral soil destabilized by wind erosion and frost action. The age of this habitat is uncertain. On the one hand, the soil profile is intensively weathered and likely ancient; on the other hand, the habitat supports all the common alpine heath and Krummholz species that also provide strong competition for the relict species. The moist meadow and alpine heath habitats surrounding Cassiope Pond contain relict taxa such as *Ligusticum calderi, Calamagrostis purpurascens* ssp. *tasuensis*, and *Carex circinata*. The pollen record (see Chapter 9) indicates that the plants of these habitats have been relatively stable for at least 11 000 years and shows a continuous record for one of the endemic species, *Ligusticum calderi*, during this interval. Habitats such as these might have persisted through glacial times.

In summary, individual plant species of specialized habitats, rather than entire plant communities, can provide insight into potential refugial conditions. High mountain habitats such as those on alpine cliffs and exposed ridges and adjacent to mountain ponds, have the highest concentrations of relict species and suggest refugial conditions.

The major categories of vegetation from Brooks Peninsula have been described. Although similar to vegetation of surrounding areas, there are numerous differences, particularly at high elevation and in lowland bogs. These differences are partly related to the hyperoceanic climate, to the small land area, and to the limited altitudinal range of Brooks Peninsula. But, some of the differences may also be related to the peninsula's glacial history. The plant communities contain species in unusual associations, similar to some of those of the Queen Charlotte Islands. A firm understanding of the vegetation can only come with further studies of the relationships of plant communities to soil and climate and their history in this remarkably diverse terrain. This paper serves as a first step towards that goal.

References Cited

Agriculture Canada Expert Committee on Soil Survey. 1987. The Canadian System of Soil Classification. 2nd edition. Can. Dept. Agric. Publ. 1646. Ottawa.

Atmospheric Environment Service. 1982. Canadian climatic normals 1951-1980. Vol. 5, Wind. Environment Canada, Victoria, BC.

Banner, A. 1983. Classification and successional relationships of some bog and forest ecosystems near Prince Rupert, British Columbia. M.Sc. thesis. Faculty of Forestry, University of British Columbia, Vancouver, BC.

______ , J. Pojar and G.E. Rouse. 1983. Postglacial paleoecology and successional relationships of a bog woodland near Prince Rupert, British Columbia. Can. J. For. Res. 13: 938-947.

______ , ______ , I. Moss and L. McCulloch. 1990. Ecosystem classification and interpretation of the coastal western hemlock zone, very wet hypermaritime subzone (CWHvh) within the mid coast, north coast, and Queen Charlotte Islands timber supply areas. Ms., Forest Sciences Section, BC Ministry of Forests, Smithers, BC.

______ , ______ , J.W. Schwab and R. Trowbridge. 1989. Vegetation and soils of the Queen Charlotte Islands: recent impacts of development. In G.G.E. Scudder and N. Gessler (eds.). The outer shores. University of British Columbia, Vancouver, BC. 21-24 August, 1984.

______ , ______ , Trowbridge, and W.J. Beese. 1990. Ecosystem classification of the coastal western hemlock zone wet hypermaritime subzone (CWHwh), Queen Charlotte Islands, British Columbia. Ms., Forest Sciences Section, BC Ministry of Forests, Smithers, BC.

______ , R.J. Hebda, J. Pojar, E.T. Oswald and R. Trowbridge. 1988. Wetlands of Pacific Canada. Pp. 305-346 in National Wetlands Working Group (eds.). Wetlands of Canada. Ecological Land Classification Series 24. Sustainable Development Branch, Environment Canada, Ottawa and Polyscience Publications, Montreal.

Bell, M.A.M. 1972. Flora and vegetation of Pacific Rim National Park: phase I, Long Beach. Ms., Canada Dept. of Indian and Northern Affairs, Ottawa.

______ and A. Harcombe. 1973. Flora and vegetation of Pacific Rim National Park: phase 2, Broken Group Islands. Ms., Canada Dept. of Indian and Northern Affairs, Ottawa.

Birks, H.J.B. 1973. Past and present vegetation of the Isle of Skye: a palaeoecological study. Cambridge University Press, London.

Brooke, R.C., E.B. Peterson, and V.J. Krajina. 1970. The subalpine mountain hemlock zone. Ecology of western North America (Dept. Bot., University of B.C., Vancouver) 2: 147-349.

Calder, J.A. and R.L. Taylor. 1968. Flora of the Queen Charlotte Islands. Part 1. Systematics of the vascular plants. Can. Dep. Agric. Res. Branch, Monogr. 4, Pt. 1, Ottawa.

Ceska, A. 1978. Vegetation classification. I. A computer method for handling vegetation data. II. Wetland plant communities in the wet Douglas fir subzone of Vancouver Island. Ph.D. thesis. Department of Biology, University of Victoria, Victoria, BC.

______ and H. Roemer. 1971. A computer program for identifying-species releve groups in vegetation studies. Vegetatio: Acta Geobotanica 23: 255-277.

Chapman, J.D. 1952. The climate of British Columbia. In D.B. Turner and H.V. Warren (eds.). Transactions of the Fifth British Columbia Natural Resources Conference, February 27-29, 1952. The British Columbia National Resources Conference, Victoria, BC.

Cordes, L.D. 1972. An ecological study of the Sitka spruce forest on the west coast of Vancouver Island. Ph.D. thesis. Department of Botany, University of British Columbia, Vancouver, BC.

______ , S.L. Hartwell and G.A. Mackenzie. 1974. Vegetation and flora of the West Coast Trail, phase III of Pacific Rim National Park. Ms., National and Historic Parks Branch, Canada Dept. of Indian Affairs and Northern Development, Calgary, AB.

Dawe, N.K. and E.R. White. 1982. Some aspects of the vegetation ecology of the Little Qualicum River estuary, British Columbia. Can. J. Bot. 60: 1447-1460.

______ and E.R. White. 1986. Some aspects of the vegetation ecology of the Nanoose-Bonell estuary, Vancouver Island, British Columbia. Can. J. Bot. 64: 27-34.

Douglas, G.W. 1972. Subalpine plant communities of the western North Cascades, Washington. Arct. Alp. Res. 4: 147-166.

Forest Inventory Division. 1969. Forest Cover Map 92-L-4-d. [map] 1" = 20 chains. BC Forest Service, Dept. of Lands, Forest and Water Resources, Victoria, BC.

Franklin, J.F. and C.T. Dyrness. 1973. Natural vegetation of Oregon and Washington. United States Forest Service Gen. Tech. Rep. PNW-417.

Hamet-Ahti, L., T. Ahti and T. Koponen. 1974. A scheme of vegetation zones for Japan and adjacent regions. Ann. Bot. Fenn. 11: 59-88.

Holland, S.S. 1976. Landforms of British Columbia, a physiographic outline. Bull. 48, BC Dept. Mines and Petroleum Resources.

Hulten E. 1969. Vascular plants. Pp. 56-95 in T.N.V. Karlstrom and G.E. Ball (eds.) The Kodiak Island refugium: its geology, flora, fauna and history. Boreal Institute, University of Alberta, Edmonton, AB.

Jungen, J.R. and Lewis, T. 1978. The Coast Mountains and islands. Pp 101-120 in W.G. Valentine, P.N. Sprout, T.E. Baker, and L.M. Lavkulich (eds.). The soil landscapes of British Columbia. Resource Analysis Branch, BC Ministry of Environment, Victoria, BC.

Klinka, K. and R.E. Carter. 1980. Ecology and silviculture of the most productive ecosystems for growth of Douglas-fir in southwestern British Columbia. Land Management Report 6. BC Ministry of Forests, Victoria, BC.

______ , F.C. Nuszdorfer, and L. Skoda. 1979. Biogeoclimatic units of central and southern Vancouver Island, BC Ministry of Forests, Victoria, BC.

______ , J. Pojar and D.V. Meidinger. 1991. Revision of biogeoclimatic units of coastal British Columbia. Northwest Science 65: 32-47.

______ , R.N. Green, P.J. Courtin and F.C. Nuszdorfer. 1984. Site diagnosis, tree species selection, and slashburning guidelines for the Vancouver Forest Region. Land Management Report 25. BC Ministry of Forests, Victoria, BC.

______ , ______ , R.L. Trowbridge and L.E. Lowe. 1981. Taxonomic classification of humus forms in ecosystems of British Columbia; first approximation. Land Management Report 8, BC Ministry of Forests, Victoria, BC.

______, W.D. van der Horst, F.C. Nuszdorfer, and R.G. Harding. 1980. An ecosystematic approach to a subunit plan: Koprino River watershed study. Land Management Report 5. BC Ministry of Forests, Victoria, BC.

Kojima, S. 1979. Biogeoclimatic zones of Hokkaido Island, Japan. J. Coll. Lib. Arts, Toyama Univ., Nat. Sci. 12: 97-141.

______ and V.J. Krajina. 1975. Vegetation and environment of the coastal western hemlock zone in Strathcona Provincial Park, British Columbia. Syesis 8, Suppl. 1.

Krajina, V.J. 1965. Biogeoclimatic zones and classification of British Columbia. Ecology of western North America (Dept. Bot., University of BC, Vancouver) 1: 1-17.

Kuramoto R.T. and L.C. Bliss. 1970. Ecology of subalpine meadows in the Olympic Mountains, Washington. Ecol. Monogr. 40: 317-347.

Lewis, T. 1982. The Ecosystems of tree-farm licence 24, Queen Charlotte Islands, B.C. Contract report. Prepared for Rayonier (Canada) Ltd., Vancouver, BC.

______ . 1985. Ecosystems of the Quatsino tree farm licence (TFL 6). Contract report. Prepared for Western Forest Products Ltd., Vancouver, BC.

Löve, D. 1970. Subarctic and subalpine: where and what? Arct. Alp. Res. 2(1): 63-73.

MacArthur, R.H. 1972. Geographical ecology: patterns in the distribution of species. Princeton Univ. Press, Princeton, NJ.

McVean, D.N. and D.A. Ratcliffe. 1962. Plant communities of the Scottish highlands. Nature Conservancy Monogr. 1 H.M. Stationery Office, London.

Mark, A.F. and G.T.S. Bayliss. 1963. Vegetation studies on Secretary Island, Fiordland. Part 6. The subalpine vegetation. New Zealand J. Botany 1: 215-220.

Meidinger, D.V. and J. Pojar (eds.). 1991. Ecosystems of British Columbia. Special Report Series No. 6. BC Ministry of Forests, Victoria, BC.

Mueller-Dombois, D. and H. Ellenberg. 1974. Aims and methods of vegetation ecology. John Wiley and Sons, NY.

Muller, J.E. 1983. Geology, Alert Bay-Cape Scott, British Columbia. Map 1552A, Geological Survey of Canada.

Numata, M. (ed.) 1974. The flora and vegetation of Japan. Elsevier Sci. Publ., London.

______, A. Miyawaki, and S. Itow. 1972. Natural and semi-natural vegetation in Japan. Blumea 20: 435-496.

Neiland, B.J. 1971. The forest-bog complex of southeast Alaska. Vegetatio: Act Geobotanica 22: 1-63.

Ogilvie, R.T. 1978. The alpine and subalpine of the Rocky Mountains of Alberta. In A. Luttmerding and A. Shield (eds.). Proceedings of the workshop on alpine and subalpine environments. Resource Analysis Branch, BC Ministry of Environment, Victoria, BC.

______ and A. Ceska. 1984. Alpine plants of phytogeographic interest on northwestern Vancouver Island. Can. J. Botany 62: 2356-2362.

Packee, E.C. 1974. The biogeoclimatic subzones of Vancouver Island and the adjacent mainland and islands. Forest Research Note. MacMillan Bloedel, Nanaimo, BC.

Pattison, A. 1980. Terrain [map]. Resource Analysis Branch, BC Ministry of the Environment, Victoria, BC. 92L/4.

Pojar, J. 1983. Forest ecology. In Forestry handbook for British Columbia. Edited by S. Watts. 4th ed. Forestry Undergraduate Society, Faculty of Forestry, University of British Columbia, Vancouver, BC. Pp. 221-318.

______ and R.M. Annas. 1980. Coastal cedars-pine-hemlock (CCPH)—a new biogeoclimatic zone for British Columbia? Abstract Bot. Soc. Am. Misc. Ser. Publ. 158: 90.

______ , F.C. Nuszdorfer, D. Demarchi, M. Fenger, T. Lea and B. Fuhr. (comps). 1988. Biogeoclimatic and ecoregion units of the Prince Rupert Forest Region [2 maps]. 1:500,000. Research Branch, BC Ministry of Forests and Lands, Victoria, BC.

Poore, M.E.D. and D.N. McVean. 1957. A new approach to Scottish mountain vegetation. J. Ecol. 45: 401-439.

Rowe, J.S. 1972. Forest regions of Canada. Publ. 1300. Canada Department of Environment, Canadian Forestry Service, Ottawa.

Tatewaki, M. 1963. Alpine plants in Hokkaido. Sci. Rep. Tohoku Univ., Ser. 4 (Biology) 29: 165-188.

Technical Committee. 1982. Biophysical resources of the Tahsish-Kwois. BC Ministry of Environment (Victoria) APD Bull. 26.

Ugolini, F.C. and D.H. Mann. 1979. Biopedological origin of peatlands in southeast Alaska. Nature 281: 366-368.

van Dieren, W. 1982. Somass River delta: a study of the flora and vegetation. Ms., Royal BC Provincial Museum, Victoria, BC.

Wade, L.K. 1965. Vegetation and history of *Sphagnum* bogs of the Tofino area, Vancouver Island. M.Sc. thesis, Department of Botany, University of British Columbia, Vancouver, BC.

Wardle, P. 1971. An explanation for alpine timberline. New Zealand J. Botany 9: 371-402.

______ . 1974. Alpine timberlines. Pp. 371-401 in J.D. Ives and R.G. Barry (eds.) Arctic and alpine environments. Methuen, London.

Wetzel, R.G. 1975. Limnology. W.B. Saunders, Philadelphia.

Williams, G.D.V. 1968. Climate. Pp. 15-49 in J.A. Calder and R.L. Taylor (eds.). Flora of the Queen Charlotte Islands. Part 1. Systematics of the vascular plants. Can. Dep. Agric. Res. Branch, Monogr. 4, Pt. 1. Ottawa.

Zach, L.W. 1950. A northern climax, forest or muskeg? Ecology 31: 304-306.

Appendix 8.1 Abbreviations for vegetation tables

Elevation	- height above sea level, in metres.
Slope	- angle of slope, recorded in degrees, percent, or in qualitative terms: flat (f), gentle (g), moderate (m) steep (st), cliff (cl), chasm (ch).
Aspect	- direction of exposure: north (N), south (S), east (E), west (W).
Stand type	- general physiognomy of vegetation: Alpine Heath (AH), Alpine Meadow (AM), Alpine Cliff - Shade (ACu), Alpine Cliff - Sun (ACs), Alpine Cliff Ledge (ACl), Alpine Chasm Floor (ACh), Beach Shrub (BS), Beach Herb (BH), Shore Headland Herb (SH), Salt Marsh Herb (SM).
Substrate	- rooting medium of the vegetation: Soil (S), Gravel (G), Rubble (R), Outcrop (O).
Analyst	- person(s) who recorded the vegetation analysis: A. Banner (B), R. Hebda (H), R.T. Ogilvie (O), H. Roemer (R).

The occurrence of the species in the stand plots is indicated by:
X - present, - - = absent; or with the following estimates of Coverage:
r = single individual; + = few individuals, less than 1% cover; 1 = 1-5%;
2 = 5-25%; 3 = 25-50%; 4 = 50-75%; 5 = 75-100%. See Mueller-Dombois and Ellenberg (1974) for coverage scales.

Appendix 8.2 Synthesis table for Forest and Scrubforest Vegetation types on Brooks Peninsula

		1	2	3	4	5	6	7	8	9	10
	elevation (m)[1]	4 4 7 6 4 6 7 3 5	6 6 6 4 3	7 7 3 5 6 7 6 6 6 5 4 8 5 5 2 5 4 3 1 6 6	2 1 2 1	1 2		1	1	1 1 2 3 2	5 1 3 2 3
		3 6 0 3 3 0 6 9 5	5 7 0 0 9	6 7 6 7 0 6 6 4 7 8 6 4 2 7 5 8 6 6 6 0 6	1 7 5 4 1 0 0 2 3	8 0 5	9	4 4 2	3 5 2 3 8 2 3 6	0 8 5 6 2 2	1 0 6 4 6
		0 0 0 0 0 0 0 0 0	0 0 0 0 0	0 0 0 0 0 0 0 0 0 0 0 0 0 0 0 0 0 0 0 0 0	0 0 0 5 0 0 0 0 0 5 0	0 0 5 5 5 0 5	3 3 0 3	5 0 5 3 0 0	0 0 0 0 0 5 0 0	0 0 0 0 0 0	5 0 0 0 0 0
	slope (deg.)[2]	1 1	3 3 3	2 2 2 3 3 4 4 2 3 2 3 2 2 3	3 3 2	3 3			1 1		3
		- g 0 - - 7 - 3 8	- 5 ■ 0 0	5 0 2 ■ 7 - - 0 0 0 0 - 2 0 ■ 7 5 5 0 0 2	- g g 2 0 0 - ■ g - 0	5 5 - - - 9 -	- - - -	- - - - 3 2	5 3 - 3 3 8 - g	- - 5 - - -	- 2 0 - g g
	aspect[3]	S S S	S N	S N N S N S S N S S N N	N S N	N S			N S N	N	S S
		- E W - c E c E E	- N E W W	W S W W N c c W S W E c E E E W E E W W W	- N N - W N - N W - W	W W - - - N -	- - - -	- - - - E S	W W - S W E - E	c c W - c -	- E E - W E
	height of stand (m)[4]			1 1 2 1 4 3 2	2 2 3 2 3 3 1 2 4	3 3	3 3 3 3	2 1 2 2 1	2 1 1	1 1	1
		1 2 3 1 6 1 2 1 1	3 1 8 9 t	7 6 7 8 2 4 5 5 0 2 9 t t t 0 9 t t 0 0 0	5 5 0 t 5 t 0 0 5 5 0	8 t t t t 0 t	5 5 3 0	0 9 t 0 0 5	0 9 2 7 6 8 5 8	s 3 8 0 s 0	t 0 t s s 1
	type[5]	K K K K T K K K K	K K T T T	T T T T K K T T T T T M M M M M M M M M M	L L L L L L L L L L L	L L S S S S S	A A A A	W W R W W W	W W B B B B B B	B B B B B P	R B B B B B
	author[6]	0		0 0 0	R R	0		0	H	H	0 H H
		R R H 0 0 R R 0 H	H H R R H	H H R R R R R R H R R H H H R R H H R R O	R R R B B 0 H R R H R	R B B B B R H	R R R R	R R H R R R	R R R R R 0 R H	B H R H B R	H B B H H H
	plot number	3 3 5 5 5 5 7 5 5	5 6 7 3 6	5 5 3 1 5 1 5 5 5 9 6 5 5 5 6 9 0 0 7 9 5	4 4 0 0 0 0 0 0 2 6 2	2 0 0 0 0 2 0	5 5 7 5	5 7 0 0 2 5	4 2 4 5 2 5 2 6	0 5 3 6 0 4	0 0 0 6 6 6
		4 5 9 1 2 1 1 0 0	1 0 7 8 3	2 7 8 8 0 5 3 2 6 8 7 3 4 5 1 7 2 3 0 9 3	9 4 9 4 1 1 1 9 7 9 5	6 6 2 3 5 3 4	3 6 3 0	9 4 1 0 0 8	7 8 5 1 9 0 1 8	1 8 9 4 7 6	2 2 2 1 2 5
		0 0 0 0 0 0 0 0 0	0 0 0 0 0	0 0 2 0 0 0 0 0 0 0 0 0 0 0 0 0 0 0 0 0 0	0 0 1 0 0 0 0 2 0 0 0	0 0 0 0 0 0 0	0 0 0 0	0 0 0 5 0 0	0 0 0 0 0 0 0 0	0 0 0 0 0 0	0 2 1 0 0 0
	table sections	1	2	3	4	5	6	7	8	9	10
	copt aspl	1 1 2	2 2 +	4 4 x 3 x 3 3 3 4 3 2 2 1 1 2 2 3 x 2				+	x x + 1	2 1 + x	+ + +
1	tsug mert	2 3 4 2 X 3 x	4 4 x 2	3 2 X x 3 x 4 3 3 4 4 5 2 2 3 x 2					2 +	2 2 2	3 2
	vera esch	+ +	x	1 1 x 1 1 2 2 + 1 1 + x					x x x 1 x		2 +
2	mone unif	+		+ + + + 1 1 + 1 r x	+ x	x					
	stre stre		+	2 x r 1 + 2 1 1 + + + x							
	tiar trif		x	x x 1 x 1 2 3 3 2 + 3 3 + 2 4 x	x x x + 1 2 +	+ x 1	1 3 x x	x + + x x			2
3	vacc alas			x 3 x 4 2 3 4 2 2 1 2 3 2 x	X X x 2 x		3 2 x	x x x	2		
	tiar laci			2 3 3 3 1 3 4 2 2 5 x	x x + 1 2 +	+ x +	+ 2 x x	+			
	list cord	x	x +	+ + x 1 x 1 + 1 + 1 1 + 2 + + x	x + +	x +		+			
4	poly muni			+	x	X 5 2 2 3 x 4	1 3 x x				
	pice sitc				x	x 3 2 4 4 x 4	4 x x				
	fest subl						1 2 x				
5	adia peda						1 x x				
	arun sylv						x				
	care obnu						+ x	x + 2 x x x	x x	x	
6	lysi amer				x		x	x + 1 x x	x		+
	alnu rubr						x x	x 1 x			
	care laev							+ x x	x		
	oinu cont	x x 2 3 1 3 4 x	3		2			4 7 x x	3 x x x 2 x 2	2 2 x 2 x x	2 3 1 3 3 2
7	linn bore	x 1 1	x	x 1 2 2				r 1 x x x	1 x x x x 2 x 2	1 1 x 1 x	2 +
	lyco clav	x +		x x 1 1 + 1 +				x x	1 x x x 1 x +	+ + + x	+ 1 1 2
	empe nigr	x 2 x 2 X 3		1					2 x x 3 2	3 3 x x x	2 + 4 2 2
	ledu groe								+ x x 5 x 2	1 1 x 2 x x	
	agro aequ							x	1 x x x x x	x x	
8	trie arct							x	1 x x x +	x	
	kalm occi								x +	+ + + x x	
	care phyl							x	x x x x	x	
	vacc ulig	x 1 2 x 3								2 2 x x	2 2 2 2
	clad pyro	2 x 2 1		2						2	2 2 1
9	faur cris	2 2 1		2						2	2 3 + 2
	vacc caes	1 x 1 x								1 1 x	2 +
	desc cesp									+ + x + x	2 + 2
	blec spic	x 2 1 1 +	x 2	2 X x 1 2 2 2 2 1 1 2 2 1 1 3 4 1 x 2	X X x 4 2 3 4 X X 2 x	x 2 3 2 X 3	3 3 x	x 3 3 x X x	4 X x x x 2 X 2	2 2 x + x	5 2 4 1
	gaul shal	x x 2 x 4 1 3 x	x 4	X x x 2 3 1 2 2 1 2 + 4 + + +	x x x 5 2 5 4 x X 4 x	2 3 5 X 5	4 x x	x 4 4 x x X	3 x x x 3 x 2	2 2 x 3 x	2 3 4 2 + +
	tsug hete	x 1	x 2	x x 3 2 2 2 3 3 2 3 2 4 2 5 x 2	x x x 3 1 4 4 x x 3 x	x 3 2 3 2 x 2	4 4 x x	x 3 2 x x x	4 x x x 3 x 1	x 2 x	2 2 2 + +
	cham noot	x x 2 3 4 4 X 2 x	4 4 x x 3	x x 4 x 4 4 3 4 4 2 4 5 2 2	2 x x 2	+		x 4 2 x x	3 x x x x 2 x +	3 2 x 3 x x	3 3 3 2 2 2
	vacc parv	x 3 1	x 2	x x 2 x 2 1 3 2 2 2 2 2 5 x	x x x 3 1 3 2 x 2 X	+ + 2 x +	3 2 x x	x 3 2 x x x	2 x x 1 x +	+ + 1	1 2 2
	corn unal	x x 2 x 2 1 x 2 2	2 2 x 1	2 x x 2 x 2 1 + r 1 + 1	x x 1 2 + x 1			x + 2 x x x	1 x x x x 2 x 2	2 2 x 1 x	2 2 +
	maia dila	x x 1 2	+ + x 1	x x r 1 + +	x x x 1 2 + +	+ 1 + 1	2 1 x x	x 1 2 x x x	+ x x x 1 x 1	+ + x x	1 1 +
	thuj plic	x	x 3	x x 2 2 4 2	x X x 4 1 3 3 x X 3	3 2 X	4 4 x x	X 1 3 x x X	4 x x x x 3 x 3	3 2 x x	4 3 4 2
	menz ferr	2	x 2	x 3 2 + 2 2 + + 1 + 1 1 1	x x x 3 1 2 2 x + x	2 x 1	4 1 x	x 1 2 x x X	2 s x 2 x	+	1 + 2
	rhyt lore	X 4 4	x	3 3 x 4 x 4 4 5 3 5 5 3 + 5 3 4	x x 4 2 x x	+ 2 3 x 2	2 + x	x 3 3 x X x	2 x x x 2 x		3
	cala nutk	x X r 3 2 +	x x 2	x x 2 2 2 2 2 1 + x	x + 1		x	+ x X	4 X X x 3 x 2	2 2 x 1 x	4 1 3 +
	hylo sple	x 4 2	2 x +	2 x 4 2 2 2 1 + 2	x x 1 1 x	1 2	x	x 1 2 x	2 x x x + x		2 x
	abie amab	1 x	x	4 4 x 3 x 2 2 3 3 2 5 2 2 5 2 4 4 x 4	x 2 2 X	X 3 3	3 3 x				
	rubu peda	2 1	+ + x	4 4 x x 2 x 3 2 2 2 1 + + 2 1 3 2 x +	x			r 1 x x			
	plag undu			x 1 + 1 1 r + + r + r	x x 1 + x x	x + 1 x	+	+ x		+	1 + x
	rhiz glab	r +		x r + 3 + + 1 4 2 x	x x x 3 1 x	x + 2 x	3 1	+ +			+ 1

stok oreg	x	x	1 1 3 4	x 2 1 x x	x + 4 4 4 x	4 3 x	+ x x	2 x x		+
ligu cald	+	x	+ + 2 1 2 + 2 1 2 x				+ x	1	x	3 + + 2
rubu spec		s	+ 1	x 1 2 x x	+ 1 2 x 2	3 4 x x	x x x			1
scap bola			x + 1 2 2 3 + 2 + 1 + 3	x +	x		1	+ x 1 x		2
pell nees		x	x 2	x x + x	x x 1	2 + x	x + x x x	x		2
phyl empe	x x x 2		2 2 + 1 1 1 2						2 2 x 2 x	3 1 1 2
vacc oval	x 2	2 2 x	4 4 x x 2 x 3 2	1 2 2		1	2		1	
ceph spp.			x 1 1 + r + 1	x + x	x x	+	r + x	r x x		
dipl albi		2	x 1 1 + 1 1 r 1 r	x +	x	+	+	x		2 1
spha girg	x	x	2 1 2 + x	x x x		2	x x x	x x		1
list caur		x	x x r 2 + 1 + 1 r +	x x + x	+		+			
apar bore	x 1 r							x x + x 1	+ + x 1 x	1 2 1
stre ampl			+ r 1 + 1 +	x +	+	x x	x r + x			
isot stol		1	+ 1 + + + + 1 2		x + 1 2		1			2
viol sko		x	+ 2 1 2 2 +	+ 1		+ 2 x	+			+
caly muel		+	+ +	x x + x	x x	+	r +	r		
taxu brev				x 2 x 2			x 1 2	x x 2 x	3	1
habe sacc			+				x	x x x + x +	x +	+ + +
alnu sinu	1 x +	x	x 2	1				2	x x	2 2
spha rube	x	x						2 x x x x x	2 x x	x
dicr maju	2		1 1 +				+ x	+ x x 2	2 2	
gent doug	2 1							1 x	+ + x	+ 1 1 1
spha papi	x	x					x x x	x x x	2 x x	
plag aspl			+ + 1 + + +		1	1 1				
hupe sela	+		r r	+		+ x		x		+
herb adun		x	+				2	+ x 2	x	2
dicr scop			1 1 1 2				+	2		2 x
myli tayl			+	x +			+ x	r x x		
dryo assi			+ + x	+	x + +					
ricc sp.			x +	x x	x		x	x		
care mert		x	1 1 +			1		x x		
hypn circ			r + + r +		x					
viol glab			+ x			1 3 x x				2
dros rotu								x x +	+ x	+
rhyt triq	x		X + + 2							x
erig pere	+							+	x + x	+
clad miti								+ x x x 1	x	
pren alat		x	+ 1 x			x				+
bazz sp.					x x		x	+ x		
viol seko		1	x x	x			x			
pleu purp	1							2	2 2 x	
habe hype		x	r r +					x		
scir caes	4								+ x	2 2
leuc menz			2	x	x	3 x				
kurz seta		+		x	x		+			
stre rose		+	x 2 1							
hook luce			+		x x	r				
loph inci			x +	x	1					
juni comm	x							+	x	2
spha squa				x	+	1	x			
spha comp								x +	x	x
dicr fusc			+ 1 +				+			
hypn diec			1 +				+		+	
anti curt			+		1 v		+			
lyco anno	1			+			+		x	
rhac lanu	2								2 x	x
bazz denu			+ +	+			+			
erio angu									x	+ + 3

Species with low constancy:

fest subl (R730:x, R530:1, R560:2), hook ovat (R230:x, R260:x, OR500:r), pelt sp. (B020:+, OH040:1, OR500:+), cass stel (H530:n, OR500:1, OR510:1), osmo chil (R990:x, R970:-2, R530:+), care anth (R210:x, R390:x, R290:x), gali trif (R230:x, R730:x, R560:1), tofi glut (H620:+, H640:+, H680:+), clad impe (HB010:2, B070:x, H580:+), adia peda (R730:x, R500:x, R560:1), spha recu (R510:x, R450:x, OH010:+), isop eleg (R970:+, R980:3, H550:+), herb saku (HB010:2, OR510:1), junc falc (R280:x, H680:+), tris cern (R450:x, R500:x), luet pect (B070:x, H650:2), calo muel (R670:+, R700:1), luzu parv (R970:r, R730:x), aste foli (H610:+, H620:+), ping vulg (R470:+, H620:+), myri gale (B070:x, H680:+), foss sp. (R210:x, R280:x), rhiz nudu (R990:x, R980:1), spha palu (R590:x, OH010:2), ricc spp. (R530:r, OH010:x), vacc oxyc (R460:x, H610:2), pyru fusc (R590:x, R500:x), pleu schr (H610:x, H680:3), spha fimb (R490:x), spha subs (R290:x), equi telm (R590:x), spha cusp (R210:x), micr seta (R700:+), arun sylv (R500:x), pogo maco (R560:2), stok prae (R560:1), tolm menz (R560:r), oplo horr (R560:1), epil alpi (R730:x), dryo aust (R530:+), spha warn (R380:x), fest subf (R730:x), menz parv (R382:-x), trau caro (R560:2), moni parv (R730:x), habe chor (R350:x), pelt cani (R670:r), boyk elat (R500:x), pogo alpi (B050:+), stac cool (R500:x), corn cana (H570:2), frit cams (R390:x), athy fili (R560:1), thel pheg (R560:1), pogo cont (R560:3), vacc viti (B070:x), rhyt robu (H600:2), clin unif (H600:+), dicr spec (H580:2), loph sp. (R740:r), calt lept (H610:3), viol palu (R005:x), caly tric (H610:x), loph cusp (H610:x), lois proc (H620:1), dode jeff (H620:2), geum calt (H620:+), pani occi (H620:+), sela sela (H620:-+), meli subu (R500:x), para iner (H620:x), camp atro (H620:x), ceph spp (H630:+), sang offi (H640:+), spha russ (H640:+), spha quin (H640:+), good oblo (H680:+), dicr sp. (H690:1).

EXPLANATION FOR VEGETATION TABLE

(A) GENERAL

Each column represents one sample plot or releve. Table entries are either presence symbols (x, X) or cover-abundance values (other entries). For reasons of uniformity different cover-abundance scales originally used by the individual authors were converted into the simplest scale used (Braun-Blanquet scale).

Presence symbols: x = present
X = present and dominant

NOTE: Species of the bryophyte/lichen layer not, or incompletely recorded for some plots.

(B) EXPLANATION OF FOOTNOTES

1] Read down column (elevation of first plot is 430 m)
2] - = flat; g = gentle slope, m = moderate slope (no quantitative values available)
3] c = convex (i.e. rounded knoll or summit); - = flat
4] Where no height is given in numbers: s = shrub size; t = tree size
5] Abbreviations of physiognomic types (compare text): K = Krummholz, T = Timberline Scrubforest, M = Mountainslope Forest, L = Lowland Forest, S = Shoreline Forest, A = Alluvial Floodplain Forest, W = Wet Lowland Forest, R = Riparian Fringe Forest, B = (Blanket) Bog Scrubforest, P = (Peat) Bog Scrubforest
6] B = A.Banner; H = R.Hebda; O = R.Ogilvie; R = H.Roemer (Combinations:surveyed by two authors).

Braun-Blanquet cover-abundance values:
r = single or very few individuals with very low total cover
+ = few individuals, low cover < 1 %
----- 1 %
1
----- 5 %
2
----- 25 %
3
----- 50 %
4
----- 75 %
5
----- 100 %

Chapter 9

Late Quaternary Paleoecology of Brooks Peninsula

Richard J. Hebda
Botany and Earth History, Royal British Columbia Museum
Victoria, BC
and
Biology and School of Earth and Ocean Sciences, University of Victoria
Victoria, BC

Abstract

Location, geomorphology, and flora suggest that part of Brooks Peninsula escaped the most recent glaciation and served as a refugium. Pollen analysis and radiocarbon dates of lake sediments reveal 13 000 years of vegetation history that is divided into five intervals. *Pinus* pollen dominates the first interval (13 000-12 000 B.P.). *Tsuga mertensiana* pollen occurs in significant amounts suggesting that it occupied moist sites within a *Pinus contorta* forest. Climate was cool and possibly moist. *Tsuga heterophylla, T. mertensiana, Picea,* and *Abies* pollen replace *Pinus* pollen in the second interval (12 000-10 500 B.P.) Mixed coniferous forest of *T. mertensiana, Abies,* and *Picea* grew on the peninsula. *T. heterophylla* was abundant on lower slopes. Cool and very moist climate prevailed. *Alnus, Picea, T. heterophylla,* and *Abies* pollen predominate in the third interval from 10 500-9000 B.P. and a significant peak of *Pseudotsuga* pollen occurs. *Picea* forest, containing occasional *Pseudotsuga* trees, grew on mesic slopes. Possibly, shrubby *Alnus sinuata* occupied dry sites, whereas *Abies* and *T. heterophylla* grew on moist low slopes. Climate was warmer and possibly drier than today. Even so, wet meadows and heath persisted on high ridges. During the fourth interval (9000-2500 B.P.), *T. heterophylla* pollen predominates and *Abies* is abundant. *T. heterophylla* forest predominated except in moist sites, where *Abies* flourished. Warm and very moist climate prevailed. In the fifth interval (2500-0 B.P.), *Cuppressaceae* pollen is codominant with *T. heterophylla* pollen. These assemblages represent modern mid-elevation forests of *T. heterophylla, Thuja plicata,* and *Chamaecyparis nootkatensis.* A moist oceanic climate prevails.

Pollen evidence reveals that *Ligusticum calderi,* a herb endemic to Brooks Peninsula, the Queen Charlotte Islands, and a few coastal islands, has occupied subalpine and lowland sites for at least the last 12 000 years. This rare species may have survived in a glacial refugium on Brooks Peninsula.

Acknowledgements

First, I thank the Friends of the Royal British Columbia Museum for generous financial support of the project—it would not have been attempted without their help.

I thank all my co-participants for their discussions and ideas that helped crystallize my interpretation. I especially thank W.H. Mathews and W.B. Schofield, veterans of the Brooks Peninsula campaign. Many decades ago Bill Mathews had the idea that Brooks Peninsula might be a special place. Wilf Schofield sponsored the first modern botanical explorations, in which I was lucky enough to participate. I am grateful to Bob Ogilvie, Allen Banner, and Hans Roemer for botanical and ecological advice.

I thank Vancouver Island Helicopters for their patience with my peculiar cargo—the coring raft—and for landing in, shall we say, "awkward" places.

I am especially grateful to those colleagues who shared the coring experience—C.C. Chinnappa, Allen Banner, W.H. Mathews, John Cooper, Bjorn Simonsen, and Ruth Kirk.

Bob Powell patiently prepared, in the lab, the hundreds of samples that resulted. Nancy Condrashoff (now Romaine) drafted and redrafted, without complaint, my numerous figures. Elaine Patterson (now Hebda) patiently typed and retyped the manuscript. I thank Bjorn Simonsen for translating from Norwegian, Mangerud's (1973) important work on refugia.

My palynological colleagues, Cal Heusser, New York University; Rolf W. Mathewes, Simon Fraser University; and Barry Warner, University of Waterloo, were kind enough to provide critical and perceptive reviews of the manuscript.

I thank Ruth Kirk for the photo of Pyrola Lake, and Allen Banner for the photo of the coring platform on Kalmia Lake.

Introduction

Paleoecological studies of late Quaternary sediments, whether on Brooks Peninsula or in other suspected unglaciated areas, are central to establishing the existence of refugia. First, such investigations can identify sediments of full-glacial[1] age—that is, sediments that are dated by relative or absolute dating techniques to span the interval during which surrounding terrain was glaciated. Second, paleoecological studies can document the existence of full-glacial plants and animals and reveal their characteristics—incontrovertible evidence that a refugium existed (Mangerud 1973). Third, paleoecological studies of continuous sedimentary records, such as those preserved in lakes, bogs, and alluvium, reveal the history of plant and animal populations and communities, and so explain extant biotic distributions. Such information is critical in the study of refugia, because suspected areas often harbour endemic or rare plants or animals. The results of paleoecological studies might indicate reasons other than the existence of a refugium for anomalous distributions of organisms.

Further, the fossil and sediment records indicate the climatic and geomorphic conditions under which refugia persisted and the manner in which these conditions changed before and after glaciation.

---

[1] Full-glacial, or pleniglacial, time is the interval during which glacial ice is at, or near, its maximum extent.

Paleoecological studies of Brooks Peninsula depend principally on the techniques of pollen and plant macrofossil analysis of sediments (see Birks and Birks 1980). Plant remains, especially pollen grains, preserve well in the generally cool, often acidic sediments of the northern part of our hemisphere. Sediments containing fossil plants are relatively abundant. Large quantities of these fossils can be recovered to provide both local and regional reconstructions. The autecology of many plant species is sufficiently known to estimate environmental conditions.

Paleoecological studies of refugia or suspected refugia are scattered. Most have been carried out in larger, "open" refugia north or south of the glacial boundary. In his publications Colinvaux (1981 and references therein) has outlined many aspects of the Bering Land Bridge area. Ager (1975), Cwynar and Ritchie (1980), and Edwards and Brubaker (1984) revealed aspects of the environments of the interior of Alaska and eastern parts of the Beringian refugium, northwest of the North American ice sheets. South of the ice margins, Heusser (1972, 1977, 1983), Barnosky (1981, 1982), and Worona and Whitlock (1995) have described climatic and vegetation history spanning full-glacial and postglacial time. Watts (1983) outlined the environmental history south of the glacial boundary in eastern North America. In Europe, there is a remarkably long record spanning full-glacial time at Grande Pile Bog in France (Woillard 1978).

Paleoecological/palynological studies of closed, partly closed, or marginal (surrounded on three sides) late Pleistocene glacial refugia are rare. There are at least two reasons. First, not many such possible refugia have been identified. Second, the nature of the terrain and the likely nature of full-glacial environmental conditions conspire against the preservation of sediments suitable for paleobotanical analysis. Areas of possible closed refugia are usually mountainous, with few sites available for continuous sediment accumulation. This is especially so in the case of mountain peak refugia, or nunataks. There is a better chance of sediment preservation in coastal closed refugia and in partly closed refugia such as the "ice-free corridor" between the Cordilleran and Laurentide ice sheets (Ritchie 1980). Unfortunately, full-glacial conditions were likely quite severe, with strong winds and repeated freeze-thaw, and resultant mixing of the soil surface and poor vegetative cover. Much silt, sand, and coarser sediment was deposited in sedimentary basins. Such materials are difficult to penetrate with conventional coring devices and are characterized by either low pollen densities (because of both low pollen productivity of local vegetation and rapid sediment accumulation) or poor pollen preservation. Research on the Queen Charlotte Islands (Clague et al. 1982; Warner 1984; Warner et al. 1982), in Washington State (Heusser 1974), and in southwest Alberta (Mott and Jackson 1982), however, has revealed sediments preserved in closed and semi-closed refugia that spanned what can be considered to be full-glacial time. Studies of suspected refugia on the coasts of Alaska and Greenland failed to turn up full-glacial biotic records (Funder 1979; Mann 1983).

Not only is the Brooks Peninsula study area located in a possible glacial refugium, but it is also part of a region—the west coast of Vancouver Island—with an unknown environmental history. The paleoecological study by Hebda and Rouse (1979) spans only the last 3000 years of the Holocene. Other work has concentrated on the east coast of Vancouver Island (see Hebda 1983, 1995).

This chapter outlines the results of paleobotanical and stratigraphic analyses of five cores and one section from sites on Brooks Peninsula. The results are used to reconstruct the late Quaternary vegetation history and outline environmental changes. The reconstructed sequence of vegetation is discussed within the context of known and conjectured regional vegetation history. Following, there is a discussion of the implications of the results to the question of a glacial refugium on Brooks Peninsula. Finally, the phytogeographic significance of the results are considered and directions for future studies are suggested.

Study Area

Regional Setting

Details of the physical and biotic features of Brooks Peninsula are described in other chapters of this volume. A brief summary of these chapters is included here to establish the setting.

Brooks Peninsula is a rectangular, mountainous block dominated by a sinuous, central ridge that ranges in elevation from ca. 500 m to 1000 m. Steep slopes descend from craggy peaks to the southwest-facing tip and parts of the northwest and southeast shores. Lowlands of irregular topography occur along parts of the northwest shore, the south tip, and the southeast shore (Figure 9.1). Climate is mild, very moist, and maritime. Extreme temperatures are rare. However, intense storms batter the peninsula, especially in the fall and winter. Strong winds, reputed occasionally to exceed 160 km/h, shape upland vegetation and deflate exposed ridge-top soils. Soils are predominantly deeply weathered humic podzols.

Forests blanket more than 95% of the peninsula. Shrubby and herbaceous vegetation is restricted to ridge tops, bogs on gentle slopes and flat terrain, and the shore zone.

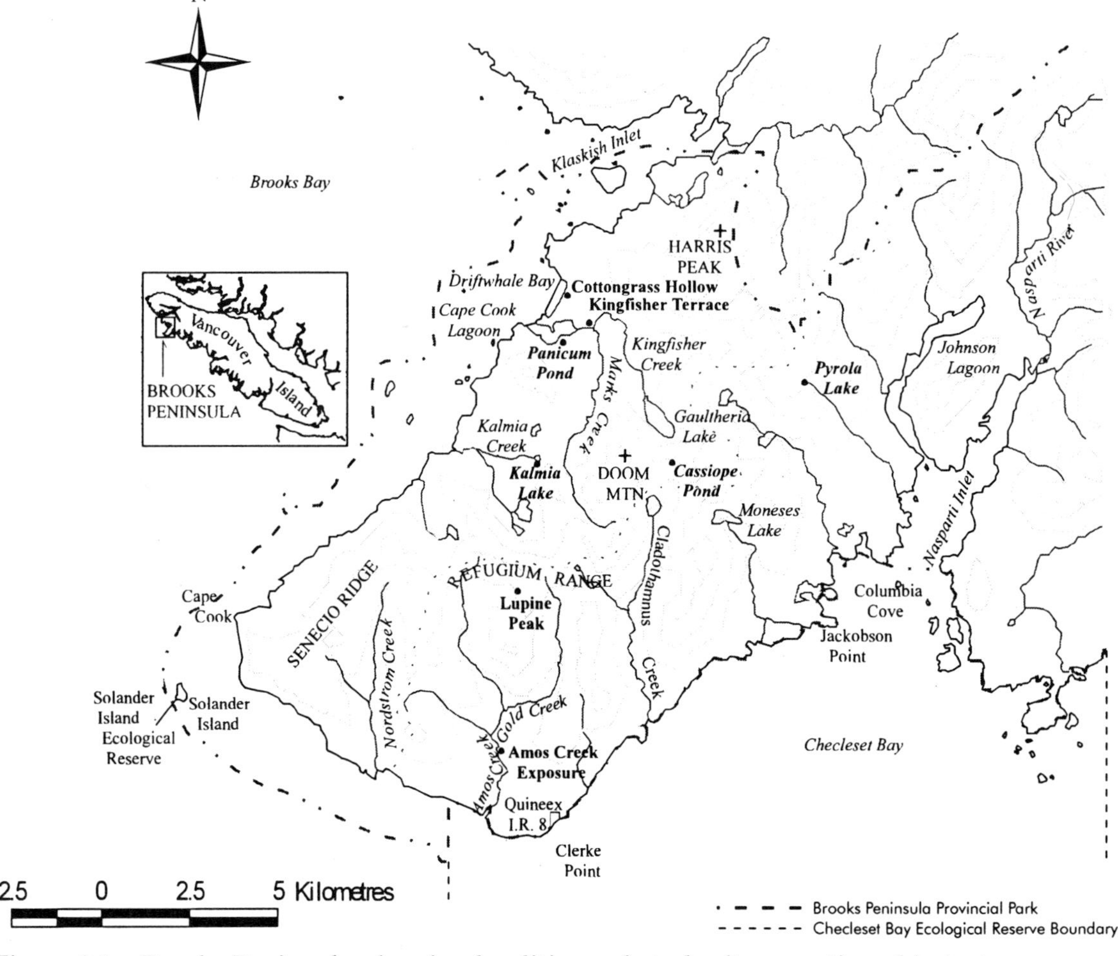

Figure 9.1 Brooks Peninsula, showing localities and study sites mentioned in text

The Shoreline Forest[2] dominated by *Picea sitchensis*[3] (Sitka spruce[4]) forms a narrow fringe along much of the shore of Brooks Peninsula. The Lowland Forest occupies lower slopes and lowland terrain. In general, *Thuja plicata* (western redcedar) and *Tsuga heterophylla* (western hemlock) form a mature, irregular forest canopy.

Three types of Lowland Forest are distinguished:

1) Wet Lowland Forest: gentle to flat terrain; dominated by *Thuja*; abundant but small *T. heterophylla*, and also *Chamaecyparis nootkatensis* (yellow cedar) and *Pinus contorta* (shore pine).

2) Mesic Lowland Forest: moderate slopes; dominated by *Thuja* and *T. heterophylla*.

3) Lowland Forest on Steep Slopes: similar to the mesic variant, but with *Abies amabilis* (Pacific silver fir) as an important species.

There are a few patches of Alluvial Floodplain Forest, which has a complex physiognomic structure with three tree strata and a diverse and rich shrubby and herbaceous understory. *Picea* dominates over *T. heterophylla*, *Thuja*, *Alnus rubra* (red alder), and the occasional *Pyrus fusca* (Pacific crab apple). Alluvial Fringe Forest occupies the banks and adjacent zones of small watercourses. The tree stratum is similar in composition to the surrounding forests, with the addition of *A. rubra*. A diverse assemblage of understory species is characteristic.

Mountain Slope Forest occurs mostly between 200 m and 400 m above sea level and is associated with steep colluvial deposits. *Abies* and *T. heterophylla* predominate. *T. mertensiana* (mountain hemlock) replaces *Thuja* with increasing elevation, and *Chamaecyparis* occurs occasionally, especially at higher elevations.

In zones where growth conditions are poor, forests are replaced by scrubforest vegetation. The tree species are the same as in the forests, except that *Pinus* is more abundant. Shoreline Scrubforest, dominated by *Picea*, grows on rocky headlands. Bog Scrubforest occupies areas of impeded drainage and those with a restricted rooting zone. *Pinus* and *Chamaecyparis* are the most common scrubby trees. Scrubforest occurs over large areas on the rolling lowlands of the northwest side of Brooks Peninsula. Timberline Scrubforest usually occupies sites above Mountain Slope Forest and grades to Krummholz vegetation, which is essentially a shrubby, wind-restricted form of Timberline Scrubforest. *T. mertensiana* and *Chamaecyparis* are the common and dominant trees. Scrubforest also occurs on rock slides and glacially rounded rock knolls.

Shrub Vegetation is distributed in scattered patches on marginal habitats. Types include Beach Shrub, Bog Shrub, Alpine Heath, and Slide Shrub. Ericaceous species and dwarfed conifers dominate these vegetation assemblages. *Gaultheria shallon* (salal) proliferates at lower elevations, especially along the shore. *Ledum groenlandicum* (common Labrador tea) and *Empetrum nigrum* (black crowberry) are common in Bog Shrub. At high elevations, *Empetrum*, *Gaultheria*, and *Phyllodoce empetriformis* (red mountain heather) grow profusely.

---

2 Vegetation classification is defined in Chapter 8.

3 Scientific nomenclature for vascular plants and bryophytes are listed, respectively, in Chapters 5 and 7.

4 Common names of plants follow Taylor and MacBryde (1977).

Herbaceous Vegetation occupies many habitats on Brooks Peninsula. In addition to the typical herbaceous communities of the strandline, lakes and ponds, and disturbed sites, there are four categories of particular interest: bogs, alpine meadows, stonefields, and cliffs.

Bog Herbaceous Vegetation is of a peculiar character. It includes not only typical bog plants such as heaths, sundews, sedges, and sphagnum mosses, but also minerotrophic (mineral requiring) species such as *Camassia quamash* (common camas) and *Dodecatheon jeffreyi* (Jeffrey's shootingstar). Mineral zones appear on the surface in bogs because of solifluction (induced by heavy rainfall) and local surface wash. Bog vegetation at higher elevations occasionally merges with, and is difficult to distinguish from, alpine vegetation.

Alpine Meadow Vegetation typically consists of heath- and grass-dominated communities, but in wetter zones some species more commonly associated with bogs, such as *Scirpus cespitosus* (tufted deer-grass), *Apargidium boreale* (apargidium), and *Gentiana douglasiana* (swamp gentian) occur. Alpine meadows and stonefields of the central ridge and wind blown headlands harbour some of the unusual plant species suspected to have survived in refugia, especially *Ligusticum calderi* (Calder's lovage) and *Calamagrostis purpurascens* subsp. *tasuensis* (purple small reed grass).

Cliff Vegetation is characterized by scattered shrubs [e.g., *Cladothamnus pyrolaeflorus* (copperbush)], herbs [e.g., *Aquilegia formosa* (Sitka columbine) and *Saxifraga punctata* (Cascade cordate-leaved saxifrage)], ferns [e.g., *Adiantum pedatum* (northern maidenhair fern)], and bryophytes. High elevation cliffs are restricted principally to small areas of the central ridge. However, other representatives of the suspected refugium grow in this habitat, including *Saxifraga taylori* (Taylor's saxifrage) and *Isopyrum savilei* (Queen Charlotte isopyrum).

Late Quaternary Vegetation History of the Region

An outline of the environmental history of British Columbia provides a framework within which to interpret the findings from Brooks Peninsula and gives a context for the possible refugium. Unfortunately, much of what we know is from sites at some distance from the study area, and only the general features of the historical sequence apply (see Hebda 1995 for a summary).

About 48 000 years ago, parts—possibly most—of southwest and coastal British Columbia were apparently recovering from a glaciation (Hebda et al. 1983; Warner et al. 1984; Hebda and Whitlock 1997). In the Fraser Lowland, the grass-herb meadows that covered the deglaciated terrain were replaced by pine (lodgepole pine) parkland or forest 48 000-46 000 years ago (Hebda et al. 1983). For the next 13 000 years Fraser Lowland forests were dominated to a varying degree by *Picea* and *Tsuga mertensiana*. The warmest interval during this non-glacial time occurred between 42 000 and 38 000 years ago when *T. heterophylla* was common in the forest. At Dashwood on Vancouver Island, similar *Picea-T. mertensiana* forests were probably extant during the later portion of this interval (Alley 1979). Similar vegetation also grew in the Queen Charlotte Islands (Warner et al. 1984).

The vegetation after 33 000 years ago seems to have been quite variable from area to area. In the Fraser Lowland, grasses and herbs replaced forests and persisted for an unknown period of time (Hebda et al. 1983). Alley (1979) infers that some kind of forest, possibly dominated by *Picea*, persisted until 29 000 years ago when it was replaced by tundra-like vegetation. *Picea-T. mertensiana* forests continued to grow on the Queen Charlotte Islands (Warner et al. 1984).

Cold climate and poor growth conditions likely were widespread from ca. 27 000 to 20 000 years ago. "Tundra," or at best parkland, covered southeastern Vancouver Island. Herbaceous communities grew in the Fraser Lowland about 25 000 years ago (Mathewes 1979). Similar vegetation, perhaps with a few more trees, grew in northwestern Washington (Heusser 1977).

Forests returned to at least part of southwestern British Columbia for a short interval between ca. 19 000 and 17 000 years ago. At the only site of this age in British Columbia investigated to date, there were forests of *Abies lasiocarpa* (Hook.) Nutt. (alpine fir) and *Picea*, with scattered parkland openings (Hicock et al. 1982). Climate was probably cold-humid-continental. Parkland, or "tundra," vegetation grew in western Washington (Barnosky 1981; Heusser 1977).

The Cape Ball cliffs on Graham Island, Queen Charlotte Islands, provide the only indication of full-glacial vegetation in British Columbia (Warner 1984). The landscape was nearly barren and was dominated by various grasses and herbs. The climate is interpreted as cool and oceanic, but not severe (Warner et al. 1982). Open, predominantly herbaceous vegetation occurred south of the glacial boundary in Washington, though there were likely also scattered trees (Barnosky 1981; Heusser 1977).

The postglacial environmental record is relatively well understood (Hebda 1995). A study at Bear Cove bog (Hebda 1983), ca. 65 km northeast of Brooks Peninsula, provides a regional setting. *Pinus contorta* woodland with *Alnus* and *Pteridium aquilinum* (western bracken) formed the pioneering postglacial plant cover during a relatively cool and dry climatic period between 14 000 and 11 500 years ago. *Picea sitchensis-T. heterophylla* forest persisted in a cool, moist, maritime climate between 11 500 and 10 000 years ago. About 10 000 years ago, temperatures warmed and *T. heterophylla* replaced *T. mertensiana*. Open *Picea-Pseudotsuga* (Douglas-fir) forests with *T. heterophylla* grew between ca. 8800 B.P. and 7000 B.P. The climate was warm and dry. Increasing moisture and possible cooling supported *Picea-T. heterophylla* forests between 7000 B.P. and 3000 B.P. Since 3000 B.P., *Thuja* and *Chamaecyparis* have shared the forest canopy with *T. heterophylla* and more or less excluded *Picea*.

Study Sites

Pyrola Lake

Pyrola Lake is contained in a bedrock depression on a flat ridge that projects southeastwards from the central spine of Brooks Peninsula (Figure 9.1). The lake was probably formed by ice-scouring as the main Vancouver Island ice mass slid across the uplands of Brooks Peninsula.

Pyrola Lake consists of two small basins separated by bedrock islands (Figure 9.2). The eastern basin is 2 m deep at its centre during the driest time of the year. The western basin is only 1 m deep. Cobble lag deposits mantle the shore on the east, south, and west sides, and active erosion produces a sharp peat/mor face above this beach zone. Along the north side, organic muck forms the shoreline, though an eroding peat face still occurs.

An intermittent stream dumps large volumes of forest floor detritus (needles, cones, twigs) into the northwest corner of the lake. At this point, a lobate delta composed of coarse organic detritus extends the lakeshore and fills approximately one-quarter of the western basin (Figure 9.2). Patches of coarse sand and small angular gravel are deposited in the creek bed at the edge of the lake, well back from the delta front. Most of the coarse mineral debris carried by the creek remains on the forested flats between Pyrola Lake and the adjacent base of the peak of Saxifraga Mountain to the north.

At high water (approximately 1.5 m higher than in late summer when this study was conducted), there are possibly as many as three outlets. One descends westwards, whereas two others drain eastwards among several bedrock blocks interspersed with peaty ponds and swales. During the

Figure 9.2 Pyrola Lake study site, seen from above the central ridge (Saxifraga Mountain) looking southwards (The square raft in the middle of the eastern basin is at the coring site. Lobate delta of organic detritus is in the lower right corner of the lake.) (Photo: Ruth Kirk)

rains, flow may be considerable, as indicated by piles of medium-sized logs in the eastward outlets.

Pyrola Lake is located within the Mountain Slope Forest of Brooks Peninsula (see Chapter 8). However, a complex mosaic of forest types occurs around the lake. On the slopes above the lake, *Chamaecyparis*, *T. mertensiana*, and *Abies amabilis* combine in various patterns to form a closed forest. On the flats north of the lake, *A. amabilis* and *T. heterophylla* form a mature stand of excellent timber. The irregular block-and-hollow topography east, south, and west of the basin supports a scrubby forest dominated by *Pinus*, *Chamaecyparis*, and *T. mertensiana*. The canopy is very open and *Thuja*, *Chamaecyparis*, *Vaccinium* spp. (blueberries and huckleberries), *Phyllodoce*, and *Gaultheria* thrive in the shrub layer. *Alnus crispa* (Sitka mountain alder) clumps occur along the lakeshore and on rocky outcrops. Peaty depressions support a mixture of forbs, grasses, and sedges. Valley slopes below Pyrola Lake are mantled in *Thuja*-*T. heterophylla* forest. *Abies* grows well in rich moist sites near the valley bottoms and on gentle slopes. A single *Picea* tree grows on the lakeshore.

The lake margin is covered by an interrupted band of forb, grass, and sedge meadow. *Deschampsia cespitosa* (tufted hair grass) and *Gentiana sceptrum* (king gentian) are notable species in this community. *Carex* spp. (sedges) and *Fauria crista-galli* (deer cabbage) also occur frequently. *Juncus oreganus* (spreading rush) stabilizes intermittently submerged mud flats at the lake's edge, whereas *Sparganium* sp. (bur-reed) forms patches in slightly deeper water (10 cm deep in summer). All but the deepest portions of the eastern basin contain scattered colonies of *Nuphar polysepalum* (yellow pond-lily). The moss *Drepanocladus exannulatus* covers the entire bottom of the lake.

Kalmia Lake

Kalmia Lake is approximately 100 m across and irregular in outline (Figure 9.3). Bedrock hills surround this basin and constrain the waters of the lake. Like Pyrola Lake, this body of water contains rocky islets. Bedrock outcrops on all but the west shore, where a stream has formed a delta. The subaerial part of the delta is partly stabilized by low scrubby vegetation that anchors peaty colluvial/alluvial gravel and sand. Ill-defined and well-defined gravel-bottomed channels cross this depositional flat. Gravels mantle coarse organic detritus in the subaqueous portion of the delta. The lakeshore is characterized by gravel lag deposits, abutting an eroding peat/mor face approximately 20-40 cm high. Along quiet portions of the lag shore, there is an organic debris line reaching 1 m above summer water level. Outflow is to the north, through an intermittent stream that has cut sharply into bedrock. The lake is deeper than 7 m at the centre.

Open Bog Scrubforest, consisting of *Pinus*, *Chamaecyparis*, and *Thuja* grows on the slopes surrounding the lake. Many openings occur along the creek and on knolls. A diverse assemblage of small shrubs and herbaceous species grows in these habitats. Most abundant are *Gaultheria*, *Phyllodoce*, *Myrica* (sweet gale), *Empetrum*, *Apargidium*, *Drosera rotundifolia* (round-leaved sundew), *Drosera anglica* (great sundew), *Fauria*, and *Gentiana* spp. Other important herbaceous plants include *Carex livida* (pale sedge), *Eriophorum angustifolium* (narrow-leaved cotton-grass), *Scirpus caespitosus*, and *Deschampsia*.

Sphagnum hummocks are restricted to seepage zones at the bases of slopes, but *Racomitrium lanuginosum* cushions are common over much of the land surface. A 2-4 m wide band of *Nuphar* grows at the margin of the lake (Figure 9.3). The shallows in the northwest corner are more extensively vegetated and include patches of *Sparganium* and *Juncus oreganus*.

Figure 9.3 Kalmia Lake study site, seen from adjacent hilltop, looking eastwards (The lower slopes of Doom Mountain are in the middle ground, the central ridge in the background. A core was taken at the deep water edge of the shallow zone in the centre of the lake [marked by white dot].) (Photo: R. Hebda)

Cassiope Pond

Cassiope Pond is perched above Gaultheria Lake, at 550 m, on a shoulder of the central spine of Brooks Peninsula (Figure 9.4). The steep slopes of the central ridge rise immediately to the south and east of this basin. North and west of Cassiope Pond very steep slopes, part of the headwalls of an abandoned cirque, plunge into Gaultheria Lake valley 450 m below. The basin seems to be, at least partly, impounded by rounded bedrock features on the north side.

Figure 9.4 Cassiope Pond study site after a light snowfall in April 1981, seen from slope of adjacent central ridge looking northwards (A core was taken at the far end of the open patch of water [white dot]. The ends of the white patches in the upper centre of the photograph mark a 300-400 m drop to Gaultheria Lake in the valley below.) (Photo: R. Hebda)

Cassiope Pond is circular, about 50 m in diameter. During the time of the field study, from late July to late August, the water level dropped 0.3 m to expose the bottom completely, but rose again after a heavy rain.

The shore consists principally of angular rocks with occasional peaty stretches. A small stream drains wet meadows on the slope above the pond and enters the basin from the south. Flow from the stream has maintained a shallow trough that follows the south and west shores.

Cassiope Pond is surrounded by a mosaic of forest, scrub, and meadow. Pockets of Mountain Slope Forest dominated by *Tsuga mertensiana* and *Abies amabilis* grow on well-drained rich sites, such as the slopes to the west, south, and east. *Chamaecyparis* favours moister sites. Timberline Scrubforest, often grading to shrubby Krummholz, occupies the shallow soils on bedrock knolls to the north. The tree species are the same as in the Mountain Slope Forest, but much smaller, ranging from miniature trees to prostrate shrubs. *Pinus* occurs irregularly.

There is a diverse association of shrubs and herbs, especially in openings. Immediately around the pond there are extensive zones of wet Alpine Meadow Vegetation, well-drained Alpine Meadow Vegetation, and Alpine Heath Vegetation. The moist margins and lower slopes around the pond are covered in species that tolerate peat and mineral substrates. *Geum calthifolium* (caltha-leaved avens), *Fauria*, *Deschampsia*, and *Scirpus cespitosus* are dominant species of this low, matted vegetation. On the somewhat deflated slopes and low ridge to the west and north of Cassiope Pond, low heath-dominated patches alternate with herbaceous patches. *Phyllodoce*, *Empetrum*, and *Vaccinium uliginosum* (bog blueberry) form the heath mats. Herbaceous species include *Luetkea pectinata* (luetkea), *Gentiana* spp., *Calamagrostis* sp. (small reed grass), *Ligusticum calderi*, and many others.

The bottom of the pond supports a well-developed plant cover of *Nuphar* in the deepest water, and also in some shallow sites. *Isoëtes* sp. (quillwort) and *Scapania undulata* (a liverwort) cover most of the shallow zones, and *Juncus oreganus* grows on the emergent margins.

Cottongrass Hollow[5]

Cottongrass Hollow sits at about 8 m above sea level in a depression between two former dune ridges abandoned by advancing Drift Whale Bay beach (Figure 9.1). This hollow is lenticular in shape, ca. 30-40 m wide, and 100-150 m long. A relatively flat sphagnum bog occupies this depression. It contains occasional small pools about 2 m across and up to 0.5 m deep.
The vegetation is mainly of the Bog Herbaceous type, with *Sphagnum* spp. predominant and associated herbaceous types such as *Eriophorum angustifolium* and *Apargidium*. The surrounding slopes and ridge tops, which rise to about 6-9 m above the hollow, are covered in Wet Lowland Forest of western red cedar, yellow cedar, western hemlock, and occasional Sitka spruce.

Panicum Pond[5]

Panicum Pond is located at about 30 m above sea level in Camassia Bog adjacent to Cape Cook Lagoon (Figure 9.1). It is set on gently sloping terrain at the margin of the forest. The pond is almost a 30 m x 10 m rectangle, with a maximum depth of 0.2-0.4 m. The shore consists of a steep, 0.3 m high bank of *Sphagnum compactum* and *Sphagnum papillosum*. Occasional boulders protrude through the bank. The shallow water of the pond is densely vegetated by *Scirpus subterminalis* (water club-rush) and scattered patches of *Nuphar* and *Juncus oreganus*. The surrounding vegetation is Bog Scrubforest of shore pine, yellow cedar, and western redcedar, and Bog Herbaceous communities (see Chapter 8).

Methods

In the field, personnel, coring equipment, and a portable raft (Figure 9.5) were lifted by helicopter to three coring sites: Pyrola Lake, Kalmia Lake, and Cassiope Pond (Figure 9.1). Coring rods were used to determine that the deepest part of Pyrola Lake is the eastern basin (Figure 9.2). The top 4.20 m of sediment were retrieved using a Livingston type piston corer. The deepest portion of core, 4.20-4.70 m, was obtained with a Hiller corer. This interval was sampled three times to obtain sufficient sedge crowns and wood fragments for radiocarbon dating.

Kalmia Lake was cored in a water depth of ca. 2-3 m, near the delta of a small stream (Figure 9.3). Other parts of the lake were too deep for our equipment (that is, deeper than 5 m), or had a gravel or rock bottom. A sandy gravel layer occurs at about 2 m depth, so it was not possible to use the Livingston corer even with a casing. The 0.00-2.00 m interval was sampled with the Livingston corer, and the 2.00-8.50 m interval with a Hiller corer.

The middle of Cassiope Pond was sampled in 1 m of water, using the Livingston sampler from 0.00 m to 0.50 m and the Hiller corer from 0.50 m to 2.65 m. The Livingston corer could not penetrate deeply into the sandy peat.

---

5 Cottongrass Hollow and Panicum Pond are names assigned by R. Hebda to study sites.

Figure 9.5 Raft and coring equipment floating in Kalmia Lake (Photo: Allen Banner)

The samples from Cottongrass Hollow were taken from the face of a pit excavated into peat. Panicum Pond was cored by driving a Livingston tube into the bottom deposits.

Cores were divided into segments ranging from 2 cm to 10 cm, depending on the rate of sediment change and overall core length. Segments were cleaned of recognizable contaminating matter and sealed in plastic bags. Selected samples were cleaned, oven-dried, packaged, and submitted for radiocarbon age determination.

Laboratory preparation for pollen analysis followed standard procedures outlined by Faegri and Iversen (1975). Briefly, organic samples were coarse-screened when necessary, boiled for 5-10 minutes in 5% potassium hydroxide and neutralized with 5% K_2CO_3 solution. Mineral samples were treated with hydrofluoric acid to remove silicates. All samples were then treated by the acetolyis procedure, which eventually left a pollen-rich residue. This residue was mounted in glycerin jelly and sealed under a coverslip on a glass microscope slide.

Palynomorphs[6] were examined under a Nikon Biophot microscope at 400X or 1000X and identified using standard keys, unpublished keys and descriptions (Hebda et al. 1982), and comparative reference material from southwestern British Columbia and Brooks Peninsula. Where necessary, detailed investigations of pollen morphology were made (e.g., Hebda 1985).

Pollen and spore frequencies were determined for all samples, but because monolete fern spores and *Isoëtes* microspores were overwhelmingly abundant in some samples, they were excluded from the sums and expressed as a per cent of the remaining pollen and spores.

---

[6] For definitions of technical terms related to pollen structure consult Kremp (1965).

Macrofossils, predominantly conifer needles, were retained from the coarse fraction of alternate samples from Kalmia Lake. These remains, as well as those from selected samples from Pyrola Lake, were examined under a dissecting microscope to determine, where possible, the conifer species represented by the pollen. Published illustrations (Hitchcock et al. 1969) and comparative material in the Royal British Columbia Museum's archaeobotanical collection were used for identification.

Stratigraphy, Radiocarbon Dates, and Pollen Density

Amos Creek

A sample of organic-rich silt was collected for pollen analysis by D. Howes and W.H. Mathews from an exposure along Amos Creek (Figure 9.1), 2 km from its mouth. This silt occurs at the top of a series of alternating beds of silty to sandy diamicton and thinly bedded lacustrine silts containing organic lenses. It is immediately underlain by 1 m of pebble-cobble gravels, which form the modern surface. An unidentifiable coniferous log from diamicton near the top of the sequence yielded an age of 30 000 ± 510 B.P. (Table 9.1). This indicates that the silt and diamicton layers were of late Olympia non-glacial interval (see Chapter 3). The pollen density of the sediment was not determined.

Pyrola Lake

Approximately 4.75 m of sediment were penetrated by corers in Pyrola Lake. Sandy gravel forms the base of the sedimentary sequence (Figures 9.6 and 9.7). Grey-blue, organic-rich silty clay containing sedge crowns and fragments of wood overlies the gravel. The clay grades to slimy, grey-brown, dense clayey gyttja between 4.45 m and 4.50 m below the surface. Scattered sedge crowns from the gyttja yielded an age of 11 400 ± 480 B.P. (Table 9.1). Dense fibrous limnic peat occurs between 4.20 m and 3.50 m. Twigs occur throughout this interval. There is a thin layer of charcoal at 4.15 m. The change in sediment type at 4.20 m, just after 11 400 years ago, implies stabilization of the surrounding landscape by well-developed vegetation (which would have reduced sediment input into the basin), as well as increasing water depth—also indicated by the disappearance of sedges. Limnic peat, or dy[7], constitutes the rest of the sedimentary column at Pyrola Lake. Fibrous layers of the aquatic moss *Drepanocladus exannulatus* occur throughout the upper part of the sequence. One especially dense layer was encountered at 1.00 m.

Pollen and spore density varies considerably throughout the sedimentary column (Figure 9.6). Basal clayey silt contains less than 2.0×10^5 grains and spores per cm^3. Density rises suddenly to ca. 1.1×10^6 grains and spores per cm^3 in the clay gyttja, but then decreases in the fibrous limnic peat to as low as 5.0×10^3 grains and spores per cm^3. Densities then fluctuate between 5.0×10^3 and ca. 3.0×10^4 per cm^3 throughout the rest of the core.

Density values in the limnic peat are similar to those found in similar sediments elsewhere in southwestern British Columbia (Hebda 1983). Those in the clay gyttja are exceptionally high for late-glacial time on the coast. These high pollen and spore densities originated during the same time that at Bear Cove much lower densities (0.1 to 0.2 times the value) were developing, albeit in a different sediment. Because the vegetation was apparently similar (see section on Pyrola Lake pollen assemblages and vegetation, this chapter), the clay gyttja sediments must represent significantly more time. Consequently, the basal date of 11 400 ± 480 B.P. for Pyrola Lake is too recent. A more realistic date is 13 000 - 14 000 B.P.

---

[7] Dy is a black-brown organic sediment, or gel-mud, which consists of microscopic and macroscopic plant fragments bound together by a dark colloidal precipitate (Faegri and Iversen 1975). Dy typically forms in nutrient-poor lakes, such as those of the coastal coniferous forests of British Columbia.

Table 9.1 Radiocarbon dates from Brooks Peninsula, Vancouver Island

Location	Description	Lab no.	Years B.P.
Pyrola Lake 50°11'20" N 127°41'40" W	1.80-2.00 m of core; limnic peat	WSU 2849	3530 ± 70
Pyrola Lake 50°11'20" N 127°41'40" W	3.50-3.60 m of core; limnic peat	SFU 217	9950 ± 260
Pyrola Lake 50°11'20" N 127°41'40" W	4.20-4.00 m of core; sedge crowns in silty gyttja and silt	SFU 214	11 400 ± 480
Kalmia Lake 50°10'20" N 127°48'00" W	1.80-2.00 m of core; watery limnic peat	WSU 2845	7910 ± 80
Kalmia Lake 50°10'20" N 127°48'00" W	5.70-5.80 m of core; limnic peat	WAT 1036	9910 ± 370
Kalmia Lake 50°10'20" N 127°48'00" W	6.25-6.40 m of core; limnic peat	WAT 927	10 390 ± 370
Kalmia Lake 50°10'20" N 127°48'20" W	8.30-8.40 m of core; limnic peat	SFU 213	12 100 ± 480
Cassiope Pond 50°10'00" N 127°45'00" W	0.80-0.95 m of core; dense limnic peat, possibly modern rootlets	WSU 2847	3845 ± 50
Cassiope Pond 50°10'00" N 127°45'00" W	1.85-1.95 m of core; dense limnic peat	WAT 1059	7990 ± 330
Cassiope Pond 50°10'00" N 127°45'00" W	2.40-2.50 m of core; dense limnic peat	SFU 215	10 460 ± 550
Cottongrass Hollow 50°12'20" N 127°47'10" W	1.40-1.50 m of section; wood near base of bog sequence	SFU 216	3900 ± 140
Cottongrass Hollow 50°12'20" N 127°47'10" W	1.45-1.50 m of excavated section; peat from base of bog sequence above sand	WAT 926	1980 ± 70
Kingfisher Creek Terrace 50°12'20" N 127°47'00" W	0.80-0.90 m of excavated section; sandy peat with sedge remains	WAT 917	8460 ± 460
Panicum Pond 50°11'40" N 127°47'20" W	ca. 0.80-0.90 m of core; organic silt at base containing twigs and seed	WAT 924	12 250 ± 790
Lupine Ridge 50°09'40" N 127°47'20" W	ca. 0.60-0.75 m below surface in excavated section; silty peat from base of soil profile, from eroding face, possible root contamination	WAT 925	690 ± 70

Table 9.1 Continued

Location	Description	Lab no.	Years B.P.
Amos Creek 2 km from mouth 50°06'10" N 127°48'30" W	conifer wood	GSC 3449	30 800 ± 510

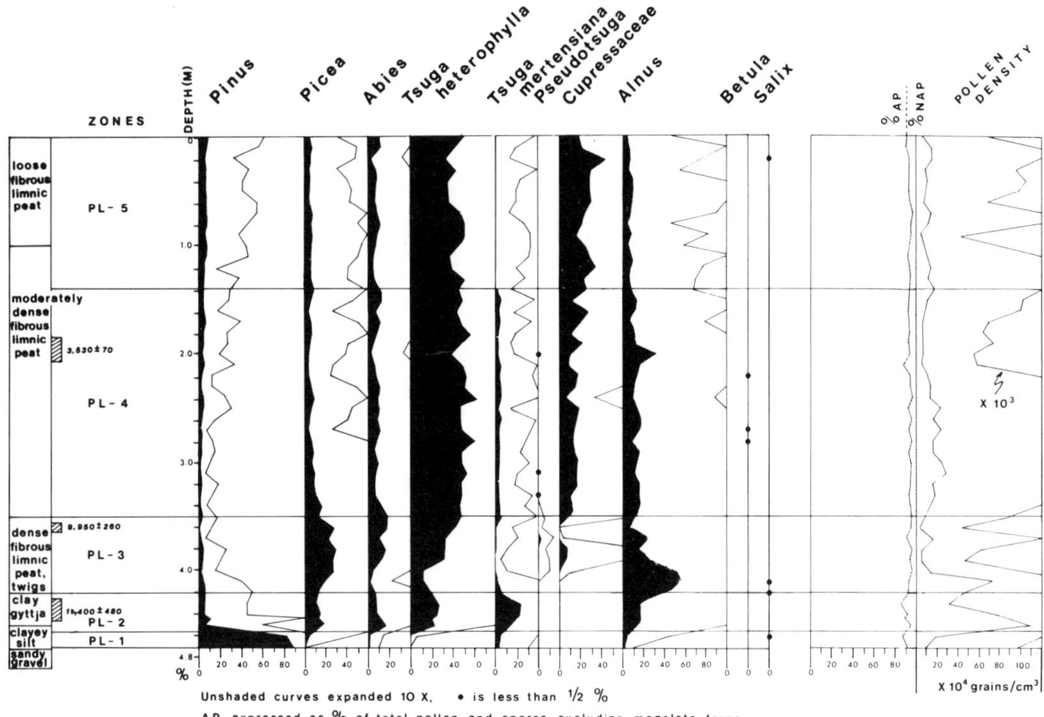

Figure 9.6 Arboreal pollen diagram for Pyrola Lake

Kalmia Lake

The depositional history revealed in the Kalmia Lake core is exceptional and likely reflects intervals of rapid sediment accumulation and periods of slow accumulation, hiatuses, or even erosion. These features are related to the location of a small delta near the coring site.

Traces of clayey silt or clayey silt with sand were recovered on the tip of the Hiller corer at a depth of 8.50 - 8.55 m (Figures 9.8, 9.9, 9.10). These sediments are overlain by 10 cm of gyttja. The sequence from 2.00 m to 8.40 m consists of a relatively uniform, brown limnic detritus (see coarse detritus dy, Faegri and Iversen 1975). The bulk of this material is composed of needles and twigs, which gives it poor cohesiveness. A series of four radiocarbon dates reveals that this 6.4 m column of sediment was deposited between 12 100 ± 480 B.P. and 7910 ± 80 B.P. This is an exceptionally rapid rate of accumulation—ca. 1.6 m per thousand years—for this interval of time on the coast of British Columbia (see Mathewes 1973). Such sedimentation rates probably resulted because of the input of large quantities of forest detritus by the nearby stream. A modern, analogous situation was observed in the western basin of Pyrola Lake. Today, the stream entering Kalmia Lake carries little organic detritus because its drainage basin is covered by sparse Bog Scrubforest and Bog Herbaceous Vegetation.

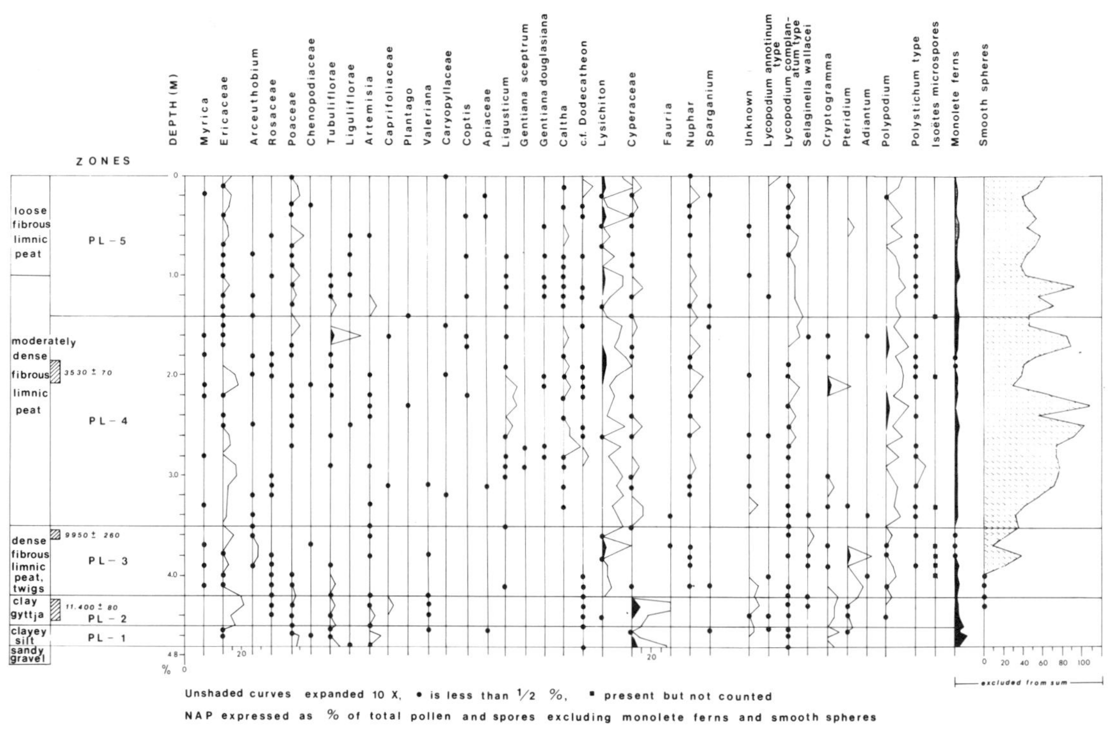

Figure 9.7 Non-arboreal pollen diagram for Pyrola Lake

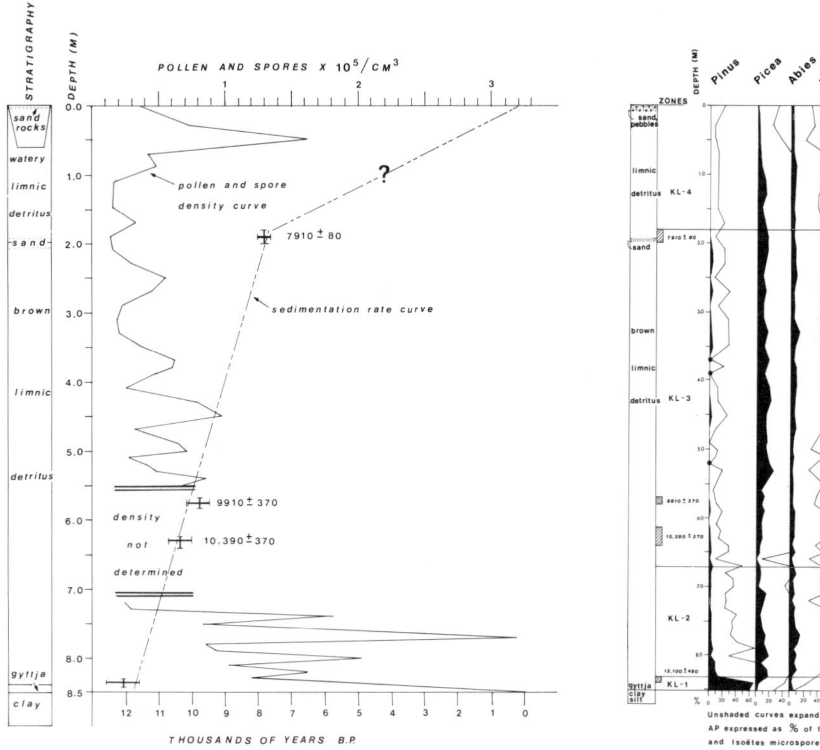

Figure 9.8 Stratigraphy, pollen density, and sedimentation rate for Kalmia Lake

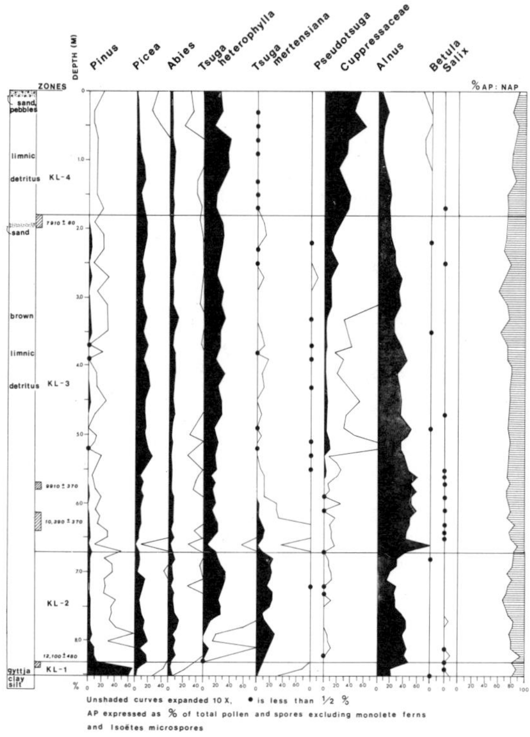

Figure 9.9 Relative arboreal pollen diagram for Kalmia Lake

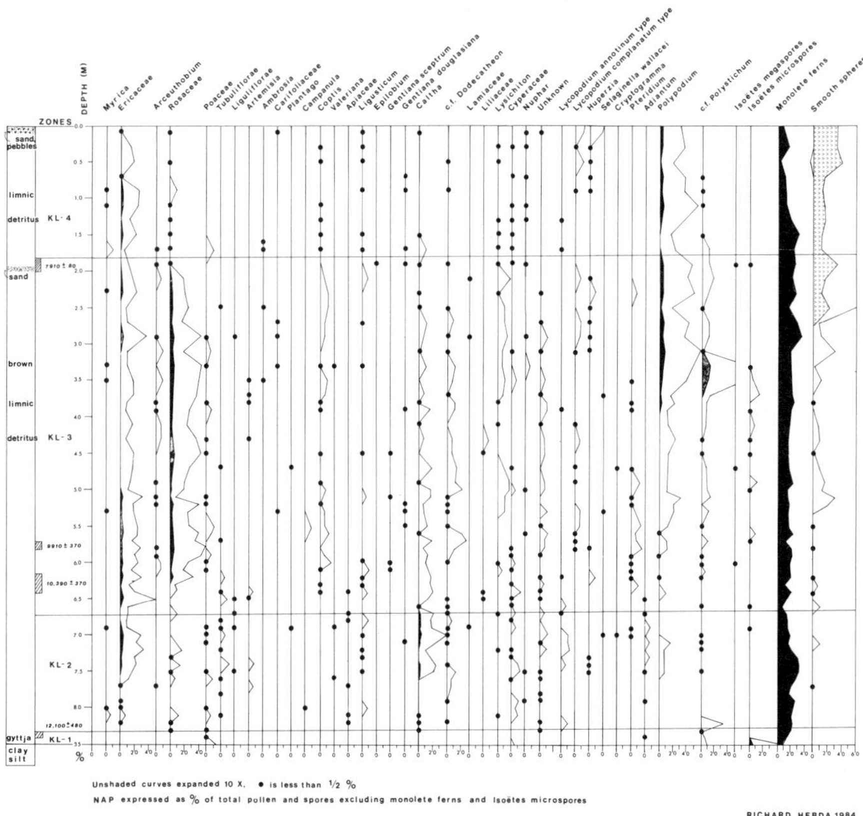

Figure 9.10 Relative non-arboreal pollen diagram for Kalmia Lake

A layer of coarse sand occurs at about 2.00 m deep and is sufficiently dense to resist penetration by a Livingston corer. From a depth of 2.00 m to the top, sediment consists of watery limnic detritus—except in the top 0.10 m, where a layer of well-sorted coarse sand with pebbles occurs.

The sand layers and the remarkably low sediment accumulation rate of ca. 0.3 m/1000 y in the top 2.0 m suggest interrupted sedimentation, or, possibly, sediment erosion and slumping into deep water. Another possibility is that organic sediment input rates greatly declined after 8000 B.P., perhaps in association with deterioration of forest cover. In any case, some disruption of sedimentation must be considered. Unfortunately, no radiocarbon dates were obtained in the 0.0 - 2.0 m interval—a date might have indicated the nature of sedimentation.

Pollen and spore densities, in general, conform to expectations. High densities, up to 3 x 10^5 pollen and spores per cm^3, occur in the gyttja at the base, and occasionally throughout the core (Figure 9.8). Lower densities typical of limnic detritus occur throughout most of the sequence. Considerable fluctuations in pollen and spore density were expected since the amount of wood and needle debris varies throughout the sequence. However, the densities of the upper 2.0 m are not particularly different from those below, which is surprising because these 2.0 m of sediment represent 8000 years. Either pollen and spore productivity dropped drastically in concert with decreases in organic sediment input, or much of the sedimentary record is absent.

Cassiope Pond

The sediments of Cassiope Pond rest on bedrock or rocks that prevented coring beyond 2.65 m. Blue clay with rocks occurs between 2.65 m and 2.50 m (Figures 9.11, 9.12, 9.13). From 2.50 m to 0.25 m the sediment consists of very dense, brown, sandy "peat." Lenses of conifer needles occur

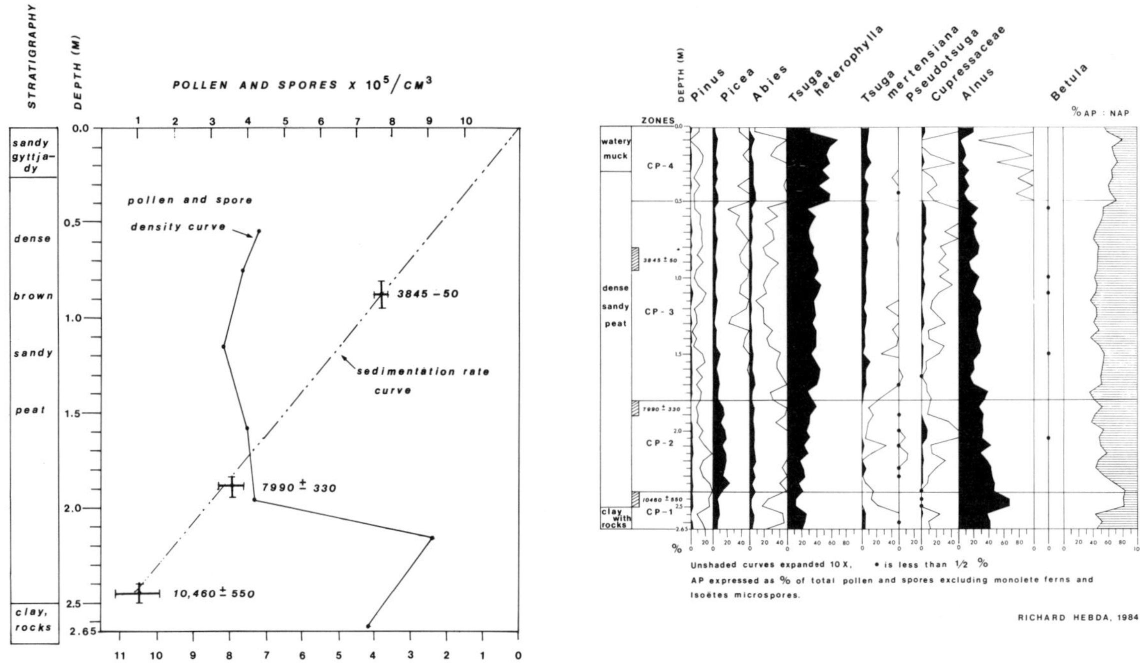

Figure 9.11 Stratigraphy, pollen densities, and sedimentation rate for Cassiope Pond

Figure 9.12 Relative arboreal pollen diagram for Cassiope Pond

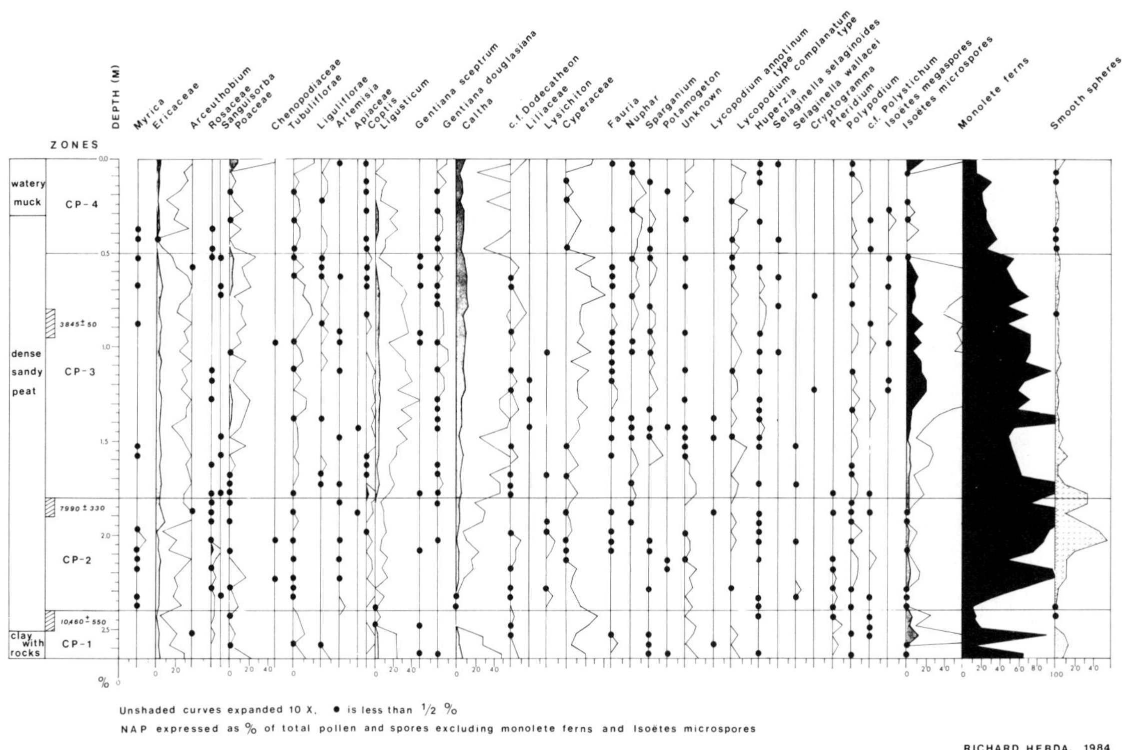

Figure 9.13 Relative non-arboreal pollen diagram for Cassiope Pond

within this material. The topmost 0.25 cm consists of slightly sandy gyttja or gyttja-dy. There are occasional plant fragments and live roots.

Sediment accumulation in Cassiope Pond began before 10 450 ± 550 years ago and continued at a constant, but slow, rate to the present (Figure 9.11). This is a remarkable feature since, as previously noted, Cassiope Pond basin is small and dries out, and interruptions in sedimentation and/or erosion would be expected. Breaks in sedimentation are either negligible, or, a less likely explanation, they occur at a constant rate. The accumulation rate of about 0.23 m is intermediate between those at subalpine and alpine sites in the Canadian Rocky Mountains (Kearney and Luckman 1980), but much lower than at low-elevation lakes on the coast. Significantly, the accumulation rate is lower than at Pyrola Lake, which is located at a similar elevation, 3 km distant. Pyrola Lake is in a larger basin and within closed forest. It is suspected that the proximity of forest to Pyrola Lake—a potential source of abundant organic sediment—explains the difference in sedimentation rates between the two sites. Pollen densities in the seven samples studied from Cassiope Pond are higher than those in limnic detritus from Pyrola and Kalmia lakes (Figure 9.11). With a range from 3.30×10^5 to 9.08×10^5 pollen and spores per cm^3, densities approach those of dense gyttja sediments at the bases of the lake cores. The higher densities at Cassiope Pond are likely the result of low sediment accumulation rates, and low palynomorph production. When the sedimentation rate-curve is extrapolated, the age of the deepest sediment is ca. 11 500 B.P.

Cottongrass Hollow

Two radiocarbon dates, 3900 ± 140 B.P. and 1980 ± 70 B.P. (Table 9.1), indicate that organic sediments amongst the middle set of dunes adjacent to Cape Cook Lagoon are recent (Figure 9.1). The incongruity of these dates—the older one from wood, the younger one from basal sedge peats—emphasizes the difficulty of obtaining actual "basal" dates. The wood estimate is likely closer to the real age, because the material does not contain younger rootlets penetrating from above, as the peat probably does. However, the wood may have yielded an exceptionally old date if it had been reworked, or had been floating around for some time, or if it came from the centre of a very old tree.

The sedimentary succession (Figure 9.14) progresses from dense, indurated, well-sorted sand, through dense woody sedge peat, to sedge peat, and finally into *Sphagnum* peat of variable character. This sequence formed as marine water retreated from dunes and succession proceeded from sedge salt-marsh/fen to *Sphagnum* bog. Sediment accumulated at a rate of ca. 0.4-0.7 m/1000 y, much more quickly than on lowland bogs that developed on till in nearby "Camassia Bog." Two different peat-forming environments are indicated in these two nearby sites.

Other Sites

Two radiocarbon dates were obtained from the bases of one section and one core at selected localities to estimate the age of the land surface and provide chronological control for two short cores. The oldest postglacial date for Brooks Peninsula, 12 250 ± 790 B.P., was obtained from the base of short core taken in a small, shallow pond (Panicum Pond) in the bogs near Cape Cook Lagoon (Figure 9.15). Small shallow ponds are scattered over the boggy lowland terrain. They usually contain less than 1.0 m of sediment, yet, as demonstrated by the date on the basal part of the section, can be quite old. The radiocarbon date was obtained from organic silts containing conifer needles. Below this, there are dense, brown organic silts that are underlain, in turn, by impenetrable silty-stony diamicton (possibly till). The reasons that these small ponds have persisted, or regenerated, since late glacial time are unclear. Normally, such small basins would have long ago filled with organic detritus and local slope wash. Sediment deposition must have been exceedingly slow and frequently interrupted. Alternatively, surrounding microtopographic features and *Sphagnum* growth may have combined to re-form the ponds.

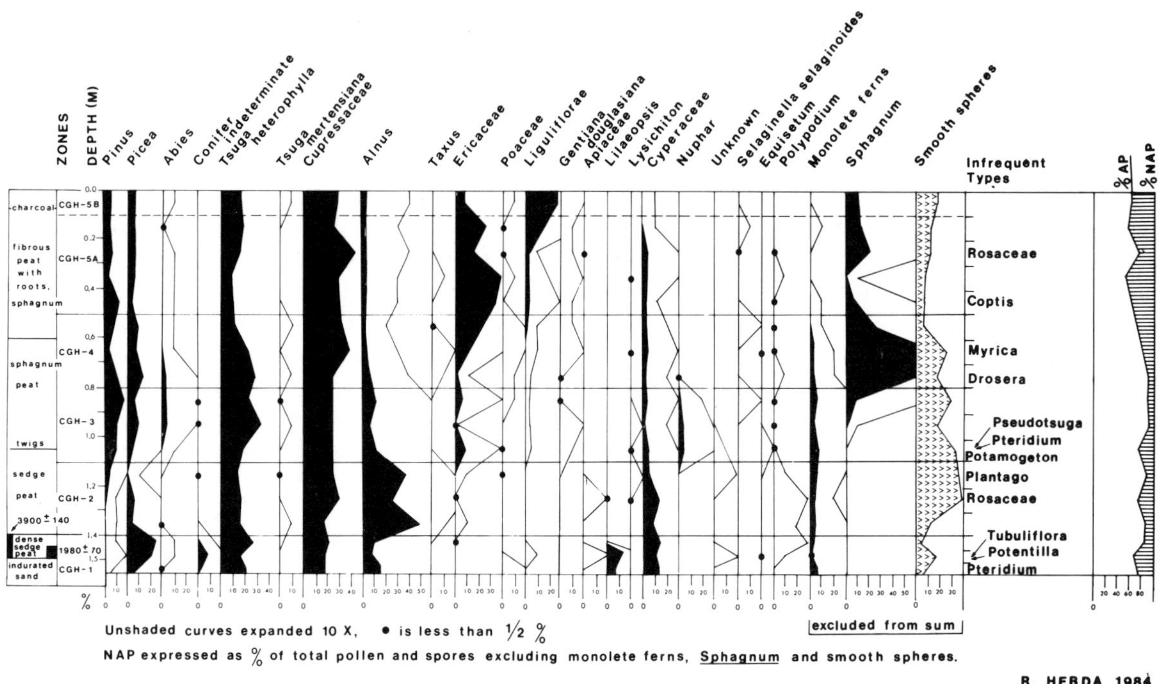

Figure 9.14 Relative pollen diagram for Cottongrass Hollow

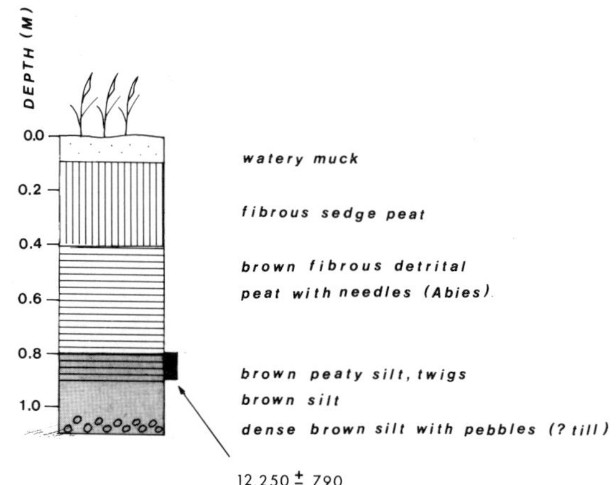

Figure 9.15 Stratigraphy of Panicum Pond

A sample of silty peat/colluvium from ca. 610 m on "Lupine Ridge" yielded a young age of 690 ± 70 B.P. This recent date may indicate that upland surfaces are not particularly stable, and that there is significant ongoing disturbance of the soil profile.

Pollen and Macrofossil Sequence

Pollen and Spore Identification

Pollen grains and spores were identified using standard keys and comparative reference material. Many of the types seen are not frequently encountered. In anticipation of this, comparative material was collected from Brooks Peninsula, and studies were made of pollen and spore morphology of selected taxa.

The most comprehensive investigation was made of Apiaceae pollen types to establish whether *Ligusticum calderi* pollen could be identified (Hebda 1985). *L. calderi* pollen is clearly distinct from other Apiaceae in the area. It has a rhomboidal equatorial outline, and pores are located at the apices of the amb (Figure 9.16).

Cupressaceae pollen is difficult to identify with certainty because it often takes the form of a clear, unornamented sphere, or a folded and deformed sphere. Many moss spores, algal cysts, and other palynomorphs are difficult to distinguish from this pollen type. The specific criteria used were: 1) patches of baculate ornament; 2) tendency towards beak-shaped splitting of the grain; 3) diameter of 17-35 µm (usually 20-30 µm) (Figure 9.16c). All similar palynomorphs that did not have baculae were classified as "smooth spheres," excluded from the sum, and included at the end of the pollen diagram. Cupressaceae pollen probably is underrepresented in the diagram; however, this narrow concept for Cupressaceae pollen eliminates spurious peaks.

Alnus pollen was not segregated into *A. rubra* and *A. crispa* types. However, the significant peaks of *Alnus* in the early Holocene, in the three major cores, are likely produced by *A. crispa*. This is

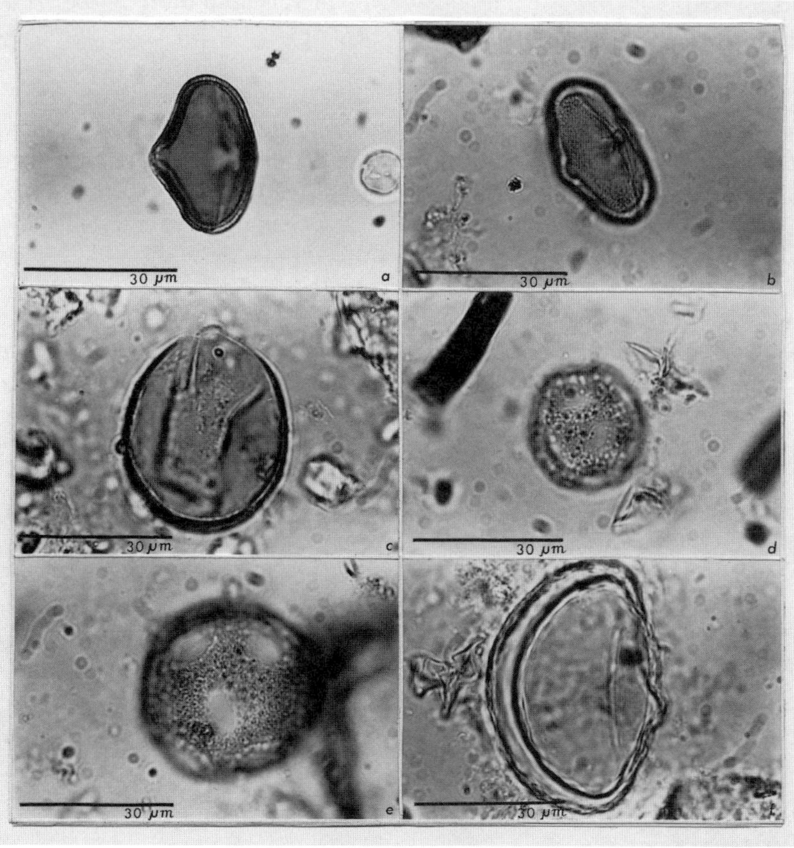

Figure 9.16 Selected modern and subfossil pollen and spore types, Brooks Peninsula: a) *Ligusticum calderi* - modern; b) *Ligusticum calderi* - sub-fossil, Cassiope Pond core; c) *Cupressaceae* - sub-fossil, Pyrola Lake core; d) *Coptis aspleniifolia* - sub-fossil, Cassiope Pond core; e) *Caltha biflora* type - sub-fossil, Cassiope Pond core; f) *Isoëtes* type - sub-fossil, Panicum Pond core

based on the presumed open, relatively dry environment at the time, and on the presence of a few *A. crispa* seeds in the samples.

The attempt to differentiate rosaceous pollen type was abandoned because of the difficulty in assigning individual pollen grains to consistent categories. A comprehensive detailed study of the group is in progress. It would be valuable to recognize indicator taxa such as *Luetkea pectinata, Geum calthifolium* (caltha-leaved avens), and *Rubus pedatus* (five-leaved creeping raspberry).

Liguliflorae (*Asteraceae*) pollen belongs to *Apargidium boreale* for the most part. This plant is widespread in all open and semi-open peaty habitats on Brooks Peninsula.

Coptis aspleniifolia (spleenwort-leaved goldthread) pollen was readily recognized by its relatively small size and periporate, almost forate, apertures (Figure 9.16d).

Caltha biflora (two-flowered white marsh-marigold) pollen was readily distinguished (Figure 9.16e) because it is large, periporate with large subcircular to oval pores and verrucate sculpture (see Warner et al. 1984).

The category cf. *Dodecatheon* includes all small tricolpate and weakly tricolporate pollen. This type most closely resembles pollen of *Dodecatheon jeffreyi*, which is abundant in open, moist environments throughout Brooks Peninsula.

Lycopodium spores were not studied in detail in the three cores. They were divided into two categories—*Lycopodium annotinum* type and *Lycopodium complanatum* type. *L. annotinum* includes all *Lycopodium* spores with a coarse reticulum, whereas *L. complanatum* includes spores with a fine reticulum. *Lycopodium* from the Amos Creek site is assigned to *L. obscurum* because some spores have faintly developed reticulum on the proximal face. Some of these spores may belong to *L. annotinum*. The plants have similar ecological requirements for acidic soil (Taylor 1971). *L. obscurum* does not grow on Vancouver Island today (Taylor 1971).

Monolete spores with an enveloping, rugulate, perispore were placed into the cf. *Polystichum* category. Spores of this morphology most likely belong to the relatively widespread *Polystichum munitum* (sword fern), but could belong to other species of ferns within the Polypodiaceae, which grow on Brooks Peninsula, but are less abundant.

Isoëtes (quillwort) microspores (Figure 9.16f) fall into another monolete spore type that is not frequently encountered elsewhere, but occurs in large quantities in sediments from Brooks Peninsula. The perispore is thin and faintly verrucate (see McAndrews et al. 1973 for comparison).

The category of monolete ferns includes all monolete ferns without a clearly distinct perispore or well-defined ornament. *Blechnum spicant* (deer fern) and *Athyrium filix-femina* (common lady fern) produce these sorts of spores. *Blechnum* spores may be separated by the presence of large, faint verrucae in the vicinity of the scar. Many of the monolete fern spores have such faint verrucae and are suspected to belong to *Blechnum*, a plant that is ubiquitous on Brooks Peninsula.

Defining Pollen Zones

Pollen diagrams were divided by inspection into zones with similar pollen and spore assemblages, as outlined by Hebda (1983). Each core was zoned independently, with no intent to produce regional pollen zones. The occurrence of *Pseudotsuga* pollen indicating warmth and relative dryness, even in small quantities, is an important characteristic in defining early Holocene zones. Changes in the Cupressaceae curve are critical to establishing late Holocene zone boundaries.

Macrofossil Identification

The study focused on the identification of conifer needles because these were abundant in many samples, especially those from Kalmia Lake. The objective was to distinguish forest tree species with pollen that could not be separated, and to compensate for the overrepresentation of certain species in the pollen rain (see Hebda 1983). Seeds and cones were identified, when possible, to supplement needle data.

Needles and, in most cases, fragments of needles can be distinguished readily for all major conifers except *Pseudotsuga*. Correct identification of *Pseudotsuga* requires complete needles. *Abies* and *T. mertensiana* needles break to produce tip, middle, and base fragments. *T. heterophylla* rarely produces middle fragments. In all cases, tip and base portions have distinct morphologies. Middle sections are separated on the basis of stomatal pattern and abaxial morphology. *Abies amabilis* needles usually have stomata on one side. The margins of the abaxial side exhibit a distinct thickened zone. *T. mertensiana* needles have stomata on both sides, and the abaxial margins do not have a well-developed marginal zone. Stomata occur only on the upper surface of *T. heterophylla*. Margins usually have minute teeth, and the abaxial (lower surface) does not exhibit a distinct marginal zone like *Abies*.

Picea middle-fragments are distinguished by the rhomboidal cross-section and, often, by a peculiar pattern of fungal decomposition. Dark bands form perpendicular to the axis of the needle. On one side of each band the cellular tissue is degraded and the interior of the needle is light coloured. On the other side of the dark band the interior of the needle is normal and dark.

Thuja and *Chamaecyparis* scales occur either singly or in branchlets of widely varying sizes. The tips of *Chamaecyparis* scales are distinctive and more elongate than those of *Thuja* scales. Because recovered conifer needles are often fragmentary, it is difficult to compare data for different taxa. Needle data from Pyrola Lake (Table 9.2) are displayed in raw form because, for many samples, the numbers of specimens are insufficient to calculate meaningful percentages.

Kalmia Lake samples contained many subfossil needles, and the results are presented as percentages (Figure 9.17). Entire needles were each scored as one unit; base, tip, and middle fragments were each scored as half a unit. Deciding upon a unit for *Thuja* and *Chamaecyparis* scales was difficult. Based on observations in the field, the unit of dispersal, roughly equivalent to the needle, is the branchlet. Hence, each branchlet scored as one unit. A branchlet can consist of two or more attached scales. Some scales become separated from branchlets during transport or within sediments. However, most of them are likely detached during screening of sediment for macrofossils. For this reason detached scales were not included in percentage calculations; the number of detached single scales is listed beside the percentage value.

Cones and seeds did not occur abundantly. Cones were easily identified by comparison with modern reference material. Seeds were identified only to generic level, except in the case of *Abies* and *Alnus*. All *Abies* seeds belong to *A. amabilis*—as might be expected, since this is the only species of *Abies* in the area. These seeds, including the wings, are larger than those of *Abies grandis* (grand fir) and *Abies lasiocarpa* (alpine fir). The kernel is large, irregular, and fusiform, whereas those of *A. grandis* and *A. lasiocarpa* are distinctly triangular (Franklin 1974: 174). *Alnus* seed macrofossils were most similar to *A. crispa* ssp. *sinuata*, which also have large wings and narrow ovoid kernels. The kernel of *A. rubra* tends to be broad near the top; wing size varies.

Small fragments of wood occurred in many of the macrofossil samples, but no effort was made to identify them.

Table 9.2 Pyrola Lake macrofossils - raw counts

DEPTH (metres)	*Pinus* E[a]	*Pinus* F	*Picea* E	*Picea* F	*Abies* E	*Abies* F	*T. mertensiana* E	*T. mertensiana* F	*T. heterophylla* E	*T. heterophylla* F	*Thuja* Branchlet	*Chamaecyparis* Branchlet	Indeterminate Fragments	Other
0-0.1	-	-	2	2	1	4	-	1	2	2	-	-	-	
0.1-0.2	-	-	5	-	-	-	2	-	1	2	-	-	1	
0.2-0.3	-	1	4	2	7	8	2	2	7	2	-	-	-	*Thuja* cone
0.3-0.4	-	-	3	1	4	7	-	-	6	-	-	-	2	
0.4-0.5	-	-	4	2	2	2	-	1	1	-	-	-	-	
0.5-0.6	-	-	1	-	29	13	2	3	24	8	1	2	4	
0.6-0.7	-	-	1	1	36	13	3	1	39	4	1	-	3	
0.7-0.8	-	-	5	-	5	14	1	-	23	5	1	-	-	*Thuja* cone
0.8-0.9	1	3	4	4	-	2	-	-	-	-	2	-	-	indet.[b] seed
0.9-1.0	-	3	2	1	3	4	1	-	2	1	-	-	-	
1.0-1.1	-	2	1	2	3	7	1	-	2	1	-	-	1	*A. amabilis* seed
1.1-1.2	-	-	-	3	3	4	4	-	2	1	1	-	-	
1.2-1.3	-	-	1	2	2	4	3	-	3	-	-	1	1	
1.3-1.4	-	-	2	1	4	5	-	1	2	1	-	-	-	
1.4-1.5	-	-	4	2	1	3	-	-	2	1	-	-	-	*A. amabilis* seed
1.5-1.6	-	-	2	3	3	2	4	-	6	-	-	-	-	
1.6-1.7	-	-	-	4	5	3	-	-	4	-	1	2	3	
1.7-1.8	-	-	3	1	6	5	1	-	4	-	-	-	1	*Chamaecyparis* cone, *Nuphar* seed
1.8-1.9	not analyzed													
1.9-2.0	-	-	2	1	8	4	1	-	6	-	2	2	1	*Chamaecyparis* cone
2.0-2.1	-	-	-	1	5	7	-	-	1	2	-	-	3	Indet. seed
2.1-2.2	-	-	2	-	5	9	-	-	7	2	-	-	2	*Nuphar* seed
2.2-2.3	-	-	3	1	6	21	-	-	4	5	6	-	8	
2.3-2.4	-	-	-	1	1	2	-	-	2	2	1	-	4	
2.4-2.5	-	-	-	-	3	7	-	-	1	6	-	-	-	
2.5-2.6	-	-	-	-	-	-	-	-	3	-	-	-	1	
2.6-2.7	-	-	-	1	1	-	-	-	-	-	-	-	-	*A. amabilis* seed
2.7-2.8	-	-	-	-	2	6	-	-	3	-	-	-	3	
2.8-2.9	-	-	-	-	-	1	-	-	-	2	-	-	-	Indet. seed
2.9-3.0	-	-	-	-	-	1	-	-	1	-	1	-	-	
3.0-3.1	-	-	-	-	-	1	-	-	-	-	-	-	1	
3.1-3.2	-	-	-	-	6	27	-	-	13	2	-	-	1	Indet. seed
3.2-3.3	-	-	-	-	-	1	-	-	-	-	-	-	-	*T. heterophylla* seed
3.3-3.4	-	-	-	-	-	-	-	-	-	-	-	-	1	*T. heterophylla* seed
3.4-3.5	-	-	-	-	1	7	-	-	-	-	-	-	-	
3.5-3.6	-	-	-	-	-	3	-	-	-	-	-	-	1	
3.6-3.7	-	-	5	-	2	4	-	-	6	-	-	-	-	
3.7-3.8	-	-	2	-	-	4	-	-	-	-	-	-	-	*A. amabilis*, two seeds *Nuphar* seed
3.8-3.9	-	-	1	-	-	2	-	-	-	-	-	-	-	
3.9-4.0	-	-	-	4	-	4	-	-	1	-	-	-	-	*A. amabilis*, seed
4.0-4.1	-	-	-	5	-	5	-	-	1	-	-	-	-	indet. seed
4.1-4.2	charcoal fragments													
4.2-4.3	-	-	-	-	-	-	-	-	-	-	-	-	1	indet. seed
4.3-4.4	none recovered													

[a] E = entire needle, F = needle fragment.

[b] indet. = indeterminate.

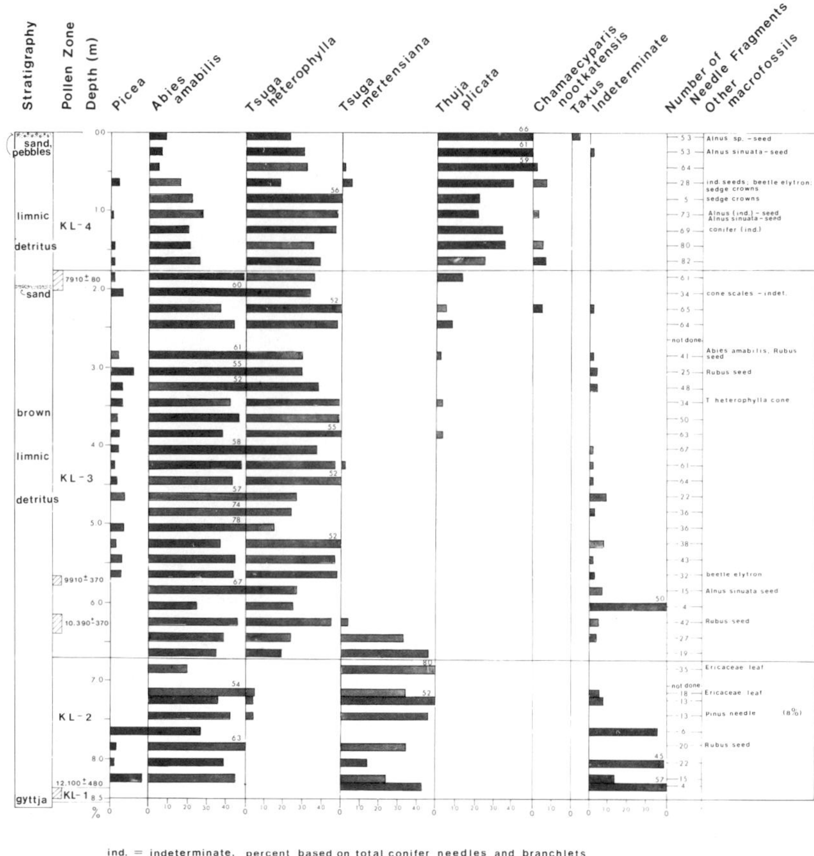

Figure 9.17 Kalmia Lake macrofossils (Conifer needles and branchlets are expressed as percentages, other macrofossils as raw counts.)

Pollen Assemblages and Vegetation

Amos Creek

A sample of organic silt from an exposure along Amos Creek yielded moderately well-preserved pollen and spores. Arboreal pollen (AP), at 56.1%, barely dominates the assemblage (Table 9.3). *Picea* pollen is most abundant, but *Tsuga mertensiana* and *Pinus* pollen also occur in significant quantities. There are numerous degraded and crumpled conifer grains that cannot be identified. These probably were reworked from older sediments or soils in the watershed. Ericaceae, Poaceae, *Caltha*, Asteraceae, and Cyperaceae pollen grains occur abundantly. Monolete fern spores and *Lycopodium* cf. *obscurum* are present in significant quantities.

Because arboreal pollen barely dominates, tree cover could not have been continuous. *Picea*, probably *Picea sitchensis* in this oceanic setting, dominated the forested patches. *Tsuga mertensiana*, a species usually underrepresented by pollen rain (Hebda 1983), occurred almost as abundantly as *Picea*. *P. contorta* may have grown on gravelly deflated sites or in boggy terrain—both habitats are present near the sample site today; under these conditions pines are scrubby and exhibit poor sexual reproduction.

Both shrubby and herbaceous communities were widespread. Ericaceae and probably *Empetrum nigrum* occupied relatively favourable sites at the margins of forested patches and in better

Table 9.3 Pollen and spore percentages at Amos Creek[a]

Type	%
Pinus	7.7
Picea	23.6
Tsuga mertensiana	8.4
Tsuga heterophylla	< 0.5
Thuja	< 0.5
Conifer, indeter.	15.4
Alnus	0.8
Ericaceae	8.4
Rosaceae	< 0.5
Poaceae	5.1
Tubuliflorae	4.5
Liguliflorae	1.3
Artemisia	< 0.5
Valeriana	0.8
Apiaceae	< 0.5
Gentiana douglasii	< 0.5
Caltha	5.1
Liliaceae	< 0.5
Cyperaceae	4.5
Unknown pollen	1.8
Lycopodium cf. obscurum	2.3
Huperzia selago	0.4
Selaginella selaginoides	< 0.5
Polypodium	0.6
Monolete fern spores	7.3

[a] Arboreal pollen = 56.1%; non-arboreal pollen = 43.9%.

drained situations. *Lycopodium* cf. *obscurum* likely grew in this community, especially on peaty substrates. At the margins of the lake in which the sample sediment was deposited (see Chapter 3), and along flowing streams, wet meadow communities of grasses, sedges, and especially *Caltha* (probably *Caltha biflora*) grew. Asteraceae may have been constituents of this community, but likely also grew along with grasses in deflated xeric sites, as they do on the headland ridge of Brooks Peninsula today. *Erigeron peregrinus* (subalpine fleabane) and *Apargidium* may have been the sources of Tubuliflorae and Liguliflorae pollen, respectively. *Valeriana sitchensis* (Sitka valerian), occupied open moist habitats.

The vegetation reconstructed from the pollen assemblage superficially resembles vegetation at elevations of 500 m and higher at the head of Brooks Peninsula today. However, western hemlock and Cupressaceae pollen are conspicuously absent from the fossil assemblage. Cupressaceae pollen may not have been preserved, but western hemlock pollen is to be expected if hemlock trees grew in the area. Unless *T. heterophylla* was absent because of physical barriers to migration, it was likely excluded by too harsh a climate. Hence, the temperature was probably cooler than today, though precipitation may have been similar. Lower temperatures than today during the Olympia non-glacial interval have been noted for the Fraser Lowland at Lynn Canyon (Hebda et al. 1983), sites on the Olympic Peninsula (Heusser 1983), and the Queen Charlotte Islands (Warner et al. 1984).

In general, the vegetation of Brooks Peninsula around 30 000 years ago, was consistent with the widespread *Picea-T. mertensiana* community types noted for this time elsewhere in coastal northwestern North America (Hebda et al. 1983; Heusser 1983; Warner et al. 1984). The vegetation on southeastern Vancouver Island was apparently different; *T. mertensiana* was nearly absent (Alley 1979). The climate there was apparently similar to that of today. In light of this wide-ranging evidence for lower temperatures, the southeastern Vancouver Island results should be reconsidered.

Pyrola Lake

Zone PL-1: *Pinus*; 4.55-4.70 m; 11 000-13 000 ± B.P.
Pinus, at 80-90%, dominates this pollen zone, with *Tsuga mertensiana* contributing an additional 5% to the arboreal pollen (Figure 9.6). Cyperaceae pollen and monolete ferns are the most abundant non-arboreal types. There are noteworthy quantities of Poaceae, Tubuliflorae (Asteraceae), and *Artemisia* pollen (Figure 9.7).

These assemblages likely represent a pine woodland or parkland, where *Pinus contorta* dominated the tree stratum and left many openings in xeric sites for grasses and herbs, especially of the aster family (Hebda 1983). *Artemisia*—possibly *A. furcata*, the only species of this genus at higher elevations on Brooks Peninsula (see Chapter 5)—occupied rocky sites and cliffs. At 5%, *Tsuga mertensiana*, a poor pollen producer compared to the notably prolific pollen producer *P. contorta* (Hebda 1983), must have been an important component of the tree stratum. Likely, *T. mertensiana* occupied moist sites with deep soils and grew near the tops of the peaks, in hollows, possibly in krummholz form.

Zone PL-2: *Tsuga mertensiana-Tsuga heterophylla*; 4.20-4.55 m; 10 500-11 000 B.P.
Four coniferous pollen types, *T. mertensiana* (20-25%), *T. heterophylla* (20-25%), *Abies* (10-20%), and *Picea* (10-20%), replace *Pinus* in this zone. *Alnus* pollen appears for the first time in significant quantities (10-20%). Cyperaceae, Ericaceae, and monolete fern spores are the most abundant non-aboreal types (NAP). A diverse collection of other NAP types, notably Tubuliflorae, *Valeriana*, and *Cryptogramma*, are also present (Figure 9.7).

Mixed coniferous forest, possibly with an ericaceous understory and containing scattered meadows, is indicated by the pollen frequencies of this zone. *T. mertensiana* and *Abies* (probably *A. amabilis*) grew in mesic sites around Pyrola Lake. *T. heterophylla* was an occasional tree at the elevation of the lake, but probably grew abundantly at lower elevations. *Picea* (probably *P. sitchensis*) likely occupied dry forest sites. *Alnus crispa* probably grew in small, very dry openings in the forest, as it does today.

Meadows were located on shallow soils over bedrock, and in unstable sites, such as talus deposits, immediately around Pyrola Lake. *Valeriana sitchensis* pollen is an indicator of these habitats (Brooke et al. 1970; Mathewes 1979). There must have been numerous open rocky knolls and cliffs around the lake to support colonies of *Cryptogramma crispa*. The occurrence of this plant indicates that the vegetation was more open then than it is today, and probably drier, or at least more "continental," or inland, in character[8].

Relatively abundant Cyperaceae pollen came from plants growing *in situ*, an indication that a fen occupied the basin bottom and margins. Ericaceous pollen was most abundant at this time, which

---

[8] Today, upland vegetation on Brooks Peninsula differs from that of sites farther inland, in the adjacent mountains (see Chapter 8). Relatively, Brooks Peninsula vegetation is more "maritime," with less extreme temperatures; inland vegetation is more "continental."

suggests that ericads were important understory species and may have crowded the edge of the basin.

Zone PL-3: *Picea-Alnus-Tsuga heterophylla-Abies*; 3.50-4.20 m; 9500-10 500 B.P.
Picea (20-30%), *Abies* (10-20%), and *Alnus* (20-60%) reach their peak values in this zone (Figure 9.6). *Alnus* pollen is extremely abundant in the first half of this interval. *T. heterophylla* pollen values decline at first from zone PL-2, but increase to more than 50% in the second half of PL-3. Small, but noteworthy, peaks of both Cupressaceae and *Pseudotsuga* occur, whereas *T. mertensiana* almost disappears. Significant features of the NAP component include peaks in *Lysichiton americanum* (American skunk-cabbage) and *Pteridium* (bracken), the appearance of *Nuphar* and *Isoëtes*, and a sudden decline in Cyperaceae (Figure 9.7). Macrofossil assemblages are characterized by needles of *Picea*, *Abies*, and *T. heterophylla* and seeds of *Abies amabilis* and *Nuphar* (Table 9.2).

On the basis of modern pollen rain studies from northern Vancouver Island (Hebda 1983), *Picea* values in this zone indicate *Picea sitchensis* was a major component of the forest around Pyrola Lake—even at 550 m, well away from the ocean. *Abies* levels are especially high and were produced by nearby stands, possibly growing on the adjacent flats. *Abies* needles are numerous in this interval, an indication that the forest may have been dominated by *Abies amabilis* (Table 9.2).

T. heterophylla became increasingly more abundant in the upper part of the zone. By the end of zone PL-3, *T. heterophylla* grew beside the lake, as indicated by fossil needles (Table 9.2). In the early part of the zone, this species was likely restricted to moist sites. *T. mertensiana* appears nearly to have disappeared around the lake, but probably it continued to grow on the peaks above. The value of 1% exhibited by *Pseudotsuga* indicates that this tree occupied slightly drier sites in the area (see Hebda 1983). The peaks of *Alnus* and *Pteridium* in PL-3 reflect sizable openings in the forest cover. *Pteridium* is well-recognized as a species favouring forest openings (Mathewes and Rouse 1975).

The *Alnus* pollen was probably contributed by *Alnus crispa*. Today, this species often grows in xeric openings within the forests of Brooks Peninsula and at the timberline. *Alnus rubra* is confined to the marine shore zone and areas along watercourses. In the relatively warm, dry climate indicated by *Pseudotsuga* and *Pteridium*, open xeric sites would have been more extensive than today; sites favoured by *A. rubra* would not have been more abundant. Moreover, *Alnus crispa* grew at Kalmia Lake on the other side of Refugium Range at about this time (Figure 9.17).

Nuphar requires several decimetres of water and a neutral to acidic organic substrate. Its presence signals permanent submergence of the coring site. The waters of Pyrola Lake increased in depth, and an oligotrophic-dystrophic nutrient status was established. The deeper water eliminated sedge communities, which explains the decline in Cyperaceae. *Isoëtes* presumably grew in seasonally emergent organic sediment at the margin of the lake.

Zone PL-4: *T. heterophylla-Abies-Cupressaceae*; 1.40-3.50 m; 2500-9500 B.P.
T. heterophylla (40-60%) dominates pollen assemblages, though noteworthy quantities of *Abies* (ca. 10%) and Cupressaceae (10-20%) occur. NAP remains low, less than 10%, but includes significant levels of *Ligusticum calderi*, *Caltha biflora*, and *Polypodium* (Figure 9.7). Needles of *A. amabilis* and *T. heterophylla* predominate, especially in the upper part of the zone (Table 9.2). *P. sitchensis* needles and *Thuja* branchlets occur throughout. *Chamaecyparis* cones and branches and *T. mertensiana* needles appear for the first time at 1.9-2.0 m.

These pollen assemblages, and macrofossil assemblages reveal that *T. heterophylla* and *A. amabilis* formed a relatively closed forest around Pyrola Lake. This is so, despite the decline of the *Abies* pollen curve from zone PL-3. This decline likely resulted from increases in absolute pollen input from *T. heterophylla* relative to the preceding zone. Both the pollen and macrofossil data indicate that Cupressaceae—first *Thuja* and later *Chamaecyparis*—were important components of the forest, presumably in moist sites. *Picea* trees grew near the lakee (despite the reduced pollen-values from the preceding zone, *Picea* needles occur throughout the upper half of the zone).

There are numerous indications that the upper half of zone PL-3 was characterized by somewhat different vegetation than the lower part, probably in response to a cooler and/or moister climate. There is little doubt that temperatures decreased and moisture became more available in comparison with PL-3. This is indicated by decline and virtual disappearance of *Pseudotsuga* pollen and *Pteridium* spores and rise in *T. heterophylla* pollen. Temperatures must have continued to decline and humidity to increase. Wet peaty areas developed adjacent to the lake and supported *Ligusticum calderi* and *Caltha biflora*. Increases in Tubuliflorae, probably from *Erigeron peregrinus* (subalpine fleabane) and cf. *Dodecatheon* pollen, further support this conclusion. By 3530 ± 70 B.P., *Chamaecyparis* and *T. mertensiana* were abundant enough in the area to contribute macrofossil remains. Both these species favour cool, moist climate. For the zone as a whole, the early climate was probably similar to that of today—that is, cool and moist. However, conditions began to get cooler beginning about 6600 years ago, a trend that agrees with results from adjacent areas (Hebda 1983, 1995; Mathewes 1973).

Zone PL-5: *T. heterophylla*-Cupressaceae; 0.00-1.40 m; 0-2500 B.P.
T. heterophylla and Cupressaceae pollen dominate this zone (Figure 9.6). *Abies* continues to occur in significant quantities, and there is a gradual rise in *Pinus*. NAP remains low with little change from PL-4—except for declines in *Ligusticum* and *Caltha* and a possibly significant rise in Poaceae (Figure 9.7). Macrofossil assemblages continue to be composed principally of *Abies* and *T. heterophylla* needles. *Pinus contorta* needles appear for the first time.

PL-5 assemblages represent more or less extant vegetation and reflect the climate of today. Mixed coniferous forest dominated by T. *heterophylla* and *Thuja* has grown around the lake since 2500 B.P. The relatively high values of *Abies* are generated by mature stands of *A. amabilis* on the flats adjacent to the lake. Macrofossils of these trees are well represented. Today, *Chamaecyparis* and *T. mertensiana* grow on the slopes above the lake. Their needles are washed into the lake by a stream. The gradual rise in the *Pinus* pollen curve, and the presence of *P. contorta* needles, indicate that *P. contorta* began to grow on the boggy terrain and rocks at the lake margin. *Picea* needles show that there has been at least one Sitka spruce next to the lake for the last 2500 years.

The tree that grows there today is a remnant of a once much larger population. The slight changes in the NAP may suggest a drying trend with the replacement of *Ligusticum* and *Caltha* by grasses near the lake margins.

Kalmia Lake

Zone KL-1: *Pinus-Alnus*; 8.40-8.55 m; 12 000-12 500 B.P.
Pinus is overwhelmingly the most abundant pollen type (60-70%) (Figure 9.9). Noteworthy quantities of *Alnus*, *Abies*, and *T. mertensiana*, and monolete fern spores occur. Needles of *T. mertensiana* are present in the macrofossil fraction (Figure 9.17).

KL-1 assemblages were produced by pine forest similar to the vegetation at Pyrola Lake during the same interval. The recovery of *T. mertensiana* needles confirms that this species grew with *P. contorta*, at least in the waning phase of its dominance. *Alnus* pollen suggests patches of open terrain nearby, but the absence of other NAP types indicates closed forest around the lake (Figure 9.10).

Zone KL-2: *T. mertensiana-T. heterophylla-Alnus*; 6.70-8.40 m; 10 500-12 000 B.P.
This zone is characterized by abundant *T. mertensiana* (10-20%) and *Alnus* (20-40%) pollen throughout (Figure 9.9). *Pinus* drops to insignificant quantities in the lower part of the zone. *T. heterophylla* reaches 30% in the upper part of the zone. *Abies* (5-10%) and *Picea* (5-20%) occur in noteworthy amounts. NAP expands almost to 30% in the middle of the zone, largely a result of increases in monolete fern spores and ericaceous pollen. Needles of *T. mertensiana* and *A. amabilis* occur throughout the zone (Figure 9.17), whereas *Picea sitchensis* needles occur in the lower part of zone KL-2 and *T. heterophylla* needles appear in the upper part.

As during the contemporaneous zone at Pyrola Lake (PL-2), mixed coniferous forest of *T. mertensiana* and *A. amabilis* grew around the lake. *Picea* trees grew near the site in the early phase, but were replaced by *T. heterophylla*. Presumably, *Alnus crispa* survived in xeric openings. Ericaceous shrubs were abundant, likely in the forest and immediately around the lake, as indicated by fossil ericad leaves (Figure 9.17). The monolete spore curve suggests abundant ferns, the same species as at Pyrola Lake. Because of the moist climate indicated by *A. amabilis* and *T. mertensiana*, and the moist local habitats indicated by *Caltha*, the fern species was probably *Blechnum spicant*.

Zone KL-3: *Alnus-T. heterophylla-Picea*; 1.80-6.70 m; 7800-10 500 B.P.
Alnus values rise abruptly from 20% in the preceding KL-2 zone to 80% in KL 3 where they dominate pollen assemblages (Figure 9.9). *T. heterophylla* levels (10-30%) decline somewhat, but remain more or less constant throughout KL-3. *Picea* increases from the end of KL-2, reaching ca. 10-20% throughout most of the zone. Cupressaceae pollen appears in significant quantities for the first time and increases to 30% near the top of the zone. *T. mertensiana*, however, almost disappears in the early phases and does not recover. Traces of *Pseudotsuga* pollen are present. NAP continues to fluctuate between about 20% and 40%. Fern spores and rosaceous pollen predominate in the NAP component (Figure 9.10).

In the macrofossil sequence, *T. mertensiana* needles give way to *T. heterophylla* needles at the base of the zone. *Abies* needles occur in abundance. *Picea* needles are scattered throughout the zone. *Thuja* scales and branchlets appear in the middle of the zone and become abundant toward the top. *Chamaecyparis* branchlets occur occasionally, in upper levels. Despite abundant *Alnus* pollen, only a single *A. crispa* seed occurs.

Although not clearly evident from the pollen diagram, the pollen and macrofossil assemblages likely represent a closed mixed coniferous forest of gradually changing composition. *A. amabilis* and *T. heterophylla* dominated the forest around Kalmia Lake throughout KL-3. *T. mertensiana* occurred as an important component in the early phases, and was replaced, presumably by *T. heterophylla*. Both pollen and needle assemblage data reveal that *Picea* was an infrequent component in early stages of KL-3, and gradually became a significant, though not major, member of the forest. *Thuja*, and later *Chamaecyparis*, contributed to the forest canopy in later phases, though they never replaced *T. heterophylla* and *Abies*. Rosaceous plants, possibly *Rubus* sp., were likely prominent understory plants. Perhaps *Rubus spectabilis* (salmonberry) grew at lake margins and along the stream that feeds Kalmia Lake. The forest interior, which supported *Coptis aspleniifolia*, appears to have been relatively moist. There are, however, indications that there were openings in the forest along the feeder streams. *Blechnum* and *Coptis* covered the forest floor, as they do today, and cf. *Dodecatheon* and *Lysichiton* grew in moist open sites.

Zone KL-4: Cupressaceae-*Tsuga*; 0.00-1.80 m; 0-7800 B.P.
Thuja-Chamaecyparis type pollen dominates this zone, displacing *Picea* and *Alnus* types, which decline from the preceding zone (Figure 9.9). *T. heterophylla* and *Abies* remain at values similar to KL-3. NAP declines slightly from preceding KL-3 because of reductions in shrubby and

herbaceous types (Figure 9.10). *Polypodium* spores and monolete fern spores remain in significant quantities. Macrofossil assemblages consist mainly of *T. heterophylla* needles and *Thuja* branchlets and scales (Figure 9.17). Numerous *Abies* needles occur at the base of the zone, but are less frequent near the top. *Picea* needles disappear. *Chamaecyparis* and *T. mertensiana* remains occur infrequently.

These fossil assemblages reflect a forest dominated by *T. heterophylla* and *Thuja*, similar to extant vegetation, though there are major differences. First, *Abies* needles and pollen occur in significant quantities to the top, that is, the present day surface. There are no *Abies* trees in the vicinity of the lake, nor along the feeder stream, today. No *Pinus* needles, and few *Pinus* pollen grains, were recovered despite the numerous scrubby *P. contorta* trees around the lake. The vegetation represented in KL-4 was probably transitional between the preceding *Abies-T. heterophylla* closed forests and today's *T. heterophylla-Thuja plicata* scrub. This implies that the uppermost recent part of the sediment sequence at the coring site has been eroded—perhaps slumped off the front of the stream delta into the lake. Although zone KL-4 has been designated to extend to the present, it more likely extends only to about 4000-5000 years ago.

Cassiope Pond

Zone CP-1: *Alnus-Tsuga heterophylla*-NAP; 2.40-2.65 m; 10 000-11 000 ± B.P.
Arboreal pollen types range from 45% to 80% in this zone, with *Alnus* pollen (40-70%) predominating (Figure 9.12). *T. heterophylla* is moderately abundant (to 25%). Significant levels of *Picea*, *Abies*, and *Tsuga mertensiana* also occur. NAP is dominated by monolete fern spores. *Ligusticum calderi*, *Caltha*, and ericaceous pollen grains also occur. There are notable numbers of *Isoëtes* microspores and monolete fern spores (Figure 9.13).

The occurrence of three important subalpine heath or meadow pollen types on Brooks Peninsula at this time, *L. calderi*, *Caltha*, and Ericaceae, suggests that heath or meadows (wet alpine meadows), similar to those of today, occupied much of the area around Cassiope Pond. Given the apparent open nature of the vegetation, *Alnus crispa* likely grew in scattered thickets near the pond, especially on well-drained shallow soils. Such thickets grow today on xeric sites on the slopes of "Senecio Ridge" on Brooks Peninsula. Groves of trees covered areas with suitably deep and well-drained mineral soils. These groves likely consisted of *T. mertensiana*, *A. amabilis*, and *T. heterophylla*, and possibly also *P. sitchensis*. Probably, most of the *T. heterophylla* pollen derived from more continuous forest stands at lower elevations. Surface spectra from high elevations on Brooks Peninsula (Hebda 1983) reveal that *T. heterophylla* pollen is transported in quantity from lowland forests. The forests at Kalmia Lake, 4 km to the west, in the lowlands, contained *T. heterophylla* trees at this time (Figure 9.9).

As is the case in many early postglacial sites of coastal British Columbia, there are numerous monolete fern spores indicating that dense fern stands, possibly composed of *Athyrium* or *Blechnum spicant*, occupied the margins of watercourses and runnels and grew on the moist forest floor. The pond was about the same size as today and approximately 1.0-1.5 m deep, as indicated by the pollen of shallow-water submerged or emergent aquatic plants such as *Sparganium*, *Isoëtes*, and Cyperaceae.

Zone CP-2: *Alnus-Tsuga heterophylla-Picea*-Monolete Spores; 1.80-2.40 m; 8000-10 000 B.P.
Alnus and *Tsuga heterophylla* pollen grains are the most abundant AP types in this zone, as they are in CP-1. But *Picea* pollen is 2 to 3 times more abundant than in the preceding zone, reaching 20% or more (Figure 9.12). *Abies* pollen occurs in approximately the same quantities, whereas *T. mertensiana* pollen almost disappears. Cupressaceae reach their highest values in this zone (approaching 10%). Only in this interval does *Pseudotsuga* occur as more than a trace (1%). NAP

values continue to be high at 50-60%, and monolete fern spores are extremely abundant, except at the bottom of the zone, where they are infrequent (Figure 9.13). Both *Caltha* and *Ligusticum* pollen curves decline to the lowest values in the core at the beginning of CP-2, though they recover in the upper part.

Zone CP-2 likely reflects more forested vegetation than CP-1. Suitable nutrient-rich sites were covered in a forest of *Picea sitchensis*, *Abies amabilis*, and *Tsuga heterophylla*, and contained occasional *Chamaecyparis* or *Thuja*. *A. crispa* still occupied margins of dry knolls and openings in the forest. Possibly, *Pseudotsuga* trees grew at this elevation, but they were infrequent. Non-forested patches around the pond were reduced in area. However, they maintained their wet-meadow character. Ferns, likely *Athyrium* sp. or *Blechnum*, thrived in moist sites. Since there is no change in sediment type, nor any major wetland indicator from the preceding zone, the character and size of Cassiope Pond appears to have remained unchanged.

Zone CP-3: *T. heterophylla-Alnus-Caltha*-Monolete Spores; 0.50-1.80 m; 2000-8000 B.P.
T. heterophylla pollen predominates (30-45%) in the AP, having increased from zone CP-2, whereas *Alnus* pollen decreases (Figure 9.12). Noteworthy quantities (5-10%) of *T. mertensiana* occur. *Picea* levels decline to less than 5% and *Abies* to 3-5%. Monolete fern spores continue to be the most abundant NAP type (more than 40%), but show a decline from CP-2 (Figure 9.13). *Caltha* and *Ligusticum* pollen and *Isoëtes* microspore curves exhibit noteworthy increases. In fact, many NAP types are more abundant than in zone CP-2.

These assemblages represent a discontinuous forest characterized by extensive open areas. *Abies amabilis*, *Tsuga mertensiana*, and probably *Chamaecyparis* or *Thuja*, formed forested patches. *Picea* and *T. heterophylla* may have grown at this elevation, but based on surface spectral studies (Hebda 1983), they were minor constituents. Open areas probably contained both heath-dominated communities and wet meadows, very much like those of today. *Caltha*, in moist sites, and *Ligusticum*, in mesic sites, must have formed luxuriant patches. Cassiope Pond supported numerous aquatic and semi-aquatic plants, including *Nuphar*, *Sparganium*, Cyperaceae, and *Isoëtes*. These indicate shallow water, no deeper than 2 m, and possible periodic exposure of the pond bottom.

CP-4: *T. heterophylla-T. mertensiana-Abies*; 0.00-0.50 m; 0-2000 B.P.
The proportion of AP rises to 60-80%. *T. heterophylla* increases to 50-60% and dominates the pollen spectra (Figure 9.12). *Abies* and *T. mertensiana* are minor, but noteworthy, constituents. NAP declines, because of decreases in *Isoëtes* microspores and monolete fern spores (Figure 9.13). Most other NAP curves decline somewhat, but many NAP types persist. *Caltha* and *Ligusticum* remain as the principal herbaceous types, except for a peak in Poaceae in the top-most sample.

These assemblages closely resemble surface spectra from the Cassiope Pond area today (Hebda 1983). On this basis, the vegetation during this interval was as it is today—large areas of wet and dry alpine meadows and shrub communities on the flat terrain adjacent to the pond, and *T. mertensiana-Abies amabilis* forest or scrubforest on slopes. However, *T. heterophylla* likely played a more important role until very recently, when, for unknown reasons, it declined. The near absence of Cupressaceae pollen is notable, because *Chamaecyparis* trees and *Thuja* scrub now grow in the area. *Thuja* may be at the limits of vigorous reproduction and thus would be poorly represented. Also, Cupressaceae pollen is not well-represented in surface spectra from large open sites (Hebda 1983). Cassiope Pond occasionally dries out, hence, there may be selective loss of the rather fragile cupressaceous pollen. For these reasons, Cupressaceae, likely *Chamaecyparis*, were a significant forest and scrubforest component near Cassiope Pond.

NAP curves indicate that the character of surrounding non-forested communities changed little from CP-3. The meadows and heaths around Cassiope Pond continued to consist of many taxa, most prominent of which was *Caltha biflora*. The decline in monolete fern spores likely reflects a decline in abundance or reproductive vigour of *Blechnum spicant*, or a change in the course of the small feeder stream.

Cottongrass Hollow

Zone CGH-1: *Picea-T. heterophylla-Lilaeopsis*-Cyperaceae; 1.40-1.55 m; 3800-4200 B.P.
Picea (20-30%) and *T. heterophylla* (20-30%) are the most important arboreal types, though *Cupressaceae* pollen also occurs abundantly (ca. 20%) (Figure 9.14). Non-arboreal pollen originates from Cyperaceae, and from *Lilaeopsis occidentalis* (western lilaeopsis), which is exceptionally abundant.

Because the arboreal assemblage is rich in *Picea*, the surrounding forest likely was dominated by this tree. *T. heterophylla* and probably *Thuja* may have been codominant with the spruce, or, more likely, they were characteristic of lowland forests away from the site. Typically, today, there is a shoreline strip of Sitka spruce (see Chapter 8), and Cottongrass Hollow was located in that strip during CGH-1. However, the possibility that regional lowland forests contained more spruce than today should not be ruled out.

Lilaeopsis pollen indicates a particular depositional environment and plant community. Today, *Lilaeopsis* grows in low-energy mid-upper intertidal habitats, at the forward edge of, and interspersed with, *Carex lyngbyei* (Lyngbye's sedge). In this habitat, sedge remains and tide-sorted sand accumulate. During zone CGH-1, therefore, Cottongrass Hollow must have been a small, quiet lagoon connected to the ocean.

Zone CGH-2: *Alnus-Cupressaceae*-Cyperaceae; 1.10-1.40 m; 3000-3800 B.P.
Alnus pollen (20-50%) increases dramatically from CGH-1. Cupressaceae pollen increases to 20-30%, whereas *Picea* declines to less than 5%. *T. heterophylla* pollen is slightly less abundant than in CGH-1. Cyperaceae pollen is the most important NAP type (Figure 9.14).

The forest stands surrounding the site no longer contained much spruce in this interval. The main shore zone and its associated spruce-dominated band had migrated well beyond the site. Presumably, a typical Lowland Forest of *T. heterophylla* and *Thuja* occupied the environs. *Alnus* pollen was derived from *Alnus rubra* that grew along the shore of this small wetland, as it does today in similar settings. Sedge meadows (salt marshes, fens), first dominated by *Carex lyngbyei*, later probably by a fresh-water sedge, grew at the site of deposition. Marine influence finally disappeared in this zone, and Cottongrass Hollow became a freshwater basin.

Zone CGH-3: *T. heterophylla*-Cupressaceae; 0.80-1.10 m; 2200-3000 B.P.
T. heterophylla (30-40%) and *Pinus* (10-20%) achieve their highest values in this zone, whereas *Alnus* declines abruptly. *Thuja* persists at 20-30%. There are significant amounts of *Nuphar* and ericaceous pollen.

By the time of CGH-3, Cottongrass Hollow was situated well into the lowland *T. heterophylla-Thuja* forest. *Alnus rubra* disappeared from the shore of the basin, because marine water no longer inundated the basin and mineral substrates disappeared below an organic blanket. The growth of *Nuphar* indicates that at this time the site was probably a shallow pond, possibly with *Sphagnum* beginning to grow at its edge.

Zone CGH-4: Cupressaceae-*T. heterophylla-Sphagnum*; 0.50-0.80 m; 1300-2200 B.P.
Arboreal assemblages change little from the preceding zone. However, *Sphagnum* spores and ericaceous pollen replace *Nuphar* pollen as the characteristic non-arboreal types (Figure 9.14).

The remarkable abundance of *Sphagnum* spores associated with *Sphagnum* peat reveal that Cottongrass Hollow changed from a shallow, acidic pond to a *Sphagnum* bog. This *Sphagnum* bog must have had enough hummocks and dry sites to support extensive patches of either *Empetrum* or ericad shrubs, which produced the 10-20% ericaceous pollen values near the top of the zone. Cyperaceous plants, possibly *Eriophorum* sp., and herbaceous plants, such as *Gentiana douglasiana* and *Apargidium boreale*, also grew in the bog.

Zone CGH-5: Cupressaceae-Ericaceae subzone (5a), Cupressaceae-Liguliflorae subzone (5b); 0.00-0.50 m; 0-1300 B.P.

Cupressaceae values remain as in the preceding zone, however, *T. heterophylla* values decline. The most prominent features of this zone are the exceptionally high percentages (to 30-40%) of Ericaceae type pollen in the early part (5a), and Liguliflorae pollen in the late part (5b). *Sphagnum* spores persist, but at reduced levels from CGH-4.

The considerable relative increase in Ericaceae type pollen would have depressed arboreal curves of *Cupressaceae* and *T. heterophylla* equally if there were no changes in tree dominance in the forest. The curve of *T. heterophylla* declines, as expected, but that of Cupressaceae does not. This could be interpreted as a decline of *T. heterophylla* in the surrounding Lowland Forest. However, a more likely explanation is that the growth of both *Thuja* and *Chamaecyparis* on the bog surface was quite vigorous. Such a local change in vegetation would be in accord with the profuse growth of ericaceous plants and *Apargidium* (Liguliflorae pollen) on the bog. These indicate some degree of humification on the bog surface and an improving nutrient regime, in comparison with the preceding phase of vigorous sphagnum growth and expansion. The assemblages reflect the vegetation as it is today, a sphagnum and heath mosaic with a diverse assemblage of herbs and graminoid plants.

Panicum Pond

The deepest sediment 0.80-1.05 m from a short core obtained at Panicum Pond (Figure 9.15) was analyzed to reconstruct vegetation associated with the oldest post-glacial date on Brooks Peninsula [12 250 ± 790 B.P. (WAT 924)]. Palynomorph assemblages (Table 9.4) in the lowest 20 cm are overwhelmingly dominated by pine pollen and *Isoëtes* microspores (see Figure 9.16f). Other noteworthy types include Poaceae, *Caltha leptosepala*, and *Lycopodium*.

Based on the same criteria used to interpret similar assemblages from other sites, the regional vegetation represented is pine forest, or pine woodland, with scattered *T. mertensiana* trees in moist sites. *Salix* trees or shrubs probably grew at the site of deposition.

The diverse and abundant NAP component suggests that there were grassy or herbaceous openings among the trees, as well as a rich wetland community at the site. Sediments accumulated in a shallow, perhaps seasonal, pond choked by *Isoëtes*. *Equisetum*, *Caltha* spp., sedges, and other herbaceous species grew at the margins. *Ligusticum calderi*, though not abundant, probably grew near the site—which extends the record of this plant earlier than 12 250 years ago. Unlike the case at the other sites of similar age on Brooks Peninsula, ferns were not prominent in the vegetation.

In the sample from 80-85 cm, pollen assemblages change suddenly. Pine declines to one-third of previous values. *Picea*, *Abies*, *T. mertensiana*, and *Alnus* pollen increase from insignificant levels to substantial percentages. Many NAP types disappear, and the aquatic plant *Nuphar* appears.

Table 9.4 Palynomorph percentages[a] - Panicum Pond, Brooks Peninsula

	DEPTH IN METRES						
POLLEN AND SPORE TYPE	.80-.85	.85-.89	.89-.91	.91-.93	.93-.95	.95-1.00	1.00-1.05
Arboreal							
Pinus	32	79	81	77	78	77	75
Picea	10	+	-	-	-	-	-
Abies	8	1	+	+	-	-	-
Tsuga heterophylla	-	-	-	-	+	-	+
Tsuga mertensiana	10	1	1	-	1	-	1
Cupressaceae	-	1	1	-	-	+	-
Alnus	30	1	-	+	1	1	1
Salix	-	+	1	2	1	-	2
Non-Arboreal							
Ericaceae	-	-	1	-	+	1	-
Poaceae	-	1	+	2	4	1	1
Tubuliflorae	-	-	-	+	1	1	1
Ambrosia	-	-	-	+	1	-	-
Artemisia	-	-	+	-	-	2	1
Caryophyllaceae	-	-	-	+	-	-	-
Apiaceae	-	-	+	+	1	+	-
Ligusticum	+	-	-	-	-	+	-
Caltha biflora	-	-	1	+	1	+	-
Caltha leptosepala type	2	-	-	3	2	11	7
Unknown	-	5	5	3	3	1	-
Cyperaceae	1	1	1	3	3	2	2
Nuphar	2	-	-	-	-	-	-
Lycopodium	2	3	1	4	1	3	1
Cryptogramma	-	-	-	+	-	-	-
Equisetum	4	3	3	-	+	4	8
Isoëtes megaspores[b]	2	2	3	2	-	-	-
Isoëtes microspores[b]	178	58	63	65	72	35	56
Monolete ferns[b]	1	4	3	1	1	2	4
Nuphar sclereids and trichomes[b]	x	-	-	-	-	-	-
TOTAL POLLEN AND SPORES IN SUM	338	368	363	449	371	388	376

[a] "+" = less than 0.5%.

[b] Excluded from sum.

We see, at this time (about 12 000 years ago), the sudden replacement of pine forest or woodland by mixed coniferous forest, probably dominated by *T. mertensiana* and *Abies*. *Alnus*, probably *A. crispa*, entered xeric openings previously occupied by grassy or herbaceous communities. The forest was likely dense and mostly continuous. Locally, the pond deepened and provided a habitat for *Nuphar*. *Isoëtes* becomes relatively more abundant, though this may reflect the decline in pine, a copious pollen producer.

Late Quaternary Environmental History of Brooks Peninsula

The information from the six paleoecological study sites contributes to a history of the changing biotic, climatic, and geomorphic patterns of the late Quaternary on Brooks Peninsula.
The single sample from Amos Creek provides a glimpse into the pre- or early-Fraser Glaciation landscape about 30 000 years ago. The vegetation consisted of parkland with patches of trees and well-developed meadows, like the extant environment on slopes and ridges a few hundred metres above the Amos Creek site. Such vegetation implies a climate perhaps slightly cooler than today. Otherwise, the setting was not very different than at the head of Brooks Peninsula now. Probably, fewer trees occurred on the upper slopes of the central ridge system.

The geological evidence reveals that sometime after 30 000 years ago ice accumulated in local cirques and flowed out of the valleys onto the floor of Brooks Bay and Checleset Bay (see Chapter 3). Presumably, the ridges above and between the cirques supported plant and animal communities. The plant communities were likely depauperate compared to those of today. Yet, many of the major species persisted. Despite the proximity of ice masses, there would have been a moderating influence from the adjacent ocean. Probably, there was much barren ground and frequent low heath communities. Scrubby patches, and, possibly, groves of stunted trees, grew on ocean-facing slopes, particularly near the head of the peninsula. At the glacial maximum, around 15 000-16 000 B.P., Vancouver Island ice covered both flanks of Brooks Peninsula and spilled through low saddles leaving only the ridges ice free. Because there is no fossil record, the plant communities of this time have to be reconstructed on the basis of indirect evidence. Three bits of information help to establish a relatively sound reconstruction. First, the oldest plant fossils recovered from cores suggest some of the species that survived and imply late glacial climatic conditions. Second, observations of plant communities from extant nunataks and ice-bordered areas (see Heusser 1954) serve as general analogues. Third, the proximity of such a large ice mass constrains the character of the environment.

The first postglacial plant communities recorded in the sediments were dominated by pine and also contained mountain hemlock. Unless these species had spread rapidly from beyond the glacial boundary, it is likely that they persisted on Brooks Peninsula during glaciation. Early plant communities were relatively open, and it can be assumed that some of the plants also grew during the climatically more severe full-glacial period. Examples of such plants include grasses, sedges, *Artemisia* and other species of the Aster family, heathers, and crowberry. Heusser (1954) reports that heath mats of *Cassiope mertensiana*, *Cassiope stellariana*, and *Empetrum nigrum* occur on the nunataks of the Juneau Ice Field in Alaska. These three species are important mat formers at high elevations on Brooks Peninsula. Heusser also reports that xeric communities occurred on nunataks. Considering that Brooks Peninsula is farther south and near the ocean, such communities likely persisted there during the period of maximum ice extent. Indeed, rich and robust plant associations would be expected.

The periglacial position of Brooks Peninsula implies that there was considerable frost action (French 1976). Repeated freeze-thaw profoundly disturbs the soil. These processes combined with wind and water erosion, resulted in the loss of fine-grained mineral materials. Such conditions do not favour extensive plant growth, and only scattered clumps or patches of low-growing herbaceous or shrubby plants persist.

We can, then, reconstruct full-glacial communities as consisting predominantly of heath-mats in moderately protected sites with patchy vegetation of grasses, sedges, and herbs in exposed sites (Figure 9.18a). Protected sites were well-vegetated by shrubby and scrubby patches of conifers,

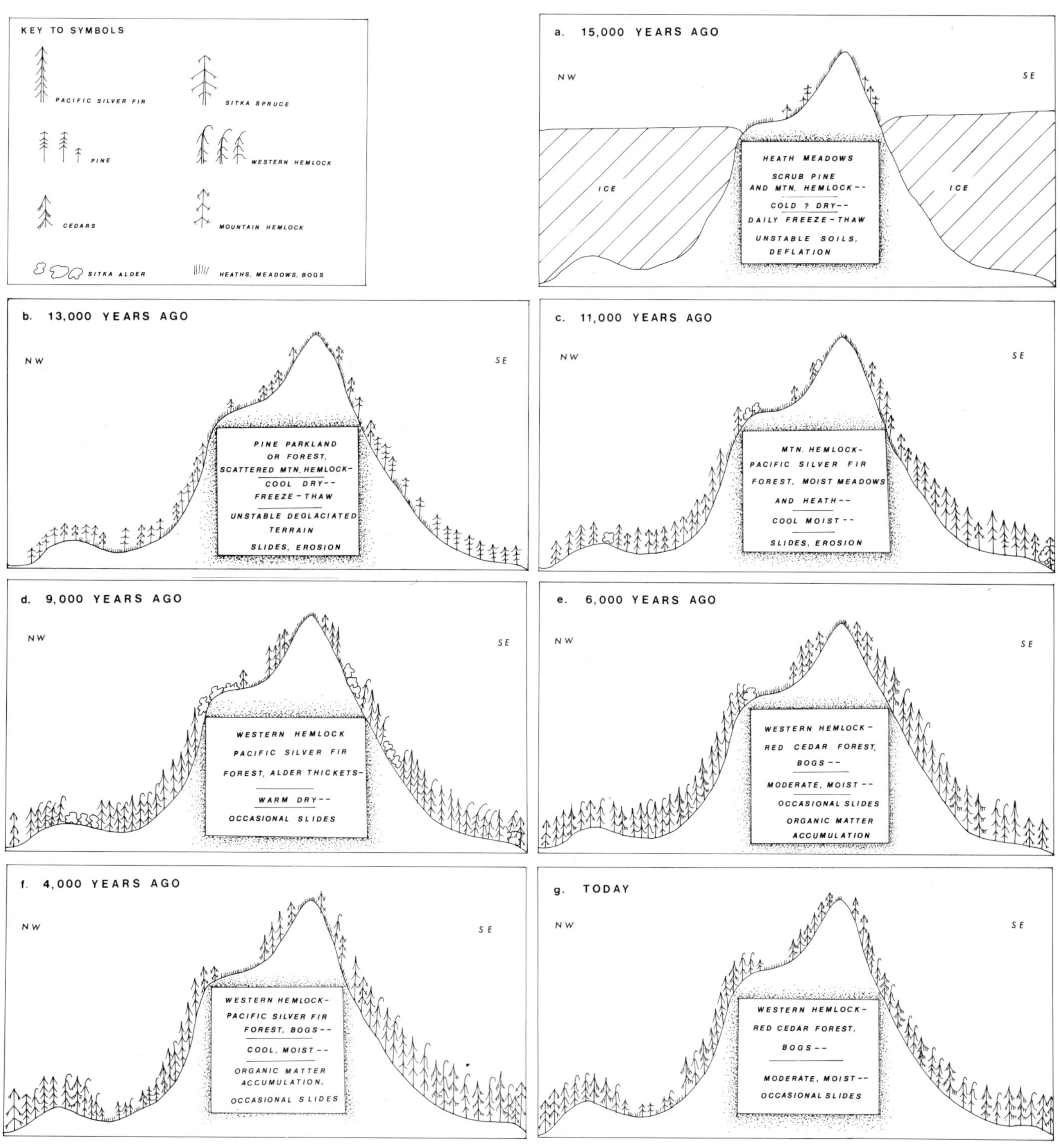

Figure 9.18 Distribution, physiognomy, and composition of principal vegetation on Brooks Peninsula: a) 15 000 B.P.; b) 13 000 B.P.; c) 11 000 B.P.; d) 9000 B.P.; e) 6000 B.P.; f) 4000 B.P.; g) present

probably pine and mountain hemlock, with well-developed adjacent heath-moss communities—precisely as occurs today on Senecio Ridge. Rich meadows and scattered trees may have grown in south-facing protected sites in the central sectors of the Refugium Range. It is possible that the climate was not so severe as to preclude such plant communities. Moist, shady cliff habitats were probably hidden among the ridges.

Three sites, Pyrola Lake, Kalmia Lake, and Panicum Pond, provide a relatively clear picture of the vegetation immediately after deglaciation. At both high and low elevations, lodgepole pine was the dominant tree (Figure 9.18b). The tree stratum appears to have been open at two sites—south-facing Pyrola Lake and low-lying Panicum Pond. Plants, such as *Artemisia* and *Cryptogramma*, that occupied open sites were able to withstand some drought. At Kalmia Lake, plants of openings do not appear to be well-represented, which suggests a partly closed forest canopy. There was abundant mountain hemlock in the forest. This species was widespread in moist settings.

Significantly, one of the plants that grew in open, or partly open, habitats is *Ligusticum calderi*. Although this species—which is endemic on Brooks Peninsula, the Queen Charlotte Islands, and adjacent coastal islands—was not abundant, its occurrence at an early time suggests that habitats similar to those of today occurred even in the first years after deglaciation.

Persisting instability in the landscape continued as the recently deglaciated terrain was washed of its glacial debris. Wind and water eroded exposed, xeric sites under the cool dry climate. Barren patches were widespread, especially at high elevations. The mineral and gyttja deposits at the lake-bottoms suggest that the ground surface was not covered by a protective humus layer. Ground water flowed over and through a mineral soil and transported nutrients. Soils were likely poorly developed brunisols. There were more ponds and puddles on the landscape than today because alluvium and organic debris had yet to fill them.

About 11 500 to 12 000 years ago the vegetation and climate altered drastically. At all elevations, mixed coniferous forest dominated by mountain hemlock and Pacific silver fir completely replaced pine stands (Figure 9.18c). Sitka spruce grew in the forests, but probably occupied dry sites on shallow soil over rock or on steep south-facing slopes. Within a thousand years or so, western hemlock joined the forest. This delay can be attributed either to the lag time necessary for western hemlock to have migrated from the south, or to an unsuitable climate. Sitka alder must have grown in patches within the forest. This shrub occupied xeric knolls and probably persisted as a successional species on landslide surfaces and other unstable substrates. During this interval the glacially oversteepened slopes continued to be adjusted to stable angles of repose. Mass wasting, such as landslides, may have been significantly more frequent than in the preceding interval because there was much more precipitation. The mountain hemlock and Pacific silver fir forest is one indication of a very moist and cool climate. The drowned sedge communities in the bottom of Pyrola Lake are another sign that there was much more water around.

The Cassiope Pond site, despite being at the same elevation as Pyrola Lake, had different plant cover. Groves of mountain hemlock and Pacific silver fir grew on the most favourable sites. However, these groves were restricted in extent because shrubby or herbaceous vegetation predominated. Sitka alder covered unstable terrain and some shallow, dry soils. Herb communities were widespread in moist habitats. These contained *Caltha* and numerous individuals of *Ligusticum calderi*, sedges, and grasses. Heath-dominated plant communities occupied dry sites near Cassiope Pond. On the basis of the results from this locality, it is possible to extrapolate to other elevated areas of Brooks Peninsula and suggest that much of the north- or northwest-facing upper slope zone was open, in contrast to the forested lowland and south-facing slopes.

During this time, organic-dominated sediment, especially organic detritus, was deposited in lakes. A well-developed plant litter and humic blanket covered the ground shaded by the forest canopy. Presumably podzols began forming.

About 10 000 to 10 500 years ago, there was a major change in Brooks Peninsula's vegetation. More or less throughout the peninsula, Pacific silver fir expanded to form extensive forests (Figure 9.18d). The forest canopy was shared with western hemlock and Sitka spruce. Mountain hemlock retreated to restricted, cool, moist sites at high elevations. At the same time, Sitka alder expanded and probably monopolized shallow dry soils, as it does today, though in only a few localities. Well-drained, warm, lowland areas supported scattered Douglas-fir. This tree has never been abundant on Brooks Peninsula, but at the time it was a conspicuous component of the vegetation, especially on the low south-facing slopes. Today, Douglas-fir is rare; with Sitka spruce it occupies well-drained ancient sand dunes near Cape Cook Lagoon and rocky headlands near Columbia Cove. There were probably scattered grassy meadows at dry sites. *Camassia quamash* (common camas) may have arrived at this time and become an important species of the open communities.

As at many other locations along the northwest coast of North America (Hebda 1983), Sitka spruce formed extensive stands, even well inland and well up the slopes. We are not familiar with such forests in British Columbia today, though a somewhat analagous vegetation grows on the west coast of the Olympic Peninsula. All together, the evidence seems to point to a warmer and drier climate than today, a situation consistent with the rest of the northwest coast (Hebda 1983, 1995; Mathewes and Heusser 1981).

Despite the warmer climate, the vegetation of the north-facing high elevations of Brooks Peninsula was not drastically affected. Based on evidence at Cassiope Pond, wet meadows and heath communities persisted from early postglacial time, with little change in character. Heaths, *Caltha*, and *Ligusticum* survived. The open vegetation was not as widespread as in the preceding thousand years or in the time that followed. Although forest crowded Cassiope Pond from below, the local microclimatic setting inhibited forest invasion. Consequently, the rare and "endemic" plants survived the warm and dry climate. It is unlikely that the climatic change of this time was sufficient to curb podzolization, so the process would have continued apace.

Between 8000 and 9000 years ago, the vegetation began to change again and to develop characteristics resembling extant plant cover. On the south flanks, western hemlock and Pacific silver fir formed dense forests (Figure 9.18e). Sitka spruce became a secondary species, but remained a conspicuous component, presumably in the drier sites. Alder thickets were restricted to the shallowest soils over bedrock knolls and landslides. In the lowlands on the northwest side, western hemlock-western redcedar forest covered the landscape. Pacific silver fir trees still grew in moist, well-drained rich sites, but they no longer dominated the forest. Sitka spruce was an infrequent member of the lowland forest, except along the shore, where it formed the typical shoreline zone. The upper slopes were covered with mountain hemlock stands and groves, mostly mixed with fir and, in some cases, with red cedar, or possibly yellow cedar. Meadow and heath communities were extensive, still maintaining the same physiognomy and characteristic species as they had during the preceding 3500 years or so.

The climate was similar to that of today, possibly a little warmer. Certainly it was much wetter than during the preceding xerothermic maximum, as indicated by the spread of cedars.

There are indications that sea levels changed at some point after 8000 years ago. Unfortunately, there is no evidence of their exact position, nor of the configuration of the shoreline. Much of Brooks Peninsula's shoreline consists of steep bluffs and cliffs, hence change in sea level has little effect on coastal configuration. In the area of Cape Cook Lagoon, however, major changes occurred. Large, coastal dunes grew and were progressively abandoned as new shorelines formed.

The last 4000 years have seen gradual adjustments in the vegetation. Also, sea level has declined with consequent shoreline adjustment. Typical coastal western hemlock-western redcedar forest developed in the lowlands, and extended up the southeast-facing slopes to at least 500 m (Figure 9.18f). The sloping bogs of the irregular, glacially derived, lowland terrain probably developed and expanded from restricted bog patches. Associated with this paludification was a decline in the vigour of lowland forests and in the spread of the poor-growth forest and scrub forests of lowland terrain. Pacific silver firs were essentially eliminated from lowland terrain and came to occupy well-drained montane sites. Meadow and heath vegetation continued to occupy much of the high elevations on the northwest-facing side. Mountain hemlock, fir, and yellow cedar formed groves on the ridges and adjacent high slopes.

The sea retreated along the entire coast, abandoning beaches and sea-carved caves. The marine communities among the dunes near Cape Cook Lagoon were replaced, first by salt marshes, then by freshwater ponds and moist lowland terrestrial communities. The ponds rapidly filled in and became basin bogs. The strip of Sitka spruces, typical of the zone adjacent to the shore, migrated seawards with the advancing coastline, and eventually reached today's position.

During the last 4000 years, the climate was moist and cool, as it is today. One of the consequences was continued intense development of podzolic soils. In boggy terrain, however, erosion may have increased. As the preceding tree cover disappeared, and inputs of organic matter declined, water would have attacked the exposed surfaces.

Landslides continued because of heavy rainfall. Streams and rivers adjusted their beds to declining sea levels. Finally, today's configuration of the land and distribution of plant communities were established.

Relationship to Regional Deglaciation, Vegetation and Climatic History

Evidence from lowlands on northeastern Vancouver Island suggests that the dates for deglaciation on Brooks Peninsula are too young. Ice left Bear Cove, near Port Hardy, by 13 630 ± 130 B.P., yet that site is much nearer the source of Cordilleran ice than is Brooks Peninsula. As suggested already, basal dates from Pyrola Lake, Kalmia Lake, and Panicum Pond are too young. The correction factor may be 1500-2000 years—if the difference between basal sediment and basal wood dates from Cottongrass Hollow can be used as a guide (see Table 9.1).

In broad terms, the vegetation and climatic history of Brooks Peninsula is similar to that of other coastal sites in British Columbia and adjacent Washington state (Figure 9.19). However, there are important differences. Throughout the region, a cool and dry late glacial climate supporting lodgepole pine forest or parkland is widespread (Hebda 1983, 1995). Only on Brooks Peninsula [possibly also on the Queen Charlotte Islands (Warner 1984)] does mountain hemlock figure in the early vegetation. Another important difference in the early vegetation is the presence of *Ligusticum calderi* (a restricted oceanic species) only on Brooks Peninsula. This suggests that *L. calderi* survived late Wisconsin glaciation on Brooks Peninsula—though *Ligusticum* might have migrated rapidly, after deglaciation, from an area such as the Queen Charlotte Islands.

Site	Pollen assemblage zones (youngest at top; Years B.P. scale 0–15,000)
PYROLA LAKE Brooks Peninsula	Tsuga heterophylla, Cupressaceae, (Abies) Tsuga heterophylla, Abies amabilis, (Cupressaceae), (Picea), (Tsuga heterophylla), (Pseudotsuga) Alnus – Picea, Abies amabilis Tsuga mertensiana, Abies amabilis, (Picea), NAP, (Tsuga heterophylla) Pinus contorta, (Tsuga mertensiana)
CASSIOPE POND Brooks Peninsula	Tsuga mertensiana, Tsuga heterophylla, Abies amabilis, NAP NAP, Tsuga mertensia, Tsuga heterophylla, (Abies), (Cupressaceae) Alnus – Picea, Abies, (Tsuga heterophylla) Alnus – NAP, (Tsuga heterophylla)
BEAR COVE BOG North Vancouver Island HEBDA 1983	Tsuga heterophylla, Cupressaceae Tsuga heterophylla, Picea Picea, Pseudotsuga, Alnus, Pteridium Picea sitchensis, Tsuga mertensiana, Tsuga heterophylla, Alnus Pinus contorta, Alnus
BOULTON LAKE Queen Charlotte Islands WARNER 1984	Cupressaceae, Tsuga heterophylla Cupressaceae, Picea, Tsuga heterophylla Tsuga heterophylla, Picea Picea, Tsuga heterophylla NAP Pinus contorta, Tsuga mertensiana
FRASER RIVER VALLEY MATHEWES 1973	Alnus rubra Tsuga heterophylla, Thuja Tsuga heterophylla, Alnus Alnus, Pseudotsuga, Pteridium, Polypodiaceae (Tsuga mertensiana), Pinus contorta, Alnus, Picea, Abies Pinus contorta, Shepherdia, Salix
HOH VALLEY west Olympic Peninsula HEUSSER 1974	Tsuga heterophylla, Thuja, Abies Tsuga heterophylla, Picea – Alnus, (Pseudotsuga), (Pteridium) Picea – Alnus, Pseudotsuga, Pteridium ----age uncertain---- (Tsuga heterophylla), (Tsuga mertensiana), Pinus – Alnus, Picea Poaceae, Cyperaceae, Asteraceae

Figure 9.19 Correlation chart of vegetation records (pollen assemblages) from selected sites of the northwest coast of North America

The onset of a cool, moist climate about 11 500-12 000 years ago, characterized by mixed conifer forest, was a widespread phenomenon (Figure 9.19). *Tsuga mertensiana* was a significant component of this forest on Brooks Peninsula and throughout the region. *T. heterophylla* was a minor component, in the wake of *T. mertensiana*. Brooks Peninsula is exceptional, however, in its clear abundance of fossil fir needles and thus, presumably, of fir trees in the forest. It is especially fortuitous that seeds of Pacific silver fir (*Abies amabilis*) were recovered, which makes it possible to identify the species (Hebda 1983). Presumably, Pacific silver fir was abundant because Brooks Peninsula is located in a very moist zone along the coast, unlike sites on the drier eastern side of Vancouver Island and on the mainland.

Findings from Cassiope Pond indicate vegetation somewhat different from the rest of the region. Non-arboreal plants were abundant; parkland, rather than forest, is indicated. At the early phase of postglacial time, this subalpine area already had distinct vegetation. Possibly, similar assemblages will be uncovered when other subalpine sites are studied. Throughout the region, about 9500 to 10 500 years ago, major changes occurred in the vegetation and are assumed to be related to a warming climate (Hebda 1983; Mathewes and Heusser 1981). Generally, the beginning of the Holocene sees the disappearance or decline of *T. mertensiana* and *T. heterophylla* and associated increases in *Alnus*, *Picea*, and *Pseudotsuga*, and, in less oceanic climates, also *Pteridium*. On Brooks Peninsula, *Alnus* and *Picea* exhibit the characteristic rise, but *Pseudotsuga* appears only as minor constituent and *Pteridium* is nearly absent. *Abies amabilis* becomes the dominant tree after this time, presumably because the oceanic climate supplies more moisture. On the Queen

Charlotte Islands, *Abies* is absent and *Tsuga heterophylla* plays a more important role than elsewhere (Warner 1984).

Precise temporal correlation of early Holocene vegetation-changes throughout the region is problematical. First, only one sequence, that from the Fraser Lowland (Mathewes 1973), is precisely dated. Second, study sites are widespread throughout different climatic zones. The same relative climatic changes trigger vegetation changes at different times in different areas because of variability in the sensitivity of plant species and communities (Faegri and Iversen 1975). Although it is significant that at the Cassiope Pond site a general trend to *Alnus* and *Picea* occurred (Figure 9.12), the non-arboreal meadow and heath component was subdued, but never obliterated.

The early to mid Holocene, 5000-9000 years ago, was a period of gradual vegetation change and establishment of stable, persistent communities. In the region, *Alnus*, *Pseudotsuga*, and *Pteridium* declined, presumably as a result of increased moisture, and possibly also lower temperature. *Tsuga heterophylla* expanded. The types that occurred with *T. heterophylla* generally include *Picea*, *Alnus*, and in the mid Holocene, Cupressaceae, presumably *Thuja plicata*. *Abies amabilis* was the principal codominant, with *T. heterophylla*, everywhere on Brooks Peninsula except at Cassiope Pond, where there was a resurgence of *Tsuga mertensiana* and non-arboreal types. In contrast to most other areas, cedars were a significant, though probably minor, constituent of the forest. This confirms previous speculations (Hebda 1983) that the moist oceanic zone of the west coast of Vancouver Island was the centre for *Thuja plicata*, which expanded into the forests of the east side of Vancouver Island and adjacent mainland in the mid to late Holocene (Hebda and Mathewes 1984).

The last major regional adjustment in vegetation took place 2000-3000 years ago. At that time, *Thuja plicata* achieved dominance, or codominance, in British Columbia's coastal forests principally in association with *Tsuga heterophylla*. *Abies amabilis* was, and is, a significant associate in oceanic areas such as Brooks Peninsula and the west side of the Olympic Peninsula (Figure 9.19).

Cassiope Pond, on Brooks Peninsula, is the only location where there were and are differences from other sites in the region. Presumably because of the local "subalpine" microclimate, *Tsuga mertensiana* and *Abies* have remained as major forest trees, whereas neither *T. heterophylla* nor *Thuja plicata* are abundant. The relatively high non-arboreal component consisting of *Caltha*, *Ligusticum*, and ericads indicates that the wet and the dry open meadows and heaths have persisted from before the Holocene to the present. This suggests that Brooks Peninsula subalpine communities have a long and distinct history, which presumably differs from that of other coastal subalpine communities that have different vegetation assemblages. The subalpine communities from adjacent areas need paleoecological study to confirm this.

Implications for a Refugium

The paleoecological studies did not produce clearly dated evidence of full-glacial-age biota, but they did reveal plant communities that probably date to 13 000-14 000 years ago. This means that either the sites studied were glaciated, or that no sediments incorporating full-glacial communities were recognized. Geomorphic evidence at the respective study sites suggests that each was glaciated and is located below the regional ice-maximum-line reconstructed for Brooks Peninsula (see Chapter 4). The steep upper slopes of Brooks Peninsula provide few, if any, sites for sediment accumulation. When this factor is combined with the likelihood that the early postglacial climate was dry (Hebda 1983; Peterson et al. 1983), it is not surprising that datable, fossiliferous full-glacial sediments were not recovered. Similar problems have been encountered elsewhere when conventional sites, such as lakes and bogs, have been examined for full-glacial records (Funder 1979; Mann 1983; Warner 1984). Even in areas clearly south of the glacial boundary, the sediment record of full-glacial time is poor, consisting of silts or silty clays (Barnosky 1981). Full-glacial sediments might be recoverable from sections of old soil horizons in gullies or in sea cliffs (e.g., Warner 1984).

The records from Brooks Peninsula, however, do provide indirect evidence of a refugium. First, and most important, is the occurrence of *Ligusticum calderi* pollen at Panicum Pond in deposits older than 12 500 years. This endemic, more or less restricted to oceanic possible-refugia, clearly has been on Brooks Peninsula from late glacial time. It seems unlikely that it originated elsewhere and migrated to Brooks Peninsula; its known modern distribution indicates little tendency for migration. Migration, however, should not be ruled out, particularly until the central coast of British Columbia is sampled and studied by pollen analysis.

Second, the late-glacial pine-dominated vegetation of Brooks Peninsula is peculiar in regard to the significant component of mountain hemlock pollen. Mountain hemlock is recorded from many sites in the mixed coniferous forests that followed the initial pine assemblage (Hebda 1983; Mathewes 1993).

Third, the peculiar plant communities of the ridges of Brooks Peninsula that harbour rare species, have persisted for at least 10 500 years, as revealed by the Cassiope Pond core. These communities did not arise in recent times, but have a long distinct history. This suggests that their origins were different from those of the surrounding glaciated areas—indirect evidence of a refugium.

The paleoecological record at Brooks Peninsula suggests that two important criteria were met to produce the "endemic" aspect of the flora. First, the botanical evidence indirectly supports geological evidence for a refugium in which endemics survived glaciation. Second, postglacial climate remained relatively stable at high elevations, ensuring that the rare plants and their associated plant communities survived to the present. This point is extremely important. For, throughout the surrounding terrain, even on Brooks Peninsula, major changes in climate and vegetation occurred that were unfavourable to the persistence of such species. In this way, parts of Brooks Peninsula have been unique, providing us with a possible glimpse of the pre-glacial and full-glacial past.

From a conservative point of view, the peculiar "endemic" component of Brooks Peninsula flora can be ascribed to a late Wisconsin glacial refugium about 14 000-17 000 years ago. However, since there is no evidence of glaciation on the highest ridges and peaks, it is possible that the "endemics" are remnants of an earlier, possibly pre-Wisconsin, flora.

Since securely dated full-glacial biotic remains were not recovered, there will be readers who will remain sceptical of the existence of a refugium. It is necessary to continue the search for sediments containing organic materials of full-glacial age. Radiometric dates may have to be obtained using the accelerator method (e.g., Mathewes et al. 1985), from tiny plant fragments, for it is unlikely that many large trees existed during the height of glaciation.

Nevertheless, the results of the paleoecological investigations, when set within a regionally consistent framework, reveal a unique vegetation history for parts of Brooks Peninsula. The fossil record of *Ligusticum calderi*, and the peculiar high-elevation open plant communities associated with the "endemic" elements of the flora, suggest that the ridges of Brooks Peninsula survived at least late Wisconsin glaciation, in a glacial refugium.

Update

No major paleoecological studies have been carried out in the vicinity of the Brooks Peninsula since the original preparation of this paper. However, several recent contributions provide a clearer framework for Brooks Peninsula results and add insight into their significance.

Two recent syntheses establish the northwest North American setting within which the Brooks Peninsula story unfolds (Hebda 1995; Hebda and Whitlock 1997). Between 25 000-14 000 years ago, the height of the last glaciation, massive continental ice sheets cooled northern mid latitudes, deflected the jet stream and winter storms far to the south of today's path and produced strong easterly and southeasterly atmospheric circulation along the south and west ice margins. This atmospheric configuration apparently resulted in a relatively cool to cold and dry climate on the west coast of Vancouver Island which extended southward into the adjacent United States (Hebda and Whitlock 1997). In response, non-forested and parkland vegetation replaced coniferous rainforests during glacial times. In ice-free Washington State, tundra and subalpine parkland occurred. Full-glacial forest communities of Engelmann spruce, lodgepole pine, true fir and mountain hemlock occurred in central Oregon (Worona and Whitlock 1995), and pine and alder grew not far south of the ice tongue in Puget Sound (Hebda and Whitlock 1997). These observations strongly support the conclusion that Brooks Peninsula full-glacial plant communities must have been strongly influenced by the relatively harsh glacial climate and consisted at best of scrubby parkland and heath.

With the waning of glacial ice, Brooks Peninsula vegetation and indeed vegetation along the northwest coast largely converted to lodgepole pine parkland and forest (Hebda 1995; Hebda and Whitlock 1997). The coast-wide, late glacial explosion of pine over a short interval strongly suggests that pine survived in coastal refugia, probably including the Brooks Peninsula and adjacent exposed continental shelves.

Most coastal sites, especially in British Columbia, passed through a mixed coniferous forest stage before the height of the warm dry (xerothermic) conditions of the early Holocene (Hebda and Whitlock 1997). This time of changing vegetation may be related to a sudden cooling event called the Younger Dryas (Mathewes 1993; Mathewes et al. 1993). Brooks Peninsula cores shed little detailed light on this question, though some of the short-duration features such as the major *Alnus* peak at about 11 000 years ago at Pyrola Lake (bottom of zone PL-3) might be related.

Though the rest of the record on the Brooks Peninsula is generally consistent with the coastal sequence, it does not exhibit the same horizons of change as more continental, drier sites on Vancouver Island (Allen 1995) and on the mainland (Hebda 1995). For example, neither the well marked increase in moisture and possibly cooling at about 7000 years ago evident in many parts of British Columbia, nor the cooling at about 3000-4000 years ago are clearly expressed by changes in vegetation on Brooks Peninsula. Instead, more recognizable changes occur earlier about 8000-9000 years ago and later 2000-3000 years ago. Such differences are likely related to the much more equable moist climate on the peninsula and a differential sensitivity of the vegetation to climate change.

A significant role for Douglas-fir in early Holocene Brooks Peninsula forests is supported by results from two other Vancouver Island studies. Allen (1995) showed that Douglas-fir clearly played a much greater role in the Island's forests in the early Holocene, dominating areas that today are included in the Coastal Western Hemlock (CWH) Biogeoclimatic zone. Early Holocene cave sediments near Gold River reveal that Douglas-fir was much more abundant even in very moist sections of the CWH (Nagorsen et al. 1995).

Allen's (1995) analysis also reveals that xeric non-arboreal communities (rocky knolls, meadows) were more widespread in the early Holocene on south Vancouver Island. This observation adds support to the suggestion that *Camassia quamash* spread to Brooks Peninsula at that time. It remains today as a relict in boggy meadows.

Recent investigations of Louise Pond in the subalpine zone on the Queen Charlotte Islands provide a comparison to the subalpine record at Cassiope Pond (Pellatt and Mathewes 1994). The Louise Pond area was well forested in the early Holocene, unlike the immediate area of Cassiope Pond. Openings with bare ground developed about 5400 years ago, soon after the expansion of subalpine yellow cedar, though the pollen diagram (Pellatt and Mathewes 1994: Fig. 4) suggests that species characteristic of open settings were present as early as 8700 years ago. The landscape around Louise Pond only took on its modern subalpine character about 4400 years ago supporting an open mountain hemlock-yellow cedar-heath community. Mathewes (1989) has provided a synthesis of vegetation and climate history for many sites on the Queen Charlotte Islands.

In summary, analyses which have appeared since this chapter was written are consistent with the general climatic and vegetation patterns interpreted from Brooks Peninsula sequences. But they suggest that the history of the peninsula has had some unique characteristics too.

References Cited

Ager, T.A. 1975. Late Quaternary environmental history of the Tanana valley, Alaska. Institute of Polar Studies, Report 54. Ohio State University. Research Foundation, Columbus, OH.

Allen, G.B. 1995. Vegetation and climate history of southeast Vancouver Island, British Columbia. M.Sc. thesis. School of Earth and Ocean Sciences, University of Victoria, Victoria, BC.

Alley, N.F. 1979. Middle Wisconsin stratigraphy and climatic reconstruction, southern Vancouver Island, British Columbia. Quat. Res. (NY.) 11: 213-237.

Barnosky, C.W. 1981. A record of late Quaternary vegetation from Davis Lake, southern Puget Lowland, Washington. Quat. Res. (NY.) 16: 211-239.

______ . 1982. Development of postglacial vegetation and climate in southwestern Washington. Abstract. In Program and abstracts, 7th biennial conference. American Quaternary Association, Seattle, WA. 65 pp.

Birks, H.J.B. and H.H. Birks. 1980. Quaternary paleoecology. E. Arnold, London.

Brooke, R.C., E.B. Peterson and V.J. Krajina. 1970. The subalpine mountain hemlock zone. Ecology of Western North America (Dept. Bot., University of British Columbia, Vancouver) 2: 153-349.

Clague, J.J., R.W. Mathewes and B.G. Warner. 1982. Late Quaternary geology of eastern Graham Island, Queen Charlotte Islands, British Columbia. Can. J. Earth Sci. 19: 1786-1795.

Colinvaux, P. 1981. Historical ecology of Beringia: the south land bridge coast at St. Paul Island. Quat. Res. (NY.) 16: 18-36.

Cwynar, L.C. and J.C. Ritchie. 1980. Arctic steppe-tundra: a Yukon perspective. Science 208: 1375-1377.

Edwards, M.E. and L.B. Brubaker. 1984. A 23,000 year pollen record from northern interior Alaska. Abstract. In Program and Abstracts, 8th biennial meeting. American Quaternary Association, University of Colorado, Boulder, CO. 35 pp.

Faegri, K. and J. Iversen. 1975. Textbook of pollen analysis. 2nd ed. Hafner, NY.

Franklin, J.F. 1974. *Abies* Mill.—fir. In Seeds of woody plants in the United States. Compiled by C.S. Schopmeyer. Part 2, Specific handling methods and data for seed of 188 genera. Forest Service, U.S. Dept. of Agriculture (Handbook 450), Washington, DC. Pp. 168-183.

French, H.M. 1976. The periglacial environment. Longman Group, London.

Funder, S. 1979. Ice-age plant refugia in east Greenland. Palaeogeogr. Palaeoclimatol. Palaeoecol. 28: 279-295.

Hebda, R.J. 1983. Late-glacial and postglacial vegetation history at Bear Cove bog, northeast Vancouver Island, British Columbia. Can. J. Botany 61: 3172-3192.

______ . 1985. Pollen morphology of *Ligusticum* (Apiaceae) in Canada. Can. J. Botany. 63: 1880-1887.

______ . 1995. British Columbia vegetation and climate history with focus on 6 KA BP. Géographie physique et Quaternaire 49: 55-79.

______ and R.W. Mathewes 1984. Holocene history of cedar and native Indian cultures of the North American Pacific coast. Science 225: 711-713.

______ and G.E. Rouse. 1979. Palynology of two Holocene cores from the Hesquiat Peninsula, Vancouver Island, British Columbia. Syesis 12: 121-129.

______ and C. Whitlock. 1997. Environmental history of the coastal temperate rain forest of northwest North America. Pp. 227-254 in P.K. Schoonmaker, B. von Hagen, and E.C. Wolf (eds.) (In press). The Rain Forests of Home: Profile of a North American Bioregion. Island Press, Covelo, CA.

______ , M.E.A. North and G.E. Rouse. 1982. Pollen and spores of British Columbia. Unpublished ms. on file at the Royal British Columbia Museum.

______ , S.R. Hicock, R.F. Miller and J.E. Armstrong. 1983. Paleoecology of mid-Wisconsin sediments from Lynn Canyon, Fraser Lowland, British Columbia. Abstract. In Program with abstracts, volume 8. Geological Association of Canada and Mineralogical Association of Canada, Victoria, BC. Pp. A31.

Heusser, C.J. 1954. Nunatak flora of the Juneau Ice Field, Alaska. Bull. Torrey Bot. Club 81: 236-250.

______ . 1972. Palynology and phytogeographical significance of a late-Pleistocene refugium near Kalaloch, Washington. Quat. Res. (NY.) 2: 189-201.

______ . 1974. Quaternary vegetation, climate and glaciation of the Hoh River valley, Washington. Geol. Soc. Am. Bull. 85: 1547-1560.

_____ . 1977. Quaternary palynology of the Pacific slope of Washington. Quat. Res. (NY.) 8: 282-306.

_____ . 1983. Vegetational history of the northwestern United States including Alaska. Pp. 239-258 in S.C. Porter (ed.). Late Quaternary environments of the United States. Vol. 1. The late Pleistocene. University of Minneapolis Press, Minneapolis.

Hicock, S.R., R.J. Hebda, and J.E. Armstrong. 1982. Lag of the Fraser glacial maximum in the Pacific Northwest: pollen and macrofossil evidence from western Fraser Lowland, British Columbia. Can. J. Earth Sci. 19: 2288-2296.

Hitchcock, C.L., A. Cronquist, M. Ownbey, and J.W. Thompson. 1969. Vascular plants of the Pacific Northwest. Part 1. Vascular cryptogams, gymnosperms and monocotyledons. University of Washington Press, Seattle, WA.

Kearney, M.S. and B.H. Luckman. 1980. Evidence for late Wisconsin-early Holocene climatic/ vegetational change in Jasper National Park, Alberta. Pp 85-105 in W.C. Mahaney (ed.). Quaternary paleoclimate. Geo Abstracts, Norwich, England.

Kremp, G.O.W. 1965. Morphologic encyclopedia of palynology. University of Arizona Press, Tucson, AZ.

Mangerud, J. 1973. Isfrie refugier i Norge under istidens. Norges geologiske undersokelse 297: 1-23.

Mann, D.H. 1983. The Quaternary history of the Lituya glacial refugium, Alaska. Ph.D. thesis. College of Forest Resources, University of Washington, Seattle, WA.

Mathewes, R.W. 1973. A palynological study of postglacial vegetation changes in the university research forest, southwestern British Columbia. Can. J. Botany 51: 2085-2103.

_____ . 1979. A paleoecological analysis of Quadra sand at Point Grey, British Columbia, based on indicator pollen. Can. J. Earth Sci. 16: 847-858.

_____ . 1989. Paleobotany of the Queen Charlotte Islands. Pp 75-90 in G.G.E. Scudder and N. Gessler (eds.). The Outer Shores. Based on the proceedings of the Queen Charlotte Islands First International Symposium, University of British Columbia, August 1984.

_____ . 1993. Evidence for Younger Dryas-Age cooling on the North Pacific Coast of America. Quaternary Science Reviews 12: 321-331.

_____ and L.E. Heusser. 1981. A 12,000 year palynological record of temperature and precipitation trends in southwestern British Columbia. Can. J. Botany 59: 707-710.

_____ and G.E. Rouse. 1975. Palynology and paleoecology of postglacial sediments from the lower Fraser River canyon of British Columbia. Can. J. Earth Sci. 12: 745-756.

_____ , L.E. Heusser and R.T. Patterson. 1993. Evidence for a Younger Dryas-like cooling event on the British Columbia coast. Geology 21: 101-104.

_____ , J.S. Vogel, J.R. Southon and D.E. Nelson. 1985. Accelerator radiocarbon date confirms early deglaciation of the Queen Charlotte Islands. Can. J. Earth Sci. 22: 790-791.

McAndrews, J.H., A.A. Berti, and G. Norris. 1973. Key to Quaternary pollen and spores of the Great Lakes region. Royal Ontario Museum (Toronto, ON) Life Sciences Miscellaneous Publication.

Mott, R.J. and L.E. Jackson, Jr. 1982. An 18,000 year palynological record from the southern Alberta segment of the classical Wisconsinan-"ice-free corridor." Can. J. Earth Sci. 19: 504-513.

Nagorsen, D.W., G. Keddie and R.J. Hebda. 1995. Early Holocene black bears (*Ursus americanus*) from Vancouver Island. Canadian Field-Naturalist 109: 11-18.

Pellatt, M.G. and R.W. Mathewes. 1994. Paleoecology of postglacial tree line fluctuations on the Queen Charlotte Islands, Canada. Écoscience 1: 71-81.

Peterson, K.L., P.J. Mehringer and G.E. Gustafson. 1983. Late-glacial vegetation and climate at the Manis Mastodon site, Olympic Peninsula, Washington. Quat. Res. (NY) 20: 215-231.

Ritchie, J.C. 1980. Towards a late-Quaternary paleoecology of the ice-free corridor. Canadian Journal of Anthropology (Dept. of Anthropology, University of Alberta, Edmonton, AB) 1: 15-28.

Taylor, R.L. and B. MacBryde. 1977. Vascular plants of British Columbia: a descriptive resource inventory. University of British Colombia Bot. Gard. Tech. Bull. 4.

Taylor, T.M.C. 1971. The ferns and fern-allies of British Columbia. Royal British Columbia Museum (Victoria, BC) Handbook 12.

Warner, B.G. 1984. Late Quaternary paleoecology of eastern Graham Island, Queen Charlotte Islands, British Columbia, Canada. Ph.D. thesis. Department of Biology, Simon Fraser University, Burnaby, BC.

______ , J.J. Clague and R.W. Mathewes. 1984. Geology and paleoecology of a mid-Wisconsin peat from the Queen Charlotte Islands, British Columbia, Canada. Quat. Res. (NY). 21: 337-350.

______ , R.W. Mathewes and J.J. Clague. 1982. Ice-free conditions on the Queen Charlotte Islands, British Columbia, at the height of late Wisconsin glaciation. Science 218: 675-677.

Watts, W.A. 1983. Vegetational history of the eastern United States 25,000-10,000 years ago. Pp. 294-310 in S.C. Porter (ed.). Late Quaternary environments of the United States. Vol. 1. The late Pleistocene. University of Minnesota Press, Minneapolis.

Woillard, G.M. 1978. Grande Pile peat bog: a continuous pollen record for the last 140,000 years. Quat. Res. (NY) 9: 1-21.

Worona, M.A. and C. Whitlock. 1995. Late Quaternary vegetation and climate history near Little Lake, central Coast Range, Oregon. Geological Society of America Bulletin 107: 867-876.

Chapter 10

Terrestrial Arthropods of Brooks Peninsula

Robert A. Cannings[a]
Sydney G. Cannings[b]

[a] Natural History Section, Royal British Columbia Museum
Victoria, BC
[b] Conservation Data Centre, Ministry of Environment, Lands and Parks
Victoria, BC

Abstract

Terrestrial arthropods were collected on Brooks Peninsula from 31 July to 14 August 1981 to meet two goals: 1) to produce a collection representative of the various habitats on the outer British Columbia coast in mid-summer; 2) to gather information on groups potentially useful in refugium studies.

About 3600 specimens were collected, representing 6 classes, 29 orders, 190 families, 438 genera, and 521 species. Both the composition of this fauna and its distribution in 17 habitat types were analyzed. Thirty-one species and 4 genera of undescribed taxa were collected, 21 species and 2 genera for the first time. Excluding new species, 34 taxa, ranging from species to families, were collected in Canada for the first time.

In general, species belong to boreal or cordilleran biotic elements, though in poorly dispersing groups the representation of Pacific coastal species is high.

The degree of endemism, disjunct distributions, and the frequency of poor dispersers (notably flightless ground beetles) suggest that a glacial refugium may have existed on Brooks Peninsula. The status of most terrestrial arthropods on the outer coast is poorly known, thus evidence of endemism and disjunction is difficult to assess. Most disjunctions are with populations in the northwestern United States (south of the extent of glaciation). Most of these species disperse easily, however, and the observed disjunctions may merely represent discontinuities in collecting.

Ground beetles show a high frequency (85%) of brachyptery (reduced wings), suggesting populations of long and stable history. However, because the species list for Brooks Peninsula is probably incomplete, the true frequency may be lower. Further collecting, especially of ground beetles at both low and high elevations, is necessary before significant statements concerning the existence of a refugium can be made.

Acknowledgements

We are grateful to all those who helped determine the large amount of material collected during this project (see Appendix 10.1). We thank the participants in the Brooks Peninsula expedition for their enthusiasm and interest in the entomological aspects of the project. Dr. David Kavanaugh (California Academy of Sciences, San Francisco) and Dr. Geoffrey Scudder (University of British Columbia, Vancouver) criticized the manuscript. Neville Winchester gave us access to the results of his more recent forest inventories so that we could compare them to our Brooks Peninsula information.

Introduction

Any faunistic study of terrestrial arthropods of a particular area of British Columbia is immediately confronted by several major constraints: the abundance of species, the difficulty of species identification, and the lack of information on the fauna of adjacent regions. This is particularly true for the central and northern coasts of the province, which have seen very little entomological activity. More particularly, biogeographical questions concerning the existence of a glacial refugium cannot be addressed in the absence of extensive collections from a wide geographical area, necessarily including areas peripheral to the proposed refugium. The lack of data concerning the arthropods of the area in question (northern Vancouver Island, the Queen Charlotte Islands, and the northern mainland coast), makes the task of placing the Brooks Peninsula fauna in context very difficult. Indeed, Kavanaugh (1980) notes that the paucity of samples from the region, especially the mainland coast, makes it the most important region for future biogeographical studies in western Canada.

Unlike botanists and vertebrate zoologists, who have, in general, a rather good idea of the gross distribution of vascular plants and vertebrates on the Queen Charlotte Islands (Calder and Taylor 1968; Foster 1965) and their significance to a suspected refugium there, entomologists and other students of arthropods have little information. The short species list of the Odonata of the Queen Charlottes (Cannings and Stuart 1977) is probably more or less complete, and the Carabidae (ground beetles) and Staphylinidae (rove beetles) are better known than other beetle families because of recent collecting (Kavanaugh 1989, 1992; J.M. Campbell personal communication, August 1983). The distribution list of British Columbia spiders published by Thorn (1967) contains 212 species, but lists only two or three species from the Queen Charlottes. More recently, West et al. (1984) list 434 species of spiders from British Columbia, but only 18 from the Queen Charlottes. Other data on terrestrial arthropods are scarce, found in scattered published records.

The record for northern Vancouver Island is similarly meagre, though for spiders there is a more substantial contribution, the S.L. Neave collection from Kyuquot listed in Thorn (1967). The terrestrial arthropods of the Scott Islands (including Triangle Island) off the northwest tip of Vancouver Island are superficially treated in Carl et al. (1951).

The main goal of the entomological effort on Brooks Peninsula was to record specimens from as many of the major habitats as possible, using collecting methods designed to sample a wide variety of taxa. Although the collections could not be exhaustive, we knew they would be representative of the outer coast fauna in midsummer. It was hoped that collecting would also produce specimens useful in refugial studies; ground beetles have been prominent in such work (Darlington 1943; Lindroth 1969, 1979; Mann 1983). (One example is the ground beetle genus

Nebria, which has been relatively well-studied along the west coast of North America [Kavanaugh 1980]). The lack of comparative data from adjacent regions meant that significant contributions to the question of a possible refugium were unlikely. Nevertheless, the planned collections would, at least, help delineate the habitats and organisms most likely to yield useful data for Brooks Peninsula. This entomological study then is mostly a pioneering one. For, even if the data do not contribute to an analysis of the glacial history of Brooks Peninsula, they will be invaluable to future zoogeographic investigations of the coastal arthropod fauna.

Figure 10.1 shows the study area and the collection localities noted in the text. Most collecting was done by Robert Cannings and Sydney Cannings between 31 July and 14 August 1981, though other expedition members, notably John Cooper, collected specimens at other times during the field project. A wide variety of areas were sampled, some more heavily than others; the Cape Cook Lagoon, Cassiope Pond, Camassia Bog, and Kalmia Lake localities were the most intensively collected. All major habitat types were covered. Examples of all aquatic habitat types, bogs, beaches, upper beach vegetation, various forest types at both low and high elevations, subalpine meadows, cliffs, and ridges above timberline were examined. The main localities visited are (letters refer to locations in Figure 10.1):

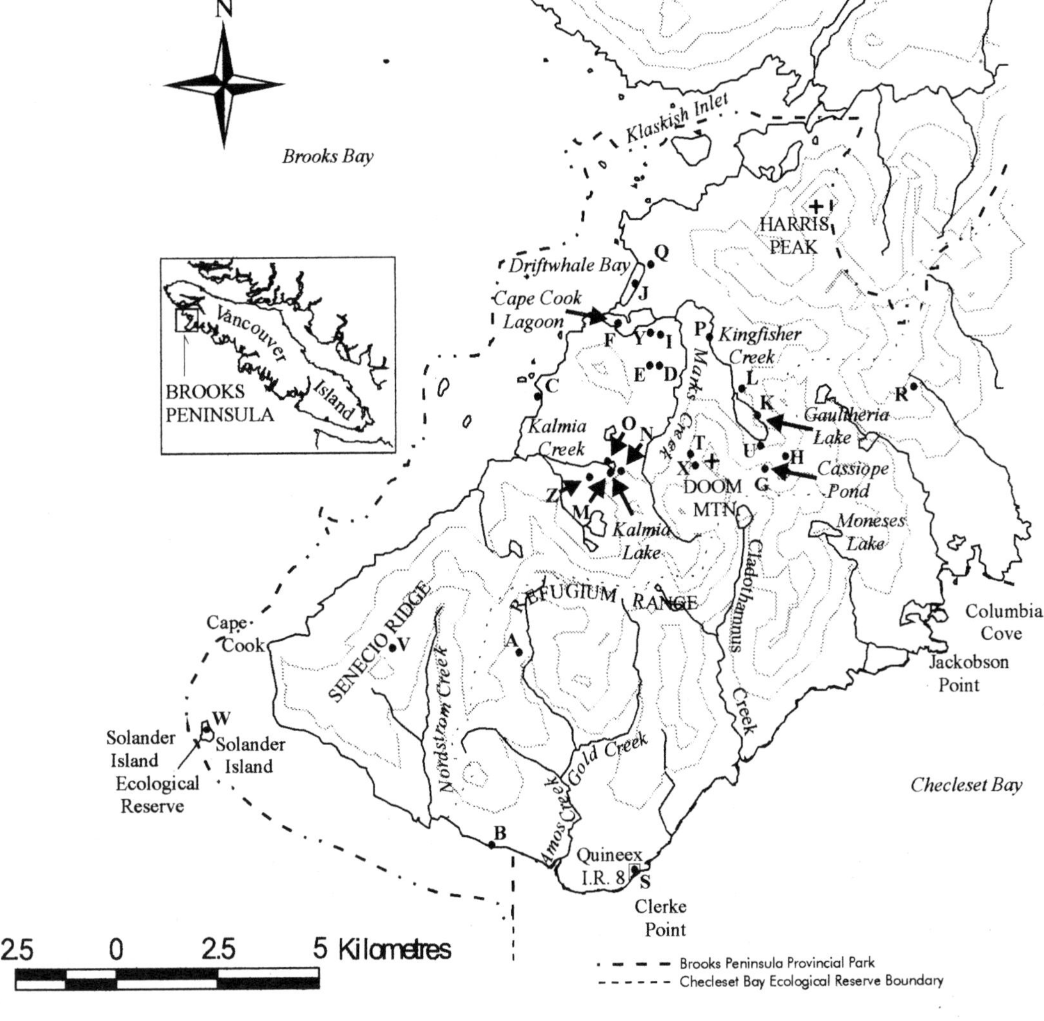

Figure 10.1 Brooks Peninsula, showing arthropod collection sites (letters refer to localities listed in Appendix 10.1)

1) Cape Cook Lagoon (F) (Figures 10.2, 10.3, 10.4),
2) Drift Whale Bay beach and bog (J) (Figure 10.4),
3) Cassiope Pond, including the ridge to the east (G, H) (Figures 10.5 and 10.6),
4) Camassia Bog, including Danae Pond and Brasenia Pond (I, D, E) (Figures 10.7, 10.8, 10.9),
5) Kalmia Lake and bog (M, N, O),
6) Gaultheria Lake valley (K, L),
7) Doom Mountain, the Throne (X) (Figure 10.9),
8) Senecio Ridge (headlands) (V) (Figure 10.10),
9) Solander Island Ecological Reserve (W) (Figure 10.11),
10) Quineex Indian Reserve 8 (S),
11) Beach seeps near Amos Creek (B),
12) Amos Creek bog (A).

Particular attention was paid to groups of insects and other arthropods that were either very abundant in particular habitats or representative of potentially non-glaciated habitats. In the latter group, stress was placed on collecting flightless species, presumed of low vagility. Thus, setting pitfall traps for beetles on high ridges was a priority, as was the collection of soil samples for the extraction of microscopic soil invertebrates. The capture of large numbers of flying species was not a priority. Thus, Malaise traps were not employed. Lentic aquatic species were collected extensively. Considerable time was spent examining the dragonfly fauna for, though the group exhibits relatively high rates of dispersal, it is a significant component of bogs. The distribution of the dragonfly fauna is the best known of any group in the region. Finally, an attempt was made to determine if any unusual insects were associated with endemic plants on Brooks Peninsula.

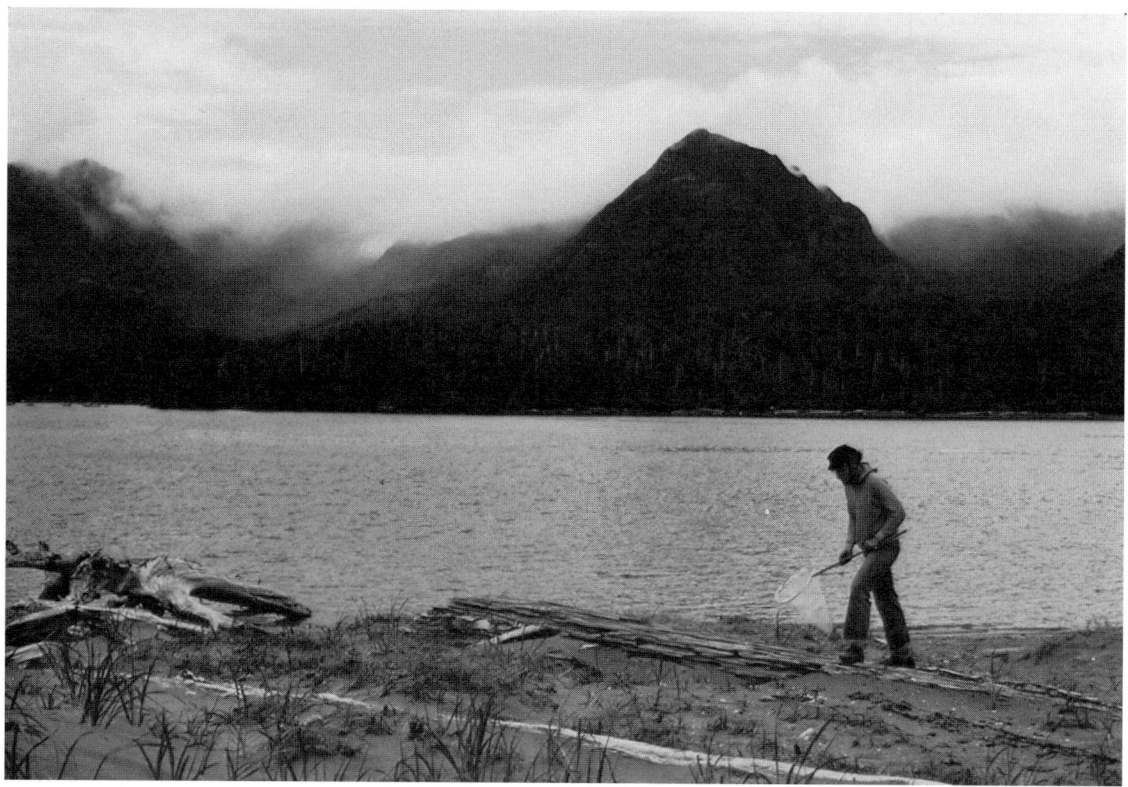

Figure 10.2 Rob Cannings stalking a new species of robber fly, *Lasiopogon* n.sp., on the upper beach of Cape Cook Lagoon (Photo: S.G. Cannings)

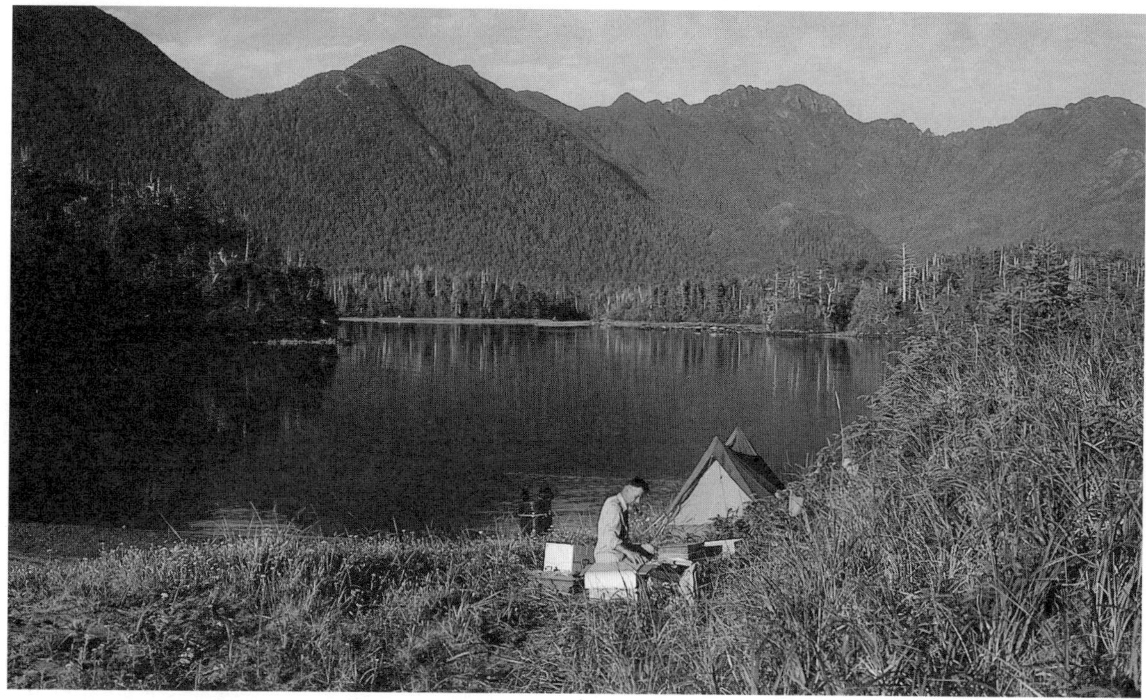

Figure 10.3 Cape Cook Lagoon; Bob Ogilvie pressing plants at his campsite (Photo: S.G. Cannings)

Figure 10.4 Cape Cook Lagoon entrance with Drift Whale Bay beach in the background (Photo: R.A. Cannings)

Figure 10.5 Cassiope Pond with Doom Mountain in the background (Photo: S.G. Cannings)

Figure 10.6 Cassiope Pond from ridge above (Photo: S.G. Cannings)

Figure 10.7 View from Doom Mountain northwest towards Cape Cook Lagoon. Camassia Bog is in the centre. (Photo: R.A. Cannings)

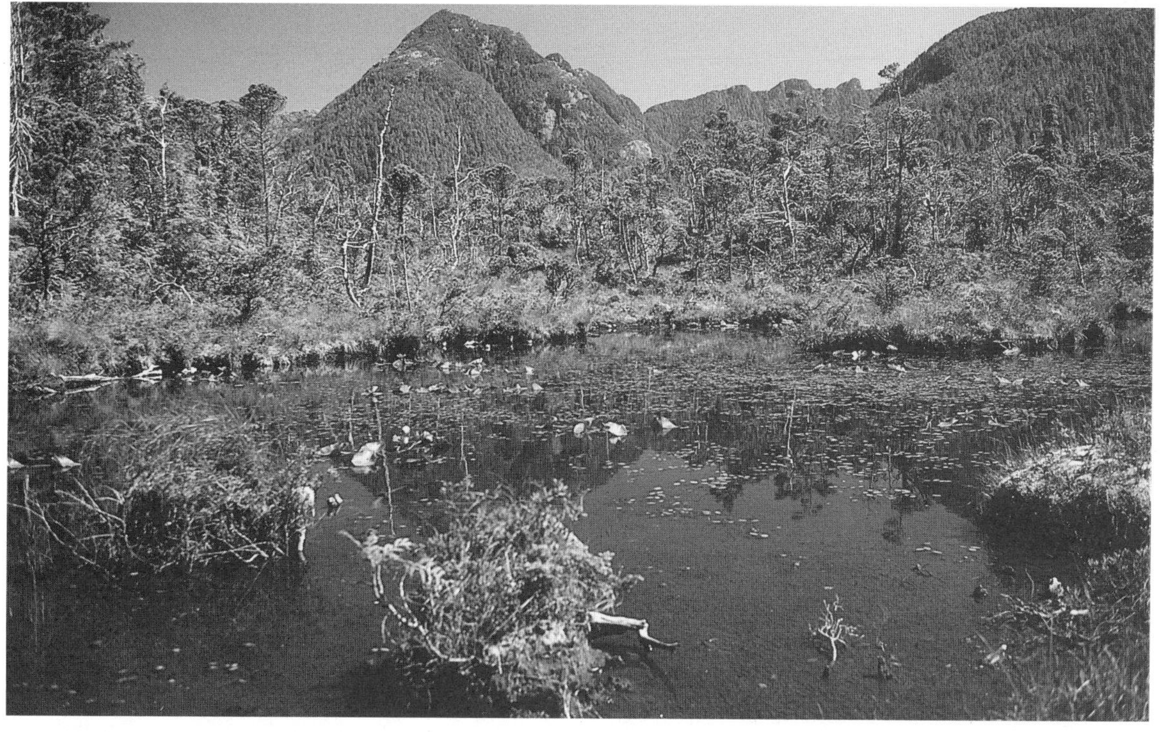

Figure 10.8 Danae Pond, Camassia Bog (Photo: R.A. Cannings)

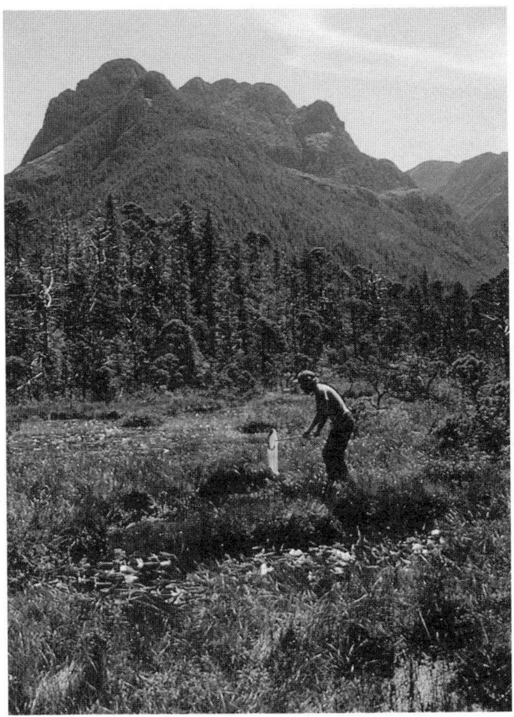

Figure 10.9 Syd Cannings collecting dragonflies in Camassia Bog. Doom Mountain is in the background. (Photo: R.A. Cannings)

Figure 10.10 Senecio Ridge (headlands) (Photo: R.A. Cannings)

Figure 10.11 Solander Island. Most arthropods collected here were associated with the burrows of seabirds (Photo: S.G. Cannings)

A number of collecting techniques were employed:

1) sweep-netting vegetation,
2) collecting, by hand or aspirator, specimens at the soil surface and in litter, moss, and rotten, logs,
3) soil and litter sampling: samples were collected on the final day of entomological, participation, sealed in plastic bags, and run through Berlese funnels two days later. Soil samples were taken from various habitats at Cape Cook Lagoon, Senecio Ridge, Doom Mountain, and Solander Island,
4) aerial netting,
5) black lighting,
6) underwater light trapping: traps consisted of 1.36 L cans suspended underwater on stakes. The open end of each can was fitted with a glass funnel, the narrow end projecting inwards. The attractant was a Cyalume light stick that glowed for eight hours after the trap was set,
7) aquatic sweep-netting,
8) pitfall trapping: traps consisted of aluminum cake pans set flush in the ground and filled with, ethylene glycol and a small amount of detergent. Specimens trapped in the fluid were transferred into 70% ethanol and later pinned or pointed[1]. Diptera were dried by the method described by Vockeroth (1966). Pitfall traps were set in various habitats at Cape Cook Lagoon, Camassia Bog, Cassiope Pond, the Cassiope Pond ridge, The Throne, Doom Mountain, and on Senecio Ridge.

---

[1] Insects too small to pin are glued to the tip of a small point of card, which is itself pinned.

The determination of collected material requires more time and energy than any other aspect of an arthropod survey. Once the collections were sorted and labelled they were sent to experts for identification (see Acknowledgements, this chapter).

Results

Approximately 3600 specimens were identified from the material collected. This represents about 1900 pinned specimens, 1500 preserved in alcohol, and 200 adult dragonflies in cellophane envelopes. The taxa are listed, with annotations, in Appendix 10.1. Six classes containing 29 orders, 190 families, 438 genera, and 521 species are represented. Of these, 15 orders, 139 families, 354 genera, and 420 species are in the Class Insecta. Numbers of taxa collected in selected orders are given in Table 10.1.

Table 10.1 Taxa collected in selected orders

Taxon	No. families	No. genera	No. species
Araneae	12	27	34
Oribatei (suborder)	15	20	22
Ephemeroptera	3	3	3
Odonata	5	8	20
Plecoptera	4	4	4
Grylloptera	1	1	1
Orthoptera	1	1	1
Hemiptera	11	35	39
Coleoptera	31	81	92
Diptera	69	143	175
Lepidoptera	9	18	19
Trichoptera	5	8	9
Hymenoptera	18	47	52
Others	6	42	50
Total	190	438	521

Despite these numbers, the collections represent mainly conspicuous forms. Sampling took place only during a two week period, and more intensive collecting would have greatly increased the number of species captured. The small aquatic Crustacea were virtually ignored; soil arthropods of all sorts were poorly collected, as were small flying insects. Malaise traps, intercept traps, and other devices for collecting large numbers of Diptera, Hymenoptera, and Coleoptera were not used. Ground and flying insects would have been better sampled had more pitfall traps been used, especially on the higher ridges. Lack of what was considered to be a comprehensive list of ground beetles is a major impediment to analysis of questions concerning refugial status of the area. The insects of the faster flowing, remote streams were not adequately collected, nor were those on coniferous trees. More intensive light trapping would have produced more taxa, especially Lepidoptera. Two people collecting for two weeks in rugged, relatively inaccessible country probably covered the wide range of potential taxa as efficiently as could be expected, but the list of specimens (Appendix 10.1) should be considered very incomplete.

Faunal Composition

Even though many small forms likely were not collected, the proportional composition of the fauna as reflected in the species list is probably relatively accurate, at least for insects. One exception is the Lepidoptera, which probably is under-represented.

The faunal composition of the collections presents no real surprises. The Diptera and Coleoptera predominate (Table 10.1), as might be expected in a region dominated by moist forest; these orders contain large numbers of species that develop in moist soil, fungi, and dead or living wood. The Diptera alone account for 69 of 139 insect families, 143 of 354 genera, and 175 of 420 species. Beetles and flies combined make up 63% of the species collected.

Arthropod Distribution and Vegetation Zonation

The species list can be divided into sections that identify selected species with particular habitat types. We have tried to delimit the arthropod associations in terms of the vegetation classification (see Chapter 8), but this has not always been possible. In some cases, plant assóciations were not sampled for their arthropod fauna, and in others samples crossed the boundaries of two or more vegetation types. Arthropod associations are outlined here, with additional information presented in Appendix 10.2. Chapter 8 should be consulted for more detailed treatments of the vegetation composition.

A. Shoreline Forest

This represents a relatively narrow strip along the coastline and is dominated by *Picea sitchensis*, with *Tsuga heterophylla* in association. The dense shrub layer consists mainly of *Gaultheria shallon* and *Rubus spectabilis*.

The spruce forest was perhaps the most thoroughly collected habitat (for insects) on Brooks Peninsula. Four pitfall traps sampled the ground fauna and a light trap was run for several nights to collect nocturnal insects. Deep shade and lack of flowers discourage insects such as butterflies and bees, but insects that thrive in dark, humid microclimates abound.

A diverse mite fauna exists in the moss and humus layers. Termites (*Zootermopsis angusticollis*) and carpenter ants (*Camponotus* sp.) burrow through rotten logs and stumps, and camel crickets (*Pristoceuthophilus celatus*) scavenge beneath logs.

Seven species of spiders were collected; the fauna is dominated by the trapdoor spider *Antrodiaetus pacificus*. There is also a diverse beetle fauna, dominated by rove beetles (e.g., *Lathrobium* sp. B, *Philonthus siegwaldi*, *Tachinus basalis*); the larger, predaceous ground beetles (*Pterostichus algidus*, *Scaphinotus angusticollis*, *Zacotus matthewsi*); and wood-feeding families such as the long-horned beetles (*Lepturopsis dolorosa*, *Plectrura spinicauda*) and bark beetles (e.g., *Gnathotrichus sulcatus*, *Hylurgops rugipennis*, *Pseudohylesinus sericeus*).

Flying insects are dominated by flies, especially nematocerous families such as crane flies (*Limonia bestigma*, *Molophilus oligocanthus*, *Tipula macrophallus*), March flies (*Bibio* sp.), sciarids (*Schwenkfeldina* sp.), and midges (*Limnophyes* sp. B, *Metriocnemus fuscipes*, *Natarsia miripes*, *Parametriocnemus* sp., *Polypedilum* sp.).

Centipedes (*Ethopolys* sp., *Scolopocryptops sexspinosus*) and millipedes (*Nearctodesmus insulans*, *Parajulidae* sp.) inhabit the damp forest floor.

B. Mountain Slope Forest

This habitat normally ranges from 200 m to 600 m above sea level; it is a dense forest, mainly of *Abies amabilis, Tsuga heterophylla,* and *Chamaecyparis nootkatensis,* with an open to absent shrub layer largely of *Vaccinium alaskaense,* V. *parvifolium,* and *Gaultheria shallon.*

The Mountain Slope Forest was sampled primarily with two pitfall traps at the base of the headwall cliffs on The Throne of Doom Mountain. Grasses and herbs were swept for insects twice at that same site, and some sweeps were also made along Salamander Creek on The Throne. Soil and humus samples were taken at the cliff base and along the creek. Overall, our samples were probably biased towards inhabitants of open, rocky areas rather than the mossy depths of the closed forest.

Of the five spider species collected, none is shared with the Shoreline Forest samples, though two were also collected along the upper beaches and dunes. The two most common spiders were *Metallina curtisi* and *Microlinyphia dana.* Only nine species of mites were collected (half the size of the shoreline forest mite fauna); one was also collected in the Shoreline Forest (*Trachytes* sp. B.).

True bugs are limited in number and are generally restricted to grasses and herbs (*Banasa sordida, Lygocoris pabulinus, Evacanthus grandipes*). The exception is the leafhopper, *Bathysmatophorus oregonensis,* which feeds on amabilis fir.

Relatively few beetles were collected: the slug-eating ground beetle *Scaphinotus angusticollis* is shared with the Shoreline Forest, but *Nebria kincaidi* is a ground beetle of the coastal and insular mountains.

Predominant flies belong to the more primitive families: crane flies (*Limnophila* sp., *Molophilus oligocanthus*), midges (*Limnophyes* sp.), and snipe flies (*Rhagio dimidiata, Rhagio incisus, Symphoromyia* spp. 1 & 2).

Hymenoptera are limited to parasitic species with the exception of a sawfly (*Tenthredo* sp nr. *semirufa*) and an ant (the widespread *Lasius pallitarsis*).

C. Bog Scrubforest

This is generally a low, open woodland of *Pinus contorta* and *Chamaecyparis nootkatensis,* with *Thuja plicata* and *Tsuga heterophylla* also common. *Gaultheria shallon* is the common shrub in the rather low, open shrub layer.

The trees of the Bog Scrubforest were not sampled extensively for their arthropod inhabitants, but two spittlebugs (*Aphrophora fulva* and *A. princeps*) fed on lodgepole pines. The leafhopper *Bathysmatophorous oregonensis,* another conifer feeder, was also found.

D. Timberline Scrubforest

This zone is generally found above the Mountain Slope Forest and below the treeless vegetation types at high elevations; in appearance, it is a miniature forest dominated by *Tsuga mertensiana* and *Chamaecyparis nootkatensis* with lesser amounts of *Abies amabilis.*

In our classification scheme, this section includes all arthropods collected along the subalpine ridge to the east of Cassiope Pond. It, therefore, includes species collected in timberline shrub and well-drained alpine meadow associations. General collecting was supplemented by two pitfall traps set from 31 July to 11 August on the open rocky spine of the ridge.

The open aspect of this habitat favours active flying insects such as the hover flies *Blera scitula, Sericomyia chalcopyga, Syrphus torvus,* and *Cynorhinella bella;* the calyptrate flies, e.g., *Scathophaga furcata, Coenosia impunctata, Limosia incisurata, Spilogona magnipunctata, Eucalliphora lilaea, Slossonaemyia angulicornis;* and the bumblebees *Bombus mixtus* and *B. terricola occidentalis* and their nest parasite *Psithyrus fernaldae.*

Seven species of spiders and two species of harvestmen were collected along the rocky ridge. *Clubiona trivialis* was also collected amongst the Deflated Ridge Herb vegetation of the lower headlands ridge. *Xysticus pretiosus* was also common in the dune vegetation at Cape Cook Lagoon.

The widespread sowbug *Ligidium gracile* and the cave cricket *Pristoceuthophilus celatus* live among the ridge rocks.

Despite the open, herbaceous nature of the habitat, only two species of true bugs were collected: the widespread spittlebug *Philaenus spumarius* and the conifer-feeding leafhopper *Bathysmatophorus oregonensis.*

There seems to be a limited beetle fauna; only six species were collected. The click beetles *Ctenicera suckleyi* and *Negastrius dispersus,* the snail-eating ground beetle *Scaphinotus marginatus,* and the rove beetle *Mycetoporus* were found only in this habitat on Brooks Peninsula, but the hister beetle *Hypocaccus bigemmeus* and the scarab *Aphodius aleutes* were also found in the dunes of Cape Cook Lagoon.

E. Shoreline Forest and Beach Shrub

In general, the vegetation represents an ecotone between the Sitka spruce forest and beach; it is usually a dense hedge of *Gaultheria shallon, Rubus parviflorus, R. spectabilis, Heracleum lanatum,* and others.

This sunny and warm habitat includes the thickly vegetated upper sand dunes and the herbs and shrubs above the high tide line in rocky areas such as Quineex Indian Reserve 8. Pitfall traps were set out at the edges of salal thickets at Cape Cook Lagoon.

The flowering herbs and grasses attract many insects, including the plant bugs *Lopida ampla, Mecomma gilvipes,* and *Orthops scutellatus;* the ladybird beetles *Coccinella johnsoni* and *C. trifasciata perplexa;* the hover flies *Blera scitula, Cheilosia hoodiana,* and *Sericomyia chalcopyga;* and the bumblebee *Bombus mixtus.* Mountain swallowtail (*Papilio zelicaon*) larvae feed on cow parsnip (*Heracleum lanatum*) and the adults fly along the sunny forest edge, feeding on various flowers.

Many of the ground species sampled by the pitfall traps are forest dwellers that hunt in open areas during the night. Examples include the spiders *Cybaeus reticulatus* and *Antrodiaetus pacificus,* the ground beetles *Pterostichus algidus* and *Zacotus matthewsi,* and the centipede *Scolopocryptops sexspinosus.*

The barklice *Phylotarsus kwakiutl* and *Polypsocus corruptus* were found in wet herbaceous areas beside a seep at the end of Drift Whale Bay beach.

F. Bog Shrub and Bog Herbaceous

This habitat is a mixture of low (less than one metre high), stunted thickets of *Thuja plicata, Chamaecyparis nootkatensis,* and *Pinus contorta,* and open bog vegetation including shrubs such as *Empetrum nigrum, Kalmia polifolia,* and *Ledum groenlandicum.* Common herbs are *Deschampsia cespitosa* and *Carex livida;* the mosses *Sphagnum* spp. and *Racomitrium lanuginosum* form hummocks.

The open bogs have a distinctive arthropod community. Spiders are common, including *Araneus trifolium*, *Pirata piraticus*, *Tibellus oblongus*, *Pellenes hoyi*, *Xysticus montanensis*, and the widespread wolf spider *Pardosa metlakatla*. These spiders are pursued by the spider-hunting wasp *Anoplius ventralis*.

There is also a diverse group of true bugs made up of the seed bugs *Ligyrocoris sylvestris* and *Nysius niger* (the latter is abundant in the dry hummocks of the moss *Racomtrium lanuginosum*), two spittlebugs, and seven leafhoppers.

The only grasshopper found on Brooks Peninsula, *Melanoplus bruneri*, lives in these bogs and in the Deflated Ridge Herb habitat of the windswept headlands.

Perhaps the most common beetle found is the tiny ground beetle *Bembidion fortestriatum*, which hunts around drying, muddy puddles in bogs. The helodid plant beetle *Cyphon variabilis* is common on marsh vegetation in and around bog pools.

The open habitat attracts sun-loving flies like the bee fly *Villa lateralis* and the hover fly *Scaeva pyrastri*, and the wet areas are home to the long-legged flies, *Hydrophorus chrysologus* and *Syntormon*. No nemotocerous flies were collected, but this is probably owing to a lack of collecting effort, for the wet sod should be inhabited by a number of these insects. The bogs are also home to the most common butterfly on Brooks Peninsula, the tiny bog copper *Epidemia mariposa*.

G. Intertidal Sand/Seaweed

This is not a vegetation type, but rather a habitat of two main components—sand at various stages of dampness and piles of decomposing seaweed.

As its name suggests, this habitat is only available to foraging arthropods at low or moderate tides, but at these times the arthropod community is distinct and abundant. Because the area is so exposed, most non-flying members of this association use it only at night.

The large amphipod *Orchestoidea californiana* is common and forms the main prey for large predaceous beetles such as the ground beetle *Nebria diversa* and the wingless rove beetle *Thinopinus picta*. Smaller predaceous and scavenging beetles include the green and red ground beetle *Dyschirius obesus* and the rove beetles *Cafius canescens*, *C. nudus johnsoni*, and *C. seminitens*. All these beetles can be abundant at low tides on summer nights.

The seaweed strand attracts several species of flies, including the distinctive dryomyzid fly *Helcomyza mirabilis* and four species of *Fucellia*.

H. Beach Herbaceous

Beach Herbaceous occupies gravel, boulder, or log debris along the shore; typical plants are *Elymus mollis* and *Vicia gigantea*. Dune Herb vegetation grows in wind-shifted sand and is dominated by *Elymus mollis*, *Ammophila arenaria*, *Carex macrocephala*, *Cakile edentula*, *Glehnia littoralis* and *Ambrosia chamissonis*.

Beach dunes are perhaps the most distinctive habitat association on Brooks Peninsula. The exposed, well-drained dunes represent an abrupt change from the closed, wet forest standing behind them. The insects are dominated by families usually associated with arid or semi-arid habitats. Tiger beetles (*Cicindela oregona*), robber flies ([*Lasiopogon* sp. nr. *willametti*], Figure 10.2), stilleto flies (*Thereva brunnea*), yellowjackets (*Vespula arenaria*), and sand wasps (*Oxybelus* sp.) hunt over the warm sand during the day; ground beetles (*Pterostichus algidus*, *P. ater*, and *P. crenicollis*) and darkling beetles (*Coelus ciliatus, Phaleromela globosa*) walk the surface at night. Three species of ants are common: *Formica neorufibarbis, F. subaenescens,* and *Lasius pallitarsis.*

The grasses and other flowering plants attract many insects such as bumblebees (*Bombus mixtus*). Flies are abundant and relatively diverse, but in contrast to the nearby forest no nematocerous species were taken. Larvae of the noctuid moth *Dargidia procincta* were found feeding on the dune grass *Elymus mollis.*

I. Salt Marsh

This habitat is subjected to flooding by salty, brackish, or fresh water; *Deschampsia cespitosa, Potentilla pacifica, Plantago maritima,* and *Carex lyngbyei* predominate.

This relatively rich habitat seems to have a limited fauna, though this may, in part, be due to limited sampling. Flies are abundant, notably the saltmarsh horsefly *Hybomitra sonomensis* and the long-legged flies *Achalcus utahensis, Dolichopus plumipes, D. xanthocnemus,* and *Gymnopternus* sp.

The wingless sphaerocerid fly *Aptilotus borealis,* included in the collections from this habitat, is usually an inhabitant of the coniferous forest floor, and those caught may have been strays from the neighbouring spruce forest.

As a larva, the rarely collected noctuid moth *Apamea maxima* is believed to live on salt marsh sedges.

Shore bugs (*Saldula* sp.) are common predators on the wet mud surface of the marsh, and plant bugs (*Mecomma gilvipes* and *Trignotylus ruficornis*) and leafhoppers (*Elymana inornata, Evacanthus grandipes,* and *Oncopsis crispae*) are numerous in the rich herbage.

J. Supra-tidal Freshwater Pools

This habitat, represented by freshwater seep pools near Amos Creek and Drift Whale Bay beach, has a very limited fauna; the small size of each pool undoubtedly restricts the number of successful colonizers. The Amos Creek pools were dominated by amphipods (*Eogammarus confervicolus*) and midge larvae (*Chironomus* sp.). Predaceous diving beetles (*Rhantus suturellus*) and dragonflies (*Aeshna palmata* and *A. umbrosa*) are the only predators documented.

K. Herbaceous Aquatic—Bog Ponds

The shallow marsh and bog pools of Brooks Peninsula's low, flat valleys contain floating or submerged aquatic plants such as *Nuphar polysepalum, Brasenia schreberi,* and *Potamogeton gramineus.* Shallow bog pools usually contain emergent *Juncus oreganus* and *Carex livida.*

These pools are surprisingly rich in aquatic insect life. The three common groups collected are aquatic bugs, diving beetles, and dragonflies. These predators must have had ample prey available, though not many potential prey species were collected—probably small crustaceans that were ignored in the collections. The aquatic bugs are dominated by the water boatmen, *Cenocorixa andersoni, Hesperocorixa vulgaris,* and *Sigara omani* in the lower bogs, and *Callicorixa alaskensis* and *S. omani* in the upper bogs and tarns. Other, larger predaceous bugs are less abundant but still common: the backswimmer *Notonecta undulata* and the giant water bug (toebiter) *Lethocerus americanus.* Skating on the water surface are large water striders (*Gerris notabilis*).

The beetles are less common. Adults of five species were collected in small numbers.

The most conspicuous insects of the bogs are the dragonflies. Nineteen species inhabit the bog pools—the larvae crawl amongst the aquatic vegetation and in the bottom muck, and the adults swarm in the air over the water and in the sunny bog clearings. This group is treated in detail in Cannings and Cannings (1983).

The larvae of many species of flies live in shallow water or in wet ground at the edges of the marshes and bogs—notable amongst these are soldier flies (*Stratiomys barbata*), long-legged flies (*Hydrophorus chrysologus*, *Syntormon* sp.), ephydrid flies (*Scatella setosa* and *S. stagnalis*), and horse flies (*Atylotus tingaureus*, *Sylvius gigantulus*, *Chrysops excitans*, and *C. noctifer*).

L. Herbaceous Aquatic—Lake Margins

The margins of lakes are usually sparsely vegetated, but stands of *Juncus oreganus* and *Scirpus subtermalis* occur. *Nuphar polysepalum* is the most prominent plant.

The insect fauna of the lakes is very similar to that of the bogs and marshes, though there are some differences in species composition. Perhaps the main difference is the addition of a number of species of caddisflies, six of which were taken in the collections.

Dragonflies are common along the lakeshores, though there are fewer species in this habitat than in the marshes and bogs. The most common large dragonfly of the lakes is probably *Aeshna eremita*, one of the blue darners (Figure 10.12).

The water boatmen *Callicorixa alaskensis* and *Sigara omani* are common in the lakes habitat as they are in the bogs and marshes, but *Notonecta kirbyi* replaces *N. undulata* as the common backswimmer.

M. Streams

Most streams sampled have little or no associated aquatic vegetation; arthropod specimens were often collected off adjacent terrestrial plants.

Figure 10.12 ***Aeshna eremita*** **is the largest dragonfly on the Brooks Peninsula and is common along the the lakeshores of the region (Photo: R.A. Cannings)**

The invertebrate fauna of streams was not well sampled in this study. Indeed, stream cobbles and gravel were not examined for insect larvae, and only limited sweeps were made of streamside vegetation for adult mayflies, stoneflies, and caddisflies.

The most common stonefly encountered was the leuctrid *Despaxia augusta*.

The bog pond inhabitants *Notonecta undulata* and *Sigara omani* were also found in the slow stream that winds through Camassia Bog.

Black flies, which live in streams as larvae, are represented by *Prosimulium dicum* and a member of the *Simulium venustum* complex.

N. Shore Headland

Rocks near the sea are sparsely vegetated just above the intertidal zone with *Potentilla villosa, Deschampsia cespitosa, Sagina crassicaulis,* and *Plantago maritima.*

The bristletails *Pedetontus* are common on the upper surfaces of the shore rocks and the isopods *Ligia pallasii* cling to the wet lower walls.

O. Cliff

Cliff habitats are varied in their vegetation, much depending on aspect and exposure. The only such habitat examined is the headwall of The Throne on Mount Doom, where the weevil *Lepidophorus inguinatus* was swept from *Geum calthifolium.*

P. Windblown Ridge Herb

On Senecio Ridge strong winds predominate and extensive barrenlands of loose stones occur. This habitat supports patches of heath or krummholz vegetation, including *Vaccinium* spp. and *Phyllodoce empetriformis; Ligusticum calderi* is the dominant herb.

The fauna of this stony, scoured habitat is very limited in comparison with the other open habitats of Brooks Peninsula. Three species of spiders (*Clubiona trivialis* and the wolf spiders *Pardosa metlakatla* and *Trochosa terricola*) and a harvestman (*Leuronychus parvulus*) hunt over the open ground, joined by the ants *Formica neorufibarbis* and *Leptothorax muscorum* and the ground beetle *Notiophilus sylvaticus.*

The grasshopper *Melanoplus bruneri* lives in the windswept grass (this species also occurs in the grass of the low bogs and beaches of Brooks Peninsula.

Perhaps the most distinctive insect is a new species of leafhopper (*Deltocephala* n. sp.), found in a litter sample taken in a clump of herbage slightly protected from the wind.

The centipede *Ethopolys sierravabus,* not previously known in Canada, was also found in this habitat.

A few flies (e.g., the hover fly *Platycheirus*) and bumblebees (*Bombus mixtus*) gather at the flowers scattered over the rocky ground and in the adjoining meadows.

Q. Solander Island

Solander Island is a steep-sided rock outcrop; much of the upper slopes is covered by tussocks of *Calamagrostis nutkaensis* and burrows of seabirds such as the tufted puffin (*Fratercula cirrhata*).

Collecting on Solander Island was limited to about two hours. Litter and loose soil samples taken at the mouth of puffin burrows revealed a healthy mite and springtail fauna, as well as the feather-winged beetle *Ptenidium* sp. (possibly *pullum*). The plant bug *Mecomma gilvipes* is common on tall grass, as is the leafhopper *Evacanthus grandipes*.

Flies are abundant, especially the blow fly *Cynomya cadaverina*. A number of species of pteromalid wasps are also common (*Chlorocytus* sp., *Seladerma* sp., *Skeloceras* sp., and *Stictomischus* sp.).

New Taxa

The following list of undescribed taxa collected on Brooks Peninsula represents 31 species and 4 genera that are probably new to science. Some of the taxa have never before been collected, whereas others (*) are known from specimens that have not been described. Additional specimens (**) are of uncertain status. Clarification of the status of such specimens will have to await examination of more material or future revision of the relevant genera. Collection data can be found in Appendix 10.1.

Class Arachnida
Order Pseudoscorpionida
Chtoniidae
    Apochthonius n. sp.

Neobisiidae
    **Microcreagris* n. sp.

Subclass Acari
Order Parasitiformes
Polyaspididae
    **Polyaspinus* sp. A
    **Trachytes* sp. B

**Trachytes* sp. C
    **Trachytes* sp. E
    **Trachytes* sp. G

Uropodidae
    **Urodiaspis* sp. A
    *New genus near *Urodiaspis*
    *New genus near *Uroobovella*+

Order Acariformes
Epilohmannidae
    **Epilohmannia* n. sp.

Liacaridae
    **Rhaphicosus* sp. near *bacillatus* Fuj. & A.

Megeremaeidae
    ***Megeremaeus* sp. near *montanus* W. & H.

Metrioppidae
**Ceratoppia* sp. near *bipilus* (Herman)
Ceratoppia n. sp.

Pelopidae
**Tenuialoides* sp. near *medialis* W. & H.

Limnocharidae
**Limnochares* sp. near *americana* Lundblad

Class Malacostraca
Order Amphipoda
Crangonyctidae
**Crangonix* sp. near *richmondensis*

Class Insecta
Order Hemiptera
Cicadellidae
Deltocephala n. sp.

Order Coleoptera
Dytiscidae
**Acilius* sp. near *semisulcatus* Aube

Order Diptera
Tipulidae
**Limnophila* (*Prionolabis*) sp. near *rufibasis*

Asilidae
Lasiopogon n. sp.

Empididae
Tachydromia sp., probably new
Empidinae n. gen.

Syrphidae
Parasyrphus sp., probably new

Agromyzidae
**Acrostilpna* sp. near *collini* Ringdahl
Paregle sp., possibly new

Order Hymenoptera
Tenthredinidae
**Tenthredo* sp. near *semirufa*

Braconidae
Aphaereta n. sp.

Ichneumonidae
Cremastinae sp. "appears not to be defined at generic level" (J. Barron personal communication, March 1983)

Class Chilopoda
Order Lithobiomorpha
Ethopolidae
  ***Ethopolys* sp. near *spectans* Chamberlin

Range Extensions

The range extensions listed here are restricted to those noted by the determiners of the various taxa, with the exception of the Diptera, which are augmented by extensions of ranges noted in Stone et al. (1965). Included are 34 taxa, ranging from species to families, that to our knowledge have not yet been recorded in the literature as occurring in Canada. In general, only significant extensions are listed; minor extensions northward from south Vancouver Island are not mentioned.

Class Arachnida
Subclass Acari
Order Parasitiformes
Polyaspidae
  Trachytes sp. E: new record for Canada; known previously from Washington south to California

Order Acariformes
Danraeidae
  Belba californica: new record for Canada; known previously from Washington south to California

Megeremaediae
  Megeremaeus sp. near *montanus*: new record for Canada; no published records of this family in Canada

Class Insecta
Order Ephemeroptera
Heptageniidae
  Cinygma sp.: new record of this genus for Vancouver Island (Scudder 1975)

Leptophlebiidae
  Paraleptophlebia sp., probably *debilis*: new record for Vancouver Island (Scudder 1975)

Order Hemiptera
Cicadellidae
  Aphrodes costatus: new record for Vancouver Island
  Bathysmatophorus oregonensis: new record for Canada; known previously from Washington, Oregon, and California

Order Coleoptera
Staphylinidae
  Bryoporus rubescens: new record for Vancouver Island
  Omalium sp.: new record for British Columbia

Ptiliidae
  Ptenidium sp., probably *pullum*: new record for Vancouver Island

Zopheridae
  Usechimorpha barberi: new record for Canada; known previously from Oregon and California

Curculionidae

Lepidophorus inguinatus: new record for Canada; known previously from coastal Alaska

Order Diptera

Tipulidae

Molophilus oligocanthus: new record for Canada; known previously from California

Mycetophilidae

Anaclileia sp.: rare, first recorded from North America in Stone et al. (1965)

Ceratopogonida

Forcipomyia mcswaini: new record for Canada; known previously from Washington to California

Chironomidae

Natarsia miripes: new record for Canada; described from California

Rhagionidae

Rhagio californicus: new record for Canada; known previously from California
Rhagio incisus: new record for Canada; known previously from Oregon and California

Empididae

Brochella monticola: new record for Canada; known previously from Washington
Chersodromia parallela: new record for Canada; known previously from Washington
Oedalea lanceolata: new record for Canada; known previously from Washington, Oregon, Idaho, and Montana

Dolichopodidae

Achalcus utahensis: new record for Canada
Argyra albiventris: new record for Canada; known previously from Alaska, Oregon, and Utah
Dolichopus convergens: new record for Canada; known previously from Washington and Oregon
Dolichopus monticola: first definite Canadian record; known from Washington; Stone et al. (1965) question an earlier British Columbia record
Tachytrechus sanus: new record for British Columbia; known previously from Washington and Alberta, south to California and Colorado

Dryomyzidae

Helcomyza mirabilis: new record for Canada; known previously from Washington and Oregon

Piophilidae

Liopiophila varipes: new record for Canada; Holarctic distribution

Sphaeroceridae

Copromyza maculipennis: new record for Canada; known previously from Washington and Idaho
Thoracochaeta brachystoma: new record for Canada; Holarctic species

Chloropidae

Tricimba brunnicollis: new record for Canada; known previously from Washington south to California

Acartophthalmidae
Acartophthalmus nigrinus: new record for Canada; Holarctic species

Heleomyzidae
Anorostoma alternans: new record for Canada; described from Washington

Muscidae
Coenosia impunctata: new record for Canada; known previously from Alaska and Washington
Spilogona sospita: new record for Canada; known previously from U.S.S.R., Alaska, and Northwest Territories

Order Trichoptera
Leptoceridae
Oecetis inconspicua: new record for Vancouver Island (Nimmo and Scudder 1979)

Order Hymenoptera
Formicidae
Formica pacifica: new record for Vancouver Island, second for British Columbia; known previously from Rosedale in the Fraser Valley

Class Chilopoda
Ethopolidae
Ethopolys sierravabus: new record for Canada

Lithobiidae
Simobius ginampus: new record for Canada; known previously from Alaska and Washington

Discussion

Dragonflies of Brooks Peninsula

Our fragmentary knowledge of terrestrial arthropod distributions in the northern coastal region of British Columbia frustrates attempts to detail the zoogeographic relationships of most groups. The distribution of the Odonata is perhaps the best known of any order on the west coast, and for this reason they received special attention. The species are relatively few and conspicuous, making identification of a large percentage of the fauna possible.

Cannings and Cannings (1983) outline the dragonfly fauna of Brooks Peninsula and briefly discuss the zoogeography on the west coast of the group. Twenty species in eight genera and five families were collected. This species total is 25% of the provincial fauna. Although the study lasted only two weeks, it encompassed the height of the probably short flying period of most local species. Consistently fine weather produced efficient collecting, and all suitable habitats were sampled. It is estimated that 80% of the species present were observed. In comparison, similar habitats in the Queen Charlotte Islands have produced to date only 13 species. On southern Vancouver Island and the Lower Mainland a greater range of habitats and much more extensive collecting account for 53 species.

The dragonfly fauna of the central and northern coasts is predominantly Boreal and Holarctic in distribution with few species having western (including southwestern) or southern transcontinental ranges. Figure 10.13 illustrates these zoogeographic patterns. The Holarctic and Boreal components decrease southwards and the percentage of species inhabiting strictly western and southern transcontinental regions increases southwards. The Queen Charlotte Islands fauna is

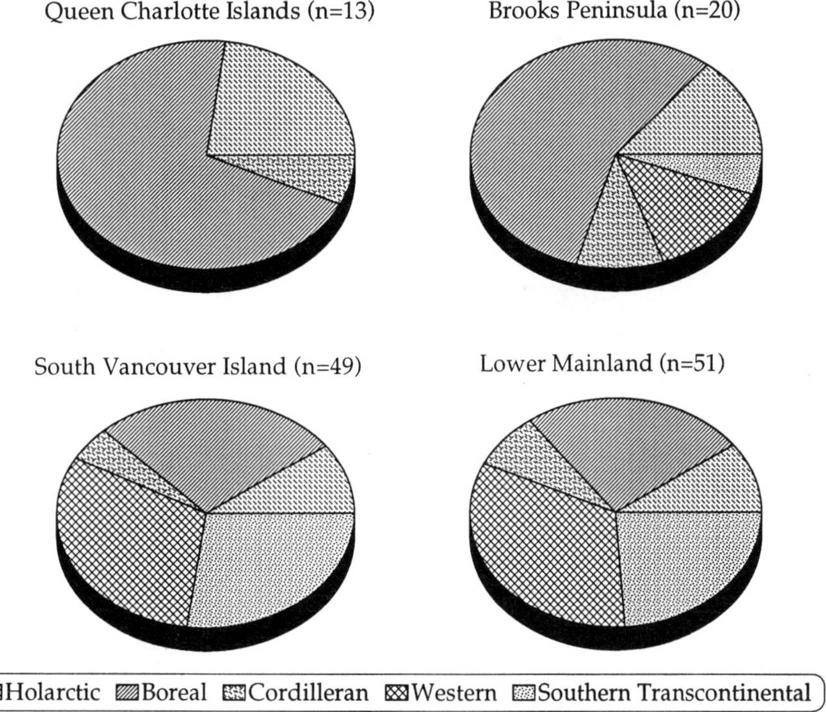

Figure 10.13 Percentage composition of the Odonata fauna of various west coast regions in British Columbia based on generalized distribution patterns of species (Faunal Elements)

completely northern in origin, whereas the Brooks Peninsula fauna is 85% so composed (Cordilleran species are a Boreal element confined to the western mountains; the Western element includes species with Great Basin, Sonoran, or Pacific Coast origins). Example species distributions for the Faunal Elements used in this zoogeographical discussion are shown in Figure 10.14. Species abundant on Brooks Peninsula, but absent from the Queen Charlotte Islands despite large amounts of suitable habitat, include the Boreal *Aeshna interrupta* and the Western *Sympetrum pallipes*. On Brooks Peninsula the three species of the Western faunal element (*Sympetrum madidum, S. occidentale*, and *S. pallipes*) are probably near their northern limit on the cool, wet outer coast.

Table 10.2 illustrates the ecological separation of species observed as adults. Some species such as *Lestes disjunctus* and *Enallagma cyathigerum*, or even *Aeshna juncea*, have wide environmental tolerances, whereas others, *Aeshna eremita, A. sitchensis*, and *Somatochlora semicircularis*, for example, are restricted to circumscribed habitats. Such spatial separation of species may be even more important in cool, often stormy climates, such as that of Brooks Peninsula, than in more clement areas to the south and east. It appears that many species (e.g., *Lestes disjunctus, Aeshna palmata, Sympetrum costiferum*) begin adult life a month or more later on Brooks Peninsula than they do on the southern B.C. coast or at the same latitude in the B.C. Interior. The total period of time that dragonflies are active on the outer west coast of Vancouver Island is thus considerably shorter than it is at low elevations elsewhere in southern B.C., and the activity of species normally flying in early summer overlaps much more than usual with that of species normally active in midsummer, late summer, or even autumn. The resulting concentration of species' activities into a relatively short period probably increases both intra- and interspecific competition.

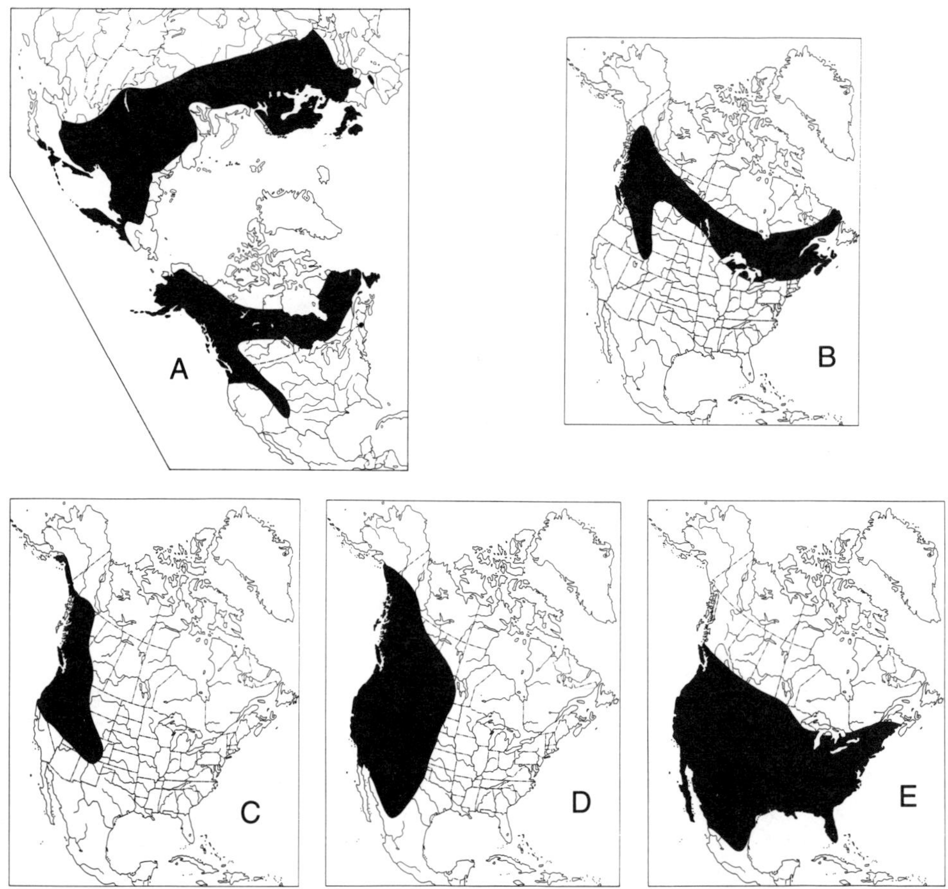

Figure 10.14 Example distribution patterns (Faunal Elements) used in the zoogeographical discussion. Ranges of individual species in each element may vary considerably. For example, many species of the Western Faunal Element, as defined here, are restricted to the lowlands of the Pacific coast. A, Holarctic; B, Boreal; C, Cordilleran; D, Western; E, Southern Transcontinental

At the same time, the mild, wet climate produces a long larval growing season. This may help to explain the large size of some adult specimens, notably those of *Somatochlora albicincta*. It has long been known that this species reaches a greater size in British Columbia than in other parts of boreal America (Walker and Corbet 1975). Specimens from high elevations in southern British Columbia and from sea level in Alaska are considerably smaller than those from sea level on the central British Columbia coast (Whitehouse 1941). Those from Brooks Peninsula are as large as, or larger than, any previously recorded.

General Zoogeographic Patterns

Using data from Stone et al. (1965), which reflect often poorly known distributions, the ranges of Diptera collected on Brooks Peninsula can be roughly compared with those noted for dragonflies, spiders, and ground beetles (Figure 10.15). The proportion of Holarctic species of Diptera is almost twice that of Odonata and four times that of spiders, whereas Boreal species are more common in dragonflies than in spiders and flies. Cordilleran species are notably more abundant in flies and spiders than in dragonflies. Strictly western, non-Cordilleran ranges are not represented to a large degree in any of these taxa.

Table 10.2 Ecological separation of dragonfly species observed as adults

Habitat	Species (in approximate order of abundance)
Bogs:	
a) large ponds	*Lestes disjunctus, Sympetrum danae, Enallagma cyathigerum, Aeshna interrupta, Libellula quadrimaculata, Aeshna juncea, Somatochlora albicincta, Leucorrhinia hudsonica, L. glacialis, L. proxima*
b) small pools, runnels, often dry	*Lestes disjunctus, Sympetrum pallipes, Aeshna sitchensis, Sympetrum danae, Somatochlora semicircularis*
c) sluggish creek pools	*Aeshna umbrosa, A. juncea, A. interrupta, A. palmata, Somatochlora semicircularis*
Lakes	*Aeshna eremita, Somatochlora albicincta, Enallagma cyathigerum*
Mountain ponds	*Lestes disjunctus, Enallagma cyathigerum, Aeshna juncea, A. interrupta, Somatochlora albicincta, Aeshna palmata*
Upper beach seepage pools	*Aeshna umbrosa*

Source: Cannings and Cannings (1983).

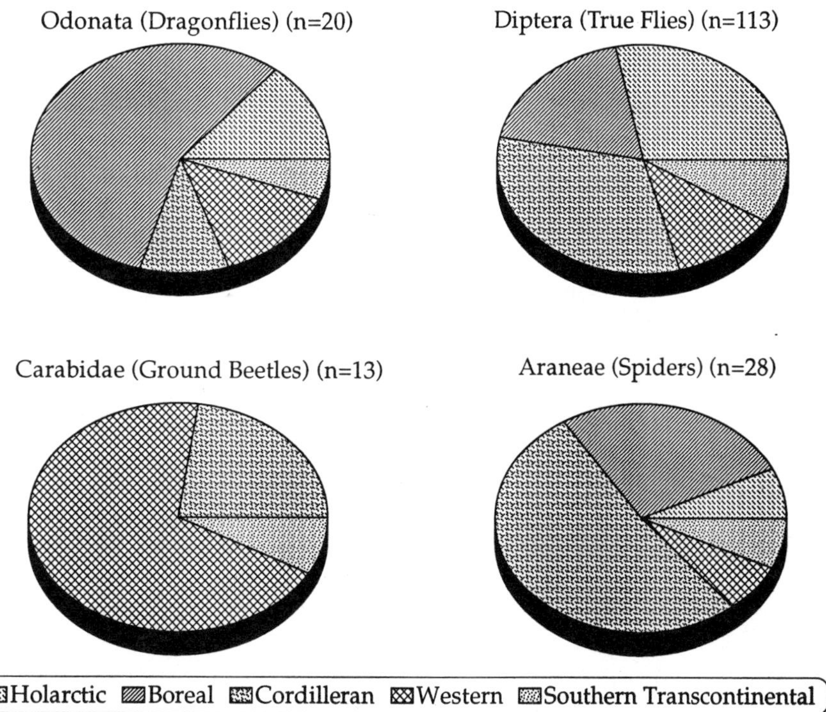

Figure 10.15 Percentage composition of selected taxa from the Brooks Peninsula based on generalized distribution patterns of species (Faunal Elements)

Brooks Peninsula ground beetles, heavily dominated by non-flying forms, consist of a majority of species restricted to the Pacific coast region west of the Coast Range divide. The remainder are transcontinental in distribution.

These data suggest that generalizations regarding the geographic derivation of the Brooks Peninsula arthropod fauna will vary widely depending on the groups under consideration. In easily dispersed groups, most species tend to have Holarctic, Boreal, or widespread Western ranges, whereas in more poorly dispersed forms, such as ground beetles, species with more restricted distributions predominate. It is not surprising that overall, most species are Boreal or Cordilleran in origin.

Only two species, both leafhoppers (Hemiptera: Cicadellidae), are introductions from Europe. *Aphrodes costatus* and *A. bicinctus*, both collected in the herbaceous upper beach vegetation at Cape Cook Lagoon, are polyphagous species first recognized as introductions in eastern North America in the early 1900s. The former was separately introduced to Agassiz, British Columbia in 1921 and in 1960 was taken at Terrace, British Columbia, probably also separately introduced. *A. bicinctus* was introduced to Vancouver, British Columbia and appeared in Victoria, British Columbia by 1950 (Hamilton 1983). Whether the Brooks Peninsula specimens have spread naturally from these populations or are the result of independent introductions, is not known.

Zoogeography and the Refugium Question

Mann (1983) examined the possible existence of a glacial refugium at Lituya Bay, Alaska. Using the ground beetle and spider faunas of the region, he tested several predictions based on endemism, disjunct distributions, frequency of poor dispersers, and evidence for age differences among the habitats within the ice-free area. Although not sufficient to test such predictions, Brooks Peninsula data can be discussed in this context.

1. Endemism

Since the presence of species restricted to a particular area can be the result of the contraction of formerly widespread ranges or the result of isolation and subsequent speciation *in situ*—both possible products of glacial activity—endemism has long been a popular argument for the existence of refugia. This is a primary premise in the botanical work of Calder and Taylor (1968) and the vertebrate studies of Foster (1965) that propose a refugium on the Queen Charlotte Islands. Arthropods have been used in the same and similar contexts. Kavanaugh (1980, 1989, 1992) using data from ground beetle collections, supports the Queen Charlotte Islands refugium concept. A refugium in the Magdalen Islands is suggested by the occurrence of an endemic grasshopper there (Scudder 1979; Vickery and Kevan 1978). Based on glaciological studies and the discovery of an endemic cave-dwelling amphipod crustacean in the Castleguard Cave of the Columbia Icefields, Holsinger (1981) proposes the cave was a subglacial refugium during glacial maxima in both Illinoisan and Wisconsin times.

Using the presence of endemism as evidence for refugial history assumes that speciation rates are too slow to account for species differentiation in post-glacial time (Mann 1983). Most endemics known from the extensive unglaciated areas of Beringia (northeastern Siberia, much of Alaska, and the northern Yukon) are apparently of the range-contraction type; there evidently has been insufficient time for speciation in populations fragmented by glaciation (Anderson 1984). In beetles, at least, most fossils from the North American Quaternary (up to 1.6 million years ago) and even some from the late Tertiary are identical to living species (Coope 1979; Matthews 1970, 1974), but those from the late Miocene (5.7 million years ago) are different enough from existing species to be considered their possible ancestors (Coope 1979; Matthews 1976). Thus, speciation during post-glacial times (the past 10 000-15 000 years) appears unlikely.

Endemism as a basis for refugial status also requires that the particular fauna of the surrounding region be well known. If it is not, the discovery of new species cannot be placed in context; one cannot be sure the species are restricted to the area in question. Of the 21 species collected only on Brooks Peninsula and thought to be undescribed, 9 are definitely, or probably, new and 12 are possibly new to science. In addition, two genera are known to be new. Ten species and two genera are undescribed but have been collected elsewhere. None of the species known only from Brooks Peninsula can be considered endemic given our relative ignorance of the fauna of surrounding areas.

Two species of ground beetles living on gravel beaches, *Nebria* (*charlottae* Lindroth and *N. louisae* Kavanaugh) (Kavanaugh 1989, 1992) are apparently endemic to the Queen Charlotte Islands. *N. haida* Kavanaugh, found on mountain tops, and once thought to be endemic, is now known from the adjacent mainland (Kavanaugh 1992). Although there is no fossil evidence for the survival of the endemics in refugia, their habitat preferences, present distributions, and phylogenetic relationships suggest they survived at least the last glacial period in the archipelago (Kavanaugh 1985, 1992). The relationships of this genus to glacial events are better understood than those of any other group of insects on the Northwest Coast.

Unfortunately, these or other closely related *Nebria* species were not collected in the present study. Only two species, *N. kincaidi*, a montane species, and *N. diversa*, a widespread species of sand beaches, were collected. Kavanaugh (1980) shows that mountain dwelling *Nebria* on Vancouver Island are probably derived from stock that re-established after Wisconsin glaciation from both the Coast/Cascade and Rocky Mountain montane regions south of the 49th parallel. *N. kincaidi* is an example of a species originating in the former area. *N. diversa* is the only lowland species known from Vancouver Island; no species occupying gravel beaches were found on Brooks Peninsula. The lack of records of *Nebria* species endemic to the peninsula, or of those known at present to be restricted to the Queen Charlotte Islands, is not evidence against the existence of a refugium, but rather an indication that more intensive collecting is needed on gravel beaches and high ridges of Brooks Peninsula.

No particular insects were found associated with the endemic plants on Brooks Peninsula.

2. Disjunct Distributions

Range disjunctions, the occurrence of isolated populations resulting from the fragmentation of formerly continuous ranges, have been used as evidence for refugia. This assumes there has been little or no establishment of disjunctions through chance dispersal in post-glacial time (Mann 1983).

Numerous significant disjunct distributions were documented by Brooks Peninsula collections. The main problem in analyzing these is, again, our poor knowledge of the fauna of coastal British Columbia. Whether these are true disjunctions or merely discontinuities in collecting cannot be established at present. Species new to British Columbia but previously known from Alaska and Washington, such as the long-legged fly *Argyra albiventris*, the muscid fly *Coenosia impunctata* and the centipede *Simobius ginampus*, no doubt represent discontinuities in collecting.

Most disjunctions are found in species previously recorded in Washington, Oregon, and California. This pattern is consistent with the refugium hypothesis since these areas are mostly south of the southern extent of maximum glaciation. However, many of the species involved are highly mobile and easily dispersed; it is difficult to envision these insects not spreading northwards from below the 49th parallel or outwards from Brooks Peninsula in the post-glacial period. Further collecting may prove their ranges are not disjunct.

Some species with low vagility also show similar disjunctions. The Brooks Peninsula records of the leafhopper *Bathysmatophorus oregonensis* are the first for Canada. It was collected on the ridge above Cassiope Pond, on Doom Mountain, and in Toebiter Bog. This polyphagous insect, the only Nearctic leafhopper known to live on fir, ranges from the forested mountains of northwestern California to the Olympic Mountains and Mount Rainier in Washington (Oman and Musgrave 1975), mostly south of the limit of Wisconsin glaciation. Oman and Musgrave (1975) note that both sexes have reduced wings and probably cannot fly. If the species does occur in the intervening forest between Brooks Peninsula and the southerly areas mentioned, it is surprising that it has not yet been collected—given the interest in forest feeding insects of the region. Its lack of mobility and distribution suggests a refugium may have been present on Brooks Peninsula. Similar disjunct distributions are shown by the tortoise mite *Trachytes* sp. E, the oribatid mite *Belba californica*, and the flightless zopherid beetle *Usechimorpha barberi*, all probably also slowly dispersed.

One disjunction focusses on the north rather than the south. The flightless weevil *Lepidophorus inguinatus* collected on *Geum* on Doom Mountain was known originally from southeastern Alaska and has recently been collected on the Queen Charlotte Islands (R.S. Anderson personal communication, January 1985). Such a distribution suggests it may have been restricted to northern coastal refugia during the last glaciation.

It should be noted that Kavanaugh (1989) feels northern glacial refugia (e.g., Lituya Bay, Kodiak Island, Aleutian Islands) have made no contribution to the ground beetle fauna of the Queen Charlottes, with the exception, perhaps, of *Nebria louisae*, which has Aleutian affinities.

3. Frequency of Poor Dispersers

Refugia, because of their age, should contain more slowly dispersing species than glaciated areas around them. This assumes flightless species have dispersed too slowly to have contributed to the present refugium fauna in post-glacial times. In the study of coastal species, however, passive dispersal over water cannot be ruled out, as drowning experiments with beetles have shown (Ball 1969; Mann 1983).

Much of the use of arthropod collections to provide evidence for the existence of glacial refugia has been restricted to studies on ground beetles (Ball 1969; Kavanaugh 1989; Lindroth 1969, 1979; Mann 1983). This is for good reason; they disperse relatively slowly for insects and preserve well in sediments (Kavanaugh 1989), thus they provide potentially useful information on past distributions. Because they are well-known taxonomically and their diverse ecological requirements are in many cases well understood, ground beetles have been used as indicators of past climate and vegetation regimes (Giterman et al. 1982; Matthews 1968, 1982).

Much stress, however, has been placed on the tendency of the group towards brachyptery, a characteristic that is genetically dominant (Lindroth 1979). The evolution of short-wingedness apparently has been prevalent in geographic areas where habitats have been stable for long periods, where flight is not advantageous or necessary for the maintenance of ranges (Darlington 1936, 1943; Kavanaugh 1989). Species are often dimorphic for wing length. Lindroth (1979) studied the Scandinavian fauna and noted that the distribution of brachypterous and macropterous populations of several species implied the existence of refugia on the Norwegian coast. Populations of *Bembidion grapei* Gyll., for example, living in old, long-occupied centres are mostly brachypterous; populations in southern and eastern areas of Scandinavia are fully winged. Lindroth believes the latter are colonizing populations originating from the coastal refugia. Examples also illustrate the reverse. Recolonization of *Calathus mollis* Marsh. from areas south of glaciation produces present distributions with mainly wingless forms in the south, larger proportions of winged forms to the north and west, and purely winged populations at the edge of the range. Lindroth has studied similar examples in North America—for example, in Newfoundland (Lindroth 1963a).

About 11% (91 species) of the ground beetles of Canada and Alaska are brachypterous (Lindroth 1979). In the Pacific Northwest coastal region, the percentage is highly variable; the mean of nine areas selected by Kavanaugh (1989) is 20%. The following data are from Kavanaugh (1989). The Vancouver, British Columbia region has 22 of 156 (14%) species brachypterous, whereas Vancouver Island (as a whole, but mostly southern collections) has 29 of 166 (17%) brachypterous. Smaller, more remote islands have high levels of brachyptery—the Aleutians, 11 of 30 (37%); Kodiak Island, 18 of 51 (31%). Both the Aleutians (Lindroth 1963b) and Kodiak Island (Ball 1969, Lindroth 1969) are considered refugia. The Queen Charlotte Islands have 21 of 59 (36%) species brachypterous and Lituya Bay on the Alaska mainland 9 of 29 (31%); both are also thought to have been partially ice-free. Some areas of the northern mainland also have high percentages of brachyptery—both the Alaska Peninsula and the Prince Rupert area have 28% rates. In general, areas considered refugia have brachyptery percentages over 30%.

Of the 13 species of ground beetles collected on Brooks Peninsula, 11 (85%) are brachypterous. Two of these, *Agonum ferruginosum* and *Notiophilus sylvaticus*, have dimorphic populations throughout their range (Lindroth 1961-69). Unfortunately, this high percentage cannot be considered accurate, because the list of species is obviously incomplete. *Bembidion* species are noticeably lacking, and these usually form a high proportion of flying forms.

Of interest is the fact that *Notiophilus sylvaticus*, which occurs along the west coast of North America and in the coastal mountains, has dimorphic populations with a peculiar distribution. From Prince Rupert and the Queen Charlotte Islands north, populations are all brachypterous, whereas to the south there is a large component of flying forms (Lindroth 1969). Southern Vancouver Island, for example, has mostly macropterous populations. Only two specimens were collected on Brooks Peninsula, both on Senecio Ridge; both were brachypterous. Lindroth states that the distribution of the species along the coast indicates that northern, brachypterous populations could hardly have originated south of the ice sheet and have immigrated in post-glacial time. Rather, he suggests they must have maintained populations in the northern regions during glaciation.

4. Age Differences in Habitats Within the Refugium

Mann (1983) suggests that if a glacial refugium existed at Lituya Bay, its vegetation was probably alpine in nature. Thus, this high altitude habitat would be the oldest and most stable in the area. He also predicts: higher altitude habitats should have accumulated more species than younger, lower ones; younger habitats may support fewer habitat endemics; inhabitants of younger habitats should be more easily dispersed than those of older habitats.

Data from Brooks Peninsula are not extensive enough to test such predictions. It is evident that not enough collecting was done at high elevations; the time spent there and the number of pitfall traps set was not sufficient to produce results comparable to those from low elevations.

Conclusions

The use of endemism and range disjunctions in arthropods as evidence for a glacial refugium on Brooks Peninsula demands that the fauna of surrounding regions be well known. Unfortunately, this requirement is not met, and the true status of the many undescribed species collected and the range disjunctions documented will have to await the results of further collecting. A more intense search for genera in which there is evidence for endemism in adjacent regions (e.g., the ground beetle genus *Nebria*) might prove fruitful.

Most species whose Brooks Peninsula populations are disjunct have the main part of their range south of the 49th parallel. Most of these are vagile species, and the disjunct distribution probably represents only disjunct collecting, not true isolation of a fragmented population. However, some non-flying, poorly dispersing forms have not been found between Brooks Peninsula and the main part of their range in the northwestern United States, even though at least some of the groups represented are relatively well-collected in southern British Columbia. This is suggestive, but not strong, evidence for a refugium on Brooks Peninsula. The flightless weevil *Lepidophorus inquinatus* has a disjunct northern distribution and if it survived the last glaciation in refugia in Alaska and the Queen Charlotte Islands, it probably also did so on Brooks Peninsula.

A high proportion of flightless species in ground beetle assemblages is indicative of isolated, stable habitats, and this phenomenon has often been used as evidence of glacial refugia show levels of wing reduction over 30%. The Brooks Peninsula proportion of 85% is considered inaccurate since the list of ground beetles is not complete; further collecting will produce more species, many of which will be macropterous. Nevertheless, as a preliminary figure it indicates the true percentage may be high.

Evidence from arthropod collections supporting the existence of a glacial refugium on Brooks Peninsula is suggestive but weak. Only further collecting on the peninsula and in adjacent regions will clarify the preliminary evidence.

Update

Since the modest inventory of the terrestrial arthropods of Brooks Peninsula described here was undertaken in 1981, there have been several relevant and noteworthy additions to our knowledge. The publication of David Kavanaugh's (1992) treatise on the carabid beetles of the Queen Charlotte Islands further clarified some of the evolutionary relationships between the fauna of the Charlottes and those of the mainland.

The detailed arthropod inventories of coastal forests initiated by Neville Winchester and Richard Ring of the University of Victoria (Winchester 1996; Winchester and Ring 1996; Ring and Winchester 1996) have provided significant new information on the presence and distribution of species in the forests of Vancouver Island. These studies have been driven by questions about the nature of the arthropod communities in the forest canopy. The most extensive study examined the fauna of the Sitka spruce groves of the Carmanah Valley. In 1991 over 612 000 specimens were collected; 150 000 were sent to various experts for identification and 1300 species were identified. Seventy-six of these are new to science. Collections were made from the old-growth canopy at 40+ metres down to the forest floor, from adjacent clearcuts, second growth sites and ecotonal areas. In 1994-95, 1.5 million specimens were collected in a canopy/forest floor study in uncut dry Douglas-fir/Garry oak habitats at Rocky Point near Victoria. Most of these specimens have yet to be identified. Other similar research has recently begun in montane sites in central and northern Vancouver Island.

Preliminary identifications of the Carmanah Valley material have not significantly affected the interpretation of the Brooks Peninsula inventory. To a large extent this is because the Brooks Peninsula inventory included many diverse environments while the Carmanah study concentrated on the Sitka spruce forest and modifications of it. However, even the number of forest species common to both locations is not high. The Carmanah study turned up only three species reported as significant range extensions in the Brooks Peninsula study: the leafhopper *Aphrodes costatus* and the rove beetle *Bryoporus rufescens*, both new to Vancouver Island; the crane fly *Molophilus oligocanthus*, new to Canada.

Much work remains to be done before we can confidently use a wide range of arthropod distribution patterns to answer questions about coastal prehistory. The efforts and difficulties inherent in the collection, preparation and identification of terrestrial arthropods will ensure that the accumulation of information occurs only slowly.

References Cited

Anderson, R.S. 1984. *Connatichela artemisiae*, a new genus and species of weevil from the Yukon Territory (Coleoptera: Curculionidae: Leptopiinae): taxonomy, paleontology, and biogeography. Can. Entomol. 116: 1571-1580.

Ball, G.E. 1969. The species of the subgenus *Cryobius* of the Kodiak archipelago (*Pterostichus*, Carabidae, Coleoptera). Pp. 156-194 in N.V. Karlstrom and G.E. Ball (eds.). The Kodiak Island refugium: its geology, flora, fauna and history. Ryerson Press, Toronto, ON.

Calder, J.A. and R.L. Taylor. 1968. Flora of the Queen Charlotte Islands, Part 1. Systematics of the vascular plants. Canadian Department of Agricultural Research Branch, Monogr. 4, part 1.

Cannings, R.A. 1982. Notes on the biology of *Aeshna sitchensis* Hagen (Anisoptera: Aeshnidae). Odonatologica 11: 219-223.

——— and S.G. Cannings. 1983. The Odonata of the Brooks Peninsula, Vancouver Island, British Columbia. J. Entomol. Soc. B.C. 80: 46-51.

——— and K.M. Stuart. 1977. The dragonflies of British Columbia. British Columbia Provincial Museum (Victoria, BC) Handbook 35.

Carl, G.C., C.J. Guiguet, and G.A. Hardy. 1951. Biology of the Scott Island group, British Columbia. Pp. 21-63 in Provincial Museum of Natural History and Anthropology report for the year 1950. British Columbia Department of Education, Victoria, BC.

Coope, G.R. 1979. Late Cenozoic fossil Coleoptera: evolution, biogeography, and ecology. Ann. Rev. Ecol. Syst. 10: 247-267.

Darlington, P.J., Jr. 1936. Variation of flying wings of carabid beetles (Coleoptera). Ann. Entomol. Soc. Am. 29: 136-179.

———. 1943. Carabidae of mountains and islands: data on the evolution of isolated faunas, and an atrophy of wings. Ecol. Monogr. 13: 37-61.

Foster, J.B. 1965. The evolution of the mammals of the Queen Charlotte Islands, British Columbia. British Columbia Provincial Museum (Victoria, BC) Occasional paper 14.

Giterman, R.E., A.V. Sher, and J.V. Matthews, Jr. 1982. Comparison of the development of tundra-steppe environments in west and east Berengia: pollen and macrofossil evidence from key sections. Pp. 43-73 in D.M. Hopkins, J.V. Matthews, Jr., C.E. Schweger, and S.B. Young (eds.). Paleoecology of Beringia. Academic Press, NY.

Hamilton, K.G.A. 1983. Introduced and native leafhoppers common to the Old and New Worlds (Rhyncota: Cicadellidae). Can. Entomol. 115: 473-511.

Holsinger, J.R. 1981. *Stygobromus canadensis*, a trogloditic amphipod crustacean from Castleguard Cave, with remarks on the concept of cave glacial refugia. Pp. 93-95 in B.F. Beck (ed.). Eighth International Congress of Speleology, Bowling Green, Kentucky, U.S.A., July 18-24, 1981.

Kavanaugh, D.H. 1980. Insects of western Canada, with special reference to certain Carabidae (Coleoptera): present distribution patterns and their origins. Can. Entomol. 112: 1129-1144.

______. 1989. The Ground-beetle (Coleoptera: Carabidae) fauna of the Queen Charlotte Islands: its composition, affinities and origins. Pp. 129-144 in G.G.E. Scudder and N. Gessler (eds.). The Outer Shores. Proc. of the Queen Charlotte Islands International Symposium (August 1984). Queen Charlotte Islands Museum Press, Skidegate. vi + 327 pp.

______. 1992. Carabid beetles (Insecta: Coleoptera: Carabidae) of the Queen Charlotte Islands, British Columiba. Memoirs of the California Academy of Sciences 16: 1-113.

Lindroth, C.H. 1961-69. The Ground-beetles (Carabidae excl. Cicindelinae) of Canada and Alaska. Parts 1-6. Opuscula Entomologicae (1961, Part 2, Supplementum 20: 1-200; 1963, Part 3, Supplementum 24: 201-408; 1966, Part 4, Supplementum 29: 409-648; 1968, Part 5, Supplementum 33: 649-944; 1969, Part 6, Supplementum 34: 945-1192; 1969, Part 1, Supplementum 35: i-xlviii).

______. 1963a. The faunal history of Newfoundland, illustrated by carabid beetles. Opuscula Entomologicae Supplementum 23: 1-12.

______. 1963b. The Aleutian Islands as a route for dispersal across the North Pacific. Pp. 121-131 in J.L. Gressitt (ed.). Pacific Basin biogeography (10th Pacific Science Congress). Bishop Museum Press, Honolulu.

______. 1969. An analysis of the carabid beetle fauna of the refugium. Pp. 195-210 in N.V. Karlstrom and G.E. Ball (eds.). The Kodiak Island refugium: its geology, flora, fauna and history. Ryerson Press, Toronto, ON.

______. 1979. The theory of glacial refugia. Pp. 385-394 in Proceedings of the First International Symposium of Carabidology, Washington, DC, August 21-25, 1976. Junk, The Hague.

Mann, D.H. 1983. The Quaternary history of the Lituya glacial refugium. Ph.D. thesis. Department of Zoology, University of Washington, Seattle, WA.

Matthews J.V., Jr. 1968. A paleoenvironmental analysis of three late Pleistocene Coleopterous assemblages from Fairbanks, Alaska. Quaestiones Entomologicae (Department of Entomology, University of Alberta, Edmonton) 4: 202-224.

______. 1970. Two new species of *Micropeplus* from the Pliocene of western Alaska with remarks on the evolution of the Micropeplinae (Coleoptera: Staphylinidae). Can. J. Zool. 48: 779-788.

______. 1974. Quaternary environments of Cape Deceit (Seward Peninsula, Alaska): evolution of a tundra ecosystem. Geol. Soc. Am. Bull. 85: 1353-1384.

______. 1976. Evolution of the subgenus *Cyphelophorus* (Genus *Helophorus*: Hydrophilidae, Coleoptera): description of two new fossil species and discussion of *Helophorus tuberculatus* Gyll. Can. J. Zool. 54: 652-673.

______. 1982. East Beringia during late Wisconsin time: a review of the biotic evidence. Pp. 127-150 in D.M. Hopkins, J.V. Matthews, Jr., D.E. Schweger, and S.B. Young (eds.). Paleoecology of Beringia. Academic Press, NY.

Nimmo, A.P. and G.G.E. Scudder. 1979. An annotated checklist of the Trichoptera (Insecta) of British Columbia. Syesis 11: 117-133.

Oman, P. and C.A. Musgrave. 1975. The Nearctic genera of Errhomenini (Homoptera: Cicadellidae). Melanderia 21: 1-14.

Ring, R.A. and N.N. Winchester. 1996. Coastal temperate rainforest canopy access systems in British Columbia, Canada. Selbyana 17: 22-26.

Scudder, G.G.E. 1975. An annotated checklist of the Ephemeroptera (Insecta) of British Columbia. Syesis 8: 311-315.

______. 1979. Present patterns in the fauna and flora of Canada. In H.V. Danks (ed.). Canada and its insect fauna. Entomological Society of Canada (Ottawa, ON). Mem. 108: 87-179.

______, D.K. McE. Kevan, and E.L. Bousfield. 1979. Higher classification. In H.V. Danks (ed.). Canada and its insect fauna. Entomological Society of Canada (Ottawa, ON). Mem. 108: 235-240.

Stone, A., C.W. Sabrosky, W.W. Wirth, R.H. Foote, and J.R. Coulson. 1965. A catalogue of the Diptera of America north of Mexico. U.S. Department of Agriculture, Washington, DC.

Teskey, H.J. 1983. A review of the *Atylotus insuetus* group from western North America including a description of a new species and immature stages (Diptera: Tabanidae). Can. Entomol. 115: 693-702.

Thorn, E. 1967. Preliminary distributional list of the spiders of British Columbia. Pp. 23-38 in Provincial Museum of Natural History and Anthropology report for the year 1966. B.C. Department of Recreation and Conservation, Victoria, BC.

Vickery, V.R. and D.K. McE. Kevan. 1978. A new species of *Melanoplus* (Orthoptera: Acrididae: Melanoplinae) from the Magdalen Islands, Quebec. Ann. Soc. Entomol. Quebec 22: 188-192.

Walker, E.M. and P.S. Corbet. 1975. The Odonata of Canada and Alaska. Vol. 3. University of Toronto Press, Toronto, ON.

West, R., C.D. Dondale, and R.A. Ring. 1984. A revised checklist of the spiders (Araneae) of British Columbia. J. Entomol. Soc. B.C. 81: 80-98.

Whitehouse, F.C. 1941. British Columbia dragonflies (Odonata) with notes on distribution and habits. Am. Midl. Nat. 26: 488-557.

Winchester, N.N. 1996. Canopy arthropods of coastal Sitka spruce trees on Vancouver Island, British Columbia, Canada. In N.E. Stork, J.A. Adis and R.K. Didham (eds.). Canopy Arthropods. Chapman and Hall, London (in press).

______ and R.A. Ring. 1996. Centinelan extinctions: extirpation of Northern Temperate old-growth rainforest arthropod communities. Selbyana 17: 50-57.

Appendix 10.1 Arthropods collected

Taxa. The higher classification scheme used in this list follows Scudder et al. (1979).

Localities. Collection localities (Figure 10.1) are represented by capital letters:

A. Amos Creek bog
B. Amos Creek, freshwater seep west of mouth
C. Aster Bay
D. Brasenia Pond
E. Brasenia Pond bog
F. Cape Cook Lagoon
G. Cassiope Pond
H. Cassiope Pond, ridge to east (700 m)
I. Danae Ponds
J. Drift Whale Bay beach
K. Gaultheria Lake
L. Gaultheria Lake, pond at outlet
M. Kalmia Lake
N. Kalmia Lake bog
O. Kalmia Lake, pond at outlet
P. Kingfisher Creek
Q. Drift Whale Bay bog
R. Pyrola Lake
S. Quineex Indian Reserve 8
T. Salamander Creek (on The Throne, Doom Mountain)
U. Scramble Creek (inlet to Gaultheria Lake)
V. Senecio Ridge (headlands)
W. Solander Island
X. Doom Mountain, The Throne
Y. Toebiter Bog
Z. Tringa Tarns

Additional habitat data. Other data are represented by lower case letters ("o" is omitted to prevent confusion with zero):

a. at light
b. *Carex/Elymus* sand dunes
c. dunes/spruce forest edge
d. dune grass/spruce forest edge
e. freshwater lagoon, sandy shore
f. freshwater supra-tidal pools
g. freshwater seep
h. from *Achillea*
i. from *Pinus*
j. from *Cakile*
k. from seaweed
l. headwall cliff
m. headwall cliff, soil, and litter
n. intertidal sand
p. pitfall trap
q. lagoon/spruce forest edge
r. litter at mouth of puffin burrow
s. moss/litter, spruce forest
t. rotten log
u. sand dunes
v. soil/grass sod
w. spruce forest
x. upper beach/forest edge
y. underwater light trap
z. wet supra-tidal meadow

Date. Collection date is indicated by a number from 0 to 31, representing 31 July 1981 (0) to 31 August 1981 (31). Dates are given in standard form where specimens from other expeditions to Brooks Peninsula are included.

Example. A sample of collection data noted as F.b,p:w.7,9 indicates specimens were collected at Cape Cook Lagoon from both *Carex/Elymus* sand dunes and a pitfall trap in the spruce forest on 7 and 9 August 1981.

Number of Specimens. The total number of specimens of each taxon is listed.

Identification. Specialists who identified specimens are indicated by their initials; names in full are listed below. Addresses given are those at time of identification (1982-83).

AB	A. Borkent, Agriculture Canada, Ottawa
AF	A. Francoeur, Dept. of Biology, Univ. du Quebec, Chicoutimi, PQ
AFj	A. Fjellberg, Tromso Museum, Tromso, Norway
AJ	A. Jansson, Dept. of Zoology, Univ. of Helsinki, Helsinki, Finland
AM	A. Mutuura, Agriculture Canada, Ottawa
AS	A. Smetana, Agriculture Canada, Ottawa
BA	B.D. Ainscough, Victoria, BC
BB	B. Bissett, Agriculture Canada, Ottawa
BC	B. Cooper, Agriculture Canada, Ottawa
BJ	B.A. Jinkinson, Agriculture Canada, Ottawa
BP	B.V. Peterson, U.S. Dept. Agriculture, Washington, DC
CD	C.D. Dondale, Agriculture Canada, Ottawa
CG	C. Guppy, Royal B.C. Museum, Victoria, BC
DB	D. Bright, Agriculture Canada, Ottawa
DC	D.S. Chandler, Dept. of Entomology, University of New Hampshire, Durham, NH
DL	D. Lemkuhl, Dept. of Biology, University of Saskatchewan, Saskatoon, SK
DO	D.R. Oliver, Agriculture Canada, Ottawa
DW	D.M. Wood, Agriculture Canada, Ottawa
EB	E. Becker, Agriculture Canada, Ottawa
EE	E. Edney, Dept. of Zoology, University of British Columbia, Vancouver, BC
EM	E.L. Mockford, Dept. of Biology, Illinois State University, Normal, IL
ER	E.W. Rockburne, Agriculture Canada, Ottawa
GB	G. Ball, Dept. of Entomology, University of Alberta, Edmonton, AB
GS	G.G.E. Scudder, Dept. of Zoology, University of British Columbia, Vancouver, BC
GW	G.B. Wiggins, Royal Ontario Museum, Toronto, ON
HG	H. Goulet, Agriculture Canada, Ottawa
HT	H.J. Teskey, Agriculture Canada, Ottawa
HW	H. Walther, Agriculture Canada, Ottawa
IA	I. Askevold, Dept. of Entomology, University of Manitoba, Winnipeg, MB
IS	I.M. Smith, Agriculture Canada, Ottawa
JC	J. Cooper, Dept. of Biology, Carleton University, Ottawa, ON
JFMcA	J.F. McAlpine, Agriculture Canada, Ottawa
JMC	J.M. Campbell, Agriculture Canada, Ottawa
JMc	J. McNamara, Agriculture Canada, Ottawa
JP	J.T. Polhemus, Englewood, CO
JR	J. Redner, Agriculture Canada, Ottawa
JV	J.R. Vockeroth, Agriculture Canada, Ottawa
JW	J. Wooley, Texas A & M University, College Station, TX
KB	K.B. Bolte, Agriculture Canada, Ottawa
KH	K.G.A. Hamilton, Agriculture Canada, Ottawa
KN	K. Neil, Dept. of Biology, Simon Fraser University, Burnaby, BC
LF	L. Forster, Agriculture Canada, Ottawa
LL	L. LeSage, Agriculture Canada, Ottawa
MR	M.E. Roussel, Agriculture Canada, Ottawa
MS	M. Sharkey, Agriculture Canada, Ottawa
PD	P.T. Dang, Agriculture Canada, Ottawa
PS	P. Shaw, Dept. of Zoology, University of British Columbia, Vancouver, BC
RA	R.S. Anderson, Texas A & M University, College Station, TX
RAC	R.A. Cannings, Royal B.C. Museum, Victoria, BC

RCr	R. Crawford, Burke Museum, University of Washington, Seattle, WA
RH	R. Holmberg, Dept. of Biology, Athabasca University, Edmonton, AB
RR	R. Roughley, Dept. of Zoology, University of Manitoba, Winnipeg, MB
RS	R. Shelley, North Carolina State Museum, Raleigh
SC	S.G. Cannings, Dept. of Zoology, University of British Columbia, Vancouver, BC
SMa	S.M. Marshall, Dept. of Biology, University of Guelph, Guelph, ON
SMi	S. Millen, Dept. of Zoology, University of British Columbia, Vancouver, BC
VB-P	V. Behan-Pelletier, Agriculture Canada, Ottawa
VV	V. Vickery, Lyman Museum, Macdonald College, Ste. Anne de Bellevue, PQ
WL	W. Lazorko, Vancouver, BC
WS	W.A. Shear, Dept. of Biology, Hampden-Sydney College, Hampden-Sydney, VA

Taxon	Collection data	No. of specimens	Identified by
SUBPHYLUM CHELICERATA			
Class Arachnida (Arachnids)			
SUBCLASS CHELONETHIDA			
Order Pseudoscorpionida (Pseudoscorpions)			
Chthoniidae			
Apochthonius n.sp.	F.s.14	8	MS
Neobisiidae			
Microcreagris n.sp.	F.s.14	1	MS
SUBCLASS LABELLATA			
Order Araneae (Spiders)			
Agelenidae (Funnel-web Spiders)	G.11	1	CD
Cryphoeca peckhami Simon	F.p:u.13	1	CD
Cybaeus morosus Simon	F.p:c.13; X.p:l.14	2	CD
Cybaeus reticulatus Simon	B.z.5; F.p:q,w.3,7,12;	10	CD
Cybaeus sp.	Q.4; X.p:l.14	1	CD
Dirksia cinctipes (Banks)	F.3	9	CD
Agelenidae sp.	F.c.2,7; W.r.14; X.m.14		
Antrodiaetidae (Folding Door Spiders)			
Antrodiaetus pacificus (Simon)	F.t,p:c.9,13,19; R.19	7	CD
Antrodiaetus sp.	F.s.14	2	CD
Araneidae (Orb Weaver Spiders)			
Araneus trifolium (Hentz)	O.10;I.6	3	CD
Araneus sp.	X.9	1	CD
Metallina curtisi (McCook)	J.22; X.p:l.14	9	CD
Clubionidae (Sac Spiders)			
Clubiona trivialis C.L. Koch	H.0; V.p.14	2	JR
Clubiona sp.	W.14	2	JR
Micaria sp.	H.p.11	5	CD
Eriogonidae (Dwarf Spiders [part])			
Ceratinops inflatus (Emerson)	F.p:w.5	1	JR
Scotinotylus sp.	H.p.11	1	CD
Tapinocyba sp.	W.r.14	1	CD

Zygottus corvallis Chamb.	F.p:q.7	1	CD
Linyphiidae (Sheet-web Spiders)			
Bathyphantes alascensis (Banks)	F.t.13	1	CD
Bathyphantes keeni (Emerton)	X.p:l.14	1	CD
Lepthyphantes alaskanus (Banks)	H.p.11	1	CD
Lepthyphantes tenuis (Blackwall)	F.s.14	3	CD
Lepthyphantes sp. poss. *zellata* Zorsch	F.p:w.5,13	3	JR
Meioneta sp.	H.p.11	1	CD
Pityohyphantes sp.	X.l.9	1	CD
Lycosidae (Wolf Spiders)			
Pardosa dorsuncata L. & D.	F.c.2; G.p.0,11	9	CD/JR
Pardosa metlakatla Em.	D.7; V.p.9,14; M.10; Q.4; Y.p.12	8	CD/JR
Pardosa sp.	D.7; F.p:c.11; H.p.11	6	CD
Pirata piraticus (Clerek)	I.6; Y.p.12	11	CD
Pirata sp.	O.10	1	CD
Trochosa terricola Thorell	V.9	1	CD
Micryphantidae (Dwarf Spiders [part[)			
Microlinyphia dana (C. & I.)	X.m.9,14	5	CD
Tachygyna vancouveri C. & I.	H.p.11	1	CD
Philodromidae (Crab Spiders [part])			
Philodromus rufus pacificus Banks	G.31	1	JR
Philodromus sp.	W.r.14	1	CD
Tibellus oblongus Walck.	D.7; I.6	2	CD
Salticidae (Jumping Spiders)			
Evarcha hoyi (Peckh. & Peckh.)	D.7; Q.4; Y.p.12	3	CD
Tetragnathidae (Long-jawed Orb Weavers)			
Tetragnatha sp. prob. *extensa* L.	D.7	1	CD
Tetragnatha laboriosa Hentz	B.z.5; G.i.0	4	CD
Tetrgnatha sp.	Q.4; I.6	2	CD
Theridiidae (Comb-footed Spiders)			
Robertus vigerens (C. & I.)	H.p.11	2	CD
Theridion agrifoliae Levi	F.b.2		CD/JR
Theridion sexpunctatum Emerton	F.11		JR
Thomisidae (Crab Spiders [part])			
Xysticus montanensis Keys	D.7	2	CD
Xysticus pretiosus G.	F.p:c,u.2,3,7,9; H.p.0	8	CD/JR
Xysticus sp.	F.p:c.11,13; V.p.14	4	CD
SUBCLASS PHALANGIDA			
<u>Order Opiliones (Harvestmen)</u>			
Ischyropsalidae			
Sabacon occidentalis (Banks)	F.p:w.2; H.0	2	RH/WS
Phalangidae			

BROOKS PENINSULA

Leiobonum paessleri Roewer	F.13; H.0; X.p:l.14	4	RH
Leuronychus parvulus Banks	V.p.14	1	RH
SUBCLASS ACARI (Mites and Ticks)			
Order Parasitiformes			
Suborder Mesostigmata			
Polyaspididae (Tortoise Mites [part])			
Polyaspinus sp. A	W.r.14	--	BA
Trachytes sp. B	F.s.14; X.m.14	--	BA
Trachytes sp. C	W.r.14; X.m.14	--	BA
Trachytes sp. E	X.m.14	--	BA
Trachytes sp. G	F.s.14	--	BA
Uropodidae (Tortoise Mites [part])			
Urodiaspis sp. A	F.s.14; W.r.14	--	BA
New Genus near *Urodiaspis*	F.s.14	--	BA
New Genus near *Uroobovella*	F.s.14; W.r.14	--	BA
<u>Order Acariformes</u>			
Suborder Oribatei (Oribatid Mites)			
Camasiidae			
Heminothrus longisetosus Willman	T.v.14	1	VB-P
Heminothrus thori (Berlese)	T.v.14	1	VB-P
Platynothrus peltifer (C.L. Koch)	F.s.14	17	VB-P
Cepheidae			
Sphodrocepheus anthelionus W. & H.	F.s.14	3	VB-P
Ceratozetidae			
Melanozetes interruptus Willman	F.s.14	1	VB-P
Danraeidae			
Belba californica (Banks)	F.p:q.7; F.l.c.s.14	14	VB-P
Epidamaeus sp.	F.s.14	3	VB-P
Epilohmannidae			
Epilohmannia n.sp.	T.v.14	20	VB-P
Haplozetidae			
Protoribates sp.	W.r.14	1	VB-P
Hermanniidae			
Hermannia gibba (C.L. Koch)	F.s.14	2	VB-P
Hypochthoniidae			
Hypochthonius rufulus C.L. Koch	W.r.14	8	VB-P
Liacaridae			
Dorycranosus acutidens Aoki	W.r.14	10	VB-P
Liacarus bidentatus Ewing	F.s.14; T.v.14; X.m.14	26	VB-P
Rhaphidosus sp. nr. *bacillatus* Fry & A.	F.s.14	3	VB-P

Megeremaeidae			
Megeremaeus sp. nr. *montanus* W. & H.	F.s.14	1	VB-P
Metrioppiidae			
Ceratoppia sp. nr. *bipilis* (Hermann)	F.s.14	6	VB-P
Ceratoppia n. sp.	F.s.14	1	VB-P
Mycobatidae			
Mycobates sarekensis Tragardh	V.v.14	1	VB-P
Nothridae			
Nothrus silvestris Nicolet	W.r.14; T.v.14	2	VB-P
Oribatulidae			
Oribatula tibialis Nicolet	V.v.14	1	VB-P
Pelopidae			
Eupelops sp.	V.v.14	1	VB-P
Tenuialoides sp. nr. *medialis* W. & H.	T.v.14	1	VB-P
Suborder Prostigmata			
Bdellidae			
Bdella sp.	H.p.11	2	IS
Bdellodes sp.	F.p:q.7	1	IS
Erythraeidae			
Balastium sp.	F.p:u.2	11	IS
Limnocharidae			
Limnochares sp. nr. *americana* Lundb.	M.y.10	2	IS
Limnochares sp.	N.10	--	IS
Pionidae			
Piona sp.	M.y.10	35	IS
Trombidiidae			
Allothrobium sp.	F.p:c,q.2,6,7,11,13; H.p.11	31	IS

Other mites unidentified owing to time and technical restraints

SUBPHYLUM CRUSTACEA
Class Malacostraca
<u>Order Isopoda (Isopods)</u>

Asellidae			
Asellus tomalensis Harford	B.f.5	5	EE
Sphaeromidae			
Exoshphaeroma oregonensis Dana	B.5; F.n.3	14	EE
Ligiidae			
Ligia pallasii Brandt	F.2	8	EE
Ligidium gracile Dana	F.p:q,w.2,11,13; H.p.11; V.p.14; W.14; X.l.9	20	EE

Porcellionidae			
Porcellio scaber Latreille	J.4; W.14	6	EE
Order Amphipoda (Amphipods)			
Anisogammaridae			
Eogammarus convervicolus (Stimpson)	B.5	10	PS
Crangonyctidae			
Crangonix sp. (*richmondensis*?)	X.9	--	PS
Taltridae			
Orchestoidea californiana Brandt	F.n.2	3	SMi
SUBPHYLUM UNIRAMIA			
Class Collembola (Springtails)			
Order Arthropleona			
Hypogastruridae			
Pseudochorates sp.	W.r.14	1	AFj
Onychiuridae			
Lephognathella choreutes Borner	F.s.14	1	AFj
Onychiurus armatus group	W.r.14	1	AFj
Isotomidae			
Folsomia picea Christiansen & Tucker	X.m.14	1	AFj
Folsomia regularis Hammer	W.r.14	1	AFj
Pseudisotoma sensibilis Tullb.	F.s.14	1	AFj
Entomobryidae			
Tomocerus dubius Christiansen	F.s.l4; F.p:w.5,7,12	13	AFj
Tomocerus flavescens (Tullb.)	F.s.l4; F.p:c,w.2,5,7,13; V.p.14; X.p:l.14; X.m.14	2	AFj
Tomocerus sp.	F.p:w.2,12	2	AFj
Order Symphypleona			
Sminthuridae			
Dicyrtoma sp.	F.p:c,w.2,7,9,12,13	34	AFj
Class Insecta (Insects)			
Machilidae			
Pedetontus sp.	J.4	7	AFj
unidentified Microcoryphia		2	
Order Ephemeroptera (Mayflies)			
Heptageniidae			
Cinygma sp.	B.5	3	DL
Leptophlebiidae			
Paraleptophlebia sp.	J.g.4	1	DL
Paraleptophlebia sp. (*debilis* Walker?)	F.p:q.2; M.11	2	DL

Siphlonuridae			
Ameletus sp.	U.1	1	DL
Order Odonata (Dragonflies)			
Lestidae			
Lestes disjunctus Selys	D.7;L.1;V.9;M.10;N.10; G.0;I.6	50	RAC
Coenagrionidae			
Enallagma cyathigerum (Charp.)	D.7;G.0;H.0;L.1;N.10;I.6	77	RAC
Aeshnidae			
Aeshna eremita Scudder	E.7; M.9,10; J.4; Z.9	20	RAC
Aeshna interrupta Walker	A.5; D.7; E.7,12; G.0; I.6;M.11;N.10	30	RAC
Aeshna juncea (L.)	A.5; E.7,12; F.x.3; G.0,11; I.6; M.10,11; V.9; X.9; Z.9	45	RAC
Aeshna palmata Hagen	A.9; B.5; D.7; E.7,12; G.0,11; I.6; M.10; T.14; V.9; X.9; Z.9	26	RAC
Aeshna sitchensis Hagen	E.7,12; I.6; N.10,11A.9; B.5;	24	RAC
Aeshna umbrosa Walker	E.7,12; F.x.6; G.0,11; I.6; N.9,10,11; T.9	27	RAC
Corduliidae			
Cordulia shurtleffi Scudder	M.10	1	RAC
Somatochlora albicincta (Burm.)	A.5; D.7; G.0,11; I.6; M.10,11	47	RAC
Somatochlora semicircularis (Selys)	A.5; E.7,8; H.0; I.6; N.10	18	RAC
Libellulidae			
Leucorrhinia glacialis Hagen	D.7; M.11	2	RAC
Leucorrhinia hudsonica (Selys)	E.12; G.0; I.6;L.1; N.10	13	RAC
Leucorrhinia proxima Calvert	M.11	1	RAC
Libellula quadrimaculata L.	A.5; D.7; E.12; I.6	27	RAC
Sympetrum costiferum (Hagen)	E.7; I.6	2	RAC
Sympetrum danae (Sulzer)	E.7,12; I.3,6; N.11	25	RAC
Sympetrum occidentale Bartenev	E.7; G.0; N.10	5	RAC
Sympetrum madidum (Hagen)	I.6	2	RAC
Sympetrum pallipes (Hagen)	D.7; E.7; I.6; N.10	26	RAC
Order Plecoptera (Stoneflies)			
Chloroperlidae			
Suwallia lineosa (Banks)	J.g.4	4	SC
Capniidae			
Mesocapnia sp. (prob. *oenone*)	X.9	1	SC
Leuctridae			
Despaxia augusta (Banks)	K.1; M.11; X.9,14	13	SC
Nemouridae			

Soyedina interrupta (Classen)	G.0	1	SC
Order Dictuoptera (Termites [part])			
Termopsidae			
Zootermopsis angusticollis (Hagen)	F.2,6,7	4	SC
Order Grylloptera (Long-horned Grasshoppers, Crickets)			
Raphidiophoridae (Cave Crickets)			
Pristoceuthophilus celatus (Scudder)	F.2,7; h.p.0	5	WS
Order Orthoptera (Short-horned Grasshoppers [part])			
Acrididae (Short-horned Grasshoppers)			
Melanoplus bruneri Scudder	D.7,12; F.11; V.9	11	VV
Order Psocoptera (Barklice)			
Psocidae			
Amphigerontia bifasciata (Latr.)	B.5; J.g.4	2	EM
Phylotarsidae			
Phylotarsus kwakiutl Mockford	J.g.4	1	EM
Amphipsociidae			
Polypsocus corruptus (Hagen)	B.x.5	1	EM
Order Hemiptera (True Bugs)			
Pentatomidae (Stink Bugs)			
Banasa sordida (Uhler)	F.2; X.14	2	GS
Lygaeidae (Seed Bugs)			
Ligyrocoris sylvestris (L.)	D.7; I.6	22	GS
Nysius niger Baker	D.7; I.6; Q.4	34	GS
Miridae (Plant Bugs)			
Lopidea ampla (Van D.)	B.x.5; S.5	12	GS
Lygocoris pabulinus (L.)	X.14	2	GS
Mecomma gilvipes (Stal)	B.x.5; F.z.4; W.14	10	GS
Orthops scutellatus Uhler	B.5; S.5	39	GS
Orthotylus sp.	M.11	1	GS
Trignotylus ruficornis (Geoffroy)	F.z.4,8	9	GS
Salididae (Shore Bugs)			
Saldula explanata Uhler	B.5; C.3; D.7; J.g.4	25	JP
Gerridae (Water Striders)			
Gerris notabilis D. & H.	D.7; E.7; G.0; I.6;M.10; N.10; O.10;Z.9	39	GS
Belostomatidae (Giant Water Bugs)			
Lethocerus americanus (Leidy)	D.7; I.4	10	RAC
Notonectidae (Backswimmers)			
Notonecta kirbyi Hung.	G.y.0	9	RAC
Notonecta undulata Say	E.7; I.6; N.10; Z.9	8	RAC

Corixidae (Water Boatmen)			
Callicorixa alaskensis Hung.	G.0; M.10; N.10; X.14; Z.9	63	AJ
Cenocorixa andersoni Hung.	D.7; Z.9	5	AJ
Hesperocorixa vulgaris (Hung.)	I.6	7	AJ
Sigara omani (Hung.)	D.7; E.7; I.6; M.10; N.11; N.y.10	27	AJ
Sigara sp.	M.y.10	1	AJ
Cercopidae (Spittle Bugs)			
Aphrophora fulva Doer	I.6; Q.4; V.i.9	7	KH
Aphrophora princeps Walley	F.11; Q.4	3	KH
Neophilaenus lineatus (L.)	D.7; M.11; Q.4	5	KH
Philaenus spumarius (L.)	B.5; F.2; H.0;M.11; Q.4; S.5	30	KH
Cicadellidae (Leafhoppers)			
Aphrodes bicinctus (Schr.)	F.b.2	5	KH
Aphrodes costatus (Pzr.)	F.p:c.11	2	KH
Balclutha neglecta (DeL. & Dav.)	F.p:b.2	1	KH
Bathysmatophorus oregonensis (Bak.)	H.0; I.6; X.14	5	KH
Deltocephala n. sp.	V.14	2	KH
Draeculacephala crassicornis Van D.	D.7; I.6; M.11; Q.4	14	KH
Elymana inornata (Van D.)	F.z.8; Q.4	9	KH
Evacanthus grandipes Hamilton	B.5; F.4; W.14; X.9,14	20	KH
Idiocerus couleanus Ball & Pkr.	Q.4	1	KH
Macrosteles fieberi (Edw.)	D.7; Q.4	8	KH
Macrosteles lineatifrons (Stal)	G.0	1	KH
Oncopsis crispae Hamilton	F.z.4; M.11	3	KH
Ophiola angustata Osb.	D.7; I.6;M.11; Q.4	15	KH
Stenocranus sp.	--	3	KH
Paraphlepsius apertus (Van D.)	D.7; I.6; Q.4	9	KH
Xestocephalus fulvocapitatus Van D.	Y.p.12	6	KH
Delphacidae (Planthoppers)			
Delphacodes sp.	B.5; G.0; H.0; Q.4; X.9,14	21	KH
Unidentified Hemiptera		15	
<u>Order Neuroptera (Lacewings, etc.)</u>			
Hemerobiidae (Brown Lacewings)			
Hemerobius ovalis Carpenter	F.2	1	JK
Hemerobius pacificus Banks	F.0,2	2	JK
<u>Order Coleoptera (Beetles)</u>			
Cicindelidae (Tiger Beetles)			
Cicindela oregona LeC.	F.8,13,14; J.4	6	WL
Carabidae (Ground Beetles)			
Agonum ferruginosum Dej.	F.z.4	1	GB
Bembidion fortestriatum Mots.	D.7; Q.4	11	GB
Bembidion zephyrum Fall	J.e.4	24	GB
Dyschirius obesus LeC.	F.0,2,3; J.4	26	GB

Nebria diversa LeC.	F.b,n.2,3,5,7,8,9,11,13; J.20,22,23	116	GB
Nebria kincaidi Sz.	X.p.14	1	WL
Notiophilus sylvaticus Esch.	V.9	2	WL
Pterostichus algidus LeC.	F.p:d,q,u.3,7,9,11,12,13	40	GB
Pterostichus crenicollis LeC.	F.5; J.22	2	WL
Pterostichus lama Men.	J.20	1	WL
Scaphinotus angusticollis (Mann.)	F.8,9,12,13; X.p.14	8	WL
Scaphinotus marginatus Fisch	H.p.11	1	GB
Zacotus matthewsi LeC.	F.p.9	2	WL
Dytiscidae (Predaceous Diving Beetles)			
Acilius sp. c.f. *semisulcatus* Aube	D.7; G.0	2	RR
Agabus tristis Aube	T.9	6	RR
Dytiscus dauricus Gebler	E.22; P.13	2	RR
Hydroporus mannerheimi J.B.-B.	R.15	3	RR
Ilybius quadrimaculatus Aube	G.0; G.y.0; M.10; N.11; RR.15	24	RR
Rhantus binotatus (Harris)	B.5	6	RR
Rhantus suturellus (Harris)	D.7; N.11; O.10	4	RR
Gyrinidae (Whirligig Beetles)			
Gyrinus sp.	M.10;Z.9	2	RR
Hydrophilidae (Water Scavenger Beetles)			
Cercyon adumbratus Mannh.	F.p:w.5,8	10	JMC/LL
Silphidae (Carrion Beetles)			
Nicrophorus defodiens Mann.	F.7,8	7	RA
Leiodidae (Round Fungus Beetles)			
Catops sp.	F.7	1	WL
Scydmaenidae (Antlike Stone Beetles)			
Stenichnus pacificus Casey	F.p:u.7	2	JMC
Scydmaenus sp.	F.p:q.7	1	JMC
Staphylinidae (Rove Beetles)			
Atheta sp.	F.p:c,w.2,5,8,13; H.p.11	14	JMC
Autalia sp.	B.5; F.p:q,w.2,5,13	30	JMC
Bledius sp.	J.4; Q.4	6	JMC
Bryoporus rubescens (Hatch)	F.p:c.13	1	JMC
Cafius canescens Makl.	F.b,n.2,3; J.4	30	JMC
Cafius nudus johnsoni Fall	F.n.2	1	JMC
Cafius seminitens Horn	F.n.2	1	JMC
Lathrobium sp. A.	N.10	1	JMC
Lathrobium sp. B.	F.w.14	3	JMC
Mycetoporus sp.	H.p.11	1	JMC
Omalium sp.	V.14	1	JMC
Oxytelus fuscipennis Mannh.	F.8	2	JMC
Philonthus siegwaldi Mannh.	F.p:w.5	7	JMC
Proteinus sp.	F.p:q.7	1	JMC

Quedius frater Smetana	X.14	1	JMC
Stenus pterobrachys Gemm. & Har.	F.14	1	AS
Stenus sp.	D.7; G.0; Q.4	4	JMC
Tachinus basalis Er.	F.p:w.2,5	5	JMC
Thinopinus pictus LeC.	F.n.3,4	17	JMC
Trigonurus dilaticollis Van D.	F.p:u.7	1	SC
Unamis sp. (possibly *fulvipes* Fall)	X.14	1	JMC
Aleocharinae	F.p:w.13	1	JMC
Staphylinidae unidentified		71	
Pselaphidae (Short-winged Mold Beetles)			
Oropus striatus (LeC.)	F.p:q.7	1	JMC
Foveoscapha terracola P. & W.	X.14	1	DC
Ptiliidae (Feather-winged Beetles)			
Ptenidium sp. (poss. *pullum* Makl.)	W.14	3	JMC
Histeridae (Hister Beetles)			
Hypocaccus bigemmeus (LeC.)	F.p:b,2,3,7; H.p.11; J.e.4	7	JMC
Lampyridae (Firefly Beetles)			
Ellychnia hatchi Fender	J.20	1	JMC
Cantharidae (Soldier Beetles)			
Podabrus sp. A.	B.5	2	JMC
Podabrus sp. B.	U.1	1	JMC
Cephaloidae (False Longhorn Beetles)			JMC
Cephaloon bicolor Horn	B.5; F.3,14	3	
			JMC
Oedemeridae (False Blister Beetles)			
Ditylus quadricollis (LeC.)	F.p:u.7; Q.4	2	JMC
Pyrochroidae (Fire-colored Beetles)			
Dendroides ephemeroides (Mann.)	F.a.6	1	JMC
Elateridae (Click Beetles)			
Athous rufiventris rufiventris (Esch.)	F.a,n,x,w.3,4,6,11; J.4; X.14	7	EB
Athous nigropilis Mots.	F.a.7	1	EB
Ctenicera suckleyi suckleyi (LeC.)	H.p.11	1	EB
Hemicrepidius morio (LeC.)	F.13	1	EB
Megapenthes stigmosus (LeC.)	B.5	3	WL
Negastrius dispersus (Horn)	H.p.11	5	EB
Negastrius sp.	H.p.11	1	EB
Helodidae (Marsh Beetles)			
Cyphon variabilis (Thunb.)	D.7; I.6	4	JMC
Byrrhidae (Pill Beetles)			
Lioligus nitidus Mots.	F.w.14	1	JMC

BROOKS PENINSULA

Nitidulidae (Sap Beetles)			
Epuraea sp.	F.2,3	4	JMC
Colydiidae (Cylindrical Bark Beetles)			
Namunaria pacifica Horn	F.3	1	WL
Coccinellidae (Ladybird Beetles)			
Coccinella johnsoni Casey	F.h.2,F.11; S.5	3	JMc
Coccinella trifasciata perplexa Muls.	S.5	1	JMc
Tenebrionidae (Darkling Beetles)			
Coelus ciliatus Esch.	F.2	4	WL
Phaleromela globosa (LeC.)	F.2,3,7,13	4	JMC
Zopheridae (Ironclad Beetles)			
Usechimorpha barberi Blaisdel	F7	1	WL
Melandryidae (False Darkling Beetles)			
Anaspis sp.	X.9	1	WL
Prothalpia holmbergi Mann.	F.a.6	1	LL
Scarabaeidae (Scarab Beetles)			
Aegialia blanchardi Horn	F.2	1	JC
Aphodius aleutes Esch.	F.8; H.0	2	JC
Polyphylla crinita LeC. (sensu lato)	F.1,6	2	JC
Cerambycidae (Long-horned Beetles)			
Lepturopsis dolorosa (LeC.)	B.5; J.4	2	JMc
Plectrura spinicauda Mann.	F.28.viii.79 (J. Van Velzen)	1	SC
Chrysomelidae (Leaf Beetles)			
Altica sp.	I.6	1	WL
Donacia hirticollis Kirby	D.7	1	IA
Plateumaris neomexicana (Schaeffer)	D.7	1	IA
Syneta hamata Horn	F.b.2	1	LL
Curculionidae (Weevils)			
Ellasoptes marinus Horn	F.2	24	WL
Geoderces horni (Van Dyke)	F.p:w.12	1	RA
Lepesoma bakeri (Van Dyke)	F.p:q.12; J.23	2	RA
Lepidophorus inguinatus (Mann.)	X.9	1	RA
Steremnius carinatus (Boh.)	F.p:w.5	1	DB
Sthereus quadrituberculatus Mots.	Q.4	1	DB
Trigonoscuta pilosa Mots.	J.20	1	DB
Scolytidae (Bark Beetles)			
Dolurgus pumilus (Mann.)	F.8	1	DB
Gnathotrichus sulcatus Blkm.	F.2,3	4	DB
Hylurgops rugipennis (Mann.)	F.3	2	DB
Pseudohylesinus sericeus (Mann.)	F.a.2,3,7	6	DB
Trypodendron lineatum (Oliv.)	F.2	1	DB

<u>Order Diptera (Flies)</u>			
Tipulidae (Crane Flies)			
Limonia (L.) *bestigma* (Coq.)	F.a.7,12	4	BC
Limonia (*Dicranomyia*) sp.	F.a.2	1	BC
Limnophila (*Prionolabis*) sp. nr. *rufibasis*	B.5; X.p:l.14	2	BC
Limnophila sp.	G.p.11; H.p.11; U.v.14; X.p:l.14	6	HT/BC
Molophilus (M.) *oligocanthus* Alex.	F.2; H.p.0,11; X.l.14	10	BC
Molophilus sp.	F.2; V.p.14; U.v.14	9	HT/BC
Ormonia sp.	F.p:u.13; H.p.11	4	BC
Pedicia (Tricyphona) tacoma Alex.	--	1	HT/BC
Pedicia sp.	F.7; U.v.14	2	HT/BC
Tipula (*Trichotipula*) *macrophallus* (Dietz)	F.a.12	2	BC
Tipula sp.	F.a.0,7,12	5	BC
Bibionidae (March Flies)			
Bibio sp.	F.0,2,3,6,13	17	BP
Anisopodidae (Wood Gnats)			
Mycetobia divergens Walker	F.a.6	1	BP
Mycetophilidae (Fungus Gnats)			
Anaclileia sp.	F.p:w.5	1	JV
Cordyla sp.	F.p:w.2	1	JV
Macrocera sp.	H.p.0	1	JV
Mycetophila sp.	H.p.0	1	JV
Neuratelia sp.	F.p:u,w.5,11; H.p.11	4	JV
Orfelia sp.	F.p:c.13	1	JV
Sciaridae (Dark-winged Fungus Gnats)			
Bradysia sp.	F.p:u,w.2,11; H.p.11; V.p.14; X.p:l.14	7	JV
Schwenkfeldina sp.	F.a,p:u.0,2,6,7,11,12,13; H.p.11	42	JV
Cecidomyiidae (Gall Midges)			
Stomatosema sp.	H.p.11	2	AB
Tribe Oligotrophini	V.p.14	1	AB
Cecidomyiinae	H.p.11	5	AB
Chaoboridae (Phantom Midges)			
Chaoborus trivittatus (Loew)	M.y.10	1	AB
Culicidae (Mosquitoes)			
Aedes aboriginis Dyar	F.a.2	1	DW
Culiseta incidens (Thomson)	F.a.2	2	DW
Culiseta minnesotae Barr	F.a.2	1	DW
Simuliidae (Black Flies)			
Prosimulium dicum D. & S.	G.0	1	DW
Prosimulium sp.	H.0	1	BP
Simulium venustum Say	G.0; H.0	2	BP

BROOKS PENINSULA

Simulium venustum complex	G.0	2	DW
Ceratopogonidae (No-see-ums)			
Culicoides sp.	F.2	18	LF
Forcipomyia macswaini Wirth	F.p:w.5	2	LF
Palpomyia sp.	F.a,p:w.2,6,7	7	LF
Chironomidae (Midges)			
Chironomus (C.) "*plumosus*" group	B.5	12	MR
Dicrotendipes modestus (Say)	G.p.0	1	MR
Limnophyes sp. A	T.v.14; X.m.14	19	DO
Limnophyes sp. B	F.s.14	5	DO
Metriocnemus fuscipes (Meigen)	F.s.14	1	DO
Micropsectra sp.	G.y.0	1	MR
Natarsia miripes (Coq.)	F.p.6	1	MR
Parametriocnemus sp.	F.2	1	DO
Paraphaenocladius sp.	T.v.14; X.m.14	20	DO
Polypedilum sp.	F.p.2	1	MR
Procladius sp.	G.y.0	1	MR
Procladius (*Psilotanypus*) sp.	D.7	1	MR
Psectrocladius (*Allopsectrocladius*) sp.	I.6	1	DO
Smittia group, near *Parasmittia*	W.r.14	22	DO
Orthocladiinae, genus unknown	G.y.0	1	DO
Tabanidae (Horse and Deer Flies)			
Atylotus tingaureus (Philip)	B.5; D.7; F.14; I.6; J.4; M.11; S.5	43	HT
Chrysops excitans Walk.	D.7; F.0; I.6; J.4; L.1; N.10	20	HT
Chrysops noctifer O.S.	D.7; G.0; L.1; N.10	5	HT
Chrysops proclivis O.S.	F.8,14; H.0; S.5	8	HT
Hybomitra captonis (Marten)	F.8	1	HT
Hybomitra sequax (Will.)	X.9	1	HT
Hybomitra sonomensis (O.S.)	D.7; F.0,2,3,8; I.6; J.4;	21	HT
Sylvius gigantulus (Loew)	L.1; M.10,11; X.9	3	HT
	I.6		
Rhagionidae (Snipe Flies)			
Rhagio californicus Leonard	F.p:q,u.7,11	1	HT
Rhagio dimidiata Loew	B.z.5; G.0; H.0; N.10; W.14; X.9	16	
Rhagio incisus (Loew)	X.p:l.14	2	HT
Rhagio sp.	T.v.14	2	HT
Symphoromyia (*Ochleromyia*) sp. 1	D.7; F.3,8; X.9	7	HT
Symphoromyia (*Ochleromyia*) sp. 2	F.3; X.9	3	HT
Symphoromyia sp.	H.p.0	1	HT
Stratiomyidae (Soldier Flies)			
Stratiomys barbata Loew	D.7,12	2	HT
Therevidae (Stilletto Flies)			
Thereva brunnea Cole	F.b.2,7,8,13	22	HT

Asilidae (Robber Flies)			
Lasiopogon n. sp. near *willametti*	F.b.2	3	RAC
Bombyliidae (Bee Flies)			
Villa lateralis (Say)	D.7,8,12; I.6	9	BC
Empididae (Dance Flies)			
Anthalia stigmalis Coq.	H.p.0	2	HT
Bicellaria sp.	X.14	2	HT
Brochella monticola Melander	F.3	1	HT
Chersodromia parallela Mel.	F.p:u.13; H.0	18	HT
Empis sp.	H.p.0; X.14	3	HT
Hilara sp.	F.b.2; H.p.0	8	HT
Microphorus atratus Coq.	H.0; V.9	3	HT
Oedalea lanceolata Mel.	F.3	1	HT
Parathalassius aldrichi Mel.	F.p:u.2,5,7,13; H.p.0	22	HT
Platypalpus sp.	B.5; F.8; X.9,14	4	HT
Rhamphomyia sp.	F.b.2; G.0; H.0; X.9	7	HT
Tachydromia sp. (probably new)	H.0	1	HT
Empidinae New Genus	F.p:u	1	HT
Empididae sp.	F.p:u.7	1	HT
Dolichopodidae (Long-legged Flies)			
Achalcus utahensis H. & M.	B.5	1	BB
Argyra albiventris Loew	F.2,4	1	JV
Argyra sp.	B.z.5	1	JV
Chrysotus sp.	D.8; G.0,11; J.4; V.p.14	13	JV
Dolichopus convergens Aldrich	G.0; V.9,14	11	JV
Dolichopus hastatus Loew	G.0; V.9	2	JV
Dolichopus monticola Van Duzee	G.0	2	JV
Dolichopus plumipes Scop.	B.z.5	2	JV
Dolichopus xanthocnemus Loew	B.z.5; F.z.8	2	JV
Dolichopus sp.	G.0; V.9; X.p:l.14	3	JV
Gymnopternus sp. A (males)	G.0	6	JV
Gymnopternus sp. B (males)	B.5; H.0	5	JV
Gymnopternus spp. (females)	B.5; F.2,4,8,12; G.0; H.0; I.6; J.4; W.14; X.14	29	JV
Hydrophorus chrysologus (Walker)	D.8	2	JV
Sympycnus sp.	F.z.8; Q.4	2	JV
Syntormon sp.	D.7	2	JV
Tachytrechus sanus O.S.	J.4	2	JV
Phoridae (Humpbacked Flies)			
Megaselia spp.	F.p:w.2,5; H.0; X.14	12	JV/BP
Syrphidae (Hover Flies)			
Blera scitula Will.	B.5; F.b.8; H.0; S.5	7	JV
Cheilosia hoodiana Bigot	B.5	7	JV
Cheilosia sp.	F.b.8	1	JV
Cynorhinella bella (Will.)	H.p.0	1	JV

Melangyna lasiophthalma Zett.	F.27.viii.1979 (J. van Velzen)	4	JV
Meliscaeva cinctella Zett.	F.b.3; F.28	2	JV
Parasyrphus sp. (new? - "cannot	B.5; F.2,8	3	JV
recognize")			JV
Platycheirus sp.	V.9	1	
Scaeva pyrastri L.	Q.4	1	JV
Sericomyia chalcopyga Loew	B.5; G.0; H.0	7	JV
Syrphus torvus O.S.	H.0	1	JV
			JV
Tephritidae (Fruit Flies)			
Paroxyna sp., possibly *americana* Her.	D.7; V.9	2	JFMcA
Paroxyna sp.	M.11; Q.4	2	JFMcA
Tephritis sp.	F.h.2	1	JFMcA
Coelopidae (Seaweed Flies)			
Coelopa nebularum Aldr.	B.5; W.14	3	JV
Dryomyzidae (Dryomyzid Flies)			
Dryomyza anilis Fall.	F.27.viii.1979 (J. van Velzen); F.2,3	8	BC
Helcomyza mirabilis Mel.	J.4	5	JV
Sciomyzidae (Marsh Flies)			
Limnia inopa (Adams)	H.0; X.9	2	BC
Chamaemyidae (Aphid Flies)			
Chamaemyia sp.	F.u,w.2,8; H.0; I.6; J.4; M.11; V.9	11	JFMcA
Piophilidae (Skipper Flies)			
Liopiophila varipes (Meigen)	F.3	12	JFMcA
Parapiophila vulgaris (Fall.)	F.3	2	JFMcA
Sphaeroceridae (Small Dung Flies)			
Aptilotus borealis Mall.	B.x.5	1	HT
Aptilotus sp.	F.p:q,w.5,7	2	HT
Copromyza maculipennis (Spuler)	X.p:l.14	2	HT
Minilimosina sp.	F.p:w.5	1	HT
Thoracochaeta brachystoma (Stenh.)	J.4	1	HT
Thoracochaeta teskeyi Marshall	F.p:u.7	1	SMa
Ephydridae (Shore Flies)			
Hydrellia griseola (Fall.)	W.14	4	BC
Limnellia sejuncta (Loew)	W.14	1	BC
Lytogaster gravida (Loew)	B.5	1	BC
Scatella setosa (Coq.)	Q.4	6	BC
Scatella stagnalis (Fall.)	Q.4	13	BC
Drosophilidae (Small Fruit Flies)			
Scaptomyza sp.	W.14	1	JFMcA

Chloropidae (Chloropid Flies)			
Chlorops sp.	D.7; G.0; I.6; Q.4; V.9	5	BP
Elachiptera sp.	F.b.2	1	BP
Oscinella sp.	W.14	1	BP
Tricimba brunnicollis (Becker)	W.14	26	BP
Agromyzidae (Leaf-miner Flies)			
Chromatomyia niger (Meigen)	W.14	1	BC
Melanagromyza sp. near *buccalis*	F.z.4,8	3	BC
Melanagromyza sp.	F.z.4	1	BC
Acartophthalmidae (Acartophthalmid Flies)			
Acartophthalmus nigrinus (Zett.)	F.p:w.2,5; H.p.0	8	JFMcA
Heleomyzidae (Heleomyzid Flies)			
Anorostoma alternans Garrett	F.p:u.2,5; H.p.0	8	JV
Borboropsis sp. (*fulviceps*) [Strobl]?)	F.p:w.5	1	JFMcA
Borboropsis puberula (Zett.)	F.p:w.5; H.p.0	2	JV
Neoleria inscripta (Meigen)	F.3	10	BP
Suilla nemorum (Meigen)	F.a.6	1	BP
Tephlochlamys rufiventris (Meigen)	F.3	1	BP
Anthomyzidae (Anthomyzid Flies)			
Anthomyza sp.	F.b.2	1	JV
Scathophagidae (Dung Flies)			
Megaphthalma pallida Fall.	F.p:q.7,9,12	12	JV
Scathophaga furcata Say	H.p.0; V.9	2	JV
Scathophaga intermedia Walker	F.z.4	1	JV
Anthomyiidae (Anthomyiid Flies)			
Acrostilpna sp. near *collini*	I.6	1	JFMcA
Delia setiventris complex	H.0	1	JFMcA
Fucellia aestum Aldrich	F.b.9	1	JFMcA
Fucellia fucorum (Fall.)	F.n.2; J.4	2	JFMcA
Fucellia rufitibia Stein	F.n.2	1	JFMcA
Fucellia separata Stein	F.n.2; J.4	6	JFMcA
Hylemya alcathoe (Walker)	F.a,b.2,5,6	5	JFMcA
Paregle sp. (possibly new)	H.0	1	JFMcA
Pegohylemyia sp.	H.0	2	JFMcA
Pegomya sp.	F.p:w.2; H.p.0	2	JFMcA
Muscidae (Muscid Flies)			
Coenosia impunctata Mall.	G.0; H.0; W.14	4	HW
Coenosia johnsoni Mall.	F.b.2; J.4	2	HW
Coenosia sp.	G.0	1	HW
Fannia abrupta Mall.	F.p:c.11	1	HW
Fannia aethiops Mall.	F.p:c.13	1	HW
Fannia glaucescens (Zett.)	F.3	2	HW
Fannia sp.	F.p:w.2; H.p.0	2	HW
Helina bicolorata (Mall.)	F.b.2	1	HW
Helina troene (Walker)	F.b.2	1	HW

Helina sp.	B.z.5	1	HW
Hydrotaea houghi Mall.	F.b,2,3	4	HW
Limosia incisurata Van der Wulp	H.p:31	2	HW
Limosia johnsoni Mall.	--	1	HW
Mydaea obscurella Mall.	F.p:q.7	1	HW
Mydaea sp.	F.p:q.12	1	HW
Schoenomyza chrysostoma Loew	G.0	1	HW
Schoenomyza dorsalis Loew	G.0; I.6	3	HW
Schoenomyza lispina Thom.	B.z.5; F.z.4,8	19	HW
Schoenomyza sp.	G.0	1	HW
Spilogona magnipunctata (Mall.)	H.p.0	1	HW
Spilogona semiglobosa (Ringdahl)	F.4	1	HW
Spilogona sospita Huck.	F.b.2	1	HW
Spilogona sp.	F.b.9	1	HW
Calliphoridae (Blow Flies)			
Calliphora terraenovae Macq.	F.3	1	BC
Calliphora vomitoria (L.)	F.3	8	BC
Cynomya cadaverina (Rob.-D.)	W.14	6	BC
Eucalliphora lilaea (authors, not Walk.)	F.b.2; H.p.0	2	BC
Lucilia illustris (Meigen)	F.3	39	BC
Tachinidae (Tachnid Flies)			
Admontia sp.	J.4	1	DW
Arctophyto borealis (Coq.)	F.8,14	2	DW
Athrycia cinerea (Coq.)	F.b.8	1	DW
Lasioneura bicolor (Curran)	F.h.2	1	DW
Mericia bicarina (Toth.)	D.7	1	DW
Phasia aenoventris (Will.)	B.z.5; F.b.2	4	DW
Phasia splendida (Coq.)	F.b.2	1	DW
Slossonaemyia angulicornis (Curran)	H.p.0	4	DW
Strongygaster triangulifer (Loew)	F.h.2	1	DW
<u>Order Lepidoptera (Butterflies and Moths)</u>			
Papilionidae (Swallowtail Butterflies)			
Papilio zelicaon Lucas	F.5	1	SC
Lycaenidae (Blues and Coppers)			
Epidemia mariposa (Reakirt)	I.6; Q.4	5	CS
Nymphalidae (Brush-footed Butterflies)			
Limenitis lorquini Boisduval	I.6	1	RAC
Noctuidae (Cutworm Moths)			
Apamea maxima Dyar	F.4	1	ER
Dargidia procincta Grt.	F.b.2	1	KN
Oligia indirecta Grt.	F.2	2	ER
Rhynchagrotis exsertistigma Morn.	F.2	1	ER
Geometridae (Geometer Moths)			
Ceratodalia queneata Pack.	F.2	1	KB
Dysstroma sobria Swett.	F.3	1	KB

Enypia venata Grt.	F.2	3	KB
Neoalcis californiaria Pack.	F.2,3,7	3	KB
Perizoma grandis Hist.	F.2,7	7	KB
Gelechiidae (Gelechiid Moths)			
Specimen too poor to name	H.p.0	2	AM/PD
Cochylidae (Webworms)			
Hysterosia sp.??	V.9	1	PD
Tortricidae (Tortricid Moths)			
Olethreutinae, unidentifiable female	H.0	1	PD
Epinotia nanana (Tr.)	H.0	1	PD
Epinotia solandriana (L.)	F.7	1	PD
Pandemis heparana (D. & S.)	F.3	1	AM
Psychidae (Bagworms)			
Psyche sp.	--	1	PD
<u>Order Trichoptera (Caddisflies)</u>			
Leptoceridae			
Oecetis inconspicua (Walker)			
Limnephilidae	M.10	1	GW
Halesochila taylori (Banks)	G.0; T.14	12	GW
Homophylax andax Ross	F.a.2,6,7	3	GW
Lenarchus vastus	F.a.6; M.10	2	GW
Limnephilus sp.	G.0	3	GW
Phryganeidae			
Ptilostomis ocellifera (Walker)	G.0	2	GW
Polycentropodidae			
Polycentropus flavus (Banks)	J.g.4; M.10	2	GW
Rhyacophilidae			
Rhyacophila grandis Banks	F.a.6	1	GW
Rhyacophila oreta Banks	J.4	4	GW
<u>Order Hymenoptera (Bees, Wasps, Ants)</u>			
Tenthredinidae (Common Sawflies)			
Pachynematus sp.	F.z.4	1	HG
Tenthredo sp. nr. *semirufa*	G.0; R.16	3	HG
Braconidae (Braconid Wasps)			
Rogas sp.	X.14	1	WM
Coelinidea sp.	G.0	4	WM
Dacnusa sp.	J.4	1	WM
Aphaereta n. sp.	B.x.5	5	WM
Glyptapanteles sp.	X.9	1	WM
Microgaster sp.	I.6; M.11	4	WM
Pholetesor glacialis (Ashmead)			
Aphidiidae (Aphidiid Wasps)			
Ephedrus sp.	W.14	4	WM
Praon sp.	F.z.8	1	WM

Ichneumonidae (Ichneumon Wasps)			
Netelia sp.	F.a.7	1	JB
Tryphon sp.	F.z.4	1	JB
Gelis sp.	F.a.2,6; H.31	3	JB
Phygadenon sp.	F.b.p:u.2,7	2	JB
Cubocephalus sp.	V.9	1	JB
Stenichneumon sp.	D.8; V.14	2	JB
Lissonota parva (Cresson)	Q.4	1	JB
Lissonota rasilis Townes	J.j.4	1	JB
Diadegma sp.	F.u.13	1	JB
Cremastinae gen.	X.p:l.14	1	JB
Homotropus sp.	X.9	1	JB
Orthocentrus sp.	F.p:w.5	1	JB
Stenomacrus sp.	F.b.2; X.14	2	JB
Pteromalidae (Pteromalid Wasps)			
Chlorocytus sp.	B.x.5; W.14	2	CY
Seladerma sp.	W.14	7	CY
Skeltoceras sp.	W.14	1	CY
Stictomischus sp.	W.14	1	CY
Eurytomidae (Seed Chalcids)			
Eurytoma sp.	F.b.2; Q.4	2	JW
Thysanidae (Thysanid Wasps)			
Chartoceras elongatus (Girault)	F.p.3	1	CY
Eulophidae (Eulophid Wasps)			
Pediobus sp.	B.x.5	1	JW
Alloxystidae (Alloxystid Wasps)			
Alloxysta sp. (*bicolor* [Baker]?)	X.p:l.14	1	CY
Diapriidae (Diapriid Wasps)			
Acropiesta sp.	X.9	1	LM
Belyta longicollis Fouts	F.p:w.2,3,5	4	LM
Belyta sp.	B.z.5; F.p:w.5; S.5	3	LM
Scelionidae (Scelionid Wasps)			
Trimorus sp.	F.p:q.7	3	LM
Platygastridae (Platygastrid Wasps)			
Platygaster sp.	H.0	1	LM
Formicidae (Ants)			
Camponotus sp.	G.0	1	RAC
Formica neorufibarbis Emery	F.b.2,11; H.0; J.4; V.9	6	AF
Formica pacifica Francoeur	B.5	1	AF
Formica subaenescens Emery	F.b.2	1	AF
Lasius pallitarsus (Prov.)	F.d,u.2,7,9,13; G.0; J.4; X.9	17	AF

Leptothorax muscorum Nylander	V.9	1	AF
Myrmica incompleta Prov.	I.6; Q.4	6	AF
Vespidae (Paper Wasps)			
Vespula (*Dolichovespula*) *arenaria* (Fab.)	F.2,11; J.4	5	LM
Pompilidae (Spider Wasps)			
Anoplius ventralis tarsatus Banks	D.7	1	HG
Pemphredonidae (Pemphredonid Wasps)			
Mimesa sp.	F.2,8	3	LM
Crabronidae (Crabronid Wasps)			
Ectemnius sp.	B.z.5;S.5	2	LM
Oxybelus sp.	F.b,h.2,9,13,14	19	LM
Apidae (Bumblebees [part])			
Bombus mixtus Cresson	B.5; F.2,8; H.0;J .j.4; M.5; S.5; V.9	16	BJ
Bombus terricola occidentalis Greene	H.0	1	BJ
Psithyrus fernaldae Franklin	B.5;F.8;H.0	5	BJ
Class Chilopoda (Centipedes)			
Order Scolependromorpha			
Cryptopidae			
Scolopocryptops sexspinosus (Say)	F.p: c,w	--	RCr
Order Geophilomorpha			
Sp. A.	X.I.9	1	RCr
Sp. B.	H.p.11	1	RCr
Order Lithobiomorpha			
Ethopolidae			
Ethopolys sierravabus (Chamberlin)	V.p.14	1	RCr
Ethopolys sp. nr. *spectans*	F.t.12,13	1	RCr
Lithobiidae			
Simobius ginampus (Chamberlin)	H.p.11	2	RCr
Lithobiidae, unidentified	X.I.9	1	RCr
Class Diplopoda (Millipedes)			
Nearctodesmidae			
Nearctodesmus insulans Chamberlin	F.p:c.7	1	RCr
Nearctodesmus sp. (*insulans* or *cochlearis* Causey)	C.3	1	RCr
Parajulidae			
Parajulidae sp.	F.7,9; X.14	5	RCr

Appendix 10.2 Arthropod associations on Brooks Peninsula

Vegetation types and associated habitats are:

A Shoreline forest
B Mountain slope forest
C Bog scrubforest
D Timberline scrubforest
E Shoreline forest and beach shrub
F Bog shrub and bog herbaceous
G Intertidal sand/seaweed
H Beach herbaceous
I Salt marsh
J Supra-tidal freshwater pools
K Herbaceous aquatic--bog ponds
L Herbaceous aquatic--lake margins
M Streams
N Shore headlands
O Cliff
P Windblown ridge herb
Q Solander Island

Additional information coded after species name:

W	=	widespread
WF	=	widespread, forest
WO	=	widespread, open areas
WT	=	widespread, timberline
WW	=	widespread, wet areas
I	=	introduced

	A	B	C	D	E	F	G	H	I	J	K	L	M	N	O	P	Q
Pseudoscorpions																	
Apochthonius n.sp.	X																
Microcreagris n.sp.	X																
Spiders																	
Cryphoeca peckhami Simon				X													
Cybaeus morosus Simon								X									
Cybaeus reticulatus Simon (WF)		X			X												
Cybaeus sp.	X	X				X			X	X							
Dirksia cinctipes (Banks)	X																
Agelenidae sp.																	X
Antrodiaetus pacificus (Simon) (WF)	X				X												
Araneus trifolium (Hentz)						X											
Araneus sp.		X															
Metallina curtisi (McCook) (W)		X						X									
Clubiona trivialis C.L. Koch (WT)				X												X	
Clubiona sp.																	X
Micaria sp.				X													
Ceratinops inflatus (Emerton)	X																
Scotinotylus sp.				X													
Tapinocyba sp.																	X
Zygottus corvallis Chamb.	X																
Bathyphantes alascensis (Banks)	X	X															
Bathyphantes keeni (Emerton)																	
Lepthyphantes alaskanus (Banks)				X													

	A	B	C	D	E	F	G	H	I	J	K	L	M	N	O	P	Q
Lepthyphantes tenuis (Blackwall) (I)	X																
Lepthyphantes sp. poss. *zellata* Zorsch	X			X													
Meioneta sp.		X															
Pityohyphantes sp.	X			X													
Pardosa dorsuncata L. & D. (W)						X										X	
Pardosa metlakatla Em. (WO)						X											
Pirata piraticus (Clerek)																X	
Trochosa terricola Thorell		X															
Microlinyphia dana C. & I.				X													
Tachygyna vancouveri C. & I.																	
Philodromus rufus pacificus Banks				X													X
Philodromus sp.						X											
Tibellus oblongus Walck.						X											
Evarcha hoyi (Peckh. & Peckh.)						X											
Tetragnatha sp. prob. *extensa* L.				X					X	X							
Tetragnatha laboriosa Hentz (W)		X		X													
Robertus vigerens (C. & I.)								X									
Theridion agrifoliae Levi																	
Theridion sexpunctatum Emerton	X																
Xysticus montanensis Keys				X		X											
Xysticus pretiosus G. (W)				X	X	X		X									
Harvestmen																	
Sabacon occidentalis (Banks) (WF)	X			X													
Leiobonum paessleri Roewer (WF)	X	X															
Leuronychus parvulus Banks				X													
Mites																	
Polyaspinus sp. A.	X																X
Trachytes sp. B (WF)	X	X															
Trachytes sp. C (WF)		X															
Trachytes sp. E		X															
Trachytes sp. G	X																
Urodiaspis sp. A (W)	X																X
New genus nr. *Urodiaspis*	X																
New genus nr. *Uroobovella*	X																X
Heminothrus longisetosus Willman		X															
Heminothrus thori (Berlese)		X															
Platynothrus peltifer (C.L. Koch)	X																
Sphodrocepheus anthelionus W. & H.	X																X
Melanozetes interruptus Willman	X																
Belba californica (Banks)	X																

	A	B	C	D	E	F	G	H	I	J	K	L	M	N	O	P	Q
Epidamaeus sp.	X																
Epilohmannia n.sp.																	
Protoribates sp.																	X
Hermannia gibba (C.L. Koch)	X																
Hypochthonius rufulus C.L. Koch																	X
Dorycranosus acutidens Aoki																	X
Liacarus bidentatus Ewing (WF)	X	X															
Rhaphidosus sp. nr. *bacillatus* Fry & A.	X																
Megeremaeus sp. nr. *montanus* W. & H.	X																
Ceratoppia sp. nr. *bipilis* (Hermann)	X																
Ceratoppia n. sp																	
Mycobates sarekensis Tragardh																X	X
Nothrus silvestris Nicolet (W)		X															
Oribatula tibialis Nicolet																X	
Eupelops sp.																X	
Tenuialoides sp. nr. *medialis* W. & H.		X															
Bdella sp.																X	
Bdellodes sp.	X																
Balastium sp.								X									
Limnochares sp. nr. *americana* Lundb.												X					
Limnochares sp.											X						
Piona sp.												X					
Allothrobium sp.	X																
Other mites unidentified owing to time and technical restraints																	
Isopods																	
Asellus tomalensis Harford										X							
Exoshphaeroma oregonensis Dana							X		X								
Ligia pallasii Brandt														X			
Ligidium gracile Dana (W)	X	X		X	X											X	X
Porcellio scaber Latreille (W)								X									X
Amphipods																	
Eogammarus convervicolus (Stimpson)										X							
Crangonix sp. (*richmondensis*?)													X				
Orchestoidea californiana Brandt							X										
Springtails																	
Pseudochorates sp.																	X
Lephognathella choreutes Borner	X																

	A	B	C	D	E	F	G	H	I	J	K	L	M	N	O	P	Q
Onychiurus armatus group																	X
Folsomia picea Christiansen & Tucker		X															
Folsomia regularis Hammer																	X
Pseudisotoma sensibilis Tullb.	X																
Tomocerus dubius Christiansen	X																
Tomocerus flavescens (Tullb.) (W)	X	X														X	
Tomocerus sp.	X																
Dicyrtoma sp.	X																
Bristletails																	
Pedetontus sp.														X			
Mayflies																	
Cinygma sp. (see Scudder 1975)										X							
Paraleptophlebia sp.													X				
Paraleptophlebia sp. (*debilis* Walker?)													X				
Ameletus sp.													X				
Dragonflies																	
Lestus disjunctus Selys											X	X					
Enallagma cyathigerum (Charp.)											X	X					
Aeshna eremita Scudder												X					
Aeshna interrupta Walker											X	X					
Aeshna juncea (L.)											X	X					
Aeshna palmata Hagen											X	X					
Aeshna sitchensis Hagen											X						
Aeshna umbrosa Walker											X	X					
Cordulia shurtleffi Scudder												X					
Somatochlora albicincta (Burm.)											X	X					
Somatochlora semicircularis (Selys)											X						
Leucorrhinia glacialis Hagen												X					
Leucorrhinia hudsonica (Selys)											X						
Leucorrhinia proxima Calvert												X					
Libellula quadrimaculata L.											X						
Sympetrum costiferum (Hagen)											X						
Sympetrum danae (Sulzer)											X						
Sympetrum occidentale Bartenev											X						
Sympetrum madidum (Hagen)											X						
Sympetrum pallipes (Hagen)											X						
Stoneflies																	
Suwallia lineosa (Banks)										X						X	
Mesocapnia sp. (prob. *oenone*)													X				
Despaxia augusta (Banks)													X				

	A	B	C	D	E	F	G	H	I	J	K	L	M	N	O	P	Q
Soyedina interrupta (Classen)													X				
Termites																	
Zootermopsis angusticollis (Hagen)	X																
Grasshoppers and crickets																	
Pristoceuthophilus celatus (Scudder) W)	X			X													
Melanoplus bruneri Scudder (WO)							X		X							X	
Barklice																	
Amphigerontia bifasciata (Latr.)					X												
Phylotarsus kwakiutl Mockford					X												
Polypsocus corruptus (Hagen)					X												
Argyra sp.										X							
Chrysotus sp.				X		X	X									X	
Dolichopus convergens Aldrich				X												X	
Dolichopus hastatus Loew				X												X	
Dolichopus monticola Van Duzee												X					
Dolichopus plumipes Scop.									X								
Dolichopus xanthocnemus Loew									X	X							
Gymnopternus sp. A (males)												X					
Gymnopternus sp. B (males) (W)				X					X								
Gymnopternus spp. (females)																	X
Hydrophorus chrysologus (Walker)						X											
Sympycnus sp.									X								
Syntormon sp.						X											
Tachytrechus sanus O.S.								X									
Megaselia spp.	X	X		X													
Blera scitula Will. (WO)				X	X			X									
Cheilosia hoodiana Bigot				X	X		X										
Cheilosia sp.								X									
Cynorhinella bella (Will.)				X													
Melangyna lasiophthalma Zett.								X	X								
Parasyrphus sp.	X																
Platycheirus sp.																X	
Meliscaeva cinctella Zett.								X									
Scaeva pyrastri L.						X											
Sericomyia chalcopyga Loew (WO)				X	X												
Syrphus torvus O.S.				X													
Paroxyna sp., poss. *americana* Her.						X										X	
Paroxyna sp.					X												
Tephritis sp.								X									
Coelopa nebularum Aldr.										X							X

	A	B	C	D	E	F	G	H	I	J	K	L	M	N	O	P	Q
Dryomyza anilis Fall.	X																
Helcomyza mirabilis Mel.							X										
Limnia inopa (Adams) (W)		X		X													
Chamaemyia sp.	X			X		X		X								X	
Liopiophila varipes (Meigen)	X																
Parapiophila vulgaris (Fall.)	X																
Aptilotus borealis Mall.										X							
Aptilotus sp.	X																
Copromyza maculipennis (Spuler)		X															
Minilimosina sp.	X																
Thoracochaeta brachystoma (Stenh.)							X										
Thoracochaeta teskeyi Marshall								X									
Hydrellia griseola (Fall.)																	X
True bugs																	
Banasa sordida (Uhler) (WF)	X	X															
Ligyrocoris sylvestris (L.)						X											
Nysius niger Baker						X											
Lopidea ampla (Van D.)					X												
Lygocoris pabulinus (L.)		X															
Mecomma gilvipes (Stal) (W)					X				X								X
Orthops scutellatus Uhler					X												
Orthotylus sp.			X														
Trignotylus ruficornis (Geoffroy)									X								
Saldula explanata Uhler									X								
Gerris notabilis D. & H.											X	X					
Lethocerus americanus (Leidy)											X						
Notonecta kirbyi Hung.												X					
Notonecta undulata Say											X		X				
Callicorixa alaskensis Hung.											X	X					
Cenocorixa andersoni Hung.											X						
Hesperocorixa vulgaris (Hung.)											X						
Sigara omani (Hung.)											X	X	X				
Sigara sp.											X						
Aphrophora fulva Doer (W)			X														
Aphrophora princeps Walley			X														
Neophilaenus lineatus (L.)						X											
Philaenus spumarius (L.) (W)						X											
Aphrodes bicinctus (Schr.) (I)								X									
Aphrodes costatus (Pzr.) (I)					X			X									
Balclutha neglecta (DeL. & Dav.)								X									
Bathysmatophorus oregonensis (Bak.) (WF)		X	X														
Deltocephala n. sp.																X	
Draeculacephala crassicornis Van D.						X											
Elymana inornata (Van D.) (WW)						X			X								

	A	B	C	D	E	F	G	H	I	J	K	L	M	N	O	P	Q
Evacanthus grandipes Hamilton (W)		X							X								X
Idiocerus couleanus Ball & Pkr.						X											
Macrosteles fieberi (Edw.)						X											
Macrosteles lineatifrons (Stal)				X													
Oncopsis crispae Hamilton (Ms name) (W)										X							
Ophiola angustata Osb.						X											
Paraphlepsius apertus (Van D.)						X										X	
Xestocephalus fulvocapitatus Van D.						X											
Delphacodes sp.		X		X	X	X											X
Lacewings																	
Hemerobius ovalis Carpenter	X																
Hemerobius pacificus Banks	X																
Beetles																	
Cicindela oregona LeC.								X									
Agonum ferruginosum Dej.									X								
Bembidion fortestriatum Mots.						X											
Bembidion zephyrum Fall										X							
Dyschirius obesus LeC.							X										
Nebria diversa LeC.							X										
Nebria kincaidi Sz.		X															
Notiophilus silvaticus Esch.																X	
Pterostichus algidus LeC. (W)	X				X			X									
Pterostichus crenicollis LeC.								X									
Pterostichus lama Men.	X							X									
Scaphinotus angusticollis (Mann.) (WF)	X	X															
Scaphinotus margiunatus Fisch				X													
Zacotus matthewsi LeC. (WF)	X																
Acilius sp. c.f. *semisulcatus* Aube												X					
Agabus tristis Aube													X				
Dytiscus dauricus Gebler													X				
Hydroporus mannerheimi J.B.-B.												X					
Ilybius quadrimaculatus Aube												X	X				
Rhantus binotatus (Harris)										X							
Rhantus suturellus (Harris)											X	X					
Gyrinus sp.																	
Cercyon adumbratus Mannh.	X																
Nicrophorus defodiens Mann.	X																
Catops sp.	X																
Stenichnus pacificus Casey							X										
Scydmaenus sp.	X																
Atheta sp.	X			X													
Autalia sp.	X									X							
Bledius sp.							X										

	A	B	C	D	E	F	G	H	I	J	K	L	M	N	O	P	Q
Bryoporus rubescens (Hatch) (WF)	X				X												
Cafius canescens Makl.							X										
Cafius nudus johnsoni Fall							X										
Cafius seminitens Horn							X										
Lathrobium sp. A.						X											
Lathrobium sp. B.	X																
Mycetoporus sp.				X													
Omalium sp.																X	
Oxytelus fuscipennis Mannh.	X																
Philonthus siegwaldi Mannh.	X																
Proteinus sp.	X				X												
Quedius frater Smetana		X															
Stenus pterobrachys Gemm. & Har.	X																
Stenus sp.				X		X											
Tachinus basalis Er. (WF)	X																
Thinopinus pictus LeC.							X										
Trigonurus dilaticollis VanD.								X									
Unamis sp. (possibly *fulvipes* Fall)		X															
Aleocharinae	X																
Oropus striatus (LeC.)	X																
Foveoscapha terracola P. & W.		X															
Ptenidium sp. (poss. *pullum* Makl.)																	X
Hypocaccus bigemmeus (LeC.) (W)				X													
Ellychnia hatchi Fender								X									
Podabrus sp. A. (WF)	X				X												
Podabrus sp. B. (WF)	X																
Cephaloon bicolor Horn	X				X												
Ditylus quadricollis (LeC.) (WO)						X		X									
Dendroides ephemeroides (Mann.)	X																
Athous rufiventris (Esch.) (W)					X		X	X	X								
Athous nigropilis Mots.	X																
Ctenicera suckleyi (LeC.)				X													
Hemicrepidius morio (LeC.)	X																
Megapenthes stigmosus (LeC.)					X												
Negastrius dispersus (Horn)				X													
Negastrius sp.				X													
Cyphon variabilis (Thunb.)						X											
Lioligus nitidus Mots.	X																
Epuraea sp.	X																
Namunaria pacifica Horn	X																
Coccinella johnsoni Casey					X			X									
Coccinella trifasciata perplexa Muls.					X						X						
Coelus ciliatus Esch.								X									

	A	B	C	D	E	F	G	H	I	J	K	L	M	N	O	P	Q
Phaleromela globosa (LeC.)								X									
Usechimorpha barberi Blaisdel	X																
Anaspis sp.		X															
Prothalpia holmbergi Mann.	X																
Aegialia blanchardi Horn	X																
Aphodius aleutes Esch.				X													
Polyphylla crinita LeC. (W)	X																
Lepturopsis dolorosa (LeC. (W)					X			X									
Plectrura spinicauda Mann.	X																
Altica sp.						X											
Donacia hirticollis Kirby											X						
Plateumaris neomexicana (Schaeffer)											X						
Syneta hamata Horn								X									
Ellasoptes marinus Horn								X									
Geoderces horni (Van Dyke)	X																
Lepesoma bakeri (Van Dyke)								X									
Lepidophorus inquinatus (Mann.)															X		
Steremnius carinatus (Boh.)	X																
Sthereus quadrituberculatus Mots.						X											
Trigonoscuta pilosa Mots.								X									
Dolurgus pumilus (Mann.)	X																
Gnathotrichus sulcatus Blkm.	X																
Hylurgops rugipennis (Mann.)	X																
Pseudohylesinus sericeus (Mann.)	X																
Trypodendron lineatum (Oliv.)	X																
True flies																	
Limonia (L.) *bestigma* (Coq.)	X																
Limonia (*Dicranomyia*) sp.	X																
Limnophila (*Prionolabis*) sp. nr. *rufibasis* (W)	X																
Limnophila sp.		X										X					
Molophilus (M.) *oligocanthus* Alex (W)	X	X															
Molophilus sp.	X	X														X	
Ormonia sp.								X									
Pedicia sp.	X	X															
Tipula (*Trichotipula*) *macrophallus* (Dietz)	X																
Tipula sp.	X																
Bibio sp.	X																
Mycetobia divergens Walker	X																
Anaclileia sp.	X																
Cordyla sp.	X																
Macrocera sp.				X													
Mycetophila sp.				X													
Neuratelia sp.	X			X				X									

	A	B	C	D	E	F	G	H	I	J	K	L	M	N	O	P	Q
Orfelia sp.					X												
Bradysia sp.	X			X				X		X						X	
Schwenkefeldina sp.	X			X				X									
Stomatosema sp.				X													
Cecidomyiinae				X													
Chaoborus trivittatus (Loew)												X					
Aedes aboriginis Dyar	X																
Culiseta incidens (Thomson)	X																
Culiseta minnesotae Barr	X																
Prosimulium dicum D. & S.					X												
Prosimulium sp.					X												
Simulium venustum Say				X													
Simulium venustum complex				X													
Culicoides sp.	X																
Forcipomyia macswaini Wirth	X																
Palpomyia sp.					X												
Chironomus (C.) "*plumosus*" group										X							
Dicrotendipes modestus (Say)												X					
Limnophyes sp. A		X															
Limnophyes sp. B	X																
Metriocnemus fuscipes (Meigen)	X																
Micropsectra sp.		X															
Natarsia miripes (Coq.)												X					
Parametriocnemus sp.	X																
Paraphaenocladius sp.	X																
Polypedilum sp.		X															
Procladius sp.	X																
Procladius (*Psilotanypus*) sp.												X					
Psectrocladius (*Allopsectrocladius*) sp.											X						
Smittia group, near *Parasmittia*											X						
Atylotus tingaureus (Philip) (W)																	X
Chrysops excitans Walk. (W)	X		X			X		X		X							
Chrysops noctifer O.S.	X					X		X									
Chrysops proclivis O.S.						X											
Hybomitra captonis (Marten)	X			X													
Hybomitra sequax (Will.)	X																
Hybomitra sonomensis (O.S.) (W)		X															
Sylvius gigantulus (Loew)	X	X				X			X			X					
Rhagio californicus Leonard						X											
Rhagio dimidiata Lowe (W)								X									
Rhagio incisus (Loew)		X		X		X			X								X
Rhagio sp.		X															
Symphoromyia (*Ochleromyia*) sp. 1		X															
Symphoromyia (*Ochleromyia*) sp. 2	X	X								X							

	A	B	C	D	E	F	G	H	I	J	K	L	M	N	O	P	Q
Symphoromyia sp.	X	X															
Stratiomys barbata Loew (WW)				X													
Thereva brunnea Cole						X					X						
Lasiopogon n. sp. near *Willametti*	X							X									
Villa lateralis (Say)								X									
Anthalia stigmalis Coq.						X											
Bicellaria sp.				X													
Brochella monticola Melander		X															
Chersodromia parallela Mel. (W)				X				X									
Empis sp.		X		X													
Hilara sp.	X			X													
Microphorus atratus Coq. (WT)				X												X	
Oedalea lanceolata Mel.	X																
Parathalassius aldrichi Mel. (W)				X				X									
Platypalpus sp.	X	X								X							
Rhamphomyia sp.	X	X		X													
Tachydromia sp. (probably new)				X													
Empidinae (new genus)	X																
Achalcus utahensis H. & M.									X								
Argyra albiventris Loew	X																
Limnellia sejuncta (Loew)																	X
Lytogaster gravida (Loew)	X								X								
Scatella setosa (Coq.)						X											
Scatella stagnalis (Fall.)						X											
Scaptomyza sp.	X																X
Chlorops sp.					X		X									X	
Elachiptera sp.								X									
Oscinella sp.																	X
Tricimba brunnicollis (Becker)																	X
Chromatomyia niger (Meigen)																	X
Melanagromyza sp. near *buccalis*						X			X								
Melanagromyza sp.									X								
Acartophthalmus nigrinus (Zett.) (WF)	X			X													
Anorostoma alternans Garrett								X									
Borboropsis sp. (*fulviceps* [Strobl]?)	X																
Borboropsis puberula (Zett.) (W)				X													
Neoleria inscripta (Meigen)	X																
Suilla nemorum (Meigen)	X							X									
Tephlochlamys rufiventris (Meigen)	X																
Anthomyza sp.								X									
Megaphthalma pallida Fall.	X																
Scathophaga furcata Say (WO)				X												X	
Acrostilpna sp. near *collini*						X											
Delia setiventris complex				X													
Fucellia aestuum Aldrich							X	X									

	A	B	C	D	E	F	G	H	I	J	K	L	M	N	O	P	Q
Fucellia fucorum (Fall.)							X										
Fucellia rufitibia Stein							X										
Fucellia separata Stein							X										
Hylemya alcathoe (Walker)								X									
Paregle sp., (possibly new)				X													
Pegohylemyia sp.				X													
Pegomyia sp.	X			X													
Coenosia impunctata Mall. (W)				X													
Coenosia johnsoni Mall.								X									
Coenosia sp.				X													
Fannia abrupta Mall.					X												
Fannia aethiops Mall.					X												
Fannia glaucescens (Zett.)	X																
Fannia sp.	X																
Helina bicolorata (Mall.)								X									
Helina troene (Walker)								X									
Helina sp.										X							
Hydrotaea houghi Mall.								X									
Limosia incisurata Van der Wulp				X													
Mydaea obscurella Mall.	X																
Mydaea sp.	X																
Schoenomyza chrysostoma Loew				X				X									
Schoenomyza dorsalis Loew (WW)						X											
Schoenomyza lispina Thom.									X								
Spilogona magnipunctata (Mall.)				X													
Spilogona semiglobosa (Ringdahl)	X																
Calliphora terraenovae Macq. (W)	X																
Calliphora vomitoria (L) (W)	X																
Cynomya cadaverina (Rob.-D.)																	X
Eucalliphora lilaea (authors, not Walk.) (W)				X				X									
Lucilia illustris (Meigen)	X																
Admontia sp.								X									
Arctophyto borealis (Coq.)								X									
Athrycia cinerea (Coq.)								X									
Lasioneura bicolor (Curran)								X									
Mericia bicarina (Toth.)						X											
Phasia aenoventris (Will.) (W)								X		X							
Phasia splendida (Coq.)								X									
Slossonaemyia angulicornis (Curran)				X													
Strongygaster triangulifer (Loew)								X									

	A	B	C	D	E	F	G	H	I	J	K	L	M	N	O	P	Q
Butterflies and moths																	
Papilio zelicaon Lucas					X												
Epidemia mariposa (Reakirt)						X											
Limenitis lorquini Boisduval (W)						X											
Apamea maxima Dyar									X								
Dargidia procincta Grt.								X									
Oligia indirecta Grt.	X																
Rhynchagrotis exsertistigma Morn.	X																
Ceratodalia queneata Pack.	X																
Dysstroma sobria Swett.	X																
Enypia venata Grt.	X																
Neoalcis californiaria Pack.	X																
Perizoma grandis Hlst.	X																
Hysterosia sp.																X	
Epinotia nanana (Tr.)				X													
Epinotia solandriana (L.)	X																
Pandemis heparana (D. & S.)	X																
Caddisflies																	
Oecetis inconspicua (Walker)										X		X					
Halesochila taylori (Banks)										X		X					
Homophylax andax Ross										X		X					
Lenarchus vastus (Hagen)										X		X					
Limnephilus sp.										X		X					
Ptilostomis ocellifera (Walker)										X		X					
Polycentropus flavus (Banks)										X		X					
Rhyacophila grandis Banks													X				
Rhyacophila oreta Banks													X				
Bees, wasps and ants																	
Pachynematus sp.									X								
Tenthredo sp. nr. *semirufa*		X															
Rogas sp.		X															
Coelinidea sp.				X													
Dacnusa sp.							X										
Aphaereta n. sp.									X								
Glyptapanteles sp.		X															
Microgaster sp.						X											
Pholetesor glacialis (Ashmead)																	X
Ephedrus sp.		X															
Praon sp.									X								
Netelia sp.	X																
Tryphon sp.									X								
Gelis sp.				X				X									
Phygadenon sp.								X									
Cubocephalus sp.																X	
Stenichneumon sp.								X									
Lissonota parva (Cresson)						X											
Lissonota rasilis Townes								X									

	A	B	C	D	E	F	G	H	I	J	K	L	M	N	O	P	Q
Diadegma sp.								X									
Homotropus sp.		X															
Orthocentrus sp.	X																
Stenomacrus sp.	X	X															
Chlorocytus sp.					X												X
Seladerma sp.																	X
Skeltoceras sp.																	X
Stictomischus sp.																	X
Eurytoma sp.						X		X									
Chartoceras elongatus (Girault)	X																
Pediobus sp.									X								
Alloxysta sp. (*bicolor* [Baker]?)		X															
Acropiesta sp.		X															
Belyta longicollis Fouts	X																
Belyta sp.	X				X				X	X							
Trimorus sp.	X																
Platygaster sp.				X													
Camponotus sp. (WF)	X																
Formica neorufibarbis Emery (W)				X				X								X	
Formica pacifica Francoeur										X							
Formica subaenescens Emery								X									
Lasius pallitarsus (Prov.) (W)		X			X			X									
Leptothorax muscorum Nylander																X	
Myrmica incompleta Prov.						X											
Vespula (*Dolichovespula*) *arenaria* (Fab.)	X							X									
Anoplius ventralis tarsatus Banks						X											
Mimesa sp.								X									
Ectemnius sp.									X	X							
Oxybelus sp.								X									
Bombus mixtus Cresson (W)				X	X			X	X							X	
Bombus terricola occidentalis Greene				X													
Psithyrus fernaldae Franklin (W)				X					X								
Myriapods																	
Scolopocryptops sexspinosus (Say) (W)	X				X												
Geophilomorpha sp. A.		X															
Geophilomorpha sp. B.				X													
Ethopolys sierravabus (Chamberlin)																X	
Ethopolys sp. nr. *spectans* Chamberlin	X																
Nearctodesmus insulans Chamberlin	X																
Simobius ginampus (Chamberlin)				X													

Chapter 11

Fishes of Brooks Peninsula

Grant W. Hughes
Curatorial Services Branch, Royal British Columbia Museum
Victoria, BC

Abstract

The fish fauna of Brooks Peninsula was surveyed in order to determine the likelihood of a fish refugium existing there when other areas of British Columbia were glaciated. One hundred and four fish specimens comprising five species were collected from freshwater habitats. The species belong to families characterized as diadromous or vicarious; they probably invaded Brooks Peninsula streams from marine or estuarine habitats at some time in the past. No endemic species were collected. Meristic and morphological characteristics of the specimens collected are within the ranges reported from other British Columbia drainages, which suggests that the fish fauna of this region is not unique. One hundred and two specimens captured from marine habitat provide documentation of the nearshore fish fauna as well as two northern extensions of known ranges.

Acknowledgements

I am grateful to Alex Peden, Royal British Columbia Museum, and Robert Carveth, University of British Columbia, for reviews of an earlier draft of this manuscript.

Introduction

As part of the multidisciplinary expedition to Brooks Peninsula in 1981, there was an opportunity to survey and collect fishes in order to determine whether endemic species live on the peninsula. Endemic species may constitute evidence for a glacial refugium—if differentiation of the new species occurred during the time that the region was isolated, or if the species, previously widely established, persisted when glaciation rendered other parts of its range inhospitable. Limited postglacial dispersal could result in a distribution that enables zoogeographers to make inferences about past glacial events.

Alternatively, natural selection, mutation, or genetic drift over a period of time could have resulted in differentiation of a new taxon since glaciation, and so it is possible that endemism is not evidence for a glacial refugium. For example, studies suggest that endemic divergent populations of threespine stickleback (*Gasterosteus aculeatus* Linnaeus) on the Queen Charlotte

Islands evolved in recent times (Moodie and Reimchen 1976). Distinct threespine stickleback variants occur in different previously glaciated lakes, and Moodie and Reimchen conclude that these populations evolved *in situ* following deglaciation and recolonization from the sea.

Species from a Brooks Peninsula refugium would need to be very different from previous colonists and from species in nearby drainages, or be closely allied to other primary freshwater fish species that do not have a mechanism for recolonizing the region after deglaciation, in order to provide conclusive evidence of isolation over a long period of time. These requirements can be illustrated with evidence for isolation of fish faunal groups in other drainages of western North America.

In western Washington, endemic species such as the Olympic mudminnow (*Novumbra hubbsi* Shultz) occur in drainages south of the previous ice boundary. The Olympic mudminnow has apparently been isolated for an extended period of time (Meldrim 1980). This species, which is intolerant of salt water and is found in quiet water, is restricted to the Chehalis and Puget Sound drainages—providing zoogeographic evidence for the non-glaciation of the area (McPhail 1967). In this same region, additional zoogeographic evidence of glacial history comes from the distribution of primary freshwater fish. They dispersed through glacial Lake Russel into tributaries farther north, but were halted at the Snohomish River—almost exactly at the point where the sea was able to enter Puget Sound (McPhail 1967). The saltwater barrier created by the sea prevented the fish from moving farther northwards into coastal drainages.

Larger regions can also be examined for zoogeographic details. Western North America is composed of seven main basins, each with some incidence of endemism (Miller 1958). The Columbia basin, the closest to Brooks Peninsula, includes the Columbia, Fraser, Skeena, and Stikine rivers. Fifty-eight per cent of the primary freshwater fish species are endemic to the basin (Miller 1958). In comparison, when all fish species are considered, the proportion of endemism drops to 19%. This difference is due to the fact that only on rare occasions are diadromous or vicarious species as restricted in distribution as primary freshwater species. The poor dispersal ability of primary freshwater species means that they are more likely to constitute contemporary clues to geographic history than are salt-tolerant species.

Although few salt-tolerant forms are endemics, there are cases where marine relicts can be used as evidence for re-invasion of previously glaciated habitats. For example, in eastern Canada coldwater lacustrine species with a limited ability to move upstream, such as the spoonhead sculpin (*Cottus ricei* [Nelson]), deepwater sculpin (*Myoxocephalus quadricornis* [Linnaeus]), ninespine stickleback (*Pungitius pungitius* [Linnaeus]), and trout-perch (*Percopsis omiscomaycus* [Walbaum]), have contemporary distributions that are essentially restricted to the previous glacial lakes in eastern Ontario and western Quebec (Dadswell 1972). In addition, the glacial history of the Ottawa valley can be deduced from the presence of the essentially marine threespine stickleback and other species. They occur there due to the incursion of the sea after the withdrawal of the last ice sheet (Dymond 1939).

These examples show how a distinctive species complement may be used to reconstruct faunal history. For this reason, an endemic species, or a species that also occurs at places from which it cannot now reach Brooks Peninsula, could be evidence for a glacial history different from that of other, nearby geographic areas.

Methodology

For logistical reasons, sampling of freshwater habitats was restricted to the lower reaches of drainages on the northwest side of Brooks Peninsula during August 1981 (Figure 11.1). These

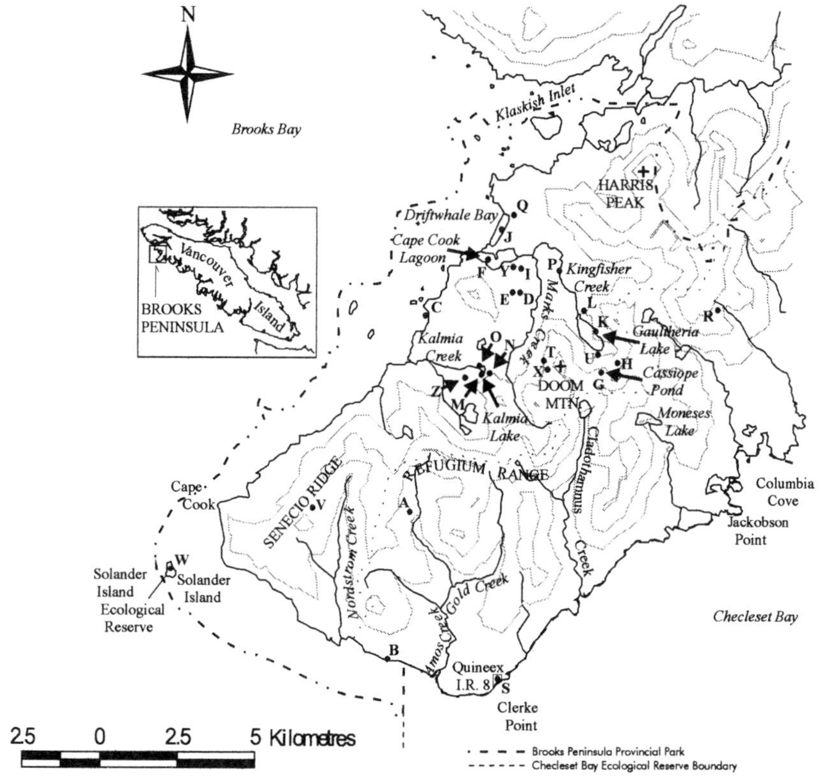

1. inside Cape Cook Lagoon Spit
2. exposed sand beach of Cape Cook lagoon spit
3. inter-tidal rocky area, just west of Cape Cook lagoon on exposed side
4. Marks Creek draining due north to the eastern end of Cooks Lagoon estuary
5. Kalmia Creek upstream of junction with stream from Menziesia
6. Amos Creek—2 km upstream from estuary

Figure 11.1 Fish collecting locations on Brooks Peninsula

areas were considered to have a high probability of being inhabited by species that might have persisted in elevated unglaciated areas throughout the Fraser maximum and then dispersed downstream during recent times. In addition, a sample from Amos Creek was collected by Dan Grant and Eero Karanta of the British Columbia Ministry of the Environment, on 6 March 1983. Fish were captured by electrofisher or minnow seines and preserved in the field.

Marine nearshore fishes were captured by gill net from surf habitat and by dip net from estuarine and tide pool habitats near Cape Cook Lagoon, in order to document which species occur along this section of the British Columbia coast.

All specimens are stored at the Royal British Columbia Museum (catalogue numbers BCPM981-68 to BCPM981-79 and BCPM983-1406). Techniques used for morphological analysis followed Hubbs and Lagler (1947).

Results

Two hundred and six specimens were captured from the six sampling locations (Tables 11.1 and 11.2). None of the species is endemic to Brooks Peninsula. Counts and measurements of diagnostic characteristics do not reveal morphological distinctions between Brooks Peninsula specimens and representatives of the same species from other areas of British Columbia (Table 11.3).

All freshwater specimens were captured from stream habitat where slow current flows over cobbles, stones, and fine gravel with filamentous algae in places. Other areas were sampled, but no fish were taken from them: (1) ponds located just south of Cape Cook Lagoon (50°12' N, 127°46'54" W), seined and sampled by minnow trap overnight, 30 July 1981; (2) Empetrum Lake (50°10'30" N, 127°42'30" W), sampled by 62 mm gill net 31 July 1981 (1.5 h set); (3) Kalmia Lake, seined by R. Wayne Campbell during August 1981. Available habitat seemed suitable for fish, and it appears that fish populations in these areas were either sparse or absent at the time of sampling. A more extensive sampling program is necessary to adequately census all areas.

Table 11.1 Freshwater fish specimens captured in Marks Creek, Kalmia Creek and Amos Creek

Common name[a]	Scientific name	No.
Coho salmon	*Oncorhynchus kisutch* (Walbaum)	41
Cutthroat trout	*Oncorhynchus clarki* Richardson	9
Rainbow trout[b]	*Oncorhynchus mykiss* Richardson	9
Coastrange sculpin[c]	*Cottus aleuticus* Gilbert	23
Prickly sculpin[c]	*Cottus asper* Richardson	22

[a] Common names as recorded by Robins et al. (1980).
[b] None from Kalmia Creek.
[c] None from Amos Creek.

Table 11.2 Marine and estuarine fish specimens captured at or near Cape Cook Lagoon

Common name[a]	Scientific name	Location[b]	No.
Starry flounder	*Platichthys stellatus* Pallas	2	1
Redtail surfperch	*Amphistichus rhodoterus* (Agassiz)	2	17
Shiner perch	*Cymatogaster aggregata* Gibbons	1	3
Silver surfperch	*Hyperprosopon ellipticum* (Gibbons)	2	3
Kelp greenling	*Hexagrammos decagrammus* (Pallas)	1	1
Smoothhead sculpin	*Artedius lateralis* (Girard)	3	1
Prickly sculpin	*Cottus asper* (Richardson)	1	6
Pacific staghorn sculpin	*Leptocottus armatus* Girard	1	4
Tidepool sculpin	*Oligocottus maculosus* Girard	1, 3	32
Fluffy sculpin	*Oligocottus snyderi* Greenley	3	1
Threespine stickleback	*Gasterosteus aculeatus* Linneaus	1	5
High cockscomb	*Anoplarchus purpurescens* Gill	3	1
Crescent gunnel	*Pholis laeta* (Cope)	1	25
Saddleback gunnel	*Pholis ornata* (Girard)	1	2

[a] Common names as recorded by Robins et al. (1980).
[b] Locations: 1, inside Cape Cook Lagoon spit; 2, exposed, sand beach of Cape Cook Lagoon spit; 3, intertidal rocky area just west of Cape Cook Lagoon, on exposed side.

Table 11.3 Diagnostic characteristics of freshwater fish species collected from Brooks Peninsula

Characteristics	Brooks Peninsula		Other Locations	
	Mean	Range (N)	Range	Source
Coho salmon				
Dorsal rays, no.	12.0	11-13 (41)	9-13	Hart 1973
Anal rays, no.	15.0	13-16 (41)	13-16	Hart 1973
Vertebrae, no.	65.6	63-68 (41)	61-69	Scott and Crossman 1973
Lateral line pores, no.	128	121-135 (35)	121-140	Hart 1973
Gill rakers, no.	21.6	20-24 (35)	19-25	Hart 1973
Standard length, in mm		38-79 (35)		
Rainbow trout				
Dorsal rays, no.	12.4	12-13 (9)	10-12[a]	Scott and Crossman 1973
Anal rays, no.	12.3	12-13 (9)	8-12[a]	Scott and Crossman 1973
Vertebrae, no.	64.6	63-66 (9)	60-66	Scott and Crossman 1973
Lateral line pores, no.	124	122-129 (9)	100-150	Scott and Crossman 1973
Gill rakers, no.	18.9	15-21 (9)	16-22	Scott and Crossman 1973
Basibranchial teeth	not evident		absent	Scott and Crossman 1973
Maxilla ratio[b]	474	451-517 (9)		
Standard length, in mm		45-123 (9)		
Cutthroat trout				
Dorsal rays, no.	11.2	10-13 (9)	10-13	Scott and Crossman 1973
Anal rays, no.	11.4	11-13 (9)	11-13	Scott and Crossman 1973
Vertebrae, no.	63	61-66 (9)	60-64	Carl et al. 1967
Lateral line pores, no.	112	110-132 (8)	116-230	Scott and Crossman 1973
Gill rakers, no.	17.7	15-19 (9)	15-22	Carl et al. 1967
Basibranchial teeth	usually visible		few small teeth	Carl et al. 1967
Maxilla ratio[2]	534	469-604 (9)		
Standard length, in mm		36-112 (9)		
Prickly sculpin				
Anal rays, no.	16.7	16-18 (21)	15-19	Carl et al. 1967
Pectoral rays, no.	15.7	14-16 (22)	15-18	Scott and Crossman 1967
Median chin pores, no.	1	1 (22)	1	Carl et al. 1967
Prickles	behind pectoral fin, and along side in some specimens		may vary from behind pectoral fin to covering most of the body except head and chest	Carl et al. 1967
Dorsal black spot	present		present	Carl et al. 1967
Posterior nostril	not tubular		may be somewhat tubular	Carl et al. 1967
Palatine teeth	present		strong	Carl et al. 1967
Standard length, in mm		46-135 (22)		Carl et al. 1967

Table 11.3 Continued

Characteristics	Brooks Peninsula		Other Locations	
	Mean	Range (N)	Range	Source
Coastrange sculpin				
Anal rays, no.	13.0	12-14 (23)	12-16	Carl et al. 1967
Pectoral rays, no.	14.1	13-15 (22)	13-16	Scott and Crossman 1973
Median chin pores, no.	1	1 (23)	1	Carl et al. 1967
Prickles	weak or absent		restricted to small patch behind pectoral fins or absent	Carl et al. 1967
Dorsal black spot	usually absent		absent	Carl et al. 1967
Posterior nostril	tubular		distinct tubes	Carl et al. 1967
Palatine teeth	absent		absent	Carl et al. 1967
Standard length, in mm		19-67 (23)		

[a] Only principal rays noted.
[b] Length from snout to end of maxilla divided by head length, multiplied by 1000.

Discussion

All five freshwater species collected are widely distributed in the coastal streams of British Columbia (Scott and Crossman 1973). Since they are tolerant to brackish, or salt water, it is likely that they rapidly re-invaded Brooks Peninsula streams after coastal ice withdrew (12 000-13 000 B.P.; see Chapter 3). It is unlikely that the higher parts of Brooks Peninsula's central ridge and Harris Peak, which remained unglaciated (see Chapter 3), harboured fish populations. High mountain refugia are not likely to contain suitable fish habitat (Moodie and Reimchen 1976). In the absence of distinct fish taxa that would have suggested a long period of isolation from other British Columbia species, a sea dispersal re-population of Brooks Peninsula streams is indicated.

Although there are four main routes (Carl et al. 1967) by which fishes have entered British Columbia (the Columbia and Fraser systems, the Peace and Liard systems, the Yukon River, and the sea), only the last is appropriate for Brooks Peninsula. In general, postglacial re-invasion along the Pacific coast by rainbow trout, prickly sculpin, and coastrange sculpin originated from the Pacific refuge south of the Cordilleran ice sheet; coho salmon dispersed from the Columbia River system (McPhail and Lindsey 1970). Coastal cutthroat trout would also likely have dispersed northwards from the Pacific refugium. These routes are appropriate for Brooks Peninsula fauna as well.

The collecting was limited in scope and should serve only as a preliminary guide to the freshwater fish fauna. Given the areas sampled to no avail, it may be that a more extensive survey will discover additional fish species. There is no conclusive evidence that species known from other Vancouver Island drainages, but not sampled in this study, are absent due to the lack of available habitat they may be found in areas not sampled to date. However, if they are species already known to occur on Vancouver Island (for example, lampreys, other salmonids, and peamouth chub) the case for a Brooks Peninsula fish refugium would not be strengthened since these species are presumed to have re-populated Vancouver Island freshwater areas after recolonization from the sea (see Carl et al. 1967).

Two marine fish species collected from Brooks Peninsula represent northern extensions of their known ranges. These records, for saddleback gunnel (*Pholis ornata*) and silver surfperch (*Hyperprosopon elliptcum*), have been reported in Peden and Hughes (1984) and Peden and Hughes (1986) respectively. The other marine species that were captured occur throughout southern British Columbia waters where suitable habitats exist. Marine inshore habitats, if they were inhospitable during the Fraser maximum, were most likely colonized very shortly after nearshore glacial melting occurred—assuming that suitable habitat and oceanographic conditions prevailed at the time.

References Cited

Carl, G.C., W.A. Clemens, and C.C. Lindsey. 1967. The fresh-water fishes of British Columbia. Royal British Columbia Museum Handbook 5. Victoria, BC.

Dadswell, M.J. 1972. Postglacial dispersal of four deepwater fishes on the basis of new distributional records in eastern Ontario and western Quebec. J. Fish. Res. Board Can. 29: 545-553.

Dymond, J.R. 1939. The fishes of the Ottawa region. Contributions of the Royal Ontario Museum of Zoology 15. Toronto, ON.

Hubbs, C.L. and K.F. Lagler. 1947. Fishes of the Great Lakes region. Cranbrook Institute of Science Bull. 26. Bloomfield Hills, MI.

McPhail, J.D. 1967. Distribution of freshwater fishes in western Washington. Northwest Sci. 41: 1-11.

——— and C.C. Lindsey. 1970. Freshwater fishes of northwestern Canada and Alaska. Bull. 173, Fish. Res. Board Canada.

Meldrim, J.W. (compiler). 1980. *Novumbra hubbsi* Schultz, Olympic mudminnow. Pp. 128 in D.S. Lee, C.R. Gilbert, C.H. Hocutt, R.E. Jenkins, D.E. McAllister, and J.R. Stauffer (eds.). Atlas of North American freshwater fishes. North Carolina State Museum of Natural History, Raleigh, NC.

Miller, R.R. 1958. Origin and affinities of the freshwater fish fauna of western North America. Pp. 187-222 in Carl L. Hubbs (ed.). Zoogeography. Am. Assoc. for the Advancement of Science, Washington, DC.

Moodie, G.E.E. and T.E. Reimchen. 1976. Glacial refugia, endemism, and stickleback populations of the Queen Charlotte Islands, British Columbia. Can. Field-Naturalist 90: 471-474.

Peden, A.E. and G.W. Hughes. 1984. Distribution, morphological variation and systematic relationship of *Pholis laeta* and *P. ornata* (Pisces: Pholididae) with a description of the related form *P. nea* n.sp. Can. J. Zool. 62: 291-305.

______ .1986. First records, confirmatory records, and range extensions of marine fishes within Canada's west coast fishing zone. Can. Field-Naturalist 100: 1-9.

Robins, C.R. and R.M. Bailey, C.E. Bond, J.R. Brooker, E.A. Lachner, R.N. Lea, and W.B. Scott. 1980. A list of common and scientific names of fishes from the United States and Canada. 4th ed. American Fisheries Society. Special Publication 12. Bethesda, MD.

Scott, W.B. and E.J. Crossman. 1973. Freshwater fishes of Canada. Bull. 184, Fish. Res. Board Canada.

Chapter 12

Vertebrates of Brooks Peninsula

R. Wayne Campbell[a]
Kenneth R. Summers[b]

[a] Wildlife Branch
BC Ministry of Environment, Lands and Parks
Victoria, BC

[b] Biological Services
Aldergrove, BC

Abstract

Reviews of early records and recent field studies revealed there are no known endemic or relict populations of mammals, birds, reptiles, or amphibians on Brooks Peninsula, British Columbia. Vertebrate evidence, therefore, does not support the suggestion that the area is a refugium. Details on habitat, migration chronology, breeding, population, and status are presented for higher vertebrates recorded in the area from 1934 through 1982. In total, 153 species have been recorded: 23 mammals, 120 birds, 2 reptiles, and 8 amphibians. Occurrences and breeding range extensions are documented for some species.

Acknowledgements

The following people have contributed records or participated in field work in the vicinity of Brooks Peninsula: M. Anderson, Ted Antifeau, D. Avline, Frank L. Beebe, Brad Beer, Michael Bigg, Donald A. Blood, D.J. Callas, R. Wayne Campbell, Robert A. Cannings, Sydney G. Cannings, G. Clifford Carl, Trudy A. Chatwin, Harry R. Carter, John M. Cooper, Rick Davies, Ben Van Drimmelin, R. Yorke Edwards, D. Elder, R.J. F. Elder, D.V. Ellis, B. Emerson, Anthea Farr, Max Findlestein, Susan Fleck, Bruce D. Ford, J. Bristol Foster, Leslie Fox, Brian Fuhr, N.W. Garrard, J. Godfrey, J.E.V. Goodwill, Charles J. Guiguet, E. Hamilton, B. Hammond, D. Hancock, Alton S. Harestad, R. Hebda, D. Hebert, Grant Hughes, Richard Inglis, Lindsy Jones, Cathy Kromm, S. Lord, B.N. Macdonald, Robin Marles, Patrick W. Martin, J.L. McGregor, Mary Morris, Rob Morris, W.T. Munro, A. Orr-Ewing, John Pinder-Moss, Jim Pojar, Ian Robertson, Michael S. Rodway, Hans

Roemer, Gordon Smith, Ian D. Smith, Karl Sturmanis, Kenneth R. Summers, Teran Synge, M. Elizabeth Taylor, M. Towsend, Neil Trenholme, Don Tretheway, Al Whitehead, R.L. Williams, Ron Williams, and R. Woodruff.

Unpublished government reports, a major source of material for this paper, were provided by Roger Hunter (BC Ministry of Environment, Lands and Parks, Terrestrial Studies Branch, Victoria); Myke Chutter, Rick Davies, Gordon Smith, and Doug Janz (BC Ministry of Environment, Lands and Parks, Fish and Wildlife Branch, Nanaimo); and J. Bristol Foster, Lynne Milnes, and J. Pinder-Moss (BC Ministry of Lands, Parks and Housing, Ecological Reserves Unit, Victoria). Data files (BC Nest Records Scheme, bibliographies, photo-records [Campbell and Stirling 1971], index cards) at the Royal British Columbia Museum were used extensively.

D.W. Nagorsen identified the *Sorex* and *Myotis* specimens. D.W. Nagorsen, R. Hebda, R.Y. Edwards, J.B. Foster and I. McT.-Cowan critically reviewed the manuscript.

We are grateful to all these people.

Introduction

Brooks Peninsula, the most prominent extension on Vancouver Island, British Columbia, has only recently been suspected to have escaped glaciation (Pojar 1980). Heusser (1960) indicates apparent evidence for the existence of glacial refugia on the Pacific Northwest coast. Foster (1965) suggests that glacial refugia existed on the Queen Charlotte Islands, but supporting evidence from other areas of coastal British Columbia is lacking. Although islands are the best known locations for refugia, headlands may also support endemic or relict populations of plants and animals (Dahl 1947, 1955).

The vertebrate fauna of Brooks Peninsula is largely unknown, though some collecting was done by field parties from the Royal British Columbia Museum on the Bunsby Islands to the south (Carl and Guiguet 1956) and the Scott Islands off the northwest tip of Vancouver Island (Carl et al. 1951). Until recently, all information available for the peninsula area was gathered by biologists and naturalists incidental to other activities.

This paper discusses Brooks Peninsula terrestrial and marine vertebrates, excluding fishes. Data have been gathered from a variety of sources, including zoological explorations by Royal British Columbia Museum staff in August 1981.

Study Area

Brooks Peninsula is located on northwestern Vancouver Island (50°10'N, 127°45' W), about 370 km northwest of Victoria and due west of Campbell River (Figure 12.1). It is a rectangular piece of land with an area of approximately 220 km^2. Much of the peninsula is mountainous with peaks (e.g., Harris Peak) reaching altitudes of 762 m (Figure 12.2). At least 12 sizeable lakes and numerous small, permanent and seasonal ponds are scattered throughout the peninsula (Figure 12.3). Two inlets, Klaskish and Nasparti, hug its base.

The maritime climate is typically mild with extremes in temperature ranging from 13.9° C to 28.9° C. Precipitation, which falls mainly during the winter months, averages 2501 mm to 3000 mm annually at Estevan Point, about 130 km to the south (Tuller 1979).

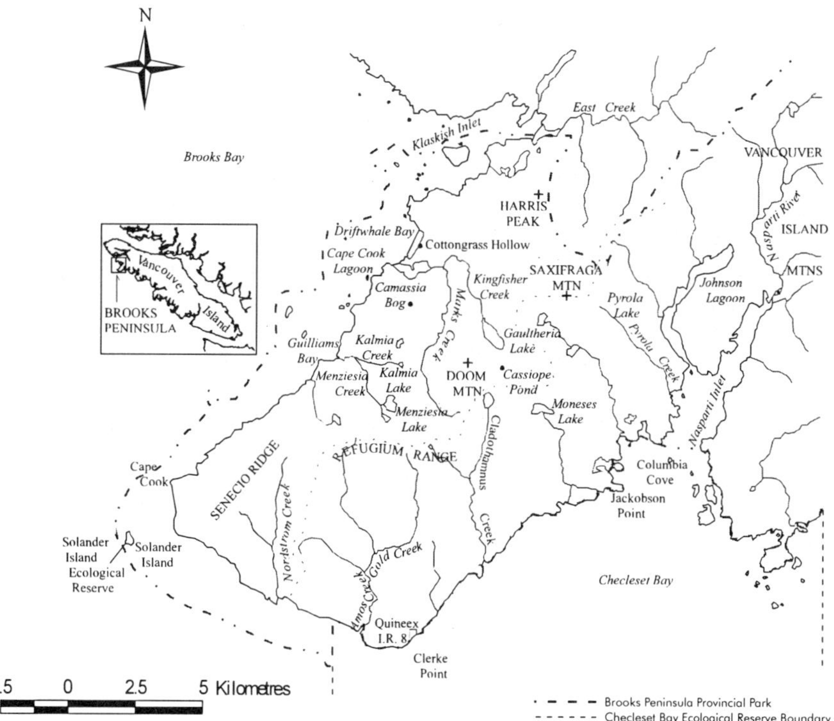

Figure 12.1 Place names and local names for Brooks Peninsula, British Columbia

Figure 12.2 Doom Mountain, Brooks Peninsula (Photo: R. Wayne Campbell)

Figure 12.3 Cassiope Pond, Brooks Peninsula (Photo: R. Wayne Campbell)

All of Brooks Peninsula lies within the Coastal Western Hemlock Biogeoclimatic Zone (Krajina 1959, 1965). Vegetative characteristics are described in detail in Chapter 8.

History of Visits

During the 18th century, European, Russian, and American explorers and traders began visiting the west coast of North America. Although routes took them past Brooks Peninsula (Ormsby 1971), they rarely stopped. The area was probably inaccessible due to lack of good anchorage and strong prevailing winds. As a result, the peninsula was not explored, even though natural historians like Juan Francisco de la Bodega Y Quadra, James Cook, Manuel Quimper, and George Vancouver explored the surrounding terrain (Pearse 1968).

The late Major Allan Brooks provides the earliest documented record for Brooks Peninsula. He collected a Cassin's Auklet (*Ptychorampus aleutica*) near Cape Cook in July 1934. The specimen, deposited in the Museum of Vertebrate Zoology at the University of California, Berkeley, was unaccompanied by field notes.

During the next 48 years, at least 69 people with some interest in vertebrates visited the vicinity of Brooks Peninsula. A summary of these visits is presented in Appendix 12.1. A total of 257 days were tallied, with a monthly breakdown, in days, as follows:

Month		Days	Month		Days
January	-	9	July	-	39
February	-	6	August	-	64
March	-	3	September	-	5
April	-	6	October	-	12
May	-	40	November	-	3
June	-	66	December	-	4

The summer months of June, July, and August account for 66% of all days and, of course, data in the species accounts that follow reflect this imbalance.

Methods

Historical data were gathered from sources listed in Appendix 12.1. All literature pertaining to the Brooks Peninsula area was extracted from bibliographies published by the Royal British Columbia Museum (Campbell, Carter et al. 1979; Campbell, Shepard et al. 1982).

During the museum's expedition in August 1981, which consisted of R.W. Campbell, J.M. Cooper, R.Y. Edwards, and M.E. Taylor, the following techniques were used:

Amphibians and Reptiles

A series of adults, metamorphosing larvae, and tadpoles were collected for most species encountered (see Appendix 12.2). Specimens were fixed in a 10% solution of formalin and preserved in 60% isopropynol. All specimens have been deposited in the Royal British Columbia Museum (Table 12.1). Species names and arrangement follow Green and Campbell (1984) and Gregory and Campbell (1984).

Birds

No birds were collected; therefore, all records are from field observations. Two references were used to put records from Brooks Peninsula in perspective, namely, Hatler et al. (1978) for the Pacific Rim National Park Reserve area to the south, and Richardson (1971) for the Grant Bay-Browning Inlet area to the north.

Other than observations in 1981, the only source of systematic data-gathering was from migration watches from Clerke Point by K.R. Summers, T. Synge, and N.S. Trenholme, from 14 May to 27 June 1973. Continuous watches were kept for an average of five hours a day, with no set pattern except that several one-to-two-hour stretches were spread over the day. With two exceptions, all watches were made between 0430 h and 2000 h pacific standard time. For the purpose of estimating total numbers and comparing daily migration notes, birds per hour were calculated for three time periods each day: 0430-1000 h, 1000-1600 h, and 1600-2000 h.

In the species accounts in this paper the following status designations are used:

Visitor - a species that visits the area to feed (e.g., shearwater, albatross), or a species with only one or two records (e.g., Golden Eagle, Caspian Tern). Does not include breeder or migrant.

Migrant - a species that passes by Brooks Peninsula on spring and/or autumn migration, but does not breed there. "Passage" refers to a migrant in both periods.

Breeder - a species for which breeding evidence has been found (eggs and/or flightless or recently fledged young).

Resident - a species present throughout the year, including non-breeder and breeder.

Season - spring is considered to be March-May; summer, June-August; autumn, September-November; winter, December-February.

The names of species and their sequence follow American Ornithologists' Union (1983, 1985). "BCNRS" refers to British Columbia Nest Records Scheme.

Table 12.1 Terrestrial vertebrate specimens collected by British Columbia Provincial Museum staff on Brooks Peninsula, August 1981

Species	No.
Amphibians and reptiles	
Ambystoma gracile	49
Plethodon vehiculum	1
Taricha granulosa	28
Bufo boreas	35
Hyla regilla	93
Rana aurora	30
Thamnophis elegans	1
Thamnophis sirtalis	11
Subtotal amphibians and reptiles	248
Mammals	
Sorex monticolus	19
Myotis lucifugus	3
Lasiurus cinereus	1
Lasionycteris noctivagans	2
Tamiasciurus hudsonicus	1
Peromyscus maniculatus	65
Microtus townsendii	4
Subtotal mammals	96

Mammals

Small mammals, insectivores and rodents, were captured in snap traps ("Museum Special" and "Victor" types). Traplines were set, from one to three days, in a variety of habitats including beach, forest edge, bog, lakeshore, and various forest types. Individual traps were spaced at 10 m intervals. Bats were shot with a .410 gauge shotgun and later preserved as study skins. Few juveniles of any species were retained as specimens. No other orders of mammals were collected (see Table 12.1), but observations were recorded. All specimens are deposited in the Royal British Columbia Museum.

Names and arrangements follow Honacki et al. (1982) for mammals, and Hart (1982) for crustaceans recovered in scats for food habit analyses.

Species Accounts

Amphibians and Reptiles

Northwestern Salamander - *Ambystoma gracile*. Found in mixed coniferous forests from sea level to 640 m. Larvae were common during daylight in lakes and slower parts of streams. The only adult located was found under logs at the forest edge. According to Nussbaum et al. (1983) larvae usually emerge at night to feed. All collecting was done during daylight. Perhaps the unusually hot weather, with resulting warm water and low water levels, accounts for this phenomenon. An adult, collected in a drying pond on Doom Mountain, was neotenic, a form that is not uncommon for this specimen (Green and Campbell 1984).

Long-toed Salamander - *Ambystoma macrodactylum*. Two adults were found between 5 August and 15 August 1981, deep within rotting Douglas-fir stumps near sea level. These are the first records for the west coast of Vancouver Island (Green and Campbell 1984). No specimens were collected.

Clouded Salamander - *Aneides ferreus*. This species (Figure 12.4) was surprisingly difficult to find, and only one adult was located, deep in a wood pile in a spruce forest, on 7 August 1981. It was not collected. Carl and Guiguet (1956) also had difficulties collecting this species on the nearby Bunsby Islands. There are unconfirmed reports for Solander Island.

Western Red-backed Salamander - *Plethodon vehiculum*. Three adults were seen (Figure 12.5) between 5 August and 15 August 1981. Habitats included soil and a large fallen log in mixed coniferous forest, and rotting wood of abandoned buildings, all at sea level.

Rough-skinned Newt - *Taricha granulosa*. This commonly encountered salamander occurred in lakes, bog ponds, seasonal creeks, and damp muskeg, from sea level to 671 m. It was found only in open areas, never in the forest. All animals seen were active in water, and most were adults.

Western Toad - *Bufo boreas*. Five adults were seen in mixed forest habitats; two were collected. Tadpoles were located only in Kalmia Lake and Amos Creek.

Figure 12.4 Clouded Salamander (*Aneides ferreus*), a rare amphibian on Brooks Peninsula (Photo: R. Wayne Campbell)

Figure 12.5 **Western Red-backed Salamander (*Plethodon vehiculum*), a common amphibian in mixed coniferous forests on Brooks Peninsula (Photo: R. Wayne Campbell)**

Pacific Treefrog - *Hyla regilla*. Adults, metamorphosing individuals, and tadpoles were common in shallow ponds (Figure 12.6), lakes, and other areas of standing water throughout Brooks Peninsula. No individuals were seen in terrestrial habitats very far from water.

Figure 12.6 R.W. Campbell collecting Pacific Treefrogs (*Hyla regilla*) on Brooks Peninsula, August 1981 (Photo: R. Wayne Campbell)

Red-legged Frog - *Rana aurora*. Few adults were seen, but all occurred within 10 m of small, slow-moving creeks. Tadpoles and metamorphosing frogs were especially abundant in shallow ponds containing submerged aquatics, at high elevations.

Common Garter Snake - *Thamnophis sirtalis*. Adults were common among drift logs around the shores of the peninsula (Figure 12.7), whereas immatures were found inland in all habitats except deep forest. Young were especially noticeable at small ponds, where we saw them gorge themselves on tadpoles and metamorphosing *Hyla regilla*. One snake, about 356 mm long, captured and swallowed four small tree frogs along the damp shores of a pond. Others were noticed resting on vegetation in the middle of several shallow ponds.

Birds

Red-throated Loon - *Gavia stellata* (summer visitor, breeder). Small numbers, usually singles or pairs, were recorded from May through August, with no pronounced spring or fall movement. At least two pairs breed on Brooks Peninsula, extending the known breeding range on Vancouver Island about 215 km northwest of Courtenay (Godfrey 1966). Two pairs of adults, each with a single young, were seen from 4 August to 5 August 1981 on Menziesia and Ledum lakes.

Pacific Loon - *Gavia pacifica* (passage migrant). Pacific Loons occur regularly throughout the year along the west coast (Richardson 1971; Hatler et al. 1978). Significant counts off Brooks Peninsula are: 100 on 29 May 1973, 100 on 8 April 1973, 60 on 5-9 August 1981, 93 in late August 1972, and 108 in early October 1972.

Figure 12.7 Drift logs, the preferred habitat for the Common Garter Snake (*Thamnophis sirtalis*) on Brooks Peninsula (Photo: R. Wayne Campbell)

From 14 May to 27 June 1973 a total of 47 081 Pacific Loons were counted off Clerke Point in northward migration; 42 020 of these were counted in 22 days (115 hours) in May, and most of the others during the first half of June. The day of heaviest migration was 21 May. Counts of reverse (southward) migrants were 1008 and 1087 for May and June respectively. The estimated net forward (northward) migration was 153 900 in May and 25 800 in June, for a total of 179 700 Pacific Loons. Offshore, Martin and Myers (1969) recorded a similar pattern.

Common Loon - ***Gavia immer*** (resident, non-breeder). Up to five individuals have been reported off Brooks Peninsula in the more shallow and protected waters of Brooks Bay and Checleset Bay. There was no pronounced movement in either spring or autumn. No adults have been recorded on inland lakes, though Godfrey (1966) includes this area in the species' breeding range on Vancouver Island. The only confirmed breeding record for Vancouver Island north of the Campbell River area (BCNRS) is an unpublished sighting by R.L. Williams of two adults with a small chick on Victoria Lake, east of Port Alice.

Horned Grebe - ***Podiceps aruitus*** (winter visitor). The only record is three birds seen on 12 March 1976 in Klaskish Inlet; it is consistent with the status reported by Richardson (1971) and Hatler et al. (1978).

Red-necked Grebe - ***Podiceps grisegena*** (resident, non-breeder). Small numbers were reported throughout the year. Four birds seen off Solander Island on 5 May 1976 and five in Johnson Lagoon on 30 October 1979 represent the largest concentrations.

Western Grebe - ***Aechmophorus occidentalis*** (summer visitor, non-breeder). Fewer than 10 birds spend the summer off Brooks Peninsula, but significantly more winter there (100 birds on 12 March 1976 in Klaskish Inlet). The only other winter concentration on the west coast was reported near Tofino by Hatler et al. (1978) where 100+ Western Grebes were seen on 4 March 1969.

Black-footed Albatross - ***Diomedea nigripes*** (visitor). This species is common in pelagic waters off Vancouver Island's west coast (Campbell and Shepard 1972; Martin and Myres 1969; Sanger 1972), so two records in littoral waters near Brooks Peninsula are noteworthy. On 27 August 1967, J.E.V. Goodwill saw four birds near Solander Island, and on 7 September 1973 P.W. Martin saw several in Brooks Bay.

Laysan Albatross - ***Diomedea immutabilis*** (visitor). On 30 October 1973, J.E.V. Goodwill recorded this species in the area of Brooks Bay. Gale force winds on the evening of 29 October may have forced the bird into the bay, though Laysan Albatrosses do forage close to land off Vancouver Island in winter (Campbell and Shepard 1973; Sanger 1965).

Pink-footed Shearwater - ***Puffinus creatopus*** (visitor). The only littoral record is of six birds, seen among a large flock of Sooty Shearwaters near Solander Island on 27 August 1967.

Sooty Shearwater - ***Puffinus griseus*** (visitor). Records from May through early September show flocks of up to 450 birds foraging in Brooks Bay and Checleset Bay in late June and July. During the spring migration watch in 1973, a total of 33 949 shearwaters (presumed to be mostly *P. griseus*) were counted. Of these, 18 680 were counted from Clerke Point in 16 days (79 hours) during the last half of May, and 15 269 were counted in 20 days (75 hours) in June. The estimated net northward movement was 56 000 birds for the last half of May and 89 800 for June. Flocks of shearwaters move in a wide path far off shore, so these figures represent only a small fraction of the total number of migrants. Shearwaters generally occur only beyond 8 km from shore. They steadily increase in numbers to at least 24 km out (Jewett et al. 1953), though they commonly occur to at least 48 km. The day of heaviest movement, 21 May 1973, when 2000 birds per hour passed by Clerke Point, coincided with two low pressure frontal systems converging on the coast.

Fork-tailed Storm-Petrel - *Oceanodroma furcata* (summer visitor, breeder). Three records are: nine counted on 27 August 1967 and two on 25 July 1968 near Solander Island, and one feeding in Checleset Bay on 10 August 1981. These birds may be from Solander Island, though breeding there has not yet been confirmed (Campbell 1976).

Double-crested Cormorant - *Phalacrocorax auritus* (visitor). Up to six birds roosted with other cormorants on low rocks off the tip of Brooks Peninsula from 5 August to 14 August 1981.

Brandt's Cormorant - *Phalacrocorax penicillatus* (visitor). Recorded from late June through August, which coincides with the northward fall movement reported off Pacific Rim National Park Reserve (Hatler et al. 1978). Eight birds, estimated on Clerke Islet on 20 August, 1981, is the largest roosting flock recorded.

Pelagic Cormorant - *Phalacrocorax pelagicus* (resident, breeder). Present in small numbers throughout the year except more numerous in summer when birds from a colony on Solander Island (Drent and Guiguet 1961), and perhaps also from elsewhere, collect to feed and roost off Brooks Peninsula. The largest concentration was 1000+ birds estimated around Solander Island on 28 May 1966.

Great Blue Heron - *Ardea herodias* (visitor). Only two records: a single bird seen on Cape Cook on 30 October 1979, and two birds seen at Nasparti Inlet on 6 August 1981 and probably again a week later in Cape Cook Lagoon.

Cattle Egret - *Bubulcus ibis* (visitor). This species, first recorded in British Columbia on southern Vancouver Island on 26 November 1973 (Campbell and Weber 1977), has spread to numerous coastal locations,.but is still very rare on the outer west coast. A single bird was flushed from the southern tip of Brooks Peninsula by B. Macdonald on 26 November 1974.

Green Heron - *Butorides virescens* (visitor). A single record by M.S. Rodway of an adult flushed at the mouth of the Klaskish River on 22 May 1978. This extends the range along the west coast of Vancouver Island about 180 km northwards from Tofino (Campbell 1972a).

Trumpeter Swan - *Cygnus buccinator* (winter visitor). During their winter survey of estuaries on Vancouver Island in 1970-71, Smith and Blood (1972) found pairs of swans at the mouths of Klaskish and Nasparti inlets. Other records are of six adults seen on 3-5 January 1973, and three adults and an immature on 5 January 1977, all on the Klaskish estuary.

Brant - *Branta bernicula* (spring migrant). In spring, this species stops, in small numbers, at both Klaskish Inlet and Checleset Bay to rest and feed on eel grass. The main movement occurs in April and May (Hatler et al. 1978; Martin and Myres 1969). During spring migration watches from Clerke Point, 4039 were counted in May and 103 in June.

Canada Goose - *Branta canadensis* (migrant, winter visitor). Spring migration occurs mainly in March and April, fall migration mainly in September and October. Fall migrants use the two estuaries on Brooks Peninsula more than do spring birds. In 1973, the main movement (1625 geese) occurred during the first five days of May. Up to 100 geese winter each year at various locations around the peninsula.

Green-winged Teal - ***Anas crecca*** (autumn migrant). Flocks of up to 20 birds were recorded in 1981, from late August through October. Lack of extensive mud flats probably accounts for the minimal use of the Brooks Peninsula area by teals.

Mallard - ***Anas platyrhynchos*** (resident, breeder). The Mallard is the only waterfowl seen in both marine and freshwater habitats around Brooks Peninsula. Up to 100 birds winter in the area. The only breeding record consists of a brood of four large, but flightless, young accompanied by a female, at the head of Nasparti Inlet on 7 August 1981.

Northern Pintail - ***Anas acuta*** (migrant). The spring migration is light. During the 1973 watch, 40 pintails were seen on eight days in May, 3 on 9 June, and 40 on 16 June. Autumn movement, however, is very conspicuous. In 1981, this movement started on 12 August (62 birds) and peaked (hundreds of birds) during the third week of August. There were no records after 25 November.

Blue-winged Teal - ***Anas discors*** (visitor). Two males were seen in a small bay near Clerke Point on 29 May 1973. Other records for the west coast of Vancouver Island are from autumn in Browning Inlet (Richardson 1971) and summer in Pacific Rim National Park (Hatler et al. 1978).

American Wigeon - ***Anas americana*** (winter visitor). Small flocks, up to 40 birds, were recorded in the Klaskish estuary in February 1975 and January 1977.

Greater Scaup - ***Aythya marila*** (migrant). The only records are from Clerke Point where 97 were counted from 14 May to 31 May 1973, and an additional 19 on the first two days of June 1973.

Harlequin Duck - ***Histrionicus histrionicus*** (summer visitor). The summer, molting population arrives in mid-May and departs by September. These birds, mostly males (139 males and 17 females in August 1981), feed in summer along the low tide line, especially near creek mouths, and roost on offshore rocky islets.

Surf Scoter - ***Melanitta perspicillata*** (resident, non-breeder). Small flocks, from 10 to 75 birds, are present throughout the year around Brooks Peninsula. The population is largest in winter, but has never been recorded as more than 200 birds.

White-winged Scoter - ***Melanitta fusca*** (resident, non-breeder). This species, associated with *M. perspicallata*, occurs in small numbers throughout the year. During the 1973 watches, 6525 scoters of both species were counted in May and another 2673 in June. The estimated net northward movement was 28 600 in May and 15 400 in June. Nearly 70% of the June migrants had passed by mid-month.

Bufflehead - ***Bucephala albeola*** (winter visitor). Flocks of up to 40 birds winter each year from November through March in Johnson Lagoon, the Nasparti River estuary, and at the Klaskish River mouth. Richardson (1971) indicates a similar situation for Grant Bay and Browning Inlet. Farther south, in Grice Bay, this species' winter population may reach 1000 (Hatler et al. 1978).

Hooded Merganser - ***Lophodytes cucullatus*** (visitor). On northern Vancouver Island this species is a winter visitant (Richardson 1971), whereas it is resident in Pacific Rim National Park Reserve (Hatler et al. 1978). There is one record for Brooks Peninsula, a flock of six male and two female adults seen on a large lake on 23 May 1978.

Common Merganser - ***Mergus merganser*** (resident, breeder). Except during the late summer months, when family flocks are common, this merganser is present throughout the year in small numbers, usually fewer than eight birds at any one location. There is only one breeding record. An adult female with a brood of 10 downy young was seen at the mouth of Nasparti Inlet on 6 August 1981.

Red-breasted Merganser - *Mergus serrator* (visitor). The only record was a flock of seven birds seen off Jackobson Point on 26 June 1975.

Waterbird Groups - Aerial surveys by personnel of the British Columbia Ministry of Environment, from 1976 to 1979, indicate that small populations of waterbirds winter near Brooks Peninsula (Table 12.2). Puddle ducks, mainly *Anas platyrhynchos*, were the most numerous group. Diving ducks (mostly *Melanitta* spp.) were next in abundance, followed by gulls (mostly *Larus canus*). *Cygnus buccinator* probably accounted for most swans, *Branta canadensis* for all geese, and *Phalacrocorax pelagicus* for most cormorants. The unprotected open waters of Brooks Bay and Checleset Bay, and the small areas of exposed estuary habitat in Nasparti Inlet and Klaskish Inlet may account for the relatively small wintering population of only 500 waterbirds. In more protected waters with extensive mud flats, such as Clayoquot Sound to the south, populations are considerably larger (Hatler 1973).

Osprey - *Pandion haliaetus* (breeder). Recorded from 8 April 1973 through 27 August 1981. It is unlikely that more than one pair frequents the area. At least two large young were seen in a small, stick nest 17 m up in a spruce snag, just west of the Klaskish River mouth, on 14 August 1981.

Table 12.2 Aerial counts of waterbirds wintering in vicinity of Brooks Peninsula[a]

	5 Jan 1977			19 Jan 1978			20 Apr 1976			30 Oct 1979		
Waterbird group	A	B	C	A	B	C	A	B	C	A	B	C
Grebes	0	0	0	0	0	0	0	0	0	0	0	11
Cormorants	0	85	1	0	0	0	0	0	0	25	1	1
Swans	4	0	0	0	0	0	0	0	0	0	0	0
Geese	30	0	20	85	0	0	0	0	0	0	0	35
Puddle ducks	109	0	0	07	0	0	0	0	0	35	0	61
Diving ducks	58	0	58	2	0	25	0	0	0	75	0	70
Gulls	4	97	28	0	0	0	0	0	0	16	59	81
Alcids	0	0	0	6	0	0	0	0	6	23	0	7
All units			494			118			6			500

[a] Census units: A, Klaskish Inlet to Cape Cook; B, Cape Cook to Clerke Point; C, Clerke Point to Nasparti Inlet.

Source: British Columbia Ministry of Environment, Lands and Parks (Terrestrial Studies Branch, Victoria; Fish and Wildlife Branch, Nanaimo)

Bald Eagle - ***Haliaeetus leucocephalus*** (resident, breeder). Nine birds seen on Solander Island on 6 May 1976 is the largest concentration recorded. Up to three birds can be seen most days throughout the year. At least three pairs breed on Brooks Peninsula. Three nests, each containing a single large young, were located: one west of Jackobson Point, one north of Quineex Indian Reserve 8, and one north of Quineex Reef. All were within 200 m of the shore and in conifers.

Prey remains collected beneath two nests included loon (1), Sooty Shearwater (1), Pelagic Cormorant (1), Surf Scoter (2), Bufflehead (1), gull (3), Mew Gull (91), Common Murre (92), Rhinoceros Auklet (5), and fish (8). Brooks (1922), in his studies on the Queen Charlotte Islands, indicated that birds are important components of the Bald Eagle's diet. Murie (1938), Hatler (1974), and Hatler et al. (1978) also indicate substantial percentages of avian prey (notably seabirds) in eagle diets on the west coast of the continent.

Northern Goshawk - *Accipiter gentilis* (visitor). An immature, seen perched in a tree near Nasparti Inlet on 7 August 1981, is the only record. Richardson (1971) did not record this species, and Hatler et al. (1978) considered it a winter bird. The nearest known breeding record (and summer occurrence) is from the south end of Vancouver Island, at Jordan River (Beebe 1974).

Red-tailed Hawk - *Buteo jamaicensis* (visitor). Only four birds (perhaps a family group) were sighted soaring over the tip of Brooks Peninsula from 6 August to 14 August 1981.

Golden Eagle - *Aquila chrysaetos* (visitor). An immature bird soaring low over Brooks Peninsula was studied carefully by J.B. Foster and T. Carson on 22 July 1978. This is the only record for the west coast of Vancouver Island. The nearest other record is 150 km east near Campbell river, where, in the summer of 1954, a pair successfully fledged three young (Laing 1956).

Peregrine Falcon - *Falco peregrinus* (resident, breeder). This species was first recorded in the area in 1949. P.W. Martin saw an adult at Solander Island on 4 July. Five years later Beebe (1960) visited the island from 29 June to 3 July and reported one adult in residence, a female in molt. Recent occupancy by a breeding pair was indicated by detached wings of auklets, dead auklets, plucking perches, and an empty, recently occupied aerie. No falcons were seen during a Royal British Columbia Museum field trip to Solander Island on 27 June 1975. J.B. Foster and R.W. Campbell visited the island on 5 May and 6 May 1976 and watched an adult falcon hunt, but did not locate an aerie. In 1981, four falcons were sighted on Brooks Peninsula. R.W. Campbell watched an adult and young of the year hunt shorebirds along the beach near Quineex Reef on 6 August and 7 August. An adult was seen by R.W. Campbell near Doom Mountain on 8 August, and an adult was seen by S.G. Cannings and R.A. Cannings on 7 August. The authors conclude that a pair probably breeds somewhere on Brooks Peninsula. Possibly, falcons on the peninsula use Bald Eagle nests for breeding sites instead of the usual cliff ledges (Campbell, Paul et al. 1977). The nearest known active Peregrine Falcon nesting site is on the Scott Islands, 130 km northwest of Brooks Peninsula (Carl et al. 1951).

Blue Grouse - *Dendragapus obscurus* (resident, breeder). An ubiquitous species found throughout Brooks Peninsula, at all elevations (including Solander Island, where an adult female was recorded on 6 May 1976). Three broods were found at high altitudes, in low shrub: two young with a female on 9 August 1981, and females with broods of one and two half-grown young on 11 August and 13 August 1981.

Ruffed Grouse - *Bonasa umbellus* (probable resident, breeder). One record, a brood of at least three young with an adult female, was flushed in open, stunted mossy forest on 22 August 1981.

Black-bellied Plover - *Pluvialis squatarola* (autumn migrant). To date, the only records are during fall migration, consistent with the August and September period recorded for the Browning Inlet area (Richardson 1971). A single bird was present at Orchard Point beach from 21 August to 23 August 1981.

Semipalmated Plover - *Charadrius semipalmatus* (autumn migrant). Recorded from 4 August to 19 August 1981 (the maximum number, 12 birds, was recorded on 4 August).

Killdeer - *Charadrius vociferus* (visitor). A single bird was seen on 7 August 1981 at the Nasparti River estuary.

Black Oystercatcher - *Haematopus bachmani* (resident, breeder). This bird occurs in singles and pairs throughout the year. Forages on Brooks Peninsula and breeds on offshore islands (e.g., Clerke Islet and Solander Island).

Greater Yellowlegs - *Tringa melanoleuca* (autumn migrant). Recorded only from 9 August to 13 August 1981, when one or two birds were seen foraging along lakeshores on Brooks Peninsula.

Lesser Yellowlegs - *Tringa flavipes* (autumn migrant). The only record, two unaged birds seen on the mouth of the Klaskish River on 27 June 1975 by C.J. Guiguet, is the earliest late-summer migration record for British Columbia. The southward movement usually commences in July and peaks in August. For the period 1970-72, first migrants were recorded on 23 July, 1 August, and 21 July for southern Vancouver Island (Tatum 1971, 1972, 1973), and on 21 July, 8 July, and 18 July for the greater Vancouver area (Campbell, Shepard and Drent 1972; Campbell, Shepard and Weber 1972; Campbell, Shepard et al. 1974). This species was not recorded in the fall on northwestern Vancouver Island (Richardson 1971), but was considered a rare autumn migrant in Pacific Rim National Park Reserve (Hatler et al. 1978).

Wandering Tattler - *Heteroscelus incanus* (summer visitor). Single birds were recorded from 5 May to 7 August on offshore islets and rocky headlands.

Spotted Sandpiper - *Actitis macularia* (summer visitor, non-breeder). Single birds were recorded in a variety of open marine and freshwater habitats throughout Brooks Peninsula from 22 May through 21 August. Nesting is suspected, but not confirmed.

Whimbrel - *Numenius phaeopus* (passage migrant). Twenty-four birds were counted flying north during migration watches from Clerke Point between 16 May and 1 June 1973. Other records are: a single bird on Clara Islet on 26 June 1975, two on Gould Rock the next day, and a flock of 12 over Orchard Point on 22 August 1981.

Long-billed Curlew - *Numenius americanus* (visitor). An adult was sighted on Solander Island on 5 May 1976 by R.W. Campbell and J.B. Foster. This species is very rare on the coast (Campbell 1972b) and was not reported by either Richardson (1971) or Hatler et al. (1978). Another unpublished coastal record, however, is of interest. Summers saw a bird on Cleland Island (off Tofino) on 3 May 1973. It is noteworthy that of 18 coastal records for British Columbia (Royal British Columbia Museum files), 15 are from the spring season in April and May.

Black Turnstone - *Arenaria melanocephala* (resident, non-breeder). Small flocks, usually fewer than 15 birds, were seen foraging along rocky beaches or on offshore islets, throughout the year. Records are too few to indicate a seasonal trend.

Western Sandpiper - *Calidris mauri* (passage migrant). Recorded in small flocks of 40 or so on sandy beaches on Brooks Peninsula, from 6 May through 26 August.

Least Sandpiper - *Calidris minutilla* (passage migrant). Usually seen with flocks of *C. mauri,* in much smaller numbers, from 6 May through 26 August.

Baird's Sandpiper - *Calidris bairdii* (autumn migrant). A single bird was noted, often associating with Western Sandpipers on sandy beaches near our field camp at Cape Cook Lagoon, from 6 August to 24 August 1981.

Short-billed Dowitcher - *Limnodromus griseus* (fall migrant). R.Y. Edwards identified a flock of 13 birds, by call, on 22 August 1981, at Cape Cook Lagoon.

Red-necked Phalarope - *Phalaropus lobatus* (spring migrant). This was the most numerous species observed during migration watches from Clerke Point. Migration was most pronounced in the first two weeks of May, and by the end of the third week species numbers dropped off sharply. By the end of the second week in June, the migration had ceased completely. In total, 43 959 birds were tallied in May and 762 in four days in June. An estimated total of 200 000 phalaropes passed by, of which 4600 moved northwards after the end of May. This represents only a small portion of the population that migrates farther offshore. The peak movement was around 14 May. Similar trends were noticed at sea by Martin and Myres (1969), with a peak movement recorded on 15 May 1969. Generally, migration did not seem to be affected by weather. On peak days (3, 14 and 15 May), however, winds were light and generally westerly.

Parasitic Jaeger - *Stercorarius parasiticus* (migrant). Eighty jaegers were counted from Clerke Point during the spring migration watches. No migrants were seen in early May, and a few passed by in late May; most observations were recorded in June. The greatest numbers were seen on or following days of strong, southeasterly winds. Single birds, both dark and light phases, can frequently be seen in June, in Brooks Bay and Checleset Bay.

Long-tailed Jaeger - *Stercorarius longicaudus* (visitor). The only record, a single bird, was seen by J.E.V. Goodwill off Solander Island on 27 August 1967.

Bonaparte's Gull - *Larus philadelphia* (migrant). The main northward movement occurs in May, the return movement peaks in August—trends already noted by Martin and Myres (1969) and Hatler et al. (1978). During 115 hours of spring migration watches, a total of 6760 gulls were counted (all in May) with an estimated total movement of 30 700 birds. This species passes northwards in large flocks at irregular intervals. For example, on 3 May, about 250 Bonaparte's Gulls were counted in 10 minutes.

Mew Gull - *Larus canus* (resident, breeder). Present in small numbers throughout the year. Two recently used nest sites were located on rocky islets in lakes (Figure 12.8). This confirms its breeding status. Freshly broken shell fragments were found in nests of mosses and sticks on Kalmia Lake (9 August 1981) and on Moneses Lake (12 August 1981). This extends the known breeding range along the west coast of Vancouver Island 200 km north from Kennedy Lake (Campbell 1970).

California Gull - *Larus californicus* (visitor). The most numerous gull in the area, recorded from 26 June to 18 September. Sandy beaches are preferred loafing sites. High counts were: 300 on 3 July 1954, 340 on 12 August 1981, and 400 on 22 August 1981.

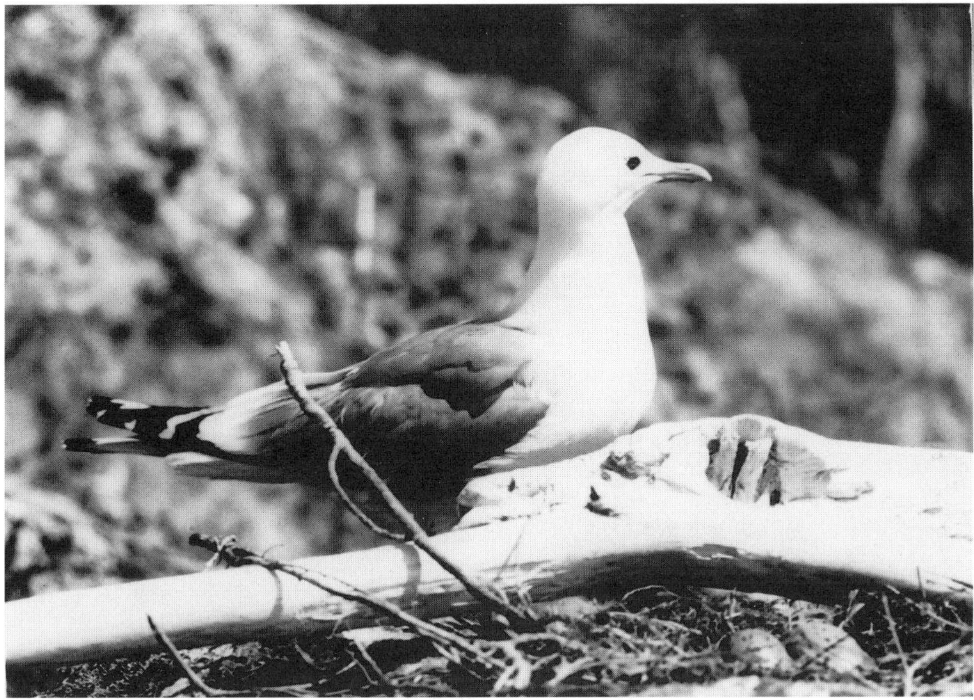

Figure 12.8 Mew Gulls (*Larus canus*) found nesting on Brooks Peninsula in August 1981, extend the breeding range 200 km north along the west coast of Vancouver Island (Photo: R. Wayne Campbell)

Herring Gull - *Larus argentatus* (visitor). Although this species is considered resident in Browning Inlet (Richardson 1971) and Pacific Rim National Park Reserve (Hatler et al. 1978), there are only 12 records for the Brooks Peninsula area. Flocks ranged in size up to 20 birds, recorded from 5 May through 14 August 1981, mostly on offshore reefs and islets.

Western Gull - *Larus occidentalis* (visitor). There is only one record: two adults roosting with California Gulls on Orchard Point beach on 22 August 1981.

Glaucous-winged Gull - *Larus glaucescens* (resident, breeder). Present throughout the year with summer populations largest because there are breeding colonies on nearby Solander Island and O'Leary Islets (Campbell 1976). From 5 August to 15 August 1981 the total population (breeding and non-breeding) for the Brooks Peninsula area was estimated at 650 birds.

Black-legged Kittiwake - *Rissa tridactyla* (visitor). Recorded in substantial numbers from 12 March through mid-September. Flocks of about 100 have been seen in March, April, and May, 600 in June, and 300 in July—usually roosting on offshore rocky islets, such as Clerke Islet and Solander Island.

This species migrates past Brooks Peninsula in large flocks at irregular intervals, though some of the birds could represent dispersal from local roosting sites. In one and one-half hours, K.R. Summers counted 750 birds passing Clerke Point on 28 May 1973.

Sabine's Gull - *Xema sabini* (visitor). A single bird, in adult plumage, was seen from Solander Island on 5 May 1976. This sighting represents an early spring arrival date (see Campbell and Shepard 1972).

Caspian Tern - *Sterna caspia* (visitor). Two birds, flying together west of Quineex Reef, were seen by R.W. Campbell on 7 August 1981. The first specimen record for British Columbia was collected in Barkley Sound on 18 August 1969 (Schick 1970). Since then, this large tern has been reported as far north as Vargas Island (Campbell 1971). The Brooks Peninsula sighting extends the species range 160 km along the west coast of Vancouver Island. On 13 June 1982, D. Thompson photographed a Caspian Tern (RBCM photo 798) near Bunsby Islands as it flew towards Brooks Peninsula.

Common Murre - *Uria aalge* (resident, non-breeder). Although present in flocks of up to 50 birds throughout the year, there is a tremendous influx of birds in Brooks Bay and Checleset Bay from mid-July through August. By late September these birds have dispersed. An aerial count on 13 August 1981, around littoral waters of Brooks Peninsula, totalled 2200 murres.

Pigeon Guillemot - *Cepphus columba* (resident, breeder). This species is widespread in coastal waters around Brooks Peninsula throughout the year. It breeds on nearby Clerke Islet and Solander Island (Campbell 1976).

Marbled Murrelet - *Brachyramphus marmoratus* (visitor). Recorded, usually in singles or pairs, from 5 May through October. J.B. Foster (personal communication April 1983) suspects this species breeds on Brooks Peninsula. His notes for 23 March 1978 show: "at 2200 hours Marbled Murrelets were heard calling in the forest (mixed conifers) north of the lake. At 0540 hours the next morning, they were heard again". As yet, no nests have been discovered in British Columbia.

Ancient Murrelet - *Synthliboramphus antiquus* (visitor). There are two records: 1 adult off Hackett island seen by R.W. Campbell and C.J. Guiguet on 27 June 1975; and 7 birds (probably family flocks) off Clerke Islet, noted by R.W. Campbell on 5 August 1981. These sightings probably represent dispersal from breeding colonies on the Queen Charlotte Islands. Sealy and Campbell (1979) document preliminary offshore movement in May and June, followed by inshore movement in July, and southward movement that continues in late fall and winter to California.

Cassin's Auklet - *Ptychorampus aleuticus* (summer visitor, breeder). A. Brooks collected an adult female off Cape Cook on 8 July 1934. This diminutive auklet has been recorded in the waters off Brooks Peninsula, from mid-May through August, where small numbers (fewer than 10) associate with mixed assemblages of feeding seabirds. A few hundred of this species breed on Solander Island (Campbell 1976).

Rhinoceros Auklet - *Cerorhinca monocerata* (visitor). Records are from 5 May through August, off Brooks Peninsula. There seem to be constant flights northwards and southwards past the tip of the peninsula in May and June, probably to and from feeding grounds. For example, from 1345 h to 1430 h (PST) on 5 May 1976, R.W. Campbell and J.B. Foster counted 16 birds flying north and 171 auklets flying south past Solander Island. This species is most noticeable in mixed feeding flocks of seabirds in Brooks Bay and Checleset Bay. C.J. Guiguet and R.W. Campbell counted 125 birds feeding off O'Leary Islets on 26 June 1975, and estimated 450 birds 3 km south of Hackett Island the next day. This species is not known to breed in the area (Campbell 1976).

Tufted Puffin - *Fratercula cirrhata* (summer visitor, breeder). This species has been recorded from 5 May to 15 August. A few thousand breed (Figure 12.9) on Solander Island (Campbell 1976).

Eight specimens have been collected there. This species is most often seen from Brooks Peninsula when feeding flocks of seabirds are present.

Horned Puffin - ***Fratercula corniculata*** (summer visitor). This species has only recently extended its range southwards into British Columbia, from Alaska (Sealy and Nelson 1973). In 1977, it was found breeding on the Queen Charlotte Islands and was first reported near Solander Island on 27 June 1975 (Campbell, Carter, and Sealy 1979). There are three additional sightings, all in August 1981—one off Quineex Reef near Solander Island. Breeding has not been confirmed.

Figure 12.9 Solander Island, off Brooks Peninsula, supports the largest colony of Tufted Puffin (*Fratercula cirrhata*) in British Columbia (Photo: R. Wayne Campbell)

Band-tailed Pigeon - ***Columba fasciata*** (summer visitor). There are five sightings: Klaskish Indian Reserve 3, 23 May 1978; Cassiope Pond, 31 July 1981; 3 at Quineex Reef, 5 August 1981; 2 at Cape Cook Lagoon, 11 August 1981; and 1 at Cape Cook Lagoon, 13 August 1981.

Western Screech-Owl - ***Otus kennicottii*** (visitor). Only one record, an adult, heard calling at 2020 h (PST) near the mouth of Nasparti River on 7 August 1981.

Great Horned Owl - ***Bubo virginianus*** (visitor). A single sighting of an adult calling, then flying along the beach, at 2010 h (PST) on 6 August 1981.

Rufous Hummingbird - ***Selasphorus rufus*** (summer visitor, probable breeder). Recorded throughout Brooks Peninsula from 5 May through 24 August. Courtship flights were witnessed on 23 May 1978, but breeding has not been confirmed.

Belted Kingfisher - *Ceryle alcyon* (resident, breeder). Recorded in singles and pairs frequenting the shores from 8 April to 25 November. There are two breeding records. M.S. Rodway located a nest hole in soil surrounding an upturned spruce root in midstream, on the Klaskish River, on 21 May 1978. The nest could not be checked, but the adults were very agitated. On 6 August 1981, R.W. Campbell observed a pair of adult kingfishers with two flying young of the year at Cape Cook Lagoon.

Red-breasted Sapsucker - *Sphyrapicus ruber* (visitor). One record only: a single bird seen in alders along the Klaskish River on 13 August 1981.

Hairy Woodpecker - *Picoides villosus* (resident, probable breeder). Single birds were recorded in all months except November to March, mostly in mixed woodlands near the mouth of the Klaskish River. This species probably breeds in the area.

Northern Flicker - *Colaptes auratus* (resident, probable breeder). Single birds were recorded in all months except December. All were *C. a. cafer*, though Richardson (1971) recorded *C. a. auratus* and hybrid forms in March, April, October, and November. This woodpecker frequents all parts of Brooks Peninsula and most likely breeds there.

Pileated Woodpecker - *Dryocopus pileatus* (visitor). A single bird was seen by BC Fish and Wildlife Branch personnel, during stream survey work along the Klaskish River, from 15 May to 25 May 1974.

Pacific-slope Flycatcher - *Empidonax difficilis* (summer visitor). The only *Empidonax* recorded were from 5 May through 15 August, at Gaultheria and Canoe lakes.

Eastern Kingbird - *Tyrannus tyrannus* (visitor). Although Godfrey (1966) includes Vancouver Island in the breeding range for this species, it is very rare, especially on the west coast. Hatler et al. (1978) list only two records, for July and August, both from Pachena Light Station; it was undetected by Richardson (1971). A sighting by R.W. Campbell, a single bird fly-catching near Quineex Indian Reserve 8 for nearly three hours on 6 August 1981, is noteworthy.

Violet-green Swallow - *Tachycineta thalassina* (summer visitor). The only sighting was five birds seen on 18 August 1981 on top of a high, open-topped ridge near Cape Cook.

Northern Rough-winged Swallow - *Stelgidopteryx serripennis* (summer visitor). The only record is of three individuals seen hawking over the exposed tidal areas at the Nasparti River mouth on 6 August, 1981. The closest breeding site is Tofino, 170 km to the south (Hatler et al. 1978).

Steller's Jay - *Cyanocitta stelleri* (resident, probable breeder). Recorded in all months except December and present in wooded areas throughout Brooks Peninsula. Breeding in the area was suspected, but not confirmed.

Northwestern Crow - *Corvus caurinus* (resident, breeder). All records are from beaches, offshore islets, and river mouths, where up to 62 crows were seen (6 August 1981) in a foraging flock. On the same date, an adult was watched feeding two large, fledged young that were begging food on the beach near Quineex Indian Reserve 8. This is the only breeding record for the area.

Common Raven - *Corvus corax* (resident). One or two birds were seen in all months except December, throughout Brooks Peninsula. Although not confirmed, a pair probably nested on Doom Mountain in 1981.

Chestnut-backed Chickadee - *Parus rufescens* (resident). Recorded in all months, throughout Brooks Peninsula, but as Hatler et al. (1978) noted, this bird is most noticeable along the forest edge of the beach.

Red-breasted Nuthatch - *Sitta canadensis* (resident). Present in most months, but recorded at irregular intervals. All records were from mixed coniferous forests. In August, this high-canopy bird associates with chickadees, kinglets, and migrating warblers and is more noticeable in lower forest strata.

Brown Creeper - *Certhia americana* (resident). Hatler et al. (1978: 130) mention that this species is "a bird of deep woods, is unconspicuous and easily overlooked". Although not recorded from October to February, this species is probably resident on Brooks Peninsula.

Winter Wren - *Troglodytes troglodytes* (resident, breeder). There are more records for this tiny bird than any other species, probably because it can be heard throughout the year. It is most common in coniferous forests, from sea level to 550 m. During the period 5 August to 15 August 1981, R.W. Campbell recorded 23 young of the year along the forest edge. Many of the fledgelings had traces of natal down and characteristic yellow gapes in their bills.

American Dipper - *Cinclus mexicanus* (summer visitor). Records were only from the months of May through August, from the Nasparti and Klaskish rivers. On 24 May 1978, M.S. Rodway watched an adult carrying food, presumably for young, but was not able to confirm breeding in the area.

Golden-crowned Kinglet - *Regulus satrapa* (visitor). This species is resident along the west coast of Vancouver Island (Hatler et al. 1978; Richardson 1971). On Brooks Peninsula, the only records are from August, when it was the most numerous species in the forest canopy.

Ruby-crowned Kinglet - *Regulus calendula* (visitor). This kinglet was only recorded in small numbers, infrequently, from 24 May through 15 August.

Swainson's Thrush - *Catharus ustulatus* (summer visitor). There are only four records, from 24 May through 7 August, though it is considered a common summer species in Pacific Rim National Park Reserve (Hatler et al. 1978).

Hermit Thrush - *Catharus guttatus* (summer visitor). This thrush is considered less common in Pacific Rim National Park Reserve than *C. ustulatus* (Hatler et al. 1978), however, on Brooks Peninsula it was the more common of the two species. Recorded from 5 May through August.

American Robin - *Turdus migratorius* (resident). Robins were present in small numbers, usually in open areas near river mouths and along beaches, in all months except December and January.

Varied Thrush - *Ixoreus naevius* (resident). This secretive thrush has been heard, or seen, in all months except December, and no doubt it breeds deep in the forests on Brooks Peninsula.

Cedar Waxwing - *Bombycilla cedrorum* (summer visitor). Flocks of six or fewer birds were recorded from 27 June through 27 August. During the last week in August, R.Y. Edwards watched this species gorge itself on red huckleberries (*Vaccinium parvifolium*).

European Starling - *Sturnus vulgaris* (summer visitor). This species was first recorded on the west coast of Vancouver Island in May 1967 at Pachena Point (Campbell 1968). During the next 15 years it spread northwards and is today (1983) well established and resident in most areas of Vancouver Island. It has only been recorded in May and June on Brooks Peninsula.

Orange-crowned Warbler - *Vermivora celata* (summer visitor). Up to three birds were recorded in mixed woodlands from 6 May through 27 August.

Yellow-rumped Warbler - *Dendroica coronata* (summer visitor, probable breeder). The subspecies *D. c. auduboni* was seen, infrequently, in deciduous woodland near river mouths from 5 May through 13 August.

Townsend's Warbler - *Dendroica townsendi* (summer visitor). This warbler was infrequently recorded from 6 May to 17 August, mostly in Sitka spruce forests, throughout Brooks Peninsula.

Wilson's Warbler - *Wilsonia posilla* (summer visitor). Recorded from 6 May to 19 August at edges of forest openings on Brooks Peninsula.

Savannah Sparrow - *Passerculus sandwichensis* (passage migrant). The main spring movement was unrecorded. Twenty-three birds counted migrating on 5 May 1976 and a single bird on 24 May 1978 were the only records. Hatler and Campbell (1975) recorded two peaks in spring migration at Cape Scott, 19-25 April and 5-24 May (for the years 1969-72). The only autumn record was a single bird, on 6 August 1981.

Fox Sparrow - *Passerella iliaca* (summer visitor, probable breeder). This species is resident to the north and south of Brooks Peninsula (Hatler et al. 1978; Richardson 1971), but has only been recorded on the peninsula from 5 May to 27 August, mostly along the beaches. At least 11 young of the year were noted along drift logs from 5 August to 14 August 1981. Most young could fly, but some still had short tails and natal down.

Song Sparrow - Melospiza melodia (resident, breeder). This sparrow has been recorded in most months along the beaches. Many young were seen above driftwood along the edge of the forest from 5 August to 14 August 1981. Usually, 2-3 birds in family flocks were seen. Most young could fly, though some only poorly, and a few still had natal down.

White-crowned Sparrow - *Zonotrichia leucophyrs* (visitor). The single record was an immature, probably an autumn migrant, seen with a mixed flock of cowbirds and blackbirds near the mouth of the Nasparti River on 6 August 1981.

Dark-eyed Junco - *Junco hyemalis* (resident, probable breeder). Recorded in flocks of up to 10 birds, in most months throughout the year. Often seen in small openings and at the edges of all forest types. Nesting was not confirmed.

Lapland Longspur - *Calcarius lapponicus* (migrant). A pair was seen on Solander Island on 5 May 1976 by R.W. Campbell and J.B. Foster. Hatler et al. (1978) only recorded this species in the fall (September and October) in Pacific Rim National Park Reserve, whereas farther north Richardson (1971) saw small flocks in the last two weeks in April and the first week in May, as well as in the second and third weeks of October.

Red-winged Blackbird - *Agelaius phoeniceus* (autumn migrant). The only record is of two immature males seen with a flock of Brown-headed Cowbirds near the mouth of the Nasparti River on 6 August and 7 August 1981. Most records for the west coast of Vancouver Island are in August (Hatler et al. 1978; Richardson 1971).

Brown-headed Cowbird - *Molothrus ater* (autumn migrant). Immatures were regularly seen around Brooks Peninsula from 2 August to 25 August 1981. The largest flock, 16 birds, was feeding in tall grasses at the mouth of the Nasparti River on 6 August and 7 August. This species appears to be uncommon in summer. It is a passage migrant on the west coast of Vancouver Island.

Red Crossbill - *Loxia curvirostra* (resident). Flocks up to 35 were seen all year throughout Brooks Peninsula. In 1973 this species was very common, as it was in Pacific Rim National Park Reserve (Hatler et al. 1978), occurrence and abundance apparently being related to conifer cone productivity.

White-winged Crossbill - *Loxia leucoptera* (visitor). There were three records for August 1981: three on the 6th, three on the 11th, and one (with eight *L. curvirostra*) on the 13th. This species was not recorded by Richardson (1971) or Hatler et al. (1978); Godfrey (1966) indicated it is "scarce on Vancouver Island".

Pine Siskin - *Carduelis pinus* (summer visitor). Flocks of up to 20 birds were recorded from 5 May through 15 August throughout the entire peninsula. Although resident in Pacific Rim National Park Reserve (Hatler et al. 1978), this species had previously only been recorded in March farther north (Richardson 1971).

Mammals

Dusky Shrew - *Sorex monticolus*. Fourteen specimens were collected (RBCM 10836-37, 10839, 10842-49, 10850-51, 10853). Habitat preference is similar to that of *Peromyscus maniculatus*, which was found in all woodland types except those associated with lodgepole pine (Table 12.3). Populations are probably small. Trapping success (animals per trap-night) was poor: 0.5% on Brooks Peninsula and 1.8% on the Bunsby Islands (Carl and Guiguet 1956).

Little Brown Myotis - *Myotis lucifugus*. This bat was widely distributed on Brooks Peninsula during August 1981. Open areas near river mouths and lagoons were preferred foraging areas. Rarely were they seen before 2140 h during the period 5-15 August. Measurements for an adult male/female are: total length, 89/75 mm; tail length, 40/34 mm; hind foot length, 9/8 mm; weight, 7.5/5.4 g.

Silver-haired Bat - *Lasionycteris noctivagans*. This bat was frequently found foraging along the forest edges from sea level to 427 m from 5 August to 17 August 1981. It was the earliest bat to appear in the evening, a habit also noticed by Guiguet (1953a) on the Goose Group Islands, British Columbia.

Two specimens collected were both adult males. Measurements are: total length, 99/95 mm; tail length, 36/35 mm; hind foot length, 9/9 mm; weight, 12.4/11.5 g.

The status, seasonal occurrence, and reproductive period are still unknown in British Columbia (Schowalter et al. 1978). Specimens from extreme southwestern British Columbia have been collected in all seasons (Cowan 1933; Schowalter et al. 1978). On Vancouver Island, spring and summer specimens were either adult males or juveniles, whereas the only autumn specimen reported was an adult female. The Brooks Peninsula specimens were probably autumn migrants, but their origin is unknown. However, this species may inhabit Brooks Peninsula during the maternity period in late spring and early summer.

Table 12.3 Small mammal trapping-success in terrestrial habitats on Brooks Peninsula in August 1981[a]

Habitat	No. of captures				Trap nights	Success rate (%)
	Sorex monticolus	*Peromyscus maniculatus*	*Microtus townsendii*	Total		
Forest - spruce/fir/cedar	1	58	0	59	663	8.9
- lodgepole pine	0	0	0	0	215	0
Seashore - high tide to beach logs	2	18	0	20	490	4.1
- beach logs to forest edge	1	35	0	36	472	7.6
- sand dunes	7	15	0	22	195	11.3
Lakeshore	0	0	0	0	90	0
Bogs	0	0	0	0	35	0
River mouth	0	1	4	5	170	2.9
Total	11	127	4	142	2330	6.1

[a] Based on M.E. Taylor's trapping results.

Hoary Bat - *Lasiurus cinereus*. This large species was found foraging over sandy beaches near Quineex Indian Reserve 8. One specimen, a female, was collected. Measurements are: total length, 142 mm; tail length, 63 mm; hind foot length, 11 mm; wing spread, 385 mm; weight, 31.1 g. This is the second record for Vancouver Island (Cowan and Guiguet 1956), though Hall (1981) includes the entire island within the species' range. Three females and one male were collected at Victoria 370 km southeast of Brooks Peninsula. All coastal specimens were collected in August and September, which indicates this bat may be an autumn migrant, as suggested by Findley and Jones (1964).

Red Squirrel - *Tamiasciurus hudsonicus*. This mammal was seldom heard or seen, and was only recorded on 12 occasions during the 253 days people visited Brooks Peninsula. All records were from mixed coniferous forests. C.J. Guiguet (personal communication May 1983) saw only two on nearby Bunsby Islands during eight days in August 1955. Measurements for a male collected are: total length, 290 mm; tail length, 110 mm; hind foot length, 50 mm.

Deer Mouse - *Peromyscus maniculatus*. This species was the most common mammal at low elevations. It preferred sand dunes, mixed coniferous forests, and beach log habitats (Table 12.2). It was not recorded in habitats associated with lodgepole pine (*Pinus contorta*). Generally, populations appeared to be small. Trapping success (animals per trap night) was 5.4%. The sex ratio of adults collected was nearly equal (18 males to 17 females). Six females were carrying fetuses (1 with four, 2 with five, and 3 with six).

Townsend's Vole - *Microtus townsendii*. Small populations of this vole were restricted to the rank grasses and sedges near river mouths (Table 12.3). This vole may inhabit alpine areas on Brooks Peninsula as it has been found at high elevations elsewhere on Vancouver Island (e.g., at 1860 m on Golden Hinde). Population levels may have been unusually low in August 1981; only four voles were taken in 170 trap nights. Alternatively, these habitats on the west coast of Vancouver Island may support only a few voles. Carl and Guiguet (1956) also report poor trapping success in August 1955 on the Bunsby Islands. During other coastal explorations, C.J. Guiguet (personal communication, May 1983) found a definite lack of small-mammal sign (i.e., fresh droppings, cuttings, and runways) in similar habitats.

Gray Wolf - *Canis lupus*. Almost everyone who spent time on Brooks Peninsula noticed wolf tracks in sand or soft mud in all terrestrial habitats. Based on tracks, the largest pack, recorded at Cape Cook Lagoon, consisted of four—two adults and two immatures, probably a family group.

Three wolves, all in dark pelage, were seen frequently by many observers during August 1981 in the vicinity of Cape Cook Lagoon. Nine scats were collected from the Cape Cook Lagoon area and analyzed following Bowen (1978). All contained hair from deer (*Odocoileus hemionus*). Scott and Shackelton (1980) indicated that deer was the major prey species for wolves on northeastern Vancouver Island and that in August deer fawns (and elk calves) constituted most of their diet.

Black Bear - *Ursus americanus*. Droppings, tracks, and other signs were recorded by most people visiting Brooks Peninsula, in all habitats. During the period 5-15 August 1981, R.W. Campbell and M.E. Taylor saw two bears and recorded fresh evidence for at least another three animals, including a bedding site at the base of a large cedar tree near the mouth of the Nasparti River. Based on the amount and ages of the droppings, the Nasparti River site was probably used all summer.

Northern Sea Lion - *Eumetopias jubatus*. This species has been recorded in all seasons on exposed, rocky islands off Brooks Peninsula. Hauling-out sites are on low islets off the north side of Solander Island (Newcombe and Newcombe 1914). In the 1970s (Table 12.4), several hundred animals hauled out on islets in Checleset Bay (Smith 1972) and, in addition, a few were seen on Clerke Islet in Brooks Bay, in August 1981.

In 1916, at least 500 sea lions were counted in the area (Newcombe et al. 1918). Subsequently, numbers declined due to control programs by the Canadian Department of Fisheries (Bigg 1984). In six years, from 1934 through 1939, a total of 551 sea lions were killed on Solander Island (Pike and Maxwell 1958); 32 755 were destroyed at various localities in British Columbia from 1922 to 1951.

From 7 August to 14 August, 1981, seven pups were counted on Solander Island. At least two pups were suckling females. They were dark in colour and non-swimmers, indicating that they were probably raised on the island. This is the first known breeding occurrences for Solander Island (Bigg 1984, 1985; Pike and MacAskie 1969; Pike and Maxwell 1958).

California Sea Lion - *Zalophus californianus*. There are two records, both from Solander Island. On 5 May and 6 May 1976, R.W. Campbell and J.B. Foster counted 29 animals hauled out on the west side of the island well above the high tide line. Most were males. Bigg (1985) reported that females were seen north of California. Portions of the group were photographed (RBCM photo 451). On 5 August 1981, R.W. Campbell counted three males, with Northern Sea Lions, near Solander Island. These records are significant since published accounts record this species only as a winter visitor off the British Columbia coast (Bigg 1973, 1985; Cowan 1936; Guiguet 1953b; Hancock 1970).

Raccoon - *Procyon lotor*. There are only three records. Fresh tracks and an adult raccoon were seen at the end of Nasparti Inlet on 6 August and 7 August 1981 and tracks were identified near Orchard Point beach on 20 August 1981.

Table 12.4 Counts of Northern Sea Lion (*Eumetopias jubata*) off Brooks Peninsula, British Columbia, 1913-1981

Date	Solander Island	Checleset Bay	Total	Source
1913 (20 July)	none	none	none	Newcombe and Newcombe (1914)
1916 (17 June)	500	?	500[a]	Newcombe et al. (1918)
1938 (20 Aug.)	200	?	200[a]	Pike and Maxwell (1958)
1954 (1 July)	16	0	16	C.J. Guiguet
1955 (Aug.)	380	?	380[a]	Pike and Maxwell (1958)
1956 (26 May)	200	?	200[a]	Pike and Maxwell (1958)
1956 (17 Aug.)	200	?	200[a]	Pike and Maxwell (1958)
1970 (27 Nov.)	0	0	0	Smith (1972)
1971 (18-20 Feb.)	35+	244+	279	Smith (1972)
1971 (8 March)	88	305	393	Smith (1972)
1971 (31 March)	0	0	0	Smith (1972)
1975 (26 June)	3	68	71	R.W. Campbell and H.R. Carter
1976 (5-6 May)	11	180	191	R.W. Campbell and J.B. Foster
1981 (7-14 Aug.)	93	68	161	R.W. Campbell and M.E. Taylor

[a] Counts for Solander Island probably include sea lions in Checleset Bay (see Smith 1972).

Mink - *Mustela vison*. Tracks and droppings were regularly seen along marine shores, especially near our field camp at Cape Cook Lagoon, Johnson Lagoon, and the mouths of both the Klaskish and Nasparti rivers. Three individuals were seen in August, 1981. No specimens were taken.

Analysis of seven fresh scats collected from 5 August to 14 August 1981 showed fragments of three species of crabs (*Cancer productus*, *Hemigrapsus nudus*, and *Pugettia producta*), as well as pieces of skin of the garter snake *Thamnophis sirtalis*. Crustaceans, especially the species found, are known to be a major part of the mink's diet in British Columbia (Cowan and Guiguet 1956; Hatler 1976). The only reference to garter snakes being eaten by mink in coastal western North America, is from Oregon (Maser et al. 1981), where the species involved was *T. ordinoides*.

River Otter - *Lutra canadensis*. This species was the most commonly seen mustelid. Most sightings were from the seashore. Of the 21 records, 16 were from lagoons, 2 from rivers, 2 offshore, and 1 from the open forest near Quineex Indian Reserve 8 where a den was located under the roots of a large spruce tree. No family groups were seen. None was seen in the Bunsby Islands in August 1955 (Carl and Guiguet 1956).

Sea Otter - *Enhydra lutris*. From 1969 to 1972 Sea Otters from Alaska were re-introduced to the Bunsby Islands (MacAskie 1971, 1975; Smith 1969). Aerial surveys of the Checleset Bay area in 1977 indicated at least 70 otters present; others were reported along the west coast of Vancouver Island (Bigg and MacAskie 1978). The following year, 1978, at least 79 Sea Otters were tallied in the Checleset Bay area (Morris et al. 1981). On 14 August 1980, 33-35 Sea Otters were counted while travelling by canoe from Kyoquot to Brooks Peninsula (Farr 1980).

The population appears to be increasing dramatically in the Checleset Bay area. In 1984, a summer survey revealed nearly 200 animals in this area (M. Bigg personal communication, January 1985).

Two adults seen on 6 August and 7 August 1981 off Quineex Indian Reserve 8 were most likely otters from the Bunsby Islands, which presently support the largest colony in British Columbia.

Harbor Seal - *Phoca vitulina*. Small numbers, usually six or less, were recorded in shallow coastal habitats (i.e., Johnson Lagoon, Nasparti River mouth) from 5 May through August. The species is probably resident in the area as Scheffer and Slipp (1944) and Spalding (1964) indicate that Harbor Seals are non-migratory. There are no known major haul-out sites located in the area.

Northern Elephant Seal - *Mirounga angustirostris*. There are only two records. Canadian Department of Fisheries personnel observed a single animal in Squally Channel, south of Brooks Peninsula, on 1 September 1958. An unaged animal (probably male) was seen by R.W. Campbell and H.R. Carter between Solander Island and Brooks Peninsula on 27 June 1975. This species was considered very rare in British Columbia as late as the mid-1940s (Cowan and Carl 1945). Due to protection, breeding populations in California and Mexico have increased from about 100 in 1900 to nearly 50 000 today (DeLong 1978). As a result, this species has now been recorded along the entire British Columbia coast, including inside waters (Fairweather 1978), in every month of the year. From 1958 to 1962 there were at least 37 sightings in British Columbia waters (Pike and MacAskie 1969; Royal British Columbia Museum files). According to Condit and LeBoeuf (1984), most animals off Vancouver Island are juveniles that have dispersed from their rookeries in California. The species is, nevertheless, more common in winter.

Mountain Lion - *Felis concolor*. This large cat was never seen, but tracks were noted along the banks of the Klaskish River by BC Fish and Wildlife Branch personnel in May 1974. In August 1981, several people at our field camp claimed to have seen fresh tracks near the mouth of Cape Cook Lagoon and the Nasparti River. Occurrence of Mountain Lions probably depends on the numbers of deer—their prey base (Cowan and Guiguet 1956).

Killer Whale - *Orcinus orca*. The earliest record was a sighting of an albino off Cape Cook on 2 May 1952 (Carl 1960). The only other sightings are: a pair of adults moving west past Clerke Point on 31 May 1973, three whales travelling south past Quineex Reef on 7 August 1981, and an adult bull off Brooks Peninsula on 22 August 1981. Records are few, but Pike and MacAskie (1969: 21) mention that from analysis of more than 5000 Killer Whale sightings from 1959 through 1964 "it has not been possible to determine any orderly pattern of movement or migration" for these mammals in British Columbia. Recently, however, Bigg (1982) indicates that the northwestern coast of Vancouver Island is frequented by pods of transient whales, as well as by two pods from the northern resident community.

Dall's Porpoise - *Phocoenoides dalli*. A pod of six animals, seen near a fish boat off Solander Island on 14 August 1981, is the only record. This species inhabits "certain channels and straits" during the summer months (Cowan 1944). The pod size (6) falls within the most common group size (5-9) listed by Pike and MacAskie (1969) for the summer period.

Gray Whale - *Eschrichtius robustus*. There are only three records: four animals off the mouth of Nasparti Inlet on 8 April 1973, a single whale off the mouth of Klaskish Inlet the following day, and two Gray Whales off Cape Cook, moving northwards, on 5 May 1976. The northward migration along coastal British Columbia, including Brooks Peninsula (Darling 1984), lasts from mid-February to mid-June and peaks in early April (Hatler and Darling 1974). There were no summer occurrences in either Brooks Bay or Checleset Bay, though Gray Whales have been sighted at this time of year near Cape Scott and Tatchu Point, to the north and south of Brooks Peninsula respectively. Darling (1984) lists several resident summer populations (e.g., at Wickaninnish Bay) along the west coast of Vancouver Island.

Elk - *Cervus elaphus*. Populations are known to exist in the drainages of the Klaskish and Nasparti rivers, but herd sizes are unknown. Abundant elk pellet groups in the Klaskish River drainage, determined by BC Fish and Wildlife Branch personnel, indicated that in 1974 and 1977 elk-use tended to focus on the valley bottom and low slopes, particularly in the estuary area.

In 1979, no elk sign was observed in either the upper or lower watershed area. According to R. Davies (personal communication, February 1984) elk densities in the Klaskish River area were comparable to those found in the Stranby and Tsitika watersheds on northern Vancouver Island.

The only record for the peninsula proper, was a single animal, seen from a helicopter, near Doom Mountain on 9 August 1981.

Mule Deer - *Odocoileus hemionus*. Deer tracks, pellets, and browse sign were abundant throughout all vegetative associations on Brooks Peninsula, but few deer were seen.

The Klaskish River supports high densities of deer (R. Davies personal communication), but their abundance and distribution vary considerably. During comparative studies in 1974 and 1979, "the number of pellet groups found per sampled area increased from 0.32 pellet groups to 0.44 per 100 square feet" (Davies 1974, 1979). Also in 1974, deer populations tended to be concentrated on the estuary (Klaskish River) and valley floor, whereas in 1979 populations were found at much higher elevations. According to pellet group densities, deer populations, at least in the Klaskish River watershed, are comparable to those found in other areas on northern Vancouver Island (i.e. Nisnak Creek, Schoen Creek, Stranby River, and Tahsish River).

Results and Discussion

A total of 153 higher vertebrates were recorded by 71 visitors to Brooks Peninsula from 1934 through 1984. These include 10 species of amphibians and reptiles, 120 species of birds, and 23 species of mammals.

Of the amphibians and reptiles, 5 species are salamanders, including 1 newt, 3 frogs and toads, and 2 garter snakes. All amphibian and reptile records are the result of the Royal British Columbia Museum's field trip in August 1981, when a total of 248 specimens of eight species was collected. At least one more species, the Northwestern Garter Snake (*Thamnophis ordinoides*), was expected, since it has been collected on the Bunsby Islands, 10 km south of Brooks Peninsula (Carl and Guiguet 1956). The only other species that may have been overlooked is Ensatina (*Ensatina eschscholtzi*). It has been found in similar habitats as far north as Tofino on the west coast of Vancouver Island (Green and Campbell 1984). No new species or major range extensions were noted for amphibians and reptiles. Rather, records from Brooks Peninsula fill in gaps in the ranges of the 10 species recorded (Green and Campbell 1984).

Of the 120 species of birds recorded, 6 are significant northward range extensions along the west coast of Vancouver Island. These include Cattle Egret, Green Heron, Long-billed Curlew, Caspian Tern, Western Kingbird, and White-winged Crossbill. Another species, the Laysan Albatross, is noteworthy because of the very few nearshore records for this species in British Columbia (Campbell and Shepard 1973). In addition, two breeding records were northern extensions for Vancouver Island, namely, Red-throated Loon and Mew Gull. Both these species breed on coastal lakes and feed at sea in protected inlets and bays (Campbell 1970, Godfrey 1966).

Table 12.5 summarizes the status for all birds. Sixty-six species (55%) are classified as visitors. For some species (e.g., Sabine's Gull, Red-breasted Sapsucker), this is a catch-all category due to single records. Forty-four species are considered non-breeding visitors (e.g., Long-billed Curlew, Western Kingbird, White-winged Crossbill). An additional 22 species probably breed on Brooks Peninsula, mostly as summer visitors (e.g., warblers, thrushes). Sixteen of these were found breeding.

Table 12.5 Total number of species, by status, of birds recorded on Brooks Peninsula, British Columbia, 1934-1982

Status	Species
Visitor	
Non-breeding	44
Breeding confirmed	6
Suspected breeding	16
Migrant	22
Resident	
Non-breeding	2
Breeding confirmed	16
Suspected breeding	14
Total	120

At least 22 species are migrants, either spring (e.g., Brant), or autumn (e.g., Baird's Sandpiper), or both (e.g., Semipalmated Plover). None of these species nests on Brooks Peninsula.

Thirty-two species (27%) are resident (throughout the year) and include mostly passerines. All (e.g., Hairy Woodpecker, Red Crossbill) probably breed on the peninsula. Breeding evidence was documented for half of these species. In total (visitors and residents), 22 species were found breeding on or in the vicinity of Brooks Peninsula.

Twenty-three species of mammals were recorded, of which 15 are terrestrial forms and 8 essentially marine. The terrestrial species are resident, with the possible exception of two bat species. All other mammals are either migrants or visitors. Significant records were obtained for Silver-haired Bat, Hoary Bat, California Sea Lion, and Northern Elephant Seal. The first recorded breeding of Northern Sea Lions (on Solander Island) is also noteworthy.

Another three species, all mustelids, probably occur on the peninsula: Marten (*Martes americana*), Ermine (*Mustela erminea*), and Wolverine (*Gulo gulo*). Fur returns form a registered trapline on the peninsula may be a noteworthy source of information for these rarely seen mammals.

Brooks Peninsula as a Refugium

Rand (1948, 1954) was one of the earliest to discuss geographical isolation of birds and mammals in terms of glacial refugia. He suggested that, over time, populations with common ancestors became separated and, in isolation, evolved to change at the species or subspecies level. More recently, Klein (1965) and Hoffman and Peterson (1967) discussed postglacial distribution patterns of mammals for coastal southeastern Alaska, in some cases showing that populations on islands were related to mainland populations. In British Columbia, there is biological evidence that refugia existed in the Queen Charlotte Islands (Foster 1965; McCabe and Cowan 1945). However, Foster (1965) suggested that some forms of mammals are not relicts, but rather the result of divergent evolution since deglaciation. The ultimate proof for refugial origin of vertebrates comes from fossils. There are no vertebrate fossils known from Brooks Peninsula. In fact, the fossil record on Vancouver Island for extant vertebrates is virtually unknown. On Vancouver Island there are 20 generally distributed endemic subspecies of mammals (Cowan and Guiguet 1956; Hall 1932). The only endemic species, however, is the Vancouver Island Marmot (*Marmota vancouverensis*).

The oldest known specimens, dated at about 2500 B.P., are from an archaeological site above Clayoquot Sound (Nagorsen, Keddie and Luszcz 1996). It has been suggested by Hoffman et al. (1979) that the Vancouver Island Marmot is a Pleistocene isolate derived from mainland populations of the Hoary Marmot (*M. caligata*). McCabe and Cowan (1945) and Heard (1977) suggested that the Vancouver Island Marmot survived the last glaciation in refugia on Vancouver Island. Nagorsen (1987), however, points out that the Vancouver Island Marmot could have colonized Vancouver Island after the Pleistocene, and until fossil evidence is obtained, its existence on Vancouver Island during the Pleistocene is only conjecture. No populations of the Vancouver Island Marmot were located on Brooks Peninsula.

Amphibians and reptiles are also good indicators of glacial refugia, because they have low mobility. We searched for refugial relicts, such as the Olympic Salamander (*Rhyacotriton olympicus*) and Red-backed Salamander (*Plethodon vehiculum*), which range to the northwestern corner of Washington state (Nussbaum et al. 1983). Although suitable habitat (see Stebbins 1985) was evident on Brooks Peninsula, neither species was found. The distribution of the Clouded Salamander, restricted to Vancouver Island in British Columbia (Green and Campbell 1984), hints at a refugial origin. Stebbins (1985), however, suggests the species may have been introduced to Vancouver Island.

The present distribution and affinities of vertebrates on Brooks Peninsula, compared with those species and/or subspecies that are more generally distributed on Vancouver Island and the adjacent southern mainland coast, still remains unknown. To differentiate vertebrate populations on the peninsula, larger series are required for select species, which would require intensive collecting over a number of years. The major shortcoming in this paper is that the time spent on the peninsula was inadequate to collect a large enough series of small mammals and amphibians for statistical comparisons.

References

American Ornithologists' Union. 1983. Check-list of North American birds. 6th ed. Allen Press, Lawrence, KS.

______. 1985. Thirty-fifth supplement to the American Ornithologists' Union check-list of North American birds. Auk 102: 680-686.

Beebe, F.L. 1960. The marine peregrines of the northwest Pacific coast. Condor 62: 145-189.

———. 1974. Field studies of the Falconiformes of British Columbia. BC Provincial Museum (Victoria, BC) Occas. Paper 17.

Bigg, M.A. 1973. Census of California sea lions on southern Vancouver Island, British Columbia. J. Mammal. 54: 285-287.

———. 1982. An assessment of Killer Whale (*Orcinus orca*) stocks off Vancouver Island, British Columbia. International Whaling Commission Rep. 32: 655-666.

———. 1984. Sighting and kill data for the Steller sea lion (*Eumetopias jubatus*) and California sea lion (*Salophus californianus*) in British Columbia, 1892-1982, with some records from Washington and southeastern Alaska. Can. Data Rep. Fish. Aquat. Sci. 460.

———. 1985. Status of the Steller Sea Lion (*Eumetopias jubatus*) and California Sea Lion (*Zalophus californianus*) in British Columbia. Can. Spec. Publ. Fish. Aquat. Sci. 77.

———. and I.B. MacAskie. 1978. Sea otters reestablished in British Columbia. J. Mammal. 59: 874-876.

Bowen, W.D. 1978. Social organization of the coyote in relation to prey size. Ph.D. thesis. Department of Zoology, University of British Columbia, Vancouver, BC.

Breen, P.A., T.A. Carson, J.B. Foster, and E.A. Stewart. 1982. Changes in subtidal community structure associated with British Columbia sea otter transplants. Mar. Ecol: Prog. Ser. 7: 13-20.

Brooks, A. 1922. Notes on the abundance and habits of the Bald Eagle in British Columbia. Auk 39: 556-559.

Campbell, R.W. 1968. European Starling at Pachena Lighthouse. Victoria Naturalist 24: 55.

———. 1970. Recent information on nesting colonies of Mew Gulls on Kennedy Lake, Vancouver Island, British Columbia. Syesis 3: 5-14.

———. 1971. Status of the Caspian Tern in British Columbia. Syesis 4: 185-189.

———. 1972a. The green heron in British Columbia. Syesis 5: 235-247.

———. 1972b. Coastal records of the Long-billed Curlew for British Columbia. Can. Field-Naturalist 86: 167-168.

———. 1976. Seabird colonies of Vancouver Island [map]. BC Provincial Museum, Victoria, BC.

——— and M.G. Shepard. 1972. Summary of 1971 offshore birding trips. Discovery (Vancouver Natural History Society, Vancouver, BC) 154: 7-8.

——— and ———. 1973. Laysan Albatross, Scaled Petrel and Parakeet Auklet: additions to the list of Canadian birds. Can. Field-Naturalist 87: 179-180.

_____ and D. Stirling. 1971. A photoduplicate file for British Columbia vertebrate records. Syesis 4: 217-222.

_____ and W.C. Weber. 1977. The Cattle Egret in British Columbia. Can. Field-Naturalist 91: 87-88.

_____, H.R. Carter, and S.G. Sealy. 1979. Nesting of Horned Puffins in British Columbia. Can. Field-Naturalist 93: 84-86.

_____, _____, C.D. Shepard, and C.J. Guiguet. 1979. A bibliography of British Columbia ornithology. BC Provincial Museum (Victoria, BC) Heritage Record 7.

_____, M.A. Paul, M.S. Rodway, and H.R. Carter. 1977. Tree-nesting Peregrine Falcons in British Columbia. Condor 79: 500-501.

_____, M.G. Shepard, and R.H. Drent. 1972. Status of birds in the Vancouver area in 1970. Syesis 5: 137-167.

_____, _____, B.A. Macdonald, and W.C. Weber. 1974. Vancouver birds in 1972. Vancouver Natural History Society, Vancouver, BC.

_____, _____, B.M. Van Der Raay, and P.T. Gregory. 1982. A bibliography of Pacific Northwest herpetology. BC Provincial Museum (Victoria, BC) Heritage Record 14.

_____, _____, and W.C. Weber. 1972. Vancouver birds in 1971. Vancouver Natural History Society, Vancouver, BC.

Carl, G.C. 1960. Albinistic killer whales in British Columbia. In Provincial Museum of Natural History and Anthropology report for the year 1959. BC Dept. Education, Victoria, BC. Pp. 29-36.

_____ and C.J. Guiguet. 1956. Notes on the flora and fauna of Bunsby Islands, B.C. In Provincial Museum of Natural History and Anthropology report for the year 1955. BC Dept. Education, Victoria, BC. Pp. 31-44.

_____, C.J. Guiguet and G.A. Hardy. 1951. Biology of the Scott Island Group, British Columbia. In Provincial Museum of Natural History and Anthropology report for the year 1950. BC Dept. Education, Victoria, BC. Pp. 21-63.

Condit, R. and B.J. LeBoeuf. 1984. Feeding habits and feeding grounds of the Northern Elephant Seal. J. Mammal. 65: 281-290.

Cowan, I. McT. 1933. Some notes on the hibernation of *Lasioncycteris noctivagans*. Can. Field-Naturalist 47: 74-75.

_____. 1936. California sea lion from British Columbia. Can. Field-Naturalist 50: 145-148.

_____. 1944. The Dall porpoise, *Phocoenoides dalli* (True), of the northern Pacific Ocean. J. Mammal. 25:295-306.

——— and C.J. Guiguet. 1956. The mammals of British Columbia. BC Provincial Museum (Victoria, BC) Handbook 11.

——— . 1947. Remarks concerning Labrador. Norsk Geologisk Tidsskrift 26: 233-235.

——— . 1955. Biogeographic and geologic indications of unglaciated areas in Scandinavia during the glacial ages. Geol. Soc. Am. Bull. 66: 1499-1519.

Darling, J.D. 1984. Gray Whales off Vancouver Island, British Columbia. Pp 207-211 in M.L. Jones, S.L. Swartz, and S. Leatherwood (eds.). The Gray Whale *Eschrichtius robustus*. Academic Press, NY.

De Long, R.L. 1978. Northern elephant seal. Pp 207-211 in D. Haley (ed.). Marine mammals of the eastern North Pacific and Arctic waters. Pacific Search Press, Seattle, WA.

Drent, R.H. and C.J. Guiguet. 1961. A catalogue of British Columbia seabird colonies. BC Provincial Museum (Victoria, BC) Occas. Paper 12.

Fairweather, N.M. 1978. Elephant seal sightings. Discovery (Vancouver Natural History Society, Vancouver, BC) 7: 125.

Farr, A. 1980. Sea otter populations stable in B.C. BC Naturalist (Federation of B.C. Naturalists) 10: 18.

Findley, J.S. and C. Jones. 1964. Seasonal distribution of the hoary bat. J. Mammal. 45: 461-470.

Foster, J.B. 1965. The evolution of the mammals of the Queen Charlotte Islands, British Columbia. BC Provincial Museum (Victoria, BC) Occas. Paper 14.

Godfrey, W.E. 1966. The Birds of Canada. Bull. 203, Nat. Mus. Can.

Gregory, P.T. and R.W. Campbell. 1984. The reptiles of British Columbia. BC Provincial Museum (Victoria, BC) Handbook 44.

Green, D.M. and R.W. Campbell. 1984. The amphibians of British Columbia. BC Provincial Museum (Victoria, BC) Handbook 45.

Guiguet, C.J. 1953a. An ecological study of Goose Island, British Columbia, with special reference to mammals and birds. BC Provincial Museum (Victoria, BC) Occas. Paper 10.

———. 1953b. California sea lion (*Zalophus californianus*) in British Columbia. Can. Field-Naturalist 67: 140.

Hall, E.R. 1932. Remarks on the affinities of the mammalian fauna of Vancouver Island, British Columbia, and with description of a new subspecies. Univ. Calif. Publ. Zool. 38: 415-423.

———. 1981. The mammals of North America Vol 1. John Wiley and Sons, NY.

Hancock, D. 1970. California sea lion as a regular visitant off the British Columbia coast. J. Mammal. 51: 614.

Hart, J.F.L. 1982. Crabs and their relatives of British Columbia. BC Provincial Museum (Victoria, BC) Handbook 40.

Hatler, D.F. 1973. An analysis of use, by waterfowl, of tideflats in southern Clayoquot Sound, British Columbia. Canadian Wildlife Service Report, Edmonton, AB.

______. 1974. Bald Eagle preys upon Arctic Loon. Auk 91: 825-827.

______. 1976. The coastal mink on Vancouver Island, British Columbia. Ph.D. thesis. Department of Zoology, University of British Columbia, Vancouver, BC.

______ and R.W. Campbell. 1975. Notes on spring migration, including sex segregation, of some western Savannah Sparrows. Syesis 8: 401-402.

______ and J.D. Darling. 1974. Recent observations of the gray whale in British Columbia. Can. Field-Naturalist 88: 449-459.

______, R.W. Campbell, and A. Dorst. 1978. Birds of Pacific Rim National Park. B.C. Provincial Museum (Victoria, BC) Occas. Paper 20.

Heard, D.C. 1977. The behaviour of Vancouver Island marmots, *Marmota vancouverensis*. M.Sc. thesis. Department of Zoology, University of British Columbia, Vancouver, BC.

Heusser, C.J. 1960. Late-Pleistocene environments of North Pacific North America. American Geographical Society, NY.

Hoffman, R.S. and R.S. Peterson. 1967. Systematics and Zoogeography of *Sorex* in the Bering Strait area. Syst. Zool. 16: 127-136.

______, J.W. Koeppl, and C.F. Nadler. 1979. The relationships of the amphiberingian marmots (Mammalia: Sciuridae). Univ. of Kansas Museum of Natural History (Lawrence, Kan.) Occas. Paper 83.

Honacki, J.H., K.E. Kinman, and J.W. Koeppl (eds.). 1982. Mammal species of the world: a taxonomic and geographic reference. Allen Press and the Association of Systematics Collections, Lawrence, KS.

Jewett, S.A., W.P. Taylor, W.T. Shaw, and J.W. Aldrich. 1953. Birds of Washington state. University of Washington Press, Seattle, WA.

Klein, D.R. 1965. Post glacial distribution patterns of mammals in the southern coastal regions of Alaska. Arctic 18: 17-20.

Krajina, V.J. 1959. Bioclimatic zones in British Columbia. University of British Columbia (Vancouver, BC) Botanical Series 1.

______. 1965. Biogeoclimatic zones and classification of British Columbia. Ecology of western North America (Department of Botany, University of British Columbia, Vancouver, BC) 1: 1-17.

Laing, H.M. 1956. Nesting of Golden Eagle on Vancouver Island. Can. Field-Naturalist 70:95-96.

MacAskie, I.B. 1971. A sea otter transplant to British Columbia. Fisheries Canada 23: 3-9.

______. 1975. Sea otters: A third transplant to British Columbia. Beaver 1975: 9-11.

Martin, P.W. and M.T. Myres. 1969. Observations on the distribution and migration of some seabirds off the outer coasts of British Columbia and Washington state, 1946-1949. Syesis 2: 241-256.

Maser, C., B.R. Mate, J.F. Franklin, and C.T. Dyrness. 1981. Natural history of Oregon coast mammals. Gen. Tech. Rep. PNW-133. (Pacific Northwest For. Range Exp. Stn.).

McCabe, T.T. and I. McT. Cowan. 1945. *Peromyscus maniculatus macrorhinus* and the problem of insularity. Trans. R. Can. Inst. 25 117-215.

Morris, R., D.V. Ellis, and B.P. Emerson. 1981. The British Columbia transplant of sea otters, *Enhydra lutris*. Biological Conservation (Eng.) 20: 291-295.

Murie, O.J. 1938. Food habits of the northern Bald Eagle in the Aleutian Islands, Alaska. Condor 42: 198.

Nagorsen, D.W. 1987. *Marmota vancouverensis*. Mammalian Species 270: 1-5.

______, G. Keddie and T. Luszcz. 1996. Vancouver Island marmot bones from subalpine caves: archaeological and biological significance. Occasional Paper No. 4. BC Parks, Victoria, BC. 56 pp.

Newcombe, C.F. and W.A. Newcombe. 1914. Sea lions on the coast of British Columbia. Pp. 131-145 in Report of the Commissioner of Fisheries for the year ending December 31, 1913. BC Dept. Fisheries, Victoria, BC

______, W.H. Greenwood, and C.M. Fraser. 1918. The sea lion question in British Columbia. Contrib. Can. Biol.: 1-39.

Nussbaum, R.A., D. Brodie, and R.M. Storm. 1983. Amphibians and reptiles of the Pacific Northwest. University of Idaho Press, Moscow, ID.

Ormsby, M.A. 1971. British Columbia: a history. MacMillan, Toronto, ON.

Pearse, T. 1968. Birds of the early explorers in the Pacific Northwest. The Close, Comox, BC.

Pike, G.C. and I.B. MacAskie. 1969. Marine mammals of British Columbia. Bull. 171, Fish. Res. Board Can.

______ and B.E. Maxwell. 1958. The abundance and distribution of the northern sea lion (*Eumetopias jubata*) on the coast of British Columbia. J. Fish. Res. Board Can. 15: 5-17.

Pojar, J. 1980. Brooks Peninsula: possible Pleistocene glacial refugium on northwestern Vancouver Island. Bot. Soc. Am. Misc. Ser. Publ. 1: 58:89.

Rand, A.L. 1948. Glaciation, an isolating factor in speciation. Evolution (Lawrence, Kan.) 2: 314-321.

———. 1954. The ice age and mammal speciation in North America. Arctic 7: 31-35.

Richardson, F. 1971. Birds of Grant Bay and Browning Inlet, northwest Vancouver Island, British Columbia: a year's phenology. Murrelet 52: 29-40.

Sanger, G.A. 1965. Observations of wildlife off the coast of Washington and Oregon in 1963, with notes on the Laysan Albatross (*Diomedea immutabilis*) in this area. Murrelet 46: 1-6.

Scheffer, V.B. and J.W. Slipp. 1944. The harbor seal in Washington state. Am. Midl. Nat. 32: 373-416.

Schick, W.J. 1970. First British Columbia specimen record of Caspian Tern. Syesis 3: 187.

Schowalter, D.B., W.J. Dorward, and J.R. Gunson. 1978. Seasonal occurrence of silver-haired bats (*Lasionycteris noctivagans*) in Alberta and British Columbia. Can. Field-Naturalist 92: 288-291.

Scott, B.M.V. and D.M. Shackelton. 1980. Food habits of two Vancouver Island wolf packs: a preliminary study. Can. J. Zool. 58: 1203-1207.

Sealy, S.G. and R.W. Campbell. 1979. Post-hatching movements of young Ancient Murrelets. Western Birds 10: 25-30.

——— and R.W. Nelson. 1973. The occurrences and status of the Horned Puffin in British Columbia. Syesis 6: 51-55.

Smith, I.D. 1969. The sea otter: a fresh start. West. Fish and Game 4:26-28, 48, 50-52.

———. 1972. Sea lions wintering along the outer coast of Vancouver Island. J. Fish. Res. Board Can. 29: 1764-1766.

——— and D.A. Blood. 1972. Native swans wintering on Vancouver Island over the period 1969-71. Can. Field-Naturalist 86: 213-216.

Spalding, D.J. 1964. Comparative feeding habits of the fur seal, sea lion and harbour seal on the British Columbia coast. Bull. 146, Fish. Res. Board Can.

Stebbins, R.C. 1985. A field guide to western reptiles and amphibians. Houghton Mifflin, Boston.

Tatum, J.B. 1971. Bird report (1970) for southern Vancouver Island. Victoria Natural History Society, Victoria, BC.

———. 1972. Annual bird report (1971) for southern Vancouver Island. Victoria Natural History Society, Victoria, BC.

———. 1973. Annual bird report (1972) for southern Vancouver Island. Victoria Natural History Society, Victoria, BC.

Tuller, S.E. 1979. Climate. In Vancouver Island: land of contrasts. Edited by C.N. Forward. Department of Geography, University of Victoria (Victoria, BC) Western Geographical Series 17: 71-91.

Appendix 12.1 Summary of visits to Brooks Peninsula, British Columbia by biologists and naturalists, 1949-1982

Year	Details of visit
1949	P.W. Martin recorded observations near Solander Island on 4 July and 1 August (Martin and Myres 1969)
1952	Fishermen off Brooks Peninsula recorded wildlife observations on 2 May (Carl 1960)
1954	C.J. Guiguet and F.L. Beebe trapped small mammals on Solander Island (Beebe 1960)
1955	G.C. Carl and C.J. Guiguet conducted biological surveys of Bunsby Islands, 3-11 August (Carl and Guiguet 1956)
1965	D. Hancock collected Tufted Puffins on Solander Island on 15 July
1966	J.E.V. Goodwill recorded seabird observations off Solander Island on 28 May
1967	J.E.V. Goodwill, near Solander Island, recorded seabird observations on 27 August and 18 September
1968	J.E.V. Goodwill, near Solander Island, recorded bird observations on 25 July
1970	Aerial counts of sea lions in waters around Brooks Peninsula by I.D. Smith on 27 November (Smith 1972); aerial survey of same area for Trumpeter Swans by I.D. Smith and D.A. Blood on 15 February (Smith and Blood 1972)
1971	Aerial counts of sea lions in vicinity of Brooks Peninsula on 18-20 February, 8 March, and 31 March by I.D. Smith (Smith 1972)
1973	Waterbirds censused around Brooks Peninsula by I.D. Smith, 3-5 January and 8 April; R. Williams recorded bird notes from a hydrographic vessel in Brooks Bay and Checleset Bay, 6-10 April; daily migration watch by K.R. Summers from Clerke Point from 11 May to 27 June; seabird observations recorded off Brooks Peninsula by P.W. Martin, 21-24 September
1974	Ungulate survey of Klaskish River by BC Fish and Wildlife Branch personnel 15-25 May. B.M. MacDonald combed Brooks Peninsula in search of glass floats 25-27 November and 13-16 December
1975	Aerial survey of waterbirds by W.T. Munro on 14 February; reconnaissance for ecological reserves by J.B. Foster on 16 June; BC Provincial Museum seabird survey of islands on 26 and 27 June by R.W. Campbell, H.R. Carter, B. Ford, C.J. Guiguet and M.S. Rodway; University of British Columbia botanical expedition on Brooks Peninsula on 15 August (R. Hebda, J.G. and G. Godfrey, J. Pinder-Moss)

BROOKS PENINSULA

1976	Aerial survey of waterbirds by I.D. Smith and R. Davies on 19 January; aerial survey of waterbirds by R. Davies on 20 April; aerial survey of waterbirds by K.R. Summers in Klaskish Inlet on 12 March; J.B. Foster and R.W. Campbell on Solander Island on 5 May and 6 May; J. Pojar on Brooks Peninsula on 24 July; aerial survey of waterbirds on 20 October by R. Davies and I.D. Smith
1977	Aerial survey of waterbirds on 5 January by R. Davies and G. Smith; wildlife reconnaissance of Klaskish River 24-25 January by BC Forest Products Ltd. personnel
1978	M.S. Rodway hiked Brooks Peninsula on 6 May and 22-26 May; University of Victoria personnel studied sea otters in Checleset Bay from 1 June to 4 July and from 12 July to 1 August; T. Carson observed wildlife in Checleset Bay 13-16 June and 25-26 July; J.B. Foster, T. Carson, and H. Roemer hiked on Brooks Peninsula for ecological reserve proposals 22-25 July.
1979	Sea otters censused in Checleset Bay on 19 February by T. Carson, R. Davis, J.B. Foster, and R. Morris; BC Fish and Wildlife personnel conducted elk survey of Klaskish River 13-17 August; research on sea otters in Checleset Bay 21-24 September (Breen et al. 1982); aerial survey by R. Davies and K.R. Summers on 30 October
1980	Aerial waterbird survey by R. Davies, K.R. Summers, and M. Townsend on 24 January; sea otter survey of Checleset Bay by A. Farr, A.S. Harestad and L. Jones on 14 July (Farr 1980); aerial waterbird survey by B. Fuhr and K.R. Summers on 25 November
1981	BC Provincial Museum collecting trip from 31 July to 27 August. Personnel included R.W. Campbell, R.A. Cannings, S.G. Cannings, J.M. Cooper, R.Y. Edwards, and M.E. Taylor
1982	A. Farr and A.S. Harestad surveyed sea otters in Checleset Bay on 9 August
1984	Pacific Biological Station census of sea otters during the summer

Appendix 12.2 Details for specimens of amphibians, reptiles, and mammals collected in August 1981 and deposited in the Royal British Columbia Museum (RBCM) collections

Amphibians and Reptiles

Ambystoma gracile, 49 specimens (1 adult, 1 neotenic adult, 47 larvae), RBCM 1471-1476; *Plethodon vehiculum*, 1 adult, RBCM 1477; *Taricha granulosa*, 28 specimens (25 adults, 2 larvae), RBCM 1451-1458; *Bufo boreas*, 35 specimens (2 adults, 33 larvae), RBCM 1449-1450, 1465; *Hyla regilla*, 93 specimens (2 adults, 91 developing larvae), RBCM 1553, 1556-1562, 1564, 1569-1570; *Rana aurora*, 30 specimens (5 adults, 25 developing larvae), RBCM 1554-1555, 1563, 1566-1567, 1580; *Thamnophis sirtalis*, 11 specimens (2 adults, 9 immatures), RBCM 1559-1565

Mammals

Sorex monticolus, 19 specimens (7 males, 8 females, 4 sex unknown), RBCM 10835-10853; *Myotis lucifugus*, 3 specimens (1 adult male, 1 adult female, 1 unknown), RBCM 10854-10856; *Lasionycteris noctivagans*, 2 specimens (adult males), RBCM 10788 and 10797; *Lasiurus cinereus*, 1 specimen (female), RBCM 10796; *Tamiasciurus hudsonicus*, 1 specimen (male), RBCM 10802; *Peromyscus maniculatus*, 66 specimens (18 adult males, 17 adult females, 31 unknown), RBCM 10726-10791; *Microtus townsendii*, 4 specimens (1 adult male, 1 immature male, 2 adult females), RBCM 10792-10795.

Chapter 13

Ethnographic History of Brooks Peninsula Region

Richard I. Inglis
Ministry of Aboriginal Affairs
Victoria, BC

Abstract

During the late 1700s and early 1800s significant political changes occurred among the peoples of the Brooks Peninsula region, brought on by disease and indigenous warfare. By the end of the 1800s only two peoples occupied the area, the Kwakwala-speaking Klaskino and the Nootka-speaking Chicklesaht. Study of limited archival records and a few interviews reveal the existence in the 19th century of at least one other independent people in the region, the Classet, a bilingual Nuu-chah-nulth people centred at Brooks Bay. The Classet were displaced from their territory when Kwakwaka'wakw people from the north end of Vancouver Island expanded southward. The Classet appear to have split, with one group moving to the area of Neah Bay, Washington; the remainder stayed in the area of Brooks Peninsula until they were absorbed by the Chicklesaht. By the end of the nineteenth century, Cape Cook on the tip of Brooks Peninsula was the recognized boundary between the Kwakwaka'wakw and the Nuu-chah-nulth.

Acknowledgements

Robert Galois, James Haggarty, Barbara Lane, and Robert Lane read and commented on an earlier version of this paper. I thank them for their critical comments. I also thank Sally Watson who typed and Kitty Bernick who edited the earlier manuscript and Ursla Masee who typed the final paper.

Introduction

A study of the ethnographic history of the Brooks Peninsula region was not included in the 1981 Brooks Peninsula refugium project, but was carried out at a later date to complement the archaeological component. The research for this study was largely archival; only a few brief interviews were conducted. Anthropological literature containing references to the aboriginal people of the Brooks Peninsula region are few and information is limited (Boas 1891, 1897, 1934; Boas and Hunt 1902; Curtis 1915, 1916; Dawson 1888; Drucker 1935, 1950, 1951; and Duff 1965). Interviews were restricted to two Nuu-chah-nulth elders and one Kwakwaka'wakw elder (Inglis

1987; John Thomas personal communication, May 1987; J.J. Wallas personal communication, January 1988).

Brooks Peninsula is considered the boundary between two ethno-linguistic groups—the Kwakwaka'wakw[1] to the north and the Nuu-chah-nulth[2] to the south. This demarcation is perhaps more a creation of academics for clarity of cultural definition than it was the reality on the landscape. Once established in the literature it has not only become generally accepted but further taken to mean that a clear demarcation always existed. The situation, however, may be much less rigid and far more complex. Borders are not areas where two cultures meet, but rather where individuals interact based on social, political and economic ties. This creates a fluid situation where individuals may access rights or citizenship in two areas. Recently, the issue of borders has become increasingly important as First Nations assert exclusivity of use and occupation of areas in the context of aboriginal rights and land claims litigation and negotiations.

The issue of the boundary was not addressed by the authors in the references cited above, in large part because of a different focus to their work. Two approaches, salvage ethnography and the Boasian historicist school of anthropology, dominated ethnographic fieldwork on the northwest coast in the late 19th and first half of the 20th centuries. Salvage ethnography was premised on the assumption that with the increasing presence of Europeans, aboriginal cultures were disappearing and being absorbed by western civilization. Historical contacts and the adoption of western ways were viewed as signalling the demise and eventual death of traditional societies. Anthropological research that followed this approach collected information and/or objects that were thought to show no acculturated elements. The goal was to reconstruct pre-contact society. This was not a time witnessed either by the informants or the ethnographer.

The Boasian approach to ethnography was predicated on the belief that the history, as well as the origin and distribution of cultural elements, was key to understanding cultures. The history of culture elements, however, could only be understood in the context of the culture studied as a whole. A culture was observed as having a core area from which elements diffused outward; the farther the elements from the centre, the greater the differences between the core area and peripheral cultures. Within the context of this model, peoples at the centre were of greater anthropological interest than those at the peripheries. Culture area studies and the mapping of cultural traits, championed by a number of Boas' students in the 1920s and 1930s (Stocking 1974: 18), developed out of this approach to history in terms of the geographical distribution of culture elements.

The following ethnographic descriptions were constructed from the archival record and a few recent interviews. Although the data is limited, the complexity of the aboriginal history of the Brooks Peninsula region is apparent.

Ethnographic Descriptions

Klaskino

The Klaskino[3], "people of the ocean" (Boas 1891: 605; Duff 1965) or "seaward tribe" (Boas and Hunt 1902: 358), are classified by anthropologists together with the Koskimo, Quatsino, and Koprino as

---

1 Formerly referred to as Kwakiutl, Kwageulth.

2 Formerly referred to as Nootka, Westcoast.

3 Variously spelled as Klas-kaino, Tla-sk'enoq, L'a'sq'enox, and LacqEnhwath in the anthropological literature and historical documents.

one of four Quatsino Sound tribes. Dawson (1888: 67) terms these tribes the "Kwakiool of the West Coast of Vancouver Island" based in part on geography, but more particularly on the practice of head deformation of female children. Boas (1897: 329) classifies these tribes together on linguistic criteria. In his scheme, they form the Koskimo subdialect of the Kwakiutl dialect. Duff (1965) describes these four tribes as the Quatsino Sound Kwakiutl who spoke the Koskimo subdialect of Kwakwala.

Others recognized the Klaskino as a bilingual people. In an 1867 newspaper article based on an interview with Captain Robinson, they are described as having "no distinct language of their own, but like border tribes speak with equal facility the language of the Kyoquot's [*sic*] on one side or that of the Koskeemo on the other, to the latter of which, however, they appear more nearly allied as they practice conical compression of the head after the Koskeemo fashion" (Victoria Daily British Colonist 1867). Drucker also noted the bilingual nature of the Klaskino, describing them as "mixed Kwakiutl and Nootkan" with most being bilingual (Drucker 1950: 158).

According to early descriptions and lists the Klaskino were not numerous. In 1867 they were "a very small...[tribe] and rapidly dying off, numbering about 40, of which 12 are adult male" (Victoria Daily British Colonist 1867). In 1889 the population was 14: 4 men, 6 women, and 4 children (Canada, Dept. of Indian Affairs 1890: 291, 292). In 1914 Jim Culteetsum was the only living Klaskino (Canada, Dept. of Indian Affairs 1914b); he died around 1940 (Malin 1961: 12). Disease is credited as the main cause for the extinction of the Klaskino people (Duff 1965).

In the anthropological literature, there are two views of the origins of the Klaskino—that the Brooks Peninsula region was their original home, and, alternatively, that they migrated from the north. According to information collected in 1885 by Dawson, the Klaskino had no traditions of being immigrants. They "came down" at five places: Oominis, located on the west coast of Vancouver Island south of the entrance to Quatsino Sound; Kwat-lim-tish, located on Klaskish Inlet; Ti-wes, a location not indicated by Dawson, but it may be Te-laise (Klaskino Indian Reserve 1), at the head of Side Bay; Ta-nilth, located at the head of Klaskino Inlet; and Tsa-wun-a-hus, located at the head of Side Bay according to Boas (1934: map 4, place 70), but on the south shore of Klaskino Inlet according to Dawson's 1887 map (Canada, Dept. of the Interior 1887). Curtis describes the Klaskino as always living "where they are now found" (Curtis 1915: 306). Boas, on the other hand, records traditions that imply an origin to the north: "According to the traditions of this people the K'oski'moq, Gua'ts'enoq, Kyo'p'enoq and Tla'sk'enoq drove tribes speaking the Nootka language from the region south of Quatsino Inlet" (Boas 1891: 608). Dawson (1888: 68-70) and Curtis (1915: 306) attribute the migration to the Koskimo and Quatsino only and date it to around the middle of the 18th century. Duff (1965) concurs with this interpretation.

There is no clear statement in the anthropological literature on the political composition of the Klaskino. Boas recorded at least four clans; in 1891 he described the Klaskino as having two gentes (clans), the T'e't'anetlenoq and the Omanitsenoq (Boas 1891: 605) and in 1897 he described them as having three clans with the addition of the Pe!pawiLenox (Boas 1897: 329). The author has identified a fourth clan, the WisEnts!a, from "Traditions of the L!a'sq'!enox" recorded by George Hunt from an unknown source sometime around 1895 (Boas 1897: 336; Boas and Hunt 1920: 355). Boas lists origin villages for three of the clans. One, O'manis, corresponds to an origin place recorded by Dawson (1888: 68). Another, Xanx", is associated with the Wi!sEnts'a (Boas 1897: 372, 1934: 37) though Boas does not give its location. GayE'mgaxts!aa, on the south shore of Quatsino Sound, is associated with the Pe!pawiLenox (Boas 1902: 365; 1934: 37). The names of the clans associated with the other four origin places noted by Dawson have not been identified.

Only one village, Tsowenachs in Klaskino Inlet, appears to have been occupied in the 19th century. It is the only village marked on the 1862 hydrographic chart "Klaskino and Klaskish Inlets and

Anchorages" (Great Britain 1865). In 1867, Captain Robinson was taken to a Klaskino village 16 km up Klaskino Sound. He did not record the name of the village, but the location of Tsowenachs approximates his description (even though the distance is incorrect). Dawson lists this village as having two houses and 14 occupants in 1885. In 1889, O'Reilly described Tsowenachs as the main village of the Klaskino (Canada, Dept. of Indian Affairs 1890: 289-291).

Klaskino territory, as defined in the anthropological literature, extends from Cape Cook on Brooks Peninsula northward to the area of Kwakiutl Point at the southern entrance to Quatsino Sound, and includes Klaskish and Klaskino Inlets and Side Bay (Dawson 1888: 70; Duff 1965). This, however, excludes the origin village of the Pe'pawiLenox, which is located on the south shore of Quatsino Sound. At one time, Klaskino territory must have included this area. Details of how it was lost have not been recorded, but may be related to the movement of the Koskimo into the region in the 18th century.

Klaskino territory was regarded as "awlis eik" or "specially favourable" (Dawson 1888: 68). According to J.J. Wallas (personal communication January 1988) their territory was "rich in sea otter, the best" and the Klaskino were noted hunters of sea otters. Drucker writes of the Klaskino: "a sea otter woman was an ancestress of theirs; consequently they had more secret rituals, magic and "medicines" for sea otter hunting than anyone else" (Drucker 1950: 243). Malin (1961: 12) claims that "at the height of the sea otter trade in the 1820s (the Klaskino) wallowed in wealth through the trading of furs with visiting foreign vessels"[4].

The Klaskino were also whalers. In "Heat-Giver", a tradition from the village of O'manis[5], the people became whale hunters after an ancestor obtained the "whale of the woods" as a charm (Boas and Hunt 1902: 362-365). Drucker recorded information on Klaskino whale ritualism from Quatsino Sam, Koskimo: "The ritualist slept in a burial cave surrounded by skulls during his training period. The ritualist then lay on a large cedar plank on the water, drifting out with the ebb tide and back ashore with the flood, to bring in whales" (Drucker 1950: 289). The same person also related a tradition about a Klaskino chief, Nimokwi'ma'lis, who obtained great numbers of drift whales through ritual observances (Drucker 1950: 289). In another tradition, the Klaskino and Chicklesaht vied for ownership of a blue whale that lived off Cape Cook. The whale would be towed to one village, then stolen and towed to the other. Eventually, the Klaskino sank the whale off Cape Cook where it turned into stone to form Solander Island. The Klaskino claimed the island as it "faces" towards their village (Wallas and Whitaker 1981: 146, 147).

In 1889, O'Reilly established three reserves for the Klaskino—the main village and the salmon fishing stations at Side Bay and Klaskish Inlet. Only one reserve, Klaskish, was confirmed in 1914 by the Royal Commission. At that time, the only surviving Klaskino person lived for most of the year with the other Quatsino Sound people at Quattishe, returning to his territory only in the summer months. Klaskino territory is unoccupied today.

Chicklesaht

The Chicklesaht[6], "small cove people" (John Thomas personal communication, June 1987) or "large

---

[4] The source of Malin's information is not known. There is little historical evidence to indicate that the Klaskino participated directly in trading with vessels. The known trading centres in the region were Nootka Sound, Nasparti (Columbia's Cove) and Newitty. The height of the otter trade in the region was the 1790s, not the 1820s.

[5] See a Hoyalas version of this tradition in Curtis (1915: 283-288).

[6] Variously spelled as Chickleset, Chaykisahts, Chiokusat, Che-wklzet, Chiklesats, and Chaic-cle-saht in anthropological and historical documents.

cut in bay people" (Boas 1891: 583), are classified by anthropologists as the northernmost of the Nuu-chah-nulth people. Sproat (1868: 308) lists them as one of 20 Aht tribes, which he divides into five groupings based on locality. He classifies the Chicklesaht as one of the "North of Nootkah Sound" tribes. Boas (1891: 583) lists 22 tribes of the Nootka divided into three groups speaking distinct dialects. The Chicklesaht are classified in group III, the tribes north of the northern entrance to Barkley Sound. Drucker (1951: 5) classifies the Chicklesaht as one of six Northern Nootka tribes, the other five being the Kyoquot, Ehattesaht, Nuchatlaht, Mowachaht, and Muchalaht. Drucker separates these tribes on the basis of their having "a much greater number of customs borrowed from the Southern Kwakiutl" than do the groups to the south (Drucker 1951: 4). Drucker's classification has been adopted by subsequent researchers in the Nuu-chah-nulth region (e.g., Arima 1983; Kenyon 1980).

The Chicklesaht were well respected by other tribes. Mrs. Olabar, a Kyoquot, described them as "good to potlatch even though not a numerous tribe. They were rich, all tyee, and invited lots of tribes" (Drucker 1935: notebook 10). Their ceremonies had several unique features. For example, at feasts the first food was not fed to the highest ranking visitor as was the custom among other Northwest Coast groups, but was thrown into the sea. This was in honour of the first white man to come to their shores (Moses Smith, personal communication June 1986)[7]. As well, a number of the dances and songs that were performed at feasts detail first contact with the white man (Kenyon 1980: 42).

The Chicklesaht were noted as warriors and for telling the "best war stories in the area" (Kenyon 1980: 44). Only one war story, however, has been recorded. In this tradition, told by Mrs. Olabar, the daughter of the Classet chief was married to the Chicklesaht chief. The marriage soured and hostilities developed between the two groups, resulting in the murder of the Chicklesaht chief. In revenge, the Chicklesaht ambushed the Classet near Cape Cook where they had gone for dogfish. Young and old, men and women, were killed. This was at a time when there "were no stores, but traders came around buying oil" (Drucker 1935: notebook 9), which dates the event to about 1850. There are two references to conflicts involving the Chicklesaht in John R. Jewitt's journal, kept at Nootka Sound from 1803 to 1805. On 29 November, 1803 he recorded: "This day our chief (Maquinna) informed us that he was going to war with the natives of Columbia's Cove[8]" (Jewitt 1976: 12). In July 1804 he recorded the arrival of a canoe of Chicklesahts who "had been to war with another tribe and killed 100 men and women" (Jewitt 1976: 12). In the 1880s the Chicklesaht were characterized by Father Nicolaye, the first missionary to work with them, as the "most aggressive [people] on the coast" (Jacobsen 1977: 66).

By the mid-19th century, the Chicklesaht were a relatively small tribe, according to available population figures. In 1855, the male population was between 50 and 60 (Banfield and Francis 1855), in 1860 the male population was 32 (Sproat 1868: 308), and in 1865 it was 30 (Torrens 1865). The population, including men, women, and children, was 144 in 1881; in 1896 it was 119, and in 1916 it was 57 (Canada, Dept. of Indian Affairs 1882, 1897, 1917). The dramatic decline revealed by these figures is due to diseases such as smallpox, measles, and whooping cough. The size of the population earlier is difficult to establish with any degree of certainty, but it was likely much larger. A 1792 estimate of 200 or 300 inhabitants in one of the three or four villages in the region (Howay 1941: 400), if extrapolated, suggests between 600 and 1200 people at the end of the 18th century.

---

[7] In 1792 Hoskins, an officer from the American trading vessel *Columbia*, visited the "head village" and noted that the entertainment included two songs in which the words "Wakush Tyee awinna", or "welcome travelling Chief", were frequently repeated (Howay 1941: 192).

[8] Located on the south shore of Brooks Peninsula.

There are two views on the political composition of the Chicklesaht. The first is from Drucker (1951: 222), who describes the Chicklesaht as a single tribe with one winter village. The second view (in Kenyon 1980: 44) is provided by an unnamed informant who describes the Chicklesaht as an amalgamation of three previously independent groups: the Malksopaht, the Ahkosaht, and an unnamed people from the other side of Cape Cook. Willie Harry (Inglis 1987) also describes the Chicklesaht as an amalgamation, but of four independent groups: the Ciq is?ath, village of Cic?ith in the Bunsby Islands; the Maqcupi?ath, village at ?apswis; the ?iqus, village at ?iqus; and the ?uwa?sa?ath, village at Naspat.

These two views are not, in the author's opinion, contradictory in that they reflect political structures at different time periods. Drucker's ethnographic horizon was the period from 1870 to 1900 (Drucker 1951: 2,3). This is nearly 100 years after first contact. We (Inglis and Haggarty 1986a, 1986b) have documented, for other Nuu-chah-nulth people, significant changes to regional political structures occurring as a result of population decline and increased warfare in the early historic period. The Chicklesaht situation appears to be analogous.

The territories of the independent groups are not recorded. The amalgamated territory of the Chicklesaht extends from Cape Cook in the north to the shoreline opposite Thomas (Whiteface) Island in the south and includes Ououkinsh and Malksope inlets and the Bunsby Islands (Drucker 1951:222).

In the mid-1800s the Chicklesaht lived together as a single political entity at Acous, a village that in 1892 consisted of 18 houses in two rows. In 1889, Peter O'Reilly, Indian Reserve Commissioner for British Columbia, visited the Chicklesaht to ascertain current land use and occupancy. He allocated seven reserves comprising two village sites, a burial ground, and four riverine salmon fishing stations (Canada, Dept. of Indian Affairs 1890: 289-291). Later, two reserves were added, including Quineex Indian Reserve 8 on the southwest corner of Brooks Peninsula near Clerke Point. In 1926, when this reserve was surveyed, it was described as a halibut station with three houses (British Columbia 1926).

Information on the economic activities of the Chicklesaht is meagre, and non-existent for the early historic period. By the late 1800s, the Chicklesaht participated actively in the new wage economy provided by commercial developments, as did many other native peoples on the coast. Men hired out to sailing schooners as fur seal hunters from May to October (Murray 1988). Others, both men and women, went to work at Wadham's Cannery at Rivers Inlet, and in the hop fields of the Fraser Valley and Puget Sound. When pelagic sealing was halted by the 1911 treaty, many of the men turned to trapping fur-bearing animals for their livelihood. Cape Cook was one of the favoured areas for trapping (Canada, Dept. of Indian Affairs 1914a; Moser 1926). The establishment of a fish camp in Walters Cove, Kyuquot Sound, provided the Chicklesaht with local employment opportunities. Many people moved to the area, at first only for the summer, but by the 1940s most were living on Mission Island Indian Reserve 2 year round (Kenyon 1980: 45, 53).

Today, the Chicklesaht live with the Kyuquot at Houpsitas Indian Reserve 6 in Kyuquot Sound. Although they are amalgamated with the Kyuquot in terms of band administration, they maintain their own hereditary chiefs, traditions, and ceremonies. Chicklesaht traditional territory is unoccupied.

Classet and Nespods

The history of the Brooks Peninsula region is more than an account of the Klaskino and the Chicklesaht. There is evidence, primarily in unpublished anthropological field notes and archival documents, that two other peoples, the Classet and the Nespods, also occupied this region. The evidence is meagre and occurs as isolated references.

The Classet[9], "coastline location people" (John Thomas personal communication, May 1987), are recorded in the first population estimates and censuses for the west coast of Vancouver Island. Banfield and Francis (1855) list the Classet as one of the tribes at the north end of the island. Helmcken (1856) lists them as a tribe located 30 miles south of Cape Scott, with a population of 75 men, 78 women, and 95 children. These writers include the Classet with Kwakwaka'wakw groups. Torrens (1865), on the other hand, lists the Classet as the northernmost of the Nootka Sound Indians, with two villages, Cla:issathus and Clo-clapp-e, and a population of 10 males. The chief was Mahulla-kinish. Sproat (1868: 308) lists the Classet as the northernmost Aht (Nuu-chah-nulth) tribe, with a population of 14 males. Boas (1891: 583) mentions the Tlahosath in parentheses at the end of a list of 22 Nuu-chah-nulth tribes noting that "even on special inquiry I [Boas] did not hear anything about this tribe".

Mrs. Olabar, Drucker's Kyuquot informant, named the Classet as one of the five tribes "going around Cape Cook" beyond Chicklesaht territory—the "Laisath, LacqEnhwath (Klaskino), Kwickimhwath (Koskimo), Ku:wp'ath (Koprino), and Qa tsinhwath (Quatsino)". The first two were bilingual, speaking both Nootka and Kwakiutl from childhood. The rest spoke Koskimo Kwakiutl (Drucker 1935: notebook 10). Mrs. Olabar also related a tradition in which the Chicklesaht attacked the Classet at Cape Cook. Many women and children were killed (Drucker 1935: notebook 9). The Classet are recorded as accompanying the first people from the east coast of Vancouver Island (the Kwakwaka'wakw) who came to trade eulachon for sea otter and dentalia with the Kyoquot (Drucker 1935: notebook 8).

What became of the Classet is unclear. Two possible scenarios are found in the unpublished anthropological notes. In a tradition collected by Alex Thomas from Kwisanishim, a Ucluelet, the Classet are described as being a people from a place "on the other side" of the Chicklesaht, drifted down to Neah Bay[10] at the time of the flood (Thomas 1914). This migration of the Classet was also noted by Drucker: "La'isath-Neah Bay—drifted down in flood from La'is[11] in Quatsino Sound, hence the name" (Drucker 1935: notebook 15). According to a tradition collected by John Thomas from Chief Charles Jones, a Pacheenaht, the Classet were from the west side of Brooks Peninsula. They left the area to search for food, that is a salmon river. They travelled down the coast until they reached the Nitinat Lake region where they found food in abundance, but the Ditidaht were already living there. They left, going next to Neah Bay where they formed an alliance with the local people to assist them in gaining the Nitinat Lake territory. The attack failed because the Ditidaht had been forewarned by a spy (John Thomas personal communication, May 1987).

There are two references to a possible second people, the Nespods, occupying the region. Grant (1857: 293) lists the Nespods as one of the tribes on the west coast of Vancouver Island south of the Koskimo. He estimates their population at 100. He does not identify them as either Nuu-chah-nulth or Kwakwaka'wakw. Nespod is also the name given by Grant to Brooks Bay (Grant 1857: 288). The other archival reference to these people is by Brown (1896: 26). He names the Neshahts of Woody Point[12] as an Aht (Nuu-chah-nulth) tribe. Naspat, referred to by Willie Harry as the village of the ?uwa?sa?ath, may be a reference to the same people (Inglis 1987).

---

[9] Variously spelled as Laisath, La'isath, Cla-issat, Tlahosath, and Klahosahts in the anthropological and historical documents. Classet is also the name recorded in the early historic period for the people of northwestern Washington.

[10] Located in Washington State.

[11] The author has not been able to identify this place or confirm its location.

[12] Cape Cook.

Both the Classet and Nespods are described as Nuu-chah-nulth from the Brooks Bay region. The explanation for this seeming overlap lies in the nature of the historical records. Both names appear in contemporaneous listings of tribes, but never in the same document. This leads the author to believe that the respective writers used different names for the same group. The author has retained the name Classet, as it is the term used in the anthropological data.

It can be concluded that the Classet, a bilingual Nuu-chah-nulth people, held territory centred in Brooks Bay. The southern boundary was in the area of Cape Cook and the northern boundary was perhaps as far north as Quatsino Sound. Around the mid-to-late 18th century, tribal distributions in this region underwent considerable change in response to people from the north end of Vancouver Island moving into Quatsino Sound. According to Kwakwaka'wakw traditions, this movement pushed out "Nootka-speaking peoples" from the area south of Quatsino Sound. These people, the author suggests, were the Classet.

The eventual fate of these people is unclear. It is possible that the Classet split as a result of conflict with the Kawkwaka'wakw. One group migrated south and settled in the area of Neah Bay where they are recorded by explorers and traders in the late 1700s. They may have become part of the Makah. The rest of the Classet remained in the southern part of their territory in the region of Cape Cook. This is where the conflict with the Chicklesaht occurred in the mid-19th century. Classet presence at the time is confirmed by population estimates that list them as one of the tribes north of the Chicklesaht. Although there is no clear documentation, it appears that the Classet were absorbed by the Chicklesaht before the end of the century.

Summary

As evident from the information presented, our knowledge of the history of the Brooks Peninsula region is sketchy. It is clear from the available data, however, that the history is complex and significant changes in respect to the number and composition of political entities occurred in the late 18th and 19th centuries. Before these changes, a number of independent people occupied the region, each with a main village and a defined territory. Population decline brought on by disease and increased warfare resulted in complete restructuring of this pattern. Previously independent people joined together in order to survive politically and economically. By the mid-1800s, perhaps earlier, two people, the Klaskino and the Chicklesaht, had come to dominate. Each had a main village and utilized the resources of their respective territory on a seasonal basis.

This was the cultural pattern witnessed by anthropologists at the end of the 19th century and assumed to be analogous to the pre-contact past. In the author's view, this was not a pre-contact pattern, but an historic-period development by previously independent peoples responding to a significant decline in population. People who did not survive to be witnessed by anthropologists became historical anecdotes in the notes and texts. The Classet are but one example.

This brief review of the aboriginal history of the Brooks Peninsula region raises many questions and suggests topics of future research. Who are the Classet referenced in the fur trade journals of the late 18th and 19th centuries? Are they people of the Neah Bay region or the Brooks Peninsula region or both? Clearly, our knowledge of political composition of the Klaskino and Chicklesaht people is limited. What is the history of these amalgamations? How do peoples in border areas interact yet remain autonomous? Research into these and other questions will greatly increase our understanding of cultures in border areas.

Update

Since this paper was written eight years ago, only one publication has dealt with the aboriginal history of the Brooks Peninsula region in any significant way. This is the major geographic study of the Kwakwaka'wakw by Galois. The Klaskino are described in the Quatsino Sound Tribes section (Galois 1994).

This work utilizes both ethnographic and historical data sources to describe the settlement changes in the region of northern Vancouver Island and adjacent mainland over the 150 years from 1775 to 1920. Galois' conclusion that the Quatsino Sound area has witnessed significant social and geographic changes supports the conclusions of this paper (Galois 1994: 347).

References Cited

Arima, E.Y. 1983. The West Coast people: the Nootka of Vancouver Island and Cape Flattery. British Columbia Museum Provincial Museum Special Publication 6. Victoria, BC.

Banfield, W.E. and P. Francis. 1855. Letter to Sir James Douglas, Governor of British Columbia and Vancouver Island, 1 July 1855. British Columbia Archives and Records Service (Victoria, BC), GR 1372 Colonial Correspondence, file 588a.

Boas, F. 1891. Second general report on the Indians of British Columbia. Pp. 562-715 in Report of the British Association for the advancement of science for 1890. London.

———. 1897. The social organization and the secret societies of the Kwakuitl Indians. Pp. 311-737 in Report of the U.S. National Museum for 1895. Smithsonian Institution, Washington, DC.

———. 1934. Geographical names of the Kwakiutl Indians. Columbia University. Contributions to Anthropology 20.

——— and G. Hunt. 1902. Kwakiutl texts. Jesup North Pacific Expedition Publications. Memoir, American Museum of Natural History, Vol. 5.

British Columbia. 1926. Field notes of B.C. government survey, Indian Reserve Quineex No. 8, lot No. 708, Rupert District by H.M.T. Hodgson, June 1926. Crown Lands, Surveyor General Branch. Victoria, BC.

Brown, R. (ed.). 1896. The adventures of John Jewitt, edited and with an introduction by R. Brown. C. Wilson, London.

Canada Department of Indian Affairs. 1882. Annual report for the year 1881.

———. 1890. Letters from Peter O'Reilly, Indian Reserve Commission, Victoria, to L. Van Koughnet, Deputy Superintendent General of Indian Affairs, Ottawa re: Chicklesaht reserves. Pp. 289-291 (14 April 1890); pp. 291, 292 (21 April 1890) in British Columbia Archives and Records Service (Victoria, BC), microfilm RG10 B-1393, file 1277.

———. 1914a. Transcript of meeting with Check-le-set band, 25 May, 1914. British Columbia Archives and Records Service (Victoria, BC) microfilm RG10 volume 11025, file AH13.

———. 1914b. Transcript of meeting with the Klaskino Band, 1914. British Columbia Archives and Records Service (Victoria, BC), microfilm RG10 volume 11025, file AH3.

——— . 1917. Annual report for the year 1916.

Canada Department of the Interior. 1887. Geological map of the northern part of Vancouver Island and adjacent coasts by George M. Dawson (map). Scale, 1 inch: 8 miles. Geological Survey of Canada, Ottawa.

Curtis, E.S. 1915. The North American Indian. Vol. 10. The Kwakiutl. Plimpton Press, Norwood, MA.

——— . 1916. The North American Indian. Vol. 11. The Nootka and the Haida. Plimpton Press, Norwood, MA.

Dawson, G.M. 1888. Notes and observations on the Kwakiool people of the northern part of Vancouver Island and adjacent coasts, made during the summer of 1885. Pp 63-98. Proc. and Transactions of the Royal Society of Canada for the year 1887. Vol. 5, section 11.

Drucker, P. 1935. Nootka field notebooks. Smithsonian Institution (.U.S.), National Anthropological Archives ms. collection 4516. Photocopy in British Columbia Archives and Records Service Add. Ms. 870. Victoria, BC.

——— . 1950. Culture element distributions: XXVI Northwest Coast. Anthropological Records, Vol. 9, No. 3. University of California Press, Berkeley, CA.

——— . 1951. The northern and central Nootkan tribes. Bureau of American Ethnology, Bull. 144. Smithsonian Institution, Washington, DC.

Duff, W. 1965. The Southern Kwakiutl. Unpublished ms. on file at the Royal British Columbia Museum, Victoria, BC.

Galois, R. 1994. Kwakwaka'wakw settlements, 1775-1920: a geographical analysis and gazetteer. UBC Press, Vancouver, BC.

Grant, W.C. 1857. Description of Vancouver Island. Journal of the Royal Geographical Society 27: 268-320.

Great Britain, Admiralty Hydrographic Office. 1865. Klaskino and Klaskish inlets and anchorages surveyed by Captain G.H. Richards in 1862. Chart 590. Scale 1:36 480. Admiralty, London, UK.

Helmcken, J.S. 1856. Indian population Vancouver Island. British Columbia Archives and Records Service (Victoria, BC), J.S. Helmcken papers, add. ms. 505, Vol. 10, folder 4.

Howay, F.W. (ed.). 1941. Voyages of the Columbia to the Northwest Coast 1787-1790 and 1790-1793. Massachusetts Historical Society, Boston, MA.

Inglis, R.I. 1987. Interview with Willie Harry, transcribed and translated by George Louie. Unpublished ms. on file at the Royal British Columbia Museum, Victoria, BC.

——— and J.C. Haggarty. 1986a. Cook to Jewitt: three decades of change in Nootka Sound. Pp. 193-222 in B. Trigger, T. Morantz, and L. Dechene (eds.). Le castor fait tout: selected papers of the fifth North American fur trade conference, 1985. Lake St. Louis Historical Society, Montreal, PQ.

——— and J.C. Haggarty. 1986b. Pacific Rim National Park ethnographic history. Parks Canada Microfiche Report Series 257. Canadian Parks Service, Ottawa, ON.

Jacobsen, J.A. 1977. Alaskan voyage 1881-1883: an expedition to the northwest coast of America. Translated by Erna Gunther from the German text of Adrian Woldt. University of Chicago Press, Chicago, IL.

Jewitt, J.R. 1976. A journal kept at Nootka Sound, 1803-1805. Garland Publishing, New York, NY.

Kenyon, S. 1980. The Kyoquot way: a study of a West Coast (Nootkan) community. National Museums of Canada, Canadian Ethnology Service Paper 61. Ottawa, ON.

Malin, E. 1961. The social organization of the Koskimo Kwakiutl. M.A. thesis, Dept. of Anthropology, University of Colorado, Boulder, CO.

Moser, C. 1926. Reminiscences of the west coast of Vancouver Island. Acme Press, Victoria, BC.

Murray, P. 1988. The vagabond fleet: a chronicle of the north Pacific sealing schooner trade. Sono Nis, Victoria, BC.

Sproat, G. 1868. Scenes and studies of savage life. Smith, Elder, and Co., London, UK.

Stocking, G.W. Jr. (ed.). 1974. The shaping of American anthropology 1883-1911: a Franz Boas reader. Basic Books, New York, NY.

Thomas, A. 1914. Origin of the Oo-oolth. Unpublished ms. on file at the Canadian Ethnology Service, Ottawa, ON. Ms. 50q.

Tolmie, W.F. and G.M. Dawson. 1884. Comparative vocabularies of the Indian tribes of British Columbia with a map illustrating distributions. Geological and Natural History Survey of Canada, Dawson Brothers, Montreal, PQ.

Torrens, R.W. 1865. Report of his explorations and proceedings at Clayoquot Sound, 19 September 1865. British Columbia Archives and Records Service Colonial Secretary Papers. Victoria, BC.

Victoria (BC). 1867. Daily British Colonist. The wreck of the Mauna Rea. 26 January 1867. Vol. 17, p. 2.

Wallas, J. and P. Whitaker. 1981. Kwakiutl legends. Hancock House, North Vancouver, BC.

Chapter 14

Archaeology of Brooks Peninsula

James C. Haggarty[a]
Richard I. Inglis[b]

[a] Shoreline Archaeological Services, Inc.
Victoria, BC

[b] Ministry of Aboriginal Affairs
Victoria, BC

Abstract

This chapter presents the results of a 1981 archaeological survey conducted on the modern shoreline of Brooks Peninsula, incorporates these results with those obtained from a 1984 overview survey of historic Chicklesaht territory, and summarizes our current knowledge of the archaeology of the Chicklesaht and Klaskino peoples who occupied the Brooks Peninsula region historically.

Ten sites were recorded on the Brooks Peninsula; nine within the historic territory of the Chicklesaht and one in Klaskino territory. Seven of the sites are classified as general activity sites, two as burial sites, and one as an isolated find site. One of the general activity sites is classified as a village site, the other six as camp sites. Two of the camp sites, including the site in Klaskino territory, are located in an open setting, three are located in caves, and one in a rockshelter. The two burial sites are located in cave settings; both contain fragments of bent-wood cedar boxes and human skeletal remains. The isolated find site contains the remains of a bent-wood cedar box. In addition, recent structures, associated with historic use of the peninsula, were observed. These sites were not recorded.

An analysis of the 38 archaeological site records for historic Chicklesaht territory indicates that as many as seven independent peoples, with a population of up to 3000 people, occupied the region. The Brooks Peninsula area was occupied by one of the seven local groups into the 20th century.

Acknowledgements

We acknowledge and thank Donald Abbott, Gay Frederick, Grant Keddie, and Bjorn Simonsen for reviewing an earlier draft of this paper. Their comments were constructive and helped to improve both the structure and content of the paper. Thanks also are due Nancy Condrashoff (now Romaine) for preparing the site map (Figure 14.11), Sally Watson for typing numerous earlier drafts, Kitty Bernick for editing an earlier draft of the manuscript, and Ursla Masee for typing the final version of the paper.

Introduction

In August 1981, at the time of the Brooks Peninsula survey, much of the historic territory of the Nuu-chah-nulth was unknown archaeologically. Although major excavation projects had been conducted in the central portion of this territory, at Yuquot or Friendly Cove (Folan and Dewhirst 1966, 1970, 1980; Folan 1969, 1972a, 1972b; Dewhirst 1969, 1978, 1980), at Coopte in Nootka Sound (McMillan 1969), and at various sites in Hesquiat Harbour (Haggarty and Boehm 1974, Cybulski 1978, Calvert 1980, Haggarty 1982), the northern region remained unexamined. Only two other excavation projects, one at Aquilar Point, a defensive site near the entrance to Bamfield Inlet in Barkley Sound (Buxton 1969), and one at the Shoemaker Bay site at the head of Alberni Inlet (McMillan and St. Claire 1975, 1982), had been conducted within historic Nuu-chah-nulth territory.

Until 1981, archaeological site surveys had been conducted only in the Estevan Point-Hesquiat Harbour area (Sneed 1972), Barkley Sound area (St. Claire 1975), Alberni Inlet and Alberni valley areas (McMillan and St. Claire 1975; McMillan 1985), Sproat Lake (Keddie 1971), and a portion of Meares Island (Brolly 1981). Although no excavation projects have been undertaken since the Brooks Peninsula survey, a number of archaeological survey projects have been conducted. These include major systematic surveys of Meares Island (Mackie 1983), the Long Beach, Broken Group Islands, and West Coast Trail units of Pacific Rim National Park Reserve (Haggarty and Inglis 1985), Bamfield Inlet and a portion of Barkley Sound (Williamson and Mackie 1985), and an archaeological reconnaissance of the northern portion of Nuu-chah-nulth territory (Haggarty and Inglis 1984b).

Prior to the Brooks Peninsula survey, a total of 250 archaeological sites had been recorded for historic Nuu-chah-nulth territory (Haggarty and Inglis 1983b). Most of the site records were incomplete and many of the sites had never been observed by archaeologists. During the past eight years, there has been a significant increase in the number of sites recorded. Approximately 1400 sites are now recorded within historic Nuu-chah-nulth territory. This figure represents, approximately, a 460% increase in the number of sites for the area. The site survey and mapping and recording methods responsible for the increase, in both the number of sites found during systematic survey and the quality of individual site records, were developed for the Brooks Peninsula project (Haggarty and Inglis 1983a) and refined on subsequent surveys (Haggarty and Inglis 1984a, 1985; Mackie 1983, 1986).

The primary objective of the Brooks Peninsula survey was to document past utilization of this landscape by human populations. Specific objectives of the project were: (1) to conduct a systematic archaeological site survey of the modern shoreline, and (2) to examine selected inland locations and river systems for evidence of earlier occupation relating to higher relative sea level stands. The second objective, although important to the overall goal of the Brooks Peninsula Refugium Project, was given lower priority than the first as the probability of locating inland archaeological sites was judged to be low until relative sea level curves were established for this area of the west coast of Vancouver Island. Intensive survey of the modern shoreline was the primary objective of the first stage of field research. Systematic inland survey would be conducted during a second field season if analysis of geological, pedological and paleoecological data indicated potential areas of investigation. Selected inland locations would be examined during the initial field phase in conjunction with planned geomorphological and paleoecological studies.

This paper presents the results of the archaeological survey conducted along the modern Brooks Peninsula shoreline and selected inland locations, incorporates them with results from more recent investigations in the area southeast of the peninsula, and summarizes our current knowledge of the archaeology of the Chicklesaht and Klaskino peoples who historically occupied the Brooks Peninsula region (see Chapter 13).

The Field Program

The site survey of the modern Brooks Peninsula shoreline was conducted from two base camps during the period 30 July to 18 August 1981. During the course of the survey, approximately 114 km of shoreline (including offshore islands and islets) were surveyed. The survey area included all of the Brooks Peninsula shoreline from the head of Klaskish Inlet to the unnamed river delta at the head of Nasparti Inlet. This shoreline was examined by boat, helicopter, or on foot, depending primarily on the character of foreshore terrain (Figure 14.1).

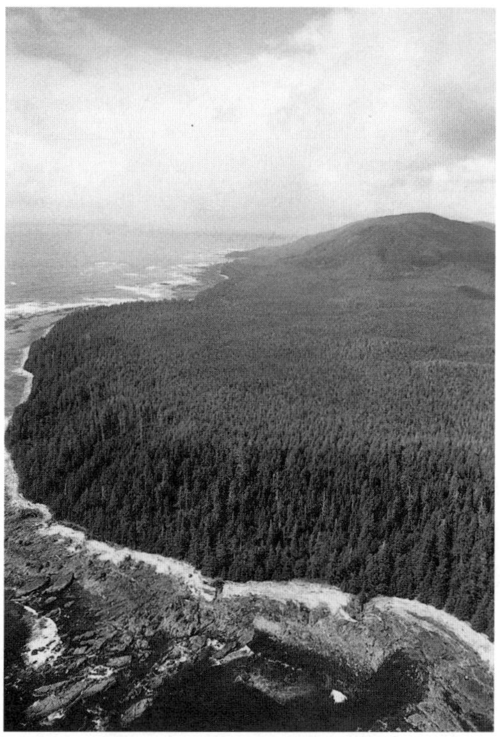

Figure 14.1 Aerial view of SW shore of Brooks Peninsula; Shelter Sheds base camp in lower right corner (Photo: Richard I. Inglis)

Research Design

In April 1981, prior to the field survey, a three-day reconnaissance trip to Brooks Peninsula was undertaken to evaluate logistical concerns. Particularly important questions concerned the feasibility and efficiency of operating out of a single base camp as opposed to two or more camps. It was apparent that two base camps were required to operate efficiently along this stretch of rugged, exposed shoreline. One camp, located near Quineex Indian Reserve 8, or "Shelter Sheds", northeast of Clerke Point, would serve as a base of operations for site survey of the southwestern and southeastern shorelines of the peninsula. This location offered a number of advantages. It was near the centre of the proposed survey unit, in the lea of prevailing summer westerly winds and swells, was accessible by boat through a natural channel in the intertidal area, and had a small cabin suitable for two-person occupancy.

A second base camp would coincide with the project field camp located at the mouth of the major lagoon on the northwestern shoreline of Brooks Peninsula. This second base camp would facilitate small boat access to the shoreline between Cape Cook and the head of Klaskish Inlet, the important beach ridge sequence northeast of the camp, and helicopter access to selected inland locations.

The base camps selected for the archaeological survey defined the three field survey units employed on the project; (1) Quineex Shoreline unit, extending from Cape Cook, east to the head of Nasparti Inlet, including Solander Island and all other offshore islands and islets; (2) Lagoon Shoreline unit, from Cape Cook northeast to the head of Klaskish Inlet, including all offshore islands and islets; and (3) Interior Terrain unit, including all potential inland terrain. The Quineex base camp was utilized first followed by the Lagoon camp. Survey of the Interior Terrain unit was undertaken from the Lagoon base camp, which also served as a base for project helicopter operations.

Within the Quineex and Lagoon shoreline units, stretches of shoreline accessible by foot were walked, whereas those accessible only by boat were spot-checked. The 18-km stretch of shoreline between Jackobson Point, on the southeastern shoreline and the small, rocky headland due west of the mouth of Nordstrom Creek on the southwestern shoreline, was surveyed on foot. All beach areas accessible by boat on the northwestern shoreline of the peninsula were also examined on foot. Using 3-cm-diameter Oakfield soil samples, all potential habitation locations were probed for evidence of human occupation.

The two major portions of the Brooks Peninsula shoreline surveyed by boat extend from the head of Nasparti Inlet to the first small headland west of the mouth of Amos Creek, excluding Johnson Lagoon, and from Cape Cook to the head of Klaskish Inlet. Along this 91-km stretch of shoreline all potential habitation locations with suitable foreshore access were examined on foot and probed. Rocky stretches of shoreline were examined closely for caves and rockshelters and these locations were examined on foot and probed for evidence of human occupation.

Areas that were not accessible by boat were examined by helicopter at slow speed and low altitude. In Johnson Lagoon the areas of the three river deltas on the western shoreline and selected areas along the rocky, exposed northwestern shoreline of the peninsula were assessed on foot while the helicopter stood by. In addition to the peninsula shoreline, the eastern shore of Nasparti Inlet and the areas of the Cuttle Islets and Acous Peninsula were surveyed.

Methodology

The field methodology employed throughout the survey was developed specifically for this project and, after some initial modifications, applied consistently in the Quineex and Lagoon shoreline survey units. Field methodology for the Interior Terrain unit was to include systematic survey of all major and selected minor river systems on Brooks Peninsula and also spot-checks of other high potential interior locations. Lack of time, however, only permitted selected investigation of the rugged interior terrain and river systems.

Site Survey

The methodology of site survey on the west coast of Vancouver Island (see Haggarty and Inglis 1984a) involves a combination of land, water, and air transport. For the two shoreline survey units, water transport was used almost exclusively for shoreline access. Air transport was used primarily for overview purposes and to check specific locations not easily accessible by boat or on foot. All stretches of shoreline accessible on foot were walked. Most other areas were investigated by boat and only a few areas were surveyed solely by helicopter.

The survey methods used in both shoreline units were standardized and applied in a uniform and consistent manner. Numerous and varied specific procedures were employed, all were applied within the context of a single overriding principle: the key to understanding past use of a particular shoreline involves accurate assessment of the intertidal zone of that landscape. This zone can only be assessed accurately when the tide is at half level or lower. A shoreline survey must, therefore, be conducted in accordance with daily tidal fluctuations. No new shoreline should be surveyed when tide levels exceed the half-tide mark. This principle was consistently adhered to during the survey.

The intertidal areas of the two shoreline survey units were observed on foot where possible. Areas virtually impassable on foot were surveyed by boat with frequent stops to investigate near-shore and forest-edge areas. As intertidal and shoreline configurations change, the range of expected site types also changes. For example, a shoreline consisting of a steep intertidal zone greatly reduces the probability of habitation sites, but increases the probability of rock art or cave/rockshelter sites suitable for burial and/or habitation. This type of shoreline was surveyed only when high tide levels precluded accurate survey of less rugged sections of shoreline. Strict adherence to this survey principle has been one of the key factors responsible for the dramatic increase in the number and variety of archaeological sites located and recorded on subsequent west coast survey projects (Haggarty and Inglis 1984a, 1985; Mackie 1983; Williamson and Mackie 1985).

All sites located during the survey were given temporary site numbers in accordance with the established site designation scheme for Canada (Borden 1952). Separate site designations were given if discrete site functions could be inferred from field observation. For example, if burials were observed on the surface of a habitation cave site, two archaeological site designations were assigned. Similarly, if two or more site locations were separated by a rocky headland, or were otherwise discontinuous even though they were relatively close together, each location was given an individual site number.

The rationale behind this approach concerns social access to, and potential control over, the use of a particular location, contemporaneity of site use, and the range of resources available for capture or collection. In the absence of detailed ethnographic data regarding the use of specific locations by specific social units, it is appropriate, during the field phase, to separate discrete site functions observed at a single location. This practice will aid interpretation. It is preferable to allow for differential use by specific social units over time than to infer that a single, unknown social unit was responsible for all observed site functions or specific sites located in proximity to one another. The assumption inherent in this approach is that specific site functions and site locations are crucial for accurate culture-historical reconstruction, particularly at the local group, household, and family levels of socio-political organization.

Site Mapping and Recording

Site mapping and recording was initiated upon completion of the site survey phase. Mapping and recording procedures, like those used in the site survey, were developed specifically for this project and applied consistently, after some initial modification, to all sites located in the study area.

The field procedures involved in mapping and recording archaeological sites varied slightly, according to the type of site being recorded (see Haggarty and Inglis 1984a, 1985). Within specific site types, however, the procedures employed were standardized and uniformly applied. The first step was to determine accurately the maximum length and width dimensions of the site. This was accomplished by using Oakfield soil samplers for general activity sites, and by direct observation for burial sites. For most general activity sites, a base line was established parallel to the long axis of the site, preferably in the high intertidal zone, clear of forest-edge vegetation. This base line must be straight, tight, free of any obstructions, and known to exceed the length of the site. With the base line set, its compass bearing relative to magnetic north was recorded. Mapping a site and associated intertidal features, such as canoe runs, proceeded by running a series of right-angle transects in both directions from the base line.

The process of drawing a detailed field map of an archaeological site requires choosing a scale appropriate for recording the site and all associated features. Once the scale for the site map was selected, the base line was plotted on graph paper so that the site and all associated features would fit, its bearing was recorded, and appropriate metric intervals were marked. A series of right-angle transects were then run from selected intervals along the base line. If the height of the tide was a factor in recording intertidal cultural features, the transects were run at low tide. Attention subsequently was directed towards mapping the main portion of the site.

The process of mapping an archaeological site was directed by the individual who drew the field map. Since site boundaries and outlines of features were interpolated between points along two adjacent transects, the number and position of transects from the base line were decided by the mapper. Sites that are generally uniform in outline required fewer transects than sites that are irregular.

Along each transect, recording certain points and their distances from the base line was mandatory. The intersections of each transect with the vegetation edge, beach edge, beginning of site deposit, beginning of front slope, top of front slope, beginning of back midden ridge, top of back midden ridge, bottom of back midden ridge, and end of deposit, were recorded, if present. As a rule, site maps were constructed by beginning at one end of the site and progressing to the other end.

On completion of the site map (including associated features such as house depressions, house platforms, and intertidal modifications) recording other information pertinent to a full site description began. Detailed notes were made on the condition of the site and the likelihood of future disturbance, on vegetation, composition and depth of both cultural and non-cultural matrices, nearest water source, location of known finds, photographs of the site or site features, possible site age and site use. In addition, numerous elevation measurements were taken with a hand-held level using the mean high tide line as the zero point of reference. Elevation measurements for all prominent site features were recorded on the site map.

Sites other than general activity sites required slight modifications to some of the mapping and recording procedures. For habitation cave and burial cave sites, the base line was positioned parallel to the long axis of the cave, beginning outside the dripline and front berm and extending the full length of the cave. Right-angle transects were then run off both sides of the base line to provide accurate measurements of the cave floor area and features. In addition, the cave walls and ceiling were measured and drawn in profile at selected intervals along the base line in order to characterize the above-surface volume of the cave.

Detailed site information was recorded on British Columbia Archaeological Site Inventory Forms.

Archaeological Site Inventory

Shoreline Survey

The intensive shoreline survey of Brooks Peninsula produced 10 mapped and recorded native archaeological sites (Figure 14.2), and information on an additional six structures associated with recent use of the study area, five of which are non-native. Seven of the native sites are classified as general activity, or shell midden sites, two as burial sites and one as an isolated find site (Table 14.1). Four of the seven general activity sites, both of the burial sites and the isolated find site occur in cave or rockshelter settings. The six recent structures were not recorded in detail.

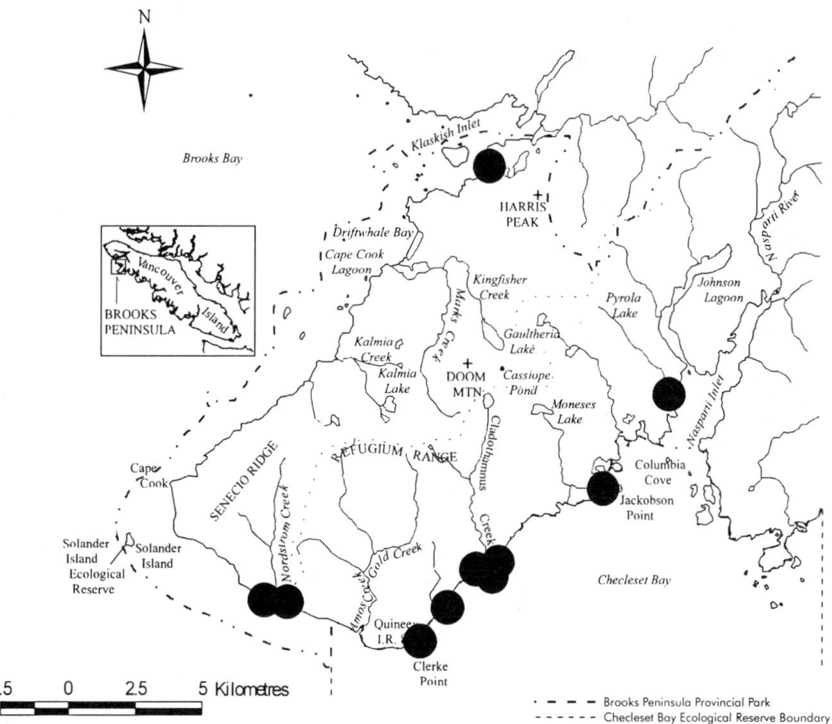

Figure 14.2 General locations of archaeological sites, Brooks Peninsula

Nine of the 10 recorded archaeological sites are located within the historic territory of the Chicklesaht, the northernmost group of the Nuu-chah-nulth people (Drucker 1951; Kenyon 1980). The remaining site on Klaskish Indian Reserve 3 is located within the historic territory of the Klaskino, the southernmost of the Kwakwaka'wakw on the west coast of Vancouver Island (Duff 1965).

The results of the archaeological survey are presented in the following major categories: general activity sites, burial sites, and an isolated find site.

General Activity Sites

Archaeological sites in this category represent a range of functions or use. At one extreme, large shell midden deposits represent major village sites; at the other extreme, small shell midden sites, including those in caves and rockshelters, represent short-term resource camps. Large, strategically placed shell midden sites, usually exceeding 100 m in length and often exhibiting well-defined house platforms, house depressions, and a back midden ridge, are classified as village sites. These sites represent the major settlement sites of distinct social units, likely local

Table 14.1 Archaeological sites on Brooks Peninsula

Major Category, Type and Sub-type	No.	% Type	% Major Category
General Activity			
Village	1	14.3	
Camps		85.7	
Open	2		
Cave	3		
Rockshelter	1		
Total	7		70.0
Burial			
Cave	2		
Total	2	100.0	20.0
Isolated Find	1		
Total	1	100.0	10.0
TOTAL	10		100.0

groups (Haggarty 1982). From these sites, local groups would have exploited specific resources within geographically-defined territories. These villages were likely occupied year-round by most members of the social unit, and would have served as the focus for winter ceremonies. Large, permanent post-and-beam or shed-roof house structures, typical of Nuu-chah-nulth culture, would have been erected at these sites.

Small, unstructured shell midden sites, including those found in relict sea caves and rockshelters, have been classified as resource camps. Generally less than under 100 m in length, these sites lack the well-defined surface features characteristic of the large village sites. Although variable in size and composition, most camp sites represent some form of resource procurement activity. Large camps may have functioned as summer resource sites and semi-permanent shelters may have been erected at them. Small resource sites include deposits associated with daily or short-term resource procurement, such as fish or shellfish collecting and processing. Temporary shelters, such as small mat huts, may have been erected at these sites. In many cases, particularly at sites used on a daily basis, no form of shelter would have been required.

The seven general activity sites are summarized by type in Table 14.1. Their distribution on Brooks Peninsula is presented in Figure 14.2. Three of the sites are located in open settings, three in caves, and one in a rockshelter. Only one, EaSw 1, is classified as a village site; the remaining six are camp sites. EaSw 1, the largest of the seven shell middens, is located adjacent to Quineex Indian Reserve 8, the only Indian reserve on Brooks Peninsula. The site is well protected from prevailing westerly winds during the summer months. As a result, air temperature along this section of Brooks Peninsula shoreline is relatively warm. It is also located as close to the end of the peninsula as possible, the extensive cobble platform and rock-strewn shoreline that characterizes the Clerke Point foreshore. Immediately in front of the site there is a natural channel in the rocky foreshore that provides for easy watercraft access to the sand and gravel beach in front of the site (Figures 14.3 and 14.4). This natural channel also reduces wave energy generated from prevailing westerly winds and swells.

Figure 14.3 Aerial view natural "canoe run" channel in front of village site EaSw 1 (Photo: Richard I. Inglis)

Figure 14.4 General view of area of village site EaSw 1 (Photo: Richard I. Inglis)

EaSw 1 is composed primarily of crushed *Mytilus californianus* (California mussel) and barnacle shell, fish remains, fire-cracked rocks and dark, charcoal-stained soil with some bird and land and sea mammal remains. The site is approximately 100 m long, 27 m wide, and 3 m deep. The relatively narrow width of the deposit is explained by the fact that wave action has eroded the front face (Figure 14.5). Originally on an old beach berm that was open to strong winds and waves coming from the southeast, the deposit is now protected by a log-gravel berm. The relatively steep front face of the midden has stabilized approximately 6 m back from the front edge of the older berm and 15 m back from the modern berm. Slumped and mixed cultural material is present in the upper levels of the exposed older berm. These materials overlie sterile beach sands and gravels. Behind the front face, the deposit is flat, forming a distinct platform. This platform is approximately 5 m above a legal survey post located immediately in front of the deposit, near the maximum high-tide line. The back edge of the deposit drops off slightly before it merges with the gently rising hillside behind the site. Large Sitka spruce trees, estimated to be 200-300 years old, grow on the flat midden platform, on the front edge of the site, and on the older beach berm in front of the site. These trees suggest a termination date of A.D. 1750 for occupation of the site. Two small, intermittent creeks drain the hillside behind the site and clearly mark the extent of the cultural deposit at either end. One bifacially utilized abrador (not collected) was found on the surface of the older beach berm in front of the site. The size and composition of the deposit suggest long-term use by a relatively small social unit.

The second open-setting midden site, EaSw 6, is much smaller than EaSw 1. This site is approximately 20 m long, 17 m wide, and only 30 cm deep. It is located at the extreme western end of the first large embayment due west of Jackobson Point (Figure 14.2). The deposit consists of dark, charcoal-stained soil, fire-cracked rocks, crushed mussel, clam, and barnacle shells, and bird, fish, land and sea mammal bones. The site is bounded by a small, intermittent stream at its western edge and by a gently sloping hillside to the south. To the east, the deposit gradually thins out on level terrain. The front edge of the deposit, approximately 7 m back from the maximum

Figure 14.5 Front face of village site EaSw 1 (Photo: Richard I. Inglis)

high-tide mark, is located on a gently sloping old beach. The deposit attains a maximum elevation of 2.7 m above the maximum high tide line. The entrance to the small bay in front of the site contains a number of small reefs that protect the bay and the site from prevailing winds and swells. The small size of the deposit and the lack of defined surface features suggest a seasonal camp rather than a village site.

The third site in this category (EbSw 1) is located on Klaskish Indian Reserve 3, due east of McDougal Island, near the entrance to Klaskish Inlet (Figures 14.2 and 14.6). The site, the only one located on the northwestern shoreline of Brooks Peninsula, is 50 m long, 27 m wide, and at least 1.2 m deep (Figure 14.7). The front edge of the deposit is being eroded by wave action assisted by a steady flow from two small streams that converge and debouch at the western margin of the site. Along its front edge, the deposit is undercut and exposed. Roots from large Sitka spruce trees growing on the front edge of the site are also exposed, extending out from the front edge of the site onto the relatively steep-sloping gravel beach in front of the site. The northernmost stream drains Canoe Lake, a relatively large and low-lying lake (less than 30 m above maximum high tide), located due east of the site. The northern edge of the site abuts a steep-faced rock outcrop. The back or eastern margin of the site merges with a relatively steep-sloping hillside. To the south, the deposit becomes shallow and terminates in what appears to be deltaic deposit associated with stream discharge. The site was utilized by Klaskino people into the 20th century.

Figure 14.6 Aerial view of Klaskish Inlet (Photo: Richard I. Inglis)

The interior of the site is relatively flat and clear of vegetation, though Sitka spruce trees are common and there are several western red-cedar trees and one hemlock tree. Salal, though not present on the site, occurs immediately south of it. Cow parsnip, nettle, fern, huckleberry, elderberry, salmonberry, grasses, and other plant species are present on the site. The cultural deposit reaches a maximum depth of 1.2 m near the middle of the front face and decreases to 25 cm in depth at its southern limit. Whole and fragmentary mussel and clam shell dominate the deposit. Fire-cracked rocks, bird, fish and mammal bones are also present in a series of dark, charcoal-stained matrices. Shell concentrations decrease towards the back of the site. Though larger than EaSw 6, the site also appears to have functioned as a seasonal camp.

Figure 14.7 Camp site EbSw 1 on Klaskish Indian Reserve 3 (Photo: Richard I. Inglis)

All three cave middens found during the survey are located within historic Chicklesaht territory. These caves, and others located on Brooks Peninsula shoreline, were formed by wave action and subsequent erosion when sea level stands were higher than at present. The first site of this sub-type, EaSx 1, one of the two sites recorded on the southern shoreline of Brooks Peninsula, is located a short distance east from the mouth of Nordstrom Creek (Figures 14.8 and 14.9). Facing southwest and located 4 m above the maximum high tide line, the case has a relatively small, rectangular entrance. Inside the cave entrance, there is a 6 m long, 6 m wide, straight-sided passageway. The cave then expands into a large, high-domed vault that is approximately 8 m long, 6 m wide, and 7 m high. A narrow, 2-m wide extension leads off from the northeast corner of the main vault. The extension is approximately 8 m long and runs in a northeastward direction. Only the entrance passageway and the central vault area contain midden deposit. The maximum floor area containing cultural deposits is 13 m long, 4 m wide in the passageway, and roughly 6 m wide in the area of the central vault. The cave floor is littered with both species of mussel and a few clam shells, fire-cracked rocks, and water-rolled gravels and cobbles.

An interesting feature noted in the central portion of the domed ceiling is a circular structure that appears to be filled with glacial till. The material is a conglomerate of rounded cobbles and gravels, cemented with sand. The position and structure of this feature suggest that it may have been a "blowhole" that once connected the domed vault area to the land surface above and was subsequently filled, possibly with glacial till. The authors were not able to inspect it closely, or to sample it. In general appearance, its composition differs markedly from the adjacent cave ceiling and walls.

There are two recent features on the surface of the midden deposit: a large, structured fire hearth, and a rough, wood-slab, fern covered sleeping platform. In addition, there are two clusters of large, water-smoothed boulders. The two clusters contain boulders that range in diameter from 0.5 m to 1.5 m. The fire hearth and sleeping platform are clearly associated with recent use of the cave.

Figure 14.8 Aerial view of the location of EaSx 1 (Photo: Richard I. Inglis)

Figure 14.9 General view of habitation cave EaSx 1 (Photo: Richard I. Inglis)

The cultural deposit is relatively homogeneous consisting of crushed mussel and clam shells, fire-cracked rocks, and some fish, bird, land and sea mammal bones. Near the entrance to the cave, the deposit is at least 1.2 m deep (maximum depth measurable with the soil auger used) with a 3-cm thick sand unit at 0.85 m below the surface. The depth of the cultural deposit decreases in depth to 0.5 m at the rear of the domed vault area, which is typical of cultural deposits in caves on the west coast of Vancouver Island. The deposit contains less cultural material towards the back of the cave, and more in angular rock concentrations in the narrow passageway that leads off from the main area of the cave. Although there is little cultural material in the passageway, shell and fish bones are present. Sterile beach sand and gravel, along with some angular rockfall fragments, occur at 0.6 m below the surface. Don Howes, a geologist on the project, collected a small sample of shell and fish bone from this area for radiocarbon dating, however, it has not been processed and no age estimates are available.

The foreshore in front of this site, and of the nearby rockshelter midden, EaSx 2, is very similar to that noted for the EaSw 1 village site near Quineex Indian Reserve 8. Both areas have a natural channel that disperses wave energy associated with westerly swells. These channels remain relatively calm while swells break and crash on adjacent reefs and rocky platforms. Access to these sites by small boat is relatively easy compared to the adjacent shoreline. Midden deposits are definitely correlated with this type of foreshore access along all stretches of beach that are exposed, even on calm days, to the turbulence of the open ocean.

The second cave midden, EaSw 2 is located in a small bay due west of a large unnamed point of land northwest of Quineex Reef. This large, relict sea cave (Figure 14.10) situated 3 m above the maximum high tide line, measures 36 m long and varies in width between 3 m and 7 m (Figure 14.11). Faunal remains, scattered over the entire floor area, include *Mytilus* species, some sea mammal and fish bones, and, at the back of the cave, a single whale phalanx.

Figure 14.10 Entrance of habitation cave EaSw 2 (Photo: Richard I. Inglis)

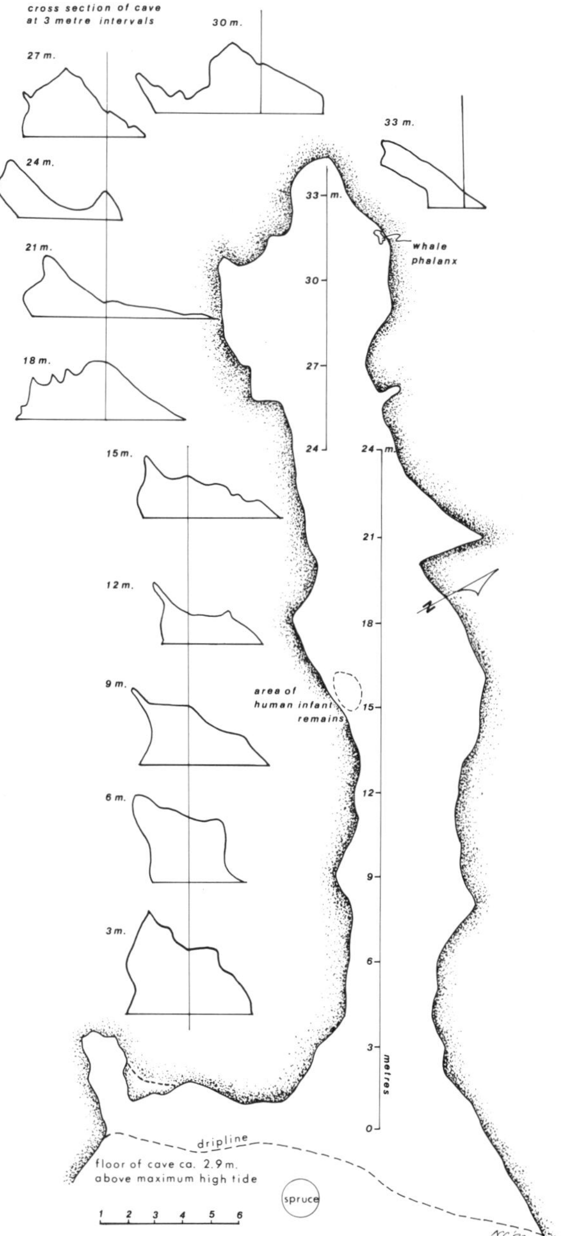

The cultural deposit, restricted to the front 10 m of the cave, reaches a depth in excess of 0.6 m. Ten metres into the cave the deposit shallows considerably, reaching a depth of 0.2 to 0.25 m with little cultural material present. Howes collected a shell sample for radiocarbon dating at this location; it yielded an estimate of 1560 ± 50 BP (GSC 3627; Howes, Chapter 3). The cobble-strewn floor of the cave is approximately 2.7 m above the maximum high tide line. Crushed and burnt fragments of *Mytilus californianus*, barnacle, some land (elk?) and sea mammal (seal?) bones, fish bones, and fire-cracked rocks were noted in the cultural deposit. A cobble layer 0.55 m below the surface at the front of the cave rises in elevation and eventually forms the floor surface toward the back of the cave.

This cave has been inhabited in recent times, a situation similar to that observed at EaSx 1. A crude structure has been erected at the entrance to the cave (Figure 14.10), probably to serve as a wind and rain screen. Inside the structure, a plank table of beach-salvaged wood has been erected, and a few china bowls and cups are scattered about. Concentrations of *Mytilus californianus* near the table are associated with this recent use of the cave. Also located in the cave are the remains of an infant, EaSw 4, which are described briefly in the next section of this chapter.

The remaining cave midden, EaSw 5, is located 600 m southwest of EaSw 2. Unlike EaSw 2, the surface of this cave is littered with storm-tossed log debris. Although the cave is extremely large, more than 100 m long and 9 m wide at the entrance, the cultural deposit, confined to the western half of the entrance, extends only 10 m into the cave and reaches a maximum depth of only 0.25 m. The deposit consists of crushed and burnt *Mytilus* species, clam, barnacle and turban shells, broken and burnt whale bones, fire-cracked rocks, and dark, charcoal-stained soil. Shells from the base of the deposit have been radiocarbon dated at 1640 ± 50 BP (GSC 3598; Howes, Chapter 3). The floor surface slopes gradually upward towards the back of the cave. The entrance is approximately 1.5 m below the surface of an older, vegetation-covered beach berm located directly in front of the cave. An estimated 200-300 year old Sitka spruce tree is growing on the berm. There is a small swale

Figure 14.11 Site map of habitation cave EaSw 2

between this older beach berm and a modern berm that marks the current maximum high tide line. The cave entrance is approximately 1 m above the maximum high tide line, protected now by the two elevated beach berms.

EaSx 2, the only rockshelter midden site recorded during the survey, is on the southern shoreline of Brooks Peninsula, approximately 40 m west of EaSx 1 (Figures 14.8 and 14.9). The site is 11 m long, 5 m wide (dripline to back of shelter), and contains less than 0.4 m of cultural deposit. The rockshelter faces south-southwest and is approximately 1.2 m above the maximum high tide line.

The deposit consists of dark, charcoal-stained soil, fire-cracked rocks, *Mytilus* species, clam, barnacle, and fish bones. An established, fully vegetated, beach berm is present between the modern beach and the site. The back slope of this berm merges with the present floor of the rockshelter. Two large Sitka spruce trees, estimated to be 200-300 years old, as well as salal and grasses, grow on the berm ridge directly in front of the site, protecting it from prevailing winds.

Burial Sites

The two sites in this category are located within historic Chicklesaht territory on the southeastern shoreline of Brooks Peninsula. The first site, EaSw 3, is a small, crevice-like cave, 3 m long, 1.5 m wide and contains human infant cranial remains and fragments of a small cedar box. The cedar box fragments consist of the bottom half of a kerfed, four-panel box and a lid or bottom fragment. The outside dimensions of the box are 41 cm long by 33 cm wide. The height measurement is incomplete and the pegged corner of the box has sprung apart. Wooden pegs and peg holes are present along the bottom edges of all four panels. Although there is no decoration on any of the panels, the box is well-made, finely adzed inside and out, and apparently smoothed and blackened on the outside. The exterior surfaces of the kerfed corners of the box were notched to prevent the cedar fibres from splitting when the panels were steamed and bent. The interior surfaces were carefully notched so that the adjoining panels at the bent corners articulate with precision.

The second fragment of the cedar box is a lid or bottom fragment. It was covered with moss and embedded in the surface matrix of the cave floor and, therefore, was left *in situ*. The fragment is approximately 45 cm long, 33 cm wide, and 4 cm thick. The width measurement is probably incomplete as there is a 2 cm wide rounded rim that would have extended beyond the perimeter of the box panels when assembled. The maximum width measurement is likely 37 cm, rather than 33 cm as recorded in the field. The rounded rim suggests a lid rather than a bottom fragment. No pegs or peg holes were detected in the fragment, which also suggests that the fragment functioned as a lid. The infant remains were covered by moss and embedded in the surface matrix of the cave floor and were, therefore, left undisturbed.

The second burial site, EaSw 4, is located inside habitation cave, EaSw 2. The infracranial remains of a human infant lie scattered along the west wall in a reasonably tight concentration. No evidence of a burial container was observed. These remains and those noted at EaSw 3 may represent the remains of a single individual.

Both burial sites found during the survey contain surface placements on cave floors. They likely represent a historic-period burial practice. Based on ethnographic documentation and personal observation in other areas of the west coast of Vancouver Island, other burial practices, including tree "burial" and non-cave/rockshelter placements, also were employed during the historic period. No evidence of these burial practices was observed in the study area.

Isolated Find Site

The remaining site, EaSv 6, is located on the rocky western shoreline of Nasparti Inlet, approximately 700 m south of the entrance to Johnson Lagoon (Figure 14.2). Situated approximately 5.5 m above the maximum high tide line, the site measures 6 m long, 8 m wide, and 1.6 m high at the cave entrance. At the dripline, the cave is approximately 8 m wide and 5 m high.

Contained in the cave were three scattered fragments of a cedar box. A fourth cedar fragment, measuring (66)[1] x (8) x 3 cm, showed no evidence of having been worked. It is mentioned only because it was the only other wood fragment found in the cave. The most complete fragment of the three recovered measures 50 x (14.5) x 1.3 cm. It is adzed on both surfaces. Both ends are squared and sewn, as is one edge, showing five sets of holes. Fibre, likely spruce branch or root, is present in some of the drilled holes. The second fragment, also adzed on both surfaces, measures (26.5) x (4.6) x 1.3 cm. This fragment shows three sets of drilled sew holes (two parallel, one diagonal) along one edge. Both ends of this fragment are missing. The remaining fragment, 50 x (3) x 1.3 cm, is adzed on both surfaces, and both ends are characteristic of bent corners. No decoration is visible on any of the surfaces. The fact that two of the fragments exhibit sewing along one edge suggests repair and a lid or bottom function for the fragments represented. The 1.3 cm thickness of these fragments suggests, however, that they may have functioned as side or end board panels. The third fragment with both ends bent is clearly a side or end board panel fragment. These fragments may be from a burial box but no human remains were observed in association or on the surface of the cave floor.

Recent Structures (Not Recorded)

During the course of fieldwork on Brooks Peninsula, six structures were observed. These structures are recent (20th century) and were not formally recorded. One structure is located on the northwestern shoreline, one on the southern end of Brooks Peninsula, three along the southeastern shoreline, and one in the Amos Creek drainage area. The last structure was observed during a helicopter reconnaissance of the peninsula in April 1981. All but one appear to be used recently by non-natives. A brief description of each structure follows.

Adjacent to the lagoon base camp on the northwestern shoreline are the remains of a log structure, now almost completely collapsed. The cabin is reported to have been the summer residence of the Ilstead family. The remains of a small frame structure were observed on the west side of the mouth of Amos Creek. No information regarding this structure was obtained. Two structures were observed at "Shelter Sheds", near Clerke Point. One of these served as the archaeological survey base camp during the first half of the project. The structure was built in 1975 by a couple from Quatsino Sound who lived in it for a couple of years and then abandoned it. It was constructed of beach-salvaged logs and beams, the roof and sides covered with cedar shakes and remains in good condition.

Nearby, on Quineex Indian Reserve 8, there are remains of three structures that are almost completely overgrown by surrounding vegetation. One other structure was observed along this stretch of shoreline. It is located in Columbia Cove, north and west of Jackobson Point. No information was obtained on the frame structure. The frame and floor, made from milled lumber, is still standing. The sixth structure, located on the large eastern tributary of Amos Creek, is a crudely constructed miner's shack made from poles and sheets of plywood. The Amos Creek drainage has been the focus of gold sluicing operations in the past (see Chapter 1), and the structure is likely associated with this activity.

---

1 ( ) indicates incomplete original dimension.

Summary

Ten archaeological sites were recorded as a result of intensive shoreline survey of the Brooks Peninsula area on the west coast of Vancouver Island. In addition, six recent structures associated with 20th century use were noted. Seven of the ten archaeological sites are classified as general activity sites, both burial sites and the isolated find site occur in caves or rockshelters. Three general activity sites occur in open settings.

Only one of the seven general activity sites, EaSw 1, is classified as a village. The other six are classified as seasonal camp sites. The two burial sites and the isolated find site contain the remains of bentwood or kerfed cedar boxes, typical of the type of burial container used on the northwest coast during the post contact period. Only two of these sites contain human skeletal remains. Archaeological evidence indicates lengthy occupation and use of this area into the 20th century.

Nine of the ten sites located and recorded during the survey occur within the historic territory of the Chicklesaht. The remaining site, EbSw 1, is located within territory occupied by the Klaskino, the southernmost of the Quatsino Sound peoples. The geographic focus of the present survey represents only a small portion of the historic territories of the Chicklesaht and Klaskino peoples.

Inland Survey

Selected inland locations were investigated in conjunction with geological and paleoecological research conducted as part of the larger study (see Chapters 3 and 9). Selected cave sites containing cultural material were investigated and samples collected for radiocarbon dating to date earliest occupation/use of these sites and to begin construction of a relative sea level curve for the region. In addition, selected open areas, including ridges, lake shorelines, and river drainages were examined for evidence of occupation or use of inland locations.

The area located immediately northeast of the lagoon base camp received particular attention as it contained a sequence of nine beach ridges formed parallel to the modern beach. Although vegetated, this series of successively older ridges were examined and probed for evidence of human occupation or use. No evidence of human occupation was found in any upland location investigated during the duration of the field program.

During a brief visit to Brooks Peninsula in 1984, Richard Hebda and Bob Powell of the Royal British Columbia Museum found what they believed to be a unifacially flaked pebble tool in the Senecio Ridge area, 375 m above sea level. On the basis of this isolated find, Hebda and Powell completed an archaeological site form. The "site" was designated EaSx 3. Several archaeologists subsequently examined the object and concluded that the item was questionable as a tool. The stone material from which it is made is not suitable for creating a cutting or chopping edge by percussion flaking. The curved end of the object is intersected by a natural fissure line, which strongly suggests unintentional or natural exfoliation. It is this process that has given the object its final form.

In July 1988, there was an opportunity to revisit Senecio Ridge and environs. Grant Keddie, a lithic technology specialist at the Royal British Columbia Museum spent three days systematically surveying Senecio Ridge (Keddie 1988), but found no evidence of human occupation or use of this area of Brooks Peninsula. Although unable to locate EaSx 3, he found no evidence in the area suggestive of human activity. On the basis of Keddie's survey and the questionable nature of the alleged pebble tool, this site has not been included in this inventory of Brooks Peninsula.

Archaeology of the Chicklesaht Area

The results of the Brooks Peninsula survey add detail but contribute little to our understanding of Chicklesaht and Klaskino settlement. To achieve this broader objective, it is necessary to include a discussion of the distribution of archaeological sites within the entire territories of the Chicklesaht and Klaskino. However, neither area had been surveyed at the time. In 1984, the authors had an opportunity to conduct an overview survey of the Chicklesaht historic territory (Haggarty and Inglis 1984b). No overview survey has yet been conducted for the Klaskino historic territory. As a result, the following section is a presentation and summary of our knowledge of the archaeology of the Chicklesaht region only.

The historic territory of the Chicklesaht, the northernmost of the Nuu-chah-nulth people of the west coast of Vancouver Island, extended from Cape Cook on Brooks Peninsula to the shoreline opposite Thomas Island in the south (see Chapter 13). The area immediately south of this boundary was recognized as belonging to the Kyuquot (Drucker 1951).

At the time of the Brooks Peninsula survey only five archaeological sites were recorded within Chicklesaht territory (four general activity shell middens and one burial site). Nine new sites were found and recorded in 1981. In 1984, as part of an overview survey of the northern regions of the west coast of Vancouver Island, another 24 sites were recorded in Chicklesaht territory. These records bring the total number of sites recorded for the Chicklesaht area to 38 (Table 14.2). Of the 38 sites recorded, 22 (58%) are classified as general activity sites; 6 (16%) as fish trap sites; 7 (18%) as burial sites; 2 (5%) as tree resource area sites; and 1 (3%) as an isolated find site. It should be stressed that these 38 sites do not represent a complete inventory for the area and will be expanded and modified as further work is completed.

Of the 22 general activity sites, 8 (36%) are classified as village sites and 14 (64%) as camp sites. It is known from research conducted in other areas of the west coast of Vancouver Island (Calvert 1980; Haggarty 1982; Inglis and Haggarty 1986, 1987) that the identification of village sites is central to understanding the distribution of independent social groups on the landscape. This site type is characteristic of local group villages, each with its own name, rights and prerogatives, and each having access to resources centered within a socially prescribed territory.

The eight village sites are comprised of seven settlement sites and one defensive site. All seven settlement sites, five of which occur on or adjacent to Chicklesaht reserves, are large (over 100 m in length), structured (with well-defined house platforms) midden deposits.

The village site of Acous, EaSv 1 (Figure 14.12), on Acous Indian Reserve 1, Acous Peninsula, consists of two distinct house platforms, structural remains of two houses and two standing poles, and a well-defined back midden ridge.

A second major village site, EaSv 3 (Figure 14.13), located on Upsowis Indian Reserve 6, at the north end of the Bunsby Islands, also contains well-defined house platforms on both sides of a small stream that dissects the deposit near the western end of the site. The remains of several collapsed houses and one unfinished, standing log structure are visible at the site. Although two carved human figures were known to have been present at the site in 1955, only one could be located during the 1984 survey. This figure stands about 2.0 m high and is badly deteriorated.

The third village site, EASv4 (Figure 14.14), located near the north end of Checkaklis Island Indian Reserve 9, consists of two distinct terraces at the north end of the site. These terraces merge to form a single terrace at the south end of the site. At least 14 well-defined house depressions are present.

Table 14.2 Archaeological sites in historic Chicklesaht territory

Major Category, Type and Sub-type	No.	% Type	% Major Category
General Activity			
Village			
Settlement	7		
Defensive	1		
Sub-total	8	36.4	
Camps			
Resource	14		
Lookout	0		
Sub-total	14	63.6	
Total	22		57.9
Fish Trap			
Stone	5	83.3	
Wood	1	16.7	
Total	6		15.8
Burial			
Surface			
Open	1		
Cave/rockshelter	6		
Sub-total	7	100.0	
Total	7		18.4
Tree Resource Area			
Bark/wood	2	100.0	
Total	2		5.3
Isolated Find			
Artifact	1	100.0	
Total	1		12.6
TOTAL	38		100.0

Figure 14.12 Aerial view of the village site of Acous, EaSv 1, with Brooks Peninsula in background (Photo: Richard I. Inglis)

Figure 14.13 Village site of Upsowis, EaSv 3 (Photo: Richard I. Inglis)

Figure 14.14 Village site of Checkaklis, EaSv 4 and defensive site EaSv 18 (Photo: Richard I. Inglis)

Another village site, EaSv 15, located on the southwestern shoreline of the middle island of the Bunsby Islands, consists of a single terrace and a well-defined back midden ridge that becomes diffuse at the south end of the site. This one is smaller in size than other village sites in the area.

The fifth village site recorded in the area, EaSv 2, is located near the southern end of Gay Passage on the southwestern shoreline of the northeasternmost of the Bunsby Islands. Although the surface and upper levels have been destroyed by logging, it is evident that this site was once a very large village, more than 100 m long and more than 2 m deep. It appears to have consisted of a single terrace. No house depressions or structural features are evident on the surface today.

Of the two remaining villages sites, EaSw 1, located near Quineex Indian Reserve 8, has been described in a previous section of this chapter. The other site, EbSu 2 (Figure 14.15), is located at the head of Ououkinsh Inlet on Ououkinsh Indian Reserve 5. At present, this is the only village known from the head of a major inlet in the region. It consists of a single terrace with three well-defined house depressions. As in the other village sites where they are evident, the house depressions are separated by ridges, which are generally 1-2 m higher than the centres of adjacent house depressions. At this site, the ridges—including the back midden ridge—are comprised primarily of fire-broken rocks with little or no shell. This contrasts sharply with the berm and back midden ridge composition of village sites located on, or near, the outer coast shoreline. A single, standing house post, associated with the middle house depression, was observed (Figure 14.16). Quantities of fire-broken rock litter the beach in front of the site. This site and, presumably, other sites situated at the heads of major inlets, are markedly different in composition from their outer-coast counterparts. This difference is due, in part, to different environmental settings and different available resources.

As mentioned earlier, this type of site is characteristic of an independent local group village. If all of these sites were occupied contemporaneously at or near the time of contact, the archaeological

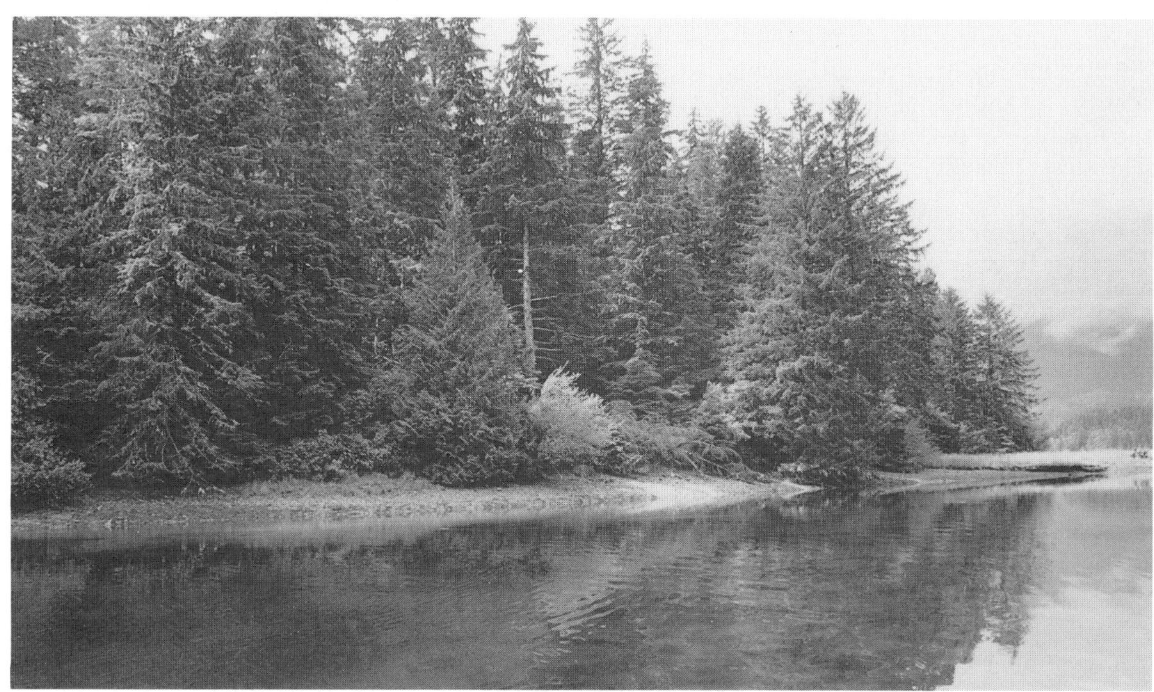

Figure 14.15 Village site EbSu 2, Ououkinsh Indian Reserve 5 (Photo: Richard I. Inglis)

Figure 14.16 House depressions at EbSu 2, Ououkinsh Indian Reserve 5 (Photo: Richard I. Inglis)

evidence suggests that at least seven local groups were established within historic Chicklesaht territory. Population is estimated at between 2000 and 3000 people. Only four local groups, however, are identified from an initial analysis of limited ethnographic sources (see Chapter 13). Further ethnographic research should add considerable detail to our knowledge of human occupation and use of the area. This research, coupled with systematic archaeological survey of the region, will provide the data necessary for full documentation of the recent past of the Chicklesaht people.

Conclusion

Current archaeological data indicates that this region of the west coast of Vancouver Island was extensively occupied and utilized well into the historic period.

The archaeological survey of Brooks Peninsula produced detailed site records for nine sites in historic Chicklesaht territory and one in Klaskino territory. Of these 10 sites, the village at Quineex (EaSw1) likely represents the year-round settlement of an independent people with a population of 200 to 400. The remaining general activity, burial, and isolated find sites are likely associated with the Quineex village site. Quineex village appears to have been occupied for a considerable period of time and abandoned as a village approximately 200 years ago, based on the estimated age of Sitka spruce growing on the house platform.

An additional six settlement sites known from historic Chicklesaht territory indicates that as many as seven independent peoples (local groups) were established in separate villages, each controlling adjacent resource territories. Population estimate, based on village size and inferred contemporaneous occupation, may be as high as 3000 people for the Chicklesaht region. The area is now unoccupied.

Today, Brooks Peninsula is unoccupied and viewed as an isolated wilderness. This is only its recent history. Both the extant archaeological and ethnographic records presented in the last two chapters document extensive occupation and use of the region, as well as the dramatic and complex changes that occurred during the last 200 years.

Update

This paper was written 12 years ago and updated in 1988. It has not been updated for publication in this volume. The paper, therefore, reflects the authors' thoughts and views on survey methodology and the archaeology of the region at the time.

References Cited

Borden, C.E. 1952. A uniform site designation scheme for Canada. Anthropology in British Columbia 3: 31-43.

Brolly, R.P. 1981. An inventory and evaluation of heritage resources on Meares Island. Unpublished ms. on file, BC Archaeology and Outdoor Recreation Branch, Victoria, BC.

Buxton, J. 1969. Earthworks of southwestern British Columbia. MA Thesis, Department of Archaeology, University of Calgary, Calgary, AB.

Calvert, S.G. 1980. A cultural analysis of faunal remains from three archaeological sites in Hesquiat Harbour, BC. Ph.D. of Anthropology and Sociology. University of British Columbia, Vancouver, BC.

Cybulski, J.S. 1978. An earlier population of Hesquiat Harbour, British Columbia: a contribution to Nootkan osteology and physical anthropology. BC Provincial Museum (Victoria, BC), Cultural Recovery Paper No. 1.

Dewhirst, J. 1969. Yuquot, British Columbia: the prehistory and history of a Nootkan village. Part 2, prehistory. Northwest Anthropological Research Notes 3(2): 232-239.

———. 1978. Nootka Sound: a 4000-year perspective. In B.S. Efrat and W.J. Langlois (eds.). Nu.tka. the history and survival of Nootkan culture. Sound Heritage 7(2): 1-30. B.C. Provincial Archives (Victoria, BC).

———. 1980. The indigenous archaeology of Yuquot, a Nootkan outside village. The Yuquot Project, Vol. 1. Environment Canada, National Historic Parks and Sites Branch (Ottawa) History and Archaeology 39.

Drucker, P. 1951. The northern and central Nootkan tribes. Bulletin of the Bureau of American Ethnology 144. Smithsonian Institution, Washington, DC.

Duff, W. 1965. The southern Kwakiutl. Unpublished ms. on file at the Royal British Columbia Museum, Victoria, BC.

———. 1972a. The community, settlement and subsistence patterns of the Nootka Sound area: a diachronic model. Ph.D. dissertation. Department of Anthropology, Southern Illinois University, Carbondale, IL.

Folan, W. 1969. Yuquot British Columbia: the prehistory and history of a Nootkan village. Part 1. Introduction and ethnohistory of the village. Northwest Anthropological Research Notes 3(2): 217-231.

———. 1972a. The community, settlement and subsistence patterns of the Nootka Sound area: a diachronic model. Ph.D. dissertation. Department of Anthropology, Southern Illinois University, Carbondale, Il.

———. 1972b. The settlement patterns of the Nootka Sound area: a diachronic model. Paper presented at the 5th annual meeting of the Canadian Archaeological Association, Burnaby, BC, 1972.

——— and J.T. Dewhirst. 1966. Yuquot: a preliminary report on excavations and site surveys; summer 1966. Unpublished ms. on file at National Historic Parks and Sites Branch, Canadian Parks Service, Ottawa.

——— and ———. 1970. Yuquot: where the wind blows from all directions. Archaeology 23(4): 276-286.

——— and ——— (eds.) 1980. The Yuquot project. Vol. 2. Environment Canada, National Historic Parks and Sites Branch (Ottawa) History and Archaeology 43.

Haggarty, J.C. 1982. The archaeology of Hesquiat Harbour: the archaeological utility of an ethnographically defined social unit. Ph.D. dissertation. Department of Anthropology, Washington State University, Pullman, WA.

_____ and G. Boehm. 1974. The Hesquiat project. The Midden (Archaeological Society of BC) 6(3): 2-12.

_____ and R.I. Inglis. 1983a. Archaeological survey of the Brooks Peninsula: Brooks Peninsula refugium project. The Midden (Archaeological Society of BC) 15(2): 1-6.

_____ and _____. 1983b. Westcoast sites: an archaeological and macroenvironmental synthesis. In R.E. Greengo (ed.). Archaeological places on the southern northwest coast. Thomas Burke Memorial Washington State Museum Research Report 4, University of Washington, Seattle WA.

_____ and _____. 1984a. Coastal site survey: theoretical implications of a new methodology. Paper presented at 17th annual meeting of the Canadian Archaeological Association, Victoria, BC.

_____ and _____. 1984b. An archaeological reconnaissance of northern Nuu-chah-nulth territory. Unpublished ms. on file at the Royal British Columbia Museum, Victoria, BC.

_____ and _____. 1985. Historical resources site survey and assessment, Pacific Rim National Park. Unpublished ms. on file at the Canadian Parks Service, Calgary, AB.

Inglis, R.I. and J.C. Haggarty. 1986. Pacific Rim National Park ethnographic history. Microfiche Report Series 257. Environment Canada, Parks Canada, Ottawa.

_____ and _____. 1987. Cook to Jewitt: three decades of change in Nootka Sound. In Trigger, B., T. Morantz, and L. Dechene (eds.). Le castor fait tout: selected papers of the fifth North American fur trade conference, 1985, Montreal, PQ.

Keddie, G. 1971. Report on the Sproat Lake highway survey. Unpublished ms. on file at the BC Archaeology and Outdoor Recreation Branch, Victoria, BC.

_____. 1988. An archaeological survey of Senecio Ridge, Brooks Peninsula, Vancouver Island. Unpublished ms. on file at the Royal British Columbia Museum, Victoria, BC.

Kenyon, S.M. 1980. The Kyuquot way: a study of a west coast (Nootkan) community. National Museum of Man Mercury Series, Canadian Ethnology Service Paper 61. National Museums of Canada, Ottawa.

Mackie, A. 1983. The 1982 Meares Island archaeological survey: an inventory and evaluation of heritage resources. Unpublished ms. on file at the BC Archaeology and Outdoor Recreation Branch, Victoria, BC.

_____. 1986. A closer look at coastal survey results. The Midden (Archaeological Society of BC). 18(1): 3-5.

McMillan, A. 1969. Archaeological investigations at Nootka Sound, Vancouver Island. MA Thesis. Department of Anthropology and Sociology, University of British Columbia, Vancouver, BC.

______ . 1985. Archaeological survey in the Alberni valley. The Midden (Archaeological Society of BC) 7(4): 6-10.

McMillan, A.D. and D.E. St. Claire. 1975. Archaeological investigations in the Alberni valley. BC Studies, 25: 32-77.

______ and ______ (eds.). 1982. Alberni prehistory: archaeological and ethnographic investigations on western Vancouver Island. Theytus Books, Penticton, BC.

St. Claire, D.E. 1975. Report on the archaeological survey of the Barkley Sound area. Unpublished ms. on file at the B.C. Archaeology and Outdoor Recreation Branch, Victoria, BC.

Sneed, P.G. 1972. Report on archaeological research activity in Hesquiat Harbour, BC. Unpublished ms. on file at the Royal British Columbia Museum, Victoria, BC.

Williamson, L. and A. Mackie. 1985. The Ohiat ethnoarchaeology project interim report. Unpublished ms. on file at the Royal British Columbia Museum, Victoria, BC.

Chapter 15

Brooks Peninsula as an Ice Age Refugium

Richard J. Hebda[a]
Don Howes[b]
Bob Maxwell[c]

[a] Botany and Earth History, Royal British Columbia Museum
Victoria, BC
and
Biology and School of Earth and Ocean Sciences, University of Victoria
Victoria, BC

[b] BC Land Use Coordination Office
Victoria, BC

[c] BC Ministry of Environment, Lands and Parks
Victoria, BC

Abstract

Brooks Peninsula's landscape exhibits a distinct trim line, ranging from 670 m to 580 m elevation above sea level, above which no evidence of glaciation occurs. High elevation soils exhibit characteristics of considerable age such as deeply weathered clasts, abundant clay and talc, and the clay mineral gibbsite, which contrast them with relatively young soils of low elevations. The flora contains Queen Charlotte Island endemic species and disjunct species, several of which occur in a diploid state. The vertebrate fauna is more or less representative of the region. The incompletely known invertebrate fauna includes disjunct species and has a high percentage of flightless ground beetles. Paleoecological studies reveal that at least one endemic species, *Ligusticum calderi,* has lived on the peninsula since the end of the last regional glaciation. Though no organic remains were found of full-glacial age, taken together physical and biotic observations provide strong evidence for a Fraser Glaciation refugium encompassing high elevations of Brooks Peninsula. Brooks Peninsula is a critical site for the study of long-term landscape processes such as soil formation, and provides indicators for identifying potential refugial sites.

Acknowledgements

We thank the participants of the Brooks Peninsula expedition whose work provided the basis for writing this synthesis. We also thank Rob Cannings, Royal British Columbia Museum, and Wilf Schofield, University of British Columbia, for reviewing drafts of this chapter.

Introduction

The scientific question addressed by this expedition was whether or not Brooks Peninsula was a glacial refugium. In this chapter the evidence for a refugium is collected, weaknesses in data and evidence are considered and a case is made for the existence of a refugium. The nature of the refugium during full glacial time is considered. The implications of a refugium are discussed and several questions considering refugia are addressed.

Refugium Pro and Con

The evidence for a glacial refugium on Brooks Peninsula comes from three sources: physical, biological and paleoecological data.

Physical Evidence

The most direct evidence supporting a glacial refugium is the physical data as documented by Quaternary Geology (Howes, Chapter 3) and Soils (Maxwell, Chapter 4).

Based on a variety of geomorphic evidence, Howes concluded that there was no evidence of glaciation on the highest portion of the central and northeastern portion of the ridge top, and the upper portion of Harris Peak, possibly extending to portions of Senecio Ridge. The size of the refugium ranged from 7.0 to 9.5 km^2. Physical evidence supporting this conclusion includes a well-defined glacial trim line, geomorphic features, Quaternary sediments and soils that occur above and below this trim line (some radiocarbon dated) and the location of Brooks Peninsula relative to continental slope.

A distinct trim line occurs on the peaks of the central ridge. The trim line decreases in elevation from 670 m in the northeast of the peninsula to 580 m, 7 km north northeast of Cape Cook and separates ice-free higher jagged and angular summits from the glaciated landscape below. The surface profile of this trim line is very similar to parabolic profiles of the Antarctic and Greenland ice caps that are grounded on their continental shelves.

Evidence supporting glaciation below this trim line includes well-preserved stoss and lee forms (whalebacks) and striations on the bedrock ridges in the saddles in the Refugium Range just below the trim line, large, ice-transported sub-rounded boulders resting on these whalebacks weathered similar to other bedrock areas overridden by Fraser Glaciation ice, the post-Fraser Glaciation age of lake bottom sediments collected from lakes on the central ridge immediately below the trim line and at lower elevations (see Chapter 9), the small volume of deltaic deposits formed by streams feeding these lakes indicating a recent origin of the lakes, and the deeply-incised cirques that occur on the northwest and southeast facing slopes of the central ridge. In addition to these features, the maximum elevation of Fraser Glaciation ice of 670 m in the northeastern part of the study area is consistent with regional ice surface elevations observed elsewhere on northern Vancouver Island.

Above the trim line the topography consists of rugged, jagged peaks with steep slopes characteristic of non-glaciated terrain. There is no evidence of cirque glaciation or glacial features such as striae and stoss and lee landforms. The strongest evidence that the peaks were unglaciated comes from observation with respect to physical and chemical properties of a podzolic soil observed at 760 m on the central ridge (see Chapter 4). The weathering of clasts, the high proportion of clay, the occurrence of gibbsite (a clay mineral largely unknown in Canadian soils), and high levels of talc in this podzolic soil suggest that this soil may be older than postglacial soils on Vancouver Island. For example, the clay in the weathered portion of the profile is about ten times as great as the clay content in soils developed on till in the lowlands of Brooks Peninsula. Although these physical and chemical features can be the result of factors other than time, the marked contrast between this soil profile and those of the lowlands favours a pre-Fraser Glaciation age of this site.

Biological Evidence

Originally, the composition of the flora, especially the occurrence of vascular plant species known as the Queen Charlotte Island endemics, led to the suggestion that Brooks Peninsula escaped the last glaciation. Ogilvie demonstrated that the flora of the peninsula contained nine of the endemic plant taxa as well as plants with unusual geographic distributions, such as *Artemisia furcata* (see Chapter 8) disjunct from populations far to the north. Based on this floristic analysis, Ogilvie concluded that the proportion of endemic and disjunct taxa with diverse geographic affinities was sufficiently high to support the concept of a refugium. Furthermore, he felt that it was only one of several refugia along the coast extending from the Olympic Peninsula to the Alexander Archipelago of Alaska (see also Heusser 1989).

Schofield (personal communication 1989) analysed the bryophyte flora and concluded that it neither supported nor refuted the idea of a refugium. He pointed out that several features of the flora, notably the distribution of disjunct species and habitat specificity, suggested a refugium of some sort. A particular feature of this flora, a considerable number of species with no sexual stages and few vegetative propagules, may indicate a relictual character. Schofield suggested that a possible explanation for the occurrence of disjunct species on Brooks Peninsula is that they may have survived in lowland coastal refugia now drowned by higher sea levels, and then spread to today's locations.

Chinnappa's study (see Chapter 6) of chromosome numbers of selected Brooks Peninsula plants provided no clear answer to the refugium question. The results, especially the occurrence of diploids in several species and chromosome numbers similar to those from Queen Charlotte Islands, however, led Chinnappa to conclude that there was a "distinct possibility that a refugium once existed...". Chinnappa recommended that chromosome studies of more species, especially of high elevation sites, focusing on the Heather Family (Ericaceae) might clarify the issue further.

Study of the vertebrate fauna shed no light on whether the peninsula was or was not a refugium (see Chapters 11 and 12). Knowledge of the region's fauna was markedly improved but no exceptional subspecies or species relevant to the refugium question were discovered. The relatively high mobility of vertebrates and the small area of the potential refugium presented circumstances in which endemic or disjunct vertebrate species would not be expected.

The terrestrial invertebrate fauna of Vancouver Island is not well known, so it is difficult to conclude whether or not Brooks Peninsula was a refugium. Nevertheless, Cannings and Cannings (see Chapter 10) identified several characteristics that suggest a refugium. Most insect species with disjunct distributions have their nearest neighbouring populations in northwest Washington State, largely beyond glacial ice limits. A preliminary estimate suggests a high percentage of flightless ground beetles, another possible indicator of a glacial refugium. Cannings and Cannings note that despite recent insights into Vancouver Island insect faunas, Brooks Peninsula insect assemblages remain distinctive. They point out that more detailed collections of insects, such as the ground beetle *Nebria*, and collection of adjacent regions are needed to strengthen the case for a refugium.

The character of high elevation plant communities provides further indications that parts of Brooks Peninsula escaped at least the last glaciation. These impoverished alpine and subalpine plant assemblages most clearly resemble those on the Queen Charlotte Islands and scattered sites on the central coast of British Columbia (see Chapter 8). In addition to containing the north coastal endemic species, the form and physical circumstances of mountain cliff, wind blown ridge, moist meadow and alpine heath habitats suggest strong adaptations to survival under the periglacial conditions that might be expected at the edge of a great ice sheet.

Cliff and ledge habitats could have persisted above, and adjacent to, nearby ice masses. Furthermore, these sites are free from competition by forest species, thus providing an opportunity for the characteristic species to persist to the present. Wind blown ridge species and plant associations would have been located above the cliffs and ledges, exposed, but well adapted to, the strong winds and unstable substrates expected near glacial ice. Just as these species and plant associations were well adapted to harsh full-glacial winds, they today resist strong winter storms that deter large woody species. Heath and meadow associations likely occupied the most favourable sites on the unglaciated landscape.

Paleoecological Evidence

Paleoecological studies did not provide the hoped-for definitive evidence of a refugium. No sediments or remains of organisms of full-glacial age were discovered and dated in lake and wetland basins (see Chapter 9). However, paleoecological results provided indirect lines of evidence for a glacial refugium. Most important, the discovery of the pollen of the coastal endemic plant *Ligusticum calderi* in late glacial sediments implies that the species survived on Brooks Peninsula during the last glaciation. It is unlikely that this species colonized immediately after glacial ice melted, since it is apparently not adapted for long distance dispersal. If it were, thriving populations should be expected on nearby peaks of Vancouver Island. Paleoecological studies also demonstrated that the suspected full-glacial moist meadow habitat persisted from late glacial time to the present around Cassiope Pond. This evidence is critical because the recognition of a refugium today depends not only on the survival of species through glacial times but the persistence of suitable habitats to the present. Refugial species then do not disappear because of postglacial competition by more vigorous species.

To a purist the only absolute proof that an area acted as a refugium is the demonstration that life, as revealed by radiocarbon-dated macro- or microfossils, survived there during full-glacial conditions. By this criterion Brooks Peninsula researchers did not find absolute proof of a refugium. However, the research showed categorically that at least the upper ridges and peaks of the peninsula escaped the last glaciation and, as far as could be observed, were never glaciated. Consequently, parts of the peninsula must have been available for life forms during the Fraser Glaciation. The occurrence of old soil profiles uninterrupted by sterile layers (see Chapter 4) suggests that living creatures occupied the landscape during full glacial time. It is difficult to imagine that this area, so near the moderating influence of the ocean, would not have supported plants and animals during maximum ice extent. To this argument must be added the fact that full-glacial conditions persisted for only the briefest interval, perhaps 2000-3000 years, if radiocarbon dates from the lowlands of western and northern Vancouver Island are accepted (Clague 1981; Hebda 1983).

Biological evidence, then, is strongly suggestive but not conclusive. Biotic affinities to the Queen Charlotte Islands, another likely, but unproven, refugial candidate (Heusser 1989), point clearly to the existence of at least a Fraser Glaciation refugium on Brooks Peninsula. The occurrence of disjunct species with affinities to populations south of the glacial limit add weight to the idea of a refugium. Other features such as vascular plant chromosome numbers and aspects of the beetle fauna further suggest a refugium. The peninsula is small and the geologically identified refugium even smaller. Species may not have survived because there was insufficient habitat to sustain them. Others may have survived only to be overwhelmed by postglacial invaders. Highly mobile groups, such as vertebrates and flying insects, may have dispersed onto the surrounding deglaciated landscape and merged with populations invading from sites south of the glacial limit. Taken together, though, the physical and biological evidence gathered by the expedition point convincingly to a glacial refugium on Brooks Peninsula.

Age of the Refugium

The age and duration of the refugium are critical to understanding the peninsula's biotic characteristics and distinctiveness. The time of the next earliest glaciation that might have covered the peninsula's peaks must be greater than 62 000 years ago (Ryder and Clague 1989). Today, Brooks Peninsula is subject to heavy precipitation and subject to intense erosional processes. Whether evidence of previous glaciations could have survived is unknown. Consequently, the length of time the refugium area was ice-free prior to 62 000 years ago cannot be determined. From this time and up to the Fraser Glaciation, climate was probably similar and at times cooler than present. The Fraser Glaciation commenced about 25 000 years ago and as this glaciation progressed, the refugium decreased in size until, at the height of glaciation, it was a small ice-free area probably surrounded by ice.

The environmental conditions prior to the establishment of the refugium appear to have been similar to those which followed, and the isolation period was brief. Under these circumstances, the biota of preglacial times might not have had time to differentiate much from its progenitors. Thus, the species that survived in the refugium may be little different from those that returned after glaciation to the surrounding terrain. As a result, Brooks Peninsula's modern biotic features may be little different from those of the surrounding terrain.

Future Studies

One problem is lack of data from adjacent glaciated sites. Brooks Peninsula collections remain among the largest from the north end of Vancouver Island. Hence, it is difficult to establish how distinct the peninsula's flora and fauna are from those of "normal" glaciated terrain. Another problem identified by several researchers is that not enough specimens and data were collected on the peninsula itself to characterize it comprehensively. So, despite all the collecting effort, much remains unknown about the peninsula.

Earth science topics meriting further attention include bedrock geology, soils and Quaternary stratigraphy with particular attention to the glacial/non-glacial boundary. A comprehensive investigation of bedrock and soil is recommended to address the age and origin of the soils above the glacial boundary. A detailed bedrock survey and map is required to assist in the verification of the soil parent material and its constituents, particularly in light of the wide variation of soil chemical analysis that resulted from this survey. Clay mineralogy studies, radiocarbon dating, the study of deep critically located soil pits should be part of any soil research program. A comprehensive investigation of soils would be invaluable to the understanding of the role of time and climate in their formation. Characterization of non-glacial soils could prove valuable to the identification of other less obvious refugia on the coast. A comprehensive study of rock weathering rates above and below the limits of glaciation would help to provide more conclusive results with respect to the Brooks Peninsula refugium. Since the survey, at least one stratigraphic section (Figure 15.1) was located in Moneses Creek valley and needs to be investigated in detail to see if it provides any further information with respect to the Quaternary History.

Though the flora and vegetation of the peninsula are relatively well documented, comprehensive studies of chromosome numbers and peculiar plant communities might shed light on the extent of

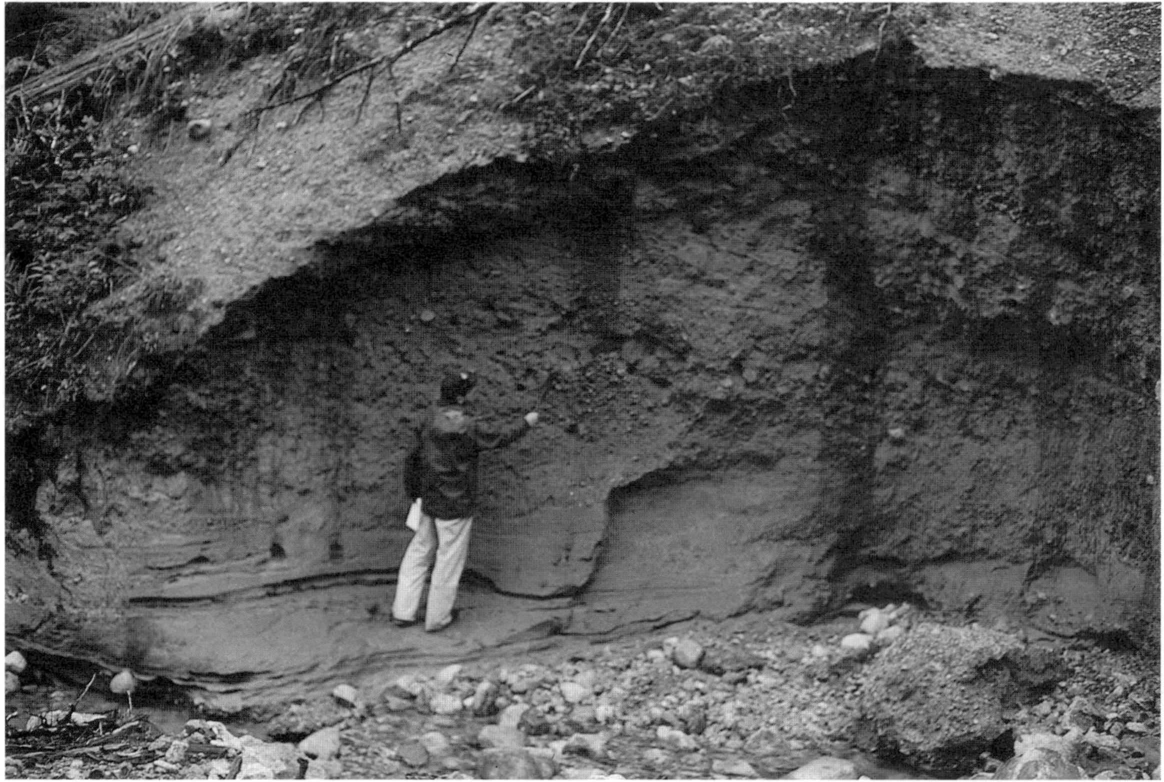

Figure 15.1 Sediment exposure in Moneses Creek Valley, Brooks Peninsula (Photo: R.J. Hebda)

the refugium and its character. In addition to more chromosome counts for more species, the newly developed DNA analysis technology could be applied to some of the more problematic taxa.

Particularly puzzling are the dwarf shore pine (Pinus contorta) stands on gradual well-drained slopes of below Senecio Ridge (Figure 15.2). These sites should support Lowland or Mountain Slope forests, but they do not. Comprehensive study of high elevation habitats might shed vital insight into the relationship of soil characteristics to vegetation in wet oceanic climates.

There remain major taxonomic groups which merit much more attention. First, the insect fauna needs to be investigated on a habitat by habitat basis, perhaps with emphasis on soil organisms. The fungi and stream and lake organisms are poorly known. Major groups of stream invertebrates were not collected.

The evidence gathered by the Brooks Peninsula expedition, despite its incomplete nature, clearly points to Brooks Peninsula as a glacial refugium. The results raise fascinating and fundamental questions about the peninsula's past and how that past has shaped its present character. The identification of the refugium leads to questions about the role of coastal refugia in the development of British Columbia's flora and fauna. Perhaps a significant part of our biological heritage is the result of the province's in-place history, not the result of invasions from the north and south. Only future studies will tell.

Figure 15.2 Open dwarf pine scrub on the slopes of Senecio Ridge, Brooks Peninsula (Photo: R.J. Hebda)

References Cited

Clague, J.J. 1981. Late Quaternary geology and geochronology of British Columbia: Part 2: summary and discussion of radiocarbon-dated Quaternary history. Geological Survey of Canada Paper, 80-35: 1-41.

Hebda, R.J. 1983. Late-glacial and postglacial vegetation history at Bear Cove Bog, northeast Vancouver Island, British Columbia. Canadian Journal of Botany 61: 3172-3192.

Heusser, C.J. 1989. North Pacific coastal refugia—the Queen Charlotte Islands in perspective. Pp. 91-106 in G.G.E. Scudder and N. Gessler (eds.). The Outer Shores. Based on the proceedings of the Queen Charlotte Islands First International Symposium, University of British Columbia, August 1984. 327 pp.

Ryder, J.M. and Clague, J.J. 1989. British Columbia (Quaternary stratigraphy and history, Cordilleran Ice Sheet). Pp. 48-58 in Quaternary Geology of Canada and Greenland R.J. Fulton (ed.). Geological Survey of Canada, Geology of Canada, No. 1.

Chapter 16

Museum Expeditions and Interdisciplinary Research

Richard J. Hebda[a]
James C. Haggarty[b]

[a] Botany and Earth History, Royal British Columbia Museum
Victoria, BC
and
Biology and School of Earth and Ocean Sciences, University of Victoria
Victoria, BC
[b] Shoreline Archaeological Services Inc.
Victoria, BC

Abstract

Multidisciplinary expeditions have played an important role in scholarly research and the development of museums. Such expeditions are logistically and financially efficient. They provide several perspectives on complex research questions and access to techniques and expertise not normally available in museums but required for rigorous research. Critical elements of planning the Brooks Peninsula expedition included setting a clear focus, recognizing researcher independence, naming the landscape and a reconnaissance trip. Three important logistical aspects were helicopter transport, regular radio communication and a camp coordinator. Publication of the results took much too long. Mechanisms for timely release of preliminary data reports should be part of planning. The expedition obtained 10 000 specimens, shed critical light on the question of a refugium and generated a collegial research atmosphere and raised public awareness of the natural values of the area.

Acknowledgements

We thank Rob Cannings and Gerry Truscott, Royal British Columbia Museum, for helpful comments on the form and content of this chapter.

Introduction

Research expeditions have a long and respectable history. Research activity, albeit for economic products, was usually included in European voyages of exploration centuries ago. Museums have played a central role in these expeditions, often providing the scientific experts for such voyages, and later processing and studying the resulting collections and data. Eventually, museums became the repositories of the collections and data so that future studies had a foundation on which to build.

Many past expeditions aimed simply to discover new places and document their human and natural histories. In this century though, expeditions, such as those sent to study dinosaurs in central Asia (Archer 1976), focused on specific research questions or issues. Although the "expedition" strategy for doing research was successful in the past, and dramatically raised public awareness of science and museums, it needed to be re-examined in the context of modern technology, specialization of scientific expertise and cost-effectiveness.

In this chapter the multidisciplinary research expedition strategy is considered from a broad perspective and from specific aspects. Elements of the Brooks Peninsula expedition, from conception to completion, are examined to help institutions and groups decide whether the expedition approach is appropriate for their purposes, and what to be aware of if the strategy is chosen.

Multidisciplinary Expeditions

Today the technical aspects of research and the characteristics of the research community are such that many broad, scholarly questions are best tackled by teams of people each using different approaches. One need only to read an issue of one of the major science journals such as *Science* or *Nature* to see that many papers are the result of the work of several scientists. The multidisciplinary approach yields data from several perspectives, which together may establish a more convincing case for an interpretation than if a single set of information was used; the more independent evidence the better. In the case of a complex question of biogeography, such as that tackled by the Brooks Peninsula expedition, this multidisciplinary approach is particularly critical. Botanists may argue on the basis of modern plant distributions that a glacial refugium existed, but other mechanisms might explain these distributions. Geological evidence might demonstrate that an area escaped glaciation, but not reveal what, if anything, survived in the refugium. Furthermore, two distinct approaches may lead to conflicting conclusions requiring yet another perspective or data set to resolve the issue.

Though museum research still relies on basic morphological and anatomical features of organisms, new analytical capabilities require access to sophisticated techniques and equipment. Such research specialization is often far beyond the skills of museum staff and requires collaboration. The chemical analysis of Brooks Peninsula soils (see Chapter 4) is a good example of this situation. The old days of descriptive field evidence for theories are long gone. Other scientists and readers of research results expect contemporary analytical techniques; such evidence comes from specialists and such specialists must be part of museum expeditions.

There is an important strategic value to multidisciplinary expeditions in today's economic and management climate. Often, support for a museum expedition can come from land or resource management agencies. Such agencies want data concerning a wide range of resources. Furthermore, in today's research management climate, a small specialized expedition is considered a luxury, focusing on insignificant or esoteric research issues. The more interest groups a project appeals to, the better its chances of being funded.

Perhaps the major advantage of large expeditions is an economic one. It is considerably cheaper, per capita, and per unit of data to use multidisciplinary teams. The most obvious benefits are logistical ones: reduced travel time, increased efficiency, greater flexibility, and improved safety. Another advantage is free or reduced cost of services contributed by co-operating agencies. These in-kind services include supplies, analyses, and logistical help that often reduce the direct costs of the expedition. Participants may also provide access to additional funding.

Finally, multidisciplinary expeditions have a major, though less obvious, benefit—synergism. During an expedition participants exchange, discuss, evaluate and expand upon ideas as they go about their daily activities. There is an opportunity to learn, to extend one's horizons. This intellectual exchange is particularly effective in the field because of the isolation from distractions. Often, new strategies or critical questions arise and lead to the gathering of unanticipated material in unexpected places. In the end, the results of the work amount to more than the sum of the parts, and participants develop new insights and contacts that serve them in future studies. This cross-fertilization is especially critical to museums that may operate at some distance from the cutting edge of modern science.

Planning

A good expedition begins with good planning. But planning should neither consume all the energy of expedition organizers nor become an end in itself. The essential elements for planning the Brooks Peninsula expedition included: setting goals and objectives and appropriate expedition format, developing a proposal (tasks, logistics, schedule, budget), making a reconnaissance trip, naming the landscape, and communication of results.

Setting a Focus

A clearly stated interdisciplinary research problem, understood and shared by all expedition participants, contributes to a constructive, co-operative enterprise. This focus leads to the development of unambiguous objectives, which lead to a list of tasks. The list of tasks assists in the selection of participants and the development of a working schedule. On the other hand, the lack of a clear focus may lead to conflicting individual or disciplinary agendas and a dysfunctional expedition hampered by interpersonal conflicts. A focus also helps promote the value of an expedition to funding agencies. If the objectives are clear, the funding agency knows what it is paying for.

At the outset, the principal objective was clear: to discover whether or not the Brooks Peninsula was a glacial refugium. The refugium focus is inherently stimulating for it beckons researchers with the possibility of discovery of organisms and phenomena new to science. The refugium question could not be addressed effectively without a second objective—establishing a base line of information on the human and natural histories of the peninsula. Before the 1981 expedition few people had studied or collected in the area. Without characterizing the region it would be difficult to establish which characteristics of the peninsula differed sufficiently from surrounding areas to provide tangible evidence to support the refugium concept. The third objective, that of testing the value of the "expedition" strategy to research, arose naturally from having an expedition. The exercise became more than a quest for knowledge because it addressed organizational questions important in the functioning of institutions such as museums.

Researcher Independence

Today's bureaucratic world is rife with controlling structures, ostensibly to promote efficiency and effectiveness. Though this approach may work well in many circumstances, it is not appropriate to scholarly endeavour. Scholars work best when they can pursue ideas and search for data within a flexible framework. A welcoming project is one that respects the knowledge and skills of all the participants as equals. The Brooks Peninsula expedition was structured to encourage independence as far as logistical considerations allowed. This approach contributed to an excellent collegial atmosphere in the field and a universally positive assessment of the enterprise.

Researchers know best what they need to work effectively—over-organization by collaborators can reduce effectiveness. Furthermore, letting individuals take responsibility for their own field needs and strategies relieves expedition organizers of those duties. Many of the participants already knew each other and some had spent time in the field together. In a heterogeneous expedition of new participants, pre-expedition workshops and seminars about the research focus could provide opportunities for expedition members to meet and share their knowledge; they also help develop effective logistical strategies.

Developing a Proposal

The proposal presented to the Friends of the British Columbia Provincial Museum (now the Friends of the Royal British Columbia Museum) contained conventional sections such as an introduction, objectives, research plan and a budget. There were also sections emphasizing the value of an interdisciplinary research, the dissemination of results and integration of research. Each participant included specific objectives. The budget section included the contribution of resources and funds from various agencies.

Integration and cooperation with other agencies were foremost elements of this successful proposal. These two features of the Brooks Expedition proposal are even more critical in the development of proposals in today's austere fiscal climate. Funding agencies, particularly those in, or associated with, government want clear indications that there is no duplication of effort and that maximum benefits accrue from a minimum of investment, particularly if large costs are involved. The budget request was for $24 000 and the total value (funds plus services) contributed by participants added about $151 000. Clearly the project was an excellent scientific investment.

The planning efforts worked well. There were few logistical problems, no personnel problems and the money for the expedition was raised. The budget turned out to be short by about 20%, however, and additional support had to be raised to cover the difference.

Reconnaissance Trip

A pre-expedition reconnaissance is a vital element of a successful expedition because it contributes to the development of logistical and research strategies. Richard Hebda, Jim Haggarty and Richard Inglis flew by helicopter to the peninsula three months before the expedition date. The reconnaissance established travel times between locations on the peninsula, investigated sites for base camp and secondary camps and tested several landing sites in the mountainous terrain. Observations of physical and biological characteristics of the landscape assisted other participants in choosing appropriate study sites. Photographs taken during the trip enhanced the proposal.

Naming the Landscape and Standardizing Habitat Names

Meaningful communication about an unknown landscape requires effective geographic designations. As described in Chapter 1, a standard method of citing localities was developed using 5 x 5 km quadrants. Each participant carried a plasticized map of the peninsula with all the quadrants clearly marked on it. Expedition participants gave their position within each quadrant using UTM coordinates. The method worked effectively for the participants and for helicopter pilots, reducing wasted flying time in search of parties on the ground.

The naming of prominent geographic features (see Chapter 1) proved especially valuable for the identification of collection localities and the subsequent write-up of results. Most of the geographic names, with some modifications, were submitted to, and accepted by, the Toponymy Section of the Province's Ministry of Crown Lands (now Ministry of Environment, Lands and Parks). These names are now marked on National Topographic Series Map 92L/4, Brooks Peninsula (Canada Centre for Mapping 1991).

A standard set of habitat names with descriptions proved valuable in the field too. Good specimen and data collections need meaningful and consistent habitat designations. The botanists and vegetation experts on the expedition provided an environmental taxonomy which later served as the basis for the classification in Chapter 8.

Logistics

Effective logistical arrangements are critical to a successful expedition in the areas of efficiency, level of analysis or study, general well-being and productivity, flexibility and safety. The three important elements of logistics of the expedition were efficient transport, good field communication, and a camp coordinator.

Efficient Transport and Helicopters

Generally, expeditions aiming to answer broad interdisciplinary questions need transport to many well-separated localities. It is important not to force people to visit the same sites as others if those sites will not provide useful data. Researchers should have the freedom to choose the best sites for their work. Furthermore, the objective of obtaining representative baseline data requires visits to many widespread sites. Helicopters proved themselves many times as the best transportation in rugged and complex landscape characteristic of Brooks Peninsula.

The most important benefit of helicopter transport is safety. Quick and pinpoint access to a site ensures rapid removal of victims in case of accident. Furthermore, helicopters reduce the need for tiring hiking over rugged landscapes. Helicopter reconnaissance allows for more effective planning of logistical deployment, and good planning in advance exposes participants to less risk.

Helicopters are economical and effective for research expeditions with large groups of people. Expeditions to remote areas often require a time-consuming ferry from the nearest helicopter base.

But with several people needing to be moved within the expedition area, the helicopter ferry time and costs decrease proportionately to the point where they become a minor factor in the overall costs of a project.

A lesson was learned about the value of helicopters during the 1981 expedition. Two members decided to walk to base camp from Cassiope Pond above Gaultheria Lake (see Chapter 1 for locations). The linear distance is approximately 5.5 km, all of it downhill. The hikers began early in the morning in good weather and descended the slopes from Cassiope Pond to Gaultheria Lake. Then, to their surprise, they encountered numerous cliffs and steep gullies slashing down to the lake. These irregularities in the landscape and the endless fallen logs were not visible from above the forest cover. The walk took eleven hours. The hikers arrived exhausted at base camp in the evening without accomplishing much scientific work. In contrast, a helicopter trip from load-up to unload took about 10 minutes!

Another important consideration concerns transportation of equipment. Though many advances have been made in the development of small compact equipment, there remain serious limitations to what a person can carry on their back. There are also limitations to the number of specimens that can be brought out safely. Helicopters can transport more field equipment of a larger size, in better condition and more frequently than hikers can. Coring of lakes would not have been possible without the use of helicopters (see Chapter 9). The machine transported a specially designed raft in a sling from study site to study site.

Communication

Effective radio communication is an essential element of good safety and transport flexibility. Sudden weather changes, often for the worse, are the norm on Brooks Peninsula. Being able to move from a site at short notice, and adjust the helicopter pick up schedule facilitated the choice of alternate sites and reduced delays.

During the expedition a system of hand-held battery powered radios for the teams working away from base camp was used. Each team reported at set times several times each day to the base camp coordinator and occasionally to adjacent teams. The base camp coordinator used a system to communicate regularly with the helicopter base and the museum. Safety regulations in many jurisdictions require that employees in remote areas must be equipped with radios. Consequently the cost of communication equipment must be part of an expedition budget.

Camp Coordinator

Perhaps the most important logistical lesson learned was the value of a camp coordinator. Often during the preparation of a budget for an expedition a camp coordinator is viewed as a luxury. It is assumed such duties can be carried out by the project researchers. But a camp coordinator is a vital element of any successful expedition.

The camp coordinator's most important role is to orchestrate the various needs of the expedition team including keeping regular communication with the outside and with field teams, organizing and receiving incoming people and supplies, making regular safety checks, responding to emergencies, maintaining security of research collections and facilities at base camp, organizing transportation, and providing an extra hand as needed. Furthermore, if time allows, the camp coordinator can cook regular meals, which is much appreciated by a group that has just returned to base camp after several days at an isolated subcamp.

The camp coordinator also can be delegated the valuable role of impartial arbitrator. Though this did not happen during our expedition, a situation may arise where one research group begins to monopolize resources, and decisions concerning equitable allocation are necessary.

Post-expedition Revisit

Often post-expedition analysis reveals intriguing questions or gaps in data that can only be resolved by another visit to the study area. Organizers of expeditions should consider the possibility of a second, scaled-down expedition. Selected participants of the 1981 Brooks Peninsula expedition had such an opportunity in 1984. By this point most analyses and identifications were complete and two items needed attention—an archaeological survey of additional upland sites and a study of bedrock geology (see Chapter 2). More sites on the peninsula were visited to collect specimens and data and mountain peaks near the peninsula were visited to make botanical observations critical for comparative purposes.

Reporting Results

Scientific results of expeditions must be reported to the research community and the interested public at large. Expedition backers must see that their investment has yielded tangible outputs. The responsibility to report results was recognized at the outset. Two vehicles were chosen for disseminating the results: a reviewed scholarly publication and programs for the public, mainly lectures. Recognizing the need for high quality visual images two photographers, Ruth Kirk and Louis Kirk, were invited to participate. Louis Kirk shot movie footage while Ruth Kirk took still photographs in colour and black-and-white. They photographed features and activities that researchers either had no time to get or did not even notice. Particularly valuable were shots of the activities of the expedition participants, and helicopter shots of study sites.

Researchers completed their analyses within 3-4 years of the 1981 expedition. Preliminary results were reported through presentations in Vancouver and Victoria and notes in newsletters. A formal publication schedule was planned. Hebda and Haggarty began editing the contributions as they came in but soon realized the task was enormous, and a technical editor (Katherine Bernick) was hired with the generous assistance of a grant from the Friends of the Royal British Columbia Museum. Most manuscripts were ready for publication by 1988 but funds for publication were not available. Only in 1995, through the BC Parks Occasional Paper Series, and with the support of Forest Renewal BC, were sufficient funds available to publish the work.

Clearly, the time from research to publication was much too long. The causes of the delay included lack of funds, busy work schedules, and an unrealistic expectation on the part of the editors to assemble a comprehensive scholarly publication. In retrospect, the most important lesson learned is that there is a need to publish preliminary or interim reports in a timely manner while work continues on the production of the definitive comprehensive volume. Some of the results of the expedition were available in published form and all were accessible as unpublished reports, but final publication proved a difficult task. A solution to this problem would have been the publishing of a preliminary summary report of results and interpretations shortly after identifications and analyses were complete, as the museum used to do in its annual reports (British Columbia Provincial Museum 1956). More detailed comprehensive treatments could have been left for later publication in reviewed journals or as part of a monographic treatment concerning a taxonomic group or large geographic areas. If this approach had been chosen, then publication costs could have been built into the original proposal.

Conclusions

The Brooks Peninsula expedition in terms of planning, data and specimen collection, and analysis was successful. However, problems were encountered with the timely production of a final comprehensive report. The design of the expedition in terms of an interdisciplinary problem, well integrated with expedition logistics, led to an efficient, inexpensive and effective exercise. Researchers collected tens of thousands of specimens, made important discoveries and cast light on the question of the peninsula as a refugium. These advancements in knowledge led to a much better understanding of the human and natural history of British Columbia, and indeed of western North America. Friendships and working relationships developed that have continued to the present day. Perhaps most importantly, the work of the expedition led to the preservation of the Brooks Peninsula in 1995 as a Class "A" provincial park. The expedition raised public awareness, with an impact a handful of people studying important issues on a smaller scale probably could not have. The peninsula is now a popular tourist destination for those looking for wilderness adventure. The expedition enhanced the Royal British Columbia Museum's leading role in human and natural history research in the province.

Museums and other institutions involved in advancing knowledge should make efforts to continue the great tradition of the scholarly expedition. It is more than an effective research tool, but also a powerful force in exciting the public imagination and advancing knowledge.

References Cited

Archer, J. 1976. From whales to dinosaurs: the story of Roy Chapman Andrews. St. Martin's Press, New York, NY.

British Columbia Provincial Museum. 1956. Provincial Museum of Natural History and Anthropology, report for the year 1955. Queen's Printer, Victoria, BC.

Canada Centre for Mapping. 1991. Brooks Peninsula 92L/4. Map 1:50 000. Department of Energy, Mines and Resources Canada, Ottawa, ON.

Index

A

C

D

E

F

G

H

I

J

K

M

N

O

P

Q

R

S

T

U

V

W

X

Y

Z

The aim of the BC Parks Occasional Paper Series is to promote interest and understanding of issues relating to the protection, planning, and management of the protected areas under BC Parks' jurisdiction. These papers contribute to scientific knowledge, and to an information base that will assist BC Parks in its stewardship of these areas.

BC Parks has statutory obligations for the protection of the natural environment; the preservation and maintenance of recreational values; and to preserve representative and special natural ecosystems, species, features and phenomena. BC Parks, therefore, has a commitment to protect, present and manage, for all time, the natural and cultural heritage conserved in provincial parks and ecological reserves, and the recreational values in provincial parks.

Researchers and authors wishing to publish in this series should contact the editor for a copy of the guidelines. Any comments and suggestions regarding this series may also be directed to:

Editor
Parks and Ecological Reserves Management Branch
BC Parks
Ministry of Environment, Lands and Parks
2nd Floor, 800 Johnson Street
Victoria, BC V8V 1X4

Denis O'Gorman
Assistant Deputy Minister
BC Parks

Occasional Paper Series

No. 1	An Investigation into the Ecology of Fallow Deer of Sidney Spit Provincial Park, March 1994
No. 2	Guidelines for Occasional Papers, March 1995
No. 3	An Inventory and Mapping of Subtidal Biophysical Features of the Goose Islands, Hakai Recreation Area, British Columbia, March 1995
No. 4	Vancouver Island Marmot Bones from Subalpine Caves: Archaeological and Biological Significance, February 1996
No. 5	Brooks Peninsula: An Ice Age Refugium on Vancouver Island, April 1997